2002

Children's Writer's & Illustrator's MARKET

THE #1 source for reaching more than 800 editors and art directors who want your work.

D1566795

Edited by
ALICE POPE

WRITER'S DIGEST BOOKS
CINCINNATI, OH

Editorial Director, Annuals Department: Barbara Kuroff
Managing Editor, Annuals Department: Douglas Hubbuch
Production Editor: Candi Cross
Writer's Digest Books websites: www.writersdigest.com, www.writersmarket.com

International Standard Serial Number 0897-9790
International Standard Book Number 1-58297-074-2

Cover design by Lisa Buchanan
Cover illustration by Dagmar Fehlau

Attention Booksellers: This is an annual directory of F&W Publications. Return deadline for this edition is April 30, 2003.

Contents

Page 58

© 2001 Janie Bynum

© 1999 Amy Walrod

Page 140

MARKETS

Page 166

RESOURCES

Page 209

Key to Symbols & Abbreviations

N Indicates a listing new in this edition.

Indicates a Canadian listing.

Indicates a publisher produces educational material.

Indicates an electronic publisher or publication.

Indicates a book packager/producer.

Indicates a change or addition to a company's contact information since the 2001 edition.

A Indicates a publisher accepts agented submissions only.

Indicates an award-winning publisher.

● Indicates a comment from the editor of *Children's Writer's & Illustrator's Market*.

ms or **mss** Stands for manuscript or manuscripts.

SASE Refers to a self-addressed stamped envelope.

SAE Refers to a self-addressed envelope.

IRC Stands for International Reply Coupon. These are required with SAEs sent to markets in countries other than your own.

b&w Stands for black and white.

Important Listing Information

- Listings are based on questionnaires, phone calls and updated copy. They are not advertisements nor are markets reported here necessarily endorsed by the editor of this book.
- Information in the listings comes directly from the companies and is as accurate as possible, but situations may change and needs may fluctuate between the publication of this directory and the time you use it.
- *Children's Writer's & Illustrator's Market* reserves the right to exclude any listing that does not meet its requirements.

Complaint Procedure

If you feel you have not been treated fairly by a listing in *Children's Writer's & Illustrator's Market*, we advise you to take the following steps:
- First try to contact the listing. Sometimes one phone call or a letter can quickly clear up the matter.
- Document all your correspondence with the listing. When you write to us with a complaint, provide the details of your submission, the date of your first contact with the listing and the nature of your subsequent correspondence.
- We will enter your letter into our files and attempt to contact the listing.
- The number and severity of complaints will be considered in our decision whether or not to delete the listing from the next edition.

From the Editor

When I was a kid in the '70s, I came home from school every day and eagerly flipped on the TV (pre-remote, pre-cable) and tuned in *The French Chef* with Julia Child. Whether Julia was preparing coq a vin or a simple potato (that's *po-TAH-to*) salad, making a fancy roast or demonstrating the ins and outs of hard cooked eggs, I was mesmerized.

One day Julia devoted her show to the most sublime of deserts, chocolate mousse. I followed my mom around the house for an hour, tugging on her shirt, begging, *Please, please, mom, please—you gotta make the chocolate mousse!* Finally, my patient mother snapped: *That's it! No more* French Chef. *You either turn on* Tom & Jerry *or go play with the other kids!* I reckon I was the first kid in the world banned from watching Julia Child.

Moving ahead 20 years . . . I got the Food Network, and lo and behold, every day at 6 p.m.: reruns of classic episodes of *The French Chef* with Julia Child! As soon as I made this discovery, I called my mom. *Guess what I'm watching right now, Mom? Julia Child—and you can't stop me!* She laughed. I hung up and learned more than I'll ever need to know about preparing tripe. I tuned in Julia's show every day. Compared to the new, slick Emerils, Marios and Wolfgangs filling up the airtime on the Food Network, Julia seems quaint, but there's something about her that I love. With a few years of constant tutoring from the Food Network and shelves full of cookbooks (I can recommend two very good ones by Julia Child), I can now hold my own in the kitchen. But it takes a lot of practice, experimentation, trial and error, and constant education.

In my interview with novelist Franny Billingsley (see page 114), she tells of quitting her work at a law practice and moving to Spain. One of the things Franny brought along was a collection of favorite children's books from her childhood. "Subconsciously I knew to bring them," she says. "I knew there was a really important part of me that was yearning for that, but I had let it go. Once I started to read those books, I thought, 'How could I have gotten so far away from what I really loved?' I think we're always drawn to create the things we love, so that's when I started to write."

We're always drawn to create the things we love. That's why I pull the TV into the kitchen to watch *Cooking Live* as I throw together my world famous spaghetti lasagna. That's why Franny spends countless hours creating amazing fantasy novels like *The Folk Keeper*. That's why you squeeze in a few minutes for writing here and there between your job and your kids' soccer practices; or take a class at the local university; or save your money for a few years to attend that week-long writing workshop you've heard so much about.

I'm glad you're doing what you love, and I'm happy you picked up a copy of *Children's Writer's & Illustrator's Market* to help you on your journey. You keep writing and illustrating, practicing and learning, revising and submitting. I'll work on perfecting my chocolate mousse.

Alice Pope
cwim@fwpubs.com

P.S. The illustration above by Barry Root is from *Brave Potatoes*, by Toby Speed. See Is It Really a Crime to Write in Rhyme? on page 77 for more about *Brave Potatoes* (*po-TAH-toes*?).

Just Getting Started? Some Quick Tips

If you're new to the world of children's publishing, buying *Children's Writer's & Illustrator's Market* may have been one of the first steps in your journey to publication. What follows is a list of suggestions and resources that can help make that journey a smooth and swift one:

1. Make the most of *Children's Writer's & Illustrator's Market*. Be sure to read How to Use This Book to Sell Your Work on page 4 for tips on reading the listings and using the indexes. Also be sure to take advantage of the articles and interviews in the book. The insights of the authors, illustrators, editors and agents we've interviewed will inform and inspire you.

2. Join the Society of Children's Books Writers and Illustrators. SCBWI, almost 12,000 members strong, is an organization for those interested in writing and illustrating for children from the beginner to the professional level. They offer members a slew of information and support through publications, a website, and a host of Regional Advisors overseeing chapters in almost every state in the U.S. and in several locations around the globe (including France, Canada, Japan and Australia). SCBWI puts on a number of conferences, workshops and events on the regional and national level (many listed in the Conferences & Workshops section of this book). For more information contact SCBWI, 8271 Beverly Blvd., Los Angeles CA 90048, (323)782-1010, or visit their website: www.scbwi.org.

3. Read newsletters. Newsletters, such as *Children's Book Insider*, *Children's Writer* and the SCBWI *Bulletin*, offer updates and new information about publishers on a timely basis and are relatively inexpensive. Many local chapters of SCBWI offer regional newsletters as well. (See Helpful Books & Publications on page 345 for contact information on the newsletters listed above and others. For information on regional SCBWI newsletters, visit www.scbwi.org and click on "publications.")

4. Read trade and review publications. Magazines like *Publishers Weekly* (which offers two special issues each year devoted to children's publishing available on newsstands), *The Horn Book*, *Riverbank Review* and *Booklinks* offer news, articles, reviews of newly-published titles and ads featuring upcoming and current releases. Referring to them will help you get a feel for what's happening in children's publishing.

5. Read guidelines. Most publishers and magazines offer writer's and artist's guidelines which provide detailed information on needs and submission requirements, and some magazines offer theme lists for upcoming issues. Many publishers and magazines state the availability of guidelines within their listings. Send a self-addressed, stamped envelope (SASE) to publishers who offer guidelines. You'll often find submission information on publishers' and magazines' websites. And while you're on the Web, visit www.writersdigest.com for a searchable database of about 1,500 guidelines.

6. Look at publishers' catalogs. Perusing publishers' catalogs can give you a feel for their line of books and help you decide where your work might fit in. Send for catalogs with a SASE if they are available (often stated within listings). Visit publishers' websites which often contain their full catalogs. You can also ask librarians to look at catalogs they have on hand. You can even search Amazon.com (www.amazon.com) by publisher and year. (Click on "book search" then "publisher, date" and plug in, for example, "Atheneum" under "publisher" and "2001" under year. You'll get a list of all the Atheneum titles published in 2001 which you can peruse.)

7. Visit bookstores. It's not only informative to spend time in bookstores—it's fun, too! Frequently visit the children's section of your local bookstore (whether a chain or an independent) to see the latest from a variety of publishers and the most current issues of children's magazines. Look for books in the genre you're writing or with illustrations similar in style to yours, and spend some time studying them. It's also wise to get to know your local booksellers—they can tell you what's new in the store and provide insight into what kids and adults are buying.

8. Read, read, read! While you're at that bookstore, pick up a few things, or keep a list of the books that interest you and check them out of your library. Read and study the latest releases, the award winners, and the classics. You'll learn from other writers, get ideas and get a feel for what's being published. Think about what works and doesn't work in a story. Pay attention to how plots are constructed and how characters are developed or the rhythm and pacing of picture book text. It's certainly enjoyable research!

9. Take advantage of Internet resources. There are innumerable sources of information available on the Internet about writing for children (and anything else you could possibly think of). It's also a great resource for getting (and staying) in touch with other writers and illustrators through listservs and e-mail, and can serve as a vehicle for self-promotion. (Visit some authors' and illustators' web pages for ideas. See Useful Online Resources on page 348 for a list of helpful websites.)

10. Consider attending a conference. If time and finances allow, attending a conference is a great way to meet peers and network with professionals in the field of children's publishing. As mentioned above, SCBWI offers conferences in various locations year round (see www.scbwi. org and click on "events" for a full calendar of conferences). General writers' conferences often offer specialized sessions just for those interested in children's writing. Many conferences offer optional manuscript and portfolio critiques as well, giving you a chance for feedback from seasoned professionals.

11. Network, network, network! Don't work in a vacuum. You can meet other writers and illustrators through a number of the things listed above—SCBWI, conferences, online. Attend local meetings for writers and illustrators whenever you can. Befriend other writers in your area (SCBWI offers members a roster broken down by state)—share guidelines, share subscriptions, be conference buddies and roommates, join a critique group or writing group, exchange information and offer support. Get online—sign on to listservs, post on message boards, visit chatrooms. (America Online offers them. Also, visit author Verla Kay's website for information on weekly workshops. See Useful Online Resources on page 348 for more information.) Exchange addresses, phone numbers and e-mail addresses with writers or illustrators you meet at events. And at conferences don't be afraid to talk to people, ask strangers to join you for lunch, approach speakers and introduce yourself, chat in elevators and hallways. Remember, you're not alone.

12. Perfect your craft and don't submit until your work is its best. It's often been said that a writer should try to write every day. Great manuscripts don't happen overnight—there's time, research and revision involved. As you visit bookstores and study what others have written and illustrated, really step back and look at your own work and ask yourself—honestly—*How does my work measure up? Is it ready for editors or art directors to see?* If it's not, keep working. You may want to ask a writer's group for constructive comments, or get a professional manuscript or portfolio critique.

13. Be patient, learn from rejection and don't give up! Thousands of manuscripts land on editors' desks; thousands of illustration samples line art directors' file drawers. There are so many factors that come into play when evaluating submissions. Keep in mind that you might not hear back from publishers promptly. Persistence and patience are important qualities in writers and illustrators working for publication. Keep at it—it will come. It can take a while, but when you get that first book contract or first assignment, you'll know it was worth the wait. (Read First Books on page 84 for proof.)

How to Use This Book to Sell Your Work

As a writer, illustrator or photographer first picking up *Children's Writer's & Illustrator's Market*, you may not know quite how to start using the book. Your impulse may be to flip through the book and quickly make a mailing list, then submit to everyone in hopes that someone will take interest in your work. Well, there's more to it. Finding the right market takes time and research. The more you know about a company that interests you, the better chance you have of getting work accepted.

We've made your job a little easier by putting a wealth of information at your fingertips. Besides providing listings, this directory includes a number of tools to help you determine which markets are the best ones for your work. By using these tools, as well as researching on your own, you raise your odds of being published.

USING THE INDEXES

This book lists hundreds of potential buyers of freelance material. To learn which companies want the type of material you're interested in submitting, start with the indexes.

The Age-Level Index

Age groups are broken down into these categories in the Age-Level Index:
- **Picture books** or **picture-oriented material** are written and illustrated for preschoolers to 8-year-olds.
- **Young readers** are for 5- to 8-year-olds.
- **Middle readers** are for 9- to 11-year-olds.
- **Young adults** are for ages 12 and up.

Age breakdowns may vary slightly from publisher to publisher, but using them as general guidelines will help you target appropriate markets. For example, if you've written an article about trends in teen fashion, check the Magazines Age-Level Index under the Young Adult subheading. Using this list, you'll quickly find the listings for young adult magazines.

The Subject Index

But let's narrow the search further. Take your list of young adult magazines, turn to the Subject Index, and find the Fashion subheading. Then highlight the names that appear on both lists (Young Adult and Fashion). Now you have a smaller list of all the magazines that would be interested in your teen fashion article. Read through those listings and decide which ones sound best for your work.

Illustrators and photographers can use the Subject Index as well. If you specialize in painting animals, for instance, consider sending samples to book and magazine publishers listed under Animals and, perhaps, Nature/Environment. Illustrators can simply send general examples of their style (in the form of tearsheets or postcards) to art directors to keep on file. The indexes may be more helpful to artists sending manuscripts/illustration packages. Always read the listings for the potential markets to see the type of work art directors prefer and what type of samples they'll keep on file, and send for art or photo guidelines if they're available.

The Poetry Index

This index lists book publishers and magazines interested in submissions from poets. Always send for writer's guidelines from publishers and magazines that interest you.

The Photography Index

You'll find lists of book and magazine publishers, as well as greeting card, puzzle and game manufacturers, that buy photos from freelancers in the Photography Index. Copy the lists and read the listings for specific needs. Send for photo guidelines if they're offered.

USING THE LISTINGS

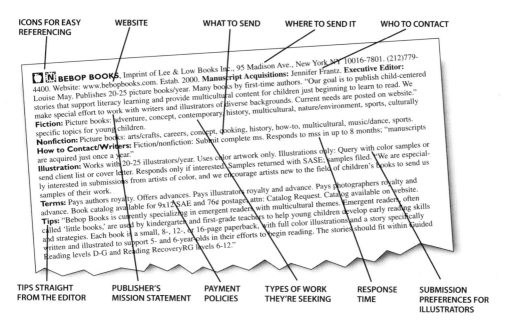

ICONS FOR EASY REFERENCING · WEBSITE · WHAT TO SEND · WHERE TO SEND IT · WHO TO CONTACT

BEBOP BOOKS, Imprint of Lee & Low Books Inc., 95 Madison Ave., New York NY 10016-7801. (212)779-4400. Website: www.bebopbooks.com. Estab. 2000. **Manuscript Acquisitions:** Jennifer Frantz. **Executive Editor:** Louise May. Publishes 20-25 picture books/year. Many books by first-time authors. "Our goal is to publish child-centered stories that support literacy learning and provide multicultural content for children just beginning to learn to read. We make special effort to work with writers and illustrators of diverse backgrounds. Current needs are posted on website." **Fiction:** Picture books: adventure, concept, contemporary, history, multicultural, nature/environment, sports, culturally specific topics for young children. **Nonfiction:** Picture books: arts/crafts, careers, concept, cooking, history, how-to, multicultural, music/dance, sports. **How to Contact/Writers:** Fiction/nonfiction: Submit complete ms. Responds to mss in up to 8 months; "manuscripts are acquired just once a year." **Illustration:** Works with 20-25 illustrators/year. Uses color artwork only. Illustrations only: Query with color samples or send client list or cover letter. Responds only if interested. Samples returned with SASE; samples filed. "We are especially interested in submissions from artists of color, and we encourage artists new to the field of children's books to send us samples of their work. **Terms:** Pays authors royalty. Offers advances. Pays illustrators royalty and advance. Pays photographers royalty and advance. Book catalog available for 9x12 SAE and 76¢ postage; attn: Catalog Request. Catalog available on website. **Tips:** "Bebop Books is currently specializing in emergent readers with multicultural themes. Emergent readers often called 'little books,' are used by kindergarten and first-grade teachers to help young children develop early reading skills and strategies. Each book is a small, 8-, 12-, or 16-page paperback, with full color illustrations and a story specifically written and illustrated to support 5- and 6-year-olds in their efforts to begin reading. The stories should fit within Guided Reading levels D-G and Reading RecoveryRG levels 6-12."

TIPS STRAIGHT FROM THE EDITOR · PUBLISHER'S MISSION STATEMENT · PAYMENT POLICIES · TYPES OF WORK THEY'RE SEEKING · RESPONSE TIME · SUBMISSION PREFERENCES FOR ILLUSTRATORS

Many listings begin with one or more symbols. (Refer to the inside covers of the book for quick reference.) Here's what each icon stands for:

- indicates a listing is new to this edition.
- indicates a listing is Canadian.
- indicates a company publishes educational material.
- indicates an electronic publisher of publication.
- indicates a listing is a book packager or producer.
- indicates a change or addition to a company's contact information since last year's edition.
- indicates a publisher only accepts submissions through agents.
- indicates a company's publications have received awards recently.

In the Book Publishers section, you'll find contact names after **Manuscript Acquisitions** and **Art Acquisitions**. Contact names in Magazines follow boldface titles such as **Fiction Editor**, **Articles Editor** or **Art Director**. Following contact information in many of these listings are mission statements. Read these to get a general idea of the aim of certain publishers and magazines to help you decide whether to explore them further.

The subheadings under each listing contain more specific information about what a company needs. In Book Publishers and Magazines, for example, you'll find such things as age levels and subjects needed under the **Fiction** and **Nonfiction** subheads. Here's an example from a listing in the Book Publishers section:

Fiction: Picture books: adventure, animal, contemporary, fantasy, humor. Young readers: animal, contemporary, humor, sports, suspense/mystery. Middle readers: adventure, humor, sports. Young adults: humor, problem novels.

Also check the listings for information on how to submit your work and response time. In Book Publishers and Magazines, writers will find this information under the How to Contact/ Writers subhead:

How to Contact/Writers: Query with outline/synopsis and 2 sample chapters. Responds to queries in 6 weeks.

For information on submission procedures and formats, turn to Before Your First Sale on page 8.

Also look for information regarding payment and rights purchased. Some markets pay on acceptance, others on publication. Some pay a flat rate for manuscripts and artwork, others pay advances and royalties. Knowing how a market operates will keep you from being shocked when you discover your paycheck won't arrive until your manuscript is published—a year after it was accepted. This information is found under **Terms** in Book Publishers, Magazines and Play Publishers. Here's an example from the Magazines section:

Terms: Pays on acceptance. Buys first North American serial rights or reprint rights. Pays $50-100 for stories/articles. Pays illustrators $75-125 for b&w or color inside; $150-200 for color cover.

Under **Tips** you'll find special advice straight from an editor or art director about what their company wants or doesn't want, or other helpful advice:

Tips: "We are looking for picture books centered on a strong, fully-developed protaganist who grows or changes during the course of the story."

Additional information about specific markets in the form of comments from the editor of this book is set off by bullets (•) within listings:

• This publisher accepts only queries and manuscripts submitted by agents.

Many listings indicate whether submission guidelines are available. If a publisher you're interested in offers guidelines, send for them and read them. The same is true with catalogs. Sending for catalogs and seeing and reading about the books a publisher produces gives you a better idea whether your work would fit in. (You should also look at a few of the books in the catalog at a library or bookstore to get a feel for the publisher's material.) Note that a number of publishers offer guidelines and catalogs on their websites, and a searchable database of more than 1,500 writer's guidelines is available at www.writersdigest.com.

Especially for artists and photographers

Along with information for writers, listings provide information for photographers and illustrators. Illustrators will find numerous markets that maintain files of samples for possible future assignments. If you're both a writer and illustrator, look for markets that accept manuscript/ illustration packages. You'll find sample illustrations from various publishers sprinkled throughout the listings. These illustrations serve as examples of the kind of art these particular companies buy. Read the captions for additional information about the artwork and the market.

If you're a photographer, after consulting the Photography Index, read the information under the Photography subhead within listings to see what format buyers prefer. For example, some want 35mm color transparencies, others want black-and-white prints. Note the type of photos a buyer wants to purchase and the procedures for submitting. It's not uncommon for a market to want a résumé and promotional literature, as well as tearsheets from previous work. Listings also note whether model releases and/or captions are required.

Especially for young writers

If you're a parent, teacher or student, you may be interested in Young Writer's & Illustrator's Markets. The listings in this section encourage submissions from young writers and artists. Some may require a written statement from a teacher or parent noting the work is original. Also watch for age limits.

Young people should also check Contests & Awards for contests that accept work by young writers and artists. Some of the contests listed are especially for students; others accept both student and adult work. These listings contain the phrase **open to students** in bold. Some listings in Clubs & Organizations and Conferences & Workshops may also be of interest to students. Organizations and conferences which are open to or are especially for students also include **open to students.**

COMMON ABBREVIATIONS

Throughout the listings, the following abbreviations are used:
- **ms** or **mss** stands for manuscript or manuscripts.
- **SASE** refers to a self-addressed, stamped envelope.
- **SAE** refers to a self-addressed envelope.
- **IRC** stands for International Reply Coupon. These are required with SAEs sent to markets in countries other than your own.

Before Your First Sale

If you're just beginning to pursue your career as a children's book writer or illustrator, it's important to learn the proper procedures, formats, and protocol for the publishing industry. This article outlines the basics you need to know before you head to the post office with your submissions.

FINDING THE BEST MARKETS FOR YOUR WORK

Researching publishers well is a basic element of submitting your work successfully. Editors and art directors hate to receive inappropriate submissions—handling them wastes a lot of their time, not to mention your time and money, and they are the main reason some publishers have chosen not to accept material over the transom. By randomly sending out material without knowing a company's needs, you're sure to meet with rejection.

If you're interested in submitting to a particular magazine, write to request a sample copy, or see if it's available in your local library or bookstore. For a book publisher, obtain a book catalog and check a library or bookstore for titles produced by that publisher. Many publishers and magazines now have websites that include catalogs or sample articles (websites are given within the listings). Studying such materials carefully will better acquaint you with a publisher's or magazine's writing, illustration and photography styles and formats.

Most of the book publishers and magazines listed in this book (as well as some greeting card and paper product producers) offer some sort of writer's, artist's or photographer's guidelines for a self-addressed, stamped envelope (SASE). Guidelines are also often found on publishers' websites. It's important to read and study guidelines before submitting work. You'll get a better understanding of what a particular publisher wants. You may even decide, after reading the submission guidelines, that your work isn't right for a company you considered. For access to a searchable database of more than 1,500 publishers' guidelines, visit www.writersdigest. com.

SUBMITTING YOUR WORK

Throughout the listings you'll read requests for particular elements to include when contacting markets. Here are explanations of some of these important submission components.

Queries, cover letters and proposals

A query letter is a no-more-than-one-page, well-written piece meant to arouse an editor's interest in your work. Many query letters start with leads similar to those of actual manuscripts. In the rest of the letter, briefly outline the work you're proposing and include facts, anecdotes, interviews or other pertinent information that give the editor a feel for the manuscript's premise—entice her to want to know more. End your letter with a straightforward request to write (or submit) the work, and include information on its approximate length, date it could be completed, and whether accompanying photos or artwork are available.

In a query letter, think about presenting your book as a publisher's catalog would present it. Read through a good catalog and examine how the publishers give enticing summaries of their books in a spare amount of words. It's also important that query letters give editors a taste of your writing style. For good advice and more samples of queries, cover letters and other correspondence, consult *How to Write Attention-Grabbing Query & Cover Letters*, by John Wood (Writer's Digest Books).

- **Query letters for nonfiction.** Queries are usually required when submitting nonfiction material to a publisher. The goal of a nonfiction query is to convince the editor your idea is perfect for her readership and that you're qualified to do the job. Note any previous writing experience and include published samples to prove your credentials, especially samples related to the subject matter you're querying about.

• **Query letters for fiction.** More and more, queries are being requested for fiction manuscripts. For a fiction query, explain the story's plot, main characters, conflict and resolution. Just as in nonfiction queries, make the editor eager to see more.

• **Cover letters for writers.** Some editors prefer to review complete manuscripts, especially for fiction. In such cases, the cover letter (which should be no longer than one page) serves as your introduction, establishes your credentials as a writer, and gives the editor an overview of the manuscript. If the editor asked for the manuscript because of a query, note this in your cover letter.

• **Cover letters for illustrators and photographers.** For an illustrator or photographer the cover letter serves as an introduction to the art director and establishes professional credentials when submitting samples. Explain what services you can provide as well as what type of follow-up contact you plan to make, if any.

• **Résumés.** Often writers, illustrators and photographers are asked to submit résumés with cover letters and samples. They can be created in a variety of formats, from a single page listing information, to color brochures featuring your work. Keep your résumé brief, and focus on your achievements, including your clients and the work you've done for them, as well as your educational background and any awards you've received. Do not use the same résumé you'd use for a typical job application.

• **Book proposals.** Throughout the listings in the Book Publishers section, publishers refer to submitting a synopsis, outline and sample chapters. Depending on an editor's preference, some or all of these components, along with a cover letter, make up a book proposal.

A *synopsis* summarizes the book, covering the basic plot (including the ending). It should be easy to read and flow well.

An *outline* covers your book chapter by chapter and provides highlights of each. If you're developing an outline for fiction, include major characters, plots and subplots, and book length.

Sample chapters give a more comprehensive idea of your writing skill. Some editors may request the first two or three chapters to determine if she's interested in seeing the whole book.

Manuscript formats

When submitting a complete manuscript, follow some basic guidelines. In the upper-left corner of your title page, type your legal name (not pseudonym), address and phone number. In the upper-right corner, type the approximate word length. All material in the upper corners should be typed single-spaced. Then type the title (centered) almost halfway down that page, the word "by" two spaces under that, and your name or pseudonym two spaces under "by."

The first page should also include the title (centered) one-third of the way down. Two spaces under that type "by" and your name or pseudonym. To begin the body of your manuscript, drop down two double spaces and indent five spaces for each new paragraph. There should be one-inch margins around all sides of a full typewritten page. (Manuscripts with wide margins are more readable and easier to edit.)

Set your computer or typewriter on double-space for the manuscript body. From page two to the end of the manuscript, include your last name followed by a comma and the title (or key words of the title) in the upper-left corner. The page number should go in the top right corner. Drop down two double spaces to begin the body of each page. If you're submitting a novel, type each chapter title one-third of the way down the page. For more information on manuscript formats, read *Formatting & Submitting Your Manuscript*, by Jack and Glenda Neff, Don Prues, and the editors of *Writer's Market* or *Manuscript Submissions*, by Scott Edelstein (both Writer's Digest Books).

Picture book formats

The majority of editors prefer to see complete manuscripts for picture books. When typing the text of a picture book, don't include page breaks and don't type each page of text on a new sheet of paper. And unless you are an illustrator, don't worry about supplying art. Editors will find their own illustrators for picture books. Most of the time, a writer and an illustrator who work on the same book never meet. The editor acts as a go-between and works with the writer and illustrator throughout the publishing process. (See Whose Book Is It Anyway? A Picture Book Illustrator's Perspective on page 52 for more insight into the subject.) *How to Write and Sell Children's Picture Books*, by Jean E. Karl (Writer's Digest Books), offers advice on preparing text and marketing your work.

If you're an illustrator who has written your own book, consider creating a dummy or story-board containing both art and text, then submit it along with your complete manuscript and sample pieces of final art (color photocopies or slides—never originals). Publishers interested in picture books specify in their listings what should be submitted. For tips on creating a dummy, refer to *How to Write and Illustrate Children's Books and Get Them Published*, edited by Treld Pelkey Bicknell and Felicity Trotman (North Light Books), or Frieda Gates's book, *How to Write, Illustrate, and Design Children's Books* (Lloyd-Simone Publishing Company).

Writers may also want to learn the art of dummy making to help them through their writing process with things like pacing, rhythm and length. For a great explanation and helpful hints, turn to Dummies Aren't for Dummies: Mocking Up a Picture Book on page 45 and see *You Can Write Children's Books*, by Tracey E. Dils (Writer's Digest Books).

Mailing submissions

Your main concern when packaging material is to be sure it arrives undamaged. If your manuscript is less than six pages, simply fold it in thirds and send it in a #10 (business-size) envelope. For a SASE, either fold another #10 envelope in thirds or insert a #9 (reply) envelope which fits in a #10 neatly without folding.

Another option is folding your manuscript in half in a 6 × 9 envelope, with a #9 or #10 SASE enclosed. For larger manuscripts use a 9 × 12 envelope both for mailing the submission and as a SASE (which can be folded in half). Book manuscripts require sturdy packaging for mailing. Include a self-addressed mailing label and return postage.

If asked to send artwork and photographs, remember they require a bit more care in packaging to guarantee they arrive in good condition. Sandwich illustrations and photos between heavy cardboard that is slightly larger than the work. The cardboard can be secured by rubber bands or with tape. If you tape the cardboard together, check that the artwork doesn't stick to the tape. Be sure your name and address appear on the back of each piece of art or each photo in case the material becomes separated. For the packaging use either a manila envelope, foam-padded envelope, brown paper or a mailer lined with plastic air bubbles. Bind non-joined edges with reinforced mailing tape and affix a typed mailing label or clearly write your address.

Mailing material first class ensures quick delivery. Also, first-class mail is forwarded for one year if the addressee has moved, and can be returned if undeliverable. If you're concerned about your original material safely reaching its destination, consider other mailing options, such as UPS or certified mail. If material needs to reach your editor or art director quickly, use overnight delivery services.

Remember, companies outside your own country can't use your country's postage when returning a manuscript to you. When mailing a submission to another country, include a self-addressed envelope and International Reply Coupons or IRCs. (You'll see this term in many Canadian listings.) Your postmaster can tell you, based on a package's weight, the correct number of IRCs to include to ensure its return.

If it's not necessary for an editor to return your work (such as with photocopies) don't include return postage. You may want to track the status of your submission by enclosing a postage-paid reply postcard with options for the editor to check, such as "Yes, I am interested," "I'll keep the material on file," or "No, the material is not appropriate for my needs at this time."

Some writers, illustrators and photographers simply include a deadline date. If you don't hear from the editor or art director by the specified date, your manuscript, artwork or photos are automatically withdrawn from consideration. Because many publishing houses and companies are overstocked with material, a minimum deadline should be at least three months.

Unless requested, it's never a good idea to use a company's fax number or e-mail address to send manuscript submissions. This can disrupt a company's internal business.

Keeping submission records

It's important to keep track of the material you submit. When recording each submission, include the date it was sent, the business and contact name, and any enclosures (such as samples of writing, artwork or photography). You can create a record-keeping system of your own or look for record-keeping software in your area computer store.

Keep copies of articles or manuscripts you send together with related correspondence to make follow-up easier. When you sell rights to a manuscript, artwork or photos you can "close" your file on a particular submission by noting the date the material was accepted, what rights were purchased, the publication date and payment.

Often writers, illustrators and photographers fail to follow up on overdue responses. If you don't hear from a publisher within their stated response time, wait another month or so and follow up with a note asking about the status of your submission. Include the title or description, date sent, and a SASE for response. Ask the contact person when she anticipates making a decision. You may refresh the memory of a buyer who temporarily forgot about your submission. At the very least you'll receive a definite "no," and free yourself to send the material to another publisher.

Simultaneous submissions

If you opt for simultaneous (also called "multiple") submissions—sending the same material to several publishers at the same time—be sure to inform each editor to whom you submit that your work is being considered elsewhere. Many editors are reluctant to receive simultaneous submissions but understand that for hopeful writers and illustrators, waiting several months for a response can be frustrating. In some cases, an editor may actually be more inclined to read your manuscript sooner if she knows it's being considered by another publisher. The Society of Children's Book Writers and Illustrators cautions writers against simultaneous submissions. The official recommendation of SCBWI is to submit to one publisher at a time, but wait only three months (note you'll do so in your cover letter). If no response is received, then send a note withdrawing your manuscript from consideration. SCBWI considers simultaneous submissions acceptable only if you have a manuscript dealing with a timely issue.

It's especially important to keep track of simultaneous submissions, so if you get an offer on a manuscript sent to more than one publisher, you can instruct other publishers to withdraw your work from consideration.

AGENTS & ART REPS

Most children's writers, illustrators and photographers, especially those just beginning, are confused about whether to enlist the services of an agent or representative. The decision is strictly one that each writer, illustrator or photographer must make for herself. Some are confident with their own negotiation skills and believe acquiring an agent or rep is not in their best interest. Others feel uncomfortable in the business arena or are not willing to sacrifice valuable creative time for marketing.

About half of children's publishers accept unagented work, so it's possible to break into children's publishing without an agent. Some agents avoid working with children's books because traditionally low advances and trickling royalty payments over long periods of time make children's books less lucrative. Writers targeting magazine markets don't need the services of an agent. In fact, it's practically impossible to find an agent interested in marketing articles and short stories—there simply isn't enough financial incentive.

One benefit of having an agent, though, is it may speed up the process of getting your work reviewed, especially by publishers who don't accept unagented submissions. If an agent has a good reputation and submits your manuscript to an editor, that manuscript will likely bypass the first-read stage (which is done by editorial assistants and junior editors) and end up on the editor's desk sooner.

When agreeing to have a reputable agent represent you, remember that she should be familiar with the needs of the current market and evaluate your manuscript/artwork/photos accordingly. She should also determine the quality of your piece and whether it is saleable. When your manuscript sells, your agent should negotiate a favorable contract and clear up any questions you have about payments.

Keep in mind that however reputable the agent or rep is, she has limitations. Representation does not guarantee sale of your work. It just means an agent or rep sees potential in your writing, art or photos. Though an agent or rep may offer criticism or advice on how to improve your work, she cannot make you a better writer, artist or photographer.

Literary agents typically charge a 15 percent commission from the sale of writing; art and photo representatives usually charge a 25 to 30 percent commission. Such fees are taken from advances and royalty earnings. If your agent sells foreign rights to your work, she will deduct a higher percentage because she will most likely be dealing with an overseas agent with whom she must split the fee.

Be advised that not every agent is open to representing a writer, artist or photographer who lacks an established track record. Just as when approaching a publisher, the manuscript, artwork or photos, and query or cover letter you submit to a potential agent must be attractive and professional looking. Your first impression must be as an organized, articulate person.

For listings of agents and reps, turn to the Agents & Art Reps section. Also refer to *Guide to Literary Agents* for listings of agents and lots more advice on finding and working with agents. For additional listings of art reps, consult *Artist's & Graphic Designer's Market*; and for photo reps, see *Photographer's Market* (all Writer's Digest Books).

The Business of Writing & Illustrating

A career in children's publishing involves more than just writing skills or artistic talent. Successful authors and illustrators must be able to hold their own in negotiations, keep records, understand contract language, grasp copyright law, pay taxes and take care of a number of other business concerns. Although agents and reps, accountants and lawyers, and writers' organizations offer help in sorting out such business issues, it's wise to have a basic understanding of them going in. This article offers just that—basic information. For a more in-depth look at the subjects covered here, check your library or bookstore for books and magazines to help you, some of which are mentioned. We also tell you how to get information on issues like taxes and copyright from the federal government.

CONTRACTS & NEGOTIATION

Before you see your work in print or begin working with an editor or art director on a project, there is negotiation. (For great advice on negotiating contracts, see Contract Savvy for Writers & Illustrators on page 21.) And whether negotiating a book contract, a magazine article assignment, or an illustration or photo assignment, there are a few things to keep in mind. First, if you find any clauses vague or confusing in a contract, get legal advice. The time and money invested in counseling up front could protect you from problems later. If you have an agent or rep, she will review any contract.

A contract is an agreement between two or more parties that specifies the fees to be paid, services rendered, deadlines, rights purchased and, for artists and photographers, whether original work is returned. Most companies have standard contracts for writers, illustrators and photographers. The specifics (such as royalty rates, advances, delivery dates, etc.) are typed in after negotiations.

Though it's okay to conduct negotiations over the phone, get a written contract once both parties have agreed on terms. Never depend on oral stipulations; written contracts protect both parties from misunderstandings. Watch for clauses that may not be in your best interest, such as "work-for-hire." When you do work-for-hire, you give up all rights to your creations.

Some reputable children's magazines, such as *Highlights for Children*, buy all rights, and many writers and illustrators believe it's worth the concession in order to break into the field. However, once you become more established in the field, it's in your best interest to keep rights

---

Contract Help from Organizations

Writers organizations offer a wealth of information to members, including contract advice:

Society of Children's Book Writers and Illustrators members can find information in the SCBWI publication Answers to Some Questions About Contracts. Contact SCBWI at 8271 Beverly Blvd., Los Angeles CA 90048, (323)782-1010, or visit their website: www.scbwi.org.

The Authors Guild also offers contract tips. Visit their website, www.authorsguild.org. (Members of the guild can receive a 75-point contract review from the guild's legal staff.) See the website for membership information and application form, or contact The Authors Guild at 31 E. 28th St., 10th Floor, New York NY 10016, (212)563-5904. Fax: (212)564-5363. E-mail: staff@authorsguild.org. Website: www.authorsguild.org.

to your work. (Note: magazines such as *Highlights* may return rights after a specified time period, so ask about this possibility when negotiating.)

When negotiating a book deal, find out whether your contract contains an option clause. This clause requires the author to give the publisher a first look at her next work before offering it to other publishers. Though it's editorial etiquette to give the publisher the first chance at publishing your next work, be wary of statements in the contract that could trap you. Don't allow the publisher to consider the next project for more than 30 days and be specific about what type of work should actually be considered "next work." (For example, if the book under contract is a young adult novel, specify that the publisher will receive an exclusive look at only your next young adult novel.)

(For more information about SCBWI, The Authors Guild, and other organizations, turn to the clubs & organizations section.)

Book publishers' payment methods

Book publishers pay authors and artists in royalties, a percentage of either the wholesale or retail price of each book sold. From large publishing houses, the author usually receives an advance issued against future royalties before the book is published. Half of the advance amount is issued upon signing the book contract; the other half is issued when the book is finished. For illustrations, one-third of the advance should be collected upon signing the contract; one-third upon delivery of sketches; and one-third upon delivery of finished art.

After your book has sold enough copies to earn back your advance, you'll start to get royalty checks. Some publishers hold a reserve against returns, which means a percentage of royalties is held back in case books are returned from bookstores. If you have a reserve clause in your contract, find out the exact percentage of total sales that will be withheld and the time period the publisher will hold this money. You should be reimbursed this amount after a reasonable time period, such as a year. Royalty percentages vary with each publisher, but there are standard ranges.

Book publishers' rates

According to the latest figures from the Society of Children's Book Writers and Illustrators, first-time picture book authors can expect advances of $2,000-3,000; first-time picture book illustrators' advances range from $5,000-7,000; text and illustration packages for first-timers can score $6,000-8,000. Rates go up for subsequent books: $3,500-5,000 for picture book text; $7,000-10,000 for picture book illustration; $8,000-10,000 for text and illustration. Experienced authors can expect higher advances. Royalties for picture books are generally about five percent (split between the author and illustrator) but can go as high as ten percent. Those who both write and illustrate a book, of course, receive the full royalty.

Advances for hardcover novels and nonfiction can fetch authors advances of $4,000-6,000 and 10 percent royalties; paperbacks bring in slightly lower advances of $3,000-5,000 and royalties of 6-8 percent.

As you might expect, advance and royalty figures vary from house to house and are affected by the time of year, the state of the economy and other factors. Some smaller houses may not even pay royalties, just flat fees. Educational houses may not offer advances or offer smaller amounts. Religious publishers tend to offer smaller advances than trade publishers. First-time writers and illustrators generally start on the low end of the scale, while established and high-profile writers are paid more.

Pay rates for magazines

For writers, fee structures for magazines are based on a per-word rate or range for a specific article length. Artists and photographers have a few more variables to contend with before contracting their services.

Payment for illustrations and photos can be set by such factors as whether the piece(s) will be black and white or four-color, how many are to be purchased, where the work appears (cover or inside), circulation, and the artist's or photographer's prior experience.

Remaindering

When a book goes out of print, a publisher will sell any existing copies to a wholesaler who, in turn, sells the copies to stores at a discount When the books are "remaindered" to a wholesaler, they are usually sold at a price just above the cost of printing. When negotiating a contract with a publisher you may want to discuss the possibility of purchasing the remaindered copies before they are sold to a wholesaler, then you can market the copies you purchased and still make a profit.

KNOW YOUR RIGHTS

A copyright is a form of protection provided to creators of original works, published or unpublished. In general, copyright protection ensures the writer, illustrator or photographer the power to decide how her work is used and allows her to receive payment for each use.

Essentially, copyright also encourages the creation of new works by guaranteeing the creator power to sell rights to the work in the marketplace. The copyright holder can print, reprint or copy her work; sell or distribute copies of her work; or prepare derivative works such as plays, collages or recordings. The Copyright Law is designed to protect work (created on or after January 1, 1978) for her lifetime plus 50 years.

If you collaborate with someone else on a written or artistic project, the copyright will last for the lifetime of the last survivor plus 50 years. The creators' heirs may hold a copyright for an additional 50 years. After that, the work becomes public domain. Works created anonymously or under a pseudonym are protected for 100 years, or 75 years after publication. Under work-for-hire agreements, you relinquish your copyright to your "employer."

Copyright notice and registration

Some feel a copyright notice should be included on all work, registered or not. Others feel it is not necessary and a copyright notice will only confuse publishers about whether the material is registered (acquiring rights to previously registered material is a more complicated process).

Although it's not necessary to include a copyright notice on unregistered work, if you don't feel your work is safe without the notice, it is your right to include one. Including a copyright notice—© (year of work, your name)—should help safeguard against plagiarism.

Registration is a legal formality intended to make copyright public record, and can help you win more money in a court case. By registering work within three months of publication or before an infringement occurs, you are eligible to collect statutory damages and attorney's fees. If you register later than three months after publication, you will qualify only for actual damages and profits.

Ideas and concepts are not copyrightable, only expressions of those ideas and concepts. A character type or basic plot outline, for example, is not subject to a copyright infringement lawsuit. Also, titles, names, short phrases or slogans, and lists of contents are not subject to copyright protection, though titles and names may be protected through the Trademark Office.

You can register a group of articles, illustrations or photos if it meets these criteria:
- the group is assembled in order, such as in a notebook;
- the works bear a single title, such as "Works by (your name)";
- it is the work of one writer, artist or photographer;
- the material is the subject of a single claim to copyright.

It's a publisher's responsibility to register your book for copyright. If you've previously registered the same material, you must inform your editor and supply the previous copyright information, otherwise, the publisher can't register the book in its published form.

For more information about the proper way to register works and to order the correct forms, contact the U.S. Copyright Office, (202)707-3000. The forms available are TX for writing (books, articles, etc.); VA for pictures (photographs, illustrations); and PA for plays and music. For information about how to use the copyright forms, request a copy of Circular I on Copyright Basics. All of the forms and circulars are free. Send the completed registration form along with the stated fee and a copy of the work to the Copyright Office.

For specific answers to questions about copyright (but not legal advice), call the Copyright Public Information Office at (202)707-3000 weekdays between 8:30 a.m. and 5 p.m. EST. Forms can also be downloaded from the Library of Congress website: www.loc.gov/copyright. The site also includes a list of frequently asked questions, tips on filling out forms, general copyright information, and links to other sites related to copyright issues. For members of SCBWI, information about copyrights and the law is available in their publication: Copyright Facts for Writers.

The rights publishers buy

The copyright law specifies that a writer, illustrator or photographer generally sells one-time rights to her work unless she and the buyer agree otherwise in writing. Many publications will want more exclusive rights to your work than just one-time usage; some will even require you to sell all rights. Be sure you are monetarily compensated for the additional rights you relinquish. If you must give up all rights to a work, carefully consider the price you're being offered to determine whether you'll be compensated for the loss of other potential sales.

Writers who only give up limited rights to their work can then sell reprint rights to other publications, foreign rights to international publications, or even movie rights, should the opportunity arise. Artists and photographers can sell their work to other markets such as paper product companies who may use an image on a calendar, greeting card or mug. Illustrators and photographers may even sell original work after it has been published. And there are now galleries throughout the U.S. that display and sell the original work of children's illustrators.

Rights acquired through the sale of a book manuscript are explained in each publisher's contract. Take time to read relevant clauses to be sure you understand what rights each contract is specifying before signing. Be sure your contract contains a clause allowing all rights to revert back to you in the event the publisher goes out of business. (You may even want to have the contract reviewed by an agent or an attorney specializing in publishing law.)

The following are the rights you'll most often sell to publishers, periodicals and producers in the marketplace:

First rights. The buyer purchases the rights to use the work for the first time in any medium. All other rights remain with the creator. When material is excerpted from a soon-to-be-published book for use in a newspaper or periodical, first serial rights are also purchased.

One-time rights. The buyer has no guarantee that she is the first to use a piece. One-time permission to run written work, illustrations or photos is acquired, then the rights revert back to the creator.

First North American serial rights. This is similar to first rights, except that companies who distribute both in the U.S. and Canada will stipulate these rights to ensure that another North American company won't come out with simultaneous usage of the same work.

Second serial (reprint) rights. In this case newspapers and magazines are granted the right to reproduce a work that has already appeared in another publication. These rights are also purchased by a newspaper or magazine editor who wants to publish part of a book after the book has been published. The proceeds from reprint rights for a book are often split evenly between the author and his publishing company.

Simultaneous rights. More than one publication buys one-time rights to the same work at the same time. Use of such rights occurs among magazines with circulations that don't overlap, such as many religious publications.

All rights. Just as it sounds, the writer, illustrator or photographer relinquishes all rights to a piece—she no longer has any say in who acquires rights to use it. All rights are purchased by publishers who pay premium usage fees, have an exclusive format, or have other book or magazine interests from which the purchased work can generate more mileage. If a company insists on acquiring all rights to your work, see if you can negotiate for the rights to revert back to you after a reasonable period of time. If they agree to such a proposal, get it in writing.

Note: Writers, illustrators and photographers should be wary of "work-for-hire" arrangements. If you sign an agreement stipulating that your work will be done as work-for-hire, you will not control the copyrights of the completed work—the company that hired you will be the copyright owner.

Foreign serial rights. Be sure before you market to foreign publications that you have sold only North American—not worldwide—serial rights to previous markets. If so, you are free to market to publications that may be interested in material that's appeared in a North American-based periodical.

Syndication rights. This is a division of serial rights. For example, if a syndicate prints portions of a book in installments in its newspapers, it would be syndicating second serial rights. The syndicate would receive a commission and leave the remainder to be split between the author and publisher.

Subsidiary rights. These include serial rights, dramatic rights, book club rights or translation rights. The contract should specify what percentage of profits from sales of these rights go to the author and publisher.

Dramatic, television and motion picture rights. During a specified time the interested party tries to sell a story to a producer or director. Many times options are renewed because the selling process can be lengthy.

Display rights or electronic publishing rights. They're also known as "Data, Storage and Retrieval." Usually listed under subsidiary rights, the marketing of electronic rights in this era of rapidly expanding capabilities and markets for electronic material can be tricky. Display rights can cover text or images to be used in a CD-ROM or online, or may cover use of material in formats not even fully developed yet. If a display rights clause is listed in your contract, try to negotiate its elimination. Otherwise, be sure to pin down which electronic rights are being purchased. Demand the clause be restricted to things designed to be read only. By doing this, you maintain your rights to use your work for things such as games and interactive software.

RUNNING YOUR BUSINESS

An important part of being a freelance writer, illustrator or photographer is running your freelance business. It's imperative to maintain accurate business records to determine if you're making a profit as a freelancer. Keeping correct, organized records will also make your life easier as you approach tax time.

When setting up your system, begin by keeping a bank account and ledger for your business finances apart from your personal finances. Also, if writing, illustration or photography is secondary to another freelance career, keep separate business records for each.

You will likely accumulate some business expenses before showing any profit when you start out as a freelancer. To substantiate your income and expenses to the IRS, keep all invoices, cash receipts, sales slips, bank statements, canceled checks and receipts related to travel expenses and entertaining clients. For entertainment expenditures, record the date, place and purpose of the business meeting as well as gas mileage. Keep records for all purchases, big and small— don't take the small purchases for granted; they can add up to a substantial amount. File all receipts in chronological order. Maintaining a separate file for each month simplifies retrieving records at the end of the year.

Record keeping

When setting up a single-entry bookkeeping system, record income and expenses separately. Use some of the subheads that appear on Schedule C (the form used for recording income from a business) of the 1040 tax form so you can easily transfer information onto the tax form when filing your return. In your ledger include a description of each transaction—the date, source of income (or debts from business purchases), description of what was purchased or sold, the amount of the transaction, and whether payment was by cash, check or credit card.

Don't wait until January 1 to start keeping records. The moment you first make a business-related purchase or sell an article, book manuscript, illustration or photo, begin tracking your profits and losses. If you keep records from January 1 to December 31, you're using a calendar-year accounting period. Any other accounting period is called a fiscal year.

There are two types of accounting methods you can choose from—the cash method and the accrual method. The cash method is used more often: you record income when it is received and expenses when they're disbursed.

Using the accrual method, you report income at the time you earn it rather than when it's actually received. Similarly, expenses are recorded at the time they're incurred rather than when you actually pay them. If you choose this method, keep separate records for "accounts receivable" and "accounts payable."

Satisfying the IRS

To successfully—and legally—work as a freelancer, you must know what income you should report and what deductions you can claim. But before you can do that, you must prove to the IRS you're in business to make a profit, that your writing, illustration or photography is not merely a hobby.

The Tax Reform Act of 1986 says you should show a profit for three years out of a five-year period to attain professional status. The IRS considers these factors as proof of your professionalism:

- accurate financial records;
- a business bank account separate from your personal account;
- proven time devoted to your profession;
- whether it's your main or secondary source of income;
- your history of profits and losses;
- the amount of training you have invested in your field;
- your expertise.

If your business is unincorporated, you'll fill out tax information on Schedule C of Form 1040. If you're unsure of what deductions you can take, request the IRS publication containing this information. Under the Tax Reform Act, only 30 percent of business meals, entertainment and related tips, and parking charges are deductible. Other deductible expenses allowed on Schedule C include: car expenses for business-related trips; professional courses and seminars; depreciation of office equipment, such as a computer; dues and publications; and miscellaneous expenses, such as postage used for business needs.

If you're working out of a home office, a portion of your mortgage interest (or rent), related utilities, property taxes, repair costs and depreciation may he deducted as business expenses—under special circumstances. To learn more about the possibility of home office deductions, consult IRS Publication 587, Business Use of Your Home

The method of paying taxes on income not subject to withholding is called "estimated tax" for individuals. If you expect to owe more than $500 at year's end and if the total amount of income tax that will be withheld during the year will be less than 90% of the tax shown on the current year's return, you'll generally make estimated tax payments. Estimated tax payments are made in four equal installments due on April 15, June 15, September 15 and January 15 (assuming you're a calendar-year taxpayer). For more information, request Publication 533, Self-Employment Tax.

The Internal Revenue Service's website (www.irs.ustreas.gov/) offers tips and instant access to IRS forms and publications.

Social Security tax

Depending on your net income as a freelancer, you may be liable for a Social Security tax. This is a tax designed for those who don't have Social Security withheld from their paychecks. You're liable if your net income is $400 or more per year. Net income is the difference between your income and allowable business deductions. Request Schedule SE, Computation of Social Security Self-Employment Tax, if you qualify.

If completing your income tax return proves to be too complex, consider hiring an accountant (the fee is a deductible business expense) or contact the IRS for assistance (look in the White Pages under U.S. Government—Internal Revenue Service or check their website, www.irs.ustrea s.gov/). In addition to numerous publications to instruct you in various facets of preparing a tax return, the IRS also has walk-in centers in some cities.

Insurance

As a self-employed professional be aware of what health and business insurance coverage is available to you. Unless you're a Canadian who is covered by national health insurance or a full-time freelancer covered by your spouse's policy, health insurance will no doubt be one of your biggest expenses. Under the terms of a 1985 government act (COBRA), if you leave a job with health benefits, you're entitled to continue that coverage for up to 18 months—you pay 100 percent of the premium and sometimes a small administration fee. Eventually, you must search for your own health plan. You may also need disability and life insurance. Disability insurance is offered through many private insurance companies and state governments. This insurance pays a monthly fee that covers living and business expenses during periods of long-term recuperation from a health problem. The amount of money paid is based on the recipient's annual earnings.

Before contacting any insurance representative, talk to other writers, illustrators or photographers to learn which insurance companies they recommend. If you belong to a writers' or artists' organization, ask the organization if it offers insurance coverage for professionals. (SCBWI has a plan available. Look through the Clubs & Organizations section for other groups that may offer coverage.) Group coverage may be more affordable and provide more comprehensive coverage than an individual policy.

Contract Savvy for Writers & Illustrators

BY DARCY PATTISON

Ring! Ring!

You answer the phone and the most amazing thing happens: You are offered a contract on your first book! What do you answer when the editor says, "Do these terms sound reasonable?"

Do yourself a favor and say, "Yes! I want to work with you, but I'm too excited to think straight right now. Let me write down these details and get back to you tomorrow."

YOU HAVE OPTIONS

Contract savvy begins with the idea that you have options.

Your first option is that you have time. Signing a publishing contract is a complicated process that you don't want to rush into: The contract you sign will govern all dealings with the publisher about this book from now on. It's too important to be impulsive about it; instead, be professional. The decision to publish your book has taken a great deal of time and thought; editors will respect that you need time to consider a contract.

Negotiating the contract

Your second option regards how you will approach the contract process: by yourself, with the guidance of a literary lawyer, or with an agent.

On your own: Many authors want to handle every aspect of their publishing career, including contracts. The main advantage of handling contracts yourself is that you will be in control: that's great if you're successful, frustrating if you aren't. But it's a conscious choice.

If you fall into this category, you need to learn everything you can about contracts. Study model contracts which are available from several authors' organizations or in books. (See sidebar on page 22.) After looking at just a few contracts, you'll see that each publisher words things slightly differently, but overall the clauses are similar. By the time you read about contracts and study model contracts, you'll start to understand what is negotiable.

In addition to studying contracts, you should read some basic business books about negotiations. Contracts are often a matter of give and take: I'll agree to world rights instead of North American rights if the advance can be increased by this much. You'll need to give reasons for your requests; learn to listen to what the editor is saying in response. Learn when to stand firm and when to agree.

One disadvantage of negotiating a contract yourself is that you begin with a boilerplate (standard) contract; literary agencies begin with the basic contract that the agency uses with that publisher, which is always a better beginning point. You can overcome this, especially if you work with the publisher on successive books, but it is something to consider when deciding how to approach a contract.

DARCY PATTISON *is the author of* The Wayfinder *(Greenwillow), which will be available in paperback in 2002. She'll have two books released in 2002—*The Journey of Oliver K. Woodman, *illustrated by Joe Cepeda (Harcourt) and* How Healthy Is Your Environment, *co-authored with Elleen Hutcheson (Millbrook). Visit her website www.darcypattison.com to read her essay about writing* The Wayfinder.

Sources of Information

Recommended Books

Guide to Literary Agents. Yearly publication listing contact information and agent's preferences.

Literary Market Place. A comprehensive guide to the publishing industry, including contact information and an alphabetized list of people working in publishing. Some information is provided free on their website: www.literarymarketplace.com.

Kirsch's Guide to the Book Contract, by Jonathan Kirsch; *Kirsch's Handbook of Publishing Law,* by Jonathan Kirsch. Good references with breakdown of clauses and a model contract.

Negotiating a Book Contract: A Guide for Authors, Agents and Lawyers, by Mark L. Levine. Good reference on contract basics.

Model Trade Book Contract and Guide, Including Electronic Rights Clauses, by the Author's Guild, Inc. This guide, which is free to members of the Author's Guild ($90 for non-members), gives a model contract, explanation of each clause, and recommendations for negotiations.

Writer's organizations

Author's Guild, Inc., www.authorsguild.org

The Author's Guild offers two services related to contracts. First, staff lawyers will review your contract and recommend changes. Second, they provide free to members their publication, *Model Trade Book Contract and Guide, Including Electronic Rights Clauses.*

Society of Children's Book Writers and Illustrators, www.scbwi.org

Members receive free *The SCBWI Publications Guide to Writing and Illustration for Children,* which includes articles about contracts and agents. Will recommend literary lawyers.

Science Fiction and Fantasy Writers of America, www.sfwa.org

SFWA offers a Handbook with several articles on contracts and negotiations. Resources on their website include model contracts for various formats and position statements on electronic rights. The SFWA maintains the "Preditors and Editors Website" which lists agents and "dares to give negative recommendations." www.sfwa.org/prededitors/pubagent.htm

The Association of Authors' Representatives, Inc., P.O. Box 237201, Ansonia Station, New York, NY 10003, www.publishersweekly.com/aar/

AAR, a not-for-profit organization of independent literary and dramatic agents, is the only monitoring group for literary agents. Members can't charge reading fees and must maintain standards of accounting. Their website has a membership list, Canon of Ethics to which their members adhere, and a list of questions to ask agents before contracting with them.

American Society of Journalists and Authors, www.asja.org/cw/cwjoin.php

The "leading organization of nonfiction writers." ASJA offers a free e-mail newsletter, *Contracts Watch,* which covers mostly contract issues for periodicals or non-fiction book publishers. See their website for an interesting series of position papers about electronic rights and other contract issues.

Using a literary lawyer: Many authors feel that their job is the creative part of publishing and they turn to lawyers for help with legal issues, including contracts. Your local lawyer is unlikely to have direct experience with the ins and outs of this type of contract: You need a literary lawyer who specializes in literary contracts. Check with various writer's groups for recommendations. A literary lawyer either just reviews the contract and suggests changes, or can negotiate the contract for you.

The advantages of this strategy are that you get expert advice and your financial costs are limited to a one-time fee. However, you don't get the ongoing advocacy of an agent.

Using an agent: When authors think of getting help with their careers, an agent is often the first place they turn. A literary lawyer helps with the legal aspects of publishing; an agent often helps with the legal and business aspects, as well as advising you about your career in general.

Agents act as matchmakers: Your story gets hooked up with an editor who loves it. Once the match is made, they read every single word of a contract. Good agents know which clauses can be negotiated with each publisher and will work to get you better terms. (First contracts are unlikely to be much larger advances, but other clauses can be improved.) Agents typically charge 15 percent commission on domestic sales and more on foreign sales because they have to split the commission with a foreign agent.

In addition to matchmaking and contract negotiations, some agents can help manage your career. They advise you which of your ideas is most lucrative, help arrange publicity, and generally act as your advocate. For help in choosing an agent, get recommendations from a friend, ask writer's organizations for a list of those who specialize in your area, and ask if the agent is a member of the Association of Authors' Representatives (AAR), which sets professional standards for their members. Also see the Agents & Art Reps section on page 284, or consult the most current edition of *Guide to Literary Agents* (Writer's Digest Books).

Can you "sell" your book, then bring in an agent? Yes, but then your response to the initial offer should be something like this: "Wow! I'm excited and I want to work with you. But I've been thinking about using an agent, and I'd like a week or ten days to work that out."

One disadvantage of agents is that they receive a percentage commission of the advance, the royalties, and any other monies—forever. If your book sells extremely well, you will always be splitting the profit with your agent. On the advantage side of the ledger is the knowledge that your agent will be your ongoing advocate with the publisher in any and all disputes.

CLAUSES, CLAUSES, CLAUSES

Your third option is negotiating clauses. Many of the confusing clauses in a contract are negotiable! These are the clauses of a typical contract, along with common changes requested by authors. The list is not all-inclusive: If you are negotiating a contract yourself, you'll want to search for other options as well.

Preamble: Gives the date, the parties involved in the agreement, and the work involved.

Grant of Rights: Specifies which rights the author is granting to the publisher.

Delivery of Works: Specifies dates for delivery of manuscript in various stages, and what other materials must be delivered such as photographs or permissions.

> *Negotiation Point:* If your book requires photographs, permissions, or other expensive materials, try to negotiate a budget to pay for these. Otherwise, you must pay for them out of your own pocket.

Author's Bill of Rights

In 2000, several writer's groups banded together to create a document that lists the Author's Bill of Rights. Groups included the Romance Writers of America, American Society of Journalists and Authors, Author's Guild, Western Writers of America, Sisters in Crime, Society of Science Fiction and Fantasy Writers, and Novelist, Inc.

The preamble begins:

"Authors of books shall have certain inalienable rights when their books are published, foremost among them the right to negotiate their contract in good faith. . . ."

The first draft of this Bill of Rights can be read online at www.sfwa.org/contracts/bor1.htm

Termination of Contract: Covers the conditions under which the contract can be terminated, including an unacceptable manuscript.

> *Negotiation Point:* Typical clauses allow publishers to terminate the contract if the manuscript is "unacceptable." The publisher should specify in writing what is unacceptable and allow the author a reasonable time to correct the work.

Warranties and Indemnities: Publisher asks you to state that you are the author of this work. Governs how lawsuits will be handled should problems arise.

> *Negotiation Point:* Publisher should include the author in their insurance protection against lawsuits.

Copyediting, Proofreading, and Correction of Proof: Specifies how and when copyediting, proofreading, and correction of proof will occur.

Options: The publisher is granted the option to your next work.

> *Negotiation Point:* Remove this clause when possible. The time frame for exercising the option should begin when a manuscript is submitted, not when the current book is published. For example, a picture book may not be published for two years. If the option begins when the current book is published, you can't submit elsewhere for those two years. Limit the option to similar books, and put time limits on the publisher. See sidebar for an alternate viewpoint.

Publication: Publisher agrees to publish the work in a specified form and within certain time limits.

> *Negotiation Point:* Specify the time limit for publication. For picture books, the illustrator's work schedule may mean a long wait. Sometimes, authors specify details of the published book. Promotion and advertising budgets can also be specified.

Advances: Specifies the amount of an advance and delivery schedule.

> *Negotiation Point:* Make sure the advances do not have to be repaid for any reason except non-delivery of a manuscript. Many books never earn out the advance, so authors try to obtain the largest advance possible, knowing that it may be the only money they receive for the work.

Royalties: Specifies the royalty schedule for various versions of the work.

> *Negotiation Point:* Royalties should be based on retail price, not wholesale price (or net receipts). Some authors are able to obtain an escalation of royalties, which means that when a certain number of books are sold, the royalty schedule increases. Typical royalties for children's hardcover is 10 percent on the first 10,000 copies, 12½ percent on the next 10,000 copies, and 15 percent on all copies in excess of 20,000. If the work is a picture book, the author and illustrator will split the royalties: 5 percent, 6.25 percent, and 7.5 percent. Paperback royalties are about half of those numbers.

First Serial Right: Specifies if an author retains these rights or grants to the publisher.

Subsidiary Rights-Print: Specifies publisher's rights and responsibilities in licensing the work to book clubs, paperback editions, abridgments, condensations, magazines, etc.

Subsidiary Rights-Non-Print: Specifies publisher's rights and responsibilities in licensing the work for dramatic, motion picture, television, audio, live theater, video games, toys, calendar, etc.

> *Negotiation Point:* Consult various model contracts for recommended percentages of division of income between the author and the publisher. In general, the author should be receiving more than the publisher.

Subsidiary Rights-Electronic: Specifies publisher's rights and responsibilities in re-issuing the work in an electronic format.

> *Negotiation Point:* Hotly debated for the last five years, this clause appears in a variety of forms. Consult various model contracts for recommendations. Avoid giving the publisher rights to "all other electronic technologies and formats, whether now existing or developed in the future."

Foreign Licenses: Specifies publisher's rights and responsibilities in licensing the work to foreign publishers.

Use of Author's Name and Likeness: Grants and/or limits the publisher's use of author's name and likeness in publicity.

Accounting and Payments: Provides procedures and time schedules for accounting and payment of monies due under the contract.

> *Negotiation Points:* Avoid "basket accounting" (also called joint accounting or cross-collateralization). Some contracts tie royalties and moneys for this contract to any other contract with wording like, "or under other contract with the publisher." These phrases, either in this clause or in the royalty clause, should be deleted.

Also, ask for a "pass through" clause for any subsidiary rights payments. This means that if your royalties have earned out, the money will be "passed on" to you within 30 days (or time period you specify) after receipt by the publisher.

More Options

Option to Accept Contract as Offered:
Vicki Grove, author of nine books, all published with Putnam:
"Let me play Devil's advocate a second. There's something, I believe, to be said in favor of not rocking the boat. I'm working under my ninth contract from Putnam, and I've never asked for a single contract change. I know some other writers have gotten higher advances, I know some like the option clause taken out, I know some like to reserve foreign rights to themselves, etc. But you do show some trust in and loyalty to the company by just plain saying "thanks," taking the ball they hand you, and running with it. I honestly think things have worked out better for me this way, by being loyal, by not asking for advances higher than they offer, by letting them do the rights haggling, by letting them assume that their faith shown in me by giving me an option clause will be repaid by my giving them that first look. Some will say I'm stupid, but I have friends who envy the relationship I've got with Putnam, and I think I've built that partly by picking my fights very, very carefully. Editorial fights, not marketing and contract ones."

Option to Choose Differently for Each Contract Offer:
Brenda Shannon Yee, author of two picture books.
"My first contract negotiation was less than ideal. I joined the Author's Guild so their lawyer could review my contract. But I handled the negotiations. Not only did none of the clauses get changed, I felt uncomfortable. Although I believe publishers and editors are honest, I wanted to 'level the playing field.' I researched and found three prospective contracts lawyers who handled children's books, then interviewed them by phone. I chose Mary Flowers, who became my advocate. Mary explained what clauses were appropriately negotiable for a new author with the house. Because of her experience, she knew what were standard terms for the industry as well as the publisher's boiler plate contract. I intend to hire Mary again when the opportunity arises."

Author's Copies: Specifies the number of free copies the author will receive.

> *Negotiation Point:* We all want as many free copies as possible. But realistically, the publisher can't give away copies, even to the author. Ask for more, but be content with what you can get.

Revised Edition Clause: Specifies how the publisher will handle a revision of a work. (Especially used in updating textbooks or books that need constant updating.)

Out of Print Provision: Specifies conditions under which a book is considered out of print.

Return of Manuscript: Specifies time frame and conditions for return of original manuscript.

Bankruptcy and Liquidation: Provides procedures for dealing with the publisher in case of bankruptcy or liquidation.

Suits for Infringement: Deals with dividing any money resulting from an infringement suit.

Governing Law: Specifies the state law which shall have jurisdiction in case of legal proceedings.

Successors and Assigns: Assures that if your publisher is bought out, the new publisher will be bound by this contract.

Waiver or Modification: Confirms that this contract is complete and binding.

Notices: Specifies that if any legal proceedings take place, there should be proper notification.

Agency Clause: If your agent negotiates the contract, they will include this clause which names the agent/agency as the receiver of monies, which the agent will then forward to the author.

Non-Compete Clause: Some publishers ask for a non-compete clause which specifies that you won't participate in any project that will compete with this work.

> *Negotiation Point:* Delete this if possible. If the publisher won't delete this, then make it as specific as possible: another early reader about Benjamin Franklin. That would still allow you to sell a picture book biography about Franklin.

Contracts are tricky; contracts are important. Whatever option you choose for negotiating your contract, you should continually be educating yourself about the clauses that govern your relationship with a publisher.

Self-Promotion for Illustrators

BY PHYLLIS POLLEMA-CAHILL

About five years ago I was laid-off my job as a graphic designer and decided to finally try pursuing my dream of illustrating for children. The first few jobless months I spent in preparing my portfolio, database and marketing materials. I really didn't know how my work would be received by children's publishers. I had heard it was a tough market to break into and I needed to either make a living at it or find another job.

After my first promotional mailing a few assignments trickled in. Thankfully, with continued marketing efforts, I developed some regular clients and work became more plentiful. In the third year I had so much work I was in my studio 60-70 hours a week. That's not a lifestyle I savor either, so I had to start turning away work. I've been fortunate enough to have enough work to choose my assignments ever since.

THE WORK & THE PORTFOLIO

When I decided to enter this field, I took an objective look at the portfolio pieces I had and realized I needed a fresh start. I had an art school portfolio and a commercial illustration portfolio and neither were going to do the job. I needed a portfolio that applied to *this* market. I read all I could find on children's publishing and learned that a good children's illustration portfolio should contain images of children of different ages and ethnicities in action and showing emotion. Animals are another popular subject. It's also good to show different settings—a cityscape, a landscape or a classroom, for example and to show adults in the proper proportion to children.

Illustrations should tell a story. In my search for good stories to illustrate for my new portfolio, I avoided well-known fairy tales or folk tales, because I can imagine how tired art buyers, whether editor or art director, get of seeing yet another *Three Little Pigs*. I started looking in back issues of children's magazines and found some gems. You can also write stories of your own. Somehow the emotional energy from a story you really like helps bring the illustrations to life. Try to find or write a story with action and drama, in order to avoid too many illustrations of kids sitting, standing or posing for an imaginary camera. Make the kids look alive, do something fresh, use a different perspective. Show you know to allow space for text.

It's also very desirable to show that you can keep a character looking consistent throughout two or three illustrations. Not everyone can do this well, and it needs to be done well in picture books. Samples in color, black and white halftone, and black and white line are good, but if your strength isn't in black and white line, don't include any samples.

Something I didn't learn from my reading was that if an art buyer is looking for an illustrator for a chicken story, they'll most likely be looking for illustration samples of chickens. It seems obvious now that they'd feel more comfortable knowing what they'll get beforehand. On the same hand, if you don't like to draw bicycles, never include one in your samples because, sure enough, you'll get a call to illustrate a dozen of them.

In your portfolio, keep your presentation clean and try to put only one large image per

PHYLLIS POLLEMA-CAHILL *lives in Colorado with her husband and two cats. She's been illustrating for children full-time for more than five years and recently finished her eighteenth picture book. Some of her clients include* Highlights for Children, Jack & Jill, *McGraw-Hill, Scott Foresman/Addison-Wesley, The Wright Group, and Star Bright Books. Her work can be seen at www.phylliscahill.com.*

Phyllis Pollema-Cahill sends mailings that appeal to a diverse roster of potential clients. As direct mail has spawned the most assignments for her, she says an 8½ × 11 introductory packet, including color printouts such as these, will grab the attention of an art director if the images are "eye-catching and appropriate to that publisher."

portfolio page. Don't go overboard with images, 10-15 are plenty. Replace the huge, black vinyl portfolio of art school days with a smaller, more professional one.

You might want to develop a logo. I created one which I put on my stationery and marketing pieces, and art buyers have remarked that they remembered it.

"How many styles?" is a question that each artist has to answer for themselves. I prefer one style because I believe it's easier for an art buyer to remember me. Using one style frees me to put my effort into other aspects of the illustration, rather than technique. If you like working in multiple styles, create different portfolios or separate one portfolio into different sections. This works very well for many artists.

CREATING A DATABASE

It's very important to study the children's publishing market. It takes time, but it's time well spent. To keep track of all the market information I was gathering, I created my own database using MyMailList software. It was about $30 at Office Depot. There are many others available, such as FileMaker Pro. You may already have software that performs the same functions.

I use my database software to print personalized letters and mailing labels and to keep track of publishing house addresses, URLs, editor and art director names, phone numbers and the type of materials they publish. I also keep track of samples I've sent and any responses my mailings receive. I categorize publishers by who seems most likely to use work similar to mine. With the sorting feature, for example, I can call up all the educational publishers in California who've responded positively to my work in the last three years and send them a new sample. I love sorting; it's like magic.

Creating your own database, rather than buying a mailing list, helps you keep up with the ever-changing marketplace. You can customize a database to your needs and make it as simple or complex as you'd like. Most importantly, you don't appear uninformed by sending inappropriate submissions or not knowing what you've already sent. Knowing the market and targeting your

As the Web becomes more popular among art directors and editors in search of fresh talent, says Phyllis Pollema-Cahill, your marketing efforts should be more expansive. Direct and thorough, her homepage includes everything the site visitor needs to know, including the various subjects she has illustrated.

mailings helps keep the slush pile down, which makes art buyers' lives easier, gives them more time to look at our submissions, and saves trees.

I gathered information for my database from *Children's Writer's & Illustrator's Market* and by sending for catalogs and sample issues of magazines. Going to the bookstore or library to see who's publishing what is another way to choose the publishers you'd like to target. I also subscribe to *Children's Book Insider* newsletter for updates to *Children's Writer's & Illustrator's Market*. The SCBWI newsletter and *Children's Writer* newsletter also contain good market information. If you want even more data, *Literary Market Place* (known as LMP) is a huge library reference which contains information on all types of publishers. In sending for catalogs, I also requested art guidelines, though they seem very similar from publisher to publisher. Art guidelines basically ask that you don't send samples larger than 8½ × 11 and NEVER send originals.

DIRECT MAIL

I'd like to cover several marketing methods in the order that they've been most effective for me. You may find that a marketing method that only works moderately well for me will work incredibly well for you. The important thing is to get your best samples into the hands of receptive art buyers. Direct mail has generated the most assignments for me. When first contacting a publisher, I send out an 8½ × 11 introductory packet. It includes about five images, a very brief cover letter, a stamped reply card and a large SASE with appropriate postage for the return of my samples, in case the publisher isn't interested in my work. Of course they're more than welcome to keep the samples, and I mention this in my cover letter. Some illustrators don't include an SASE, but I prefer to learn which art buyers aren't interested so I can note it in my database and save myself time and postage by not sending them future mailings.

A self-addressed, stamped reply postcard has been very helpful to me in getting feedback. I make it as easy as possible for the art buyer by putting checkboxes in front of brief statements such as:

☐ I like your illustration samples.
☐ Please send me a full portfolio.
☐ I'll keep your samples on file.
☐ Please send me new samples periodically.
☐ I'm returning your samples, they're not appropriate for our current needs.

Direct Mail Misconceptions

There's something to be said about plunging into a career head-on with enthusiasm. But when successful illustrators look back on the beginnings of their careers they invariably wish they could have been a little more prepared for the realities of the market place. There are some common misconceptions about marketing illustrators should be aware of. Here's a list of traps to avoid as you start your direct mail campaign.

1. *The "I'll change their mind" misconception.* If a publication doesn't use the type of illustration I do they'll see my work, fall in love with it and change their mind. It's very unlikely this will happen.

2. *The "savior" misconception.* A publication would really benefit from my help. I could "save" them from mediocre art. That may be true, but chances are they just don't have the budget to pay for higher-quality art.

3. *The "shotgun" misconception.* I'll send my samples to everyone and see which ones stick. It's so much better to save your postage and concentrate your efforts on sending samples to those publications for whom your work is really appropriate. When there are huge slush piles it hurts us all.

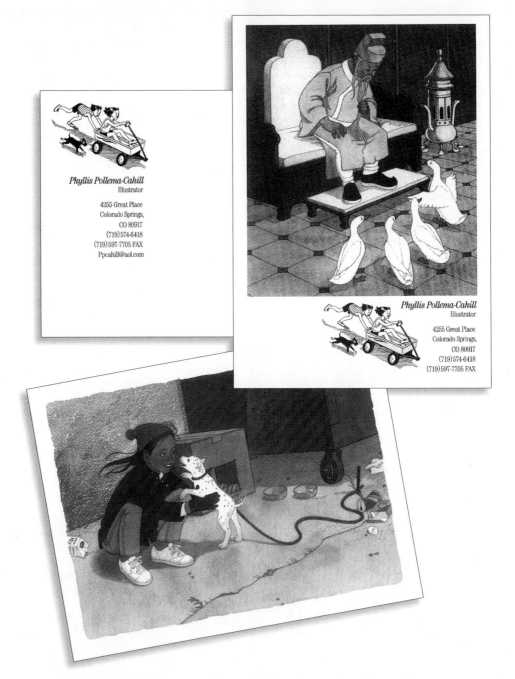

"Consistency and recognizability in your mailers will make them more memorable," says Phyllis Pollema-Cahill. Whether sending color, black and white halftone, or simply black and white line, it's important to be inventive and present your talent professionally. With these postcards, Pollema-Cahill proves she can create characters of different ethnicities in distinct settings. And she offers clear contact information.

It's best to avoid cleverness in reply cards and cover letters because you don't know how it will be received by an art buyer. Be professional and you can't go wrong.

I also adhere a mailing label to the reply postcard, with the art buyer's name, title and address so I'll know who returned the card. Below it I include the sentence, "If this mailing label is incorrect, could you please write in the correct information?" I also include a few blank lines on which they can write comments. Many art buyers do correct the mailing label or write a brief note.

A résumé isn't really necessary in a mailing, but you can include it. A brief paragraph in your cover letter about yourself and your work might be more readable. Of course, the most important element in a mailing is your illustrations. Only send your very best samples, not those you have doubts about.

When preparing a mailing, it's most enlightening to put yourself in the place of an art buyer. They may have a 12-foot-tall stack of mailings from illustrators that has accumulated in their office while they've been busy with other aspects of their job. When they do find time to attack the pile, each submission may get three to five seconds of their attention. Your samples have to stand on their own because you won't be there to explain anything. Make sure they're eye-catching and appropriate to that publisher. Show you've done your homework. Many samples go directly in the trash because the artist didn't take the time to learn what kind of art the publisher buys.

In my experience it can take anywhere from a week to four years (seriously) to get a reply card or samples back. Most publishers seem to take about three months. No response doesn't necessarily mean they don't like your work or haven't kept it. I've gotten calls with assignments from publishers I had assumed weren't interested.

What to send and when

You can send color copies of your samples. I prefer Canon color copiers for their accurate color reproduction. Modern Postcard will print 500 full-color postcards for only $95. Color printouts from a quality ink-jet printer will work. Epson is a brand of color printer that many illustrators use. Art buyers understand the limitations of color copiers and printers, but do your best to send accurate reproductions of your work. Be sure to label every sample with your name and contact info. You don't want your sample to be the one an art buyer likes, but they don't recall who sent it and it's not labeled.

If you buy an ad in a sourcebook (more about them later) you'll also get a box of additional copies called tearsheets. These make great direct mail pieces. Magazines will also send you a few tearsheets of assignments you've done. You can make additional color copies of these to have a quantity to mail.

Some artists do more elaborate pieces that are cut, folded or glued. I prefer promotions that are quick, simple, cost-effective and that emphasize the image rather than the presentation. I'd avoid sending gifts like chocolates, T-shirts or tea bags with your samples in the hope that they'll make your mailing stand out. They may, but not necessarily in a positive way.

When to send samples? It depends on your work flow. A quarterly postcard seems to work well. Once a year it's good to send updated samples to publishers who keep your work on file. Repetition of your name over time will help art buyers remember you, but don't send them the same illustration over and over.

REFERRALS, WHO YOU KNOW, NETWORKING

Children's publishing is a small world. It helps to make as many connections as you can. Get to know children's writers and other illustrators. You never know who might give you a recommendation. Go to conferences and workshops and meet art buyers in person. SCBWI puts on conferences around the world.

There are also conferences hosted by the American Library Association, the American Bookseller Association and the International Reading Association. BookExpo, Bologna Children's Book Fair, Kindling Words and Keene Children's Literature Festival are also events for those in the children's book field.

It applies to illustration too—one of the best advertisements is word-of-mouth from satisfied clients. Keep your clients happy, meet your deadlines, and be cooperative. Stand up for yourself when appropriate, but don't throw a fit if your art is criticized or if minor corrections are requested. Make sure your final art for an assignment looks like your samples. If you find the style you've chosen is too time-consuming, don't switch styles without the knowledge of the art buyer. Keep the lines of communication open. There's nothing more positive than one art buyer recommending you to another art buyer.

PORTFOLIO CRITIQUES & DISPLAYS

Often portfolio critiques or displays are part of a conference. I'd participate in them whenever possible. They can be a good opportunity to make contact with an art buyer and get feedback on your work. Plus, you never know who might see your work and remember you. Be sure to bring sample pieces that art buyers can take and that you can give to people you meet. Take every opportunity to show your work.

AGENTS & ART REPS

Connecting with the right agent or rep can be wonderful for your career. Making that connection isn't always easy, nor does it always happen on the first try. Agents do have advantages to offer illustrators. They have connections that might be difficult for most illustrators to make and maintain. Because they have established relationships with art buyers, they can more easily get your work in front of them. Art buyers know that represented artists have met an agent's criteria. Agents usually get reduced rates on sourcebook ads and the cost savings is passed on to their illustrators. A good agent should know the marketplace, how to best market your work, and be able to negotiate fair pricing and contracts for you. These are skills artists can (and should) develop themselves, but if you prefer to spend your time illustrating, an agent can free you up to do that.

Getting an agent is not always the quickest route to marketing success—there are disadvantages. A good agent can be very difficult to find. The best have full stables and are very particular about who they represent. It's also practical for them to represent artists who'll make them money, or they'll soon be out of business. Some agents may sign you on, but not get you any work. Worst of all is an agent whose actions reflect badly on you. The 25-30 percent commission for an illustration agent (literary agents take less) can be substantial. Hopefully they earn their commission by freeing up your time and by negotiating higher fees. You may not like the possible loss of control over your own marketing. If you're thinking of going the agent route, choose carefully. Don't be afraid to ask for references. Also ask other illustrators what they may know about the agent you're considering.

SOURCEBOOKS

Sourcebooks are full-color books in which illustrators buy ads. These books are then distributed to art buyers. They can reach a large audience you may not be able to connect with through other means. Art buyers usually save sourcebooks, so they may have a longer shelf life than individual samples.

I don't think anyone can predict whether a sourcebook will work for you or not. You just have to try it and see. Before you buy an ad, learn as much as you can about the particular sourcebook. Request a copy and evaluate its distribution. You may get lost among all the other illustrators. There's a chance your ad may not work at all. Even though you'd be out a lot of money, the tearsheets can be used for direct mail.

I've had good success with *Picturebook*. It's a sourcebook targeted to the children's book market. Check out their site at www.picture-book.com for rates and a lot more great information.

THE WEB

More and more illustrators are getting their own websites. I have two—one which I created and maintain myself and one with an online portfolio. My sites aren't my most effective marketing tool, but I think as modem speeds increase and the Web becomes a more popular method of searching for new talent, they will become more helpful.

I include the URL of the site I maintain on my marketing materials. If an art buyer is interested in my work, they can go online and see my portfolio in a matter of minutes. They can also learn how I work, who my clients are and more.

At first I was reluctant to learn web page building and decided to have someone else do it for me—thus the creation of my online portfolio web page. There are several online portfolio sites. Some charge more than others. The quantity of artists can be a draw to art buyers because it offers a kind of one-stop-shopping. Agents and sourcebooks now have sites too.

If you learn web page building, you can control your own site, which is a definite advantage. I use Quark and Adobe Illustrator software, so when I bought Adobe Pagemill to build web pages I found it quite easy to use. Having a personal website allows you to show many samples and change them whenever you'd like without paying a fee for someone else to do it. You can include more information about yourself. It's a good investment to buy your own domain name. It gives you a URL that's short and easy to remember and it seems more professional. There are several sites and search engines to which you can link your site, such as scbwi.org, picture-book.com and yahoo.com.

THE NEW YORK TRIP

Since so many trade publishers are located in New York City, some children's illustrators go there to show their portfolios. I made the trip about three years ago. Visiting New York gives you face-to-face contact with art buyers, which is very valuable. I know some artists who have been offered book assignments while showing their portfolios. Though it's a very exciting place to visit, it is an expensive way to see only a handful of art buyers. Because of the quantity of artists and the busy schedules of art buyers, many publishing houses now only allow portfolio drop-offs. My trip was quite an experience so I wrote an article about it, which is on my site at www.phylliscahill.com/faq/faq.html.

BOOK DUMMIES

Some illustrators write their own stories, make them into book dummies and market them. I haven't tried this yet because it seems like such a large amount of time to invest in a speculative project. If you want to do a book dummy on spec, I'd suggest doing rough sketches throughout and only do final art for one or two pages. Chances are great that what you submit will be changed. With your dummy you should include a typewritten manuscript, formatted according to manuscript guidelines, and an SASE with the appropriate postage.

If writing isn't your strength, seek help. It takes a lot of skill and talent to write a good children's book. There are many how-to books on the subject. Read them and practice writing. Get critiques and consider enrolling in a writing for children course.

CONTESTS

Another way to get your work noticed is to win contests, for example the SCBWI Magazine Merit Award contest. For a large listing of contests see the Contest & Awards section of this book.

ELEMENTS OF SUCCESS

As an overview, there are several things I believe help illustrators succeed in children's publishing. The most important is a good knowledge of the market. Another is the awareness that art buyers like to see samples similar to what they need. Directing your focus totally on your goal of illustrating for children, even for only an hour a day, will make a difference.

Consistency and recognizability in your mailers will make them more memorable. And, of course, the four "P's": persistence, patience, professionalism and postage.

On my site, at www.phylliscahill.com/greatsites/sites.html, you'll find listings of online portfolios, agents, sourcebooks, conference sites, critique services and more.

Helpful Marketing Books

The following books offer tips, advice, and ideas for marketing your artwork.

Children's Writer's & Illustrator's Market, Writer's Digest Books, (Published annually in November). Read the back issues for good articles.

The Graphic Artist's Guide to Marketing and Self-Promotion, by Sally Prince Davis, North Light Books, 1991. Contains a lot of tricky promotional ideas.

Creative Self-Promotion on a Limited Budget, also by Sally Davis, North Light Books, 1992. More tricky ideas.

The Barnes & Noble Guide to Children's Books. An inexpensive overview of children's books in print.

How to Write and Illustrate Children's Books and Get Them Published, by Treld Bicknell and Felicity Trottman, North Light Books, 1988. Contains a small section on marketing and portfolio preparation.

Are E-Books an E-Z Sale?

BY LINDA JOY SINGLETON

My experience as an e-book author began with a trip to a historical castle during the last century (April 1999, to be exact). I attended a writing conference held in Manresa Castle, in Port Townsend, Washington. In this setting from the past, I heard wondrous tales of futuristic paperless books and illuminated devices that turn pages with the push of a button. Fascinated, I longed to join this pioneer world of publishing.

So I journeyed to my computer and submitted two young adult magical romances to Hard Shell (www.hardshell.com). These books had sold to a print publisher, only to be canceled a few months before their publication date. Fortunately, I'd gotten the rights back and was free to sell them again.

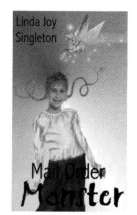

While I waited to hear from Hard Shell, I learned New Concepts Publishing was interested in middle grade books, so I sent them two humorous novels: *Mail-Order Monster* (about a monstrous delivery from Specialty Fiends) and *Melissa's Mission Impossible* (a gold medallion plus a historical Spanish mission equals mystery!).

New Concepts responded first. Unlike print publishers' modus operandi, I didn't receive The Call. Instead I had an e-mail saying my books were in the "contract pending" file. Contract! That meant a sale! Months later, I was e-mailed the contracts. My first two e-books, *Mail-Order Monster* and *Melissa's Mission Impossible* were 2001 releases from New Concepts Publishing.

While the e-book market offers exciting opportunities, there are also risks. Lynne Hansen (www.LynneHansen.com), author of *The Return*, a YA e-book, points out some issues to keep in mind when considering e-publishing:

- E-publishing is a much easier sale for cross-genre works because the low initial material costs make an e-publisher more likely to take on a book that's not easily categorized.
- Independent e-publishers come and go quickly, like most e-businesses. When one goes under, the market is flooded with books looking for new homes.
- Authors have to be very willing to promote their e-books. The initial sale might be easier, but if you're not out there spreading the word, you won't see good sales figures.

Submitting to e-publishers is slightly different than submitting to print publishers—e-publishers want e-mail submissions, whereas most print publishers will not accept manuscript submissions through e-mail. In some cases e-publishers respond quickly, and the publishing process can be swift. However, some e-publishers are backlogged with submissions, and the response time can be just as long as with print publishers, if not longer.

E-books are published in all juvenile genres, from picture books to young adult novels. For the real scoop on e-publishing, I talked to three e-book authors with a variety of experiences.

LINDA JOY SINGLETON *is the author of more than twenty-five middle grade and young adult books, including Berkley's mystery series about teen clones, Regeneration (under L.J. Singleton), two midgrade e-books, and two YA e-books in the works. She lives near Sacramento, California, and works as a full-time author. For e-book news, fan letters, covers, excerpts, writing tips and more, see her website, www.ljsingleton.com.*

Dotti Enderle is an award-winning writer and storyteller who draws on her warm and adventurous childhood growing up in Texas to shape her stories. She has published numerous children's stories and poems over the last seven years. Her picture e-book, *Making Cents*, is available through Kudlicka Publishing (www.kudlickapublishing.com). Enderle chose to explore e-publishing "to experiment. It's in its early stages and I wanted to get in on the ground floor," she says. (Read more about her at www.ourcreativespace.com/dottienderle.)

After selling two juvenile books to print publishers, **Betty Jo Schuler** found the market tight but continued to write. "I'd written a pick-a-path book, and print publishers said they weren't selling," she says. "My book *Camp Cheer*, with its interactive format, was perfect for e-publishing." Schuler sold seven juvenile books and four adult romances to e-publishers in less than a year. Her children's books *Baby for Sale* and *Secret 'Till We're Grown*, and one young adult title *Second Chance at Love*, were published by DiskUs (www.diskuspublishing.com). Her YA interactive mystery, *Camp Cheer*, a 2001 Eppie Award finalist (see sidebar on page 38), was published by Wordbeams (www.wordbeams.com) as are her other titles *Brain Man*, *Double-Trouble Ditto Box*, and an upcoming YA anthology, *No Rain, No Rainbows*. (Her website is http://home.webworks2000.net/bschuler/bettyjo.html.)

Eloise Barton's foray into e-publishing was the result of a contest. "Publication by Hard Shell Word Factory was the prize—I won and was published." After selling more than 100 stories and articles, Barton's first book, *Finding Mariah*, a YA suspense novel, was published by Hard Shell Word Factory in April 2000. In 2001, the book was a finalist for the Eppie Award for best YA from an electronic publisher. Her book's teaser: "Small towns hold secrets. So do families. Finding out those secrets will change Mariah's life forever—if she survives." (Her website is www.EloiseBarton.com.)

How did you research e-book publishers?

Enderle: I checked out the e-publishers that were referred by friends. If I'd hear about a particular e-publisher, I'd go to the site and look at what genre of books they published, the percentage of royalties, and read a sample contract.

Schuler: I went with publishers recommended by fellow writers whose judgment I trust. I didn't research because I didn't know how to do it. I was very fortunate in making excellent choices, but I'd advise people to research more widely.

Barton: I talked to other writers who were published electronically, read several e-books, and went online to the various e-publishers to check out their web pages and to download and read their contracts.

Is it easier to sell an e-book?

Enderle: That all depends on the e-publisher. Reputable e-publishers can be as picky as print publishers, accepting only quality work. E-publishing is perfect for authors with great manu-

On E-Books: Editor, ipicturebooks

Harold Underdown has been working in the world of children's book publishing for the past decade with editorial positions at Macmillan, Orchard, and most recently Charlesbridge. He's recently taken the title of Vice President, Editorial for ipicturebooks.com, a children's e-book publisher offering original work, e-book editions of out-of-print books, and e-book versions of children's books from a number of print publishers. Here Underdown shares his thoughts on children's e-book publishing and where it's going. To learn more about ipicturebooks turn to the Insider Report with Underdown on page 157 and check the website, www.ipicturebooks.com.

There are a number of online publishers who do children's books and picture books. The quality of their material varies greatly. What's your take on e-publishing in general?

One of the problems with e-publishing is anybody can do it. The cost of entry is low, the need to produce quality is lower. It's like what happened with desktop publishing ten years ago. People started to be able to design on screen so everybody thought they could. Actually, you need skill to do it. It's the same thing with e-publishing. This is going to continue to be true, simply because someone can set themselves up as an e-publisher with a smaller amount of capital than they would have needed to set themselves up as a print publisher.

On my personal website I've received questions from people: How do I approach an e-publisher? How do I figure out if I should be working with them? I think it's not necessarily that difficult. You need to ask questions of them. What are the backgrounds of the people working at this publisher? Do they have experience publishing children's books? Do they have a marketing team? Do they have a production team? Or is it one person who's scanning images and typing up text at home?

Do you think the existence of lower-quality online publishers has created a stigma towards e-publishers like ipicturebooks?

No, I think it's pretty obviously different than what we do. And I'm not saying that they're all bad. I've seen some really interesting stuff being done. It's runs the gamut. Writers should use their critical judgment. The thing that makes it so difficult is that e-books are so new. Sometimes you wonder, do the same standards apply here? And I totally think they do. The original books that we're going to do at ipicturebooks are of the quality I would be doing at any trade house here in New York. They have to be, because we're not going to get anywhere with them if they're not.

What do you predict for the future of e-books?

I really don't know. I don't think anybody does. There are some people making sniffy predictions that e-books will never go anywhere because who wants to read books on computers? And there are other people, including Microsoft, who say this is going to be 20 percent of the market in three years. I think both of them are wrong. I see e-books as another format in the same way that trade paperbacks were starting in the 1960s. And there are two parts of that. There are e-books that are simply books in electronic form, which will probably, in terms of sheer volume, be the larger part of the market pretty much indefinitely. And then there are e-books to which you've added special features like sound and animation or hyperlinking. Those are important elements we're pursuing. We already have some titles available with those features, but whether or not that will become more important than simply e-books as books, I don't know.

—Alice Pope

On E-Books: Editor, New Concepts Publishing

Editor Madris Gutierrez established New Concepts Publishing in the spring of 1996 as the first e-book company in continuous operation in the world. The company went online with their first books in October of the same year.

Gutierrez is a published author herself. Her background also includes an earlier career in computer science, and previous hands-on experience in building a company from the ground up. Here she discusses juvenile e-books. For more information about New Concepts Publishing, visit their website, www.newconceptspublishing.com.

What are the advantages of selling a juvenile e-book?
The main advantage of selling any book as an e-book, if we're speaking of author-to-publisher sales, is that e-publishers are all relatively new to the publishing industry and building their businesses from the ground up. They're more open-minded and they're looking to build both their stock of books and establish their own authors as future household names.

If the question pertains to sales to customers, then, as with anything else, there are advantages and disadvantages. The biggest advantage is that the very newness of the market means less competition. The object of the children's market has always been two-fold. It's a market unto itself, and has obviously proven a profitable one. But it works to build tomorrow's adult readers, and since it seems fairly certain by now that tomorrow's readers will be e-book readers, getting in on the ground floor has obvious advantages for authors looking to establish a career in writing.

The main disadvantage at this point, of course, is that it is so new that building the reader market is a work in progress and thus authors cannot expect to see the number of sales that they might expect if they went with a traditional publisher with a long established market.

What's the future of juvenile books in the e-book market?
I think it's a far brighter one than the traditional market can offer. I think one of the biggest problems publishers have faced in recent years is the decline of the number of readers. Young people are more oriented toward high tech, and less likely to read. The e-book, in my opinion, gives publishers and authors the best shot at capturing the younger generations by combining technology with good old-fashioned stories.

—Linda Joy Singleton

scripts that don't quite fit a specific genre. Because there is no cost for printing and paper, e-publishers will take a chance on a manuscript that might seem risky to a print publisher.

Schuler: It isn't any easier if you sell to a respected publisher. You must still write an excellent story, proof carefully, etc. There are companies that aren't picky and will publish books of substandard quality, just as there are print publishers of this sort.

Barton: Yes, but getting harder as more people selling increases competition.

What benefits and drawbacks have you experienced with e-publishing?
Enderle: I did have one nightmare with my first e-book. I had a picture book manuscript accepted by a popular e-publisher who

promptly told me I had to find my own illustrator. I found an artist who, after working on my e-book for a few weeks, fell upon great times! He suddenly got several contracts from major publishers, and although he never said he wouldn't illustrate my book, I knew it would be put on the back burner for a long time. I found a new illustrator, who not only did a great job, but also became a very close friend. After waiting nearly a year, my e-book became a reality. Three weeks later, the e-publisher decided to shut down her site. Luckily a small print publisher picked up that book. My next e-published book, *Making Cents*, was a much smoother and happier experience.

Schuler: Benefits: a close working relationship with my editor-publishers, instant feedback when I have questions, openness to ideas that cross genres, less emphasis on trends, and books that are easier to store and carry. Also, my publisher offers opportunities to take part in anthologies, cookbooks, etc., which helps promote and establish authors' names and works. I'm in on the ground floor of what I believe will become a booming industry.

Drawbacks: Many people don't understand e-publishing, so you must "sell" the medium at the same time you're promoting your work. And authors don't receive advances, but the much larger royalty helps offset this.

Barton: Benefits: I'm published, and I have a book to sell. Drawbacks: very little respect, and very little money.

E-book authors must be prepared to promote their books. How do you market your titles?
Enderle: My e-book, *Making Cents*, is fiction and it's educational. My primary goal was to target preschool and kindergarten teachers. I wrote an article with tie-in activities for teachers, ending with a plug for *Making Cents*. I've sent postcards to schools and daycares, and I'm working on an electronic postcard with my book cover. I offer coloring pages on my website. Once my e-book was available, my publisher sent out press releases, and made sure it got reviewed.

Schuler: I sent promo packets to schools and libraries, and I frequently book engagements to talk about e-publishing and my releases. I send an e-mail newsletter to friends and people who sign up through my site. I sign up at various online sites that offer free publicity such as Authors-Den (www.authorsden.com). I had bookmarks made and create my own flyers. I submit my work to reviewers. I sometimes offer prize drawings at my website. I sent promo material to a newspaper and was interviewed and photographed for an article.

Barton: Most effective were speaking to writers' groups, and selling my books (disks) after speaking; reviews arranged by my publisher, and requested by me; e-mail notices to everyone I've ever met; postcards to family, friends, and writers in six writers' groups I belong to; promo cards (business cards with blurb, book cover, and email address for order, etc.); postcards and promo cards handed out and sent to writers' conferences; paid-for Author's Page on eBooks Rock! with bio and interview.

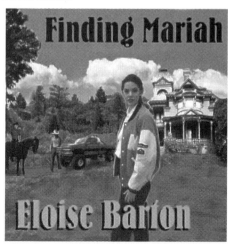

I entered the Eppie contest and made finalist (and the finalist logo goes on everything now). I created return address labels with book covers to put on all outgoing mail. I also took part in a YA

Sampler disk with fifteen other YA authors pro-
duced by Lynne Hansen. The disk will be handed out at various writers' conferences.
There's a picture of my book cover and blurb on my door at work, along with the Eppie Finalist logo. There's also a copy of eBook Connections June 2000 Bestseller List, with my book highlighted.

I took part in the RWA Literacy Booksigning in Washington D.C. in July 2000. I had a great time, and it generated great publicity for both Hard Shell and me. My publisher donated ten books for the signing.

How do e-book royalty payments compare to print publishers?

Enderle: Sadly, the e-book market hasn't taken off yet, and total royalty dollars are low. I once heard that if someone makes $100 off her e-book, it's considered successful. Of course, I've heard from authors who've made much more, but their e-books were published by established print publishers who ventured into the e-book market.

Schuler: E-publishers pay a much higher royalty percentage. Most offer about 35 percent. I have made several hundred dollars on school and library talks, telling people about this new medium, as well as promoting my books.

Barton: I have no personal experience with print publishers to draw on. However, e-books offer no advance. I suspect royalty payments are much smaller for e-books than for print books.

So can you make money in selling an e-book?

Enderle: Not yet, but I think a little time and new technology will change that.

Schuler: Yes. Write a good book and put effort into the promotion and you can make money. As time goes on, I believe sales will increase.

Barton: Not much. I heard on one of the e-author lists that the average income for each book is approximately $100. This was quite a shock but so far, in the year since my book was published, this has been true for me. My contract gives a royalty rate of 30 percent, but bookstores get a 40 to 55 percent discount on the books they sell, so royalties on those books are based on the balance that Hard Shell gets. I made a total of about $35 on the 40 books sold through Hard Shell and other sources. I also get a 40 percent discount on books I buy from Hard Shell, so I made $80 on the 40 books I hand-sold to friends, family, co-workers, writers groups, and at speaking engagements. The total income of $115 I earned from my book is abysmal, but it is still out there, still earning. It will continue to earn for another year. Longer, if I can get a sequel done and accepted, and my contract is extended. Other writers have said their royalties increase each year, as word-of-mouth increases their readership.

Where do you see the future of e-books going?

Enderle: Once a universal e-book reader is available at a reasonable cost, e-books will have a better shot. Pocket-sized e-book readers that let you adjust the font size and have built in lighting

---

What's an Eppie?

Electronically Published Internet Connection (EPIC) gave the first Eppie Awards in August 2000. Eppies honor the best e-books in fifteen categories. Any e-book published before January 1, 2000 was eligible for the award and almost 200 authors entered. The categories were judged by published authors, all members of EPIC. To learn more about the award and see a list of winners, visit www.eclectics.com/epic/eppies.html.

and bookmarks could solve a world of problems for today's readers. I also think e-books could be the perfect replacement for text books in our educational system. Students today are electronically adept and studying from an e-book could give them a world of options; pop-up windows, interactive quizzes, etc.

Schuler: I see students downloading their textbooks all into one handheld reader. I see kids reading fiction on pocketsize readers. I believe the only thing that's slowing down the industry is the electronic reader technology and price. As these improve, more people will read e-books. I also believe handheld reader companies aren't promoting their products enough. When Palm Pilots ™ and other personal digital assistants are advertised, their capability of being used as an electronic reader should be played up. As it is, this aspect isn't being mentioned.

Barton: E-books are the wave of the future. As more readers come on the market, and prices come down, more people will try them, and will get hooked on the immediacy of ordering the books online, and the ease of reading a handheld reader. Students may be able to carry all their books on a reader, instead of in a heavy backpack. One law school is providing textbooks on readers. Some libraries are experimenting with loaning readers and e-books. Newspapers and magazines can be downloaded into readers—much easier to read on commuter trains.

Some e-publishers are going to simultaneous publication as downloads and POD (print on demand). I'm looking forward to my book being available in POD form. I won't feel like a real author until I can hold an actual book in my hand. That may be an old-fashioned and emotional attitude, but in their hearts, I think many authors feel, as I do, that e-books are only a step toward print publication.

Perhaps the next generation will consider only e-books "real," with print books a quaint anachronism, like eight-track tapes and papyrus scrolls, and we'll be the pioneers of this new way of reading!

A Peek Into the Canadian Children's Book Market

BY ALMA FULLERTON

Comparing the Canadian and U.S. children's publishing industries is like comparing a sprout planted next to a full-grown tree. Like the sprout, the Canadian market is young and is struggling to grow in the shade of the enormous U.S. market.

Over the last few years the Canadian market has changed drastically. When financial difficulties bombarded Canada's super-bookstore, Chapters, several Canadian publishers found themselves scrambling to stay afloat. Some of them asked for government assistance, while others looked toward alternate (international) markets to protect themselves in the future. Even with the new obstacles, writers are still submitting, and Canadian publishers will continue to produce excellent children's books and do their best to compete with the vast U.S market.

Here an editor, an agent and a publisher share their views of the market. **Leona Trainer** is currently an associate agent with Transatlantic Literary Agency in Toronto. She's served on the boards of several publishing industry organizations and was formerly editor and president of Stoddart Kids. **Jane Pavanel** is the picture book and chapter book editor at Lobster Press in Montreal. **Valerie Hussey** has almost 30 years of publishing experience behind her. She's currently the president and CEO of Kids Can Press Ltd.

LEONA TRAINER, Transatlantic Literary Agency

At Transatlantic you deal with both U.S. and Canadian publishers. Can you tell us the biggest differences between the two markets?

The largest difference between the markets is, as you might imagine, one of size. In the Canadian market it's easier to know all the players. Editors in the Canadian publishing houses wear many hats. In the larger U.S. houses, there are more specialists, sub categories and imprints, so tracking down the exact person you need can be difficult. Major houses already have stables of authors and illustrators they have spent years developing and promoting for their lists. With this large talent pool of established authors and illustrators available to them, newcomers must be very special indeed to attract attention.

You've been in the children's publishing business for several years. How has the Canadian market changed?

Beginning in the '70s, the school and public library budgets designated for purchasing children's books were increased substantially across Canada. The action prompted some of the large publishing houses like Penguin and Doubleday Canada to develop library and education divisions with dedicated children's personnel and focused publishing programs.

Some independent houses like Tundra and Kids Can Press began to specialize in Canadian material for the school and library marketplace. As other small presses emerged, each found its own niche market. Aided by government subsidies and programs, publishers gained access to

---

ALMA FULLERTON *is a writer based in Ontario, Canada.*

the U.S. and other foreign markets. Many independent children's bookstores sprang up in cities across Canada, and general bookstores began purchasing more books for a designated children's section in their stores.

Over the last ten years the children's book business has changed dramatically. There are still some new small publishing houses starting up, but major stumbling blocks are now inhibiting expansion. School and public library book budgets have been cut. Many small public library branches have been closed. Trained personnel no longer staff school libraries and some of those have been closed. The cost of books has accelerated so rapidly over the last few years, budgets can no longer cover the demands for needed materials.

The advent of the superstores has had an adverse effect on the independent booksellers and only a few have survived the downswing of sales. Merging of major publishing houses has

Canadian or U.S. Publishers? Two Authors' Choices

Here two Canadian authors talk about their decision to either work with the Canadian children's book market or look elsewhere for publication.

Trina Wiebe is author of the Abbey and Tess Pet Sitters series published by Canadian publisher Lobster Press.

What made you decide to stay in Canada to publish?
Although the exchange rate in the U.S. is quite enticing, I always knew getting published in Canada was my goal. I wanted to be part of Canadian children's literature. We have so much to offer our children these days. Much more than when I was a child. I'm thrilled to be part of it.

I don't know if it's easier to get published in Canada. I've never submitted to the U.S. In some ways it might be harder to get published in Canada. There are fewer publishers here and a manuscript really has to stand out to be considered.

I'm pleased to be working with Lobster Press. They're enthusiastic about children's books and have been working hard to promote my series. Lobster Press has made sure the Abbey and Tess series is available all over the world. I feel lucky to have a Canadian publisher with a global view.

Mary McKenna Siddals's list of picture book credits includes *Tell Me a Season*, *Millions of Snowflakes*, *I'll Play with you* (all Clarion Books) and *Morning Song* (Henry Holt).

What made you turn to the U.S. for publication?
When I first began researching publishers nearly ten years ago, it quickly became evident there were many more publishing opportunities in the U.S. Not only were there far fewer Canadian publishers to begin with, there were even fewer who were accepting unsolicited submissions, and fewer still once I eliminated those whose requirements I did not meet—regional authors only, no picture books, specific "Canadian content," etc. In fact, in my case—writing concept picture books with a more "universal" than "Canadian" focus—I managed to narrow it down to one. Yes, I did try that one Canadian house first, but soon moved on to targeting my submissions to the many more U.S. publishers specifically seeking the types of books I was writing.

Of course there are other advantages to publishing with a U.S. house, particularly a larger one—higher advances, bigger print runs and wider distribution. However, the most compelling reason for going with a U.S. publisher, in my experience, is the greater opportunity to find the right house for your work.

resulted in the production of more merchandise-type book products and series material rather than high-end books.

The dwindling Canadian market has increased publishers' attempts to make inroads in the U.S. Some have successfully penetrated the school and library market. The hiring of U.S. sales forces and publicity people has also allowed Canadian publishers to have more access to the trade market.

With so few Canadian agents representing children's literature, many authors and illustrators are looking to the U.S. to find agents. How would one go about finding a reputable Canadian agent?

Most agencies in Canada focus on adult material mainly because it generates more revenue than children's material. Also, there are few agents who have knowledge of children's books and the authors and illustrators who create them.

To find a reputable agent in Canada (or the U.S.) research the agency to find out about the people who are involved in the business. Listings of Canadian agents are available in *Quill & Quire*'s *The Book Trade in Canada* directory; and letters of inquiry about representation can be sent directly to each firm.

Five Fast Facts about Book Publishing in Canada

1. More than 80 percent of Canadian-authored titles are published by Canadian houses.
2. Export of Canadian books has tripled since 1989.
3. The average print run for a work of first-time (trade) fiction in Canada is about 1,500 compared to 10,000 in the U.S., making the cost per Canadian book much higher.
4. Canadian authors regularly win international acclaim. In recent years Canadians have won several major literary prizes, including the Pulitzer Prize, the Booker Prize, the Commonwealth Writer's and First Writer's Prizes.
5. Canadian book publishers are on the leading edge of multimedia development and actively market their books on the Internet.

JANE PAVANEL, Lobster Press

Approximately how many manuscripts do you receive a year?

I get over 1,400 picture book and chapter book manuscripts a year. My assistant reads every one and I read the 60 percent she passes on to me.

How do you choose which stories to publish?

We narrow them down over several reads until we have about 20 good ones then we narrow those down to about 10 or 12. To make the last cut, the story has to read well and have something special about it. When a story moves me and I can't really tell why, I *know* the author has talent. Often I'll send the last ten manuscripts to my publisher with a write-up. We'll send them around the office and if we still need help we'll send them to six readers who fill out an evaluation form. We look for stories with a wonderful plot, charming characters and multiple-readability.

Canadians are internationally known for their excellence in literary adult fiction. Do you believe that's the case with children's fiction as well?

I'm constantly amazed by the literary power of some of the children's fiction produced in this country. Have you read *A Screaming Kind of Day*, by Rachna Gilmore (Fitzhenry & Whiteside)?

One thing I'm not so keen on is the proliferation of beautiful picture books with absolutely gorgeous illustrations that hold mediocre stories. It seems that many publishers are getting away with creating books for art. I think it's worth it to make the stories as good as the art.

Does Lobster Press have a list of Canadian illustrators they prefer to work with?

When we decide on a story, we look at every illustrator we can get our hands on. We find out whose style or touch will match the story well and lift it higher. We're looking for someone who is comfortable working as part of a team.

VALERIE HUSSEY, Kids Can Press

If Kids Can Press had been launched in 2000 instead of 1973 do you feel they would have had as much success as they have?

In the early days, government grants were the basis on which many companies were founded and existed. Without grants Kids Can Press would not have been launched. But today grants are a small portion of total revenue—less than eight percent—and are basically used as capital for research and development in riskier areas of publishing. In 1973 there was little publishing history for kids' books here, and each book contributed to a newly developing list. Growing from nothing is a fairly dynamic process. But as the industry grew, and more competition entered the market, one had to become better and better. It is a well-developed industry today that one enters. It would be much more difficult to enter as a new player, and one would require far greater financial resources today than 30 years ago.

How are Canadian houses able to compete with the larger U.S. houses?

We compete through excellence. There is always a demand for originality in publishing, and smaller independent houses—whether Canadian, American or British—offer new, fresh voices and vision. When 75 or 80 percent of the market is dominated by fewer than ten publishers, there is a serious need for what the independent publishers have to offer.

How do Canadian-produced books fare in the market here and abroad?

Our books have been well accepted in the U.S. market from the beginning. For 15 years we licensed our books to U.S. publishers who produced them under their own imprint. We were a "publisher's publisher" but we knew from that experience the content of our books traveled well. The publishers to whom we sold succeeded with our titles. When we launched our list under our own imprint three years ago, we didn't have to sell anyone on the quality or content, but we did have to establish ourselves as a reliable, credible supplier to the marketplace. The customers with whom we now had to deal were different than the publishers to whom we had previously sold rights. And those customers had to learn that we were as professional and reliable as any publisher.

Internationally, selling licenses has always been very important to Canadian publishers. Our market is so much smaller than the U.S. and that forces one to look beyond one's own borders. Over 30 percent of our revenue comes from international sales. American publishers don't need that kind of international reach to be financially successful, but we do.

Why do Canadian publishers produce a high percentage of their books by Canadian authors?

When KCP was founded, and through the early years of its development, it addressed the lack of an indigenous Canadian publishing industry for children's books. Canadian children were, before the 1980s raised on British and U.S. children's books. Since the Canadian children's industry began in the '70s—or even earlier in the '60s, if you consider the launch of Tundra—there have been limited opportunities for Canadian children's writers at home. The formation of strong cultural policy in the '70s created the climate and opportunities for an industry to exist and grow, enabling us to give voice to Canadian creators.

KCP does plan to expand our creator base to include Americans, which will advance our place in the U.S. market.

How did the recent takeover of Canadian super-bookstore, Chapters, affect the publishing industry?

The history of Chapters, from the point at which the government permitted the merger of three chains, has had a major impact on the industry. After the initial consolidation of the original chains, the next difficulty was the creation of the poorly conceived wholesale division, Pegasus. Last year's operation of Chapters created great uncertainty and instability in the industry. It's been a challenging time. It's too early to know what the future will be, but if it's not successful, the industry as we know it now probably won't exist for long. So, one needs to be cautiously optimistic, work as effectively as possible with the new owners, and at the same time set a strategy that mitigates against the negative potential of the future unknown.

Candian Children's Book Authors & Illustrators

Check out work by these favorite Canadian authors and illustrators:

Young Adult and Mid-Grade Writers

Deborah Ellis	Janet Lunn
Gayle Friesen	Lucy Maude Montgomery
Linda Holeman	Kenneth Oppel
Rukhsana Khan	Kit Pearson
Julie Lawson	Eric Walters
Jean Little	Tim Wynne-Jones

Picture Book Writers

Andrea Beck	Phoebe Gilman
Jo Ellen Bogart	Don Gillmor
Paulette Bourgeois	Marilyn Helmer
Sheree Fitch	Loris Lesynski
Mary-Louise Gay	Robert Munsch
	Gilles Tibo

Illustrators

Carol Biberstein	Katy Macdonald Denton
Gina Calleja	Michael Martchenko
Brenda Clark	Pascal Milelli
Mary-Louise Gay	Gilles Tibo
Phoebe Gilman	Janet Wilson

Dummies Aren't for Dummies: Mocking Up a Picture Book

BY SUE BRADFORD EDWARDS

To write the best possible picture book, dummy your manuscript. While you've probably heard editors give this advice at a writer's conference, explanations on how to do it are seldom more complete than, "Read good picture books and you will know." Unfortunately, without a strong knowledge of the elements of picture book structure, many authors read for character and entirely miss the importance of the picture book's physical structure.

In dummying, knowledge of physical structure is a must. "It is the ability to physically turn the page that gives a dummy its power," says Kathryn O. Galbraith, author of *Look! Snow!* (Margaret McElderry), *Roommates and Rachel* (Macmillan), and *Holding Onto Sunday* (Simon & Schuster). "The author can really 'see' the manuscript as a book." Before you can create such a powerful dummy, you must understand the effects of a picture book's physical structure on the text.

JUST SO LONG

Most picture books are limited to 32 pages. Within this space, the author must tell a complete story and leave the editor room for front matter—half title page, title page, dedication, and copyright.

The amount of space devoted to front matter varies according to the design of the individual book. In trade picture books, this material often takes the first 4 pages of the book, leaving 28 pages for text. In supplemental educational publishing, says Nina Hess, senior editor at Wright Group/McGraw-Hill, "We reserve one page for front matter, with copyright information appearing on the inside front cover. The remaining pages are devoted to text." This means that when you construct a dummy, you will have from 28 to 31 pages to lay out your story.

To make a blank dummy, take 8 sheets of paper, fold them in half, and staple them together along the crease, yielding a 32 page mockup picture book. For a dummy with larger pages, take 16 blank pages and staple them at one edge. Decide how many pages will be devoted to front matter and mark these with a large "X."

The remaining pages are reserved for text. Each page or set of facing pages that will take text is a spread. A double-page spread consists of facing pages, such as pages 6 and 7, when these pages include one illustrated scene and accompanying text. Single page sets of illustrations and text are single-page spreads. This means that to fill the dummy you will need to break your manuscript into at least 14 spreads—2 single-page (page 5 and page 32) and 12 double-page

---

SUE BRADFORD EDWARDS creates picturebook dummies from home in St. Louis, Missouri. Her book reviews appear in the St. Louis-Post Dispatch *and she's a frequent contributor to* Children's Writer *and the* SCBWI Bulletin. *Find out more about her and her course on writing children's nonfiction through her website http://SueBradfordEdwards.8m.com.*

(pages 6 through 31). But how should you break your text for a well-planned spread? To do this, you have to know how a spread functions.

When to Dummy

When is the best time to dummy a manuscript?

Some writers find it best to polish the manuscript in standard form before working it up as a dummy. As Atheneum Senior Editor Caitlin Dlouhy advises, "The development of character and the story itself are so important. The dummy won't help if the rest doesn't work." If it is easiest to concentrate on the story itself in normal manuscript form, wait until your work is fairly polished to dummy.

Other writers find it best to use a dummy early in the process. "To make sure the pacing works over 14 spreads," says author Deborah DeSaix, "I write a story a spread at a time."

You can also go back and forth between dummy and manuscript. "Rereading the dummy leads me back to the manuscript and more editing/polishing, and those alterations lead me back to the dummy," says author Kathryn O. Galbraith. "I see the dummy as an integral part of creating and shaping the manuscript."

THE SPREAD

At its most basic, a spread is a combination of text and art. Explains G.P. Putnam's Sons' Senior Editor, Kathy Dawson, "Picture books get a lot of their magic from the process of two 'wholes' coming together to create something bigger than the sum of its parts. That's why it's often called a 'marriage' between art and text." To create such a marriage, the text for a spread must include an illustration possibility. In the cinematic terms of Dutton President and Publisher Stephanie Owens Lurie, "Each spread should contain a different scene or action." This brings movement and motion to the manuscript.

Look at your manuscript. Do you have at least 14 unique scenes of action to provide the illustrator with a variety of illustration possibilities? If you frequently duplicate scenes, character combinations or actions, you may need to rewrite. If you have more than 14 scenes, remember that double-page spreads can be split into single-page spreads.

Break your text into these scenes, assuming you have at least 14, and tape them into your dummy.

Now, back to structure. Each scene must contribute to the development of the story as a whole. When she is rewriting a manuscript, Galbraith seeks to develop a sense of movement on every page either through the character, or by a change in action, mood or setting. It isn't enough for a spread to encompass a new scene or an exciting action. It must also be necessary to the development of the plot or to bring the reader to a deeper understanding of the character yet must still be new and non-repetitive. "If there is no reason to turn the page," says Galbraith, "if nothing new is revealed or developed, then that spread is where the author must turn her/his attention for revision."

Check your spreads. Do they reveal something new in both plot/character and scene/action/mood? Or should you rewrite?

ONE PAGE OR TWO?

At this point, you may still think the only difference between a double-page spread and a single-page spread is the number of pages involved. Actually, each functions differently in terms of picture book pacing. While single-page spreads contain less space for the illustrator to work, they offer the opportunity for a cinematic close-up. "Single pages have a more intimate feel," explains Hess. "They work well for showing details, cozy moments between characters, or for a final coda or punch line at the end of a book." Though it happens rarely in trade publishing, educational picture books are sometimes composed entirely of single-page spreads. Zoom in with a single page and keep your pacing fast.

Variations on a Theme

Some writers turn to tools other than a standard text dummy to revise their work.

With a storyboard, a single page that shows every spread of a picture book simultaneously, author Deborah DeSaix views her entire manuscript at once. "That's so useful because I can see how it flows from beginning to end. How it's going to work from spread to spread. This is useful when setting up layout."

Mary Whittington, author of *The Patchwork Lady* (Harcourt) and *Winter's Child* (Atheneum), uses the storyboard almost to the exclusion of the dummy. On her office wall, Whittington has a 3-foot by 2-foot melamine board indelibly inked with 32 numbered squares, each a picture book page. With a dry-erase marker, Whittington fills each page or spread with identifying words or stick-figure thumbnail sketches. "I'm able to step back and view the whole . . . and easily make changes if I need to. For example, if the story's climax comes too soon or too late, I can identify the problem almost immediately, erase and place the climax in a better position—before going back to revise the story."

Although a dummy can help writers judge text distribution, some writers find flipping back and forth between spreads distracting. To avoid this, Linda Johns, author of *To Pee or Not to Pee* (Infinity Plus One) and *Sarah's Secret Plan* (Troll Associates), produces an "exploded dummy." Each page spread is the same size as a regular dummy, but instead of being "bound," the pages are loose. Johns lays the spreads out on her dining room table. "I let my eyes kind of relax and I take a look at it again, seeing if there is any area that looks 'too gray.' It gives me a quick visual idea of where the text might be too dense. Or if page breaks and page turns look too unbalanced." To quickly move text from spread to spread, Johns recommends double-stick tape.

Because a double-page spread encompasses two whole pages, it takes longer to view. In this way, "it can function as a 'rest stop' for the reader before the story moves on again," says Galbraith. This is because "the reader's eye lingers longer over a double-page spread," says Lurie. Such a respite may be necessary after several scenes of intense action or after a character fails to solve a problem.

Because the reader does pause at a double-page spread, Lurie says, "it should be used for dramatic effect" when a scene carries emotional weight. These types of scenes include important moments such as when the character has an epiphany or when something epic occurs. Think of the double-page spread as offering more room for development or to make an emotional impact, a cinematic long shot.

Look at the scenes you have taped into your dummy. Do you have a large number of single-page spreads? If so, the pacing of your manuscript may be too fast for too long. Your reader may need a double-page breather. Is the text on your double-page spread weighty enough to fill this much space? If not, rewrite.

THE PAGE TURN

Another structural element is the page turn. Page turns should occur "where a natural break in the manuscript happens," says Hess. You can identify these natural breaks, adds Deborah DeSaix, author/illustrator of *Returning Nicholas* (Farrar, Straus & Giroux) and *In the Back Seat* (Farrar, Straus & Giroux), as "natural places to take a breath," as the place you would pause when reading aloud. If your page breaks feel forced, shift your text to utilize the natural pauses in your work.

In some picture books, page turns build suspense. "Surprises and punch lines should come after the turn of a page," recommends Lurie. Use the page turn to surprise the reader with the unexpected, such as Rick Walton does in *Once There Was a Bull . . . Frog* (Gibbs Smith).

To evaluate page turns, force yourself to slow down when viewing your dummy. This is especially hard to do when familiar with a manuscript. Sit down and read it out loud as you would to a child. Do you want to turn the page before you are done reading the text? Do you need a break that doesn't come? Then shift the text in your dummy for another rewrite.

THROUGH THE PACES

As you review the text on each spread, you begin to sense your manuscript's pacing. Some authors and editors maintain a general sense of pacing, using a dummy to see if things happen too late or too early. "You want your pacing to pick up toward the climax and then come down again, so you need the space to do both," says Atheneum senior editor Caitlyn Dlouhy. "The dummy can help you see if this peak happens too soon—for example, does it happen after only four spreads."

Others think of pacing in specific terms. "I use the general rule of thumb," explains Lurie, "that you have about three spreads to introduce your character and set up his/her situation, and three spreads to conclude the story. The rest is for the ups and downs."

Using a specific approach, Esther Hershenhorn, author of *Chicken Soup by Heart* (Simon & Schuster), *The Confe$$ion$ and $ecret$ of Howard J. Fingerhut* (Holiday House), and *There Goes Lowell's Party* (Holiday House), quickly hooks the reader to take advantage of the limited space available in a picture book manuscript. "It is crucial that the reader know why the character wants what he wants, so the reader cares about the character as he turns the pages," says Hershenhorn. To accomplish this, she allots the first two two-page spreads to her hook.

Look at your dummy. How many spreads are spent introducing your character and his situation? Do you devote enough time to make the reader care? Or do things drag on?

The middle of the picture book fills the greatest number of pages but has a lot to accomplish. In this section, your character must make several, typically three, attempts to solve their problem. In her own work Hershenhorn allows three double-page spreads for each of her character's

---

Caution

Manufacturing a dummy can turn your concentration from the manuscript itself as you strive for the perfect dummy. It can also lead you to plan specifics over which you ultimately won't have control.

When dummying a manuscript, Atheneum senior editor Caitlin Dlouhy reminds authors to "think of the pacing of the story. Leave the actual planning of illustrations, including wordless spreads, to the illustrator."

After doing the work required to produce a text dummy, authors may be mistakenly tempted to submit it with their manuscript. Don't, warns Putnam editor Kathy Dawson. "If authors get too involved with planning the visual aspects of the book, they risk getting hurt in the end, because ultimately they have no control over how the book looks. I have often said that picture book writing is all about learning how to 'let go.' It's a very difficult emotional process."

Instead, she recommends leaving the illustrator's job to the illustrator and writing a picture book manuscript that is open-ended enough to provide a wealth of visual possibilities.

attempts, enough space to set up the attempt, make the attempt and fail. This level of action keeps the story interesting as well as providing the illustrator with fodder for her contributions.

Examine your dummy again. How much space is devoted to each attempt and subsequent failure, complication or resolution? Too much time spent on the introduction may limit these attempts, giving the story a rushed feeling. Expand each attempt into the space it needs.

The space that is left, roughly the same as devoted to the beginning or introduction, remains for the climax. In Hershenhorn's work, the climax often begins on the last spread of the third attempt and then continues on the last two two-page spreads. Combining the final portion of the third attempt with the beginning of the climax gives Hershenhorn "room for a twist, when the reader thinks, 'Oh . . . it's working out okay, but . . . wait a minute . . . ' " The last spread contains the "inevitable yet surprising, satisfactory resolution."

Look at the final spreads in your dummy. Do you wrap things up in about three spreads? Does your conclusion include a twist or an "ah-ha" moment? If not, you may want to rewrite.

Now you have an understanding of how a double-page spread, a single-page spread, a page turn and pacing work within a picture book manuscript. Dummy several pieces of your work to see how they function within the limits of a picture book. You may find you have a specific area that needs improvement.

Once you know how it works, a dummy is a great way to create a better picture book manuscript.

Read, Right? Read, Write!

BY LINDA SUE PARK

Finding time to read is a problem for many writers, both aspiring and established. Most people have very busy lives, and finding time to write is hard enough—how on earth can anyone find time to *read* as well?

I'm not talking here about reading for factual research. I hope most serious writers take for granted the need to research certain topics or angles in their work. What I'd like to address here is the *general* need for reading to write: reading children's or young adult books because you want to write them. From the larger issues of plot and character to the nuances of rhythm and word use, reading *a lot* exposes the serious reader to the patterns of story and language, which emerge transformed and renewed when that reader sits down to write.

ATTITUDE & STRATEGY

Making reading a priority is a question of two things: *Attitude* and *Strategy*.

Attitude is the most important. Suppose I want to be an Olympic athlete in track and field. I love the sport, and I dream of seeing myself on the medal stand someday, or at least wearing the uniform of my country. It's been my dream for years . . .

. . . but I can't find the time to train.

Ludicrous, yes? No serious athlete would ever say or think such a thing. Indeed, training would be their *top* priority.

Reading children's books is "training" for a children's writer. To continue the analogy: "I dream of being published someday . . . of seeing my work as a beautiful book . . . maybe even of winning awards . . .

. . .but I can't find the time to read.

If this sounds uncomfortably familiar, the first step is changing your attitude toward reading. Athletes don't "find time" to train any more than you "find time" to brush your teeth or take a shower. It's simply built into the day. Automatically, without a second thought. If an athlete doesn't train for a few days, he or she feels all "wrong." That's exactly how I feel if I go a few days without reading.

And this is where *Strategy* comes in. How can we read more without taking away from our writing time? Most of us have incredible demands to meet in our daily lives. Some of us are working full-time at non-writing jobs, most have families, and families with small children are the most demanding of all. So it's difficult for me to offer specific suggestions on how to put your new "attitude" into daily practice.

But I do have one tip that will work for a great number of people.

Turning off the tube

Most of us watch more TV than we'd like to admit—even to ourselves. Try this: Keep a pad of paper by the television. For one week, do an honest accounting of the number of hours you

---

LINDA SUE PARK, *the author of three middle-grade novels,* A Single Shard, The Kite Fighters *and* Seesaw Girl *(all Clarion Books), reads at least half a dozen mid-grades every month. Visit her website—which includes several pages of booklists—at www.lindasuepark.com. (Read more about Park and her work in the Insider Report on page 130.)*

watch. The next week, take at least *half* of those hours and *read* instead.

For me personally, it means choosing a small list of shows I want to watch each week and *not watching at any other time*. I make exceptions for special events (like the Olympics). But otherwise, no channel-surfing, no sitting down and getting engrossed in a movie that's half over, etc.

My family watches a lot more TV than I do. In the evenings I sit with them—they're all watching TV while I'm curled up with a terrific book. (This in itself took some practice, to concentrate on reading while the box is on—but a good book is better than 99 percent of television anyway!)

It might not be TV that's getting in the way; for many folks nowadays, it's surfing the Internet. You can apply the same strategy there. The point is, I believe most people *do* have at least some time to read. What they lack is the attitude that reading is important.

WHAT TO READ?

Deciding which books to read can be overwhelming. With some 5,000 new children's books published every year, many of us feel lost and uncertain when we go to the library or bookstore to pick out titles. Here are a few tips to make it easier:

- A solid background in the classics is like making sure you're in good health before you even begin your "training." If you're a picture book writer, the Caldecott and Zolotow lists are a terrific place to start. Likewise, novel writers should peruse the list of Newbery Medal and Honor winners and choose among those. Other major award lists are the Boston Globe-Horn Book Award and the National Book Award. I've also enjoyed several titles that won the Carnegie Medal or the Guardian Prize in England. A comprehensive list of the major awards can be found at the Children's Literature Web Guide.

- For recent titles, the review journals are an invaluable resource. Reading a brief review of a book can help you decide whether it's something you'd like to read. These reviews often "give away" parts of the plot, but I find that if the writing is stellar I get completely caught up in the story anyway! Reviews of titles in every genre are available at the *ALA Booklist* site. The YALSA lists are a gold mine for those interested in YA literature. Other sources include: *School Library Journal*; *The Horn Book*; the *Bulletin of the Center for Children's Books*; *Kirkus Reviews*; *Publishers Weekly*; *VOYA*; *Christian Library Journal*, and many more. It isn't always necessary to subscribe to these magazines; most of them have websites that include a selection of reviews and/or book lists. They can also be found at most libraries, although you may have to beg for recent issues, as the library staff usually circulates those among themselves.

- Most states have a "children's choice" award with a reading list of new and newish titles for various reading levels. Many of these can be accessed through the *School Library Journal* website.

- Special-interest groups often maintain websites with booklists; for example, I know of a kite-fighting website linked to a bookstore that lists dozens of books exclusively about kites! There are also sites for just about every ethnicity you can imagine—an important consideration for those writing books from or about diverse cultures. Search engines and the search tools at major online bookstores can be a writer's best friend. In this way you can often combine general reading with research reading.

I never go to the library without a list. If a certain title isn't available, I ask for it via inter-library loan. In my local library, new books are shelved separately, and I also spend a few moments during each visit checking those shelves.

Back to that would-be Olympian. Training to be a world-class athlete is often painful and difficult. That's where the analogy falls apart—because while reading good books is a vital part of a writer's training, it *isn't* about pain and pressure and going for the burn. It's about losing yourself in a wonderful story—about escaping into pleasure. Who wouldn't want a little more of that in their day?

Whose Book Is It Anyway? A Picture Book Illustrator's Perspective

BY JANIE BYNUM

In a business full of artists and big egos, how does one even address the question of ownership? Of course it's the author's book. She came up with the concept; she wrote it. A particular book wouldn't have existed if it weren't for that author. But, wait. Could it be the illustrator's book? She spent months, maybe even years, bringing this picture book to fruition with her exceptional art. Her artwork could make or break sales of this picture book. Or could it be the editor's book? After all, she put all the talent together and orchestrated the concert. And, don't forget the art director. She commandeered the design of the book, and she had to please marketing and everyone else involved.

So, whose book is it anyway? It's everybody's.

Each contributor must develop a sense of ownership in order for a book to succeed. I've tried to track where, in the process, this occurs for me. Of course I know that the story came from an outside source, another author, but when I begin to page-break the manuscript, that story is *mine*. It has to be. Otherwise I couldn't fully connect and do my best work. I don't know the author personally, other than through her words. So, until I release the final art, the story is me. I am the story. Very Zen. And, very true.

Several authors I know have voiced concerns or asked questions about what happens once a manuscript is contracted and the editor contacts the desired illustrator for the book. I can't speak for the entire industry (nor would I want to), but I can tell you what I know first-hand and what I've gleaned from very reliable sources (who shall remain nameless to protect the innocent and even the not-so-innocent).

One question that comes up from time to time is: *Why can't authors have more contact with the artists illustrating their book?* (Many authors haven't realized the secret to this equation yet—that it's not *their* book anymore.) I'm not an editor and certainly not qualified to make a general statement on behalf of all editors, but I do know that some editors prefer to keep the process more "traditional" (no direct contact), while others have no problem with collaboration. I think whether or not collaboration occurs depends mostly on how the editor and artist like to work. I hate to keep sounding like I'm cutting the author out of the deal (I remember who wrote the story), but with fiction picture books, unless the author has a lot of clout (and some do) the story she's written takes on a life of it's own once it's sold. It's pretty much out of the author's hands.

When I work on fiction illustration, author notes are sufficient. I like to read how an author envisioned something if it's important to the story, but I reserve the right to completely ignore these notes if I feel that my vision for the story is stronger. One prolific picture book author I

JANIE BYNUM, *originally from the Dallas area, lives in southwest Michigan with her teenage son, Taylor, an Aussie/hound mix, Sydney, and two cats, Will and Grace. She is the author and illustrator of Harcourt titles* Altoona Baboona *(1999),* Otis *(2000),* Altoona Up North *(2001) and an upcoming book,* Pig Enough *(2003). Other upcoming titles include* Too Big, Too Small, Just Right *by Frances Minters, (Harcourt, 2001);* Moose Tracks *(Simon & Schuster/McElderry, 2002);* Ooh La La, Edna, *a brand new reader series from Candlewick Press;* Porcupining, A Prickly Love Story, *by Lisa Wheeler, and* Rock-A-Baby Band, *by Kate McMillan—both from Little, Brown & Co./Megan Tingley Books, 2003.*

know supports this with her comments: *I know I am not a visual person, so I have never had very definite ideas about how my books should be illustrated. And the times when illustrators have departed from my expectations, they have often improved on what I was imagining.*

Recently I've been illustrating two fiction picture books for authors I know personally. We have even critiqued each other's stories over the years. Some friends have asked me: *Isn't that strange, to be illustrating for a friend?* It could be strange, but it hasn't been. I think the process could have been uncomfortable if the authors told me what they expected to see and if I listened to them. But they didn't; and I didn't. Other than a couple of comments from one author (who just couldn't contain herself), we didn't even discuss their books when I was in the sketching stages. I purposely kept my distance, respecting the traditional process of submitting to our editor, not tossing ideas back and forth directly with the author. There were several reasons for this.

One, I am a fairly autonomous illustrator by nature. And, remember this is now *my* book; I don't want more input than I'm already sure to get from our editor.

The title character of Janie Bynum's *Otis*, is a pig who just can't stand mud. Like a manuscript without a publisher, "Otis was lonely." He finally finds a friend in a mud-hating frog, and the two form a unique relationship just as a picture book author and illustrator do.

Two, if the author and I think some idea we've conceived is absolutely wonderful and I proceed with sketches in that vein, then, if the editor hates the idea, she will have to reject the illustrator and the author. That puts the editor in an awkward position. Imagine dealing with two artist-egos at that point. I have enough faith in my editor to trust that she knows what she's doing.

And, thirdly, the editor can "protect" me from an author's need for control since some authors have trouble letting go during this part of the process. I know authors don't intend to "scare" the illustrator. Their passion for their story is appreciated, but it's time to let the artist's passion develop.

I'm sure some authors would be wonderful collaborators, knowing when to comment and, more importantly, when not to. When an author (or an editor, for that matter) interjects too much during the sketch phase, it can backfire. Instead of enhancing the process, such involvement can hinder the artist's creativity. This is why I prefer notes to actual collaboration on fiction books.

Working with friends was helpful in that I had a connection with their senses of humor and wit, and I knew that I could capture in the art a certain "attitude" in the characters that they would appreciate. Also, both authors had incredible editors working on their books, so I knew these books would be growth opportunities for me as an illustrator and as a children's book professional.

While I'm creating, I don't want to think about pleasing anyone other than myself and my editor. Frankly, I'd prefer not to have to please her! But, this is a team effort and a business, not some individual creative endeavor such as painting for personal enjoyment—although, hopefully, that kind of joy is also involved. And, at this point in my career, as painful as it is to admit, my editors know more about producing books than I do. So I have to trust my editors to guide the process, knowing that the creation of a memorable and marketable picture book is their primary goal.

For nonfiction, though, I believe the author and illustrator should be married—almost literally! One nonfiction author writes: *My editor talked to me about the artist's work prior to signing him. Once he decided to do the project, I sent him a huge box of primary materials, everything from newspapers to family photos to videos. I then had an opportunity to review the sketches at each stage of the artwork. I didn't point out anything having to do with artistic sensibilities, but there were a few factual things that needed correcting. The illustrator graciously agreed to make the changes with the understanding that ultimately that decision was up to him. On several occasions, he expressed appreciation that I was available as a research resource. My editor seemed to think that our collaboration (author and illustrator) was in the best interest of the book.*

However, I've heard horror stories of books going to press with inaccurate information in the illustrations. These kinds of mistakes or oversights can render such a book unmarketable if the mistake is integral to the work. Not too many librarians or teachers are willing to use materials with known inaccuracies.

According to one author, she was more or less forbidden to talk to the artist for her nonfiction book: *I sent many semi-technical drawings and photos to my editors to pass on to the artist. He never received any of the materials I'd sent. This totally explained why one of the major illustrations didn't look at all like the real thing. And, it was too late to fix the art. The book had already gone to press by the time I saw the proofs.*

As if authors don't have enough opportunity for humility with their editors, they can be rejected by the illustrator as well. A picture book author recently asked me this question: *How can illustrators turn down my stories? As a writer, I take on some of the least exciting assignments because I need to work! So when an illustrator turns down my story, I think: I'd like to be in such a position to say "no." I figure they must be making a lot more money than me to be able to turn down work!*

Until this writer put the question to me, I never really considered how an author might feel

Author/illustrator Janie Bynum's debut picture book *Altoona Baboona* is a fun, rhyming tale of an ape who takes a jaunt in a hot air balloon—and makes some new friends. "Bynum's watercolors have a breezy ocean air feel to them, as light and bouyant as her simian heroine," says *Kirkus Reviews* of Bynum's work. A sequel, *Altoona Up North* was released in fall 2001 from Harcourt.

when an artist turns down the opportunity to illustrate their manuscript, or what the author might conclude from the "rejection." But there are many reasons an artist might reject a manuscript, most of them having nothing to do with the quality of the story.

Rejection Reason #1: The artist can't work the book into her schedule to accommodate the publisher's schedule for getting the book to market.

For trade books, artwork must be completed and approved by the publisher at least one year before the book is scheduled to arrive in stores. The rough sketch approval stage begins at least nine to eighteen months before that date, depending on how long it takes an artist to paint the book. On average, the printing process of picture books takes around six to eight months. Marketing materials also need to be produced—adding to the timeline. So, if an editor wants to get a book out in August 2003, first sketches will be required by January 2002.

More than likely that big name, oh-so-perfect-artist-for-this-book is, well, booked—into the next five years or more. It seems outrageous, but think about the previously mentioned production timeline and how long it can take an artist to illustrate a 32 (or more)-page book. For artists working in a lighter, more humorous style, it's possible to complete a book from thumbnails to finish in nine months or less (provided editorial goes smoothly). But for art created with oil paints or rendered in a more complicated or realistic style the painting process alone can take well over a year. That doesn't include rough sketches, revised sketches, finished sketches, and editorial sessions with the editor and art staff.

Some artists must concentrate on one book at a time, limiting the number of books they can produce in a year. But, other artists work on several books at once—all in different stages. So,

Too Big, Too Small, Just Right

Frances Minters
Illustrated by Janie Bynum

Illustrator Janie Bynum knows creating a picture book is a team effort. Bynum illustrated Frances Minters' text for *Too Big, Too Small, Just Right* with the guidance of Harcourt editorial director Allyn Johnston and the collaboration of designer Linda Lockowitz and production specialist Ginger Boyd. Their book turned out . . . *just right!*

Illustration © 2001 Janie Bynum. Reprinted with permission of Harcourt, Inc.

say the illustrator (one who generally takes a year to complete a book, and works on several books at a time) has four books contracted to illustrate when a new manuscript arrives for her to review (the famous illustrators have even more stories lined up). It could easily be two to three years before she could even begin the art process for a new book.

Rejection Reason #2: The artist may connect with the manuscript but feels that her particular style doesn't quite fit the story. This isn't necessarily a judgment about the quality of the story—or the artist's abilities. For whatever reason, the artist can't envision spending the next six months to a year living and breathing the art for this book. Maybe she could produce a few illustrations she would love, but for the most part the book would be a strain, or seem to require a different approach that the illustrator isn't comfortable reaching for.

Rejection Reason #3: The artist just can't connect with the story. I know artists who have taken on such projects out of flattery (*"But you're so good at creating subtext with your art!"*) or out of the need for work. The latter being absolutely acceptable; artists have to work (see

Reason #5). But, without the connection, the process is agonizingly difficult. Thirty-two-page picture books require, on average, from 16 to 24 illustrations, depending on the number of single-page illustrations versus full-spread art. That's a lot of painting. For the most part, the artist has to love the manuscript (or create their own subtext to fall in love with) to sustain the level of excitement required for that much painting!

Rejection Reason #4: There just isn't enough story to illustrate. Many manuscripts may, indeed, have a great concept, some wonderful "moments," but there just doesn't seem to be enough happening in the story. Maybe another artist can illustrate it, but the one holding the manuscript can't envision it, so the story is rejected and passed along to the next illustrator. This is why the editor has *at least* two or three illustrators in mind when she starts scouting for an available artist.

Rejection Reason #5: The manuscript is questionable. Amazing as it is, poorly-written manuscripts do find editors who love them enough to want to publish them. And artists may have to reject them. Or not—depending on an artist's financial need and/or immediate desire to be published. Inevitably, if the artist accepts the manuscript, a better, more suitable manuscript will arrive within weeks after she's committed to the first one!

Rejection Reason #6: The publisher won't pay enough. Oops. There it is, again. That business thing. But, when an artist is busy, booked through the next four years or so, it can take more than a publisher is willing to pay to convince them to give up weekends and evenings to add another book to their schedule. And, lest anyone think artists get paid exorbitant fees, perish the thought. Some do. Most don't.

As an artist, I sometimes forget that we are all working toward the same goal. I can get temporarily stymied by what initially appears to be negative criticism from the editor or author. But, usually, if I step back from these editorial sessions without reacting, and give the comments a few days to "gel," I can see their value and proceed with a new gusto for the revision process. Just like any artist who puts her heart into her work, I can get frustrated with the process, this business of children's books. Who *are* all these people? Isn't this *my* book?

But this is a business, and cooperation is part of my job. When that printed and bound picture book arrives on my doorstep, I don't see only my artwork, or the author's words, or the art director's design. I see our book. Everybody's glorious book.

Writing Humor (in Five Easy Steps!)

BY GREG R. FISHBONE

Before I started writing my mid-grade humor novel, *How To Become A Superhero (In Ten Easy Steps!)*, I sent an e-mail to Scott Adams. Adams writes and draws "Dilbert," a comic strip that comes pre-mounted to office cubicle walls, and that also appears in many newspapers. I figured that if anyone knew the secret to humor writing, it would be a man whose main character owns a talking dog that wants to rule the world.

Sure enough, Adams wrote back with the most brilliant advice since Mom warned me not to stick my tongue in the blender. Even better, he has given me permission to share that advice with you! If you want to write humor, all you need to do is . . .

"Be funny."

The rest of this article is just commentary on what "being funny" means to me.

I think humor writing, like most activities, can best be described in an "X easy steps" format, where X is the required length of this article divided by the number of words before the readers start nodding off. As you can see from the title, X is equal to 5.

Writing Humor, Step One: Requisition a Sense of Humor

In your efforts to "be funny," a sense of humor is almost a necessity. If you don't already own a sense of humor, I highly recommend you pick one up, or assemble one from common items you have lying around your home.

I trace my sense of humor back to afternoons watching classic Warner Brothers cartoons on TV. If you ever see me drop a grand piano onto an unsuspecting animated coyote, now you'll know why. Bugs Bunny and his friends made me laugh, but they also gave me a lifetime ambition to work toward. The more I experienced the joy of watching those lovable cartoon comedians, the more I wanted to grow up to become . . . a guy who watches cartoons all day.

Then I discovered that I also could make people laugh, just like Bugs, simply by chewing on a carrot and asking, "Eh . . . what's up, Doc?" What a thrill! With only a simple prop and a silly voice, I could create laughter! My world was transformed, and I would never again be satisfied to just watch cartoons all day. Instead, I dedicated my life to becoming . . . a *sarcastic wisecracker* who watches cartoons all day.

The problem was, I wasn't sure why my Bugs impression was so amusing. Were people laughing because I was clever and endearing, like Bugs himself? Or was it because I was making a fool of myself, like Elmer Fudd? Why should it be so funny for a little kid to imitate a talking cartoon rabbit? I had to find out.

So I studied the cartoons, and books of old "Peanuts" comic strips, and a joke book as thick as the phone directory. I experimented on my friends and family like a scientist in a humor lab. Sometimes my friends all cracked up at a joke that made my parents wince. Other times I could make my parents chuckle at something that left my friends scratching their heads. Once, I came up with the most wonderful joke in the history of the world—except that nobody thought it was

---

GREG R. FISHBONE *is a children's author, freelance writer, Web designer, attorney, and former editor of* Mythic Heroes *magazine. (Whew!) Visit his website at gfishbone.com for more discussion about humor, writing, and classic Warner Brothers cartoons.*

funny but me. Getting everyone to laugh at the same joke seemed impossible, but I learned to target certain kinds of humor to certain kinds of people.

Slowly, I developed and refined my sense of humor in a process that's made me more than just an ordinary humor writer. Today I'm a sarcastic wisecracking humor writer who loves to watch cartoons all day, and don't you ever forget it!

The bottom line: Your sense of humor, or lack thereof, is the product of every experience you've ever had and every joke you've ever heard.

Writing Humor, Step Two: Understand the Mechanics of Writing

Do you enjoy metaphors? Are they the champagne and caviar in the all-you-can-eat buffet of your life? Do they illuminate the dark shadows of your existence? Then have I got a metaphor for you.

If you wanted to build a funny-looking house, you could make it out of aluminum cans, Silly Putty, and cheesecloth. Passersby would laugh and gawk until their eye-sockets ached, but you would not be able to live there, and your friends would not want to visit. In order to make your funny-looking house safe and functional, and obtain the necessary building permits, you would need a strong foundation, solid structure, and competent construction skills.

Writing a humorous story is like building that funny-looking house. You are creating an environment functional enough for characters to live in, and safe enough to make readers want to drop by for tea and scones. The standard toolbox of writing still applies—grammar, syntax, character building, and dramatic structure—but instead of hammering nails into lumber, you're pounding aluminum cans into Silly Putty.

Problems I had while writing *How to Become a Superhero* involved plot and characterization. I wrote some amusing situations that didn't advance the plot, and funny dialogue that wasn't consistent with the characters as I had written them. Against all mathematical logic, the book became stronger and funnier when certain jokes were removed, and the characters became funnier when they reacted like people instead of "joke machines." (See What an Editor Looks For in Humor Writing sidebar below.)

The bottom line: Good humor writing is good writing first, and also just happens to be funny.

What an Editor Looks For in Humor Writing

Let me start by admitting that I am not a joke person and have occasionally been accused of having no sense of humor. That said, the most important thing I look for in humorous writing is "funny stuff" that feels real, not obvious. This happens when the humor naturally arises from the story and characters, rather than an author sitting around thinking "how can I make this funny" and twisting the plot in order to create the humor.

My favorite funny books that I've edited are a first chapter book quartet by Jackie French Koller about two characters named Mole and Shrew, where the laughs come from misunderstandings often related to word play. For example, in *Mole and Shrew Find a Clue*, Mole overhears Buzzard in the grocery store planning on having Rabbit and his family for dinner. Of course, Buzzard means having Rabbit's family *over* for dinner, but the misunderstanding sets off a chain of events that are both plausible and very funny.

That's the kind of thing I like. Luckily, not all editors are amused by the same things. It's just a matter of an author finding an editor on her or his wavelength.

—Mallory Loehr, *Random House Books for Young Readers*

Writing Humor, Step Three: Understand the Mechanics of Humor

Back in my days of doing Bugs Bunny impressions, I got steady laughs, and probably could have put together a standup comedy monologue something like this:

"Good evening ladies and gentlemen, and what's up Doc! What's up, Doc? What's . . . up . . . Doc! Yo, Doc, what's up? Hickory, Dickory, What's-Up-Doc! The mouse ran up the What's-Up-Clock! Doc, Doc, Doc, Doc, Goose! Whassup! You've been a wonderful audience, and I'll be here through next Thursday!"

It was funny, but I didn't understand *why* it was funny. Like a babbling infant, I was just repeating a language I barely understood. That's what humor is, a language with its own syntax and usage rules, just like English or Spanish. Let's call it "Humorish." In English, every sentence is built around a noun (the subject) and a verb (the predicate). In Humorish, every joke is built around a setup (the straight road) and a punchline (the unexpected curve).

Setup: A horse walks into a bar and the bartender says . . .
Punchline: "Why the long face?"

Setup: Did you ever wonder . . .
Punchline: . . . why we drive on parkways and park on driveways?

Setup: Take my wife . . .
Punchline: . . . please!

The humor in humor writing doesn't need to come from one-liners and puns. Often it comes from your characters and the situations you put them into. The setup might be a character's personality, and the punchline something that character does or says. Or the setup might be a situation you describe, and the punchline something unexpected that happens as a result. Or the setup might be a description in the first chapter of the book, and the punchline might happen twelve chapters later. The best way to learn the vocabulary of Written Humorish is to read funny books (like the ones listed in the sidebar on page 61).

Keep in mind that although Humorish is a nearly universal language among humans, we each have our own individual Humorish dialects. Don't be discouraged when one of your jokes falls flat—it may be that you're trying to speak Knock-Knock Humorish when your audience prefers Satire Humorish or Toilet Humorish. You also need to realize that Written Humorish differs greatly from Visual Humorish.

The "speakers" of Visual Humorish can use gestures, actions, facial expressions, costumes, makeup, props, and images to help create their setups and punchlines. They can tell jokes without using any words at all! You, as a practitioner of Written Humorish, do not have any of these things unless you construct them from the 26 letters of the alphabet and an assortment of punctuation marks. Some successful jokes in Visual Humorish can not be told in Written Humorish. On the other hand, the Visual Humorist will run out of props and special effects long before you run out of alphabet, and then who will have the last laugh, hmm?

The bottom line: Behind the laughter, humor is all about rules and structure and junk like that.

Writing Humor, Step Four: Develop Your Voice

Remember when I said that all you had in Written Humorish were 26 letters and some punctuation marks? I lied! You also have the numerals 0-9. And, oh yeah, there's this little thing called "style."

Think of your two favorite humor writers. I might pick Mark Twain and Dave Barry. If you were presented with 500 words from a story you had never seen before, would you be able to identify which of the two had written it? Sure you would. Each writer has his or her own catch phrases, rhythms, preferred subject matter, and language usage—in shorthand, "style."

Some people will tell you not to mimic the style of a writer you admire, but to develop your own style from scratch instead. Yeah, right, as if that were such an easy thing to do. Fortunately for me, I didn't receive any advice of this kind back when I was in high school and writing short stories in a badly-mimicked imitation of Douglas Adams. At the time, the highest praise I aspired to was, "Wow, this is like something Douglas Adams would write if he were a pimple-faced American teenager like you!"

So here's what I want you to do. Choose an author you admire and study his or her style of writing and humor. Understand how the setups and punchlines are put together. Are they short and punchy, elaborate and involved, or an unpredictable mix? Are they based on character, situation, or language? How do the humor style and writing style complement each other? Get into that author's head until you can produce a 500-word story in the same style, and then . . . never write in that style again!

Repeat until you've eliminated all styles but your own. Not only will you get the urge to mimic out of your system, but you might learn a thing or two in the process.

My style, when I finally found it, was a synthesis of everything I had seen, heard, and read. Douglas Adams continues to influence my writing, as all my favorite authors and best-loved

Funny Books I Like

These are some funny books and comic strips I like, which you might also like if you and I happen to share a similar sense of humor. If not, feel free to ridicule my (in your view) horrible taste in book selection. Either way you have something to laugh at, so it's win-win!

Books for Kids
 Tales of a Fourth Grade Nothing, by Judy Blume
 Charlie and the Chocolate Factory, by Roald Dahl
 Pippi Longstocking, by Astrid Ericsson Lindgren
 The Gashlycrumb Tinies: Or, After the Outing, by Edward Gorey
 The Shrinking of Treehorn, by Florence Parry Heide
 The Phantom Tollbooth, by Norton Juster
 Mrs. Piggle-Wiggle, by Betty MacDonald
 In the Night Kitchen, by Maurice Sendak
 Where the Sidewalk Ends, by Shel Silverstein
 The Bad Beginning (A Series of Unfortunate Events, Book 1), by Lemony Snicket

Books for Adults
 The Hitchhiker's Guide to the Galaxy, by Douglas Adams
 Various collected "Dilbert" volumes, by Scott Adams
 A Spell for Chameleon, by Piers Anthony
 Another Fine Myth, by Robert Asprin
 Dave Barry's Only Travel Guide You'll Ever Need, by Dave Barry
 Various collected "Bloom County" volumes, by Berkeley Breathed
 The Princess Bride: S. Morgenstern's Classic Tale of True Love and High Adventure,
    by William Goldman
 Various collected "Far Side" volumes, by Gary Larson
 The Onion Presents Our Dumb Century, by The Onion staff
 The Color of Magic, by Terry Pratchett
 The Westing Game, by Ellen Raskin
 Various collected "Peanuts" volumes, by Charles Schulz
 Various collected "Calvin & Hobbes" volumes, by Bill Watterson

books continue to influence my writing—because I have taken them into my heart, not because I am actively trying to imitate them.

The bottom line: Don't strive to be "the next Douglas Adams" or "the next Dr. Seuss"—be yourself.

Humor Writing, Step Five: Get a life!

When I took martial arts classes at the Chung Moo dojo, Instructor Dave always warned us not to "telegraph our punches." When an opponent figures out, from your positioning and body language, that you are about to throw a punch, the next thing you're likely to see is a close-up of the dojo floor.

The first humor writing lesson I took from this is that telegraphing punchlines is like telegraphing punches, except that a reader isn't likely to rub your face into the mat. When the reader recognizes your setup and anticipates the punchline before it happens, a good part of the impact is lost. On the other hand, can you telegraph one punchline and deliver a completely different punchline? Yes, you can!

The second humor writing lesson I took from Instructor Dave was even more useful than the first. It was the fact that I could learn humor writing lessons from getting punched, kicked, and tossed to the floor. It made me wonder, what other writing lessons are out there? Could I learn about rhythm and timing by playing an instrument? Could a basic knowledge of mathematics help me with structure? Could the study of Stanislavski method acting lead to more interesting and expressive characters? Yes, yes, yes!

I can do something I enjoy, other than writing, and not feel guilty about the unfinished manuscript on my computer. I can look that manuscript in the title page and tell it that I haven't been procrastinating, at least not entirely, because I've also been picking up hidden lessons that apply directly to writing, or to humor, or to both!

And as an added bonus, the martial arts might come in handy against book critics.

The bottom line: Mine your life experiences for writing lessons as well as story material.

I ask you to think of these "five easy steps" as the start of an infinite staircase, where "being funny" is the process of climbing ever upward without ever reaching a destination. Either that, or "being funny" is an infinite staircase where you slip on a banana peel, tumble downward your entire life, and land in a big vat of cream pie filling at the end.

The choice is up to you.

Traveling Companions: Making Connections Online

BY LISA WHEELER

In 1997, I hit the information highway in search of knowledge that might lead to my heart's desire: becoming a children's author. What I found on the journey was fortuitous opportunity, amazing friendship, and ultimate success.

HOOKING UP
In the Driver's Seat

Five years ago, my husband insisted I "go online" to help my writing career. I had been writing seriously for more than two years and had chalked up a decent amount of magazine sales.

"Why in the world do I need the Internet?" I asked.

"Try it, you'll like it," hubby said, quoting the old '70s TV commercial. So I did—and I *did!* Like it, that is. In fact, the Internet opened up a whole world of writing possibilities that I never anticipated.

With no road map to guide me, I searched for a children's writer's website. I finally got my search engine in gear and found www.Write4kids.com, a site belonging to Jon Bard and Laura Backes. Along with great information for new writers, interviews with famous authors, and tons of how-to's for those of us in between, Write4kids also features an active message board, fondly known as Old Yeller.

I parked at Old Yeller, hoping to get my writing questions answered and to find a worthwhile critique group. After a month or so of making connections, (most of which stalled) a new post caught my eye.

Linda Smith posted that she was looking for someone "serious" about her picture-book writing and wanted to share critiques. Her tone was friendly and her sense of humor apparent as she mentioned her eight children and an assortment of pets. She also mentioned that her manuscript won first place in one of *Byline* magazine's Children's Picture Book contests (www.bylinemag.com). My interest was piqued! I'd been entering *Byline*'s contests for several years and could never make it to the number one position. I wanted to see what a winning manuscript looked like. I also wanted to find out how a mother of eight had time to write!

During the summer of '97, Linda and I wrote to each other on a daily basis. E-mails became phone calls and a friendship was born.

LISA WHEELER*'s first book,* Wool Gathering: A Sheep Family Reunion, *illustrated by Frank Ansley (Richard Jackson/Atheneum) was released October 2001. Her upcoming titles include* Sixteen Cows, *illustrated by Kurt Cyrus (Harcourt, March 2002),* Sailor Moo: Cow at Sea, *illustrated by Ponder Goembel (Richard Jackson/Atheneum, summer 2002), and* Porcupining: A Prickly Love Story, *illustrated by Janie Bynum (Little, Brown, February 2003). (Ten other picture books and an easy reader series—Fitch & Chip—follow.) Lisa says she owes much of her success to her critique groups, both online and in person.*

With the help and support of her critique groups, author Lisa Wheeler has more than a dozen upcoming books under contract. Her first release, *Wool Gathering: A Sheep Family Reunion*, illustrated by Frank Ansley, is a collection of delightful poems published by Richard Jackson/Atheneum.

Here is how Linda answered a question on the Children's Writer's Listserve (CW List). This post is typical of Linda's sense of humor.

Date: 6-3-98

Q: Linda—do you write full-time or part-time?

A: I have eight kids, all home for summer vacation, a large Golden Retriever who loves puncturing baby pools and eating pies off the counter, a hugely messy never-ending pile of laundry, dirt, scattered toys, snotty noses, bloody knees, ringing phone, banging door, bedraggled husband, and always, always something burning on the stove, something spilling, someone crying, and a toilet that overflows three times out of four flushes (I think the dog put his ball in it) and yes, I write full-time.

The humor and camaraderie between Linda and other new Internet pals developed into lasting relationships. I've had the opportunity to meet some of these folks in person at conferences. It is always like a reunion when we get together. If I'd refused my husband's suggestion, I truly believe I would still be sitting in the virtual garage, waiting for a jump-start.

CRITIQUE GROUPS

Since going online, I have become involved with four different critique groups. There is no such thing as a one-size-fits-all group. Like cars, crit groups come in many shapes, sizes, and colors.

The test drive

My first critique group was a lemon. The group formed when someone on a message board put out a call. Like a bad carpool, we were overcrowded and bad writing "personality" matches. There were young adult, mid-grade and picture book writers vying to ride shotgun and play navigator. As you can imagine, we ended up in a wreck: some dropped out before submitting anything; others detoured after a couple weeks. Eventually, everyone drove off in her own direction. This is what happens when you set off too eagerly and without a map.

A first set of wheels

In the fall of 1997 Linda encouraged me to join *STARS*. This critique group formed when folks on the CW List communicated a desire to connect. Author Verla Kay took on the task of getting everyone "hooked up." She sorted groups by genre, and kept them small. Out of our new group of eight "rhyming picture book writers," Verla was the only one with contracted book sales. All that would soon change.

> Linda got the idea for her picture book, *When Moon Fell Down*, from an NYC childhood memory. She remembered waking in the middle of the night and seeing searchlights glowing against the building, floating up and down the street. At the time, she assumed the moon fell out of the sky, rolled down her street, and was shining into her bedroom window.

> *Date: 6-3-98*
> *Subject: YIPPEEEEEEEEEEEEEE!!!!!*
> *Date: 6-4-98*

> *I am too excited to type right now!!*
> *Alix Reid, the editor at HarperCollins, called back this morning and said she couldn't get WHEN MOON FELL DOWN out of her mind. She took it home with her last night and said she read it beneath a New York moon, the same one I thought so long ago had fallen down. This morning she called and said she didn't want that poem to go anywhere else, and wanted to make an offer.*
> *She did!!!!!*
> *Linda, who is way too excited to do ANY housework today!!*

When Moon Fell Down was released in April 2001, almost three years later.

Six months after Linda sold her first book (and second, third, fourth, and fifth!) I sold mine. Three months later, two other *STARS* members sold first picture books. Over the course of time, new members came. Old ones left. Group dynamics changed. One member went on to write YA articles and another sold a MG novel. As a critique group, we were driven . . . we were successful! We achieved excellence because we cared enough to be honest with each other. Eventually, as all good things must come to an end, the group scattered. Each of us had grown and moved on to do our own things. Today, we rarely critique as a group, but we still keep in touch and champion each other's successes. In total, the *STARS* have sold over 40 books!

By Linda Smith ★ Illustrated by Kathryn Brown

When Moon Fell Down

A portion of the proceeds from the sale of this book will be donated to breast cancer research, in memory of the author.

Late author Linda Smith was a beloved and supportive critique partner for writer Lisa Wheeler. Even now, "Linda's unwavering confidence in my abilities inspires me to work hard," says Wheeler. "She's that invisible 'editor' looking over my shoulder." Smith's first book *When Moon Fell Down*, illustrated by Kathryn Brown (HarperCollins), was released posthumously in 2001. Several more titles written by Smith will be published in the next few years.

Driving instructor

I came to my third group as a mentor. *Wordplay* was comprised of new writers, eager to learn the rules of the road. I volunteered to stay on for a few months until they could maneuver on their own. As with most online groups, membership wavers. Only three of the original members are still with *Wordplay*. But on the whole, I have seen their writing grow, and there have been many successes along the road including book sales by members Kelly DiPucchio, Margaret O'Hair, and Hope Vestergaard. And even though they can easily find their way without me, I find myself unwilling to get out of the car.

A sensible vehicle

I now belong to an online group appropriately called *Nitpickers*. This group, founded by author Dori Chaconas (who is interviewed for First Books on page 82), consists of children's picture book authors. We've paid our tolls, stowed our rejections in the glove compartment, and operate with the precision of a well-oiled machine. I don't kid myself that this group will run forever, but for now it is rolling along nicely.

NETWORKING

When I tell people how important it is to make online connections, I speak from personal experience. Oh sure, you get the occasional cranky-pants or obnoxious flamer, but the good friends I've made, and good connections, far outweigh the bad.

Opportunities on the horizon

In 1997, I read online that an educational software company was looking for experienced writers to write stories for their curriculum. I sent in my résumé and magazine writing clips, and after a test run was assigned four stories. The money I made from those assignments was better than anything I had previously earned. The experience also taught me to write "tight." The stories had to be 300 words or less and include vocabulary terms, a challenge that seriously revved up my editing skills.

Another great opportunity presented itself in Verla Kay's chat room. Author Lindy Rymill, who at the time was also the SCBWI Michigan regional advisor, invited me to attend a schmooze that was only an hour's drive from my home. I wasn't a member of SCBWI—I didn't yet realize the wealth of information and opportunities they offered. After attending the schmooze and meeting others who shared my love of children's books, I gladly sent off a check for membership.

Pass it on

You never know where online roads will lead. In 1997, Linda Smith met author/illustrator Janie Bynum on the CW Listserv. (See Janie's article Whose Book Is It Anway? A Picture Book Illustrator's Perspective on page 52.)Janie had just sold her picture book *Altoona Baboona* to Harcourt. Janie recognized Linda's talent and encouraged her to submit her manuscript *The Inside Tree* to literary agent, Steven Malk. Linda hesitated because the manuscript was with an editor in New York who had asked for a rewrite. When this editor sent the manuscript back, Linda sent it to *STARS*. After a nip and tuck, off it went to Steven in California.

> Date: 4-17-98
> Subject: YIPPEE!!!!!!
>
> I have such good news. The agent (Steven Malk) called. He was very, very excited about my work, and I just stood there with my mouth open. I can't believe it . . . my good luck and fortune . . . and am so nervous about living up to this now. I am really, really happy, but a little disbelieving too. I think maybe my Murphy's Law life may take a small turnabout. And of course, I feel like pinching myself. He said he was going to send my work to the cream of the crop, and said, "You have a

Shopping Smart

New writers are often concerned their ideas, words, and stories will be carjacked by strangers on the information highway. Although this has never been my experience, people, unlike cars, come with no guarantees. Before you jump behind the wheel, here's a checklist to keep you on track while you shop for a critique group.

- **Do your homework.** Lurk on a children's writers message board or listserv for several days, or weeks, or even months to get a feel for the posters' personalities and interests. A few shining individuals are sure to catch your eye.
- **Know what you want.** Try to find a group that specializes in one genre. If you write novels and picture books, join two groups, one for each genre. You wouldn't go to an RV dealership to buy a sports car, so don't expect a picture book group to critique your novel.
- **Read the fine print.** Approach people professionally. You are entering into a contract of sorts: You promise to give a service (your critique) in exchange for receiving that same service. If you are joining an established group, ask if they have guidelines. Your group will run more smoothly if everyone knows the rules.
- **Ask about a warranty.** Ensure that other members' goals and commitments are in line with your own. Is this a vehicle that will stay reliable for the long haul? Can it help you reach your destination?
- **Check the performance level.** There are many levels of challenge between riding a tricycle and professional racecar driving. If you have logged many miles in your writing career, look for a group who can keep pace.
- **Read the speedometer.** If you expect fast critiques, and everyone in your group works full time, you may find yourself spinning your wheels. Likewise, if you have difficulty critiquing in a timely manner, you may want to move out of the fast lane.
- **Go for a test drive.** Everything looks great, but you still may not be sure if this is the group for you. There's nothing like getting behind the wheel to test a vehicle's performance. Ask if you can "try out." Critique a few manuscripts. Submit one of your own and read everyone's responses. This will give you a feel for the overall quality of the group.
- **Enjoy the ride.** If you find a great online critique group, buy it! If not, keep shopping. Your dream vehicle is worth waiting for. Even critique groups that don't work out will help you learn something from the trip and become a smarter shopper. In the meantime, enjoy the ride.

fantastic career ahead of you." I just can't believe it. I felt like not telling anyone, because if I did I would wake up and find I was dreaming. All smiles :) Linda

Shortly after, Linda encouraged me to send a few things to Steven Malk, who accepted me as a client on the basis of a chapter book I had written. Months later, he accepted two other *STARS*, not because of Linda's referral, but because their books were excellent. Since then, I have also referred other good writers who had excellent manuscripts. Those connections on the Internet highway can lead to exciting places!

SUPPORT

Now you're in the driver's seat, buckled in and ready to go. But traveling by yourself can get lonely. You need great companions for the trip!

If you live in a rural area, or a community with few bookstores, colleges, or public libraries, finding critique groups and making connections may prove difficult. Perhaps you have small children at home, or the only writing groups in your area meet during times you are at work. In cases like these, Internet writing companions can be invaluable.

The long road

Besides sharing our rejections and disappointments, Linda and I shared our joys and successes in our personal life as well.

This was in response to my tongue-in-cheek suggestion that Linda and I get Glamour Shots for our author photos.

> *Date: 11-7-98*
> *Subject: Author Photo*
>
> *Hahahahaaha! You crack me up, Lisa! Of COURSE I've thought of that!*
> *What the heck ya think Glamour shots are for!*
> *And then when we go to our book signings and everyone will say . . . "Gee, I wonder where the author is?" And we'll say, "It's me! Here I am!" and they'll think, "What a weirdo! Trying to impersonate the author!"*

Not long after that happy e-mail, I received this one.

> *Date: 11-20-98*
> *Subject: Hello—I Miss You!*
>
> *Lisa,*
> *I am so sick tonight I can hardly sit up, so what do I do? Get my heating pad and sit HERE because at least it gives me something "busy" to do (rather than lay in bed). I have gall bladder woes really bad, and will probably have to have surgery or some other godawful treatment. But I was SO happy to see you back . . . and learn you had a wonderful time, I just had to write to you.*
> *I've missed our e-mail chats.*
> *God, what misery. I'm telling you this depressing stuff so you'll know where I "disappeared to" if I'm not too fast to write back. I'm just four feet away from the computer . . . in bed!*
> *Talk soon*
> *Linda*

And then . . .

> *Date: 11-23-98*
>
> *Lisa, I'm going in to the doc today for more tests.*
> *I'll let you know what happens. Sorry I have been so unavailable . . .*
> *I have really been feeling rotten.*
> *I'll be in touch!!*
> *Linda*

And ultimately . . .

> *Date: 12-1-98*
>
> *Lisa,*
> *The news is bad. I found out today that I have breast cancer . . .*

My dear friend, Linda Smith, lived another year and a half after this diagnosis. By the time her cancer was found, it had already spread to her liver and that is why she had been misdiagnosed with a gall bladder problem. I had the opportunity to fly out to San Diego and visit with Linda

Great Places To Connect

WEBSITES

Children's Writing Resource Center, www.write4kids.com
Hosts a message board dedicated to children's writing. Offers free information for children's writers as well as a bookshop where you can purchase informative children's writing material.

The Children's Literature Web Guide, www.ucalgary.ca/~dkbrown/index.html
Discussion board on children's books, links to author sites, and much more.

The Writers Bbs, www.writersbbs.com/
Hosts chatrooms, discussion forums, and more. Many genres. Great place to connect!

The Drawing Board for Illustrators, http://members.aol.com/thedrawing/
Contains articles, interviews, FAQ's and more for illustrators.

LISTSERVES

Children's Writer's Listserv
To subscribe to the CW List, send a blank email to childrens-writers-subscribe@egroups.com. This is a very active listserv and you can expect to get around 30 or more e-mails per day. Digest version available.

Wrt4kdz
An online community of children's writers (about half of them are published), 100-member limit with a waiting list. Go to www.sandbaggers.8m.com where moderator will announce openings when/if they become available.

Utah Children's Writers
To subscribe, e-mail utahchildrenswriters-subscribe@yahoogroups.com. This is a community for children's writers with a tie to Utah. Some members also live in Idaho and belong to the Utah/Idaho region of SCBWI.

Scbwi State/Regional Listservs
Unless otherwise stated, listservs are open to state/regional members only.
Canada: http://groups.yahoo.com/group/scbwicanada
Illinois: e-mail thebrandon@aol.com
Michigan: e-mail marienkafer74@aol.com
Rocky Mountain (Wyoming/Colorado): e-mail lroberts@ecentral.com
Mid-South (Tennessee): e-mail scbwi.midsouth@juno.com
Wisconsin: e-mail Catchne@aol.com

CHAT ROOMS

Verla Kay's Website, www.verlakay.com
Author Verla Kay offers book reviews, authors talks, workshops, and a very busy children's writing chat room.

AuthorChats.com, www.authorchats.com
AuthorChats is dedicated to bringing children's books and authors together with parents, teachers and children since 1999. Online chats between authors and school children, as well as a wealth of information about children's books and teaching children about reading and writing.

for four wonderful days in August of 1999. She was pretty sick, but she donned a turban to cover her hairless head and we hit The White Rabbit children's bookstore in La Jolla, a place we had always dreamed of going together. We shared a hotel room and talked deep into the night about books and stories, family and friends. It was such a precious time for me.

Because Linda had given so much of herself and her talents to her Internet friends, we all rallied to support her in her time of need. Folks in the online writing community, who had never met Linda face-to-face, donated money when she had no health insurance. Many wrote to media and government officials to try and get Linda the help she needed. Peter Davis set up a list-serve to share information. Marti Anderson put together a website where folks could honor Linda with testimonials and get information (www.execpc.com/~marti/). These folks only knew Linda from her e-mails and online posts. I wish I could name every person who helped, but it would take pages. This is the information highway at its finest, with roadside angels waiting with outstretched hands. I know Linda's family and friends are eternally grateful.

The end of the journey?

Folks who have witnessed my heartache at the loss of my traveling companion have asked if I regret my trip on the Internet. My answer now and always will be "No."

I truly believe that Linda and I were brought together for a reason. We needed each other for more than just networking and critiquing. We both needed a friend and since, as writers, we communicate better through the written word, our friendship was probably deeper than it would have been if we had met in any other way.

I learned so much from Linda. She was my friend and my mentor. Since knowing her, I have achieved things in my writing that may have taken me years to learn on my own. She taught me to trust my instincts, break some rules, and above all else, pass it on.

> *Date: 4-30-98*
> *Lisa,*
>
> *I talked to my agent about referring people and he said, "If you think they're good, send them along." I mentioned your name, of course. I can't promise you anything, Lisa, as you know. Janie did this for me, and I will always be very grateful to her. Now the agent has said he would love to see a referral, so I am grabbing this opportunity to pass the favor along. Nothing would make me happier. I do mean that.*
> *Linda*

To Crit or Not to Crit? A Spotlight on Critique Groups

BY VICTORIA J. COE

So you want to be a critter. You're thinking that a critique group can help improve your writing skills, give new life to your stories and encourage creativity. Right? Not necessarily. The wrong attitude or the wrong group can do just the opposite. Sound scary? It doesn't have to be. A few ins and outs can help you avoid potential pitfalls and get the most out of your critique group experience.

Can we talk?

It all boils down to good communication—starting with yourself. Take a long, hard look at that writer in the mirror. What does she *really* want from a critique group? Friendship and support? A pat on the back? Validation? Objective eyes? Tips on how to improve? In fact, you may have many desired outcomes. But if your number one goal is growth as a writer, read on.

No pain, no gain

Let's be honest. It can be very intimidating to read your work to a group of strangers and hear unbiased feedback. What if they say you stink? What if you lack one original thought? What if they tell you to pack it in and forget about writing altogether?

Before you decide if you're ready to take that plunge, think! If you're at the place where you feel you've done all you can on your own, and you are willing to listen to others' opinions, even if they're tough to hear, then and only then should you consider joining a group.

On the lookout

Before setting out to find a group, make a list of your personal goals as a writer. Use this list as a guideline in evaluating potential groups in terms of how they can help you reach those goals.

When contacting a group, remember it's a two-way street. The members will evaluate you and your "fit" with the group, just as you will with them. Present yourself honestly and openly. Anything less will do everyone a disservice.

Communicate your writing interests, history and goals. Tell them why and how you think a critique group might help you reach those goals.

Ask questions. Aside from basic logistics, learn all you can about how the group works and the interest and experience that each member offers. (See sidebar on page 22.) If your initial contact is positive, try it out. In addition to your comfort level, pay attention to the writing the other members share. You will probably benefit most from writers who are better than you.

VICTORIA J. COE *has been sharing, learning, and growing with her San Francisco-based critique group for two and a half years. She's an SCBWI member, and a frequent contributor to the "Read to Write" column at www.writejourney.com, where this article first appeared.*

Critter Do's and Don'ts

Do's

- Do keep an open mind!
- Do offer something positive about someone's work and keep the tone encouraging, even if the criticism has to be a little harsh to be honest.
- Do put your name on your crit so the writer can follow up with you later if something requires further explanation.
- Do offer positive suggestions for improvement where appropriate.
- Do read lots of recently published books in the genre you write and crit.

Don'ts:

- Don't ask the group to crit your first draft. Only submit a manuscript or chapter that you've taken as far as you can on your own.
- Don't revise in order to please the group. If a suggestion doesn't feel right, don't take it.
- Don't believe excessive praise absent of constructive criticism. Everything can be improved.
- Don't defend. Ask questions to clarify a critique, but defending isn't helpful because you can't defend something that is unclear to an editor or reader. Accept that whatever you had in mind isn't coming across to the reader and try again.

Now stand there naked

That's what it will feel like the first time you submit your writing for critique! Keep a receptive attitude and open your mouth.

Tell the other critters what you're looking for from this particular critique. If you're open to general feedback, say so. If you're looking for something more specific, tell the group which areas you're unsure about and ask for their ideas. Guide them, so they can offer you the greatest possible assistance. You might want to know if your plot seems plausible or tight. The areas that overwhelm the reader or slow her down. The consistency of the voice. Is the main character sympathetic, three-dimensional, engaging?

Respect the group's time and effort by telling them what you don't want. If you don't want a line-by-line grammar and spelling check in favor of a more general evaluation, speak up. Help them help you!

When listening to feedback, ask questions if you need clarification, but don't offer explanations. If the reader didn't connect with what you were trying to say, consider that your written word may not adequately convey your vision. Note any and all suggestions for later assessment.

Take a day or two, if possible, to digest your critique. Some reactions that may have seemed unsettling at first make sense after the critique has cooled. Others may seem overwhelming or conflicting. Evaluate suggestions in light of whether they make the work stronger, consistent with your own vision. If you don't, you run the risk of losing your individuality and writing to please the group.

Be a good critter

Read widely in your group's genre(s). Let various writers' strengths touch and shape you, not only as a reader, but as a critter.

When it's your turn to critique, recognize the trust the writer places in you. It's your responsibility to be supportive, yet as honest and helpful as possible. Holding back in order to spare someone's feelings helps no one.

Realize that writing is subjective. Encourage each writer to find and develop her own unique style, not to write the way you would. Be open to originality, uniqueness and experimentation.

Follow any guidelines the writer has offered. In addition, look for both strengths and weaknesses in the work. Don't forget to point out inconsistencies in story, setting, character or voice.

Think of a critique as a sandwich. Start out with something positive, layer on observations, questions, improvements for the writer to consider, then end with another positive comment. Remember that the best part of any sandwich is the "meat," so don't skimp!

But if it's just not working . . .

Okay, you've made an earnest effort trying out the group, but despite everyone's best efforts, it's not right for you. If so, you owe it to your writing and to the other members to keep looking.

Once you do locate a group where you feel comfortable, give yourself a certain time period, say six months or a year, to decide if you're any closer to your goals. If you feel you're going around in circles, move on. If it's not working, don't waste your time in a holding pattern when your goal is to fly.

If the critique group experience doesn't give you what you need, one-on-one critiques, whether from a swap with another writer or a paid professional, can be the way to go. Whatever you decide, measure its success or failure against your personal goals.

The prize

With the right attitude and the right group, the critique experience can be an invaluable tool in helping you achieve your goals. Many critique groups support each other in ways that extend far beyond writing, not only commiserating over rejections and celebrating sales, but forming strong friendships. I always smile when I crack open a new book to see that the author has dedicated the story to the "Tuesday Night Group." This is what it's all about, folks.

Finding the right group can be like searching for treasure: the pursuit may be tough and tedious, but when you finally behold the brilliance of the prize, you realize that the toil was well worth the reward!

Matchmaker, Matchmaker

Here's a list of questions to consider when checking out an existing group:
1. What is the goal of the group?
2. Are the members seeking to improve their writing?
3. Are they seriously seeking publication?
4. How many members are published?
5. In what genres are the members writing?
6. Are the members expected to bring writing for critique each meeting?
7. How successful do the members seem in reaching their goals?
8. Imagine yourself as part of the group. Do you see the group helping you to meet your goals?

Is It Really a Crime to Write in Rhyme?

BY BARBARA J. ODANAKA

Is it really a crime
To write in rhyme?
. . . So many say it's true.
But born with the curse of compulsive verse,
What else can a rhymer do?

Ah, the lament of the rhyming writer.

Told from the get-go that verse is a no-no, this misguided creature actually believes the rumors swirling around conferences and Internet chats:

Editors despise rhyme. Serious writers write in prose. Writing in verse is a one-way ticket to the rejection pile . . .

Oh, what a bucket of balderdash.

I know because, until recently, I was this misguided creature. When an editor told me she didn't buy rhyme because "children deserve better," I nodded reverently. You could have plastered a big, scarlet R on my chest. *Rhyme = Crime* was my mantra.

Trouble was, I could barely write *without* rhyming. Nearly every line that popped from my brain did so with a distinctive beat—a boogie-woogie, a rumba, a cha cha cha—that was impossible to ignore. The heck with the naysayers, I decided. Win or lose, I'd give in to the muse. I sold my first book soon after.

After interviewing more than two dozen editors, agents and authors, I've come to believe the odds of selling a rhyming picture book manuscript increase substantially if one follows a few simple guidelines:

RHYME RIGHT

Sure, it sounds obvious, but editors often complain that the bulk of rhyming manuscripts they receive are just plain stinky. Mangled meter, forced rhyme, inverted sentences to accommodate rhyme . . . the pet peeves go on and on.

"Some of the worst manuscripts I've ever read have been in rhyme," says Liz Bicknell, associate publisher/editorial director of Candlewick Press. "I don't mean to discourage serious writers, but anyone who thinks they can dash off a great rhyming picture book text in a couple of afternoons is either a genius or deluded."

Messy meter is a prime cause for rejection. Learning to scan your verse can certainly help—prime rhymer Sarah Weeks, author of the popular Mrs. McNosh books, calls herself a "scansion maven." Newcomer Lisa Wheeler (see sidebar on page 76) says while she feels she has a natural

BARBARA J. ODANAKA *is the author of the forthcoming* Skateboard Mom *(G. P. Putnam's Sons, 2003) and* Smash, Mash, Crash—There Goes the Trash! *(Margaret K. McElderry, 2004), both picture books in rhyme. A former staff writer for the* Los Angeles Times*, Odanaka covers the children's book industry and reviews children's books for a number of publications. For more about the author, glide on over to www.skateboardmom.com.*

Profile of a Rhymer: Lisa Wheeler

Lisa Wheeler says she wakes up every morning feeling grateful—with good reason. Over a three-year stretch, the Michigan author sold 18 books, most of them in rhyme.

"I am doing *exactly* what I was meant to do with my life," Wheeler says. "How many people can say that?"

Wheeler, a mother of three, started dabbling in children's books in the late 1980s when her children were young. In 1995, she vowed to get serious. Today, Wheeler is definitely one to watch in the world of prime rhymers. Her *Wool Gathering: A Sheep Family Reunion*, illustrated by Frank Ansley and published by Richard Jackson/Atheneum, debuted last fall. Four more Wheeler books will be published this year. (See Wheeler's article Traveling Companions: Making Connections Online on page 63.)

Did you rhyme often as a kid?

In 4th grade, I won a poetry contest and the prize was reading my poem over the school's PA system. When the other winners read their poems, I noted places where the meter was off (in my head, of course). Even though I didn't know what meter was, I knew something was "off" about some of their poems. Rhyme came easily to me and I thought it was something everyone did. It took me years to realize that wasn't true.

What were your earliest efforts like?

In 1987, while I was still "dabbling," my mother decided I should send my rhyming manuscript to publishers. She took it upon herself to make copies of my story—titled *Smelly* which was appropriate because the manuscript stunk—and send it out. She included my horrible artwork and she didn't send a SASE. She sent it to four houses, three of which didn't take unsolicited material and did not include a cover letter. A year later, I got back four manuscripts with form rejections—one from Harcourt. Eleven years later, Harcourt bought my first book (which was not *Smelly* and did not stink). I guess they forgot all about my first lame effort.

You've said stories need a reason to rhyme. How do you know whether one should be in rhyme or not?

I ask myself questions like: "Does the rhyme hinder the story? Help the story? Would the story be clearer, more cohesive, without rhyme? Does the rhyming aspect make it more readable? More fun? How much would be lost if the story were in prose? How much would be gained?"

Why, despite negative marketing rumors, do you think so many writers choose to write in rhyme?

Rhyming picture books are deceptive. They look much easier than they truly are. Though I always had a knack for rhyme, I joined a local chapter of the Poetry Society of Michigan, where octogenarian Gwen Funston (a retired English teacher) helped me to learn about poetry. Just because the end words rhyme, does not make it poetry! I studied with Gwen's group for two years. I still haven't "mastered" anything. I think it takes a lifetime to fully appreciate and learn the nuances of good poetry. But there are so many elements that go into good rhyme . . . and a good story.

—*Barbara J. Odanaka*

Megan Tingley, editorial director of her own imprint with Little, Brown, cites David T. Greenberg's *Bugs!* as a superior example of a rhyming picture book. "Anyone can find a rhyme for 'bear' or 'bug'," says Tingley. "But the true masters, such as Greenberg, create hilarious rhymes with more unusual language."

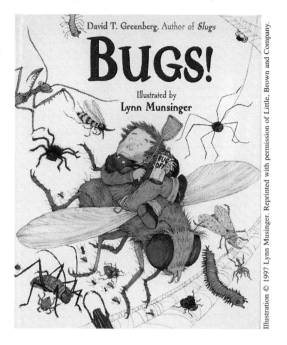

ear for rhythm, she always scans her verse to be sure. Reading your manuscript out loud is a good idea, but don't stop there. Have someone (an *objective* someone) read it aloud. If you hear glitches in the rhythm, or feel the urge to coach the reader in any way, you probably have more work to do.

"It must flow off the tongue," says Victoria Wells, Editorial Director of Bloomsbury USA. "If I have trouble reading it out loud—or worse, have trouble just reading it silently—forget it."

Consider taking a poetry class. A slew of award-winning authors—Janet Wong, Ann Whitford Paul and Kristine O'Connell George among them—were taught and inspired by the late, great Myra Cohn Livingston. Author Leslea Newman (*Cats, Cats, Cats!*) studied under the legendary Allen Ginsberg.

Most importantly, immerse yourself in verse. *Great* verse, that is.

"The advice I would give to aspiring writers," says Christy Ottaviano, Executive Editor at Henry Holt, "is to study the masters—Prelutsky, Silverstein, Kuskin, Seuss, and Florian, for starters."

PUT STORY FIRST

As many editors know, a manuscript written in rhyme, even when the rhyme and meter are perfect, does not guarantee a good story. A bee and a flea can sit by a tree, but if that's the whole of your plot, well . . .

"A dull story is a dull story whether it's written in rhyme or prose," says Grace Maccarone, executive editor of Scholastic's Cartwheel Books, and author of *Itchy, Itchy Chicken Pox*, among others.

Maria Modugno, editorial director of Little, Brown, agrees: "It's important for the book to say something—either tell a story or describe an incident or person or place."

In other words, don't let rhyme be your guide. A story must have *story*. Author Anastasia Suen says her trick is to "storyboard" her books before she begins writing them.

"A line or two comes to mind," says Suen, author of *Window Music*. "If it feels like it's a picture book, then I plot it out. If I have enough story, *then* I write the rest of the rhyme. It took

Profile of a Rhymer: Mary Ann Hoberman

For nearly a half century, Mary Ann Hoberman has entertained scores of youngsters with her delightful, insightful verse. The award-winning author of *The Seven Silly Eaters, One of Each* and the classic *A House Is A House for Me* has more than 30 books to her credit.

And Hoberman, of Greenwich, Conn., shows no signs of slowing down.

"People who learned my poems as children are now reciting them to their own children," Hoberman says. "And to meet a child whose classroom you visited three or four years ago, and hear that child with great excitement recite one of your poems back to you letter perfect— it doesn't get better than that!"

What shaped you as a writer today?
From as far back as I can remember, I loved words, sounds, rhythms, tunes. And well before I learned to write, I "wrote," making up songs and verses and stories in my head, telling them to myself and to my first audience, my little brother. As for rhyme, it is the most obvious element in a whole range of linguistic qualities shared with music. For me the heart of poetry is the lyric . . . the song. Rhythm, repetition, rhyme are key lyrical elements . . . and rhyme contains the others. By now, after a lifetime of writing in rhyme, I am myself a rhyming dictionary!

Do you start with a story idea first, or does a line of verse or a rhythm usually inspire you?
Rhythm, rhythm, rhythm! Usually with some words/sounds attached, but not always. I have found that walking is a great stimulus to writing in rhythm/verse. And I'm not the only one . . . Wordsworth made this discovery centuries ago as he trod the Lake District!

Outside of talent, hard work and persistence, why do you think you've succeeded so?
Thank you for crediting me with these three elements! But also, importantly, I was in the right place at the right time. I submitted my first book (*All My Shoes Come in Two's*, Little, Brown, 1957) to an editor, the late great Helen Jones, who was open to publishing children's verse. This was a rare situation at that time and I, all unknowingly, happened to send my manuscript to just the right editor and the right publisher.

The second factor is simple longevity! Building a body of work over a long period of time creates an audience of both children and adults (and children who become adults) familiar with your writing and open to more of it. And a third reason is simply that children love poetry made to their measure and respond enthusiastically when they hear it.

—Barbara J. Odonaka

me years to learn this: story first, then rhyme. You can have the best rhyme in the world, but if you don't have a story, why would an editor want to see it?"

The challenge, of course, is to blend all the ingredients—captivating plot, unforgettable characters, etc.—with seamless rhythm and rhyme. Susan Middleton Elya, author of a dozen rhyming picture books including *Eight Animals on the Town*, does this with an additional twist. Elya weaves English and Spanish in her verse.

"The key," Elya says, "is telling a story so effortlessly that the rhyming seems secondary."

Mary Ann Hoberman (*One of Each*) agrees: "The rhyme," she says, "should feel inevitable."

BE *EXTRA* CREATIVE
"Rhyming picture books should introduce children to a few delicious new words and have some clever, surprising rhymes," says Megan Tingley, editorial director of Megan Tingley

Books, an imprint of Little, Brown. "Anyone can find a rhyme for 'bear' or 'bed.' But the true masters, such as David Greenberg, create hilarious rhymes with more unusual language."

Like this, from Greenberg's *BUGS!*:

> *There isn't any question,*
> *They're infestin' your intestine.*

Several editors noted that predictable end rhymes—cat/bat, frog/log, and so on—are a turn-off. Some resist end rhyme altogether.

"I think it's extremely difficult to write a book with regular rhyme that doesn't drone and that isn't exhausting to read," says Kathy Dawson, executive editor of G.P. Putnam's Sons. "For me, the best picture books use rhythm and rhyme but don't often have end rhymes. I love books that feel great in your mouth when you read them."

Toby Speed's *Brave Potatoes*, which Dawson edited, is a prime example. The story, about a squad of spuds evading a malicious chef's soup pot, features an intoxicating mix of alternating rhythms, alliteration—Maldonada mushrooms, Bastaboola beets—and various forms of rhyme, all woven into a raucous read-aloud. An excerpt:

> *Over at the Fair,*
> *potatoes in the air!*
> *See them flip, flip, flip on the wild and wooly Zip!*
> *See the fearless aviators in their aviating duds*
> *going over, going under in an aerial display.*
> *What a trip, trip, trip! What a perilous ballet*
> *for the mamas and the papas and the wee potato buds.*
> *See the mesmerizing,*
> > *death-defying*
> > > *spuds!*

> © 2000 Toby Speed. Reprinted with permission of G.P. Putnam's Sons

Like Speed, Nancy Van Laan (*A Tree for Me, When Winter Comes*) emphasizes rhythm over rhyme, with fabulous results.

"The only advice I can offer is this: Don't intentionally set out to write in rhyme," Van Laan says. "If it starts to become overworked as the verse progresses, perhaps it shouldn't be written in rhyme after all. Settle for a nice, rhythmic prose instead."

Whatever you do, don't aim to be the "next Dr. Seuss." (That is something editors despise.) Develop your own style, perfect it, and strive for the freshest, most wonderful stories your muse can muster.

As Ottaviano of Holt put it, writing in verse "isn't just about 'turning a rhyme.' It's about developing a poetic voice and taking the form to another level."

RHYME FOR A REASON

I'll admit, this one used to drive me batty. *There has to be a reason? Can't I rhyme just because it sounds good?*

Well, no. Most of the editors interviewed said there needs to be a compelling reason for rhyme, especially for books aimed at children older than four.

Modugno, of Little, Brown, is supportive of picture book verse (she edited Jane Yolen's *Off We Go!*) but says rhyme schemes ought to become more sophisticated as the target age gets older.

Tingley believes picture books should only be written in rhyme if the use of the rhyme is integral to the telling of the story.

"In *One of Each*," Tingley says, "Mary Ann Hoberman wrote a refrain, 'One plum and one apple, one pear and one peach. Just one, only one, simply one, one of each,' that carries throughout the book and grows into "two of each" by the end. This creates tension and drama and the story wouldn't work without it."

Of course, some authors let the work decide for itself.

"For me, the best picture books use rhythm and rhyme but don't often have end rhymes," say Kathy Dawson, executive editor of G.P. Putnam's Sons. Tody Speed's *Brave Potatoes*, which Dawson edited, employs these techniques. "I love books that feel great in your mouth when you read them."

"The books themselves demand whether they'll be written in rhyme or prose," Jane Yolen says. "I just listen to what they say."

Author Bonny Becker was listening, too, when she decided to bail on her rhyming version of *The Christmas Crocodile* ("There once was a Christmas crocodile/A crocka-a-crocka-a-crocodile . . ."). Becker had worked hard on the rhyming text, but when a new opening line suddenly popped into her brain ("The Christmas Crocodile didn't mean to be bad, not really,") Becker knew it was a tell-tale sign to switch gears.

"It set up a whole different story and different voice for the story," Becker says. "And that voice was in prose, not in rhyme."

AIM FOR THE BULLS-EYE

We've all heard it's important to target our submissions. With rhyming manuscripts, it's downright critical.

Comb the shelves of bookstores and libraries; analyze catalogs. Note which publishers support rhyme—and which do not. You'll save time, postage, and spare yourself an insta-ject if you avoid sending verse to publishers who rarely buy it.

Some houses, like Candlewick, aim for an international market, meaning they strive to translate their books into many languages. Prose translates easier than verse, so prose is what they tend to acquire. (Says Bicknell: "You can be sure that if we do acquire a rhyming text, it will be because we are besotted with it!")

If you find books in rhyme you particularly enjoy, or seem somewhat similar to your style, call the publishers' marketing departments and ask who edited them. At conferences, ask editors to list their favorite picture books, especially those they enjoyed as a child. If they loved rhyme as a child, chances are they're probably still receptive to it. Better yet, ask them how they feel about rhyme in general.

If you're seeking an agent, target accordingly. Andrea Brown, a 25-year industry veteran, had the pleasure of working with Ted Geisel, a.k.a. Dr. Seuss, while at Random House. Now president of her own literary agency, Brown has a closed-door policy on rhyming manuscripts.

"Editors are looking to get manuscripts off their desks," Brown explains. "If writers give them an off-word or off-rhythm, that's an instant, easy rejection."

Agent Steven Malk of Writers' House agrees some editors have an aversion to rhyme. But when it's done well, and elevates a story, he says "it's just as marketable as prose."

Just as marketable as prose.

Now there's a mantra I can live with.

First Books

BY CANDI LACE

Anaïs Nin, often criticized for exercising too much "emotion" and "melodrama" in her writing, once said, "I will not be just a tourist in a world of images I cannot create and change, and possess as permanent sources of joy and ecstasy." Not only did she create her own world of images—she masterfully shared it in books such as *Ladders to Fire*, *Cities of the Interior* and *Children of Albatross*, among other abstruse tales.

For most writers, the instinct to record something is simply not satisfactory. Like Nin, they harbor a smoldering desire to share their newly invented world with others, no matter how bizarre, fantastical *or* melodramatic it may be. Here, four writers and illustrators discuss what it was like to get published for the first time, and invite an audience into the distinctive realms of their imagination—talking Valentine cards and houses included!

RACHEL COHN
Gingerbread (Simon & Schuster Books for Young Readers)

"If I'm not hungry for food, then I'm hungry for something bigger: answers to the secrets of the universe, true love, a more substantial bustline," declares Rachel Cohn's leading *Gingerbread* character, Cyd Charisse. Inquisitive and adventurous, Cyd is a 16-year-old girl in search of destiny. Named after the famous sleek dancer of the musical era, she defies most conceptions of a teenager from an affluent upbringing. Cyd stays away from malls, glittery makeup, boy bands, and television, for instance, and her best friend, Sugar Pie, is a senior citizen who resides in a nursing home. Cyd proudly carries around her doll Gingerbread everywhere she goes—even on shoplifting ventures—and her passions include caffeine, sweets, Mexican fare, and a boy named Shrimp.

Cohn's character was inspired by the front of a greeting card given to her by a close friend. "The figure on the card was wearing monster-sized black boots and toting a doll," says Cohn. "She was nothing like other characters I created, but I became a vehicle for who she was instantly."

Cohn's book, *Gingerbread* takes place in San Francisco and New York City, where both locations are almost as substantiated as the characters throughout. Drawing on culture, Cohn highlights the essence of the two cities through her portrayal of Cyd Charisse. At home in San Francisco, Cyd spends most of her time on the beach and in cafes with Shrimp and Sugar Pie. In between jaunts, she argues with her high society mother, imagines knowing her real father and struggles with the emotional scars her past relationship at boarding school generated. As she visits her natural father in New York City, Cyd peruses art museums, dines on pizza with her Italian escort and explores Greenwich Village, among other trendy East Coast spots. "I relied on my exposure to these places while writing the book," says Cohn. "Cyd Charisse was the first character I materialized who had nothing to do with me; therefore, I felt a need to

---

CANDI LACE *is the production editor and staff writer for* Children's Writer's & Illustrator's Market *and* Artist's & Graphic Designer's Market. *Her writing has been published in* Clamor, Art Papers, Alternative Cinema, *and* Sojourner: The Women's Forum, *among other venues.*

"Cyd Charisse was the first character I created who had nothing to do with me," says Rachel Cohn. "but I became a vehicle for who she was instantly." *Gingerbread* carries Cohn's lead character Cyd from San Francisco to New York City in this dynamic book about a teen who wears combat boots and befriends a doll.

Book design by Anahid Hamparion. © Simon & Schuster Books for Young Readers.

provide realistic detail to her surroundings in order to make her more believable."

Before *Gingerbread,* Cohn wrote two adult books that remain unpublished. Frustrated by all the rejections and criticism she received, Cohn decided to embark on an entirely different genre and complete a novel for her own satisfaction, not a potential agent's or editor's. While she was hanging out in youth-filled coffeehouses in the Richmond section of San Francisco, the characters in *Gingerbread* blossomed. Thereafter, Cohn says the writing process was more fulfilling than ever before, and everything about the book simply fell into place. For instance, life as a teenager, which had not been the foundation of her other books, naturally emerged from her environment. Accordingly, Cohn doesn't skimp while describing the many facets of a 16-year-old girl's existence: parental relations, sexuality, drug usage, spirituality, political choices, self-esteem, and cultural identity.

The first draft of the book impressed her Writer's House agent enough that it was solicited and picked up by Simon & Schuster Books for Young Readers within a month. Cohn never dreamed *Gingerbread* would be published without pages of changes and the inclusion of "stale" characters to lighten the subject matter. Instead, her editor merely suggested subtle alterations, and remained encouraging every step of the way. "I don't want to sound too joyous or overly ecstatic, but I really don't have any complaints about the development of the book," says Cohn. "I was at ease during every minor adjustment, and I wish every writer had the same positive experience to boast about!" Cohn's first published book has spawned a world of exciting ideas for a second, third and fourth young adult novel. A Cyd Charisse or Sugar Pie continuum? Cohn doesn't specify, but although she has no plans to dismiss her day job, she insists that writing has enveloped her future permanently. She says she trusts her agent implicitly, and no matter how ridiculous the publishing process seems sometimes (as in pre-*Gingerbread* days), Cohn has assured herself the future is well positioned. As for *your* future, remain "hungry for something bigger" and write your own "answers to the secrets of the universe."

THERESA SMYTHE
The Runaway Valentine (Albert Whitman & Company)

In elementary school, Theresa Smythe sold her sketches of Peanuts characters for five cents each. In between reading about the planets, learning multiplication tables and marketing her drawings, this busy girl also assembled collages. Big and bright, the paper creations became her grandmother's treasures and the foundation of Smythe's career many years later.

Considering all the cards and collage gifts her grandmother harbored in closets, drawers and keepsake boxes, Smythe knew she would be overjoyed about *The Runaway Valentine*, her first collage-illustrated book. Published by Albert Whitman & Company, the book is written by Tina Casey. Because of a recent promotional mailing she sent to the company, Whitman asked her to examine Casey's manuscript. "That promotional image of two snowmen continues to acquire assignments for me," says Smythe. "I was rather excited that the publisher was confident I could successfully complete this book assignment based on my mailings."

The Runaway Valentine amplifies the life of Victor, a dazzling Valentine card. Once he falls off a crowded shelf and skids into a corner, his independent journey begins. Draped in glitter and sparkles, he attracts many people who have a use for him. In the end, all the characters appear at the same Valentine's Day Party, and Victor finds a home.

Smythe says personifying a Valentine's Day card was not easy. As she read the manuscript during a flight to Las Vegas, she scrambled for ideas. "I was terrified when I read *The Runaway Valentine*. The writing was so clever, but it was a story about a card—what kind of face would I give it, after all?" As a result, she says visiting a city like "glittery, lacy, colorful" Las Vegas at that time really offered perspective about the characters she would create. Thus, she got started on the illustrations immediately after the trip.

During the book's creation, Smythe's ongoing interaction with the publisher was lively and beneficial. Since Whitman had never published a book with cut-paper collage as illustration, the editor often asked her for input on the process and was very receptive to her ideas. Because *The Runaway Valentine* was also her first book, she submitted extra sketches, consulted her critique group, and read guides to negotiating book contracts.

Upon the book's completion and receiving an appreciative letter from Tina Casey, Smythe says she felt more comfortable defining herself as a professional paper collagist. Influenced by hand-made toys and decorative crafts, she has always expressed herself through creative means, but she certainly didn't plan on cutting out paper figures for a living.

While working as an animator, Smythe woke up one morning from a dream that conveyed she should pursue collage. "As ridiculous as it sounds, it's absolutely true," says Smythe. "This voice shouted 'Do Collage!' I was stunned and half asleep, but acutely aware . . . or *awakened* you might say." As a result, she left her position at a top-notch company, and purchased the necessary materials to get started.

In the beginning, she promoted herself by sending out 400 mailings to adult- and children-oriented companies including magazines and record companies. She received her first assignment from *Folio* magazine, and has been busy ever since. After *The Runaway Valentine* was published, she condensed her mailing list to 125 children-specific companies. Because of the book's success, Smythe's phone didn't stop ringing for some time, and she was booked with more than a year's assignments. Additionally, Cartoon Network in California exhibited *The Runaway Valentine* illustrations.

Considering how bustling her agenda is every day, Smythe frowns at the thought of working with an agent. She admits that answering the phone and weeding out assignments takes a lot of time away from other aspects of her life, but she enjoys being in charge of her own career.

"I trust my own judgement, even through rejections," says Smythe. "The most important part is that I'm having fun doing what I do, and the results continue to amaze me—what an ideal job!"

The Runaway Valentine, Theresa Smythe's first collage-illustrated book, chronicles the life of an abandoned Valentine's Day card—don't worry though, the ending is as glittery and happy as the illustrations. "The writing was so endearing, after all, I couldn't kill off the lead character!" says Smythe. In recognition of her work, Cartoon Network exhibited Smythe's illustrations from the book, including this cover.

JENNIFER THERMES
When I Was Built (Henry Holt and Company)

Whether you're embarking on an educational manual about birds and insects or a venturesome novel about teenage alcoholics, writing a book is challenging and time-consuming. Add layers of drawing and illustrating to the project, and you may have set yourself up for exhaustion before presenting it to an audience. Writer and illustrator Jennifer Thermes confirms that the rewards of enduring the hefty schedule may even be worth doing it again.

"When I was invited to read the book to my son's second grade classroom, I was on razor edge all morning," says Thermes, who wrote and illustrated her first book, *When I Was Built*, published by Henry Holt. "As every student in that room became entranced by the story and lifted all my anxieties, I was overcome by inspiration and happiness."

Thermes, a professional illustrator with a credit list longer than a full address book (*The Wall Street Journal*, *Modern Bride*, *Trinity Communications*, and *Spectator*, to name a few of her clients), was warmly influenced by her house enough to give it a voice. While the house was built around 1720 and owned by the acclaimed poet Louis Untermeyer, its narration in the book is contemporary and dexterous. Addressing subjects such as the evolution of transportation, fashion, recycling, and electricity, for instance, *When I Was Built* teaches history from the house's point of view. Through clever illustrations and uncomplicated language, the book invites kids to examine the differences between old-fashioned survival and modern amenities.

As the book idea was proposed and Thermes sketched some images, Henry Holt accepted the concept within two weeks. "I was overjoyed that someone else could relate to the idea with enthusiasm," says Thermes. "With a unique personality and perspective, I wanted to share the many renovations of the house and of the world."

While designing illustrative maps for a variety of corporations, Thermes imagined stories to accompany them, but this was the first idea she brought to fruition. After her proposal was accepted, she collaborated with an editor for approximately a year. Thermes soaked up every suggestion their critiques offered, eager to explore her newfound career in writing. She says she fell in love with the possibility of creating a whole world within in a book, using her experience in visual application. As it was difficult to maintain a balance between writing and illustrating the book at first, Thermes insists the visual concepts were primary. Once she applied the images, she wrote the complementary sections. Overall, Thermes maintains the process was most trying when she took a break from generating ideas. Simultaneously, she read about the technical process of writing and how to structure a story, while also drawing motivation from other creative professionals around her.

As humble as it sounds, the most imperative thing Thermes remembered while juggling tasks, attaining small goals and adhering to a deadline was that she was constantly a beginner, vulnerable but always aware, open to more possibilities each day—and her muse was a house.

DORI CHACONAS
On a Wintry Morning (Viking)

Some writers enliven their innate creativity by candlelight during a rainstorm (Flannery O'Connor and Edgar Allen Poe produced their best works on drenched evenings). Others retreat in the woods or near the ocean to fuel inventiveness. Dori Chaconas conceives stories while hovering over an ironing board and a rumpled pile of laundry. Ever since she wrote her first book, *On a Wintry Morning*, she has continued to materialize other stories in the same fashion.

"I was ironing, so while my hands were busy, my mind played words about wintry mornings," says Chaconas, whose book was

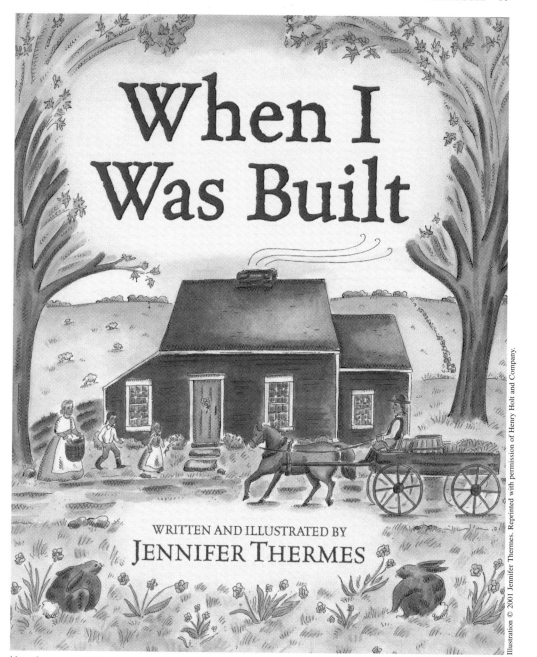

WRITTEN AND ILLUSTRATED BY
JENNIFER THERMES

How do you teach kids history without confusing them too much or boring them? Jennifer Thermes teaches everything from the evolution of transportation and recycling to fashion in her first book, *When I Was Built*, which is narrated by her house. Through unique illustrations and simple dialogue, Thermes invites children to be proud of their ancestors *and* the advantages of living in a modern-day society.

sold to Viking Children's Books within the month it was completed. "A first draft was finished along with the last pillowcase."

Undoubtedly, the mother of four had no way of knowing *On a Wintry Morning* would line library shelves, sweep pre-school classroom reading lists and receive the 2000 Archer/Eckblad Award for best picture book published by a Wisconsin author. The book tenderly portrays a father-daughter relationship on a brisk, snow-filled day. Exploring the outdoors, they lovingly bond as a sleigh glides them through mountains of snow and the white ground becomes their decorative canvas. Children's book discussion groups and teachers everywhere have praised *On a Wintry Morning* for its compassionate nature. Meanwhile, the book received a number of favorable reviews. Fans may have found it most appealing because of the father-daughter connection rarely seen in children's picture books. Mothers or entire families are primarily described in books such as this one, which makes the theme more original in *On a Wintry Morning*, even if the subject is rudimentary.

Chaconas says she didn't plan on writing a children's book about a man and his baby daughter. Drawing from the relationship her husband had with their four daughters while making reference

Illustration © 2000 Stephen T. Johnson. Reprinted with permission of Viking, a division of Penguin Putnam.

Dori Chaconas' first book *On A Wintry Morning* headlines a father and daughter who cherish snow people, sleighs and puppies as they share an afternoon together. Praised for its compassionate nature, *On A Wintry Morning* won the 2000 Archer/Eckblad Award for best picture book.

to her own cherished father, Chaconas simply wrote the story because that's what she knew. Additionally, the temperature was rather low and the snow indeed draped the landscape around her as she bounced verses on the paper next to her iron.

A "self-trained" writer, Chaconas has always had a passion for picture books. For encouragement, she belongs to writers' listservs, attends conferences and meets with other writers in her community. "For me, writing is a craft more than it is an inborn talent that guarantees automatic success," asserts Chaconas. "When you feel passionate about anything, the work involved in learning comes with much pleasure."

Working with pleasant agents and editors helps too!

Chaconas met renowned agent Steven Malk through a referral from another writer. Their alliance was established right away, as Malk offered to represent one of her short stories before she wrote *On a Wintry Morning*. Since the success of the first, Malk has uncompromisingly supported Chaconas' second and third forthcoming books every step of the way. Likewise, she has no complaints about the book's editor, Melanie Cecka.

"The editing process, thanks to Melanie Cecka and the staff at Viking, was as enjoyable as ice cream on chocolate cake," beams Chaconas.

Considering all the success Chaconas savors, the results must be just as delicious!

First Books Follow-up: Sonya Sones

Photo by: Ava Tramer

After receiving swarms of positive reviews and literary achievement awards for her first novel-in-verse, *Stop Pretending: What Happened When My Big Sister Went Crazy*, (among them a Christopher Medal, the Claudia Lewis Award for Poetry, the Myra Cohn Livingston Poetry Award, the Gradiva Award for Best Poetry Book and a nomination for a Los Angeles Times Book Prize) author Sonya Sones didn't waste much time before delivering a second young adult book. *What My Mother Doesn't Know* (Simon & Schuster Books for Young Readers), is another story told in poems. This one is about a 14-and-a-half-year-old girl named Sophie, who's having a hard time trying to figure out the difference between love and lust. "Unlike the poems in *Stop Pretending*," Sones says, "These poems are not autobiographical. Especially not the embarrassing ones."

We caught up with Sones recently, and found her hard at work on yet another novel-in-verse for teens.

How was the writing process different for you during the creation of *What My Mother Doesn't Know*?

When I was writing *Stop Pretending*, I didn't realize that I was writing a novel. I thought I was writing a themed collection of poems. So I tried to keep it short. It didn't turn into a novel until I began working with my editor. She asked me lots of great questions, and these questions inspired me to flesh out the story with 50 additional poems.

But when I was writing *What My Mother Doesn't Know*, I knew right from the start that I was writing a novel. So I didn't try to shorthand anything. And, of course, since this second book wasn't autobiographical, I had a lot more freedom with the direction the story could take.

Did you find yourself more eager and ambitious, or nervous and apprehensive after all the attention you received for your first book?

All of the above. I was excited to be writing a new story, but a bit intimidated by all the praise I'd received for *Stop Pretending*. I was worried that I might turn out to be one of those "one-book-wonders"-that nothing I wrote would ever be as good as my first book. But I just pushed those nasty, paralyzing fears to one side and forced myself to forge ahead.

You received prestigious awards for *Stop Pretending.* **Did you imagine that the book would be so successful?**
I hadn't dared to dream quite that big, so I was very pleasantly surprised, to say the least!

In your first book, the focus is on mental illness. The second embraces sexuality, and the tone is lighter. How did the themes shift for you?
Stop Pretending was inspired by the true story of what happened on the eve of my thirteenth birthday, when my older sister had a nervous breakdown and had to be hospitalized. There are some poems, towards the end of that book, about my first love, a boy named John. I had such a good time writing about those first feelings of overwhelming passion that I knew I wanted to delve into them more deeply. That's when the poems for *What My Mother Doesn't Know* began bubbling to the surface.

Your character, Sophie, often makes statements that are truly great monologue material. Can you characterize her briefly?
Sophie's an artist, with a deeply romantic and passionate nature. Inspite of being saddled with a guiltifying mother and a cold father, she's got a great sense of humor, and this is what helps her to pull through, when the going gets rough.

What outside influences matter while composing your books? Pop culture, television shows, teen publications, fashion trends perhaps?

Sonya Sones' second YA novel.

I'm not quite as "with it" as I'd like to be, in terms of being up on current pop culture. This became apparent to me a few years ago, when I noticed that I was recognizing fewer and fewer of the groups on the cover of *Rolling Stone* magazine. And I don't watch very much television. To compensate for my inherent lack of knowledge in this area, I tune in to teen radio stations, look through teen magazines, cruise teen web sites, and keep an eye out for what kids are wearing and how they're speaking when I go on school visits.

I also eavesdrop shamelessly on my 14-year-old daughter and her friends when I'm chauffeuring them around town. And when I'm not sure about whether teens would get certain references, or say certain things, I run them by my daughter and her friends to find out.

You used to be an animator, and eventually became a film editor. Have your earlier professions affected your work as a poet?
What I liked best about making animated films was that I could make my wildest dreams come true. And now that I'm an author, that same freedom is mine. But even more so, because now that I've begun painting my pictures with words, I'm no longer limited to what I'm able to draw, only to what I'm able to imagine.

It turns out that film editing was an excellent preparation for becoming a poet. Both film and poetry use images to tell stories. As an editor, you're choosing when to move in for a closeup, when to hang back in a longshot. As a poet, you're essentially doing the same thing- choosing when to go in close and study a detail, when to pull back and show the big picture. Editing is all about rhythm and pacing. And poetry is, too. So it turns out that the years I spent editing films were great practice for becoming a poet. Who woulda thunk it?

But being an author is far more satisfying. When I was editing, I always felt like I was doing the final rewrite on someone else's story. When I'm writing my novels, *I'm* the story teller. And I've got lots more stories to tell.

David Almond: A Sense of Coming Home

BY ANNE BOWLING & ALICE POPE

British author David Almond is a star member of the growing group of U.K. writers whose books are charming young adult audiences and critics alike in both the U.K. and the U.S. Almond, a former postman, brush salesman and teacher, has earned a number of prestigious literary awards including a Michael L. Printz Honor Award for his debut YA novel *Skellig* and the Printz Award for its follow-up *Kit's Wilderness*. (See sidebar on page 94 for more about the Printz Award.)

David Almond

Alex Telfer Photography

Skellig's critical reception was a happy surprise for Almond. In addition to the Printz Honor, the book earned the 1998 Carnegie Medal and the Whitbread Award. It received plaudits from *Publishers Weekly*. And *The New York Times* compared his novels to the work of C.S. Lewis and *The Indian in the Cupboard* author Lynne Reid Banks.

Readers who enjoyed *Skellig* and *Kit's Wilderness* will find Almond's trademark magical realism in his third novel. *Heaven Eyes* is the story of runaway orphans Erin, January and Mouse. It follows their escape and journey down a twisting river in northeast England during which they learn something about themselves and their missing parents. Their journey leads them to a mysterious girl called Heaven Eyes, who finally teaches them much more than they had hoped to learn in what Almond calls a story about redemption.

Here Almond talks about writing *Skellig* and *Kit's Wilderness*, shares his thoughts on the YA audience, discusses young adult authors he admires, and offers his advice to writers trying to break into the exciting world of YA.

How did your writing change when you switched from writing adult material to writing young adult novels?

When I suddenly found myself writing for younger people, I had a sense of coming home. This is where my style worked best. I'd been dealing with young voices when I'd been writing for adults, and I'd been working toward quite a clear syntax, and a very direct style. And the dialogue seemed to be a natural element of that.

When I made the change, I found the narrative was moving much more quickly—I didn't have time to rest. Young people have minds that are very active and forward moving—it's important to keep the pages turning. But in writing YA, I'm also able to take on more meditative aspects of life. Young people have more time than adults do, so I don't think the need to keep the pages turning means you don't have time to take on more meditative aspects, and I think young people are quite capable of grasping them.

When I switched to YA I found I was writing better than I ever had before, and the demands of writing for young people meant that my writing had to be better, more fluid and better honed.

Heaven Eyes, the third novel by award-winning U.K. based novelist David Almond, follows the journey of those runaway orphans. "Possessing a rare understanding of human frailties, impulses, desires and fears, the author boldly explores the gray area between reality and imagination," says *Publishers Weekly* of the book.

The Michael L. Printz Award: A New Honor for YA Authors

The Young Adult Library Services Association (YALSA) established the Michael L. Printz Award in 1999 to honor "excellence in literature written for young adults." The award is named in honor of the late Michael L. Printz, "longtime YALSA member and Topeka, Kansas school librarian, known for discovering and promoting quality books for young adults." Printz served on both the Best Books for Young Adults and the Margaret A. Edwards Award Committees, and was a winner of the Grolier Award. He died in 1996 at the age of 59. The first Printz Award was given in 2000.

For more information on Michael L. Printz and his namesake award, visit www.ala.org/yalsa/printz/. See the sidebar on page 98 to learn about Printz Honor Award winner Terry Trueman and his book *Stuck in Neutral*.

The Printz Honorees:

2000 Michael L. Printz Award

Monster, by Walter Dean Myers (HarperCollins)

2000 Printz Honor Awards

Hard Love, by Ellen Wittlinger (Simon & Schuster)

Skellig, by David Almond (Delacort)

Speak, by Laurie Halse Anderson (Farrar, Strauss & Giroux)

2001 Michael L. Printz Award

Kit's Wilderness, by David Almond (Delacorte)

2001 Printz Honor Awards

Angus, Thongs, and *Full Frontal Snogging: Confessions of Georgia Nicolson*, by Louise Rennison (HarperCollins)

The Body of Christopher Creed, by Carol Plum-Ucci (Harcourt)

Many Stones, by Carolyn Coman (Front Street)

Stuck in Neutral, by Terry Trueman (HarperCollins)

And I think it is obvious that you have to be enormously respectful of your reader, to treat them as human beings.

How did you come up with the narrative style you used in *Skellig*?

Skellig really did kind of write itself. I was walking down the street one day, and the story just began to come to me. *Skellig* took hardly any redrafting, just a little touching up at the end. It was incredible. It'll happen once in my life, and it was that sense of, "Oh yes, I'm at home." This is the kind of story I should be writing, and this is the style in which I should be writing.

I spent years working as a short story writer, where the purpose is to have most effect with limited resources, so I've been working toward that style, one that moved quickly but was able to carry a lot of meaning and implication. And then when I wrote *Skellig* it began to happen almost of itself. It didn't become easy, but the story and the style came together, and it was one of the reasons I was very happy to be writing for young people, because I found that my style and the things I was interested in came together.

Since *Skellig* came so easily, was your follow-up novel *Kit's Wilderness* more difficult to write?

Yes. After *Skellig*, which had been so fluid to write, *Kit's Wilderness* was a monster. I rewrote the first third of the book about seven times, and threw it away each time. I knew what I was looking for and it began to take on its own life. I just knew this was the next book I had to write, and it had such power for me. The imagery was just pouring out and it was pushing me to find its proper shape. After the first third I did, and off it went.

The Horn Book called the final portions of Kit's Wildnerness "not for the timid." Did you ever worry it would be too much for your YA audience?

By the time I was well into the book, into that last section, I was quite happy the story had taken on its own pace and dynamic and I trusted the audience to go with it. I didn't think it was too much for them. In writing for young people, you re-experience the imaginative lives young people have, which is often not taken seriously by society at large. I felt I was very much in a young person's world, and I didn't feel it was too much for the audience, no.

Have you gotten much feedback about your books from young readers? How have they reacted to your novels?

One of the great things about writing for young people is that they are very enthusiastic and demanding readers. I get lots of mail, not just from children and young adults, but from adults, too. After reading these books, some parents have really opened their hearts to me about the joys and fears of their family lives. The questions and observations of my young readers really put to shame those who say, "kids don't read any more"—and they often lead me to understand my own work better.

For instance, they see connections between the books that I wasn't aware of, for example, the connection between my characters Askew and Jax and also Mina and Whisper. Their explorations and suggestions about the nature of Skellig himself are often very complicated and fascinating—for example, that he has been sent by Mina's dead father, or by Ernie Myers; that he is from the past or the future or another dimension. Children often refer to the quality of friendship in the books, for example, between Erin Law and January Carr. My favorite letters are those that say the reader really felt as if he or she was there in the book, experiencing the events along with the characters. One boy wrote, "I really was Kit Watson."

Was it necessary to edit your books for the American audience before they were released in the U.S.?

That really was not an issue. *Kit's Wilderness* is set deeply in the north of England and yet it's been read all over the world. I suppose that says the local really is the universal. When I was in the states, people would come up to me and say, "Oh it was just like West Virginia." Or "It was just like Pennsylvania." The issues that were raised in the book, even down to the landscape, struck a chord with readers. We all like to read about other places.

The book was very lightly edited for American audiences. If a book's well written, it has an international appeal. I think children enjoy running across words they don't know—it makes them want to find things out, instead of having things laid out on a plate for them. It's respect for the audience, and acknowledging that some things are different, and they can find out about them if they really want to.

Is this a good time for young adult literature?

It certainly seems to be a good time. I'm a newcomer but I suddenly find myself in a world that seems very vibrant and creative, and it's having a big impact on booksellers and readers. Here in the U.K. YA is being taken more seriously, and I found the same was true when I was in the states.

People say kids don't read anymore, but that's absolute nonsense. Children are avid readers, and there seem to be many fine writers writing books for them.

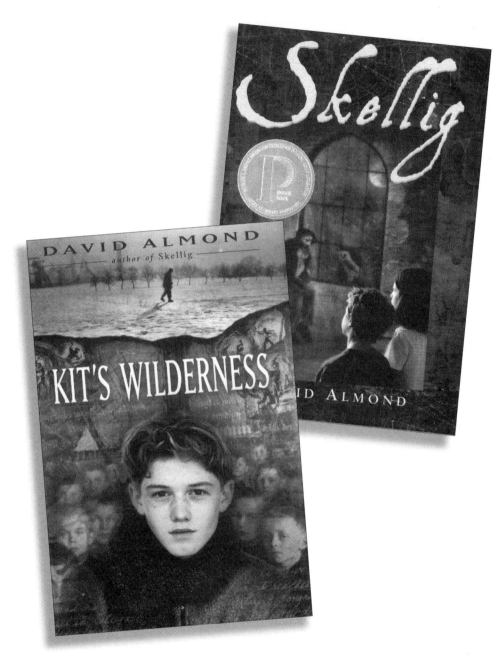

Called a "master imagist," and "the most exciting new voice in children's books of this decade," novelist David Almond's first two books, *Kit's Wilderness* and *Skellig*, captured critics and readers alike, and earned several awards including a Printz Honor, a Printz Award, and England's Whitbread Award for best children's book.

Terry Trueman: The Price of Honor

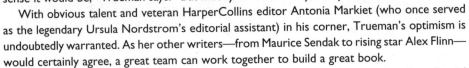

With steady sales and advice from mentors Chris Crutcher (*Whale Talk*) and Terry Davis (*Vision Quest*) to encourage him, 54-year-old first-time novelist Terry Trueman felt confident he could brave the pressure of writing a second book. Then came the American Library Association's 2000 Michael L. Printz Honor Award announcements.

In the twinkling of an eye, Trueman's novel *Stuck in Neutral* became much more than a proud debut. The Spokane, Washington author's first stab at young adult literature was suddenly awash in ALA acclaim. Trueman and his second novel now stood in the shadow of unexpected Printz Honor fame.

Has the weight of success been overwhelming? "If I had any sense it would be," Trueman says. "But mostly it's been really, really fun."

With obvious talent and veteran HarperCollins editor Antonia Markiet (who once served as the legendary Ursula Nordstrom's editorial assistant) in his corner, Trueman's optimism is undoubtedly warranted. As her other writers—from Maurice Sendak to rising star Alex Flinn—would certainly agree, a great team can work together to build a great book.

How did a teacher from the Pacific Northwest win the Printz Honor and stellar editorial assistance? Trueman credits hard work, good solid advice, and an extra helping of beginner's luck for his good fortune.

When did you first realize you wanted to be a writer?
I'm not sure I've ever been more clear about wanting to be a writer than when, at 17, my high school creative writing teacher, Kay Keyes, told me I had talent. It was the first time a teacher had ever said such a thing. But I didn't give writing a serious "professional" until I started writing *Stuck in Neutral*, at the age of 48. I got up every morning at 6 a.m. and worked hard until somehow the writing twisted and turned its way into pure pleasure. That's when I knew I wanted to be a writer—when I became one.

When did you begin to recognize you could be a "successful" writer, and is there a distinction?
To me the distinction has more to do with having the time to do what you want to do with your time. If what you want to do more than anything else is write, and you get that gift through the writing you undertake, you're a success. In other words, whether I make $24,000 a year or $50 million (no, I've never seen anything like that kind of money), if I can pay for my writing habit/addiction, I'm a success.

Was *Stuck in Neutral* your first novel or did others actually come before it?
I wrote a number of bad novels before I reached the emotional, spiritual and intellectual maturity to finish *Stuck in Neutral*. Each effort taught me something about what not to do. One of them, a terrible story entitled *Confessions of a Balding Boy*, taught me the greatest secret of all—find some way to tell the truth. *Stuck in Neutral* came about because I am the father of a profoundly developmentally disabled son, like the character Shawn in the story. Living through this "worst-thing-that-ever-happened-to-me" experience gave me insights into the story that I would not have otherwise had. Would I trade the success of *Stuck in Neutral* for my son

Shawn to have a normal life? Of course. I'd trade my life for that (although that's easy to say because it's not a real possibility). But that's not how life works. So instead of saving my son, I had to settle for saving myself. *Stuck in Neutral* has been an enormous step towards doing that.

When did you know you'd been nominated for the Printz Award?

I knew I was on the list of "final nominations"—-more than 250 titles—a few weeks before the January 15 vote. I didn't figure I had a snowball's chance in hell of actually taking home an award. The competition was incredibly stiff. There were all these amazing writers—Gary Paulson, Walter Dean Meyers, Jerry Spinelli; and all of these terrific books—the newest Harry Potter, the late Tupac Shakur's poems, Lance Armstrong's courageous book. I figured if that was the competition, I was extremely unlikely to win a medal or honor.

Has it been tough fine-tuning your second novel, after the overwhelming success of *Stuck in Neutral*?

If I had any sense it would be. But mostly it's been really, really fun. I do think *Stuck in Neutral* set the bar rather high. But David Almond's *Skellig* only won an honor in 1999 then came back and won the gold medal in 2000. I could live with that!

Where do you hope to be in ten years?

I hope to be healthy and sharp enough to be writing better than I am today, better than I ever have. I hope to be like the poet Bukowski, who didn't start earning his living as a writer until he was fifty either. I'm only afraid of death because I'll miss some people, and because I won't be able to write anymore. But ten years from now? I don't know. Ask me the same question then.

—*Kelly Milner Halls*

Art © 2000 Cliff Nielsen

Stuck in Neutral is Terry Trueman's Printz Honor-winning debut novel.

What are the special considerations for writing compelling fiction for young adults? How do you advise writers tackle the task?

I think the obstacles are the same in all fiction: getting the story to take on a powerful rhythm, getting the language to flow, creating believable characters, getting the story started, pressing on through the middle, moving towards an authentic ending. The only advice really is to believe you can do it, then begin to do it. Don't worry about the obstacles and the problems. Just write and keep on writing, page after page, building up the book. It's helpful to see writing as a kind of play, rather than as a burden. Enjoy the language you use. Enjoy developing your characters. Enjoy throwing away the things that don't work and putting in new things that help the story to live. Trust yourself, respect your audience and be brave with your language and themes.

Which YA authors do you admire? Who would you recommend?

Gary Paulsen. Robert Cormier. Melvin Burgess in the UK is very good. Philip Pullman, of course. Jannie Howker. It's all in the language. These people are writing fantastically powerful, poetic stories dealing with the major themes of literature, and they're not being skeptical and ironic. They're writing the best stories they possibly can. There's a power and integrity to these writers that I absolutely love.

Authors like Gary Paulsen and Robert Cormier do well here in the U.K. Maybe the UK's just catching up. J.K. Rowling is having a big effect on everyone. Her Harry Potter books have made it cool to read, and helped to show that children do read, and that sort of easy skepticism about children as readers can't hold water anymore.

What are your upcoming projects?

I'm going to write a shorter novel for the six- to eight-year-old range. I'm finding picture books are a big challenge, because they are so few words. It's like poetry. I keep avoiding them, and writing long novels. It's easier. That's another great thing about writing for young readers—publishers encourage you to experiment and write for other audiences, in contrast to adult writers who have more set expectations of what they're supposed to do.

My story collection called *Counting Stars* (Delacorte) will be released in the U.S. in early 2002. I'd written those stories over a period of a couple of years, and it was during that time I made the change in audience. In the process of writing them I began to experience writing from the emotional mindset of a child. When I was writing those stories I felt I was coming toward what I was meant to write, what was waiting for me.

Counting Stars will be followed by the novel *Secret Heart* in fall 2002.

What's your advice to writers trying to break in to the young adult fiction market?

For me, when I wrote *Skellig*, it paradoxically helped to know nothing at all about the young adult market. I just wrote the best story I could in the best way I could. There's always a danger in "researching the market" and trying to fit into it. By the time you've written your book, the "market" has changed. Write your own story in your own voice. Then try it out on the market. Don't fall victim to fashion or try to be too topical. I suppose I simply try to write the kind of books I like to read now and I feel would have appealed to me when I was a young adult.

One Voice (in a Million)

BY KELLY MILNER HALLS

From the free flow of popular fiction to the staunch rigors of academia, one elusive quality makes or breaks a writer's ability to connect with a reader: voice. And yet definitive direction on that subjective magic is nearly impossible to find. What is voice? How is it mastered? What makes one writer's voice more spellbinding than the next? Perhaps it's impossible to define and answer these without a waver. Perhaps our worship of words, when it comes to voice, does not allow for absolutes.

If explaining voice requires near mystic wizardry, successful writers and their editors are our best hope for accurate divining. So open your minds and your spirits to some of the finest professionals in the young adult universe, as they explore the wonders and weaknesses of a writer's most intimate tool—the authorial voice.

Lurlene McDaniel has written dozens of inspirational novels for young readers including *Until Angels Close My Eyes*, a USA Today national bestseller, and her latest short story collection for Bantam Doubleday Dell, *How Do I Love Thee?* Her editor, **Beverly Horowitz**, also vice president, publisher and editor-in-chief at Bantam Doubleday Dell deftly guides her creative endeavors, after decades at her craft.

Terry Davis, author of the much-heralded *Vision Quest*, and two other works of literary YA fiction once studied under John Irving at the prestigious University of Iowa's Writer's Workshop. "Davis is a wonderful storyteller," Irving wrote. "And *Vision Quest* is the truest novel about growing up since *The Catcher in the Rye*." That novel and If *Rock and Roll Were a Machine* will be re-released by Eastern Washington University Press this spring (of 2002).

"**Alex Flinn** is not yet a staple of young adult literature," says *The Washington Post* (May 13, 2001). "In fact *Breathing Underwater* (HarperCollins) is the former Miami-Dade County attorney's first novel. But if this intimate look at the contagious nature of physical abuse is any indication, she's on her way." Flinn credits her strong start to veteran editor **Antonia Markiet**, who once worked under children's book legend Charlotte Zolotow, and has since become legend herself.

John H. Ritter softly took his place in the world of YA literature when his debut novel, *Choosing Up Sides*, (Philomel) won the 1999 IRA Children's Book Award. The remarkably focused story centers on a left-handed pitcher raised under the fear of God and examines the struggle between a son who loves the game, and a father who believes it's a pastime of the Devil. His follow-up novel *Over the Wall* also explored the parallel wonders of adolescent life and baseball. Philomel Senior Editor **Michael Green** partnered with Ritter, after ten years of editorial experience, guided by his mentor, Patricia Lee Gauch.

Each of these respected artisans was asked the same questions. Their responses are represented side-by-side, as you see them here. With faith and careful study, perhaps a little of their collective magic will rub off. Perhaps you'll capture a glimpse of your own writer's voice between their well-considered lines.

KELLY MILNER HALLS *is a freelance writer living in Spokane, Washington. Her work has appeared in* Writer's Digest, Booklist, BookPage, Book Magazine, Teen PEOPLE, FamilyFun, Highlights for Children, Fox Kids, Boys' Life, The Washington Post, The Chicago Tribune, The Atlanta Journal Constitution, The Denver Post *and dozens of other publications. Her fifth and latest children's book is* I Bought a Baby Chicken, *published by Boyds Mills Press in 2000.*

If you had to define "voice," how would you define it?

Lurlene McDaniel: To me, voice is the distinctive way a writer has of laying down words and phrases, of manipulating language to create plot and characters to tell a story in a special way. As we all know, there is nothing new under the sun, no "new" stories to tell. What sets every story apart is the writer's voice, or unique way of telling the story. A friend of mine defines voice as plot + characters + style. But for me, voice is more a quality of a writer's writing than a learned craft, and yet, paradoxically, it often takes lots of writing effort for a writer's voice to emerge. A writer's voice stamps his/her work indelibly, and if a reader especially likes a particular writer, he/she can "hear" the favored writer's "voice" even if passages are read blind—without knowing who wrote the words beforehand.

Beverly Horowitz: Voice is selecting the best way to tell a story that reaches the greatest number of people with the most interesting perspective. One of the problems for new writers is that they think first person is the most intimate choice they can make. I do not agree. I think with the first person POV—and certainly with first person present—you have to be so skilled that it takes an incredible amount of talent and training. But I think people assume if they use the "I" voice, there is an intimacy there, which I'm not denying exists, however it limits the depths and texture of what you can know about and learn about and develop in the other characters because it's filtered through this one person.

Terry Davis: I've always thought of voice as the writer's—or the character's—personality captured in the words. Often the word "natural" comes with voice. Among the things we mean when we say this, I think, is that the voice in the words seems unusually real, that it sounds more like a person talking than any kind of writing.

Alex Flinn: A good *young adult* voice consists of three elements: how the author speaks, how the character speaks, and how teenagers speak. There's no generic teen voice. But it is important to listen to how they speak, the words they choose and, more importantly, the words they *don't* choose. I try to avoid what I call "grandpa" words—any word my father would have used. Likewise, I try to avoid current slang that will become dated. Then, there is the rhythm of teen speech, which is something different.

How the author speaks is what makes his or her voice different. I'm sure I could read a new book by Rob Thomas or Francesca Lia Block and know who had written it. Rhythm is a big part of that too.

Finally, how the character speaks. I honestly believe this is different from how the author speaks. I gave Nick, the main character in *Breathing Underwater*, humor to make him more likable. When I started my second novel (*Blown Away*, HarperCollins, 2002), I was surprised that the main character did not have the same cynical wit. I tried and tried to make him funnier, but I couldn't. Finally, I just let him talk, and the voice was better for it.

Antonia Markiet: To me, voice is really an expression of the character—what the character thinks, what the character feels. It is as unique as every individual is. It's harder to master in books for younger people because we're no longer 12 or 13 or 14. We've really got to put aside how we think now and express ourselves now and go back to how we thought about things at 14. We have to look at the world through 14-year-old eyes, notice the kinds of things a 14-year-old would notice and react to them the way a 14-year-old would react.

John H. Ritter: To me, voice is a combination of rhythm, attitude, and personality. Just as in singing, it comes from phrasing, pacing, tone, timbre, and heart. The difference is that the vocalist generally uses the same, recognizable voice for all songs (think of Neil Diamond), whereas a good writer is more like a good method actor (think of Meryl Streep), who changes voice to suit the character and the story being told.

Michael Green: It's the sensual climate that greets a reader the second he enters through the door of a book. It's the current—fast and strong, or gentle and cradling—that carries the reader past the landscape that is the author's story. It's the author's persona, the most direct link he has with the reader. It is perhaps the most imperceptible element of a story, yet it is the most important. Strong voice can breathe life into a dull story, while weak voice can render even the most exciting of tales limp and tasteless.

What makes one voice stronger than another?

McDaniel: Practice. The more a writer creates and hones his/her skills, the more his/her distinctive voice comes through. In today's market, especially in genre fiction, there is often a blandness and new writers don't always get to develop strong voices. Editors and publishing companies want to keep the flavor of books as uniform as possible, so writers aren't encouraged to "stray" from tried and true formulas. Hence, the gap between genre/mass market and "literary" fiction where the rules are broader. Different voices are more accepted on the literary side. I hate that there is a distinction, but I really do believe it's there. I also believe that life experiences contribute to the strength of a writer's voice. The more a writer brings to the table, i.e. novel he/she is writing, the more singular his/her voice becomes.

Horowitz: It is extremely hard to step back as an adult and write the voice of a teenager honestly, because you are an adult. As much as you think you remember, as much as teenagers are experiencing things today as we did then, there is *still* a difference. It's the falseness of dialogue that makes a reader slam the book shut and say, "Oh come on . . . nobody talks like this." I am not saying one needs to include obscenities or vulgarity. I'm talking about emotional honesty. That's the difference. Kids can spot a fake a mile away.

Davis: At the heart of it is probably the writer's commitment to credibility, to make the character real. And not just "real," of course, but a little *more* real than real. The writer lives inside the character and tries to become him in the words. If we know our characters well, for example, we'll hear their voices in our heads. We'll hear the colloquial expressions they use, maybe if they end sentences before actually delivering the last word. When we work with a strong voice we're probably trying to entertain in the best sense, which means we're trying to make the voice so real that a real character comes alive in and with it, and the reader is forced to "engage." The reader just cannot help the character coming alive in his head and meshing—*engaging* his life with the character's life like the cogs of a gear so that they run along together.

Flinn: I suppose that depends on your definition of "strong" — whether it's synonymous with good ("He's a strong swimmer") or with in your face ("What a strong odor") or just powerful ("He's a strong guy") because, of course, the most obvious voice is not necessarily the best. My early writing was *so* in-your-face, lots of metaphors, lots of sarcasm, too much humor (because this is the sort of thing that makes a voice "strong" odor-wise). Finally, I cut about half the stuff. Toni then cut half of what was left. I hope it has the right balance now.

I think that balance is what makes a voice good. It should be distinctive enough that it sounds like a real person talking, but it should be subtle enough that it doesn't sound like the author talking. Above all, the author's individuality should shine through. When I first started writing, I read Richard Peck and set out to write like him. I did okay, except that I *wasn't* Richard Peck. It's better to have your own special voice than to copy someone else's.

Markiet: Going somewhere no one else has gone in a way that's distinctive. It's all been said, but it's how you say it—the voice. With Alex and *Breathing*, what struck me was one, she was a first time writer. And two, I liked Nick at the start, and at the end, I still liked him. It was not contrived. What also surprised me was the adult part knew he was doing more than he *told* you he was doing. But you still uncovered the truth as *he* uncovered it. When it hit him, it hit you.

Ritter: Again, as in singing and acting, the strength comes from how distinct, vital, and accurate the storyteller's voice is for that particular story.

Green: Creativity and aggressiveness with language certainly help. Consistency does, too. Some people confuse dialect with voice, but a dialect can't mask a passive voice, and it can easily overwhelm the author's own voice and feel artificial if over-used. I suppose the ultimate answer sounds a bit subjective: What makes one voice stronger than another is its hold on the reader. What some may find poetic, others may find too flowery. What some may find powerfully succinct, others may find blunt. It is my job to make certain the author's voice feels authentic at all times, and that it works in unison with the story as a whole.

What are the most common mistakes new writers make when it comes to voice?

McDaniel: Underdeveloped voices are common, as is trying to copy someone else's voice. Neither work. A simple love of your story and your characters will help develop your voice along with rewriting, rewriting, rewriting.

Horowitz: New writers forget to include what I call the "Nancy Drew, here are the keys to the car" syndrome. Teenagers, no matter how much they exist in a world of peers and peer pressure, still deal with adults in all parts of their life. Too many books for teenagers present adults as absent or buffoons or mean spirited and I think we need better adult involvement in a teenager's story. That's not to say an adult should be there to preach or solve the problem, but teenagers exist in a world with adults, even if it's just saying, "My mother would scream if she knew what I was doing."

Davis: Inexperienced writers so often try too hard with voice, so it sounds forced. When we're just starting out we're working hard to be good, and we push and push. If our skills aren't high, the reader hears our intentions, hears us working hard to be effective as opposed to actually being effective. In the case of voice, our best intentions often take us too far. The characters sound too youthful, for example, or too sinister, too everything. If we read writers who work well with voice, we'll discover that balance between filling the words with life and filling them so full they pop and sink rather than float. Voice can be tough. We need to listen to our own voices—our voices aloud and the voices in our heads. It might be fundamental to know ourselves—all of ourselves, including our voices—before we're going to be able to create other characters with much success.

Flinn: Trying too hard. This usually takes the form of trying to write in a voice that bears no relation to their own voice or that they've only heard on television. I was in a workshop with a 50-ish whitewoman who decided to write a novel in the voice of an African-American teenager from a tough background. She used all these buzz words from TV—lots of "the hoods" and "my posses" but the language *around* the buzzwords had the wrong flavor. Similarly (and something I hear a lot), I don't think one can approximate Southern speech by tacking on a few "I reckons" or dropping some consonants. I guess it's a variation on "Write What You Know." Except it's "Write How You Know."

Another thing—too many people who try to write YA think they have to use some stunted vocabulary because a kid wouldn't know such hard words. But I think it depends on the character. A boy like Nick, who takes honors classes, does well in school, writes poetry—well, of course he would know lots of SAT vocabulary and he could use it if he felt like it. Call it a complex, from sitting in my critique group, having people ask stuff like, "Would a 15-year-old boy know what a philosopher was?" I always want to scream back, "I don't know. Did you know when you were 15?" Richard Peck calls it "not writing down to readers."

Markiet: If voice is weak, it's because it's the mouthpiece of the author instead of the character. I had this argument with Alex about Paul's voice. I said, "This is *you* saying this, Alex. You've got to get rid of this." That's what makes voice strong or weak. If you're telling me, I'm going to be bored and angry. Show me by their thoughts, by what they do, by what they don't do. But don't tell me.

Ritter: Inconsistency. Often a writer tries too hard, especially at the beginning of a story, then the voice lapses later on. That's okay in early drafts, because an author has to discover and refine the voice as the story progresses. But it's important for the writer to go back and ensure that the voice at the end is the same voice that began the story. Another mistake is trying to be too cute or too clever. This one is harder for the author to spot, and so one has to rely on good, honest feedback from other readers or an editor. Again, it has to be worked out in the earlier drafts.

Green: Overwriting. They feel they have to cram in every bit of narrative exposition and physical descriptions, rather than letting the information reveal itself naturally.

Are there any classics in YA literature that stand out as being exceptionally strong in voice—books new authors could study?

McDaniel: I think S.E. Hinton's voice spoke so strongly in *The Outsiders* that it's become the classic for teens that it is today.

Horowitz: Cormier novels that broke new ground because they presented teenagers in a world that did not necessarily paint a pretty picture of adults. Lurlene is a certain kind of voice of a certain genre. Caroline Cooney; David Almond; Walter Dean Myers has been writing honestly about different parts of life. But no matter what anybody says, one of the most honest and certainly right-on books is *Harriet the Spy*, by Louise Fitzue. Harriet is a kid who's observing, thinking, and breaking the boundaries. Jerry Spinelli's *Stargirl*—there's a voice that's quite interesting and honest. Kids get taken in, in a positive way, when they realize somebody who gets it.

Davis: All of Chris Crutcher's books are awfully successful with voice. Crutcher often uses first-person narration, where voice is so evident. But he doesn't always use first-person, so you can look to him for examples of third-person narration, too. Many writers are wonderful with voice. Carl Hiasson; John Irving; Tim O'Brien in *The Things They Carried*. There are so many good writers. What we need to do is find the ones who do what we want to do, then we need to study them with more care than we've ever employed before in our lives.

Flinn: *Speak*, by Laurie Halse Anderson; *Slot Machine*, by Chris

Lynch; and *Slave Day*, by Rob Thomas. Though not YA, *The Great Santini* and *The Lords of Discipline*, by Pat Conroy show a beautiful, rich voice that is still definitely masculine.

Markiet: How about Barbara Robinson's, *The Best Christmas Pageant Ever; Sarah Plain and Tall*, by Patricia MacLauchlin; *The Pigman*, by Paul Zindel. There are so many great examples.

Ritter: Off the top of my head, I'd say, *Winnie the Pooh*, by A.A. Milne; *The Adventures of Huckleberry Finn*, by Mark Twain; *Are You There God? It's Me, Margaret*, by Judy Blume; and any of the Alice books, by Phyllis Reynolds Naylor.

Green: This may be the hardest question to answer. So many authors have done a good job when it comes to voice. A few that come to mind include: *A Long Way from Chicago*, by Richard Peck; *The Giver*, by Lois Lowry; and *Staying Fat for Sarah Byrnes*, by Chris Crutcher. I just finished an adult novel that I found to have a lovely voice: *Memoirs of a Geisha*, by Arthur Golden.

Does voice have anything to do with the rhythms of human language and translating them to the written page?
McDaniel: It does for me.

Horowitz: I think so, quite often. A multilingual household may make the person a better listener. If you're a better listener, even as you're writing, the false notes of what you're trying to say are more obvious because you're used to listening.

Davis: Voice has *everything* to do with this. If our characters are to be credible and to come alive inside readers' heads and hearts, we must hear them with all the qualities of human language, one of the most important and distinctive of which is the rhythm of their words and sentences. As we think of the people we most love to hear speak, specific qualities of their speech come to mind. We need to study this speech and these qualities in real life as much as we study all those things we find in the life of literature.

Flinn: Absolutely. It is one of the most fun parts of writing fiction, and especially, of writing YA. I love the ability to defy all the rules of grammar and write the way people really speak. Sometimes, I feel like calling up my eleventh grade English teacher and saying, "Hey, Miss Sheridan, I'm using sentence fragments! I'm starting a sentence with *And*! I'm using PAREN-THESIS!" That said, I think it is important for writers to be well versed in the grammatical rules before they defy them.

Ritter: Partly, yes. But voice is more than that. It also comes from the rhythms of motion, of interaction, of gesture. That's why I say voice is something that is best learned by observation. It's song, it's rhythm, it's nuance. It's not something you'd get out of an academic book. Voice is something you get from walking in the hills or down city streets, from lurking dockside watching a team of stevedores unload 25 tons of coal. You get it from listening. From the whistle of a meadow lark, from the rhyme patterns of a river delta blues, from the hard, breath-bursts of a girl in soccer silks darting after a ball. It's poetic in nature, musical, and it's pure right brain. It doesn't come from having lots of knowledge. It comes from having a good ear.

Green: Certainly a strong voice mirrors these rhythms when it comes to dialogue, but that isn't always the case when it comes to narrative. Sometimes the best narrative voices are the ones that sound fresh to our ears, rather than mimicking the ones we hear every day.

What tips do you have for writers struggling with the understanding of voice?

McDaniel: Read your favorite books and ask yourself *why* they're your favorites. Can you "hear" the writer's voice as you read? How do you define it? What makes it distinctive to you? And most important, write!

Horowitz: One of the things I always say to an editor at a meeting, when we're trying to decide on a cover concept is, "If you have only five words to describe this book, what would they be?" The point is *focus*. We are not standing at the bookshelf, next to the book to tell the prospective reader what it's all about. That book goes into the world all by itself. More than an orphan, it's a birthday cake that everybody wants a piece of. The same is true for authors. Your book can be whatever you want it to be, but it can't be all things to all people. You must have focus.

Davis: I would probably try to find some commentary on voice to get a scholarly or academic take on it—a definition and explanation by some thoughtful person. But I would also begin a careful and long study of how people speak in life and in literature. I'd remind myself of those books I love and admire, and I'd force myself to understand exactly what it was about those books that touched me so. When I realized the ones that struck me because of the way a character or characters talked—of how the narrator talked—I would study those so hard that I would force them to yield the secrets of their composition. We need to monitor our responses as we read (as we react to situations and people in life), as we need to discover exactly what is going on in the literature that creates the specific responses in us. When we learn how the writers create these effects on the page and the reactions in us as we read, then we can begin teaching ourselves to create similar effects in our own material.

Flinn: Spend a lot of time really listening to people speak. Use your own speaking voice—and your characters'—as a jumping-off point, rather than trying to invent a voice wholesale or copy anyone else's. And read a lot. Read books in your genre by a lot of different authors. Then, read some plays or, better yet, take a drama class—much more useful than a writing class.

Markiet: A decent human being is a successful person because they have memories. If someone can't access that teenager, I tend to think it'll be hard because successful books are about authenticity. So new writers need to put aside any preconceived notions they have on what is "right for kids" and just go back into their own memories and feelings to get to the heart of what mattered to them at that age and what matters to them now. The big question they need to ask themselves is why do I want to write for kids? Is it for the money? (forget it). Is it because they think it's easy writing for kids? (ha!). Or do they have something to share? Only they have the answer to those questions.

Green: 1. Be natural. 2. Don't think of yourself as Writer; think of yourself as an observer, recording the world around you. 3. Read your work aloud. Often you will hear quirks in your own writing that you would otherwise miss.

Ritter: Again, I'd stay away from trying to understand it. You learn to hit a 90-mile-an-hour fastball by having someone throw you hundreds of 60-, then 70-, then 80-mile-an-hour fastballs. You learn to hit a high "C" two or three octaves above middle "C" by working your way up to it, expanding your range. Same thing with your authorial voice. I'd say, start easy. Get out of your mind a little bit, see how that works. Then go a little further, expand your range. Become goofy, become gentle, become stern. But most of all, realize that building a writer's voice is an organic process. It takes time.

Markets

Book Publishers

There's no magic formula for getting published. It's a matter of getting the right manuscript on the right editor's desk at the right time. Before you submit it's important to learn publishers' needs, see what kind of books they're producing and decide which publishers your work is best suited for. *Children's Writer's & Illustrator's Market* is but one tool in this process. (Those just starting out, turn to Just Getting Started? Some Quick Tips, on page 2.)

To help you narrow down the list of possible publishers for your work, we've included several indexes at the back of this book. **The Subject Index** lists book and magazine publishers according to their fiction and nonfiction needs or interests. **The Age-Level Index** indicates which age groups publishers cater to. **The Photography Index** indicates which markets buy photography for children's publications. **The Poetry Index** lists publishers accepting poetry.

If you write contemporary fiction for young adults, for example, and you're trying to place a book manuscript, go first to the Subject Index. Locate the fiction categories under Book Publishers and copy the list under Contemporary. Then go to the Age-Level Index and highlight the publishers on the Contemporary list that are included under the Young Adults heading. Read the listings for the highlighted publishers to see if your work matches their needs.

Remember, *Children's Writer's & Illustrator's Market* should not be your only source for researching publishers. Here are a few other sources of information:

- The Society of Children's Book Writers and Illustrators (SCBWI) offers members an annual market survey of children's book publishers. (Members send a SASE with $3 postage. SCBWI membership information can be found at www.scbwi.org.)
- The Children's Book Council website (www.cbcbooks.org) gives information on member publishers.
- If a publisher interests you, send a SASE for submission guidelines *before* submitting. For a searchable database of over 1,500 publishers' guidelines, visit www.writersdigest.com.
- Check publishers' websites. Many include their complete catalogs which you can browse. Web addresses are included in many publishers' listings.
- Spend time at your local bookstore to see who's publishing what. While you're there, browse through *Publishers Weekly, The Horn Book* and *Riverbank Review.*

SUBSIDY AND SELF-PUBLISHING

Some determined writers who receive rejections from royalty publishers may look to subsidy and co-op publishers as an option for getting their work into print. These publishers ask writers to pay all or part of the costs of producing a book. We strongly advise writers and illustrators to work only with publishers who pay them. For this reason, we've adopted a policy not to include any subsidy or co-op publishers in *Children's Writer's & Illustrator's Market* (or any other Writer's Digest Books market books).

If you're interested in publishing your book just to share it with friends and relatives, self-publishing is a viable option, but it involves a lot of time, energy and money. You oversee all book production details. Check with a local printer for advice and information on cost.

Whatever path you choose, keep in mind that the market is flooded with submissions, so it's important for you to hone your craft and submit the best work possible. Competition from thousands of other writers and illustrators makes it more important than ever to research publishers before submitting—read their guidelines, look at their catalogs, check out a few of their titles and visit their websites.

ADVICE FROM INSIDERS

For insight and advice on getting published from a variety of perspectives, be sure to read the Insider Reports in this section. Subjects include authors **Franny Billingsley** (page 114) and **Linda Sue Park** (page 130); illustrator **Amy Walrod** (page 139); and editors **Harold Underdown** of ipicturbooks (page 157), and **Phillip Lee** of Lee & Low Books (page 164).

Information on book publishers listed in the previous edition but not included in this edition of *Children's Writer's & Illustrator's Market* may be found in the General Index.

ABINGDON PRESS, The United Methodist Publishing House, 201 Eighth Ave. S., Nashville TN 37203. (615)749-6384. Fax: (615)749-6512. E-mail: paugustine@umpublishing.org. **Acquisitions:** Peg Augustine, children's book editor. Estab. 1789. "Abingdon Press, America's oldest theological publisher, provides an ecumenical publishing program dedicated to serving the Christian community—clergy, scholars, church leaders, musicians and general readers—with quality resources in the areas of Bible study, the practice of ministry, theology, devotion, spirituality, inspiration, prayer, music and worship, reference, Christian education and church supplies."
Fiction: Picture books, middle readers, young readers, young adults/teens: multicultural, religion, special needs.
Nonfiction: Picture books, middle readers, young readers, young adults/teens: religion.
How to Contact/Writers: Query; submit outline/synopsis and 1 sample chapter. Responds to queries in 3 months; mss in 6 months.
Illustration: Uses color artwork only. Reviews ms/illustration packages from artists. Query with photocopies only. Samples returned with SASE; samples not filed.
Photography: Buys stock images. Wants scenics, landscape, still life and multiracial photos. Model/property release required. Uses color prints. Submit stock photo list.
Terms: Pays authors royalty of 5-10% based on retail price. Work purchased outright from authors ($100-1,000).

□ ABSEY & CO., 23011 Northcrest Dr., Spring TX 77389. (281)257-2340. Fax: (281)251-4676. E-mail: abseyandco@aol.com. Website: www.absey.com. **Publisher:** Edward Wilson. "We are looking primarily for education books, especially those with teaching strategies based upon research." Publishes hardcover, trade paperback and mass market paperback originals. Publishes 5-10 titles/year. 50% of books from first-time authors; 50% from unagented writers.
Fiction: "Since we are a small, new press, we are looking for good manuscripts with a firm intended audience. As yet, we haven't explored this market. We feel more comfortable starting with nonfiction—educational. A mistake we often see in submissions is writers underwrite or overwrite—a lack of balance."
Nonfiction: Recently published *Amazing Jones*, by Deanna Cera; and *Ancient Egyptian Jewelry*, by Carol Andrews.
How to Contact/Writers: Fiction: Query with SASE. Nonfiction: Query with outline and 1-2 sample chapters. Will consider simultaneous submissions. Responds to queries in 3 months.
Illustration: Reviews/ms illustration packages. Send photocopies, transparencies, etc.
Photography: Reviews ms/photo packages. Send photocopies, transparencies, etc.
Terms: Pays 8-15% royalty on wholesale price. Publishes book 1 year after acceptance of ms. Ms guidelines for #10 SASE.

ADVOCACY PRESS, P.O. Box 236, Santa Barbara CA 93102. (805)962-2728. Fax: (805)963-3580. E-mail: advpress@impulse.com. Website: www.advocacypress.com. Division of The Girls Incorporated of Greater Santa Barbara. Book publisher. **Editorial Contact**: Ruth Vitale, curriculum specialist. Publishes 2-4 children's books/year.
Fiction: Picture books, young readers, middle readers: adventure, animal, concepts in self-esteem, contemporary, fantasy, folktales, gender equity, multicultural, nature/environment, poetry. "Illustrated children's stories incorporate self-esteem, gender equity, self-awareness concepts." Published *Father Gander Nursery Rhymes*, by Doug Larche, illustrated by Carolyn Blattel; *Minou*, by Mindy Bingham, illustrated by Itoko Maeno; *Time for Horatio*, by Penelope Paine, illustrated by Itoko Maeno. "Most publications are 32-48 page picture stories for readers 4-11 years. Most feature adventures of animals in interesting/educational locales."
Nonfiction: Middle readers, young adults: careers, multicultural, self-help, social issues, textbooks.
How to Contact/Writers: "Because of the required focus of our publications, most have been written in-house." Responds to queries/mss in 2 months. Include SASE.

Illustration: "Require intimate integration of art with story. Therefore, almost always use local illustrators." Average about 30 illustrations per story. Reviews ms/illustration packages from artists. Submit ms with dummy. Contact: Ruth Vitale. Responds in 2 months. Samples returned with SASE.

Terms: Authors paid by royalty or outright purchase. Pays illustrators by project or royalty. Book catalog and ms guidelines for SASE.

Tips: "We are not presently looking for new titles."

ALADDIN PAPERBACKS, 1230 Avenue of the Americas, 4th Floor, New York NY 10020. Fax: (212) 698-2796. Website: www.simonsays.com. Paperback imprint of Simon & Schuster Children's Publishing Children's Division. Vice President/Editorial Director: Ellen Krieger. **Manuscript Acquisitions:** Stephen Fraser, executive editor. **Art Acquisitions:** Debra Sfetsios, art director. Publishes 130 titles/year.

• Aladdin publishes primarily reprints of successful hardcovers from other Simon & Schuster imprints. They accept query letters with proposals for middle grade series and single-title fiction, beginning readers, middle grade mysteries and commercial nonfiction.

 **ALL ABOUT KIDS PUBLISHING**, 6280 San Ignacio Ave., Suite C, San Jose CA 95119. (408)578-4026. Fax: (408)578-4029. E-mail: mail@aakp.com. Website: www.aakp.com. Estab. 1999. Specializes in fiction, educational material, multicultural material, nonfiction. Book publisher. **Manuscript Acquisitions:** Linda L. Guevara. **Art Acquisitions Editor:** Nadine Takvorian, art director. Publishes 20-30 picture books/year. 80% of books by first-time authors.

Fiction: Picture books, young readers: adventure, animal, concept, fantasy, folktales, history, humor, multicultural, nature/environment, poetry, religion, special needs, suspense/mystery. Average word length: picture books—450 words. Recently published *Jake the Barbarian*, by Jackie Leigh Ross (picture book); *The Flight of the Sunflower*, by Melissa Bourbon-Ramirez (picture book).

Nonfiction: Picture books, young readers: activity books, animal, biography, concept, history, multicultural, nature/environment, religion, special needs, textbooks. Average word length: picture books—450 words. Recently published *Fishes, Flowers & Fandangles*, by Hua Tao Zhang; *Activity Book to Teach Children Ages 5-12 Art For Teachers & Parents*.

How to Contact/Writers: Fiction: Submit complete ms. Nonfiction: Submit complete ms for picture books; outline synopsis and 2 sample chapters for young readers. Responds to mss in more than 3 months. Publishes a book 1-2 years after acceptance. Manuscript returned with SASE.

Illustration: Works with 20-30 illustrators/year. Uses both color and b&w artwork. Reviews ms/illustration packages from artists. Submit ms with dummy or ms with 2-3 pieces of final art. Contact: Linda L. Guevara, editor. Illustrations only: Arrange personal portfolio review or send résumé, portfolio and client list. Contact: Nadine Takvorian, art director. Responds in 3 months. Samples returned with SASE; samples filed.

Photography: Works on assignment only. Contact: Linda L. Guevara, editor. Model/property releases required. Uses 35mm transparencies. Submit portfolio, résumé, client list.

Terms: Pays author royalty of 5% based on retail price. Offers advances (Average amount: $2,500). Pays illustrators by the project (range: $3,000 minimum) or royalty of 3-5% based on retail price. Pays photographers by the project (range: $500 minimum) or royalty of 5% based on wholesale price. Sends galleys to authors; dummies to illustrators. Originals returned to artist at job's completion. All imprints included in a single catalog. Writer's, artist's and photographer's guidelines available for SASE.

Tips: "Write from the heart and for the love of children. Submit only one manuscript per envelope. Only one per month please."

ALYSON PUBLICATIONS, INC., P.O. 4371, Los Angeles CA 90078. (323)860-6065. Fax: (323)467-0173. Book publisher. **Acquisitions:** Editorial Department. Publishes 1-3 picture books/year and 1-3 young adult titles/year.

Fiction: All levels: adventure, animal, contemporary, fantasy, history, humor, multicultural, nature/environment, science fiction. Young readers and middle readers: suspense, mystery. Teens: anthology.

Nonfiction: Teens: concept, social issues. "We like books that incorporate all racial, religious and body types. Books should deal with issues faced by kids growing up gay or lesbian." Published *Heather Has Two Mommies*, by Lesléa Newman; and *Daddy's Wedding*, by Michael Willhoite.

How to Contact/Writers: Submit outline/synopsis and sample chapters (young adults). Responds to queries/mss within 3 months. Include SASE.

**FOR EXPLANATIONS OF THESE SYMBOLS,
SEE THE INSIDE FRONT AND BACK COVERS OF THIS BOOK**

Sheila Bailey knows what finicky young readers are drawn to—color, action, and humor, above all. All About Kids Publishing chose Bailey to illustrate the book, *Spaghetti and Peas*, because of her proficient drawing skills and uncompromising manipulation of colors. Bailey is currently working on a second book for All About Kids entitled *Ty's Ordinary Day*.

Terms: Pays authors royalty of 8-12% based on wholesale price. "We *do* offer advances." Pays photographers per photo (range: $50-100). Book catalog and/or ms guidelines free for SASE.

AMIRAH PUBLISHING, P.O. Box 541146. Flushing NY 11354. Phone/fax: (718)321-9004. E-mail: amira hpbco@aol.com. Website: www.ifna.net. Estab. 1992. Specializes in fiction, educational material, multicultural material. **Manuscript Acquisitions:** Yahiya Emerick. **Art Acquisitions:** Yahiya Emerick, president. Publishes 2 young readers/year; 5 middle readers; 3 young adult titles/year. 25% of books by first-time authors. "Our goal is to produce quality books for children and young adults with a spiritually uplifting application."
Fiction: Picture books, young readers, middle readers, young adults: adventure, animal, history, multicultural, religion, Islamic. Average word length: picture books—200; young readers—1,000; middle readers—5,000; young adults—5,000. Recently published *Ahmad Deen and the Curse of the Aztec Warrior*, by Yahiya Emerick (ages 8-11); *Burhaan Khan*, by Qasim Najar (ages 6-8); *The Memory of Hands*, by Reshma Baig (ages 15 to adult).
Nonfiction: Picture books, young readers, middle readers, young adults: history, religion, Islamic. Average word length: picture books—200; young readers—1,000; middle readers—5,000; young adults—5,000. Recently published *Color and Learn Salah*, by Yahiya Emerick (ages 5-7, religious); *Learning About Islam*, by Yahiya Emerick (ages 9-11, religious); *What Islam Is All About*, by Yahiya Emerick (ages 14 +, religious).
How to Contact/Writers: Query. Nonfiction: Query. Responds to queries in 2 weeks; mss in 3 months. Publishes a book 6-12 months after acceptance. Will consider electronic submissions via disk or modem.
Illustration: Works with 2-4 illustrators/year. Reviews ms/illustration packages from artists. Query. Contact: Qasim Najar, vice president. Illustrations only: Query with samples. Contact: Yahiya Emerick, president. Responds in 1 month. Samples returned with SASE.
Photography: Works on assignment only. Contact: Yahiya Emerick, president. Uses images of the Middle East, children, nature. Model/property releases required. (31) Uses 4×6, matte, color prints. Submit cover letter.
Terms: Work purchased outright from authors for $1,000-3,000. Pays illustrators by the project (range: $20-40). Pays photographers by the project (range: $20-40). Sends galleys to authors; dummies to illustrators. Originals returned to artist at job's completion. Book catalog available for SASE and 2 first-class stamps. All imprints included in a single catalog. Catalog available on website.
Tips: "We specialize in materials relating to the Middle East and Muslim-oriented culture such as stories, learning materials and such. These are the only types of items we currently are publishing."

ATHENEUM BOOKS FOR YOUNG READERS, 1230 Avenue of the Americas, New York NY 10020. (212)698-2715. Website: www.simonsayskids.com. Imprint of Simon & Schuster Children's Publishing Division. Book publisher. Vice President and Editorial Director: Ginee Seo. Estab. 1960. **Manuscript Acquisitions:** Send queries with SASE to: Ginee Seo, Anne Schwartz, editorial director of Anne Schwartz Books; Richard Jackson, editorial director of Richard Jackson Books; Marcia Marshall, executive editor; Caitlyn Dlouhy, senior editor. "All editors consider all types of projects." **Art Acquisitions:** Ann Bobco. Publishes 15-20 picture books/year; 4-5 young readers/year; 20-25 middle readers/year; and 10-15 young adults/year. 10% of books by first-time authors; 50% from agented writers. "Atheneum publishes original hardcover trade books for children from pre-school age through young adult. Our list includes picture books, chapter books, mysteries, biography, science fiction, fantasy, middle grade and young adult fiction and nonfiction. The style and subject matter of the books we publish is almost unlimited. We do not, however, publish textbooks, coloring or activity books, greeting cards, magazines or pamphlets or religious publications. Anne Schwartz Books is a highly selective line of books within the Atheneum imprint. The lists of Charles Scribner's Sons Books for Young Readers have been folded into the Atheneum program."
 • Atheneum does not accept unsolicited manuscripts. Send query letter only. Atheneum title *Olivia*, by Ian Falconer, won a 2001 Caldecott Honor Medal; *Dovey Coe*, by Frances O'Roark Dowell won an Edgar Award.
How to Contact/Writers: Send query letter and 3 sample chapters. Responds to queries in 1 month; requested mss in 3 months. Publishes a book 18-24 months after acceptance. Will consider simultaneous queries from previously unpublished authors and those submitted to other publishers, "though we request that the author let us know it is a simultaneous query."
Illustration: Works with 40-50 illustrators/year. Send art samples résumé, tearsheets to Ann Bobco, Design Dept. 4th Floor, 1230 Avenue of the Americas, New York NY 10020. Samples filed. Reports on art samples only if interested.
Terms: Pays authors in royalties of 8-10% based on retail price. Pays illustrators royalty of 5-6% or by the project. Pays photographers by the project. Sends galleys and proofs to authors; proofs to illustrators. Original artwork returned at job's completion. Ms guidelines for #10 SAE and 1 first-class stamp.
Tips: "Atheneum has a 40-year tradition of publishing distinguished books for children. Study our titles."

A/V CONCEPTS CORP., 30 Montauk Blvd., Oakdale NY 11769. (631)567-7227. Fax: (631)567-8745. E-mail: info@edcompublishing.com. Educational book publisher. **Manuscript Acquisitions:** Laura Solimene, editorial director. **Art Acquisitions:** President: Phil Solimene. Publishes 6 young readers/year; 6 middle readers/year; 6 young adult titles/year. 20% of books by first-time authors. Primary theme of books and multimedia is classic literature, math, science, language arts, self esteem.

Award-winning fantasy novelist shares her process

When novelist Franny Billingsley was a kid, she loved to read more than anything else, "but it never occurred to me that I could be a writer," she says. Then what happened to her is what happens to a lot of kids. "You sort of get away from reading. And there I was, 16 or so, and not really interested in adult books, but it wasn't okay to still be reading children's books. So I left them behind."

Billingsley went on to become a lawyer, a career she came to despise, so much so that she finally quit and moved to another country. "I had taken a two-week sort of yuppie vacation to visit my sister who was living in Spain. She had a completely different life than I did. She had so much time and no money; I had so much money and no time. When I got back to my desk, I thought,

Franny Billingsley

'What am I doing?' And I decided right then to quit and go live in Spain."

She brought all her favorite children's books with her, thinking that they would be a relief from all that awful law stuff she'd been reading. "But I think subconsciously I knew to bring them. I knew there was a really important part of me that was yearning for that, but I had let it go. I hadn't been in touch with it for 13 or 14 years. Once I started to read those books, I thought, 'How could I have gotten so far away from what I really loved?' " Then she started to write them.

Having worked with the late, legendary editor Jean Karl at Athenuem, Billingsley has penned two well-received novels, *Well Wished* and *The Folk Keeper*, a Boston Globe-Horn Book Award-winner for fiction. *The Horn Book*'s review of *The Folk Keeper* says, "The intricate plot, vibrant characters, dangerous intrigue, and fantastical elements combine into a truly remarkable novel steeped in atmosphere." Billingsley took a break from working on her third fantasy novel to talk about her process of weaving those elements into a cohesive web. "A novel is not linear," she says, "but a weave of interconnected filaments."

When you returned to the U.S. from Spain, you became a bookseller. That must have been a nice change from your much-hated lawyering.
Oh, I loved that. It was a bit of a struggle at first to find a job, and once I found it . . . I remember the first night I was working just sitting in the children's book section looking at the books, and tears coming to my eyes because I was so happy. I thought, "I'm going to be working with these books—they're going to pay me to do this!" It was amazing. It was fantastic.

You started writing in the late '80s. Your first book, *Well Wished*, wasn't published until 1997. Had you been submitting to publishers in the meantime?
I didn't submit much. I wrote a few really awful novels. I didn't think they were awful then, but

one never does. I sent one to an agent, and I sent it out to a few publishers and got polite rejections.

I audited a class in children's literature with Betsy Hearne at the University of Chicago, then I audited a young adult literature class. I don't know how I got up the guts to do this, but I asked Betsy if she would read one of my manuscripts. She graciously said she would. This manuscript was one of the awful ones. She was very kind, and said, "I think you have a lot of promise, here are some of the problems I see," etc. She made me feel as though I could be a writer. I will always thank her for that. I was this novice, nobody—I didn't quite realize just who she was in the world of children's books. I didn't have a writing group and felt pretty isolated at that point.

I think Betsy also gave me a perspective on my writing that helped me realize it wasn't ready yet. Then I started writing *Well Wished* in 1988.

You've said it took a great deal of time and several drafts for you to come up with the elements that would become the cruxes of your novels: the well and the folk. New writers may not grasp that novel writing is a long process of revision. I'd like to hear about your process.

My process is very messy. I start with the idea. Ideas for my novels have presented themselves as the idea for the complication for the novel. I had the idea of two kids switching bodies for *Well Wished*. I started *The Folk Keeper* with the idea of a half-selkie girl looking for her skin. But I don't know how I'm going to get them into the complication; I don't know how I'm going to get them out of the complication. That's the journey my process takes me through.

For her first novel *Well Wished*, Franny Billingsley worked with the late, well-respected editor Jean Karl. "When Jean found my manuscript, it was far from being the manuscript for *Well Wished* which is now published. It was clunky and it was at least 50 pages longer. But she saw the glimmering in it."

Illustration © 1997 Kimberly Bulcken Root. Reprinted with permission of Atheneum.

I jump into it and I swim around in it, and I write way too much. In my new novel, I have so many pages that I'm never going to use. Then I may write it again. I do this in a right-brained way, in an intuitive, just-float-through-it way. Two or three drafts in, I may sit down and try to look at it in a left-brained way, and say, "Okay, what do I have here? What elements, if any, am I excited about? What elements work? Is there any narrative force here?"

I tend to make a messy outline, often on note cards that I place on a bulletin board in my office, and try to get a conscious idea for how I might revise it. Then I dive into it again. And I do look at those note cards, but usually they're pretty different from my idea. I'm not an organizer. I know some people organize like crazy, and they do fewer drafts because they're able to do more thinking. Somehow my thinking comes to me as the ink is leaking out the tip of my pen. I can't think in the abstract very cleary.

It sounds like an exhaustive task. It's interesting to hear the process you go through.
It is really a huge thing. And at the beginning of a novel, I think it's going to be easy, because I really see it clearly, then I just flail around like crazy. When I was writing *The Folk Keeper*, I thought, "Oh my God, I'll never write a book that's as good as *Well Wished*." Now I'm saying that with this one—"*The Folk Keeper* is the best novel I'll ever write." In some place in my brain, I hope it's not true, and believe it's not true; but in another place, I think it is true. Because it's so hard. Because I have no real control—the only control I have over the process is just doing it. I can't sit there and make the story come, but it is only by sitting there that the story will come. I can bring myself to the process; that's all I can do.

I've recently been re-reading *David Copperfield*, and have been struck by the brilliance of Dickens' characterizations, trying to figure out what he does to make his characters spring to life in such an extraordinary way. I've been typing out pages from *David Copperfield* for myself, trying to analyze them, and saying. "Okay, he gives the person these adjectives, and these physical attributes, and these things that he cares about, and they all connect in an interesting way." I'm trying to do that with my new book—seeing if I can give my characters something that can really define them, in a way that's organic to the book, not just pasted on. That's left-brained, so I do that then I dive back into the book and forget about it, but maybe it's waiting there for me and it will surface when I need it.

Do you feel any added pressure to write a really wonderful novel after winning The Boston Globe-Horn Book Award for *The Folk Keeper*?
I really do. The book I'm working on has been hard. I have asked myself if it's so hard because now the bar has been raised. I find myself wanting to imitate *The Folk Keeper*, and I really have to struggle against that. I want that same kind of voice. I want that same kind of clipped format. I started out writing it in the third person, and then I decided I really love first person. I rewrote it in the first person. Then I thought, hmmm, maybe I'll write it in a document, the way Corinna's folk record is a document, and I find I'm getting perilously close to imitating myself. I need to do the thing that works, but it's not clear to me what's going to work.

You're working with Richard Jackson on your current novel, but you worked with Jean Karl on your first two. Will you comment on working with her?
I think I was very, very lucky to find Jean. When she found my manuscript, it was pretty far from being the manuscript for *Well Wished* which is now published. It was clunky and it was

at least 50 pages longer. But she saw the glimmering in it. And she was willing to take a book that had a glimmer and was not necessarily particularly marketable. Now, in these post-Harry Potter days, it would be more marketable as a first novel, but then it didn't have a clear market niche. It's a book with sophisticated literary language, complicated plot, and it's dense in a way.

She was willing to take that and guide me in making it the best book I could make it. Maybe the market pressures are such that a lot of editors can't do that. If an editor has a working relationship with someone who has already successfully published, then he or she will invest a lot of time and energy into a manuscript. Editors spend a huge amount of time editing people's manuscripts. Other novelists I know love their editors, and their editors put a tremendous amount of time into their work. I'm lucky I found Jean insofar as maybe she had the luxury that not every editor does.

What advice can you share with aspiring novelists?

In one of his books, John Gardner said something that I found really useful. He said, in a way, you can't really learn to write—you can just catch on. I found that consoling. Writing a novel is a huge thing and it's so visceral. But I think if you keep at it, you can catch on. Don't give up. Just don't give up. Just keep writing. It's really 99.9 percent determination. If you read a book that's great, try to figure out what makes it great, in the same way I'm trying to figure out how Charles Dickens creates fabulous characters. I really, truly believe that almost anyone can write a good novel if they stick to it.

—*Alice Pope*

Franny Billingsley's second novel *The Folk Keeper* earned the author the Boston Globe-Horn Book Award for fiction in 2001. In *The New York Times Book Review*, Betsy Hearne wrote, "The story of Corinna's survival sustains a lyrical narrative. There's poetry not only in the style but also in the story elements themselves." Almost a decade before her first book contract, Billingsley took a class from Hearne at the University of Chicago. "Betsy gave me perspective on my writing that helped me realize it wasn't ready yet."

Illustration © 1999 Leonid Gore. Design by Angela Carlino. Reprinted with permission of Atheneum.

Fiction: Middle readers: hi-lo. Young adults: hi-lo, multicultural, special needs. "We hire writers to adapt classic literature."

Nonfiction: All levels: activity books. Young adults: hi-lo, multicultural, science, self help, textbooks. Average word length: middle readers—300-400; young adults—500-950.

How to Contact/Writers: Fiction: Submit outline/synopsis and 1 sample chapter. Responds to queries in 1 month.

Illustration: Works with 4-6 illustrators/year. Reviews ms/illustration packages from artists. Submit ms with 3-4 pieces of final art. Illustrations only: Query with samples. "No originals; send non-returnable material and samples only." Responds in 1 month. Samples returned with SASE; samples filed.

Photography: Submit samples.

Terms: Work purchased outright from authors (range $50-1,000). Pays illustrators by the project (range: $50-1,000). Pays photographers per photo (range: $25-250). Ms and art guidelines available for 9×12 SASE.

AVISSON PRESS, INC., 3007 Taliaferro Rd., Greensboro NC 27408. (336)288-6989. Fax: (336)288-6989. Estab. 1995. Specializes in multicultural material, nonfiction. **Manuscript Acquisitions:** Martin Hester, publisher; Stephanie Todd. Publishes 8-10 young adult titles/year. 70% of books by first-time authors.

Nonfiction: Young adults: biography. Average word length: young adults—25,000. Recently published *Mum Bet: The Life and Times of Elizabeth Freeman*, by Mary Wilds; *Young Superstars of Tennis: The Venus and Serena Williams Story; Here Comes Eleanor: A New Biography of Eleanor Roosevelt for Young People*, by Virginia Veeder Westervelt.

How to Contact/Writers: Nonfiction: Submit outline/synopsis and 2 sample chapters. Responds to queries in 2 weeks; mss in 2 months. Publishes a book 9-12 months after acceptance. Will consider simultaneous submissions.

Terms: Pays author royalty of 8-10% based on wholesale price. Offers advances (Average amount: $500). Sends galleys to authors. Book catalog available for #10 SAE and 1 first-class stamp; ms guidelines available for SASE.

Tips: "We don't use illustrated books."

AVON BOOKS/BOOKS FOR YOUNG READERS, 1350 Avenue of the Americas, New York NY 10019. (212)261-6800. Fax: (212)261-6668. Website: www.harperchildrens.com. A division of The Hearst Corporation. Book publisher. Mass market paperback publisher. **Acquisitions:** Julie Richardson, senior editor and Abigail McAden, associate editor. Art Director: Barbara Sitzsimmons. Publishes 12 hardcovers, 25-30 middle readers/year, 20-25 young adults/year. 10% of books by first-time authors; 80% of books from agented writers.

Fiction: Middle readers: comedy, contemporary, problem novels, sports, spy/mystery/adventure. Young adults: contemporary, problem novels, romance. Average length: middle readers—100-150 pages; young adults—150-250 pages. Avon does not publish preschool picture books.

Nonfiction: Middle readers: hobbies, music/dance, sports. Young adults: "growing up." Average length: middle readers—100-150 pages; young adults—150-250 pages. Recent publications: *Nightmare Room*, by R.L. Stine (middle reader).

How to Contact/Writers: "Please send for guidelines before submitting." Fiction/nonfiction: Submit outline/synopsis and 3 sample chapters. Reports on mss in 2-3 months. Publishes a book 18-24 months after acceptance. Will consider simultaneous submissions.

Illustration: Will not review ms/illustration packages.

Terms: Pays authors in royalties of 6% based on retail price. Average advance payment is "very open." Book catalog available for 9×12 SAE and 4 first-class stamps; ms guidelines for #10 SASE.

Tips: "Our list primarily includes series, with the emphasis on high quality recreational reading—a fresh and original writing style; identifiable, three-dimensional characters; a strong, well-paced story that pulls readers in and keeps them interested." Writers: "Make sure you really know what a company's list looks like before you submit work. Is your work in line with what they usually do? Is your work appropriate for the age group that this company publishes for? Be aware of what's in your bookstore (but not what's in there for too long!)" Illustrators: "Submit work to art directors and people who are in charge of illustration at publishers. This is usually not handled entirely by the editorial department. Do *not* expect a response if no SASE is included with your material."

N: AZRO PRESS, PMB 342 1704 Llano St. B, Santa Fe NM 87505. (505)989-3272. Fax: (505)989-3832. E-mail: books@azropress.com. Website: www.azropress.com. Estab. 1997. **Manuscript/Art Acquisitions:** Gae Eisenhardt. Imprints: Green Knees (Jaenet Guggenheim, acquisitions editor). Publishes 6 picture books/year. 90% of books by first-time authors. "We publish illustrated children's books with a southwestern flavor."

Fiction: Picture books: animal, humor, multicultural. Average word length: picture books—1,000; young readers—1,500. Recently published *Moon Rabbit Builds A Fine House*, by Terry Avery (ages 2-5, fiction/legend); *Those Toes*, by Marie McLaughlin, illustrated by Roni Rohr (2-5 years counting rhyme); and *One Bullfrog*, by Sid Hausman (age 5-10, illustrated song book with CD).

Nonfiction: Picture books: activity books, animals, science.

How to Contact/Writers: Fiction/nonfiction: Submit complete ms or outline/synopsis. Responds to queries in 2 weeks; mss in 2-3 months. Publishes a book 2 years after acceptance. Will consider simultaneous submissions, electronic submissions via disk or modem.

Illustration: Works with 3-4 illustrators/year. Reviews ms/illustration packages from artists. Submit ms with 2-3 pieces of final art. Contact: Gae Einsenhardt, editor. Query with samples. Samples filed.

Terms: Pays authors royalty fo 5-10% based on wholesale price. Pays illustrators by the project (range: $3,000-4,000) or royalty of 5%. Sends galleys to authors; dummies to illustrators. Originals returned to artist at job's completion. Book catalog available for SASE. All imprints included in a single catalog. Manuscript guidelines available for SASE. Catalog available on website.

Tips: Read our submission guidelines. Go to your local bookstore and library to see what is available.

BANTAM DOUBLEDAY DELL, Books for Young Readers, imprints of Random House, Inc., 1540 Broadway, New York NY 10036. (212)354-6500. Website: www.randomhouse.com. Book publisher. Imprints: Delacorte Press for Young Readers, Doubleday Books for Young Readers, Dell Laurel Leaf, Skylark, Starfire, Dell Yearling Books and Dell Dragonfly. President/Publisher: Craig Virden. Vice President/Publisher: Beverly Horowitz. **Manuscript Acquisitions:** Craig Virden, publisher; Françoise Bui, executive editor, series; Wendy Lamb, vice president, publisher Wendy Lamb Books; Karen Wojtyla, executive editor. **Art Acquisitions:** Art Director. Publishes 16 picture books; 35 middle reader hardcover books; 35 young adult hardcover titles/year. 10% of books by first-time authors; 70% of books from agented writers. "Bantam Doubleday Dell Books for Young Readers publishes award-winning books by distinguished authors and the most promising new writers."

• Delacorte title *Kit's Wilderness*, by David Almond, won the 2001 Printz Award. See David Almond: A Sense of Coming Home on page 93 to learn more about the author. Delacorte title *Nory Ryan's Song*, by Reilly Giff, won a Golden Kite Honor Award for Fiction in 2001.

Fiction: Picture books: adventure, animal, contemporary, fantasy, humor. Young readers: contemporary, humor, fantasy, sports, suspense/mystery. Middle readers: adventure, contemporary, humor, easy-to-read, fantasy, sports, suspense/mystery. Young adults: adventure, contemporary issues, humor, coming-of-age, suspense/mystery. Recently published *Bud, Not Buddy*, by Christopher Paul Curtis; *Nory Ryan's Song*, by Patricia Reilly Giff.

Nonfiction: "Bantam Doubleday Dell Books for Young Readers publishes a very limited number of nonfiction titles."

How to Contact/Writers: Submit through agent; accepts queries from published authors. "All unsolicited manuscripts returned unopened with the following exceptions: Unsolicited manuscripts are accepted for the Delacorte Press Prize for a First Young Adult Novel contest (see Contests & Awards section) and the Marguerite de Angeli Prize for a First Middle Grade Novel contest (see Contests & Awards section)." Responds to queries in 4 months; mss in 3 months. "Simultaneous submissions must be stated as such."

Illustration: Number of illustrations used per fiction title varies considerably. Reviews ms/illustration packages from artists. Query first. Do not send originals. "If you submit a dummy, please submit the text separately." Responds to ms/art samples only if interested. Cannot return samples; samples filed. Illustrations only: Submit tearsheets, résumé, samples that do not need to be returned. Original artwork returned at job's completion.

Terms: Pays authors advance and royalty. Pays illustrators advance and royalty or flat fee.

Tips: "Writers can submit to Delacorte Contest for a First Young Adult Novel or Marguerite de Angeli Contest for Contemporary or historical fiction set in North America for readers age 7-10. Send SASE for contest guidelines or see website."

BAREFOOT BOOKS, 3 Bow St., Cambridge MA 02138. (617)576-0660. Fax: (617)576-0049. E-mail: Alison @barefootbooks.com. Website: www.barefoot-books.com. Estab. 1993 in the UK; 1998 in the US. Specializes in fiction, trade books, multicultural material, nonfiction. **Manuscript Acquisitions:** Alison Keehn, associate editor. **Art Acquisitions:** Alison Keehn, associate editor. Publishes 35 picture books/year; 10 anthologies/year. 40% of books by first-time authors; 60% subsidy published. "The Barefoot child represents the person who is in harmony with the natural world and moves freely across boundaries of many kinds. Barefoot Books explores this image with a range of high-quality picture books for children of all ages. We work with artists, writers and storytellers from many cultures, focusing on themes that encourage independence of spirit, promote understanding and acceptance of different traditions, and foster a life-long love of learning."

Fiction: Picture books, young readers: animal, anthology, concept, fantasy, folktales, multicultural, nature/environment, poetry, spirituality. Middle readers, young adults: anthology, folktales. Average word length: picture books—500-1,000; young readers—2,000-3,000; anthologies—10,000-20,000. Recently published *The Gigantic Turnip*, by Aleksei Tolstoy, illustrated by Niamh Sharkey (ages 1-7, picture book); *One, Two, Skip a Few*, by Roberta Arenson (ages 2-7, picture book); *Grandmothers' Stories: Wise Woman Tales from Many Cultures*, by Burleigh Mutén, illustrated by Sian Bailey (ages 6 to adult, anthology).

Nonfiction: Picture books, young readers, middle readers, young adults: multicultural, spirituality/inspirational. Average word length: young readers—3,000-20,000. Recently published *The Genius of Leonardo*, by Guido Visconti, illustrated by Bimba Landmann; *Daughters of Eve: Strong Women of the Bible*, by Lillian Hammer Ross, illustrated by Kyra Teis.

How to Contact/Writers: Fiction: Submit complete ms for picture books; outline/synopsis and 1 sample story for collections. Nonfiction: Query. Responds to queries in 1 month; mss in 2 months. Will consider simultaneous submissions and previously published work.

Illustration: Works with 45 illustrators/year. Uses color artwork only. Reviews ms/illustration packages from artists. Query for anthology/collections or send ms with dummy for picture books. Contact: Alison Keehn, associate editor. Illustrations only: Query with samples or send promo sheet and tearsheets. Contact: Alison Keehn, associate editor. Responds only if interested. Samples returned with SASE.

Terms: Pays author royalty of 5% based on retail price. Offers advances. Sends galleys to authors. Originals returned to artist at job's completion. Book catalog available for 9×12 SAE and 5 first-class stamps; ms guidelines available for SASE. Catalog available on website.

Tips: "We are looking for books that inspire, books that are filled with a sense of magic and wonder. We also look for strong stories from all different cultures, reflecting the ways of the individual culture while also touching deeper human truths that suggest we are all one. We welcome playful submissions for the very youngest children and also anthologies of stories or poems for older readers, all focused around a universal theme. We encourage writers and artists to visit our website and read some of our books to get a sense of our editorial philosophy and what we publish before they submit to us. Always, we encourage them to stay true to their inner voice and artistic vision that reaches out for timeless stories, beyond the momentary trends that may exist in the market today."

BARRONS EDUCATIONAL SERIES, 250 Wireless Blvd., Hauppauge NY 11788. (631)434-3311 or (800)645-3476. Fax: (631)434-3723. Website: www.barronseduc.com. Book publisher. Estab. 1945. "Barrons tends to publish series of books, both for adults and children." **Acquisitions:** Wayne R. Barr, acquisitions manager. Publishes 20 picture books/year; 20 young readers/year; 20 middle reader titles/year; 10 young adult titles/year. 25% of books by first-time authors; 25% of books from agented writers.

Fiction: Picture books: animal, concept, multicultural, nature/environment. Young readers: Adventure, multicultural, nature/environment, suspense/mystery. Middle readers: adventure, horror, multicultural, nature/environment, problem novels, suspense/mystery. Young adults: horror, problem novels. Recently published *Sports Success: Winning Women in Soccer*, by Marlene Targ Brill; *Word Wizardry* by Margaret and William Kenda.

Nonfiction: Picture books: concept, reference. Young readers: how-to, reference, self help, social issues. Middle readers: hi-lo, how-to, reference, self help, social issues. Young adults: how-to, self help, social issues.

How to Contact/Writers: Fiction: Query. Nonfiction: Submit outline/synopsis and sample chapters. "Submissions must be accompanied by SASE for response." E-mailed or faxed proposals are not accepted. Responds to queries in 1 month; mss in 6-8 months. Publishes a book 1 year after acceptance. Will consider simultaneous submissions.

Illustration: Works with 10 illustrators/year. Reviews ms/illustration packages from artists. Query first; 3 chapters of ms with 1 piece of final art, remainder roughs. Illustrations only: Submit tearsheets or slides plus résumé. Responds in 3-8 weeks.

Terms: Pays authors in royalties of 10-14% based on wholesale price or buys ms outright for $2,000 minimum. Pays illustrators by the project based on retail price. Sends galleys to authors; dummies to illustrators. Book catalog, ms/artist's guidelines for 9×12 SAE.

Tips: Writers: "We are predominately on the lookout for preschool storybooks and concept books. No YA fiction/ romance or novels." Illustrators: "We are happy to receive a sample illustration to keep on file for future consideration. Periodic notes reminding us of your work are acceptable." Children's book themes "are becoming much more contemporary and relevant to a child's day-to-day activities. We have a constant interest in children's fiction (ages 7-11 and ages 12-16) with New Age topics."

BEACH HOLME PUBLISHERS, 2040 W. 12th Ave., Suite 226, Vancouver, British Columbia V6J 2G2 Canada. (604)733-4868. Fax: (604)733-4860. E-mail: bhp@beachholme.bc.ca. Website: www.beachholme.bc.ca. Book publisher. **Manuscript Acquisitions:** Michael Carroll, publisher. **Art Acquisitions:** Michael Carroll. Publishes 5-6 young adult titles/year and 7-8 adult literary titles/year. 40% of books by first-time authors. "We publish primarily regional historical fiction. We publish young adult novels for children aged 8-12. We are particularly interested in works that have a historical basis and are set in the Pacific Northwest, or northern Canada. Include ideas for teacher's guides or resources and appropriate topics for a classroom situation if applicable."

• Beach Holme *only* accepts work from Canadian writers.

Fiction: Young adults: contemporary, folktales, history, multicultural, nature/environment, poetry. Multicultural needs include themes reflecting cultural heritage of the Pacific Northwest, i.e., first nations, Asian, East Indian, etc. Does not want to see generic adventure or mystery with no sense of place. Average word length: middle readers—15-20,000; young adults/teens—30,000-40,000. Recently published *Tiger in Trouble*, by Eric Walters (ages 9-13, young adult fiction); *A Miracle for Maggie*, by Stephen Eaton Hume (ages 9-13, young adult fiction); and *Viking Quest*, by Tom Heningham (ages 9-13, young adult fiction).

"PICTURE BOOKS" are for preschoolers to 8-year-olds; "Young readers" are for 5- to 8-year-olds; "Middle readers" are for 9- to 11-year-olds; and "Young adults" are for ages 12 and up. Age ranges may vary slightly from publisher to publisher.

How to Contact/Writers: Fiction: Submit outline/synopsis and 3 sample chapters. Responds to queries/mss in 6 months. Publishes a book 6 months-1 year after acceptance. No electronic or multiple submissions.
Illustration: Works with 4-5 illustrators/year. Responds to submissions in 1-2 months if interested. Samples returned with SASE; samples filed. Originals returned at job's completion. Works mainly with Canadian illustrators.
Terms: Pays authors 10% royalty based on retail price. Offers advances (average amount: $500). Pays illustrators by the project (range: $500-1,000). Pays photographers by the project (range: $100-300). Sends galleys to authors. Book catalog available for 9×12 SAE and 3 first-class Canadian stamps; ms guidelines available with SASE.
Tips: "Research what we have previously published and view our website to familiarize yourself with what we are looking for. Please, be informed."

BEBOP BOOKS, Imprint of Lee & Low Books Inc., 95 Madison Ave., New York NY 10016-7801. (212)779-4400. Website: www.bebopbooks.com. Estab. 2000. **Manuscript Acquisitions:** Jennifer Frantz. **Executive Editor:** Louise May. Publishes 20-25 picture books/year. Many books by first-time authors. "Our goal is to publish child-centered stories that support literacy learning and provide multicultural content for children just beginning to learn to read. We make a special effort to work with writers and illustrators of diverse backgrounds. Current needs are posted on website."
Fiction: Picture books: adventure, concept, contemporary, history, multicultural, nature/environment, sports, culturally specific topics for young children.
Nonfiction: Picture books: arts/crafts, careers, concept, cooking, history, how-to, multicultural, music/dance, sports.
How to Contact/Writers: Fiction/nonfiction: Submit complete ms. Responds to mss in up to 8 months; "manuscripts are acquired just once a year."
Illustration: Works with 20-25 illustrators/year. Uses color artwork only. Illustrations and photographs: Query with color samples and send client list or cover letter. Responds only if interested. Samples returned with SASE; samples filed. "We are especially interested in submissions from artists of color, and we encourage artists new to the field of children's books to send us samples of their work."
Terms: Pays authors royalty. Offers advances. Pays illustrators royalty and advance. Pays photographers royalty and advance. Book catalog available for 9×12 SAE and 76¢ postage, attn: Catalog Request. Catalog available on website.
Tips: "Bebop Books is currently specializing in emergent readers with multicultural themes. Emergent readers, often called 'little books,' are used by kindergarten and first-grade teachers to help young children develop early reading skills and strategies. Each book is a small, 8-, 12-, or 16-page paperback, with full color illustrations and a story specifically written and illustrated to support 5- and 6-year-olds in their efforts to begin reading. The stories should fit within Guided Reading™ levels D-G and Reading Recovery™ levels 6-12."

BENCHMARK BOOKS, Imprint of Marshall Cavendish, 99 White Plains Rd., Tarrytown NY 10591. (914)332-8888. Fax: (914)332-1888. E-mail: knunn@marshallcavendish.com. Website: www.marshallcavendish.com. **Manuscript Acquisitions:** Joyce Stanton and Kate Nunn. Publishes 90 young reader, middle reader and young adult books/year. "We look for interesting treatments of primarily nonfiction subjects related to elementary, middle school and high school curriculum."
Nonfiction: Most nonfiction topics should be curriculum related. Average word length for books: 4,000-20,000. All books published as part of a series. Recently published *Life in the Middle Ages* (series), *The City, The Countryside, The Church, The Castle*, by Kathryn Hinds; *Lifeways: The Abache, The Cheyenne, The Haida, The Huron*, by Raymond Bial.
How to Contact/Writers: Nonfiction: submit complete ms or submit outline/synopsis and 1 or more sample chapters. Responds to queries and mss in 3 months. Publishes a book 2 years after acceptance. Will consider simultaneous submissions.
Photography: Buys stock and assigns work.
Terms: Pays authors royalty based on retail price or buys work outright. Offers advances. Sends galleys to authors. Book catalog available. All imprints included in a single catalog.

BETHANY HOUSE PUBLISHERS, 11400 Hampshire Ave. S., Minneapolis MN 55438-2852. (952)829-2500. Fax: (952)829-2768. Website: www.bethanyhouse.com. Book publisher. **Manuscript Acquisitions:** Rochelle Glöege, Natasha Sperling. **Art Acquisitions:** Paul Higdon. Publishes 4 young readers/year; 18 middle-grade readers/year; and 8 young adults/year. Bethany House Publishers is a non-profit publisher seeking to publish imaginative, excellent books that reflect an evangelical worldview without being preachy. Publishes picture books under Bethany Backyard imprint.
Fiction: Series for early readers, middle readers, historical and contemporary adventure, history, humor, multicultural, suspense/mystery, religion, sports and current issues. Will consider sophisticated novels for young adults with older characters. Does not want to see poetry or science fiction. Average word length: early readers—4,000; young readers—20,000-40,000; young adults—75,000-90,000. Published *Until Tomorrow*, by Robin Jones; *The Ghost of KRZY*, by Bill Myers (middle-graders, suspense/adventure/humor series); and *The Mystery of the Dancing Angels*, by Elspeth Campbell Murphy (young readers, mystery series).

Nonfiction: Young readers, middle readers, young adults: religion/devotional, self-help, social issues. Published *Get God*, by Kevin Johnson (young teen; discipleship); and *Hot Topics, Tough Questions*, by Bill Myers (young adult/teen, Biblically based advice).

How to Contact/Writers: Fiction/Nonfiction: Send synopsis with first three chapters. Query. Responds in 4 months. Picture Books: does not accept unsolicited mss. Publishes a book 12-18 months after acceptance. Will consider simultaneous submissions.

Illustration: Works with 12 illustrators/year. Reviews illustration samples from artists. Illustrations only: Query with samples. Responds in 2 months. Samples returned with SASE.

Terms: Pays authors royalty based on net sales. Pays illustrators by the project. Pays photographers by the project. Sends galleys to authors. Book catalog available for 11 × 14 SAE and 5 first-class stamps.

Tips: "Research the market, know what is already out there. Study our catalog before submitting material. We look for an evangelical message woven delicately into a strong plot and topics that seek to broaden the reader's experience and perspective."

☑ BEYOND WORDS PUBLISHING, INC., 20827 N.W. Cornell Rd., Hillsboro OR 97124-1808. (503)531-8700. Fax: (503)531-8773. E-mail: beyondword.com. Website: www.beyondword.com. Book publisher. Director, Children's Division: Michelle Roehm. **Acquisitions:** Michelle R. McCann. Publishes 6-10 picture books/year and 2 nonfiction teen books/year. 50% of books by first-time authors. "Our company mission statement is 'Inspire to Integrity,' so it's crucial that your story inspires children in some way. Our books are high quality, gorgeously illustrated, meant to be enjoyed as a child and throughout life."

Fiction: Picture books: adventure, animal, contemporary, fantasy, feminist, folktales, history, multicultural, nature/environment, spiritual. "We are looking for authors/illustrators; stories that will appeal and inspire." Average length: picture books—32 pages. Recently published *Turtle Songs*, by Margaret Wolfson, illustrated by Karla Sachi (ages 5-10, South Pacific myth).

Nonfiction: Picture books, young readers: biography, history, multicultural, nature/environment. *The Book of Goddesses*, by Kris Waldherr (all ages, multicultural historic reference); and *Girls Know Best* (compilation of 38 teen girls' writing—ages 7-15).

How to Contact/Writers: Fiction: Submit complete ms. Nonfiction: Submit outline/synopsis. Responds to queries/mss in 6 months. Will consider simultaneous submissions and previously published work.

Illustration: Works with 4-6 illustrators/year. Reviews ms/illustration packages from artists. Submit ms with 2-3 pieces of final art. Illustrations only: Send résumé, promo sheet, "samples—no originals!" Responds in 6 months only if interested. Samples returned with SASE; samples filed.

Photography: Works on assignment only.

Terms: Sends galleys to authors; dummies to illustrators. Book catalog for SAE; ms and artist's guidelines for SASE.

Tips: "Please research the books we have previously published. This will give you a good idea if your proposal fits with our company."

BLACKBIRCH PRESS, INC., P.O. Box 3573, Woodbridge CT 06525. Fax: (203)389-1596. E-mail: staff@blackbirch.com. Website: www.blackbirch.com. Book publisher. Editorial Director: W. Scott Ingram. **Manuscript Acquisitions:** Kristen Woronoff. **Art Acquisitions:** Calico Harington. Publishes 20 middle readers and 70 young adult titles/year. 15% of books by first-time authors.

Nonfiction: Picture books: animal, concept, geography, history, nature/environment, science. Young readers: animal, biography, geography, multicultural, nature/environment, special needs. Middle readers and young adults: geography, nature/environment, reference, special needs. Does not want to see dogs, spiritual, medical themes. Average word length: young adult readers—8,000-10,000; middle readers—5,000-7,000. Recently published *Wild Marine Animals* (ages 8-10); and *Giants of Science* (biography series).

How to Contact/Writers: Nonfiction: Query. Materials will not be returned. Publishes a book 1 year after acceptance. Will consider simultaneous submissions.

Illustration: Works with 10 illustrators/year. Uses color artwork only. Reviews ms/illustration packages from artists. Submit query. Illustrations only: Query with samples; send résumé, promo sheet. Samples not returned; samples filed.

Photography: Buys photos from freelancers. Buys stock and assigns work. Uses animal, human culture, geography. Captions required. Uses 35mm, 2¼ × 2¼, 4 × 5 transparencies. Submit cover letter, published samples and promo piece.

Terms: Pays authors royalty or work purchased outright from author. Offers advances. Pays illustrators by the project or royalty. Pays photographers by the project, per photo or royalty. Original artwork returned at job's completion. Book catalog available for 8 × 10 SAE and 3 first-class stamps. Ms guidelines available for SASE.

▼ BLUE SKY PRESS, 555 Broadway, New York NY 10012. (212)343-6100. Website: www.scholastic.com. Book publisher. Imprint of Scholastic Inc. **Acquisitions:** Bonnie Verburg. Publishes 15-20 titles/year. 1% of books by first-time authors. Publishes hardcover children's fiction and nonfiction including high-quality novels and picture books by new and established authors.

• Blue Sky is currently not accepting unsolicited submissions due to a large backlog of books. Blue Sky title *The Rain Came Down*, illustrated by David Shannon, won the Golden Kite Award for Picture Book Illustration in 2001.

Fiction: Picture books: adventure, animal, concept, contemporary, fantasy, folktales, history, humor, multicultural, nature/environment, poetry. Young readers: adventure, contemporary, fantasy, folktales, history, humor, multicultural, nature/environment, poetry. Young adults: adventure, anthology, contemporary, fantasy, history, humor, multicultural, poetry. Multicultural needs include "strong fictional or themes featuring non-white characters and cultures." Does not want to see mainstream religious, bibliotherapeutic, adult. Average length: picture books—varies; young adults—150 pages. Recently published *To Every Thing There Is a Season*, illustrated by Leo and Diane Dillon (all ages, picture book); *Bluish*, by Virginia Hamilton; *No, David!*, by David Shannon; *The Adventures of Captain Underpants*, by Dav Pilkey; and *How Do Dinosaurs Say Goodnight?*, by Jane Yolen, illustrated by Mark Teague.

How to Contact/Writers: "Due to large numbers of submissions, we are discouraging unsolicited submissions—send query with SASE only if you feel certain we publish the type of book you have written." Fiction: Query (novels, picture books). Responds to queries in 6 months. Publishes a book 1-3 years after acceptance; depending on chosen illustrator's schedule. Will not consider simultaneous submissions.

Illustration: Works with 10 illustrators/year. Uses both b&w and color artwork. Reviews illustration packages "only if illustrator is the author." Submit ms with dummy. Illustrations only: Query with samples, tearsheets. Responds only if interested. Samples returned with SASE. Original artwork returned at job's completion.

Terms: Pays 10% royalty based on wholesale price split between author and illustrators. Advance varies.

Tips: "Read currently published children's books. Revise—never send a first draft. Find your own voice, style, and subject. With material from new people we look for a theme or style strong enough to overcome the fact that the author/illustrator is unknown in the market."

BOYDS MILLS PRESS, 815 Church St., Honesdale PA 18431. (800)490-5111. Fax: (570)253-0179. Website: www.boydsmillspress.com. Imprint: Wordsong (poetry). Book publisher. **Manuscript Acquisitions:** Beth Troop. **Art Acquisitions:** Tim Gillner. 5% of books by agented writers. Estab. 1990. "We publish a wide range of quality children's books of literary merit, from preschool to young adult."

Fiction: All levels: adventure, contemporary, history, humor, multicultural, poetry. Picture books: animal. Young readers, middle readers, young adult: problem novels, sports. Multicultural themes include any story showing a child as an integral part of a culture and which provides children with insight into a culture they otherwise might be unfamiliar with. "Please query us on the appropriateness of suggested topics for middle grade and young adult. For all other submissions send entire manuscript." Does not want to see talking animals, coming-of-age novels, romance and fantasy/science fiction. Recently published *Mr. Beans* by Dayton O. Hyde (novel, ages 10 and up); and *An Alligator Ate My Brother*, by Mary Olson (picture book, ages 5-8).

Nonfiction: All levels: nature/environment, science. Picture books, young readers, middle readers: animal, multicultural. Does not want to see reference/curricular text. Recently published *Uncommon Champions*, by Marty Kaminsky (ages 12 and up) and *St. Nicholas*, by Ann Tompert (ages 6 and up).

How to Contact/Writers: Fiction/Nonfiction: Submit complete ms or submit through agent. Query on middle reader, young adult and nonfiction. Responds to queries/mss in 1 month.

Illustration: Works with 25 illustrators/year. Reviews ms/illustration packages from artists. Submit complete ms with 1 or 2 pieces of art. Illustrations only: Query with samples; send résumé and slides. Responds only if interested. Samples returned with SASE. Samples filed. Originals returned at job's completion.

Photography: Assigns work.

Terms: Authors paid royalty or work purchased outright. Offers advances. Illustrators paid by the project or royalties; varies. Photographers paid by the project, per photo, or royalties; varies. Mss/artist's guidelines available for #10 SASE.

Tips: "Picture books—with fresh approaches, not worn themes—are our strongest need at this time. Check to see what's already on the market before submitting your story."

BROADMAN & HOLMAN PUBLISHERS, LifeWay Christian Resources, 127 Ninth Ave. N., Nashville TN 37234. Fax: (615)251-5026. Book publisher. **Senior Acquisitions & Development Editor:** Gail Rothwell. Publishes 25-30 titles/year with majority being for younger readers. Only publish a few titles/yr. for ages 0-3 or 9-11. 10% of books by first-time authors. "All books have Christian values/themes."

Fiction: Middle readers, young readers: adventure, concept, contemporary, religion.

Nonfiction: Picture books: religion. Young or middle readers: self-help, social issues, religion, contemporary. Recently published: *Manners Made Easy: A Workbook for Student Parent and Teacher*, by June Hines Moore, illustrated by Jim Osborn (ages 7-12); *The Great Adventure* and *Thank You*, by Stephen Elkins, illustrated by Ellie Colton (children's storybook with CD based on Dove-Award winning songs, age 5 and up); *Which Came First, the Chicken or the Egg?*, by Leslie Eckard, illustrated by Judy Sakaguchi (children's songbook, ages 5-8).

How to Contact/Writers: Responds to queries in 2 weeks; mss in 2 months. Publishes a book 1 year after acceptance. Will consider simultaneous submissions.

Illustration: Works with 5-6 illustrators/year. Samples returned with SASE; samples filed.

Terms: Pays authors royalty 10-18% based on wholesale price. Offers variable advance. Original artwork returned at job's completion. Book catalog available for 9 × 12 SAE and 2 first-class stamps. Ms guidelines available for SASE.

Tips: "We're looking for picture books with good family values; Bible story re-tellings; modern-day stories for younger readers based on Bible themes and principles. Write us to ask for guidelines before submitting."

CANDLEWICK PRESS, 2067 Massachusetts Ave., Cambridge MA 02140. (617)661-3330. Fax: (617)661-0565. E-mail: bigbear@candlewick.com. Children's book publisher. Estab. 1991. **Manuscript Acquisitions:** Liz Bicknell, editorial director; Joan Powers, editorial director (novelty); Amy Ehrlich, editor-at-large; Mary Lee Donovan, executive editor; Yolanda Leroy, editor; Kara LaReau, editor; Sarah Ketchersid, editor; Cynthia Platt, associate editor; Deborah Wayshak, associate editor; Jamie Michalak, associate editor; Erin Postl, assistant editor. **Art Acquisitions:** Anne Moore. Publishes 175 picture books/year; 5 middle readers/year; and 5 young adult titles/year. 10% of books by first-time authors. "Our books are truly for children, and we strive for the very highest standards in the writing, illustrating, designing and production of all of our books. And we are not averse to risk."
- Candlewick Press is accepting queries and unsolicited mss at this time. Send one manuscript at a time; allow at least three months for a reply, and do not call. Candlewick title *Because of Winn-Dixie*, by Kate DiCamillo, won a 2001 Newbery Honor Medal.

Fiction: Picture books, young readers: animal, concept, contemporary, fantasy, history, humor, multicultural, nature/environment, poetry. Middle readers, young adults: animal, anthology, contemporary, fantasy, history, humor, multicultural, poetry, science fiction, sports, suspense/mystery. Recently published: *Because of Winn Dixie* (middle grade fiction); *A Poke in the I* (concrete poetry collection).

Nonfiction: Picture books: concept, biography, geography, nature/environment. Young readers: biography, geography, nature/environment. Recently published *Castle Diary* (nonfiction).

Illustration: Works with 20 illustrators/year. "We prefer to see a variety of the artist's style." Reviews ms/illustration packages from artists. "General samples only please." Illustrations only: Submit résumé and portfolio to the attention of Design Dept. Responds to samples in 6 weeks. Samples returned with SASE; samples filed.

Terms: Pays authors royalty of 2.5-10% based on retail price. Offers advances. Pays illustrators 2.5-10% royalty based on retail price. Sends galleys to authors; dummies to illustrators. Photographers paid 2.5-10% royalty. Original artwork returned at job's completion.

CAPSTONE PRESS INC., P.O. Box 669, Mankato MN 56002. (507)388-6650. Fax: (507)388-1227. Website: www.capstone-press.com. Book publisher. **Acquisitons:** Helen Moore. Imprints: Capstone Press, Bridgestone Books, Pebble Books, Blue Earth Books, Life Matters (all Helen Moore, acquisitions).

Nonfiction: Publishes only nonfiction books for emergent, early, challenged and reluctant readers. Currently looking for experienced authors to write on vehicle and sport topics; also science, social studies, and pleasure reading areas. All levels: animals, arts/crafts, biography, geography, health, history, hobbies, special needs. Young adults only: Hi-lo, cooking, self help.

How to Contact/Writers: Does not accept submissions. Do not send mss. Instead, send query letter, résumé and samples of nonfiction writing to be considered for assignment.

Photographers: Buys stock and assigns work. Contact: Photo Research Manager. Model/property release required. Uses 35mm slides, 4 × 5, 8 × 10 transparencies. Submit slides, stock photo list.

Terms: Photographers paid by the project or per photo. Originals returned to artist at job's completion. Authors paid flat fee. Book catalog available for large format SAE.

Tips: "See catalog prior to submitting."

CAROLRHODA BOOKS, INC., Division of the Lerner Publishing Group, 241 First Ave. N., Minneapolis MN 55401. (612)332-3344 or (800)328-4929. Fax: (612)332-7615. Website: www.lernerbooks.com. Imprint of Lerner. Lerner's other imprints are Runestone Press, Lerner Sports, LernerClassroom and First Avenue Editions. The acquisition editor for Lerner is Jennifer Zimian, who handles fiction and nonfiction for grades 5-12. Book publisher. Estab. 1969. **Acquisitions:** Rebecca Poole, submissions editor. Carolrhoda Books is a children's publisher focused on producing high-quality, socially conscious nonfiction and fiction books for young readers K through grade 4, that help them learn about and explore the world around them. List includes picture books, biographies, nature and science titles, multicultural and introductory geography books and fiction for beginning readers. Recently published *Sybil Ludington's Midnight Ride*, by Marsha Amstel, illustrated by Ellen Beier (On My Own History series, grades 1-3, nonfiction); *Totally Uncool*, by Janice Levy, illustrated by Chris Monroe (picture book); *Polar Bears*, by Dorothy Hinshaw Patent, photographs by William Muñoz (Nature Watch series, grades 3-6, nonfiction).

How to Contact/Writers: Submissions are accepted in the months of March and October only. Submissions received in any month other than March or October will be returned unopened to the sender. The Lerner Publishing group does not publish alphabet books, puzzle books, songbooks, textbooks, workbooks, religious subject matter or plays. A SASE is required for all submissions. Please allow 2-6 months for a response.

CARTWHEEL BOOKS, for the Very Young, Imprint of Scholastic Inc., 555 Broadway, New York NY 10012. (212)343-6100. Fax: (212)343-4444. Website: www.scholastic.com. Book publisher. Executive Director:

Grace Maccarone. **Manuscript Acquisitions:** Jane Gerver, easy readers. **Art Acquisitions:** Edie Weinberg, art director. Publishes 25-30 picture books/year; 30-35 easy readers/year; 15-20 novelty/concept books/year. "With each Cartwheel list, we strive for a pleasing balance among board books and novelty books, hardcover picture books and gift books, nonfiction, paperback storybooks and easy readers. Cartwheel seeks to acquire novelties that are books first; play objects second. Even without its gimmick, a Cartwheel novelty book should stand alone as a valid piece of children's literature. We want all our books to be inviting and appealing, and to have inherent educational and social value. We believe that small children who develop personal relationships with books and grow up with a love of reading, become book consumers, and ultimately better human beings."
Fiction: Picture books: adventure, animal, anthology, concept, contemporary, fantasy, folktales, history, humor, multicultural, nature/environment, poetry, science fiction, sports, suspense/mystery. Easy readers: adventure, animal, concept, contemporary, fantasy, history, holiday, humor, multicultural, nature/environment, poetry, science fiction. Average work length: picture books—1-3,000; easy readers—100-3,000.
Nonfiction: Picture books, young readers: animal, biography, concept, history, multicultural, nature/environment, sports. "Most of our nonfiction is either written on assignment or is within a series. We do not want to see any arts/crafts or cooking." Average word length: picture books—100-3,000; young readers—100-3,000.
How to Contact/Writers: Cartwheel Books is no longer accepting unsolicited mss; query. All unsolicited materials will be returned unread. Fiction/nonfiction: For previously published or agented authors, submit complete ms. Responds to queries in 1-2 months; mss in 3-6 months. Publishes a book 18-24 months after acceptance. Will consider simultaneous submissions; electronic submissions via disk or modem; previously published work.
Illustration: Works with 100 illustrators/year. Reviews ms/illustration packages from artists. Send ms with dummy. Illustrations only: Query with samples; arrange personal portfolio review; send promo sheet, tearsheets to be kept on file. Responds in 2 months. Samples returned with SASE; samples filed.
Photography: Buys stock and assigns work. Uses photos of kids, families, vehicles, toys, animals. Submit published samples, color promo piece.
Terms: Pays authors royalty of 2-8% based on retail price or work purchased outright for $600-5,000. Offers advances (Average amount: $3,000). Pays illustrators by the project (range: $2,000-10,000); flat fee; or advance against royalties (royalty of 1-3% based on retail price). Photographers paid by the project (range: $250-10,000); per photo (range: $250-500); or royalty of 1-3% of wholesale price. Sends galley to authors; dummy to illustrators. Originals returned to artist at job's completion. Book catalog available for 9 × 12 SAE and 2 first-class stamps; ms guidelines for SASE.
Tips: "Know what types of books we do. Check out bookstores or catalogs to see where your work would fit best."

CHARLESBRIDGE, 85 Main St., Watertown MA 02472. (617)926-0329. Fax: (617)926-5720. E-mail: tradeeditorial@charlesbridge.com. Website: www.charlesbridge.com. Book publisher. Estab. 1980. Imprints: Talewinds and Whispering Coyote. Publishes 60% nonfiction, 40% fiction titles and picture books. Publishes nature, science, multicultural social studies and fiction picture books and board books. Charlesbridge also has an educational division. **Contact:** Trade Editorial Department, submissions editor or School Editorial Department.
Fiction: Picture books: "Strong, realistic stories with enduring themes." Considers the following categories: adventure, concept, contemporary, health, history, humor, multicultural, nature/environment, special needs, sports, suspense/mystery. Recently published: *Scatterbrain Sun*, by Ellen Jackson; *Hello Ocean*, by Pam Muñoz Ryan.
Nonfiction: Picture books: animal, biography, careers, concept, geography, health, history, multicultural, music/dance, nature/environment, religion, science, social issues, special needs, hobbies, sports. Average word length: picture books—1,500. Recently published: *The Coin Counting Book*, by Rozanne Lanczak Williams; and *The Egg*, by Shelley Gill.
How to Contact/Writers: Send ms and SASE. Accepts exclusive submissions only. Responds to mss in 3 months. Full ms only; no queries.
Illustration: Works with 5-10 illustrators/year. Uses color artwork only. Illustrations only: Query with samples; provide résumé, tearsheets to be kept on file. "Send no original artwork, please." Responds only if interested. Samples returned with SASE; samples filed. Originals returned at job's completion.
Terms: Pays authors and illustrators in royalties or work purchased outright. Ms/art guidelines available for SASE. Exclusive submissions only.
Tips: Wants "books that have humor and are factually correct. See our website for more tips."

CHICAGO REVIEW PRESS, 814 N. Franklin St., Chicago IL 60610. (312)337-0747. Fax: (312)337-5985. E-mail: publish@ipgbook.com. Website: www.ipgbook.com. Book publisher. Estab. 1973. **Manuscript Acquisitions:** Cynthia Sherry, executive editor. **Art Acquisitions:** Joan Sommers, art director. Publishes 3-4 middle readers/year and "about 4" young adult titles/year. 33% of books by first-time authors; 30% of books from agented authors. "Chicago Review Press publishes high-quality, nonfiction, educational activity books that extend the learning process through hands-on projects and accurate and interesting text. We look for activity books that are as much fun as they are constructive and informative."
Nonfiction: Picture books, young readers, middle readers and young adults: activity books, arts/crafts, multicultural, history, nature/environment, science. "We're interested in hands-on, educational books; anything else probably will be rejected." Average length: young readers and young adults—175 pages. Recently published *Shake-*

speare for Kids, by Margie Blumberg and Colleen Aagesen (ages 9 and up); *Civil War for Kids*, by Janis Herbert (ages 9 and up); and *Bite-Sized Science*, by John H. Falk and Kristi Rosenberg, illustrated by Bonnie Matthews (ages 3-8).

How to Contact/Writers: Enclose cover letter and no more than table of contents and 1-2 sample chapters. Send for guidelines. Responds to queries/mss in 2 months. Publishes a book 1-2 years after acceptance. Will consider simultaneous submissions and previously published work.

Illustration: Works with 6 illustrators/year. Uses primarily b&w artwork. Reviews ms/illustration packages from artists. Submit 1-2 chapters of ms with corresponding pieces of final art. Illustrations only: Query with samples, résumé. Responds only if interested. Samples returned with SASE.

Photography: Buys photos from freelancers ("but not often"). Buys stock and assigns work. Wants "instructive photos. We consult our files when we know what we're looking for on a book-by-book basis." Uses b&w prints.

Terms: Pays authors royalty of 7½-12½% based on retail price. Offers advances of $1,000-4,000. Pays illustrators by the project (range varies considerably). Pays photographers by the project (range varies considerably). Original artwork "usually" returned at job's completion. Book catalog/ms guidelines available for $3.

Tips: "We're looking for original activity books for small children and the adults caring for them—new themes and enticing projects to occupy kids' imaginations and promote their sense of personal creativity. We like activity books that are as much fun as they are constructive. Please write for guidelines so you'll know what we're looking for."

N: CHILD WELFARE LEAGUE OF AMERICA, Child & Family Press, 440 First St., NW, 3rd Floor, Washington DC 20001-2085. (202)942-0263. Fax: (202)638-4004. E-mail: www.ptierney@cwla.org. Website: www.cwla.org. The Child & Family Press imprint was created in 1990. **Acquisitions:** Peggy Porter Tierney. Publishes 5 picture books/year; 1 middle reader/year. 50% books by first-time authors. "CWLA is the nation's oldest and largest membership-based child welfare organization. We are committed to engaging people everywhere in promoting the well-being of children, youth, and their families, and protecting every child from harm."

Fiction: Picture books: animal, concept, contemporary, health, multicultural, special needs. Recently published *Glenna's Seeds*, by Nancy Edward (picture book, ages 4-11); *Imagine*, by Angela Lamanno (picture book, ages 4-9); and *An American Face*, by Jan Czech (picture book, ages 4-11).

Nonfiction: Picture books, young readers, middle readers, young adults: concept, multicultural, self-help, social issues, special needs (anything relating to child welfare). Recently published *Being Adopted*, by Stephanie Herbert (picture book, ages 4-8); *I Miss My Foster Parents*, by Stefan Herbert (picture book, 4-8); and *The Visit*, by Latisha Herbert (picture book, ages 4-8).

How to Contact/Writers: Fiction/nonfiction: Submit complete ms or submit outline/synopsis and 3-4 sample chapters. Responds in 3 months. Publishes a book 1 year after acceptance. Will consider simultaneous submissions.

Illustration: Works with 5 illustrators/year. Reviews ms/illustration packages from artists. Send ms with dummy or submit ms with 3-4 pieces of final art. Contact: Jennifer Geanakos, lead designer. Illustrations only: Query with samples. Contact: Peggy Porter Tierney, acquisitions. Responds in 3 months. "We prefer to keep samples on file in case suitable for future job." Samples returned with SASE.

Photography: Buys stock. Contact: Peggy Porter Tierney, acquisitions. Uses photos of children and families. Uses color or b&w prints and 35mm, 2¼×2¼, 4×5 transparencies. Submit slides, client list, promo piece, published samples, stock photo list.

Terms: Pays authors royalty of 9-12% based on retail price. Pays illustrators by the project up to $5,000. Pays photographers by the project or per photo. Sends galleys to authors; dummies to illustrators. Writer's guidlines for SASE. Catalog available on website.

Tips: "We are looking for upbeat, imaginative children's stories, particularly with some kind of message. Authors do not need to worry about illustrations or formatting. In fact, a plain text to me is preferable to a manuscript set out in pages with very amateurish drawings. Do not call to propose an idea."

☑ CHILDREN'S BOOK PRESS, 2211 Mission St., San Francisco CA 94110. (415)821-3080. Fax: (415)821-3081. E-mail: info@cbookpress.org. Website: www.cbookpress.org. **Acquisitions:** Submissions Editor. "Children's Book Press is a nonprofit publisher of multicultural and bilingual children's literature. We publish folktales and contemporary stories reflecting the traditions and culture of minorities and new immigrants in the United States. Our goal is to help broaden the base of children's literature in this country to include more stories from the African-American, Asian-American, Hispanic and Native American communities as well as the diverse Spanish-speaking communities throughout the Americas."

Fiction: Picture books, young readers: contemporary, folktales, history, multicultural, poetry. Average word length: picture books—800-1,600.

Nonfiction: Picture books, young readers: multicultural.

How to Contact/Writers: Submit complete ms to Submissions Editor. Responds to mss in roughly 4 months. Publishes a book 1-2 years after acceptance. Will consider simultaneous submissions.

Illustration: Works with 4-5 illustrators/year. Uses color artwork only. Reviews ms/illustration packages from artists. Send ms with 3 or 4 color photocopies. Illustrations only: color copies preferable, slides if you must, no original artwork. Send slides. Responds only of interested. Samples returned with SASE.

Terms: Original artwork returned at job's completion. Book catalog available; ms guidelines available via website or with SASE.

© Maya Christina Gonzalez

My Very Own Room (Mi Propio Cuartito), written in both English and Spanish, is characteristic of the multicultural, bilingual picture books Children's Book Press has published for 25 years. Specializing in tales from diverse Spanish-speaking communities especially, the editor sought award-winning painter and graphic artist Maya Christina Gonzalez to create engaging visuals for Amada Irma Perez's autobiographical story.

Tips: "Vocabulary level should be approximately third grade (eight years old) or below. Keep in mind, however, that many of the young people who read our books may be nine, ten, or eleven years old or older. Their life experiences are often more advanced than their reading level, so try to write a story that will appeal to a fairly wide age range. We are especially interested in humorous stories and original stories about contemporary life from the multicultural communities mentioned above by writers *from* those communities."

CHINA BOOKS & PERIODICALS, 2929 24th St., San Francisco CA 94110. (415)282-2994. Fax: (415)282-0994. E-mail: info@chinabooks.com. Website: www.chinabooks.com. Book publisher, distributor, wholesaler.

Estab. 1960. **Acquisitions:** Greg Jones, editor. Publishes 1 picture book/year; 1 middle readers/year; and 1 young adult title/year. 50% of books by first-time authors. Publishes only books about China and Chinese culture. Recently published *Sing Chinese! Popular Children's Songs & Lullabies*, by Ma Baolin and Cindy Ma (children—adults/song book); and *The Moon Maiden and Other Asian Folktales*, by Hua Long (children to age 12/folktales). "China Books is the main importer and distributor of books and magazines from China, providing an ever-changing variety of useful tools for travelers, scholars and others interested in China and Chinese culture."
Fiction: All levels: animal, anthology, folktales, history, multicultural, nature/environment.
Nonfiction: All levels: activity books, animal, arts/crafts, cooking, how-to, multicultural, music/dance, reference, textbooks. Recently published *West to East: A Young Girl's Journey to China*, by Qian Gao (young adult nonfiction travel journal).
How to Contact/Writers: Fiction/Nonfiction: Query. Responds to queries and mss in 2 months. Publishes a book 1 year after acceptance. Will consider simultaneous submissions, electronic submissions via disk or modem, previously published work.
Illustration: Works with 4-5 illustrators/year. Reviews ms/illustration packages from artists. Query. Illustrations only: Query with samples. Send résumé, promo sheet, tearsheets. Responds in 1 month only if interested. Samples returned with SASE; samples filed.
Terms: Pays authors 4-10% royalty based on wholesale price or work purchased outright. Pays illustrators and photographers by the project (range $400-1,500) or royalty based on wholesale price. Sends galleys to authors; dummies to illustrators. Originals returned to artist at job's completion. See website for guidelines.

✓ CHRISTIAN PUBLICATIONS, INC., 3825 Hartzdale Dr., Camp Hill PA 17011. (717)761-7044. Fax: (717)761-7273. E-mail: dfessenden@christianpublications.com. Website: www.christianpublications.com. Managing Editor: David Fessenden. **Art Acquisitions:** Marilynne Foster. Imprints: Christian Publications, Horizon Books. Publishes 2 young adult titles/year. 50% of books by first-time authors. The missions of this press are promoting participation in spreading the gospel worldwide and promoting Christian growth. Does not publish fiction.
Nonfiction: Young adults: religion. Does not want to see evangelistic/new Christian material. "Children and teens are too often assumed to have a shallow faith. We want to encourage a deeper walk with God." Average word length: young adults—25,000-40,000 words. Recently published *Grace and Guts to Live for God*, by Les Morgan (Bible study on Hebrews, 1 and 2 Peter); and *Holy Moses! And other Adventures in Vertical Living*, by Bob Hostetler. (Both are teen books which encourage a deeper commitment to God. Both illustrated by Ron Wheeler.) "Not accepting unsolicited material for age levels lower than teenage."
How to Contact/Writers: Nonfiction: Submit outline/synopsis and 2 sample chapters (including chapter one). Responds to queries in 6 weeks; mss in 2 months. Publishes a book 8-16 months after acceptance. Will consider simultaneous submissions, electronic submissions via disk or modem ("a one page, please").
Illustration: Works with 1-3 illustrators/year. Query with samples. Contact: Marilynne Foster, promotions coordinator. Responds only if interested. Samples returned with SASE; samples filed.
Terms: Pays authors royalty of 5-10% based on retail price. Offers advances. Pays illustrators by the project. Sends galleys to authors; dummies to illustrators (sometimes). Originals returned to artist at job's completion (if requested). Ms guidelines available for SASE or via website.
Tips: "Writers: Only opportunity is in teen market, especially if you have experience working with and speaking to teens. Illustrators: Show us a few samples. View website for an electronic book submissions form."

✓ CHRONICLE BOOKS, 85 Second St., 6th Floor, San Francisco CA 94105. (415)537-4422. Fax: (415)537-4420. Website: www.chroniclekids.com. Book publisher. **Acquisitions:** Victoria Rock, associate publisher, children's books. Publishes 35-60 (both fiction and nonfiction) books/year; 5-10 middle readers, young adult nonfiction titles/year. 10-25% of books by first-time authors; 20-40% of books from agented writers.
Fiction: Picture books: animal, folktales, history, multicultural, nature/environment. Young readers: animal, folktales, history, multicultural, nature/environment, poetry. Middle readers: animal, history, multicultural, nature/environment, poetry, problem novels. Young adults: multicultural needs include "projects that feature diverse children in everyday situations." Recently published *Red is a Dragon*, by Roseanne Thong, illustrated by Grace Lin; *Bintou's Braves*, by Sylviane A. Dionf, illustrated by Shane W. Evans; *Twinkle Twinkle Little Star*, by Sylvia Long.
Nonfiction: Picture books: animal, history, multicultural, nature/environment, science. Young readers: animal, arts/crafts, cooking, geography, history, multicultural and science. Middle readers: animal, arts/crafts, biography, cooking, geography, history, multicultural and nature/environment. Young adults: biography and multicultural. Recently published *Story Painter: The Life of Jacob Lawrence*, by John Duggleby; *Seven Weeks on an Iceberg*, by Keith Potter (Doodlezoo series).
How to Contact/Writers: Fiction/Nonfiction: Submit complete ms (picture books); submit outline/synopsis and 3 sample chapters (for older readers). Responds to queries/mss in 4 months. Publishes a book 1-3 years after acceptance. Will consider simultaneous submissions, as long as they are marked "multiple submission." Will not consider submissions by fax or e-mail. Must include SASE or projects will not be returned.
Illustration: Works with 15-20 illustrators/year. Wants "unusual art, graphically strong, something that will stand out on the shelves. Either bright and modern or very traditional. Fine art, not mass market." Reviews ms/illustration packages from artists. "Indicate if project *must* be considered jointly, or if editor may consider text

and art separately." Illustrations only: Submit samples of artist's work (not necessarily from book, but in the envisioned style). Slides, tearsheets and color photocopies OK. (No original art.) Dummies helpful. Résumé helpful. "If samples sent for files, generally no response—unless samples are not suited to list, in which case samples are returned. Queries and project proposals responded to in same time frame as author query/proposals."
Photography: Purchases photos from freelancers. Works on assignment only. Wants nature/natural history photos.
Terms: Generally pays authors in royalties based on retail price "though we do occasionally work on a flat fee basis." Advance varies. Illustrators paid royalty based on retail price or flat fee. Sends proofs to authors and illustrators. Book catalog for 9×12 SAE and 8 first-class stamps; ms guidelines for #10 SASE.
Tips: "Chronicle Books publishes an eclectic mixture of traditional and innovative children's books. We are interested in taking on projects that have a unique bent to them—be it in subject matter, writing style, or illustrative technique. As a small list, we are looking for books that will lend our list a distinctive flavor. Primarily we are interested in fiction and nonfiction picture books for children ages infant-8 years, and nonfiction books for children ages 8-12 years. We are also interested in developing a middle grade/YA fiction program, and are looking for literary fiction that deals with relevant issues. Our sales reps are witnessing a resistance to alphabet books. And the market has become increasingly competitive. The '80s boom in children's publishing has passed, and the market is demanding high-quality books that work on many different levels."

CLARION BOOKS, 215 Park Ave. S., New York NY 10003. (212)420-5889. Website: www.houghtonmifflinbooks.com/trade/. Imprint of Houghton Mifflin Company. Book publisher. Estab. 1965. **Manuscript Acquisitions:** Dinah Stevenson, editorial director; Michele Coppola, editor; Virginia Buckley, contributing editor; Jennifer Green, editor; Julie Strauss-Gabel, associate editor. **Art Acquisitions:** Joann Hill, art director.
• Clarion title *Kite Fighters*, by Linda Sue Park, won a Notable Books for a Global Society Award. See the Insider Report with Park on page 130.
How to Contact/Writers: Fiction and picture books: Send complete mss. Nonfiction: Send query with up to 3 sample chapters. Must include SASE. Will accept simultaneous submission if informed.
Illustration: Send samples (no originals).
Terms: Pays illustrators royalty; flat fee for jacket illustration. Pays royalties and advance to writers; both vary.

CLEAR LIGHT PUBLISHERS, 823 Don Diego, Santa Fe NM 87505. (505)989-9590. Fax: (505)989-9519. Website: www.clearlightbooks.com. Book publisher. **Acquisitions:** Harmon Houghton, publisher. Publishes 4 middle readers/year; and 4 young adult titles/year.
Nonfiction: Middle readers and young adults: multicultural, American Indian and Hispanic only.
How to Contact/Writers: Fiction/Nonfiction: Submit complete ms with SASE. "No e-mail submissions. Authors supply art. Manuscripts not considered without art or artists renderings." Will consider simultaneous submissions. Responds in 3 months. Only send *copies*.
Illustration: Reviews ms/illustration packages from artists. "No originals please." Submit ms with dummy and SASE.
Terms: Pays authors royalty of 10% based on wholesale price. Offers advances (average amount: up to 50% of expected net sales within the first year). Sends galleys to authors.
Tips: "We're looking for authentic American Indian art and folklore."

COLONIAL WILLIAMSBURG FOUNDATION, P.O. Box 1776, Williamsburg VA 23168. Fax: (757)220-7325. Website: www.colonialwilliamsburg.org. Estab. 1926. **Manuscript Acquisitions:** Donna Sheppard, senior book editor/writer. **Art Acquisitions:** Helen Mageras, senior book designer. Publishes 1 young readers/year; 2 middle readers/year. 15% of books by first-time authors. Our editorial mission is "That the future may learn from the past." (John D. Rockefeller, Jr.).
Fiction: Picture books, young readers, middle readers, young adult/teens: history.
Nonfiction: Picture books, young readers, middle readers, young adults/teens: history.
How to Contact/Writers: Only interested in agented material. Fiction/nonfiction: submit outline/synopsis. Responds in 3 months to queries.
Illustration: Only interested in agented material. Query. Illustrations only: Query with samples. Resonds in 3 months only if interested. Samples returned with SASE; samples filed.

CONCORDIA PUBLISHING HOUSE, 3558 S. Jefferson Ave., St. Louis MO 63118. (314)268-1187. Fax: (314)268-1329. Website: cphmall.com. Book publisher. **Manuscript Acquisitions:** Jane Wilke. **Art Acquisitions:** Ed Luhmann, art director. "Concordia Publishing House produces quality resources which communicate and nurture the Christian faith and ministry of people of all ages, lay and professional. These resources include curriculum, worship aids, books, multimedia products and religious supplies. We publish approximately 30 quality children's books each year. All are nonfiction based on a religious subject. We boldly provide Gospel resources that are Christ-centered, Bible-based and faithful to our Lutheran heritage."
Nonfiction: Picture books: concept, poetry, contemporary, religion. Young readers, middle readers, young adults: concept, contemporary, religion. "All books must contain explicit Christian content." Recently published *The Very First Christmas*, by Paul L Maier (picture book for ages 6-10); and *Running the Race of Faith*, by Pam Ausenhus (ages over 12, youth nonfiction).

insider report

Author explores her cultural roots through historical fiction

When author Linda Sue Park was ten years old, her parents gave her a beat up copy of Frances Carpenter's book *Tales of a Korean Grandmother*. "I suppose this was in some way a stand-in for the fact that they didn't tell us very many stories about Korea as we were growing up. We ate Korean food and celebrated some holidays with Korean traditions, and I now realize that many of the values we were raised with were traditionally Korean. But I didn't know much about Korea until I began research for *Seesaw Girl*."

Seesaw Girl became Park's first published novel, a middle grade book set in 17th-century Korea. "That book grew directly out of a single line in Carpenter's book—an image of a girl jumping on a seesaw to see over the walls of the courtyard. I wrote the

Linda Sue Park

book relatively quickly—in about six months or so—but it had been in my head for almost 25 years!"

Clarion editor Dinah Stevenson signed Park's first novel after pulling her query from the slush pile. "I've been fortunate to work with her on three subsequent novels as well as a picture book," Park says. She followed-up *Seesaw Girl* with *The Kite Fighters* and *A Single Shard*, all historical fiction set in Korea.

Her fourth novel, a spring 2002 Clarion title called *When My Name Is Keoko*, is set in Korea during World War II. "At that time, Korea was occupied by Japan. The story is about the terrible difficulties faced by a people who want to maintain their cultural identity when the dominant forces are making every effort to erase it," says Park. "This sounds like a 'heavy' topic—which it is—but I hope it will be accessible to young readers through the narrators, a young girl and her brother. Much of the material in the book is based on the experiences of my parents."

Park maintains a terrific website, www.lindasuepark.com, which includes information about her and all her books as well as articles, links and reading lists. (See her article Read, Right? Read, Write! on page 50.) Here she talks about working with her editor, getting ideas and doing research for her novels.

How did you find your agent Ginger Knowlton? Why did you decide that having an agent was right for you?

I asked around a lot, mostly online, and Ginger's name was suggested by a writer-friend of mine. Before that, I had seen her name in the reference books and marked her as a "possible" to submit to; when my friend said she was highly regarded, I decided to submit to her. Having an agent is right for me because I don't have very much time for writing—I have a part-time teaching job and a busy family, so I'm only writing three days a week as it is. I didn't want to spend that time on marketing my work and deciphering contracts. Ginger does all that for me; she's worth every cent of her commission and then some!

You've worked with editor Dinah Stevenson on all your books. What's the advantage of building a relationship with an editor? Do you feel your working relationship strengthens as you continue to work together?
Most writers adore their editors and I'm no exception. If, as I hope, my work is getting stronger

SEESAW GIRL

BY LINDA SUE PARK

ILLUSTRATED BY JEAN AND MOU-SIEN TSENG

Illustration © 1999 Jean and Mou-sien Tseng. Reprinted with permission of Clarion Books.

The idea for Linda Sue Park's first book, *Seesaw Girl*, was sparked from Frances Carpenter's *Tales of a Korean Grandmother*, a book Park read as a girl. "That book grew directly from a single line—an image of a girl jumping on a seesaw to see over the walls of the courtyard," Park says. "I wrote the book in about six months—but it had been in my head for almost 25 years!"

as I go, a large part is due to Dinah's guidance. What I love most is the way she edits. Rarely does she make changes; instead she'll simply say what she thinks the problem is—whether it's as small as a word or punctuation choice, as big as a character, scene, chapter—and leave the answer to me. There's no doubt that the long-term nature of our relationship has been a boon; I now feel I can ask her the dumbest questions, confident that she'll always forgive my stupidity!

What are some of the difficulties of writing about other cultures?
I would say the biggest difficulty is balancing authenticity with accessibility. I want readers to be able to relate to the characters, but at the same time I want the characters to be grounded in their place and time. As an example, the brothers in *The Kite Fighters* have a sibling rivalry, yet not in the way American boys today might. No fistfighting, no screaming at each other, no outright meanness—because brothers would not have treated each other that way in their time. Does this make their portrayal less effective to today's readers? I hope not. I try to concentrate on the emotions—the feelings that remain the same over time and define our being human—even if the outward expression of those emotions might not be the same.

As far as names go, I'm lucky there. Korean names are fairly easy to pronounce, and they read phonetically. But I am careful to choose names that hopefully won't cause the reader to stumble.

It almost seems as if the ideas for your books have started from objects (a seesaw, a kite, celadon pottery) and then fiction bubbled up around them. Is there any truth to that? Do story ideas develop as you research?
The idea for *Seesaw Girl* came not so much from the object as the concept—what would it be like to be a girl who could never leave her home, who could only glimpse the outside world in flashes? *The Kite Fighters* came from hearing my father mention his participation in the sport as a boy. But *A Single Shard* did grow directly out of my research. When I was reading books for *Seesaw Girl*, I came across several references to the fact that in the 11th and 12th centuries, Korean pottery was considered the finest in the world. I liked that—the idea of a little tiny country being the best at something. So I took notes on those pages, tucked them away for a while (more than a year, as it turned out), and eventually went back to them.

What do you like most and least about doing research? Any tips for doing historical research?
What I like most: Reading well-written sources that take me to another world for hours at a time—and being able to call that 'work'! Also, of course, finding a gem of information that is either exactly what I was looking for, or else fits perfectly into the story in some way.

What I like least: Reading long, dry, boring books and not being able to stop because the very next page might have what I need.

Tip: It's very easy to get caught up in research and find something interesting that may be appropriate to the time and place, but simply doesn't fit the story. The danger there is the writer tries to put it in anyway. Bad idea—either the story gets contorted and twisted to accommodate the detail, or the detail simply sticks out and isn't integrated. The story comes first. If it doesn't fit—no matter how fascinating—I won't put it in. But I won't throw it away either. I'll save it for another book!

Is there any particular reason you write middle grade novels? Was this a conscious decision?

When I first began writing the story that became *Seesaw Girl*, I didn't know what it was going to be. At first I thought maybe it would be a picture book. Then, as it grew longer, I thought, hmm, adult short story? When I finally finished it, the length and the age of the protagonist fit the mid-grade genre. But the decision was not made until after I'd completed the story.

In retrospect, it's not surprising, because mid-grade novels have always been my favorite reading material. The pace and structure of mid-grade are sort of built into my brain because I've read so many of them.

All of your titles have done well in the book review circuit. What was it like to read that first starred review? How has your critical success affected your writing life?

The good reviews are always a thrill, and my first starred review (for *The Kite Fighters*, from *School Library Journal*) was no exception. But it's important to me to keep "external forces" from affecting me too much—because you never know for certain how things are going to play out. For example, *Seesaw Girl* didn't receive any starred reviews. Yet it was chosen for the Texas Bluebonnet Master List and other "best" lists as well.

When *A Single Shard* first came out, I was working on revisions for my next novel, *When My Name Was Keoko*. *Shard* received starred reviews from several publications—and paradoxically, I started to worry. What if the next book isn't as good? What if it completely disappoints everyone who liked *Shard*? My editor helped me tremendously there. She reminded me that to this point my motivation had always been internal—my desire to write the best book possible. She said I had to concentrate on that and keep the other stuff where it belongs—on the "outside," not inside my head while I'm writing. I try hard to remember her advice.

—Alice Pope

A Single Shard, the story of a 12th-century homeless Korean boy who works for a master potter, is Linda Sue Park's latest novel with Clarion. "When I was reading books for *Seesaw Girl*, I came across several references to the fact that in the 11th and 12th centuries, Korean pottery was considered the finest in the world," says Park. "I liked the idea of a little tiny country being the best at something." She went back to her notes on pottery and wrote *A Single Shard*.

Illustration © 2001 Jean and Mou-sien Tseng. Reprinted with permission of Clarion Books.

Nonfiction: Picture books, young readers, middle readers: activity books, arts/crafts, religion. Young adults: religion.

How to Contact/Writers: Submit complete ms (picture books); submit outline/synopsis and sample chapters for longer mss. May also query. Responds to queries in 1 month; mss in 3 months. Publishes a book 2 years after acceptance. Will consider simultaneous submissions. "No phone queries."

Illustration: Works with 50 illustrators/year. Illustrations only: Query with samples. Contact: Ed Luhmann, art director. Responds only if interested. Samples returned with SASE; samples filed. Originals not returned at job's completion.

Terms: Pays authors in royalties based on retail price or work purchased outright ($750-2,000). Sends galleys to author. Ms guidelines for 1 first-class stamp and a #10 envelope. Pays illustrators by the project ($1,000).

Tips: "Do not send finished artwork with the manuscript. If sketches will help in the presentation of the manuscript, they may be sent. If stories are taken from the Bible, they should follow the Biblical account closely. Liberties should not be taken in fantasizing Biblical stories."

☑ COOK COMMUNICATIONS MINISTRIES, (formerly Cook Communications), 4050 Lee Vance View, Colorado Springs CO 80918. (719)536-0100. Fax: (719)536-3296. Website: www.cookministries.org. Book publisher. **Acquisitions:** Mary McNeil, product manager. Publishes 15-20 picture books/year; 6-8 young readers/year; and 6-12 middle readers/year. Less than 5% of books by first-time authors; 15% of books from agented authors. "All books have overt Christian values, but there is no primary theme." Recently published *Sun Song*, by Susan Sutton (age 4-7); *What Difference Does It Make?*, by Debi Little Brazzali (age 8-12); *Field of Dreams* (Noah's Park Series), by Richard Hays (age 4-7).

● Cook does not read unsolicited mss. Writers must query, except board books and picture books.

Illustration: Works with 15 illustrators/year. "Send color material I can keep." Query with samples; send résumé, promo sheet, portfolio, tearsheets. Responds in 3-6 months only if interested. Samples returned with SASE; samples filed.

Terms: Pays illustrators by the project, royalty or work purchased outright. Sends dummies to illustrators. Original artwork returned at job's completion. Ms guidelines available for SASE. Call ms hotline at (719)536-0100, ext. 3930.

☒ COTEAU BOOKS LTD., 401-2206 Dewdney Ave., Regina, Sasketchewan S4R 1H3 Canada. (306)777-0170. E-mail: coteau@coteaubooks.com. Website: www.coteaubooks.com. Thunder Creek Publishing Co-op Ltd. Book publisher. Estab. 1975. **Acquisitions:** Geoffrey Ursell, publisher. Publishes 3-4 juvenile and/or young adult books/year, 12-14 books/year. 10% of books by first-time authors. "Coteau Books publishes the finest Canadian fiction, poetry, drama and children's literature, with an emphasis on western writers."

● Coteau Books publishes Canadian writers and illustrators only; mss from the U.S. are returned unopened.

Fiction: Young readers, middle readers, young adults: adventure, contemporary, fantasy, history, humor, multicultural, nature/environment, science fiction, suspense/mystery. "No didactic, message pieces, nothing religious. No picture books. Material should reflect the diversity of culture, race, religion, creed of humankind—we're looking for fairness and balance." Recently published *Angels in the Snow*, by Wenda Young (ages 11-14); *Bay Girl*, by Betty Dorion (ages 8-11); and *The Innocent Polly McDoodle*, by Mary Woodbury (ages 8-12).

Nonfiction: Young readers, middle readers, young adult: biography, history, multicultural, nature/environment, social issues.

How to Contact/Writers: Fiction: Submit complete ms to acquisitions editor. Include SASE or send up to 20-page sample by e-mail, as an attached file, in the Mime protocol. Responds to queries in 3-4 months; mss in 3-4 months. Publishes a book 1-2 years after acceptance. Send for guidelines.

Illustration: Works with 1-4 illustrators/year. Illustrations only: Submit nonreturnable samples. Responds only if interested. Samples returned with SASE; samples filed.

Photography: "Very occasionally buys photos from freelancers." Buys stock and assigns work.

Terms: Pays authors in royalties based on retail price. Pays illustrators and photographers by the project. Sends galleys to authors; dummies to illustrators. Original artwork returned at job's completion. Book catalog free on request with 9×12 SASE.

Tips: "Truthfully, the work speaks for itself! Be bold. Be creative. Be persistent! There is room, at least in the Canadian market, for quality novels for children, and at Coteau, this is a direction we will continue to take."

☑ CRICKET BOOKS, (formerly Front Street/Cricket Books), Imprint of Carus Publishing Company, 332 S. Michigan, Suite 1100, Chicago IL 60604. (312)939-1500. E-mail: cricketBooks@caruspub.com. Website: www.cricketbooks.net. Imprint estab. 1999; Company estab. 1973. **Manuscript Acquisitions:** Carol Saller. **Art Acquisitions:** Tony Jacobson. Publishes 5 young readers, 5 middle readers and 2 young adult/year. 50% ob books by first time authors. "For 25 years we've published the best children's literary magazines in America, and we're looking for the same high-quality material for our book imprint."

● Publisher Marc Aronson is launching a new Cricket Books imprint, Marcato, to publish fiction and nonfiction for teenagers. Look for news on the new imprint in industry publications.

Fiction: Young readers, middle readers, young adult/teen: adventure, animal, contemporary, fantasy, history, multicultural, humor, sports, suspense/mystery, science fiction, problem novels. Recently published *John Riley's Daughter*, by Vezi Matthews; *Two Suns in the Sky*, by Miriam Bat-Ami.

How to Contact: Fiction: submit complete ms. Responds to queries in 3 months; mss in 3 months. Publishes a book 18 months after acceptance. Will consider simultaneous submissions.

Illustration: Works with 4 illustrators/year. Use color and b&w. Illustration only: submit samples, tearsheets. Contact: Tony Jacobson. Responds only if interested. Samples returned with SASE; sample filed.

Terms: Authors paid royalty of 7-10% based on retail price. Offers advances. Illustrators paid royalty of 3% based on retail price. Sends galleys to authors; dummies to illustrators. Originals returned to artist at job's completion. Writer's guidelines available for SASE. Catalog available at website.

Tips: "At this time we are only considering chapter book and middle-grade submissions. No nonficiton or picture books. Study *Cricket* and *Spider* magazines to get an idea of our approach and to learn more of what we're looking for."

CROCODILE BOOKS, 46 Crosby St., Northampton MA 01060. (413)582-7054. Fax: (413)582-7057. E-mail: interpg@aol.com. Imprint of Interlink Publishing Group, Inc. Book publisher. **Acquisitions:** Pam Thompson, associate publisher. Publishes 4 picture books/year. 25% of books by first-time authors.

• Crocodile does not accept unsolicited mss.

Fiction: Picture books: animal, contemporary, history, spy/mystery/adventure.

Nonfiction: Picture book: history, nature/environment.

Terms: Pays authors in royalties.

CROSSWAY BOOKS, Good News Publishers, 1300 Crescent, Wheaton IL 60187-5800. (630)682-4300. Fax: (630)682-4785. Book Publisher. Estab. 1938. Editorial Director: Marvin Padgett. **Acquisitions:** Jill Carter. Publishes 3-4 picture books/year; and 1-2 young adult titles/year. "Crossway Books is committed to publishing books that bring Biblical reality to readers and that examine crucial issues through a Christian world view."

Fiction: Picture books: religion. Middle readers: adventure, contemporary, history, humor, religion, Christian realism. Young adults: contemporary, history, humor, religion, Christian realism. Does not want to see horror novels, romance or prophecy novels. Not looking for picture book submissions at present time. Recently published *With You All the Way*, by Max Lucado, illustrated by Chuck Gilles; *You Are Mine*, by Max Lucado, illustrated Sergio Martinez.

How to Contact/Writers: Fiction: Query with outline/synopsis and up to 2 sample chapters. Responds to queries/mss in 2 months. Publishes a book 12-18 months after acceptance. Will consider simultaneous submissions.

Illustration: Works with 3-4 illustrators/year. Reviews ms/illustration packages from artists. Query. Illustrations only: Query with samples; provide résumé, promo sheet and client list. Responds to artists' queries/submissions in 2 months. Samples returned with SASE; samples filed. Originals returned at job's completion.

Terms: Pays authors royalty based on wholesale price. Pays illustrators by the project. Sends galleys to authors; dummies to illustrators. Book catalog available; ms guidelines available for SASE.

 CSS PUBLISHING, 517 S. Main St., P.O. Box 4503, Lima OH 45802-4503. (419)227-1818. Fax: (419)222-4647. E-mail: acquisitions@csspub.com. Website: www.csspub.com. Book publisher. Imprints include Fairway Press and Express Press. **Manuscript Acquisitions:** Stan Purdum. Publishes books with religious themes. "We are seeking material for use by clergy, Christian education directors and Sunday school teachers for mainline Protestant churches. Our market is mainline Protestant clergy."

Fiction: Picture books, young readers, middle readers, young adults: religion, religious poetry and humor. Needs children's sermons (object lesson) for Sunday morning worship services; dramas for Advent, Christmas or Epiphany involving children for church services; activity and craft ideas for Sunday school or mid-week services for children (particularly pre-school and first and second grade). Does not want to see secular picture books. Published *That Seeing, They May Believe*, by Kenneth Mortonson (lessons for adults to present during worship services to pre-schoolers-third graders); *What Shall We Do With This Baby?*, by Jan Spence (Christmas Eve worship service involving youngsters from newborn babies-high school youth); and *Miracle in the Bethlehem Inn*, by Mary Lou Warstler (Advent or Christmas drama involving pre-schoolers-high school youth and adult.)

Nonfiction: Picture books, young readers, middle readers, young adults: religion. Young adults only: social issues and self help. Needs children's sermons (object lesson) for Sunday morning worship services; dramas for Advent, Christmas or Epiphany involving children for church services; activity and craft ideas for Sunday school or mid-week services for children (particularly pre-school and first and second grade). Does not want to see secular picture books. Published *Mustard Seeds*, by Ellen Humbert (activity/bulletins for pre-schoolers-first graders to use during church); and *This Is The King*, by Cynthia Cowen.

How to Contact/Writers: Responds to queries in 2 weeks; mss in 3 months. Publishes a book 9 months after acceptance. Will consider simultaneous submissions.

● **SPECIAL COMMENTS** by the editor of *Children's Writer's & Illustrator's Market* are set off by a bullet.

Terms: Work purchased outright from authors. Ms guidelines and book catalog available for SASE and on website.

☑ ▥ **MAY DAVENPORT, PUBLISHERS**, 26313 Purissima Rd., Los Altos Hills CA 94022-4539. (415)948-6499. Fax: (650)947-1373. E-mail: mdbooks@earthlink.net. Website: www.maydavenportpublishers.c om. Independent book producer/packager. Estab. 1976. **Acquisitions:** May Davenport, editor/publisher. Publishes 1-2 picture books/year; and 2-3 young adult titles/year. 99% of books by first-time authors. Seeks books with literary merit. "We like to think that we are selecting talented writers who have something humorous to write about today's unglued generation in 30,000-50,000 words for teens and young adults in junior/senior high school before they become tomorrow's 'functional illiterates.' We are interested in publishing literature that teachers in middle and high schools can use in their Language Arts, English and Creative Writing courses. There's more to literary fare than the chit-chat Internet dialog and fantasy trips on television with cartoons or humanoids." This publisher is overstocked with picture book/elementary reading material.
Fiction: Young adults (15-18): contemporary, humorous fictional literature for use in English courses in junior-senior high schools in US. Average word length: 40,000-60,000. Recently published *To Touch the Sun*, by Andrea Ross (for ages 15-18); *A Taste of the Elephant*, by Robert Norman Farley (ages 12 and up).
Nonfiction: Teens: humorous. Published *Just a Little off the Top*, by Linda Ropes (essays for teens); *Surviving Sarah*, by Dinah Leigh (15-18); *Wind Shadow*, by Lynn A. Morrison bio (12-18).
How to Contact/Writers: Fiction: Query. Responds to queries/mss in 3 weeks. "We do not answer queries or manuscripts which do not have SASE attached." Publishes a book 6-12 months after acceptance.
Illustration: Works with 1-2 illustrators/year. "Have enough on file for future reference." Responds only if interested. Samples returned with SASE; samples filed. Originals returned at job's completion.
Terms: Pays authors royalties of 15% based on retail price; negotiable. Pays "by mutual agreement, no advances." Pays illustrators by the project (range: $75-350). Book catalog, ms guidelines free on request with SASE.
Tips: "Create stories to enrich the non-reading high school readers. They might not appreciate your similies and metaphors and may find fault with your alliterations, but show them how you do it with memorable characters in today's society. Just project your humorous talent and entertain with more than two sentences in a paragraph."

DAWN PUBLICATIONS, P.O. Box 2010, Nevada City CA 95959. (530)478-0111. Fax: (530)478-0112. E-mail: glenn@dawnpub.com. Website: www.dawnpub.com. Book publisher. Publisher: Muffy Weaver. **Acquisitions:** Glenn J. Hovemann, editor. Publishes works with holistic themes dealing with nature.
Nonfiction: Picture books: animal, nature/environment. Biographies of naturalists recently published *John Muir: My Life With Nature*, by Joseph Cornell (80-page biography); and *Do Animals Have Feelings Too?*, by David L. Rice (32-page picture book).
How to Contact/Writers: Nonfiction: Query or submit complete ms. Responds to queries/mss in 3 months maximum. Publishes a book 1 year after acceptance. Will consider simultaneous submissions.
Illustration: Works with 5 illustrators/year. Will review ms/illustration packages from artists. Query; send ms with dummy. Illustrations only: Query with samples, résumé.
Terms: Pays authors royalty based on wholesale price. Offers advance. Pays illustrators by the project or royalties based on wholesale price. Book catalog available for 8½×11 SASE; ms guidelines available for SASE.
Tips: Looking for "picture books expressing nature awareness with inspirational quality leading to enhanced self-awareness. Usually no animal dialogue."

☑ **DIAL BOOKS FOR YOUNG READERS**, Penguin Putnam Inc., 345 Hudson St., New York NY 10014. Website: www.penguinputnam.com. Publisher: Nancy Paulsen. Editorial Director: Lauri Hornik. **Acquisitions:** Toby Sherry, editor; Cecile Goyette, editor; Karen Riskin, editor. Art Director: Atha Tehon. Publishes 30 picture books/year; 3 young reader titles/year; 8 middle reader titles/year; and 6 young adult titles/year.
  • Dial prefers submissions from agents and previously published authors. Dial title *A Year Down Yonder*, by Richard Peck won the 2001 Newbery Medal.
Fiction: Picture books: adventure, animal, contemporary, folktales, history, poetry, sports, suspense/mystery. Young readers: contemporary, easy-to-read, fantasy, folktales, history, poetry, sports, mystery/adventure. Middle readers, young adults: animal, contemporary, folktales, history, poetry, sports, mystery/adventure. Published *A Year Down Yonder*, by Richard Peck (ages 10 and up); *The Magic Nesting Doll*, by Jacqueline K. Ogburn and illustrated by Laurel Long (all ages, picture book); *The Missing Mitten Mystery*, by Steven Kellogg (ages 2-6, picture book).
Nonfiction: Will consider query letters for submissions of outstanding literary merit. Picture books: animals, biography, history, sports. Young readers: animals, biography, history, sports. Middle readers: biography, history. Young adults: biography, history, contemporary. Recently published *Thanks to My Mother*, by Schoschana Rabinovici (ages 12 and up, YA) and *Dirt on their Skirts*, by Doreen Rappaport and Lyndall Callan (ages 4-8, picture book).
How to Contact/Writers: Prefers agented material (but will respond to queries that briefly describe the ms and the author's writing credits with a SASE). Responds to queries/mss. in 2 months. "We do not supply specific guidelines, but we will send you a recent catalog if you send us a 9×12 SASE with four 34¢ stamps attached. Questions and queries should only be made in writing. We will not reply to anything without a SASE." No e-mail queries.

UNDER ONE ROCK
Bugs, Slugs and other Ughs

By Anthony D. Fredericks
Illustrated by Jennifer DiRubbio

Dawn Publications wants "first-class, awe-inspiring" artwork only. Dedicated to teaching children about the environment, the publisher strives to showcase realistic and emotionally appealing imagery. For *Under One Rock (Bugs, Slugs and other Ughs)*, Jennifer DiRubbio Lubinsky employed watercolor and her own personal love of nature. Lubinsky sent samples to Dawn two years ago. The publisher gave her file a star, keeping her in mind until the "right" project was chosen for her.

Illustration: Works with 25 illustrators/year. To arrange a personal interview to show portfolio, send samples and a letter requesting an interview. Art samples should be sent to Ms. Toby Sherry and will not be returned without a SASE. "No phone calls please. Only artists with portfolios that suit the house's needs will be interviewed."

Terms: Pays authors and illustrators in royalties based on retail price. Average advance payment "varies."

DK INK, Imprint of Dorling Kindersley Publishing, Inc., 95 Madision Ave., New York NY 10016.
● The DK Ink imprint is being phased out.

DOG-EARED PUBLICATIONS, P.O. Box 620863, Middletown WI 53562-0863. (608)831-1410. (608)831-1410. Fax: (608)831-1410. E-mail: field@dog-eared.com. Website: www.dog-eared.com. Book publisher. Estab. 1977. Art Acquisitions: Nancy Field, publisher. Publishes 2-3 middle readers/year. 1% of books by first-time authors. "Dog-Eared Publications creates action-packed nature books for children. We aim to turn young readers into environmentally aware citizens and to foster a love for science and nature in the new generation.

Nonfiction: Middle readers: activity books, animal, nature/environment, science. Average word length varies. Recently published *Leapfrogging Through Wetlands*, by Margaret Anderson, Nancy Field and Karen Stephenson, illustrated by Michael Maydak (middle readers, activity book); *Ancient Forests*, by Margaret Anderson, Nancy Field and Karen Stephenson, illustrated by Sharon Torvik (middle readers, activity book); *Discovering Wolves*, by Nancy Field, Corliss Karasov, illustrated by Cary Hunkel (activity book).

How to Contact/Writers: Nonfiction: Currently not accepting unsolicited submissions.

Illustration: Works with 2-3 illustrators/year. Reviews mss/illustration packages from artists. Submit query and a few art samples. Contact: Nancy Field, publisher. Illustrations only: Query with samples. Contact: Nancy Field, publisher. Responds only if interested. Samples not returned; samples filed. "Interested in realistic, mature art!"

Photography: Works on assignment only.

Terms: Pays authors royalty based on wholesale price. Offers advances(amount varies). Pays illustrators royalty based on wholesale price. Sends galleys to authors. Originals returned to artist at job's completion. Brochure available for SASE and 1 first-class stamp. Brochure available on website.

Ⓐ DORLING KINDERSLEY PUBLISHING, INC., 95 Madison Ave., New York NY 10016. (212)213-4800. Fax: (212)689-1799. Website: www.dk.com. **Acquisitions:** submissions editor. Publishes 30 picture books/year; 30 young readers/year; 10 middle readers/year; and 5 young adult titles/year.

Nonfiction: Picture books: animal, concept, nature/environment. Middle readers: activity books, geography, history, nature/environment, reference, science, sports. Young adults: biography, careers, history, reference, science, social issues, sports. Average page count: picture books, middle readers: 32 pages; young readers: 128 pages. Recently published *Children Just Like Me: Our Favorite Stories*, by Jamila Gavin (for all ages); and *Stephen Biesty's Cross-Sections Castle* (for ages 8 and up).

How to Contact/Writers: Only interested in agented material. "Due to high volume, we are unable to accept unsolicited mss at this time. We will review policy in the future."

Illustration: Only interested in agented material. Uses color artwork only. Reviews ms/illustration packages from artists. Query with printed samples. Illustrations only: Query with samples. Send résumé and promo sheet. Responds only if interested. Samples filed.

Photography: Buys stock and assigns work. Uses color prints. Submit cover letter, résumé, published samples, color promo piece.

Terms: Pays authors royalty. Offers advances. Book catalog available for 10×13 SASE and $3 first-class postage.

Tips: "Most of our projects are generated in London where authors and illustrators are solicited."

DUTTON CHILDREN'S BOOKS, Penguin Putnam Inc., 345 Hudson St., New York NY 10014. (212)366-3700. Website: www.penguinputnam.com. Book publisher. President and Publisher: Stephanie Owens Lurie. **Acquisitions:** Lucia Monfried, editor-in-chief. **Art Acquisitions:** Sara Reynolds, art director. Publishes approximately 60 picture books/year; 4 young reader titles/year; 10 middle reader titles/year; and 8 young adult titles/year. 10% of books by first-time authors.
● Dutton is temporarily not accepting new manuscripts.

Fiction: Picture books: adventure, animal, folktales, history, multicultural, nature/environment, poetry. Young readers: adventure, animal, contemporary, easy-to-read, fantasy, pop-up, suspense/mystery. Middle readers: adventure, animal, contemporary, fantasy, history, multicultural, nature/environment, suspense/mystery. Young adults: adventure, animal, anthology, contemporary, fantasy, history, multicultural, nature/environment, poetry, science fiction, suspense/mystery. Recently published *The Little Red Hen (Makes A Pizza)*, by Philemon Sturges, illustrated by Amy Walrod (picture book).

Nonfiction: Picture books: animal, history, multicultural, nature/environment. Young readers: animal, history, multicultural, nature/environment. Middle readers: animal, biography, history, multicultural, nature/environment. Young adults: animal, biography, history, multicultural, nature/environment, social issues. Recently published *Sitting Bull*, by Albert Marrin; *Croodiles, Camels and Dug Out Canoes*, by Bob Zounder, illustrated by Roxie Munro.

insider report

Illustrator's characters come to life in cut paper collage

In the bio for her first picture book *Horace and Morris but Mostly Dolores*, it says illustrator Amy Walrod "enjoys collecting toys, cupcake ornaments, lunch boxes, sparkly things, and stuff she finds on the ground." Walrod also collects paper. Lots of paper. Beautiful paper in an array of colors, textures, weights and patterns. Paper that she uses to create what *Kirkus Reviews* calls "stunningly inventive paper collages."

Amy Walrod

© John McLaughlin

Horace and Morris but Mostly Dolores and its upcoming sequel *Horace and Morris Join the Chorus*, both written by James Howe and featuring mouse characters, are illustrated in acrylic with collage mixed in. Walrod's latest book *How Hungry Are You?*, written by Donna Jo Napoli and Richard Tchen, and her Golden Kite Award winner *The Little Red Hen (Makes a Pizza)*, by Philemon Sturges, are illustrated entirely in delightfully detailed cut paper collage.

Walrod had already begun collecting paper when she was a student at Rhode Island School of Design. At RISD, Walrod's teacher and mentor was agent Judy Sue Goodwin Sturges. "Judy Sue was someone who really supported and encouraged my work." She became Walrod's agent, and asked her to join Studio Goodwin Sturges (www.studiogoodwinsturges.com). "There were a few years where I was doing samples, and eventually got my first book," *Horace and Morris but Mostly Dolores*.

"When I got out of school, I wanted to do just cut paper. I had done some painting and collage when I was in school, and that's the style sample Judy Sue had in the portfolio that Atheneum art director Ann Bobco saw. It was a little mouse. James Howe was looking for someone to illustrate his picture book. He saw the piece and decided my work was the style of illustraton he wanted. When I found out, I was kind of disappointed because I wanted to do cut paper only, but I was very excited because it was an opportunity to illustrate a children's book."

In hindsight, Walrod is glad she's been able to work on books in two styles, both painting with collage and cut paper. "Working in one style can make you feel stuck. I like to think if I wanted to take off and do a something a little different from here, I could."

In the meantime, Walrod works in *Horace and Morris* style, and also creates clever collage work like the illustrations in *The Little Red Hen (Makes a Pizza)*. Much like her painting work, Walrod begins the collage process by sketching. "I do really detailed sketches for the whole book, so I know everything that's happening and where the characters fall in relation to the text. I try to do character sketches before each book, and figure out how I'll put each character together. From there, I usually use the sketches as templates."

And thus Walrod's quirky cut-paper characters evolve, like the foursome in *The Little Red Hen*: the title character, who wears high heels with purple bows, sips chickweed tea, and reads books about dream vacations; a hep blue cat who plays the blues on his sax; a goofy yellow duck sporting a bathing cap and innertube; and a dog donning a big cardboard biscuit box and party hat.

"When I started *The Little Red Hen*, and I was doing my samples for the characters, it was really difficult to make things look interesting. I had some really beautiful sheets of paper, but it was all the same texture and all the same sort of color consistencies. I attempted to make texture. I knew it was really awful." So Walrod began adding diverse papers to her stash. She learned that she must utilize texture as much as she can and try to make the characters transcend just being paper.

"When I look at papers, I think about what textures seem interesting to me and how I can use them throughout. It can be frustrating, though, because I'll find a paper and fall in love with it and decide, 'Forever and a day, this will be my sidewalk material. Now every book I have a sidewalk in, I'll never have to worry about the material.' Then I get another book with a sidewalk and the paper is discontinued."

In creating her illustrations, Walrod uses scissors most of the time. "When I use X-Acto®,

Amy Walrod used cut paper collage to illustrate *The Little Red Hen (Makes a Pizza)*, by Philemon Sturges. The book earned Walrod a Golden Kite Award for Illustration from SCBWI in 2000.

I tend to bear down, and I actually did get an illustration-related injury working on *The Little Red Hen*." It was likely worth the boo-boo—*The Little Red Hen (Makes a Pizza)* earned plaudits from reviewers and a Golden Kite Award for Illustration from the Society of Children's Book Writers and Illustrators, which Walrod accepted at SCBWI's annual summer conference in Los Angeles in 2000. "The award was really exciting, but it was also great being there in a community of people who are doing the same thing, and being able to talk shop," she says. ."The way I work is very solitary. When I talk to other illustrators, it's a tremendous bonding experience for me. I found myself almost crying several times. I had to go hide in the corner for a while."

Walrod does get away from her desk for occasional book signings and school appearances, including a recent whistle stop tour of sorts to a number of Vermont schools when *The Little Red Hen* was nominated for Vermont's Red Clover Book Award. "That was really interesting. You get a cross section and see different ways schools work. I really love talking to kids. Once you get into the whole creative process, you get blinders on. Kids really have a sense of how things should be."

Walrod has a number of upcoming projects in the works. In addition to *Horace and Morris Join the Chorus*, she'll be illustrating a third book by James Howe featuring the same group of mice. "James really knows how I work. He writes stories that allow me to pull out all the little tricks in my illustrations. Dolores is growing on me. At first she was just Dolores. It's kind of weird how involved I get with my characters. The way he writes Dolores makes me fall in love with her."

In another repeat collaboration, Walrod is illustrating a Philemon Sturges tale called *This Little Pirate*, an adaptation of the "This Little Piggy Went to Market" rhyme. "Right now, I've been collecting a lot of pink paper for the pigs, but I'm changing my mind—they're probably not going to be all pink."

In her latest release, *How Hungry Are You?*, by Donna Jo Napoli and Richard Tchen, Amy Walrod created cut-paper characters (including ants, frogs, bunnies and monkeys) whose picnic antics teach young readers about math.

For illustrators who want to work in picture books, Walrod confesses it's tough to give them advice on breaking in. "I meet people who are fellow illustrators who come to children's book illustration with several years' experience under their belts working freelance. I came right out of school and was offered the opportunity, and it worked out. It was exciting, but everybody doesn't get into it that way.

"I think you really have to love what you're doing and really want to put energy into it. Whether you're an illustrator or a writer, you can't just jump in and think you'll know exactly how to do things. People often think I jump right into final illustrations, that there isn't this whole process. It's hard for them to understand that there are steps.

"As far as agents go, for me having one is ideal. Judy Sue has people at the studio who are able to look over my contracts and she's able to articulate things and speak up and be my 'tough guy.' She is really more to me than just my agent—she is truly a friend and an advocate for my work. That isn't an easy thing to find in an agent in my opinion."

Thanks to her agent and her own award-winning, well-received work, in addition to cupcake ornaments and stuff she finds on the ground, Walrod has a nice collection of book contracts. She's also started to collect Fisher- Price® Little People®, "the ones that are choking hazards, not the new vinyl ones. My collecting is kind of frustrating for my husband. We live in a very small house, and he ends up building shelves that go up to nowhere. Many of the once sparse surfaces that existed in his bachelor days are now covered with Little People®, snow globes (the kind you buy at airport gift shops) and weird stuff I find at garage sales or Goodwill."

—*Alice Pope*

How to Contact/Writers: Query only. Does not accept unsolicited mss. Reports on queries in 2-3 months. Publishes a book 12-18 months after acceptance. Will consider simultaneous submissions.
Illustration: Works with 40-60 illustrators/year. Reviews ms/illustration packages from artists. Query first. Illustrations only: Query with samples; send résumé, portfolio, slides—no original art please. Reports on art samples in 2 months. Original artwork returned at job's completion.
Photography: Will look at photography samples and photo-essay proposals.
Terms: Pays authors royalties of 4-10% based on retail price. Book catalog, ms guidelines for SASE with 8 first-class stamps. Pays illustrators royalties of 2-10% based on retail price unless jacket illustration—then pays by flat fee.
Tips: "Avoid topics that appear frequently. In nonfiction, we are looking for history, general biography, science and photo essays for all age groups." Illustrators: "We would like to see samples and portfolios from potential illustrators of picture books (full color), young novels (b&w) and jacket artists (full color)." Foresee "even more multicultural publishing, plus more books published in both Spanish and English."

E.M. PRESS, INC., P.O. Box 336,, Warrenton VA 20188. (540)349-9958. E-mail: empress2@erols.com. Website: www.empressinc.com. Book publisher. **Acquisitions:** Beth Miller, publisher/editor (nonfiction manuscripts and children's books). "We're now publishing illustrated children's books." 50% of books by first-time authors.
Fiction: Children, young adults: folk tales, nature/environment, special needs. Recently published *New Shoes*, by Ming Wah Chien.
Nonfiction: Children, young adults: animal, arts/craft, health, history, multicultural, music/dance, nature/environment, religion, self-help, social issues. Recently published *Can You Come Here Where I Am: The Poetry and Prose of Breast Cancer Survivors*, by Rita Busch.
How to Contact/Writers: Query with outline/synopsis and SASE for novel-length work and complete ms for shorter work. Reports on ms/queries in 3 months. Publishes a book 18 months after acceptance. Will consider simultaneous submissions.
Illustration: Works with 4 children's illustrators/year. Illustration packages should be submitted to Beth Miller, publisher. Responds in 3 months. Samples returned with SASE; samples kept on file. Original artwork returned at job's completion.
Terms: "We've used all means of payment from outright purchase to royalty." Offers varied advances. Sends galleys to authors. Book catalog for SASE.
Tips: "Present the most professional package possible. The market is glutted, so you must find a new approach."

EERDMAN'S BOOKS FOR YOUNG READERS, an imprint of Wm. B. Eerdmans Publishing Company, 255 Jefferson Ave. SE, Grand Rapids MI 49503. (616)459-4591. Website: www.eerdmans.com/youngreaders. Book publisher. **Manuscript Acquisitions:** Judy Zylstra, children's book editor. **Art Acquisitions:** Jesse Josten. Publishes 10-12 picture books/year; and 3-4 middle readers/year.
Fiction: Picture books, middle readers: parables, religion, retold Bible stories, child or family issues, historical fiction, art/artists, poetry. No science fiction.
Nonfiction: All levels: biography, religion.
How to Contact/Writers: Fiction/Nonfiction: Query with sample chapters (novels) or submit complete ms (picture books). Responds to queries in 6 weeks; mss in 2 months.
Illustration: Works with 14-16 illustrators/year. Reviews ms/illustration packages from artists. Responds to ms/art samples in 3 months. Illustrations only: Submit résumé, slides or color photocopies. Samples returned with SASE; samples filed.
Terms: Pays authors and illustrators royalties of 5-7% based on retail price. Sends galleys to authors; dummies to illustrators. Original artwork returned at job's completion. Book catalog free on request with SASE (4 first class stamps, 9×12 envelope); ms and/or artist's guidelines free on request, with SASE.
Tips: "We are looking for material that will help children build their faith in God and explore God's world. We accept all genres."

ENSLOW PUBLISHERS INC., Box 398, 40 Industrial Rd., Berkeley Heights NJ 07922-0398. Website: www.enslow.com. Estab. 1978. **Acquisitions:** Brian D. Enslow, vice president. Publishes 100 middle reader titles/year; and 100 young adult titles/year. 30% of books by first-time authors.
Nonfiction: Young readers, middle readers, young adults: animal, biography, careers, health, history, hobbies, nature/environment, social issues, sports. "Enslow is moving into the elementary (Grades 3-4) level and is looking for authors who can write biography and suggest other nonfiction themes at this level." Average word length: middle readers—5,000; young adult—18,000. Published *Louis Armstrong*, by Patricia and Fredrick McKissack (grades 2-3, biography); and *Lotteries: Who Wins, Who Loses?*, by Ann E. Weiss (grades 6-12, issues book).
How to Contact/Writers: Nonfiction: Send for guidelines. Query. Responds to queries/mss in 2 weeks. Publishes a book 18 months after acceptance. Will not consider simultaneous submissions.
Illustration: Submit résumé, business card or tearsheets to be kept on file.
Terms: Pays authors royalties or work purchased outright. Sends galleys to authors. Book catalog/ms guidelines available for $2, along with an 8½×11 SAE and $1.67 postage or via website.

☑ 🏠 **EVAN-MOOR EDUCATIONAL PUBLISHERS**, 18 Lower Ragsdale Dr., Monterey CA 93940-5746. (831)649-5901. Fax: (831)649-6256. E-mail: main@evan-moor.com. Website: www.evan-moor.com. Book publisher. **Manuscript Acquisitions:** Marilyn Evans, editor. **Art Acquisitions:** Joy Evans, production director. Publishes 30-50 books/year. Less than 10% of books by first-time authors. " 'Helping Children Learn' is our motto. Evan-Moor is known for high-quality educational materials written by teachers for use in the classroom and at home. We publish teacher resource and reproducible materials in most all curriculum areas and activity books (language arts, math, science, social studies). No fiction or nonfiction literature books."
Nonfiction: Recently published *Literacy Centers* (4-color book with directions and patterns for 17 centers); *Ten-Minute Activities* (2 books grades 1-3, 4-6); *Math Practice at Home* (full-color book for each grade K-4); *Scienceworks for Kids* (6 books for grades K-1).
How to Contact/Writers: Query or submit complete ms. Responds to queries in 2 months; mss in 2 months. Publishes a book 12-18 months after acceptance. Will consider simultaneous submissions if so noted. Send SASE for submission guidelines. Authors' updated submissions guidelines available on our website. E-mail queries are responded to quickly. View our materials on our website to determine if your project fits in our product line.
Illustration: Works with 8 illustrators/year. Uses b&w artwork primarily. Illustrations only: Query with samples; send résumé, tearsheets. Contact: Joy Evans, production director. Responds only if interested. Samples returned with SASE; samples filed.
Terms: Work purchased outright from authors, "dependent solely on size of project and 'track record' of author." Pays illustrators by the project (range: varies). Sends galleys to authors. Artwork is not returned. Book catalog available for 9×12 SAE; ms guidelines available for SASE.
Tips: "Writers—know the supplemental education or parent market. (These materials are *not* children's literature.) Tell us how your project is unique and what consumer needs it meets. Illustrators—you need to be able to produce quickly and be able to render realistic and charming children and animals."

EXCELSIOR CEE PUBLISHING, P.O. Box 5861, Norman OK 73070-5861. (405)329-3909. Fax: (405)329-6886. E-mail: ecp@oecadvantage.net. Website: www.excelsiorcee.com. Book publisher. Estab. 1989. **Manuscript Acquisitions:** J.C. Marshall.
How to Contact/Writers: Nonfiction: Query or submit outline/synopsis. Responds to queries in 1 month. Publishes a book 1 year after acceptance. Will consider simultaneous submission.

☑ **FACTS ON FILE**, 132 W. 31st St., New York NY 10001. (212)967-8800. Fax: (212)967-9196. Website: www.factsonfile.com. Book publisher. Editorial Director: Laurie Likoff. **Acquisitions:** Frank Darnstadt, science and technology/nature; Nicole Bowen, American history and studies; Anne Savarese, language and literature;

Owen Lancer, world studies; Jim Chambers, arts and entertainment. Estab. 1941. "We produce high-quality reference materials for the school library market and the general nonfiction trade." Publishes 25-30 young adult titles/year. 5% of books by first-time authors; 25% of books from agented writers; additional titles through book packagers, co-publishers and unagented writers.

Nonfiction: Middle readers, young adults: animal, biography, careers, geography, health, history, multicultural, nature/environment, reference, religion, science, social issues and sports.

How to Contact/Writers: Nonfiction: Submit outline/synopsis and sample chapters. Responds to queries in 8-10 weeks. Publishes a book 10-12 months after acceptance. Will consider simultaneous submissions. Sends galleys to authors. Book catalog free on request. Send SASE for submission guidelines.

Terms: Submission guidelines available via website or with SASE.

Tips: "Most projects have high reference value and fit into a series format."

FARRAR, STRAUS & GIROUX INC., 19 Union Square W., New York NY 10003. (212)741-6900. Fax: (212)633-2427. Book publisher. Imprints: Frances Foster Books, Melanie Kroupa Books. Children's Books Editorial Director: Margaret Ferguson. **Acquisitions:** Frances Foster, publisher, Frances Foster Books; Beverly Reingold, executive editor; Wesley Adams, senior editor; Robbie Mayes, editor; Janine O'Malley, assistant editor. Estab. 1946. Publishes 30 picture books/year; 15 middle reader titles/year; and 15 young adult titles/year. 5% of books by first-time authors; 20% of books from agented writers.

- Farrar title *Joey Pigza Loses Control*, by Jack Gantos, won a 2001 Newbery Honor Medal. Farrar/ Francis Foster Books title *The Longitude Prize*, by Joan Dash, won the 2001 Boston Globe-Horn Book Award for Nonfiction. Farrar title *Everything on a Waffle*, by Polly Horrath, won a 2001 Boston Globe-Horn Book Honor Award for Fiction and Poetry. Their title *Five Creatures*, by Emily Jenkins, illustrated by Tomek Bogacki, won a 2001 Boston Globe-Horn Book Honor Award for Picture Books. Their title *The Boxer*, by Kathleen Karr, won a Golden Kite Award for Fiction in 2001.

Fiction: All levels: all categories. "Original and well-written material for all ages." Recently published *Joey Piaza Loses Control*, by Jack Gantos (ages 10 up).

Nonfiction: All levels: all categories. "We publish only literary nonfiction."

How to Contact/Writers: Fiction/Nonfiction: Query with outline/synopsis and sample chapters. Do not fax submissions or queries. Responds to queries/mss in 3 months. Publishes a book 18 months after acceptance. Will consider simultaneous submissions.

Illustration: Works with 30-60 illustrators/year. Reviews ms/illustration packages from artists. Submit ms with 1 example of final art, remainder roughs. Do not send originals. Illustrations only: Query with tearsheets. Responds if interested in 2 months. Samples returned with SASE; samples sometimes filed.

Terms: "We offer an advance against royalties for both authors and illustrators." Sends galleys to authors; dummies to illustrators. Original artwork returned at job's completion. Book catalog available for 9 × 12 SAE and $1.87 postage; ms guidelines for 1 first-class stamp.

Tips: "Study our catalog before submitting. We will see illustrator's portfolios by appointment. Don't ask for criticism and/or advice—it's just not possible. Never send originals. Always enclose SASE."

FENN PUBLISHING CO., 34 Nixon Rd., Bolton, Ontario L7E-1W2 Canada. Phone: (905)951-6600. Fax: (905)951-6601. E-mail: fennpubs@hbfenn.com. Website: www.hbfenn.com. Estab. 1982. **Manuscript/Art Acquisitions:** C. Jordan Fenn, publisher. Publishes 35 books/year.

Fiction: Picture books: adventure, animal, folktales, multicultural, religion, sports. Young readers: adventure, animal, folktales, multicultural, religion. Middle readers: adventure, animal, health, history, multicultural, religion, special needs, sports. Young adults: adventure, animal, contemporary, folktales, health, history, multicultural, nature/environment, religion, science fiction, sports.

Nonfiction: Picture books, young readers, middle readers, activity books, animal, arts/crafts, geography, health, history, hobbies, how-to, multicultural, nature/environment, religion.

How to Contact/Writers: Fiction/Nonfiction: Query or submit complete ms. Responds to queries/mss in 2 months.

Illustration: Reviews ms/illustration packages from artists. Contact: C. Jordan Fenn, publisher. Responds only if interested. Samples not returned or filed.

FIESTA CITY PUBLISHERS, Box 5861, Santa Barbara CA 93150-5861. (805)733-1984. E-mail: fcooke3924 @aol.com. Book publisher. **Acquisitions:** Frank Cooke, president. **Art Director:** Ann H. Cooke. Publishes 1 middle reader/year; 1 young adult/year. 25% of books by first-time authors. Publishes books about cooking and music or a combination of the two. "We are best known for children's and young teens' cookbooks and musical plays."

Fiction: Young adults: history, humor, musical plays.

Nonfiction: Young adult: cooking, how-to, music/dance, self-help. Average word length: 30,000. Does not want to see "cookbooks about healthy diets or books on rap music." Published *Kids Can Write Songs, Too!* (revised second printing), by Eddie Franck; *Bent-Twig*, by Frank E. Cooke, with some musical arrangements by Johnny Harris (a 3-act musical for young adolescents); *The Little Grammar Books*, by F. Cooke.

How to Contact/Writers: Query. Responds to queries in 4 days; on mss in 1 month. Publishes a book 1 year after acceptance. Will consider simultaneous submissions.

Illustration: Works with 1 illustrator/year. Will review ms/illustrations packages (query first). Illustrations only: Send résumé. Samples returned with SASE; samples filed.
Terms: Pays authors 5-10% royalty based on retail price.
Tips: "Write clearly and simply. Do not write 'down' to young adults (or children). Looking for self-help books on current subjects, original and unusual cookbooks, and books about music, or a combination of cooking and music." Always include SASE.

☑ **FIRST STORY PRESS**, Imprint of Rose Book Group, 1800 Business Park Dr., Clarksville TN 37040. (931)572-0806. Fax: (931)552-3200. Publisher/Editor in Chief: Judith Pierson. Contact: Acquisitions Editor. Publishes 4 books/year. 50% of books by first-time authors. Publishes books on quilt themes.
Fiction: Picture books. Average word length: picture books—700-1,500. Recently published *The Much Too Loved Quilt*, by Rachel Waterstone.
How to Contact/Writers: Fiction: Submit complete ms. Send hard copy. Responds to queries/mss in 3 months.
Illustration: Works with 3 illustrators/year. Reviews ms/illustration packages from artists. Send ms with dummy. Contact: Editor. Illustrations only: Send résumé, promo sheet and tearsheets to be kept on file. Contact: Editor. Responds only if interested. Samples returned with SASE; samples filed.
Terms: Pays authors royalty of 4-5% based on retail price or work purchased outright. Offers advances. Pays illustrators royalty of 4-5% based on retail price. Originals returned to artist. Ms guidelines available for SASE.
Tips: "SASE is always required. Do not send original artwork. Guidelines available—send SASE. Take a look at our books. We do not send out catalogs."

☐ ☐ **FIVE STAR PUBLICATIONS, INC.**, P.O. Box 6698, Chandler AZ 85246-6698. (480)940-8182. Fax: (480)940-8787. E-mail: info@fivestarsupport.com. Website: www.fivestarsupport.com. Estab. 1985. Specializes in educational material, nonfiction. Independent book packager/producer. Publishes 7 middle readers/year.
Nonfiction: Recently published *Shakespeare for Children: The Story of Romeo & Juliet*, by Cass Foster; *The Sixty-Minute Shakespeare: Hamlet*, by Cass Foster; *The Sixty-Minute Shakespeare: Twelfth Night*, by Cass Foster.
How to Contact/Writers: Nonfiction: Query.
Illustration: Works with 3 illustrators/year. Reviews ms/illustration packages from artists. Query. Contact: Sue DeFabis, project manager. Illustrations only: Query with samples. Responds only if interested. Samples filed.
Photography: Buys stock and assigns work. Works on assignment only. Contact: Sue De Fabis, project manager. Submit letter.
Terms: Pays illustrators by the project. Pays photographers by the project. Sends galleys to authors; dummies to illustrators.

FOREST HOUSE PUBLISHING COMPANY, INC., P.O. Box 738, Lake Forest IL 60045. (847)295-8287. Fax: (847)295-8201. E-mail: info@forest~house.com. Website: www.forest~house.com. Estab. 1989. **Acquisitions:** Dianne L. Spahr, president. Imprints: HTS Books. Published 40 titles in 2001. "We are not accepting any unsolicited manuscripts, until 2003."

FORWARD MOVEMENT PUBLICATIONS, 412 Sycamore St., Cincinnati OH 45202. (513)721-6659. Fax: (513)721-0729. E-mail: orders@forwarddaybyday.com. Website: www.forwardmovement.org. **Acquisitions:** Edward S. Gleason, editor.
Fiction: Middle readers and young adults: religion and religious problem novels, fantasy and science fiction.
Nonfiction: Religion.
How to Contact/Writers: Fiction/Nonfiction: Query. Responds in 1 month. Does not accept mss via e-mail.
Illustration: Query with samples. Samples returned with SASE.
Terms: Pays authors honorarium. Pays illustrators by the project.
Tips: "Forward Movement is now exploring publishing books for children and does not know its niche. We are an agency of the Episcopal Church and most of our market is to mainstream Protestants."

🆕 **WALTER FOSTER PUBLISHING**, 23062 La Cadena Dr., Laguna Hills CA 92653. (949)380-7510. Fax: (949)380-7575. Website: www.walterfoster.com. Estab. 1922. **Manuscript Acquisitions:** Sydney Sprague. **Art Acquisitions:** Pauline Foster, art director. Publishes 3-6 picture books/year; 3-6 young readers/year; 10-12 middle readers/year; 0-6 young adult titles/year. "We seek to provide quality art- and craft-related activity products that are instructional, innovative and competitively priced."
Fiction: All levels: anything art/craft/activity-oriented.

A SELF-ADDRESSED, STAMPED ENVELOPE (SASE) should always be included with submissions within your own country. When sending material to other countries, include a self-addressed envelope (SAE) and International Reply Coupons (IRCs).

Nonfiction: Picture books, young readers, middle readers, young adults: activity books, arts/crafts, hobbies, how-to. Recently published *Create Your Own Slimy Gooey Gunk*, illustrated by Jim Paillot (age over 8, children's craft book and kit); *How to Draw Disney's Atlantis* (age over 8, licensed how-to-draw instruction book); and *Create Your Own 3-D Extinct Animals* (age over 6, craft and activity book).

How to Contact/Writers: Fiction/nonfiction: Query or submit outline/synopsis. Responds only if interested. Publishes a book 6-9 months after acceptance. Will consider simultaneous submissions.

Illustration: Works with 10-12 illustrators/year. Reviews ms/illustration packages from artists. Query with samples. Contact: Sydney Sprague, associate publisher. Illustrations only: Query with samples. Contact: Pauline Foster, art director. Responds only if interested. Samples not returned; samples filed.

Terms: Work purchased outright from authors. Pays illustrators by the project; varies. Originals returned to artist at job's completion. Catalog available on website.

Tips: "Walter Foster Publishing—producer of instructional art books, kits, and specialty products—has been providing quality art instruction for people of all ages and skill levels for almost 80 years. Today the company continues to offer products that challenge the imaginations of children and adults throughout the world."

FREE SPIRIT PUBLISHING, 217 Fifth Ave. N., Suite 200, Minneapolis MN 55401-1299. (612)338-2068. Fax: (612)337-5050. E-mail: help4kids@freespirit.com. Website: www.freespirit.com. Book publisher. **Acquisitions:** Editor. Publishes 18-22 titles/year for children and teens, teachers and parents. "We believe passionately in empowering kids to learn to think for themselves and make their own good choices."

• Free Spirit no longer accepts fiction or story book submissions.

Nonfiction: "Free Spirit Publishing specializes in SELF-HELP FOR KIDS® and SELF-HELP FOR TEENS®, with an emphasis on self-esteem and self-awareness, stress management, school success, social skills, violence prevention, creativity, friends and family, social action, and special needs (i.e., gifted and talented, children with learning differences). We prefer books written in a natural, friendly style, with little education/psychology jargon. We need books in our areas of emphasis and prefer titles written by specialists such as teachers, counselors, and other professionals who work with youth." Recently published *What Do You Really Want? How to Set A Goal and Go For It*, by Beverly Eachel; *What In the World Do You Do When Your Parents Divorce? A Survival Guide For Kids*, by Kent Winchester and Roberta Beyer.

How to Contact/Writers: Send query letter or proposal. Responds to queries/mss in 4 months. "If you'd like materials returned, enclose a SASE with sufficient postage." Write or call for catalog and submission guidelines before sending submission. Accepts queries only by e-mail. Submission guidelines available online.

Illustration: Works with 5 illustrators/year. Submit samples to acquisitions editor for consideration. If appropriate, samples will be kept on file and artist will be contacted if a suitable project comes up. Enclose SASE if you'd like materials returned.

Photography: Submit samples to acquisitions editor for consideration. If appropriate, samples will be kept on file and photographer will be contacted if a suitable project comes up. Enclose SASE if you'd like materials returned.

Terms: Pays authors in royalties based on wholesale price. Offers advance. Pays illustrators by the project. Pays photographers by the project or per photo.

Tips: "Prefer books that help kids help themselves or that help adults help kids help themselves; that complement our list without duplicating current titles; and that are written in a direct, straightforward manner."

FREESTONE/PEACHTREE, JR., Peachtree Publishers, 1700 Chattahoocher Ave., Atlanta GA 30318-2112. (404)876-8761. Fax: (404)875-2578. Website: www.peachtree-online.com. Estab. 1997. **Manuscript Acquisitions:** Lyn Deardorff (children's, young adult). Art Acquisitions: Loraine Balsuk (all). Publishes 3-4 young adult titles/year. Peachtree Jr. publishes 3-4 juvenile titles/year (ages 8-12) and Peachtree Publishers, Ltd. publishes 10 books a year. "We look for very good stories that are well-written, and written from the author's experience and heart with a clear application to today's young adults."

• Freeston & Peachtree, Jr. are imprints of Peachtree Publishers. See the listing for Peachtree for submission information. No e-mail or fax queries, please.

☑ ♟ **FRONT STREET BOOKS**, 20 Battery Park Ave., #403, Ashville NC 28801. (828)236-3097. Fax: (828)236-3098. Fax: (828)236-3098. E-mail: contactus@frontstreetbooks.com Website: www.frontstreetbooks.com. Book publisher. Estab. 1995. **Acquisitions:** Stephen Roxburgh, publisher; Joy Neaves, editor; Nancy Zimmerman, associate publisher. Publishes 10-15 titles/year. We are a small independent publisher of books for children and young adults. We do not publish pablum: we try to publish books that will attract, if not addict, children to literature and art books that are a pleasure to look at and a pleasure to hold, books that will be revelations to young minds."

• See Front Street's website for submission guidelines and their complete catalog. Front Street focuses on fiction, but will publish poetry, anthologies, nonfiction and high-end picture books. They are not currently accepting unsolicited picture book manuscripts. Front Street title *Carver: A Life in Poems*, by Marilyn Nelson, won the 2001 Boston Globe-Horn Book Award for Fiction and Poetry. Their title *Many Stones*, by Carolyn Coman, won a 2001 Printz Honor Medal.

Fiction: Recently published: *Many Stones*, by Carolyn Coman; *Cut*, by Patricia McCormic; *A Step from Heaven*, by An Na; *Carver: A Life in Poems*, by Marilyn Nelson; *The Comic Book Kid*, by Adam Osterweil.

How to Contact/Writers: Fiction: Submit cover letter and complete ms if under 30 pages; submit cover letter, one or two sample chapters and plot summary if over 30 pages. Nonfiction: Submit detailed proposal and sample chapters. Poetry: Submit no more than 25 poems. Include SASE with submissions if you want them returned. "It is our policy to consider submissions in the order in which they are received. This is a time-consuming practice, and we ask you to be patient in awaiting our response."
Illustration "If you are the artist or are working with an artist, we will be happy to consider your project." Submit ms, dummy and a sample piece of art "rendered in the manner and style representative of the final artwork."
Terms: Pays royalties.

✔ ☐ **FULCRUM KIDS**, Imprint of Fulcrum Publishing, 16100 Table Mountain Parkway, #300, Golden CO 80403. (303)277-1623. Fax: (303)279-7111. E-mail: fulcrum@fulcrum-resources.com. Website: www.fulcrum-resources.com. Estab. 1984. Specializes in nonfiction and educational material. **Manuscript Acquisitions:** Susan Zernial, acquisitions editor. Publishes 4 middle readers/year. 25% of books by first-time authors. "Our mission is to make teachers' and librarians' jobs easier using quality resources."
Fiction: Looking for fiction with an educational focus.
Nonfiction: Middle and early readers: activity books, multicultural, nature/environment. Recently published *In Search of the Perfect Pumpkin*, by Gloria Evangelista (grades K-4, gardening picture book); *That's Weird! Awesome Science Mysteries*, by Kendall Haven (grades 4 and up-science mystery); *Smart Start II: Why Standards Matter*, by Patte Barthe and Ruth Mitchell (educational book for teachers/college).
How to Contact/Writers: Submit complete ms or submit outline/synopsis and 2 sample chapters. Responds to queries in 3 weeks; mss in 2 months. Publishes a book 12-18 months after acceptance. Will consider simultaneous submissions.
Illustration: Works with 10 illustrators/year. Reviews ms/illustration packages from artists. Send ms with dummy or submit ms with 3 pieces of final art. Send résumé, promotional literature and tearsheets. Contact: Patty Maker, creative director, education. Responds only if interested. Samples not returned; samples filed.
Photography: Works on assignment only.
Terms: Pays authors royalty based on wholesale price. Offers advances (Average amount: $1,500). Pays illustrators by the project (range: $300-2,000) or royalty based on wholesale price. Sends galleys to authors; dummies to illustrators. Originals returned to artist at job's completion. Book catalog available for 9×12 SAE and 77¢ postage; ms guidelines available for SASE. Catalog available on website.
Tips: "Research our line first. We are emphasizing science and nature nonfiction. We look for books that appeal to the school market and trade. Be sure to include SASE."

GIBBS SMITH, PUBLISHER, P.O. Box 667, Layton UT 84090. (801)544-9800. Fax: (801)544-5582. E-mail: staylor@gibbs-smith.com. Website: gibbs-smith.com. Imprint: Gibbs Smith. Book publisher; co-publisher of Sierra Club Books for Children. Editorial Director: Madge Baird. **Acquisitions:** Suzanne Taylor, acquisitions editor. Publishes 2-3 books/year. 50% of books by first-time authors. 50% of books from agented authors.
Fiction: Picture books: adventure, contemporary, humor, multicultural, nature/environment, suspense/mystery, western. Average word length: picture books—1,000. Recently published *Bullfrog Pops!*, by Rick Walton, illustrated by Chris McAllister (ages 4-8); and *The Magic Boots*, by Scott Emerson, illustrated by Howard Post (ages 4-8).
Nonfiction: Middle readers: activity, arts/crafts, cooking, how-to, nature/environment, science. Average word length: up to 10,000. Recently published *Hiding in a Fort*, by G. Lawson Drinkard, illustrated by Fran Lee Kirby (ages 7-12); and *Sleeping in a Sack: Camping Activities for Kids*, by Linda White, illustrated by Fran Lee (ages 7-12).
How to Contact/Writers: Fiction/Nonfiction: Submit several chapters or complete ms. Responds to queries and mss in 2 months. Publishes a book 1-2 years after acceptance. Will consider simultaneous submissions. Ms returned with SASE.
Illustration: Works with 2 illustrators/year. Reviews ms/illustration packages from artists. Query. Submit ms with 3-5 pieces of final art. Illustrations only: Query with samples; provide résumé, promo sheet, slides (duplicate slides, not originals). Responds only if interested. Samples returned with SASE; samples filed.
Terms: Pays authors royalty of 2% based on retail price or work purchased outright ($500 minimum). Offers advances (average amount: $2,000). Pays illustrators by the project or royalty of 2% based on retail price. Sends galleys to authors; color proofs to illustrators. Original artwork returned at job's completion. Book catalog available for 9×12 SAE and postage. Ms guidelines available.
Tips: "We target ages 5-11."

DAVID R. GODINE, PUBLISHER, 9 Hamilton Place, Boston MA 02108. (617)451-9600. Fax: (617)350-0250. Website: www.godine.com. Book publisher. Estab. 1970. Publishes 1 picture book/year; 1 young reader title/year; 1 middle reader title/year. 10% of books by first-time authors; 90% of books from agented writers. "We publish books that matter for people who care."
● This publisher is no longer considering unsolicited mss of any type.
Fiction: Picture books: adventure, animal, contemporary, folktales, nature/environment. Young readers: adventure, animal, contemporary, folk or fairy tales, history, nature/environment, poetry. Middle readers: adventure,

animal, contemporary, folk or fairy tales, history, mystery, nature/environment, poetry. Young adults/teens: adventure, animal, contemporary, history, mystery, nature/environment, poetry. Recently published *Roma and Sita*, by David Weitzman (picture book); *Ultimate Game*, by Christian Lehmann (received the Batchelder Honor Book for the American Library Association).

Nonfiction: Picture books: alphabet, animal, nature/environment. Young readers: activity books, animal, history, music/dance, nature/environment. Middle readers: activity books, animal, biography, history, music/dance, nature/environment. Young adults: biography, history, music/dance, nature/environment.

How to Contact/Writers: Query. Responds to queries in 2 weeks. Reports on solicited ms in 2 weeks (if not agented) or 2 months (if agented). Publishes a book 2 years after acceptance.

Illustration: Only interested in agented material. Works with 4-6 illustrators/year. Reviews ms/illustration packages from artists. "Submit roughs and one piece of finished art plus either sample chapters for very long works or whole ms for short works." Illustrations only: "After query, submit slides, with one full-size blow-up of art." Please do not send original artwork unless solicited. Reports on art samples in 2 weeks. Original artwork returned at job's completion. "Almost all of the children's books we accept for publication come to us with the author and illustrator already paired up. Therefore, we rarely use freelance illustrators." Samples returned with SASE; samples filed (if interested).

Terms: Pays authors in royalties based on retail price. Number of illustrations used determines final payment for illustrators. Pay for separate authors and illustrators "differs with each collaboration." Illustrators paid by the project. Sends galleys to authors; dummies to illustrators. Originals returned at job's completion. Book catalog available for SASE. "No phone calls please!"

Tips: "Always enclose a SASE. Keep in mind that we do not accept unsolicited manuscripts and that we rarely use freelance illustrators."

GOLDEN BOOKS, 888 Seventh Ave., New York NY 10106-4100. (212)547-6700. Imprint of Golden Books Family Entertainment Inc. **Editorial Directors:** Diane Arico, trade publishing; Lori Haskins, Road to Reading and Road to Writing; Ellen Stamper, vice president, editorial. **Art Acquisitions:** Paula Darmofal, vice president, creative department.

How to Contact/Writers: Send unsolicited ms to: Submissions. Does not accept queries. No multiple submissions.

Fiction: They publish board books, novelty books, picture books, workbooks, series (mass market and trade).

GREENE BARK PRESS, P.O. Box 1108, Bridgeport CT 06601-1108. (203)372-4861. Fax: (203)371-5856. E-mail: greenebark@aol.com. Website: www.greenebarkpress.com. Book publisher. **Acquisitions:** Michele Hofbauer; associate publisher. Thomas J. Greene, publisher. Publishes 4-6 picture books/year. 40% of books by first-time authors. "We publish quality hardcover picture books for children. Our books and stories are selected for originality, imagery and colorfulness. Our intention is to capture a child's attention; to fire-up his or her imagination and desire to read and explore the world through books."

Fiction: Picture books, young readers: adventure, fantasy, humor. Average word length: picture books—650; young readers—1,400. Recently published *The Day Lenny the Leopard Lost His Spots*, by Carm Boeffy; *Couldn't We Make A Difference*, by Michele Hofbauer; *Empty Pockets*, by Faye Van Wert; *To Know the Sea*, by Frances Gilbert.

How to Contact/Writers: Responds to queries in 1 month; ms in 2-4 months. Publishes a book 18 months after acceptance. Will consider simultaneous submissions. Prefer to review complete mss with illustrations.

Illustrations: Works with 1-2 illustrators/year. Uses color artwork only. Reviews ms/illustration packages from artists. Submit ms with 3 pieces of final art (copies only). Illustrations only: Query with samples. Responds in 2 months only if interested. Samples returned with SASE; samples filed. Originals returned at job's completion.

Terms: Pays authors royalty of 10-12% based on wholesale price. Pays illustrators by the project (range: $1,500-3,000) or 5-7½% royalty based on wholesale price. No advances. Send galleys to authors; dummies to illustrators. Book catalog available for $2.00 fee which includes mailing. All imprints included in a single catalog. Ms and art guidelines available for SASE or per e-mail request.

Tips: "As a guide for future publications do not look to our older backlist. Please no telephone, e-mail or fax queries."

☑ **GREENHAVEN PRESS**, Lucent Books, P.O. Box 289009, San Diego CA 92198-9009. (858)485-7424. Website: www.greenhaven.com. Book publisher. Estab. 1970. **Acquisitions:** Scott Barbour, managing editor. Publishes 300 young adult titles/year. 35% of books by first-time authors. "Greenhaven continues to print quality nonfiction for libraries and classrooms. Our well known opposing viewpoints series is still highly respected by students and librarians in need of material on controversial social issues. In recent years, Greenhaven has also branched out with a new series covering historical and literary topics."

• Greenhaven accepts no unsolicited mss. All writing is done on a work-for-hire basis.

Nonfiction: Middle readers: biography, controversial topics, history, issues. Young adults: biography, history, nature/environment. Other titles "to fit our specific series." Average word length: young adults—15,000-25,000.

How to Contact/Writers: Query only.

Terms: Buys ms outright for $1,500-3,000. Offers advances. Sends galleys to authors. Writer's guidelines available with SASE. Book catalog available for 9 × 12 SAE and 65¢ postage.

Tips: "Get our guidelines first before submitting anything."

■ **GREENWILLOW BOOKS**, 1350 Avenue of the Americas, New York NY 10019. (212)261-6500. Website: www.harperchildrens.com. Imprint of HarperCollins. Book publisher. Vice President/Publisher: Virginia Duncan. **Manuscript Acquisitions:** Submit to Editorial Department. **Art Acquisitions:** Ava Weiss, art director. Publishes 50 picture books/year; 5 middle readers books/year; and 5 young adult books/year. "Greenwillow Books publishes picture books, fiction for young readers of all ages, and nonfiction primarily for children under seven years of age. We hope you will read many children's books (especially those on our list), decide what you like or don't like about them, then write the story *you* want to tell (not what you think we want to read), and send it to us!"

   • Greenwillow title *Rocks in His Head*, by Carol Otis Hurst, illustrated by James Stevenson, won a 2001 Boston Globe-Horn Book Honor Award for Nonfiction.

Fiction: Will consider all levels of fiction; various categories.
Nonfiction: Will consider nonfiction for children under seven.
How to Contact/Writers: Submit complete ms. "If your work is illustrated, we ask to see a typed text or rough dummy, and a *copy* of a finished picture. Please do not send original artwork with your submission." Do not call. Reports on mss in 10-12 weeks. Publishes a book 18-24 months after acceptance. Will consider simultaneous submissions. For novels/YA, submit synopsis and sample chapters.
Illustration: Reviews ms/illustration packages from artists. Illustrations only: Query with samples, résumé.
Terms: Pays authors royalty. Offers advances. Pays illustrators royalty or by the project. Sends galleys to authors. Book catalog available for 9 × 12 SASE with $2.20 postage (no cash or checks); ms guidelines available for SASE.
Tips: "You need not have a literary agent to submit to us. We accept—and encourage—simultaneous submissions to other publishers and ask only that you so inform us. Because we receive thousands of submissions, we do not keep a record of the manuscripts we receive and cannot check the status of your manuscript. We do try to respond within ten weeks' time."

■ **GRYPHON HOUSE**, P.O. Box 207, Beltsville MD 20704-0207. (301)595-9500. Fax: (301)595-0051. E-mail: kathyc@ghbooks.com. Website: www.gryphonhouse.com. Book publisher. **Acquisitions:** Kathy Charner, editor-in-chief.
Nonfiction: Parent and teacher resource books—activity books, textbooks. Recently published *Preschool Art: Painting*, by MaryAnn F. Kohl; *Gems to Play with Babies Third Edition*, by Jackie Silberg; *Creating Readers*, by Pam Schiller.
How to Contact/Writers: Query. Submit outline/synopsis and 2 sample chapters. Responds to queries/mss in 3 months. Publishes a book 18 months after acceptance. Will consider simultaneous submissions, electronic submissions via disk or modem.
Illustration: Works with 3-4 illustrators/year. Uses b&w artwork only. Reviews ms/illustration packages from artists. Submit query letter with table of contents, introduction and sample chapters. Illustrations only: Query with samples, promo sheet. Responds in 2 months. Samples returned with SASE; samples filed.
Photography: Buys photos from freelancers. Buys stock and assigns work. Submit cover letter, published samples, stock photo list.
Terms: Pays authors royalty based on wholesale price. Offers advances. Pays illustrators by the project. Pay photographers by the project or per photo. Sends edited ms copy to authors. Original artwork returned at job's completion. Book catalog and ms guidelines available via website or with SASE.
Tips: "Send a SASE for our catalog and manuscript guidelines. Look at our books, then submit proposals that complement the books we already publish or supplement our existing books. We are looking for books of creative, participatory learning experiences that have a common conceptual theme to tie them together. The books should be on subjects that parents or teachers want to do on a daily basis."

GULLIVER BOOKS, 15 E. 26th St., New York NY 10010. (212)592-1000. Imprint of Harcourt, Inc. **Acquisitions:** Elizabeth Van Doren, editorial director, Garen Thomas, senior editor. Publishes 25 titles/year.
   • Gulliver only accepts mss submitted by agents, previously published authors, or SCBWI members.
Fiction: Emphasis on picture books. Also publishes middle grade and young adult.
Nonfiction: Publishes nonfiction.
How to Contact/Writers: Fiction/Nonfiction: Query or send ms for picture book.

HACHAI PUBLISHING, 156 Chester Ave., Brooklyn NY 11218-3020. (718)633-0100. Fax: (718)633-0103. E-mail: info@hachai.com. Website: www.hachai.com. Book publisher. **Manuscript Acquisitions:** Devorah Leah Rosenfeld, submissions editor. Publishes 3 picture books/year; 3 young readers/year; 1 middle reader/year. 75% of books published by first-time authors. "All books have spiritual/religious themes, specifically traditional Jewish content. We're seeking books about morals and values; the Jewish experience in current and Biblical times; and Jewish observance, Sabbath and holidays."
Fiction: Picture books and young readers: contemporary, history, religion. Middle readers: adventure, contemporary, problem novels, religion. Does not want to see animal stories, romance, problem novels depicting drug use

or violence. Recently published *As Big As An Egg*, by Rachel Sandman, illustrated by Chana Zakashanskaya (ages 3-6, picture book); and *Red, Blue, and Yellow Yarn*, by Miriam Kosman, illustrated by Valeri Gorbachev (ages 3-6, picture book); *A Thread of Kindness*, by Leah Shollar, illustrated by Shoshana Meribel.

Nonfiction: Published *My Jewish ABC's*, by Draizy Zelcer, illustrated by Patti Nemeroff (ages 3-6, picture book); *Nine Spoons* by Marci Stillerman, illustrated by Pesach Gerber (ages 5-8).

How to Contact/Wrtiers: Fiction/Nonfiction: Submit complete ms. Responds to queries/mss in 6 weeks.

Illustration: Works with 4 illustrators/year. Uses primary color artwork, some b&w illustration. Reviews ms/ illustration packages from authors. Submit ms with 1 piece of final art. Contact: Devorah Leah Rosenfeld, submissions editor. Illustrations only: Query with samples; arrange personal portfolio review. Responds in 6 weeks. Samples returned with SASE; samples filed.

Terms: Work purchased outright from authors for $800-1,000. Pays illustrators by the project (range: $2,000-3,500). Book catalog, ms/artist's guidelines available for SASE.

Tips: "Write a story that incorporates a moral . . . not a preachy morality tale. Originality is the key. We feel Hachai is going to appeal to a wider readership as parents become more interested in positive values for their children."

HAMPTON ROADS PUBLISHING COMPANY, INC., 1125 Stoney Ridge Road, Charlottesville VA 22902. (804)296-2772. Fax: (804)296-5096. E-mail: hrpc@hrpub.com. Website: www.hrpub.com. Estab. 1989. **Manuscript Acquisitions:** Pat Adler, Grace Pedalino. **Art Acquisitions:** Jane Hagaman. Publishes 3 picture books/year. 50% of books by first-time authors. Mission Statement: "to work as a team to seek, create, refine and produce the best books we are capable of producing, which will impact, uplift and contribute to positive change in the world; to promote the physical, mental, emotional and financial well-being of all its staff and associates; to build the company into a powerful, respected and prosperous force in publishing in the region, the nation and the world in which we live."

Fiction: Picture books, young readers, middle readers, young adult titles: metaphysical and spiritual. Average word length: picture books—100-200; young readers—1,000-5,000; middle readers—500-4,000. Recently published *The Legend of Wings*, by Timothy Green (5-9); *The Little Soul and the Sun*, by Neale Donald Walsch (ages 7-12); *OBO*, by Robert Anderson (preschool-age 8); *Coyote Bead*, by Gerald Hausman (ages 9-14).

Nonfiction: Picture books, young readers, middle readers, young adult titles: metaphysical and spiritual. Average word length: picture books—100-200; young readers—1,000-5,000; middle readers—500-4,000.

How to Contact/Writers: Fiction/nonfiction: submit complete ms. Responds to queries in 1 month; mss in 6 months. Publishes a book 6-12 months after acceptance. Will consider simultaneous submissions.

Illustration: Works with 2-3 illustrators/year. Reviews ms/illustration packages from artists. Submit ms with 2-3 pieces of final art (copies). Contact: Pat Adler, associate editor. Illustration only: query with samples. Contact: Jane Hagaman, art director. Responds in 1 month. Samples returned with SASE; samples not filed.

Terms: Pays authors royalty of 10-20% based on retail price. Offers advances (average amount: $1,000). Pays illustrators by the project. Occasionally pays by royalty based on retail price. Sends galleys to authors. Original returned to artist at job's completion. Book catalog available for SASE. Writer's guidelines available for SASE.

Tips: "Please familiarize yourself with our mission statement and/or the books we publish. Preferably send manuscripts that can be recycled rather than returned. If there is no SASE, they will be recycled."

Ⓐ 🏆 HARCOURT, INC., 525 B St., Suite 1900, San Diego CA 92101-4495. (619)231-6616. Fax: (619)699-6777. Children's Books Division includes: Harcourt Children's Books (Allyn Johnston, editorial director), Gulliver Books (Elizabeth Van Doren, editorial director), Silver Whistle Books (Paula Wiseman, editorial director), Voyager Paperbacks, Odyssey Paperbacks, and Red Wagon Books. Book publisher. **Art Acquisitions:** Art Director. Publishes 50-75 picture books/year; 5-10 middle reader titles/year; 10 young adult titles/year. 20% of books by first-time authors; 50% of books from agented writers. "Harcourt, Inc. owns some of the world's most prestigious publishing imprints—which distinguish quality products for the juvenile, educational and trade markets worldwide."

● The staff of Harcourt's children's book department is no longer accepting unsolicited manuscripts. Only query letters from previously published authors and manuscripts submitted by agents will be considered. Harcourt title *Troy*, by Adéle Geras, won a 2001 Boston Globe-Horn Book Honor Award for Fiction and Poetry. Their title *The Body of Christopher Creed*, by Carol Plum-Ucci, won a 2001 Printz Honor Medal. Their title *Let It Shine*, by Andrea Davis Pinkney, won a 2001 Coretta Scott King Author Honor Award.

Fiction: All levels: Considers all categories. Average word length: picture books—"varies greatly"; middle readers—20,000-50,000; young adults—35,000-65,000. Recently published *Home Run*, by Robert Burleigh, illustrated by Mike Wimmer (ages 6-10, picture book/biography); *Cast Two Shadows*, by Ann Rinaldi (ages 12 and up; young adult historical fiction); *Tell Me Something Happy Before I Go to Sleep*, by Joyce Dunbar, illustrated by Debi Gliori (ages 4-8, picture book).

Nonfiction: All levels: animal, biography, concept, history, multicultural, music/dance, nature/environment, science, sports. Average word length: picture books—"varies greatly"; middle readers—20,000-50,000; young adults—35,000-65,000. Recently published *Lives of the Presidents*, by Kathleen Krull; illustrated by Kathryn Hewitt (ages 8-12, illustrated nonfiction).

How to Contact/Writers: Only interested in agented material. Fiction: Query or submit outline/synopsis. Nonfiction: Submit outline/synopsis. Responds to queries/mss in 2 months.

A Bikur Cholim Story

by Dina Rosenfeld • illustrated by Rina Lyampe

Many children's book publishers seek illustrators who will capture the essence of a star character with ease and unyielding precision. Like other acclaimed publishers working under rigid schedules, Hachai does not want to spend a lot of time "coaching" artists to materialize their specific vision for a book. According to Yossi Leverton of Hachai, artist Rina Lyampe "perfectly" illustrated *Get Well Soon* without much coaching or reinventing. The publisher contacted Lyampe immediately after the author's mother spotted one of her drawings in a friend's home.

Illustration: Works with 150 illustrators/year. Reviews ms/illustration packages from artists. "For picture book ms—complete ms acceptable. Longer books—outline and 2-4 sample chapters." Send one sample of art; no original art with dummy. Illustrations only: Submit résumé, tearsheets, color photocopies, color stats all accepted. "Please DO NOT send original artwork or transparencies." Samples are not returned; samples filed. Responds to art samples only if interested.

Photography: Works on assignment only.

Terms: Pays authors and illustrators in royalty based on retail price. Pays photographers by the project. Sends galleys to authors; dummies to illustrators. Original artwork returned at job's completion. Book catalog available for 8×10 SAE and 4 first-class stamps; ms/artist's guidelines for business-size SASE. All imprints included in a single catalog.

Tips: "Become acquainted with Harcourt's books in particular if you are interested in submitting proposals to us."

HARPERCOLLINS CHILDREN'S BOOKS, 1350 Sixth Ave., New York NY 10019. (212)261-6500. Website: www.harpercollins.com. Book publisher. Senior Vice President/Associate Publisher/Editor-in-Chief: Kate Morgan Jackson. **Art Acquisitions:** Harriett Barton, Barbara Fitzsimmon, directors. Imprints: Laura Geringer Books, Joanna Cotler Books, Greenwillow Books. Paperback Imprints: Harper Trophy, Harper Tempest, Avon. Merchandise Imprint: Harper Festival.

- HarperCollins is not accepting unsolicited and/or unagented mss not addressed to a specific editor. Harper/Joanna Cotler Books title *The Wanderer*, by Sharon Creech, won a 2001 Newbery Honor Medal. HarperCollins title *The Stray Dog*, retold and illustrated by Marc Simont, won a 2001 Boston Globe-Horn Book Honor Award for Picture Books. Their titles *Angus, Thongs*, and *Full-Frontal Snogging: Confessions of Georgia Nicolson*, by Louise Rennison, and *Stuck in Neutral*, by Terry Trueman, won 2001 Printz Honor Medals. See the sidebar on page 98 for an interview with Trueman.

Fiction: Picture books: adventure, animal, anthology, concept, contemporary, fantasy, folktales, hi-lo, history, multicultural, nature/environment, poetry, religion. Middle readers: adventure, hi-lo, history, poetry, suspense/mystery. Young adults/teens: fantasy, science fiction, suspense/mystery. All levels: multicultural. "Artists with diverse backgrounds and settings shown in their work."

Nonfiction: Picture books: animal, arts/crafts, biography, geography, multicultural, nature/environment. Middle readers: how-to.

Illustration: Works with 100 illustrators/year. Responds only if interested. Samples returned with SASE; samples filed only if interested.

How to Contact/Writers: Nonfiction: Query with SASE only.

Terms: Ms and art guidelines available for SASE.

HARVEST HOUSE PUBLISHERS, 1075 Arrowsmith, Eugene OR 97402-9197. (541)343-0123. Fax: (541)342-6410. Book publisher. Publishes 1-2 picture books/year and 2 young reader titles/year. Books follow a Christian theme.

- Harvest House no longer accepts unsolicited manuscripts.

HAYES SCHOOL PUBLISHING CO. INC., 321 Pennwood Ave., Wilkinsburg PA 15221-3398. (412)371-2373. Fax: (800)543-8771. E-mail: chayes@hayespub.com. Website: www.hayespub.com. **Acquisitions:** Mr. Clair N. Hayes. Estab. 1940. Produces folders, workbooks, stickers, certificates. Wants to see supplementary teaching aids for grades K-12. Interested in all subject areas. Will consider simultaneous and electronic submissions.

How to Contact/Writers: Query with description or complete ms. Responds in 6 weeks. SASE for return of submissions.

Illustration: Works with 3-4 illustrators/year. Responds in 6 weeks. Samples returned with SASE; samples filed. Originals not returned at job's completion.

Terms: Work purchased outright. Purchases all rights.

HEALTH PRESS, P.O. Box 1388, Santa Fe NM 87504. (505)474-0303 or (800)643-2665. Fax: (505)424-0444. E-mail: goodbooks@healthpress.com. Website: www.healthpress.com. Book publisher. **Acquisitions:** Contact Editor. Publishes 4 young readers/year; 4 middle readers/year. 100% of books by first-time authors.

Fiction: Young readers, middle readers: health, special needs. Average word length: young readers—1,000-1,500; middle readers—1,000-1,500. Recently published *Pennies, Nickels and Dimes*, by Elizabeth Murphy.

Nonfiction: Young readers, middle readers: health, special needs.

How to Contact/Writers: Submit complete ms. Responds in 1 month. Publishes a book 9 months after acceptance. Will consider simultaneous submissions.

Terms: Pays authors royalty. Sends galleys to authors. Book catalog available.

FP HENDRIKS PUBLISHING, 4806 53rd St., Stettler, Alberta T0C 2L2 Canada. (403)742-6483. Fax: (403)742-6483. E-mail: editor@fphendriks.com. Website: www.fphendriks.com. Estab. 1995. Specializes in trade books, educational material. **Manuscript/Art Acquisitions:** Faye Boer, managing editor. Imprints: LifeS-port Books (Faye Boer, acquisitions editor). 100% of books by first-time authors. "We will begin a young adult publishing program in next few years. We're looking for fiction suitable for educational purposes with clear elements of plot, good characterization."

Fiction: Young adults: adventure, fantasy, science fiction, sports, suspense/mystery.

Nonfiction: Sports.

How to Contact/Writers: Fiction/nonfiction—query or submit outline/synopsis and 2-3 sample chapters. Responds in up to 1 year; to mss in up to 18 months. Publishes a book 18 months after acceptance. Will consider simultaneous submissions, electronic submissions via disk or modem.

Illustration: Works with 1 illustrator/year. Uses primarily b&w artwork. Reviews ms/illustration packages from artists or send ms with dummy. Contact: Faye Boer, managing editor. Illustrations only: Query with samples. Contact: Faye Boer, managing editor. Responds only if interested. Samples returned with SASE.

Photography: Buys stock and assigns work. Contact: Faye Boer, managing editor. Model/property releases required; captions required. Uses color or b&w prints. Submit cover letter.

Terms: Pays authors royalty 7-10% based on wholesale price. Pays illustrators by the project. Pays photographers by the project. Sends galleys to authors; dummies to illustrators. Book catalog available for 9×12 SASE. Manuscript guidelines available for SASE. Catalog available on website.

HOLIDAY HOUSE INC., 425 Madison Ave., New York NY 10017. (212)688-0085. Fax: (212)421-6134. Book publisher. Estab. 1935. Vice President/Editor-in-Chief: Regina Griffin. **Acquisitions:** Suzanne Reinochl, associate editor. Publishes 35 picture books/year; 3 young reader titles/year; 10 middle reader titles/year; and 3 young adult titles/year. 20% of books by first-time authors; 10% from agented writers.

- Holiday House title *Darkness Over Denmark*, by Ellen Levine, won a Golden Kite Award for Nonfiction in 2001. Their title *Fireflies in the Dark: The Story of Freidl Dicker-Brandeis and the Children of Terezin*, by Susan Goldman Rubin, won a golden Kite Honor Award for Nonfiction in 2001.

Fiction: All levels: adventure, contemporary, ghost, historical, humor, school. Picture books, middle readers, young adults. Recently published *A Child's Calendar*, by John Updike, illustrated by Trina Schart Hyman; *I Was a Third Grade Science Project*, by M.J. Auch; and *Darkness Over Denmark*, by Ellen Levine.

Nonfiction: All levels: animal, biography, concept, contemporary, geography, historical, math, nature/environment, science, social studies.

How to Contact/Writers: Send queries only to Associate Editor. Responds to queries in 2 months. If we find your book idea suited to our present needs, we will notify you by mail. Once a ms has been requested, the writers should send in the exclusive submission, with a S.A.S.E., otherwise the ms will not be returned.

Illustration: Works with 35 illustrators/year. Reviews ms illustration packages from artists. Send ms with dummy. Do not submit original artwork or slides. Color photocopies or printed samples are preferred. Responds only if interested. Samples returned with SASE or filed.

Terms: Pays authors and illustrators an advance against royalties. Originals returned at job's completion. Book catalog, ms/artist's guidelines available for a SASE.

Tips: "Fewer books are being published. It will get even harder for first timers to break in."

HENRY HOLT & CO., LLC, 115 W. 18th St., New York NY 10011. (212)886-9200. Fax: (212)645-5832. Website: www.henryholt.com. Book publisher. **Manuscript Acquisitions:** Laura Godwin, editor-in-chief/associate publisher of Books for Young Readers dept.; Nina Ignatowicz, executive editor; Christy Ottaviano, executive editor, Reka Simonsen, editor. **Art Acquisitions:** Martha Rago, art director. Publishes 20-40 picture books/year; 4-6 chapter books/year; 10-15 middle grade titles/year; 8-10 young adult titles/year. 15% of books by first-time authors; 40% of books from agented writers. "Henry Holt and Company Books for Young Readers is known for publishing quality books that feature imaginative authors and illustrators. We tend to publish many new authors and illustrators each year in our effort to develop and foster new talent."

- Holt title *Uptown*, by Bryan Collier, won the 2001 Coretta Scott King Illustrator Award. See First Books to read about Henry Holt author/illustrator Jennifer Thermes and her book *When I Was Built*.

Fiction: Picture books: animal, anthology, concept, folktales, history, humor, multicultural, nature/environment, poetry, special needs, sports. Middle readers: adventure, contemporary, history, humor, multicultural, special needs, sports, suspense/mystery. Young adults: contemporary, multicultural, problem novel, sports.

Nonfiction: Picture books: animal, arts/crafts, biography, concept, geography, history, hobbies, multicultural, music, dance, nature/environment, sports. Middle readers, young readers, young adult: biography, history, multicultural, sports.

How to Contact/Writers: Fiction/Nonfiction: Submit complete ms with SASE. Responds in 3 months. Will not consider simultaneous or multiple submissions.

Illustration: Works with 50-60 illustrators/year. Reviews ms/illustration packages from artists. Random samples OK. Illustrations only: Submit tearsheets, slides. Do *not* send originals. Responds to art samples in 1 month. Samples returned with SASE; samples filed. If accepted, original artwork returned at job's completion.

Terms: Pays authors/illustrators royalty based on retail price. Sends galleys to authors; proofs to illustrators.

HOUGHTON MIFFLIN CO., Children's Trade Books, 222 Berkeley St., Boston MA 02116-3764. (617)351-5000. Fax: (617)351-1111. E-mail: childrensbooks@hmco.com. Website: www.houghtonmifflinbooks. com. Book publisher. **Manuscript Aquisitions:** Hannah Rodgers, submissions coordinator. Kim Keller, assistant managing editor; Ann Rider, Margaret Raymo, senior editors; Amy Flynn, editor; Eden Edwards, Sandpiper Paperback editor; Walter Lorraine, Walter Lorraine Books, editor. **Art Acquisitions:** Bob Kosturko, art director. Averages 60 titles/year. Publishes hardcover originals and trade paperback reprints and originals. Imprints include Clarion Books. "Houghton Mifflin gives shape to ideas that educate, inform, and above all, delight."

● Houghton title *Uncommon Traveler: Mary Kingsley in Africa*, by Don Brown won the 2001 Boston Globe-Horn Book Award for Nonfiction.

Fiction: All levels: all categories except religion. "We do not rule out any theme, though we do not publish specifically religious material." *The Strange Egg*, by Mary Newell DePalma (ages 4-8, picture book); *Gathering Blue*, by Lois Lowry (ages 10-14, novel); and *The Circuit*, by Francisco Jimenez (ages 10 and up).

Nonfiction: All levels: all categories except religion. Recently published *Slap, Squeak, and Scatter*, by Steve Jenkins (ages 6-10; picture book); *The Man-Eating Tigers of Sundarbans*, by Sy Montgomery (ages 4-8, photo); *Girls Think of Everything*, by Catherine Thimmesh, illustrated by Melissa Sweet (ages 8-12).

How to Contact/Writers: Fiction: Submit complete ms. Nonfiction: Submit outline/synopsis and sample chapters. Always include SASE. Response within 4 months.

Illustration: Works with 60 illustrators/year. Reviews ms/illustration packages from artists. Ms/illustration packages or illustrations only: Query with samples (colored photocopies are fine); provide tearsheets. Responds in 4 months. Samples returned with SASE; samples filed if interested.

Terms: Pays standard royalty based on retail price; offers advance. Illustrators paid by the project and royalty. Ms and artist's guidelines available for SASE.

HUNTER HOUSE PUBLISHERS, P.O.Box 2914, Alameda CA 94501-0914. Fax: (510)865-4295. E-mail: acquisitions@hunterhouse.com. Website: www.hunterhouse.com. Book publisher. **Manuscript Acquisitions:** Jeanne Brondino. Publishes 0-1 titles for teenage women/year. 50% of books by first-time authors; 5% of books from agented writers.

Nonfiction: Young adults: health, multicultural, self-help (self esteem), social issues, violence prevention. "We emphasize that all our books try to take multicultural experiences and concerns into account. We would be interested in a social issues or self-help book on multicultural issues." Books are therapy/personal growth-oriented. Does *not* want to see books for young children; fiction; illustrated picture books; autobiography. Published *Turning Yourself Around: Self-Help Strategies for Troubled Teens*, by Kendall Johnson, Ph.D.; *Safe Dieting for Teens*, by Linda Ojeda, Ph.D.

How to Contact/Writers: Query; submit overview and chapter-by-chapter synopsis, sample chapters and statistics on your subject area, support organizations or networks and marketing ideas. "Testimonials from professionals or well-known authors are crucial." Responds to queries in 3 months; mss in 6 months. Publishes a book 18 months after acceptance. Will consider simultaneous submissions.

Photography: Purchases photos from freelancers. Buys stock images.

Terms: Payment varies. Sends galleys to authors. Book catalog available for 9 × 12 SAE and $1.25 postage; ms guidelines for standard SAE and 1 first-class stamp.

Tips: Wants therapy/personal growth workbooks; teen books with solid, informative material. "We do few children's books. The ones we do are for a select, therapeutic audience. No fiction! Please, no fiction."

HYPERION BOOKS FOR CHILDREN, 114 Fifth Ave., New York NY 10011. (212)633-4400. Fax: (212)633-4833. Website: www.hyperionchildrensbooks.com. Trade imprint of Disney Publishing Worldwide. Book publisher. **Manuscript Acquisitions:** Andrea Davis Pinkney, editorial director. **Art Acquisitions:** Ken Geist, associate publisher and creative director. 10% of books by first-time authors. Publishes various categories.

● Hyperion/Jump at the Sun title *Freedom River*, illustrated by Bryan Collier (text by Doreen Rappaport), won a 2001 Coretta Scott King Illustrator Honor Award.

Fiction: Picture books, young readers, middle readers, young adults: adventure, animal, anthology (short stories), contemporary, fantasy, folktales, history, humor, multicultural, poetry, science fiction, sports, suspense/mystery. Middle readers, young adults: commercial fiction. Recently published *Emily's First 100 Days of School*, by Rosemary Wells (ages 3-6, *New York Times* bestseller); *Artemis Fowl*, by Eoin Colfer (YA novel, *New York Times* bestseller); *Dumpy The Dump Truck*, series by Julie Andrews Edwards and Emma Walton Hamilton (ages 3-7).

Nonfiction: All trade subjects for all levels.

How to Contact/Writers: Only interested in agented material.

Illustration: Works with 100 illustrators/year. "Picture books are fully illustrated throughout. All others depend on individual project." Reviews ms/illustration packages from artists. Submit complete package. Illustrations only: Submit résumé, business card, promotional literature or tearsheets to be kept on file. Responds only if interested. Original artwork returned at job's completion.

Photography: Works on assignment only. Publishes photo essays and photo concept books. Provide résumé, business card, promotional literature or tearsheets to be kept on file.

Terms: Pays authors royalty based on retail price. Offers advances. Pays illustrators and photographers royalty based on retail price or a flat fee. Sends galleys to authors; dummies to illustrators. Book catalog available for 9 × 12 SAE and 3 first-class stamps.

◆ **HYPERION PRESS LIMITED**, 300 Wales Ave., Winnipeg, Manitoba R2M 2S9 Canada. (204)256-9204. Fax: (204)255-7845. E-mail: tamos@escape.ca. Website: www.escape.ca/~tamos. Book Publisher. **Acquisitions:** Dr. M. Tutiah, editor. Publishes authentic-based, retold folktales/legends for ages 4-9. "We are interested in a good story or well researched how-to material."

Fiction: Young readers, middle readers: folktales/legends. Recently published *The Wise Washerman*, by Deborah Froese, illustrated by Wang Kui; *The Cricket's Cage*, written and illustrated by Stefan Czernecki; and *The Peacock's Pride*, by Melissa Kajpust, illustrated by Jo'Anne Kelly.

How to Contact/Writers: Fiction: Query. Responds in 3 months.

Illustration: Reviews ms/illustration packages from artists. Ms/illustration packages and illustration only: Query. Samples returned with SASE.

Terms: Pays authors royalty. Pays illustrators by the project. Sends galleys to authors; dummies to illustrators. Book catalog available for 8 1/2 × 11 SAE and $2.00 postage (Canadian).

ILLUMINATION ARTS, P.O. Box 1865, Bellevue WA 98009. (425)644-7185. Fax: (425)644-9274. E-mail: liteinfo@illumin.com. Website: www.illumin.com. Book publisher. Estab. 1987. "All of our books are inspirational/spiritual. We specialize in children's picture books, but our books are designed to appeal to all readers, including adults." **Acquisitions:** Ruth Thompson, editorial director. "We publish high quality children's picture books with enduring inspirational and spiritual values. We are so selective and painstaking in every detail that our company has established a reputation for producing fine quality books. Additionally we are known for our outstanding artwork."

Fiction: Average word length: picture books—500-2,000. Recently published *What If . . .* , by Regina Williams, illustrated by Doug Keith; *Cassandra's Angel*, by Gina Otto, illustrated by Trudy Joost; *Little Square Head*, by Peggy O'Neill, illustrated by Denise Freeman.

How to Contact/Writers: Fiction: Submit complete ms. Responds to queries in 1-2 months. Publishes a book 2 years after acceptance. Will consider simultaneous submissions.

Illustration: Works with 3 illustrators/year. Uses color artwork only. Reviews ms/illustration packages from artists. Query or send ms with dummy. Illustrations only: Query with samples; send résumé and promotional literature to be kept on file. Contact: Ruth Thompson, editorial director. Responds in 1 week. Samples returned with SASE or filed.

Terms: Pays authors royalty based on wholesale price. Sends galleys to authors; dummies to illustrators. Originals returned to artist at job's completion. Book fliers available for SASE.

Tips: "Follow our guidelines. Expect considerable editing. Be patient. The market is tough. We receive 10-15 submissions a week and publish two-three books a year."

▣ **IMPACT PUBLISHERS, INC.**, P.O. Box 6016, Atascadero CA 93423-6016. (805)466-5917. Fax: (805)466-5919. E-mail: info@impactpublishers.com. Website: www.impactpublishers.com. Estab. 1970. Nonfiction publisher. **Manuscript Acquisitions:** Melissa Froehner, children's editor. **Art Acquisitions:** Sharon Skinner, art director. Imprints: Little Imp Books, Rebuilding Books, The Practical Therapist Series. Publishes 1 young reader/year; 1 middle reader/year; and 1 young adult title/year. 50% of books by first-time authors. "Our purpose is to make the best human services expertise available to the widest possible audience."

Nonfiction: Young readers, middle readers, young adults: self-help. Recently published *The Divorce Helpbook for Kids*, by Cynthia MacGregor (ages 8-12, children's/divorce/emotions).

How to Contact/Writers: Nonfiction: Query or submit complete ms, cover letter, résumé. Responds to queries in 8-10 weeks; mss in 10-12 weeks. Will consider simultaneous submissions or previously published work.

Illustration: Works with 1 or less illustrator/year. Uses b&w artwork only. Reviews ms/illustration packages from artists. Query. Contact: Children's Editor. Illustrations only: query with samples. Contact: Sharon Skinner, production manager. Responds only if interested. Samples returned with SASE; samples filed. Originals returned to artist at job's completion.

Terms: Pays authors royalty of 10-12%. Offers advances. Pays illustrators by the project. Sends galleys to authors. Book catalog available for #10 SAE with 2 first-class stamps; ms guidelines available for SASE. All imprints included in a single catalog.

◐ **INCENTIVE PUBLICATIONS, INC.**, 3835 Cleghorn Ave., Nashville TN 37215-2532. (615)385-2934. Fax: (615)385-2967. E-mail: info@incentivepublications.com. Website: www.incentivepublications.com. Estab. 1969. "Incentive publishes developmentally appropriate instructional aids for tots to teens." **Acquisitions:** Jean Signor. Approximately 20% of books by first-time authors. "We publish only educational resource materials (for teachers and parents of children from pre-school age through high school). We publish *no fiction*. Incentive endeavors to produce developmentally appropriate research-based educational materials to meet the changing needs of students, teachers and parents. Books are written by teachers for teachers for the most part."

Nonfiction: Black & white line illustrated books, young reader, middle reader: activity books, arts/craft, multicultural, science, health, how-to, reference, animal, history, nature/environment, special needs, social issues, supplemental educational materials. "Any manuscripts related to child development or with content-based activities and innovative strategies will be reviewed for possible publication." Recently published *Romeo & Juliet Curriculum Guide*, by Laura Maravilla ESL Games, Puzzles and Inventive Exercises Series, by Imogene Forte and Mary Ann Pangle.

How to Contact/Writers: Nonfiction: Submit outline/synopsis, sample chapters and SASE. Usually responds to queries/mss in 1 month. Responds to queries in 6 weeks; mss in 2 months. Typically publishes a book 18 months after acceptance. Will consider simultaneous submissions.

Illustration: Works with 2-6 illustrators/year. Responds in 1 month if reply requested (send SASE). Samples returned with SASE; samples filed. Need 4-color cover art; b&w line illustration for content.

Terms: Pays authors in royalties (5-10% based on wholesale price) or work purchased outright (range: $500-1,000). Pays illustrators by the project (range: $200-1,500). Pays photographers by the project. Original artwork not returned. Book catalog and ms and artist guidelines for SAE and $1.78 postage.

Tips: Writers: "We buy only educational teacher resource material that can be used by teachers and parents (home schoolers). Please do not submit fiction! Incentive Publications looks for a whimsical, warm style of illustration that respects the integrity and age of the child. We work primarily with local artists, but not exclusively."

N ▪ **ipicturebooks**, Website: www.ipicturebooks.com. Online book publisher. "ipicturebooks is the #1 brand for children's e-books on the Internet. It is designed to appeal to parents, children, teachers and librarians seeking in-print, out-of print and original enhanced e-books for use on home computers, school and library networked computers, proprietary and open hand-helds and dedicated e-book readers. It will sell e-books by individual downloaded copy, site licenses and subscription models. ipicturebooks will also introduce a variety of 'enhanced' e-books, ranging from original ebooks illustrated digitally, to 'custom' e-books in which a child's name appears to 'e-pop up books' to e-books with spoken text to e-books with music and animation." See website for submission information for writers and illustrators, as well as sample e-books.

☐ ☐ **JAYJO BOOKS, L.L.C.**, A Guidance Channel Company, 135 Dupont St., P.O. Box 760, Plainview NY 11803-0760. (516)349-5520. Fax: (516)349-5521. E-mail: jayjobooks@guidancechannel.com. Website: www .jayjo.com. Estab. 1993. Specializes in educational material. Independent book packager/producer. **Manuscript Acquisitions:** Sally Germain. Publishes 3-5 picture books/year; 3-5 young readers/year. 25% of books by first-time authors. "Our goal is to provide quality children's health education through entertainment and teaching, while raising important funds for medical research and education."

Fiction: Picture books, young readers, middle readers, young adults: health, special needs, chronic conditions. Average word length: picture books—1,800; young readers—1,800; middle readers—1,800. Recently published *There's a Louse in My House*, by Cheryl Hayes (ages 3-9); *Taking Cancer to School*, by Cynthia Henry and Kim Gosselin (ages 5-10); *Taking Autism to School*, by Andreanna Edwards (ages 5-10).

Nonfiction: Picture books, young readers, middle readers: health, special needs, chronic conditions. Average word length: picture books—1,500; young readers—1,500; middle readers—1,500.

How to Contact/Writers: Fiction/Nonfiction: Send query. Responds in 3 months. Publishes a book 2 years after acceptance. Will consider simultaneous submissions.

Illustration: Works with 2 illustrators/year. Uses color artwork only. Illustrations only: Query with samples. Responds in 3 months. Samples returned with SASE; samples filed.

Terms: Work purchased outright from authors. Pays illustrators by the project. Book catalog and guidelines available for #10 SAE and 1 first-class stamp. Manuscript guidelines for SASE.

Tips: "Send query letter. Since we only publish books adapted to our special format, we conatct appropriate potential authors and work with them to customize manuscripts."

JEWISH LIGHTS PUBLISHING, P.O. Box 237, Rt. 4, Sunset Farm Offices, Woodstock VT 05091. (802)457-4000. Fax: (802)457-4004. E-mail: everyone@longhillpartners.com. Website: www.jewishlights.com. A division of LongHill Partners, Inc. Book publisher. Imprint: Sky Light Paths Publishing. President: Stuart M. Matlins. **Manuscript Acquisitions:** Submissions Editor. **Art Acquisitions:** Bridget Taylor. Publishes 1 picture book/year; 1 young reader/year. 50% of books by first-time authors; 50% of books from agented authors. All books have spiritual/religious themes. "Jewish Lights publishes books for people of all faiths and all backgrounds who yearn for books that attract, engage, educate and spiritually inspire. Our authors are at the forefront of spiritual thought and deal with the quest for the self and for meaning in life by drawing on the Jewish wisdom tradition. Our books cover topics including history, spirituality, life cycle, children's, self-help, recovery, theology and philosophy. We do *not* publish autobiography, biography, fiction, *haggadot*, poetry or cookbooks. At this point we plan to do only two books for children annually, and one will be for younger children (ages 4-10)."

Fiction: Picture books, young readers, middle readers: spirituality. "We are not interested in anything other than spirituality." Recently published *God Said Amen*, by Sandy Eisenberg Sasso, illustrated by Avi Katz (ages 4-9, picture book); and *For Heaven's Sake*, by Sandy Eisenberg Sasso, illustrated by Kathryn Kunz Finney (ages 8 and up).

Nonfiction: Picture book, young readers, middle readers: activity books, spirituality. Recently published *When a Grandparent Dies: A Kid's Own Remembering Workbook for Dealing with Shiva and the Year Beyond*, by Nechama Liss-Levinson, Ph.D. (ages 7-11); and *Sharing Blessings: Children's Stories for Exploring the Spirit of the Jewish Holidays*, written by Rabbi Michael Klayman and Rahel Musleah, illustrated by Mary O'Keefe Young (ages 6-10, picture book).

insider report

Editor, author, webmaster enters the exciting world of e-publishing

In 1994, when the Internet was in its infancy, Harold Underdown created the beginnings of what would become his well-known website about children's publishing, The Purple Crayon (www.underdown.org). "It literally grew from a one-page list of links and a couple of articles to what it is now, by a kind of organic process. I had new ideas for it; people sent me materials. I've followed my nose with it."

Harold Underdown

In 2000, Underdown once again got in on the ground floor of an electronic innovation. He left his editorial position at Charlesbridge to become Vice President, Editorial, of ipicturebooks.com, a new kind of children's book publisher.

Launching in February 2001, ipicturebooks, an affiliate of Time Warner Trade Publishing, is "a user-friendly place to find and buy e-book versions of children's books from some of the best children's book publishers in the world." The site offers high-quality e-books, both original material and online "reprints" of out-of-print books, as well as e-book versions of titles from a variety of publishers, and even a few "enhanced" books, offering animation or sound.

Here Underdown talks about ipicturebooks.com, his website The Purple Crayon, and his new book *The Complete Idiot's Guide® to Publishing Children's Books*. For more of his thoughts on e-publishing, read the sidebar on page 35. For more information on ipicturebooks, visit www.ipicturebooks.com.

Why did you decide to take the job at ipicturebooks and leave Charlesbridge? What made you confident enough in the company and the product?
I had some very personal reasons for doing this. When I was working at Charlesbridge I was commuting. I was in Boston every other week. My family needs me in New York fulltime.

As for my confidence, there was one major factor that really helped. Even before it was publicly announced, I knew ipicturebooks was going to be funded by Time Warner. If I'd been looking at a situation where there wasn't funding or there was funding from venture capitalists that had to be used in six months and we had to be profitable in a year, I wouldn't have gone near this with a ten-foot pole.

I basically decided that this was something worth trying out and that meshed with my personal needs to get me back to New York.

Do you have any original books available yet?

We have three original books that are spin-offs from the *Shrek* movie. We've got others in development, several of which will be in print next year with Little, Brown in addition to being e-books. The e-book editions of those will probably appear on our website well before the print books come out. In most cases, when we're doing originals, we're doing both a print and an e-book. Our first list with Little, Brown appears in Spring 2002 with two books, growing to four a season.

What advice can you offer on submitting to your company?

It's important to note that we don't accept submissions by mail. On the submissions page of our website, we don't even post our address. Writers should visit our website and look at our submission guidelines online. I don't think we're ever going to start sending them out by mail either. We want an e-mail query. The website gives advice as to what you might want to include. It's the same kind of thing you would do in any query letter—avoid spelling mistakes, avoid being vague. If we say yes to the query, writers receive an e-mail requesting the manuscript through the mail.

What kind of reactions have you gotten from visitors to your site? Have there been any technical difficulties? Are people having any problem grasping the concept of what an e-picture book is?

Once somebody downloads the free samples we have on the site, it's pretty obvious what an e-book is. You don't have to buy a special hand-held device to look at our books. Getting that across to people has been a tough hill to climb. Once people realize all they need is to have Acrobat Reader or Microsoft Reader on their computer, we're two-thirds of the way there.

Having said that, there is a second difficulty. The systems of digital rights management that both Adobe and Microsoft have created (and they're slightly different systems) are a little complicated. Getting them set up on your computer takes a little work, and some people have had trouble with that. That's something we have to deal with. I think a year or two from now when we've got some improved software, the whole system will work a lot more smoothly. At this point we're working with very early versions of the software and the people who are using it are the early adopters.

So you think just two years down the line things will change dramatically?

Two years down the line things will be very different. Right now, I think we'll be spending most of the next year just getting the point across to people in general and to people in publishing and libraries and schools in particular, that e-books are available now, that they're easy to use now, and that they're inexpensive now.

The International Reading Association convention was the first show where we exhibited to the public. We set up our booth at IRA to be a place for teachers to come and learn about e-books. We did a couple hundred demonstrations—whoever we could get into the booth. Some people seemed intimidated by the whole idea of e-books and would not even look at what we were doing. There were also a lot of people who were very open to the idea of learning something new. Fortunately, demonstrating an e-book takes about one minute, so we were very easily able to show them how it works. A lot of them said, "Oh! I bet the kids in my class would love these!"

Are adults more the obstacle than kids? Kids are so computer savvy now.
Kids would be like, "Oh, this is just something else on the computer." It's adults who come to it with a lot of preconceptions and anxieties about what it might mean or how difficult it might be to deal with. Actually, once you've got the software set up, you "open a book" by double clicking on it, then you can just read through it by using the arrow keys on your keyboard. It's easy.

Do you think once you get more established and do original books and kind of set a standard, print publishers will follow suit and do similar online picture books?
Already larger publishers seem to be exploring e-books primarily as a marketing tool, both for picture books and books for older readers. Scholastic did a free download of a new Kristina Applegate book, for example. Publishers like Simon & Schuster and Random House are experimenting with e-books for older kids, because they think that's where the market is to start with. I'm not sure that's true. The neat thing about picture books is they're short and they're visual. I would much rather look at a picture book on screen than read a 100-page novel on screen, even with some of the new clear-type technology.

I think some of the other companies are watching us. But even if publishers like them decide to do their own picture books as e-books, those will simply be another offering from that particular company. We'll still be the place where there will be an aggregation of material from different sources. We'll still be the place where you've got everything.

Let's talk about your new book, *The Complete Idiot's Guide® to Publishing Children's Books.* How did the project come about?
Actually, the publisher came to me. They published a book in their series called *The Complete Idiot's Guide® to Getting Published* and it was quite successful for them. Then they thought, "What other areas of the market can we divide this up into?" One they settled on was children's books.

They came to me because they did some searching online and found The Purple Crayon. It seemed like a really interesting idea to me. I do spend a lot of time giving people basic information, so a lot of the stuff was already in my head. And yet, I knew there were areas I didn't have information about on my website or I had not talked about at conferences. It was an intriguing challenge to think about how to write a complete guide to this world that I've been living in for ten years.

The book covers a lot of areas, and it's a lot different from *Children's Writer's & Illustrator's Market* and books that are more about the craft of writing.
That's exactly it. When I was thinking about it initially, it seemed to me there was no point in doing something that was already out there. And there were two kinds of books out there— there were market guides like yours, and there were tons of craft books about how to write. I wanted to focus on everything else—on the personnel at a publishing company, on the basics of how to format a manuscript, on query letters, on marketing, on different kinds of publishers and how you figure out what they do, on how to analyze a catalog.

Why did you decide to create your personal website, The Purple Crayon?
It's a combination of things that made it possible. I was downsized at Orchard at the end of 1994, and that was just at the point when the Web was starting to exist. It had only been active about six months. And there was very little on the Web—nothing like all the commercial stuff you find now. In that first year or so, it was very much a place of universities and individuals

and a few fledgling companies setting things up. I had some time on my hands. I also had some material that I had written for SCBWI newsletters and other things, and they were just sitting in a drawer.

I started setting up a website, just to play around with it. In its first stages, it was nothing more than my booksmarks turned into an HTML page. Then I realized I could convert some of the materials I'd written and put them online.

Do you plan on keeping it going for some time?
I plan on keeping it going indefinitely. The difficulty is that the more material that's on it, the more time I have to spend keeping that material up-to-date. There are sections on my website I have not updated in a year or two that need to be updated. There are other sections that are fairly timeless. "Getting out of the Slush Pile" I originally wrote almost ten years ago as a presentation at a small SCBWI conference. The basic information in that really hasn't changed. The beginner mistakes that I warn about are still beginner mistakes. Everybody makes them when they first get started and probably will forever.
—*Alice Pope*

Hide, Clyde!, by Russell Benfanti, is the first book in ipicturebooks print and e-book program, published through the ipicturebooks imprint at Little, Brown. "We expect to do eight books a year through this imprint," says Harold Underdown, "focusing on titles that in some way work particularly well in electronic form or can be extended or enhanced."

How to Contact/Writers: Fiction/Nonfiction: Query with outline/synopsis and 2 sample chapters; submit complete ms for picture books. Include SASE. Responds to queries/mss in 3-4 months. Publishes a book 6 months after acceptance. Will consider simultaneous submissions and previously published work.
Illustration: Works with 2 illustrators/year. Reviews ms/illustration packages from artists. Query. Illustrations only: Query with samples; provide résumé. Samples returned with SASE; samples filed.
Terms: Pays authors royalty of 10% of revenue received. Offers advances. Pays illustrators by the project or royalty. Pays photographers by the project. Sends galleys to authors; dummies to illustrators. Book catalog available for 6½×9½ SAE and 59¢ postage; ms guidelines available for SASE.
Tips: "Explain in your cover letter why you're submitting your project to *us* in particular. (Make sure you know what we publish.)"

☑ BOB JONES UNIVERSITY PRESS, 1700 Wade Hampton Blvd., Greenville SC 29614. (803)242-5100, ext. 4350. E-mail: jb@bjup.com. Website: www.bjup.com/books/FreelanceOpportunities. Book publisher. Estab. 1974. **Acquisitions:** Mrs. Nancy Lohr, editor. Publishes 4 young reader titles/year; 4 middle reader titles/year; and 4 young adult titles/year. 30% of books by first-time authors. "Our books reflect the highest Christian standards of thought, feeling, and action, are uplifting or instructive and enhance moral purity. Themes advocating secular attitudes of rebellion or materialism are not acceptable. We are looking for books that present a fully developed main character, capable of dynamic changes, who experiences the central conflict of the plot, which should have plenty of action and not be didactic in tone."
Fiction: Young readers, middle readers, young adults: adventure, animal, concept, contemporary, easy-to-read, fantasy, history, multicultural, nature/environment, sports, spy/mystery. Average word length: young readers—10,000; middle readers—30,000; young adult/teens—50,000. Published *The Treasure of Pelican Cove*, by Milly Howard (grades 2-4, adventure story); and *Over the Divide*, by Catherine Farnes (young adult, contemporary).
Nonfiction: Young readers, middle readers: concept, history, multicultural. Young readers, middle readers, young adults: biography, history, nature/environment. Young adults/teens: biography, history, nature/environment. Average word length: young readers—10,000; middle readers—30,000; young adult/teens—50,000. Published *With Daring Faith*, by Becky Davis (grades 5-8, biography); and *Someday You'll Write*, by Elizabeth Yates (how-to).
How to Contact/Writers: Fiction: "Send the first five chapters and synopsis for these genres: Christian biography, modern realism, historical realism, regional realism and mystery/adventure, fantasy. Do not send stories with magical elements. We are not currently accepting picture books. We do not publish these genres: romance, science fiction, poetry and drama." Nonfiction: Query or submit complete ms or submit outline/synopsis and sample chapters. Responds to queries in 3 weeks; mss in 3 months. Publishes book "approximately one year" after acceptance. Will consider simultaneous submissions.
Illustration: Works with 4 illustrators/year. Responds only if interested. Samples returned with SASE; samples filed.
Terms: Pays authors royalty based on wholesale price. Or work purchased outright. Pays illustrators by the project. Originals returned to artist at job's completion. Book catalog and ms guidelines free on request. Send SASE for book catalog and mss guidelines.
Tips: "Writers—give us original, well-developed characters in a suspenseful plot that has good moral tone. Artists—we need strong color as well as black & white illustrations. Looking for quality illustrations of people in action in realistic settings. Be willing to take suggestions and follow specific directions. Today's books for children offer a wide variety of well-done nonfiction and rather shallow fiction. With the growing trend toward increased TV viewing, parents may be less interested in good books and less able to distinguish what is worthwhile. We are determined to continue producing high-quality books for children."

KAEDEN BOOKS, P.O. Box 16190, Rocky River OH 44116-6190. (440)356-0030. Fax: (440)356-5081. E-mail: curmston@kaeden.com. Website: kaeden.com. Book publisher. **Acquisitions:** Creative Vice President. 50% of books by first-time authors. "Kaeden Books produces high quality, pre-reader, emergent and early reader books for classroom and reading program educators."
Fiction: Young readers: adventure, animal, concept, contemporary, health, history, humor, multicultural, nature/environment, science fiction, sports, suspense/mystery. Average word length: picture books—20-150 words; young readers—20-150 words. Recently published *Moose's Loose Tooth*, by Nancy Louise Spinelle; *Another Sneeze, Louise!*, by Cheryl A. Potts; *Sammy's Moving*, by Kathleen Urmston and Karen Evans—all three titles illustrated by Gloria Gedeon.
Nonfiction: Young readers: activity books, animal, biography, careers, geography, health, history, hobbies, how-to, multicultural, music/dance, nature/environment, religion, science, sports. Multicultural needs include group and character diversity in stories and settings. Average word length: picture books—20-150 words; young readers—20-150 words.
How to Contact/Writers: Fiction/nonfiction: Query or submit complete ms. Do not send original transcripts. Reports on mss in 6-12 months. Will consider simultaneous submissions, electronic submissions via disk or modem.
Illustration: Works with 30 illustrators/year. Reviews ms/illustration packages from artists. Query. Submit art samples in color. Can be photocopies or tearsheets. Illustrations only: Query with samples. Send résumé, promo sheet, tearsheets, photocopies of work, preferably in color. Responds only if interested. Samples are filed.

Terms: Work purchased outright from authors. "Royalties to our previous authors." Offers negotiable advances. Pays illustrators by the project (range: $50-150/page). Book catalog available for 8½×11 SAE and 2 first-class stamps.

Tips: "Our books are written for emergent and fluent readers to be used in the educational teaching environment. A strong correlation between text and visual is necessary along with creative and colorful juvenile designs."

KAMEHAMEHA SCHOOLS PRESS, 1887 Makuakane St., Honolulu HI 96817. (808)842-8880. Fax: (808)842-8895. E-mail: kspress@ksbe.edu. Website: www.ksbe.edu/pubs/KSPress/catalog.html. Estab. 1933. Specializes in educational and multicultural material. **Manuscript Acquisitions:** Henry Bennett. "Kamehameha Schools Press publishes in the areas of Hawaiian history, culture, language and studies."

Nonfiction: Middle readers, young adults: biography, history, multicultural, Hawaiian folklore. Recently published *From the Mountains to the Sea: Early Hawaiian Life*, by Julie Stewart Williams, illustrated by Robin Yoko Racoma (pre-contact Hawaiian life and culture).

How to Contact/Writers: Query. Responds to queries in 2 months; mss in 3 months. Publishes a book 12-18 months after acceptance.

Illustration: Uses b&w artwork only. Illustrations only: Query with samples. Responds only if interested. Samples not returned.

Terms: Work purchased outright from authors. Pays illustrators by the project. Sends galleys to authors. Book catalog available for #10 SASE and 1 first-class stamp. All imprints included in a single catalog. Catalog available on website.

Tips: "Writers and illustrators *must* be knowledgeable in Hawaiian history/culture and be able to show credentials to validate their proficiency. Greatly prefer to work with writers/illustrators available in the Honolulu area."

KAR-BEN COPIES, INC., 6800 Tildenwood Lane, Rockville MD 20852-4371. (301)984-8733. Fax: (301)881-9195. E-mail: karben@aol.com. Website: www.karben.com. Book publisher. Estab. 1975. **Manuscript Acquisitions:** Madeline Wikler, vice president. Publishes 5-10 picture books/year; 20% of books by first-time authors. All of Kar-Ben Copies' books are on Jewish themes for young children and families.

Fiction: Picture books, young readers: adventures, concept, contemporary, fantasy, folktales, history, humor, multicultural, religion, special needs, suspense/mystery; *must be* on a Jewish theme. Average word length: picture books—2,000. Recently published *Once Upon a Shabbos*, by Jacqueline Jules; *Baby's Bris*, by Susan Wilkowski; *Too Many Cooks*, by Edie Zolkowe; and *Sammy Spiders First Tu B'Shevat*, by Sylvia Rouss; *Clap and Count, Action Rhymes for the Jewish Year*, by Jacqueline Jules.

Nonfiction: Picture books, young readers: activity books, arts/crafts, biography, careers, concept, cooking, history, how-to, multicultural, religion, social issues, special needs; must be of Jewish interest. Average word length: picture books—2,000. Published *Jewish Holiday Games for Little Hands*, by Ruth Brinn; *Tell Me a Mitzvah*, by Danny Siegel; *All About Hanukkah*, and *Come Let Us Welcome Shabbat*, by Judith Grones and Madeline Wikler; and *My First Jewish Word Book*, by Roz Schanzer.

How to Contact/Writers: Fiction/nonfiction: Submit complete ms. Responds to queries/ms in 6 weeks. Publishes a book 1 year after acceptance. Will consider simultaneous submissions. "Story should be short, no more than 3,000 words."

Illustration: Works with 3-4 illustrators/year. Prefers "four-color art in any medium that is scannable." Reviews ms/illustration packages from artists. Submit whole ms and sample of art (no originals). Illustrations only: Submit tearsheets, photocopies, promo sheet or anything representative that does *not* need to be returned. "Submit samples which show skill in children's book illustration." Enclose SASE for response. Responds to art samples in 2 weeks.

Terms: Pays authors in royalties of 8-10% based on wholesale price or work purchased outright (range: $500-2,000). Offers advance (average amount: $1,000). Pays illustrators royalty of 8-10% based on wholesale price or by the project (range: $500-3,000). Sends galleys to authors. Original artwork returned at job's completion. Book catalog free on request. Ms guidelines for 9×12 SAE and 2 first-class stamps.

Tips: Looks for "books for young children with Jewish interest and content, modern, non-sexist, not didactic. Fiction or nonfiction with a *Jewish* theme—can be serious or humorous, life cycle, Bible story, or holiday-related."

KEY PORTER BOOKS, 70 The Esplanade, Toronto, Ontario M5E 1R2 Canada. (416)862-7777. Fax: (416)862-2304. Website: www.keyporter.com. Book publisher. Publishes 4 picture books/year; and 4 young readers/year. 30% of books by first-time authors.

Fiction: Young readers, middle readers, young adult: animal, anthology, concept, health, multicultural, nature/environment, science fiction, special needs, sports, suspense/mystery. Does not want to see religious material. Average word length: picture books—1,500; young readers—5,000.

Nonfiction: Picture books: animal, history, nature/environment, reference, science. Middle readers: animal, careers, history, nature/environment, reference, science and sports. Average word length: picture books—1,500; middle readers—15,000. Recently published *New Animal Discoveries*, by Ronald Orenstein (ages 8-12); *Footnotes: Dancing the World's Best Love Ballads*, by Frank Augustyn and Shelley Tanaka (ages 8-10).

How to Contact/Writers: Only interested in agented material from Canadian writers; *no unsolicited mss.*

Photography: Buys photos from freelancers. Buys stock and assigns work. Captions required. Uses 35mm transparencies. Submit cover letter, résumé, duplicate slides, stock photo list.

KIDS CAN PRESS, 2250 Tonawanda Rd., Tonawanda NY 14150. (800)265-0884. E-mail: info@kidscan.c om. Estab. 1973. Specializes in fiction, trade books, nonfiction. **Contact:** Acquisitions Editor. **Contact:** Art Director. Publishes 6-10 picture books/year; 10-15 young readers/year; 20-30 middle readers/year; 2-3 young adult titles/year. 10-15% of books by first-time authors.
Fiction: Picture books, young readers: concept. All levels: adventure, animal, contemporary, fantasy, folktales, history, humor, multicultural, nature/environment, poetry, special needs, sports, suspense/mystery. Average word length: picture books—1,000-2,000; young readers—750-1,500; middle readers—10,000-15,000; young adults — over 15,000. Recently published *Oma's Quilt*, by Paulette Bourgeois, illustrated by Stéphane Jorlisch (picture book); *The Secret of Sagawa Lake*, by Mary Labatt (early novel-mystery); and *The Best Figure Skater in the Whole Wide World*, by Linda Bailey, illustrated by Alan and Lea Daniel (picture book).
Nonfiction: Picture books: activity books, animal, arts/crafts, biography, careers, concept, health, history, hobbies, how-to, multicultural, nature/environment, science, social issues, special needs, sports; young readers: activity books, animal, arts/crafts, biography, careers, concept, history, hobbies, how-to, multicultural; middle readers: cooking, music/dance. Average word length: picture books—500-1,250; young readers—750-2,000; middle readers—5,000-15,000. Recently published *The Kids Winter Handbook*, by Jane Drake and Ann Love, illustrated by Heather Collins (informational activity); *Animals at Work*, by Etta Kaner, illustrated by Pat Stephens (animal/nature); and *Quilting*, by Biz Storms, illustrated by June Bradford (craft book).
How to Contact/Writers: Fiction/nonfiction: Query or submit outline/synopsis and 2-3 sample chapters. Responds in 3-6 months. Publishes a book 18-24 months after acceptance. Will consider simultaneous submissions and previously published work.
Illustration: Works with 40 illustrators/year. Reviews ms/illustration packages from artists. Send color copies of illustrtion portfolio. Contact: Art Director. Illustrations only: Send tearsheets, color photocopies. Contact: Art Director. Responds only if interested. Samples returned with SASE; samples filed.
Photography: Buys stock. Contact: Photo Editor. Uses color or b&w prints and 35mm, $2\frac{1}{4} \times 2\frac{1}{4}$, 4×5, 8×10 transparencies. Submit cover letter, résumé published samples, stock photo list, color copies.
Terms: Pays authors royalty of 2-10% based on retail price. Offers advances. Pays illustrators royalty of 2-10% based on retail price. Pays photographers 2-4% royalty based on retail price. Sends galleys to authors. Originals returned to artist at job's completion. All imprints included in single catalog. Manuscript and art guidelines available for SASE. Catalog available on website.
Tips: Know our approach.

KINGFISHER, Imprint of Larousse Kingfisher Chambers, 85 Maiden Lane, New York NY 10016. (212)686-1060. Fax: (212)686-1082. Website: www.lkcpub.com.
 • Kingfisher is not currently accepting unsolicited mss. All solicitations must be made by a recognized literary agent. Kingfisher is an award-winning publisher of nonfiction and fiction for children of all ages. They publish high-quality books with strong editorial content and world class illustration at a competitive price, offering value to parents and educators.

LEE & LOW BOOKS INC., 95 Madison Ave., New York NY 10016-7801. (212)779-4400. Website: www.leea ndlow.com. Book publisher. Estab. 1991. **Acquisitions:** Philip Lee, publisher; Louise May, executive editor. Publishes 12-14 picture books/year. 50% of books by first-time authors. Lee & Low publishes only picture books with multicultural themes. "One of our goals is to discover new talent and produce books that reflect the multicultural society in which we live."
 • Lee & Low Books is dedicated to publishing culturally authentic literature. The company makes a special effort to work with writers and artists of color and encourages new voices. See listing for their new imprint BeBop Books.
Fiction: Picture books: concept. Picture books, young readers: anthology, contemporary, history, multicultural, poetry. "We are not considering folktales, animal stories and chapter books." Picture book, middle reader: contemporary, history, multicultural, nature/environment, poetry, sports. Average word length: picture books—1,000-1,500 words. Recently published *Love to Mamá*, edited by Pat Mora, illustrated by Pauls S. Barragán M., *The Secret to Freedom*, by Marcia Vaughan, illustrated by Larry Johnson, and *DeShawn Days*, by Tony Medina, illustrated by R. Gregory Christie.
Nonfiction: Picture books: concept. Picture books, middle readers: biography, history, multicultural, science and sports. Average word length: picture books—1,500. Recently published *¡Béisbol! Latino Baseball Pioneers and Legends*, by Jonah Winter.
How to Contact/Writers: Fiction/Nonfiction: Submit complete ms. Responds in 4 months. Publishes a book 12-24 months after acceptance. Will consider simultaneous submissions.
Illustration: Works with 12-14 illustrators/year. Uses color artwork only. Reviews ms/illustration packages from artists. Submit ms with dummy. Illustrations only: Query with samples, résumé, promo sheet and tearsheets. Responds only if interested. Samples returned with SASE; samples filed. Original artwork returned at job's completion.

insider report

Multicultural publisher encourages new authors

Growing up in Hong Kong, Philip Lee was a voracious reader—of comic books. Batman. Superman. Chinese comic books . . . "I read books, but not for pleasure," says Lee. But "when it came to comic books, I read everything I got my hands on."

Today, as the publisher and editor-in-chief of Lee & Low Books, Lee's literary sights are loftier, indeed. When he and Thomas Low founded their small, multicultural publishing company in 1991, they had two main goals in mind: to offer top-quality multicultural children's books with contemporary settings, and to encourage new talent—especially authors and illustrators of color.

Philip Lee

The results have been impressive. Award-winning titles include Stephanie Stuve-Bodeen's *Elizabeti's Doll*, illustrated by Christy Hale; Ken Mochizuki's *Baseball Saved Us*, illustrated by Dom Lee; and the much-hailed poetry anthology *In Daddy's Arms I Am Tall*, which earned illustrator Javaka Steptoe the 1998 Coretta Scott King award. The company's website (www.leeandlow.com) offers a wealth of insights regarding Lee & Low's editorial policies, plus information on writing contests and its new emergent reader imprint, Bebop Books.

The affable Lee, who moved to the United States with his family in 1974, has definitely found his niche. Read on.

How did you first get into publishing?
I worked in bookstores since I was in high school, then at the university bookstore when I was in college at University of California, Berkeley, and at several independent bookstores after I graduated. I would say the people I met through working in bookstores were the greatest influence in my career. Some of my bookstore friends moved to New York to work in publishing. I visited them and learned about their work. Sure enough, I liked what I saw. I enrolled in the Radcliffe Publishing Procedures Course, and ended up working in magazine publishing afterwards. I was on the staff of *GQ* (as marketing manager) in 1989 when I met Tom Low.

You went from GQ to publishing children's books?
At the time I met Tom, I'd been in magazine publishing for six years, and wanted to make a change to something that was more meaningful. Tom and I started talking and it turned out he shared my interests. We spent a year just doing research, took publishing courses at New York University, and met with teachers and librarians and booksellers to see what was being published.

This was in 1990—a boom period for children's books, including multicultural books. People told us, "Well, everyone else is doing multicultural books, why would you want to do it?"

But when we started investigating further, we learned that what was published was mostly folklore. We wanted to do stories about people here, people now, stories set in the U.S. That's one angle we felt was not being addressed. We also thought the circle of talent was too narrow, too small. The same established authors and artists were being published everywhere, but it was very hard for a new talent to get published. So it is one of our missions to introduce new authors and artists to the field of children's books.

Have you met your goals?

Since our first list in 1993, we've published 83 authors and illustrators. Out of those, 57 were new to the field. That's two-thirds of our list. That is very exciting to us. Our list continues to grow and we now have over 100 titles in print, in English and Spanish, hardcovers and paperbacks.

However, the field of multicultural children's books has been in a bit of a decline. The number of these books published has decreased three years in a row. That's a great concern to me. Asian-American books have been kind of steady, but there's been a significant decline of African-American, Latino, and Native American books.

Roughly about 5,000 children's books are published each year. The CCBC (Cooperative Children's Book Center) at the University of Wisconsin tracks data on multicultural children's books. They say of all children's books published in 2000, 147 were by or about African-Americans, 54 were Asian-American, 39 were Native American, and 42 were Latino American. That's a total of 288 books out of more than 5,000 published.

Lee & Low title *DeShawn Days*, by Tony Medina, illustrated by R. Gregory Christie, received a starred review in *School Library Journal*: "Told in verse and segmented into descriptive passages . . . Medina's story introduces readers to the world of an African-American boy who lives in the projects. Happy, sad, or scary, the experiences DeShawn shares are vivid, thought-provoking, and insightful." Author Tony Medina came from a world similar to DeShawn's. "I was a skinny brown boy from the projects with asthma, an active imagination, and a grandmother who was there for me."

How do you feel about that?

It's shocking. And disappointing, I have to say. I want people to be more aware of the continued need of multicultural books. It is not a fad. The census data tells us that the U.S. is getting more diverse and publishers need to provide more materials that reflect this diversity. The industry has to do a better job serving this market. We have to start with publishing good books, but also have better distribution systems, finding better markets. A lot of times multicultural books don't sell well because they're sold through traditional markets. Your average Barnes & Noble and Borders are not located in African-American communities, so the readers these books are intended for don't even know they exist. So when mainstream publishers say, "Oh, these books don't sell," it's because the books' primary audiences aren't being reached.

Tell us about the Bebop imprint.

With Bebop Books, we continue our mission, this time applying it to books in the educational market. These are leveled books to fill the needs of teachers. Many of our books are sold in the educational market anyway, so it really made us aware of how we can service that area. We launched these books in November 2000, with 23 titles in English and Spanish. In 2001, we introduced 19 more. These books are still new, but response has been really great. We're very excited about them.

Author Pat Mora edited a collection of poems celebrating the maternal bond for Lee & Low Books. *Love to Mama: A Tribute to Mothers*, illustrated by Paula S. Barragán M., offers poetry from 13 Latino writers, ranging from humorous to poignant. "Although the voices are Latino, the poems and the experiences they encompass will speak to all," says *Kirkus Reviews*, in a starred review. "Abrazos (hugs) for Mora and all the contributors for this one."

Illustration © 2001 Paula S. Barragán M. Reprinted with permission of Lee & Low Books Inc.

Any other new concepts on the horizon?
Well, there's our New Voices Award. Again, it's aimed at continuing our mission of growth and outreach. We started the award specifically to bring in new authors to the field. Last year, we got just around 200 submissions of which we have one winner and two honorees. And in addition, we found a good handful of authors we'll work with on other projects. We're really happy about that. Those interested can learn more about it on our website.

Another thing we're looking into is books about biracial families, or adoptive families—families who adopt children of different races.

Any plans to publish novels?
Not right now, but certainly it's possible at a later time.

Is it more difficult for first-time authors to break in with your company if they are not from the culture they're writing about?
At this point, one third of our authors and artists are not from the culture that they write about. So, certainly, that is not a policy for us. But one of the most important issues for us is authenticity. This comes from authors doing diligent research and showing great sensitivity to the culture that he or she writes about. This does not automatically mean one has to be from that culture to write about it authentically. But we do ask the question, "Why does an author want to write about another culture?" We don't want writers to send us stories just because they think there is a market for them. There has to be a genuine interest and knowledge of the culture before they can write convincingly about it.

It's tricky. It's not that we think race doesn't matter. It does matter. We believe people writing about or illustrating from their own culture are often able to bring something personal to the story that others can't easily research. But we're just not judging a person's ethnic background as the only factor in our selection.
—*Barbara J. Odanaka*

Photography: Buys photos from freelancers. Works on assignment only. Model/property releases required. Submit cover letter, résumé, promo piece and book dummy.
Terms: Pays authors royalty. Offers advances. Pays illustrators royalty plus advance against royalty. Photographers paid royalty plus advance against royalty. Sends galleys to authors; proofs to illustrators. Book catalog available for 9 × 12 SAE and $1.43 postage; ms and art guidelines available via website or with SASE with 34¢ postage.
Tips: "We strongly urge writers to visit our website and familiarize themselves with our list before submitting. Materials will only be returned with SASE."

LEGACY PRESS, Imprint of Rainbow Publishers, P.O. Box 261129, San Diego CA 92196. (858)271-7600. Book publisher. Estab. 1997. **Manuscript/Art Acquisitions:** Christy Allen, editor. Publishes 3 young readers/year; 3 middle readers/year; 3 young adult titles/year. Publishes nonfiction, Bible-teaching books. "We publish growth and development books for the evangelical Christian—from a non-denominational viewpoint—that may be marketed primarily through Christian bookstores."
Nonfiction: Young readers, middle readers, young adults: reference, religion. Recently published *God's Girls* (devotions and crafts for girls age 9-12) and *Gotta Have God* (3-book series of devotionals for boys ages 2-12) both illustrated by Aline Heiser.
How to Contact/Writers: Nonfiction: Submit outline/synopsis and 3-5 sample chapters. Responds to queries in 6 weeks; on ms in 3 months. Publishes a book 18 months after acceptance. Will consider simultaneous submissions and previously published work.
Illustration: Works with 5 illustrators/year. Reviews ms/illustration packages from artists. Submit ms with 5-10 pieces of final art. Illustrations only: Query with samples to be kept on file. Responds in 6 weeks. Samples returned with SASE.

Terms: Pays authors royalty or work purchased outright. Offers advances. Pays illustrators by the project. Sends galley to authors. Book catalog available for business size SASE; ms guidelines for SASE.

Tips: "Get to know the Christian bookstore market. We are looking for innovative ways to teach and encourage children about the Christian life. No fiction, please."

LERNER PUBLICATIONS CO., 241 First Ave. N., Minneapolis MN 55401. (612)332-3344. Fax: (612)332-7615. E-mail: info@lernerbooks.com. Website: www.lernerbooks.com. Book publisher. Estab. 1959. **Manuscript Acquisitions:** Jennifer Zimian, submissions editor. Primarily nonfiction for readers of all grade levels. List includes titles encompassing nature, geography, natural and physical science, current events, ancient and modern history, world art, special interest, sports, world cultures, and numerous biography series. Some YA and middle grade fiction.

How to Contact/Writers: Submissions are accepted in the months of March and October only. Lerner Publications does not publish alphabet books, puzzle books, song books, textbooks, workbooks, religious subject matter or plays. Work received in any month other than March or October will be returned unopened. An SASE is required for authors who wish to have their materials returned. Please allow 2-6 months for a response. No phone calls please.

✓ ▭ ▨ **LIGHTWAVE PUBLISHING**, 26275 98th Ave., Maple Ridge, British Columbia V2W 1K3 Canada. (604)462-7890. Fax: (604)462-8208. E-mail: mikal@lightwavepublishing.com. Website: www.lightwav epublishing.com. **Assistant:** Mikal Marrs. Estab. 1991. Independent book packager/producer specializing in Christian material. Publishes over 30 titles/year. "Our mission is helping parents pass on their Christian faith to their children."

Fiction: Picture books: religion adventure, concept. Young readers: concept, religion. Middle readers: adventure, religion. Young adults: religion.

Nonfiction: Picture books, young readers: activity books, concept, religion. Middle readers, young adults: concept, religion. Average word length: young readers—2,000; middle readers—20,000; young adults—30,000. Recently published *Focus On The Family's Guide to Spiritual Growth of Children*, edited by Osborne, Bruner, Trent; *The Memory Verse Bible*, by K. Christie Bowler.

How to Contact/Writers: Fiction/Nonfiction: Does not accept unsolicited mss. Only interested in writers who will work for hire. Query. Responds to queries in 6 weeks; mss in 2 months. Publishes book 1 year after acceptance.

Illustration: Works with 5-10 illustrators/year. Reviews ms/illustration packages from artists. Submit ms "any way the artist wants to." Contact: Terry Van Roon, art director. Responds only if interested. Samples not returned; samples filed.

Photography: Buys stock and assigns work. Model/property releases required. Uses color prints and digital.

Terms: Work purchased outright from authors. Amount varies. Pays illustrators by the project. Amount varies. Pays photographers by the project. Amount varies. Book catalog available for SASE (Canadian postage or IRC). Writer's guidelines available for SASE (Canadian postage or IRC). Catalog available on website.

Tips: "We only do work-for-hire writing and illustrating. We have our own projects and ideas then find writers and illustrators to help create them. No royalties. Interested writers and illustrators are welcome to contact us. Please don't put U.S. stamps on SASE."

▣ **LINNET BOOKS**, Imprint of The Shoe String Press Inc., 2 Linsley St., North Haven CT 06473-2517. (203)239-2702. Fax: (203)239-2568. E-mail: books@shoestringpress.com. Website: www.shoestringpress.com or www.linnetbooks.com. Estab. 1952. Specializes in nonfiction, educational material, multicultural material. **Manuscript Acquisitions:** Diantha C. Thorpe. Imprints: Linnet Books, Linnet Professional Publications, Archon Books—Diantha C. Thorpe, acquisitions for all. Publishes 12-15 books/year.

Nonfiction: Young readers: activity books, animal. Middle readers: animal, biography, geography, history, multicultural, music/dance, nature/environment, reference, science. Young adults: biography, history, multicultural, nature/environment, reference. Recently published *Chaucer's England*, by Diana Childress; *Four to The Pole! The American Women's Expedition to Antarctica 1992-93*, by Nancy Loewen and Ann Bancroft; *Tragic Prelude: Bleeding Kansas*, by Karen Zeinert.

How to Contact/Writers: Manuscript guidelines on website. Nonfiction: Query or submit outline/synopsis and 3 sample chapters. Responds to queries in 6 weeks; mss in 4 months. Publishes a book 1 year after receipt of edited ms. Will consider simultaneous submissions "only if, when we indicate serious interest, the author withdraws from other publishers."

Illustration: Uses mainly b&w artwork. Illustrations only: Query with samples. "We keep on file—send only disposable ones."

Photography: Buys stock. "We keep work on file, but generally our authors are responsible for photo illustrations." Uses 5×7 glossy b&w prints. Send "anything that tells us what you specialize in."

Terms: Pays authors variable royalty. Offers advances. Sends galleys to authors. Book catalog available annually.

N LION BOOKS, PUBLISHER, Suite B, 210 Nelson, Scarsdale NY 10583. (914)725-2280. Fax: (914)725-3572. Imprint of Sayre Ross Co. Book publisher. **Acquisitions:** Harriet Ross. Publishes 5 middle readers/year; 10 young adults/year. 50-70% of books by first-time authors. Publishes books "with ethnic and minority accents for young adults, including a variety of craft titles dealing with African and Asian concepts."
Nonfiction: Activity, art/crafts, biography, history, hobbies, how-to, multicultural. Average word length: young adult—30,000-50,000.
How to Contact/Writers: Query, submit complete ms. Responds to queries in 3 weeks; ms in 2 months.
Illustration: Responds in 2 weeks.
Terms: Work purchased outright (range: $500-5,000). Average advance: $1,000-2,500. Illustrators paid $500-1,500. Sends galleys to author. Book catalog free on request.

A LITTLE, BROWN AND COMPANY CHILDREN'S BOOKS, Three Center Plaza, Boston MA 02108-2084. (617)227-0730. Website: www.twbookmark.com. Book publisher. Estab. 1837. **Editorial Director:** Maria Modugno. Art Director: Sheila Smallwood. Editorial Director of Megan Tingley Books: Megan Tingley; Senior Editor: Cynthia Eagan; Managing Editor: Ann-Marie Simundson. Publishes picture books, board books, pop-up and lift-the-flap editions, chapter books and general fiction and nonfiction titles for middle and young adult readers.
● Little, Brown does not accept unsolicited mss. See the listing for their newest imprint Megan Tingley Books.
Fiction: Picture books: adventure, animal, contemporary, fantasy, folktales, history, humor, multicultural, nature/environment. Young adults: contemporary, health, humor, multicultural, nature/environment, suspense/mystery. Multicultural needs include "any material by, for and about minorities." Average word length: picture books—1,000; young readers—6,000; middle readers—15,000-25,000; young adults—20,000-40,000. Recently published *Cirque du Freak: The Vampire's Assistant*, by Darren Shan (ages 10 and up); *The Magical, Mystical, Marvelous Coat*, by Catherine Ann Cullen (ages 4-8; picture book); *Toot and Puddle: I'll be Home for Christmas*, by Holly Hobbie (ages 4-8; picture book).
Nonfiction: Picture books: nature/environment, sciences. Middle readers: arts/crafts, biography, history, multicultural, nature, self help, social issues, sports. Young adults: multicultural, self-help, social issues. Average word length: picture books—2,000; young readers—4,000-6,000; middle readers—15,000-25,000; young adults—20,000-40,000. Recently published *Baby on the Way*, by Dr. William Sears (ages 4-8); *The Big Dig: Reshaping An American City*, by Peter Vanderwarker (ages 9 and up; photo essay).
How to Contact/Writers: Only interested in agented material. Fiction: Submit complete ms. Nonfiction: Submit cover letter, previous publications, a proposal, outline and 3 sample chapters. Do not send originals. Responds to queries in 2 weeks. Responds to mss in 2 months.
Illustration: Works with 55 illustrators/year. Illustrations only: Query art director or managing editor with samples; provide résumé, promo sheet or tearsheets to be kept on file. Responds to art samples in 2 months. Original artwork returned at job's completion.
Photography: Works on assignment only. Model/property releases required; captions required. Publishes photo essays and photo concept books. Uses 35mm transparencies. Photographers should provide résumé, promo sheets or tearsheets to be kept on file.
Terms: Pays authors royalties based on retail price. Pays illustrators and photographers by the project or royalty based on retail price. Sends galleys to authors; dummies to illustrators. Artist's and writer's guidelines for SASE.
Tips: "Publishers are cutting back their lists in response to a shrinking market and relying more on big names and known commodities. In order to break into the field these days, authors and illustrators research their competition and try to come up with something outstandingly different."

LOBSTER PRESS, 1620 Shererooke St. W., Suite C&C, Montréal, Quebec H3H 1C9 Canada. (514)904-1100. Fax: (514)904-1101. E-mail: editorial@lobsterpress.com. Website: www.lobsterpress.com. Estab. 1997. **Editorial Assistant:** Maria Simpson. Publishes 4 picture books/year; 4 young reader/year. Encourages books by first-time authors.
Fiction: Picture books, young readers, middle readers: adventure, animal, contemporary, health, history, multicultural, special needs, sports, suspense/mystery. Average word length: picture books—200-1,000. Recently published *From Poppa*, by Anne Carter, illustrated by Kasia Charko; *How Cold Was It*, by Jane Barclay, illustrated by Janice Donato; *Smarty Pants*, by Colleen Syder, illustrated by Suzane Lanelois; *When Pigs Fly*, by Valerie Coupman, illustrated by Rogé.
Nonfiction: Young readers, middle readers and adults/teens: animal, biography, careers, geography, health, history, hobbies, how-to, multicultural, nature/environment, references, science, self-help, social issues, sports, travel. Average word length: middle readers—40,000. Recently published *The Lobster Kids' Guide to Exploring Montréal*, by John Symon; *The Lobster Kids' Guide to Exploring Ottawa-Hull*, by John Symon; *The Sex Book*, by Jane Pavanel.
How to Contact/Writers: Fiction: submit complete ms. Nonfiction: submit complete ms or submit outline/synopsis and 2 sample chapters. Responds to queries in 4 months; mss in 1 year. Publishes a book 18 months after acceptance.

Illustration: Works with 5 illustrators/year. Uses line drawings and color artwork. Reviews ms/illustration packages from artists. Query with samples. Contact: Maria Simpson. Illustrations only: query with samples. Samples not returned; samples kept on file.

Terms: Pays authors 5-10% royalty based on retail price. Offers advances (average amount: $750-1,000). Pays illustrators by the project (range: $1,000-2,000) or 2-7% royalty based on retail price. Sends galleys to authors; dummies to illustrators. Originals returned to artist at job's completion. Writer's and artist's guidelines available for SASE.

Tips: "Do not send manuscripts or samples registered mail or with fancy envelopes or bows and ribbons—everything is received and treated equally. Please do not call and ask for an appointment. We do not meet with anyone unless we are going to use their work."

MAGINATION PRESS, 750 First Street NE, Washington DC 20002-2984. Website: www.maginationpress.com. Book publisher. **Acquisitions:** Darcie Conner Johnston, managing editor. Publishes up to 15 picture books and young reader titles/year. "We publish books dealing with the psycho/therapeutic treatment or resolution of children's serious problems and psychological issues, many written by mental health professionals."

● Magination Press is an imprint of the American Psychological Association.

Fiction: Picture books, young readers, middle readers, young adult/teens: concept, health, mental health, multi-cultural, special needs. Recently published *Maybe Days: A Book for Children in Foster Care* (ages 4-8), by Jennifer Wilgocki; *What Can I Do? A Book for Children of Divorce* (ages 8-12), by Danielle Lowry; *Mom, Dad, Come Back Soon* (ages 3-8), by Debra Pappas; *Oho Learns About His Medicine, 3rd Ed.*, by Matthew Galvin M.D.

Nonfiction: Picture books, young readers: concept, health, mental health, multicultural, psychotherapy, self-help, social issues, special needs.

How to Contact/Writers: Fiction/nonfiction: Submit complete ms or query. Responds to queries/mss in 6 months. Materials returned only with a SASE. Publishes a book 12-18 months after acceptance.

Illustration: Works with 10-15 illustrators/year. Reviews ms/illustration packages. Will review artwork for future assignments. We keep all samples on file.

How to Contact/Illustrators: Illustrations only: Query with samples. Original artwork returned at job's completion.

Terms: Pays authors 5-15% in royalties based on receipts minus returns. Pays illustrators by the project. Book catalog and ms guidelines on request with SASE.

⃞N⃞ MAVAL PUBLISHING, INC., Imprint of Editora Maval, 567 Harrison St., Denver CO 80206. (303)320-1035. Fax: (303)320-1546. E-mail: maval@maval.com. Website: www.maval.com. Book publisher. Estab. 1991. **Acquisitions:** George Waintrub, manager; Mary Hernandez, manuscripts coordinator. Publishes 10 picture books/year. 50% of books by first-time authors.

Fiction: Picture books, young readers, middle readers: adventure, animal, anthology, contemporary, fantasy, health, history, multicultural, nature/environment. Picture books, young readers: concept. Picture books: folktales, sports.

Nonfiction Picture books, young readers, middle readers: adventure, animal, anthology, contemporary, fantasy, health, history, multicultural, nature/environment. Picture books, Young readers: concept. Picture books: folktales, sports.

How to Contact/Writers: Fiction/Nonfiction: Submit outline/synopsis and 1-2 sample chapters. Responds to queries/mss in 2-3 months. Publishes a book 6-12 months after acceptance. Will consider simultaneous submissions and previously published work.

Illustration: Works with 2 illustrators/year. Reviews ms/illustration packages from artists. Submit manuscript with 1-2 pieces of final art. Contact: George Waintrub, manager. Illustrations only: Query with samples. Contact: George Waintrub, manager. Responds in 1-2 months. Samples not returned.

Photography: Buys stock.

Terms: Pays authors royalty of 5-7% based on retail price. Pays illustrators royalty of 5-7%. Book catalog and writer's guidelines available for SASE. All imprints included in a single catalog. Catalog available on website.

MARGARET K. McELDERRY BOOKS, 1230 Sixth Ave., New York NY 10020. (212)698-2761. Fax: (212)698-2796. Website: www.simonsays.com/kidzone. Imprint of Simon & Schuster Children's Publishing Division. Editor at Large: Margaret K. McElderry. **Manuscript Acquisitions:** Emma D. Dryden, editorial director. **Art Acquisitions:** Ann Bobco, executive art director. Publishes 10-12 picture books/year; 2-4 young reader titles/year; 8-10 middle reader titles/year; and 5-7 young adult titles/year. 10% of books by first-time authors; 33% of books from agented writers. "Margaret K. McElderry Books publishes original hardcover trade books for children from pre-school age through young adult. This list includes picture books, easy-to-read books, and fiction for eight to twelve-year-olds, poetry, fantasy and young adult fiction. The style and subject matter of the books we publish is almost unlimited. We do not publish textbooks, coloring and activity books, greeting cards, magazines and pamphlets or religious publications."

● Margaret K. McElderry Books is not currently accepting unsolicited mss. Send queries only for picture books. Send queries and 3 sample chapters for middle grade and young adult projects; also looking for strong poetry.

Fiction: Young readers: adventure, contemporary, fantasy, history. Middle readers: adventure, contemporary, fantasy, humor, mystery. Young adults: contemporary, fantasy, mystery, poetry. "Always interested in publishing humorous picture books and original beginning reader stories." Average word length: picture books—500; young readers—2,000; middle readers—10,000-20,000; young adults—45,000-50,000. Recently published *Mrs. McTats and Her Houseful of Cats*, by Alyssa Capscalli and Joan Rankin; *Understanding Buddy*, by Marc Kornblatt, *Ghandhi*, by Demi; *The Year of Miss Agnes*, by Kirkpatrick Hill.

Nonfiction: Young readers, young adult teens, biography, history. Average word length: picture books—500-1,000; young readers—1,500-3,000; middle readers—10,000-20,000; young adults—30,000-45,000. *Shout, Sister, Shout!*, by Roxane Orgill.

How to Contact/Writers: Fiction/nonfiction: Submit query and sample chapters with SASE; may also include brief résumé of previous publishing credits. Responds to queries in 3 weeks; mss in 4 months. Publishes a book 18 months after contract signing. Will consider simultaneous submissions (only if indicated as such).

Illustration: Works with 20-30 illustrators/year. Query with samples; provide promo sheet or tearsheets; arrange personal portfolio review. Contact: Ann Bobco, executive art director. Responds to art samples in 3 months. Samples returned with SASE or samples filed.

Terms: Pays authors royalty based on retail price. Pay illustrators royalty based on retail price. Pays photographers by the project. Sends galleys to authors; dummies to illustrators. Original artwork returned at job's completion. Ms guidelines free on request with SASE.

Tips: "We're looking for strong, original fiction. We are always interested in picture books for the youngest age reader."

MEADOWBROOK PRESS, 5451 Smetana Dr., Minnetonka MN 55343. (952)930-1100. Fax: (952)930-1940. Website: www.meadowbrookpress.com. Book publisher. **Manuscript Acquisitions:** Angela Wiechmann, submissions editor. **Art Acquisitions:** Paul Woods, art director. Publishes 1-2 middle readers/year; and 2-4 young readers/year. 20% of books by first-time authors; 10% of books from agented writers. Publishes children's activity books, arts-and-crafts books and how to books.

● Meadowbrook does not accept unsolicited children's picture books, short stories or novels. They are primarily a nonfiction press. The publisher offers specific guidelines for children's poetry. Be sure to specify the type of project you have in mind when requesting guidelines.

Nonfiction: Young readers, middle readers: activity books, arts/crafts, hobbies, how-to, multicultural, self help. Average word length: varies. Recently published *Storybook Parties* (party book); *Free Stuff for Kids* (activity book); and *Picture Book Activities*.

How to Contact/Writers: Nonfiction: Query or submit outline/synopsis with SASE. Responds to queries in 3 months. Publishes a book 1-2 years after acceptance. Send a business-sized SASE and 2 first-class stamps for free writer's guidelines and book catalog before submitting ideas. Will consider simultaneous submissions.

Illustration: Works with 10-12 illustrators/year. Reviews ms/illustration packages from artists. Submit ms with 2-3 pieces of nonreturnable samples. Illustrations only: Responds only if interested. Samples filed.

Photography: Buys photos from freelancers. Buys stock. Model/property releases required. Submit cover letter.

Terms: Pays authors in royalties of 5-7½% based on retail price. Offers average advance payment of $2,000-4,000. Pays illustrators per project. Pays photographers per photo. Originals returned at job's completion. Book catalog available for 5×11 SASE and 2 first-class stamps; ms guidelines and artists guidelines available for SASE.

Tips: "Illustrators and writers should send away for our free catalog and guidelines before submitting their work to us. Also, illustrators should take a look at the books we publish to determine whether their style is consistent with what we are looking for. Writers should also note the style and content patterns of our books. For instance, our children's poetry anthologies contain primarily humorous, rhyming poems with a strong rhythm; therefore, we would not likely publish a free-verse and/or serious poem. I also recommend that writers, especially poets, have their work read by a critical, objective person before they submit anywhere. Also, please correspond with us by mail before telephoning with questions about your submission. We work with the printed word and will respond more effectively to your questions if we have something in front of us."

MERIWETHER PUBLISHING LTD., 885 Elkton Dr., Colorado Springs CO 80907-3557. Fax: (719)594-9916. E-mail: merpeds@aol.com. Website: www.meriwetherpublishing.com. Book publisher. Estab. 1969. Executive Editor: Arthur L. Zapel. **Manuscript Acquisitions:** Ted Zapel, educational drama; Rhonda Wray, religious drama. "We do most of our artwork in-house; we do not publish for the children's elementary market." 75% of books by first-time authors; 5% of books from agented writers. "Our niche is drama. Our books cover a wide variety of theatre subjects from play anthologies to theatrecraft. We publish books of monologs, duologs, short

THE SUBJECT INDEX, located in the back of this book, lists book publishers and magazines according to the fiction and nonfiction subjects they seek.

one-act plays, scenes for students, acting textbooks, how-to speech and theatre textbooks, improvisation and theatre games. Our Christian books cover worship on such topics as clown ministry, storytelling, banner-making, drama ministry, children's worship and more. We also publish anthologies of Christian sketches. We do not publish works of fiction or devotionals."

Fiction: Middle readers, young adults: anthology, contemporary, humor, religion. "We publish plays, not prose-fiction."

Nonfiction: Middle readers: activity books, how-to, religion, textbooks. Young adults: activity books, drama/theater arts, how-to church activities, religion. Average length: 250 pages. Recently published *Grammar Wars* by Tom Ready (language arts) and *Worship Sketches 2 Perform* by Steven James.

How to Contact/Writers: Nonfiction: Query or submit outline/synopsis and sample chapters. Responds to queries in 3 weeks; mss in 2 months. Publishes a book 6-12 months after acceptance. Will consider simultaneous submissions.

Illustration: Works with 2 illustrators/year. Query first. Query with samples; send résumé, promo sheet or tearsheets. Samples returned with SASE. Samples kept on file. Originals returned at job's completion.

Terms: Pays authors in royalties of 10% based on retail or wholesale price. Outright purchase $200-1,000. Royalties based on retail or wholesale price. Book catalog for SAE and $2 postage; ms guidelines for SAE and 1 first-class stamp.

Tips: "We are currently interested in finding unique treatments for theater arts subjects: scene books, how-to books, musical comedy scripts, monologs and short plays for teens."

MILKWEED EDITIONS, 1011 Washington Ave. S., Suite 300, Minneapolis MN 55415-1246. (612)332-3192. Fax: (612)215-2550. E-mail: editor@milkweed.org. Website: www.milkweed.org. Book Publisher. Estab. 1980. **Manuscript Acquisitions:** Emilie Buchwald, publisher; Elizabeth Fitz, manuscript coordinator. **Art Acquisitions:** Dale Cooney. Publishes 3-4 middle readers/year. 25% of books by first-time authors. "Milkweed Editions publishes with the intention of making a humane impact on society, in the belief that literature is a transformative art uniquely able to convey the essential experiences of the human heart and spirit. To that end, Milkweed Editions publishes distinctive voices of literary merit in handsomely designed, visually dynamic books, exploring the ethical, cultural, and esthetic issues that free societies need continually to address."

Fiction: Middle readers: adventure, contemporary, fantasy, multicultural, nature/environment, suspense/mystery. Does not want to see anthologies, folktales, health, hi-lo, picture books, poetry, religion, romance, sports. Average length: middle readers—90-200 pages. Recently published *The $66 Summer*, by John Armistead (multicultural, mystery); *The Ocean Within*, by V.M. Caldwell (contemporary, nature); *No Place*, by Kay Haugaard (multicultural).

How to Contact/Writers: Fiction: Submit complete ms. Responds to mss in 6 months. Publishes a book 1 year after acceptance. Will consider simultaneous submissions.

Illustration: Works with 2-4 illustrators/year. Reviews ms/illustration packages from artists. Query; submit ms with dummy. Illustrations only: Query with samples; provide résumé, promo sheet, slides, tearsheets and client list. Samples filed or returned with SASE; samples filed. Originals returned at job's completion.

Terms: Pays authors royalty of 7½% based on retail price. Offers advance against royalties. Illustrators' contracts are decided on an individual basis. Sends galleys to authors. Book catalog available for $1.50 to cover postage; ms guidelines available for SASE or at new www.milkweed.org. Must include SASE with ms submission for its return.

THE MILLBROOK PRESS, P.O. Box 335, 2 Old New Milford Rd., Brookfield CT 06804. (203)740-2220. Fax: (203)775-5643. Website: www.millbrookpress.com. Book publisher. Estab. 1989. **Manuscript Acquisitions:** Editorial Assistant. **Art Acquisitions:** Associate Art Director. Publishes 20 picture books/year; 40 young readers/year; 50 middle readers/year; and 10 young adult titles/year. 10% of books by first-time authors; 20% of books from agented authors. Publishes nonfiction, concept-oriented/educational books. Publishes under Twenty-First Century Books imprint also.

Nonfiction: All levels: animal, arts/craft, biography, cooking, geography, how-to, multicultural, music/dance, nature/environment, reference, science. Middle readers: hi-lo, social issues, sports. Young adults: careers, social issues. No poetry. Average word length: young readers—5,000; middle readers—10,000; young adult/teens—20,000. Published *Wildshots: The World of the Wildlife Photographer*, by Nathan Aaseng (grades 5-8, nature and photography); *Meet My Grandmother: She's A Children's Book Author*, by Lisa Tucker McElroy, photographs by Joel Benjamin (grades 2-4, current events/history); *Little Numbers*, by Edward Packard, illustrated by Sal Murdocca (grades K-3, math/concepts); *Crafts From Your Favorite Children's Songs*, by Kathy Ross, illustrated by Vicky Enright (grades K-3, arts and crafts); *Adoption Today*, by Ann E. Weiss (grade 7-up, social studies). No fiction, picture books, activity books or other novelty submissions.

How to Contact/Writers: Send for guidelines w/SASE *before* submitting. We do not accept certain manuscripts, guidelines give specific instructions.

Illustration: Work with approximately 30 illustrators/year. Illustrations only: Query with samples; provide résumé, business card, promotional literature or tearsheets to be kept on file. No samples returned. Samples filed. Responds only if interested.

Photography: Buys photos from freelancers. Buys stock and assigns work.

Implementing her capricious signature style for Millbrook Press, illustrator Sharon Hawkins Vargo designed *Señor Felipe's Alphabet Adventure* with expert renderings of highly animated people and animals. Perhaps taking inspiration from her four children and parakeet, she also illustrated *Make Yourself A Monster* and the Play-Doh™ crafts series by Kathy Ross, which were recently published by Millbrook Press.

Terms: Pays author royalty of 5-7½% based on wholesale price or work purchased outright. Offers advances. Pays illustrators by the project, royalty of 3-7% based on wholesale price. Sends galleys to authors. Manuscript and artist's guidelines for SASE. Address to: Manuscript Guidelines, The Millbrook Press . . . Book catalog for 9×11 SASE. Address to: Catalogues, The Millbrook Press . . .

MIRACLE SOUND PRODUCTIONS, INC., 1560 W. Bay Area Blvd., Suite 110, Friendswood TX 77546-2668. (281)286-4575. Fax: (281)286-0009. E-mail: imsworldwd@aol.com. Website: www.storyangel.com. Book publisher. **Acquisitions:** Trey Boring, director of special projects. Estab. 1997. Publishes 2 young readers/year. 100% of books by first-time authors. Miracle Sound Productions is best known for "positive family values in multimedia products."
Fiction: Young readers. Average word length: young readers—500. Recently published *CoCo's Luck*, by Warren Chaney and Don Boyer (ages 3-8, Read-A-Long book and tape).
Illustration: Only interested in agented material. Works with 1 illustrator/year. Uses color artwork only. Reviews ms/illustration packages from artists. Submit ms with dummy. Contact: Trey W. Boring, director, special projects. Illustrations only: Send résumé and portfolio to be kept on file.
Photography: Works on assignment only. Contact: Trey W. Boring, director, special projects.
Terms: Payment negotiable for authors, illustrators and photographers.

■ MITCHELL LANE PUBLISHERS, INC., P.O. Box 619, Bear DE 19701. (302)834-9646. Fax: (302)834-4164. E-mail: mitchelllane@eclipsetel.com. Website: www.angelfire.com/biz/mitchelllane/index.html. Book publisher. **Acquisitons:** Barbara Mitchell, president. Publishes 20 young adult titles/year. "We publish multicultural biographies of role models for children and young adults."
Nonfiction: Young readers, middle readers, young adults: biography, multicultural. Average word length: 4,000-50,000 words. Recently published *Marc Anthony*, by John Torres; *Dr. Seuss*, by Ann Gaines (real-life reader biographies); and *The Development of the Web Browser*, by Kathleen Tracy (Unlocking the Secrets of Science series).
How to Contact/Writers: Nonfiction: Query or submit outline/synopsis and 3 sample chapters. Responds to queries only if interested. Publishes a book 18 months after acceptance. Most assignments are work-for-hire.
Illustration: Works with 2-3 illustrators/year. Reviews ms/illustration packages from artists. Query. Illustration only: query with samples; arrange personal portfolio review; send résumé, portfolio, slides, tearsheets. Responds only if interested. Samples not returned; samples filed.
Photography: Buys stock images. Needs photos of famous and prominent minority figures. Captions required. Uses b&w prints. Submit cover letter, résumé, published samples, stock photo list.
Terms: Pays authors 5-10% royalty based on wholesale price or work purchased outright for $250-2,000. Pays illustrators by the project (range: $40-250). Sends galleys to authors.
Tips: "Most of our assignments are work-for-hire. Submit résumé and samples of work to be considered for future assignments."

Ⓐ MONDO PUBLISHING, 980 Avenue of the Americas, New York NY 10018. (212)268-3560. Fax: (212)268-3561. Website: www.mondopub.com. Book publisher. **Acquisitions:** editorial staff. Publishes 60 picture and chapter books/year. 10% of books by first-time authors. Publishes various categories. "Our motto is 'creative minds creating ways to create lifelong readers.' We publish for both educational and trade markets, aiming for the highest quality books for both."
  ● Mondo Publishing only accepts agented material.
Fiction: Picture books, young readers, middle readers: adventure, animal, contemporary, fantasy, folktales, history, humor, multicultural, nature/environment, poetry, sports. Multicultural needs include: stories about children in different cultures or about children of different backgrounds in a U.S. setting. Recently published *You Don't Look Like Your Mother*, by Aileen Fisher (ages 4-8) and *A Lion for Michael*, by Uri Orley.
Nonfiction: Picture books, young readers, middle readers: animal, biography, geography, how-to, multicultural, nature/environment, science, sports. Recently published *Touch the Earth*, by Jane Baskwill (ages 6-10); and *Thinking About Ants*, by Barbara Brenner (ages 5-10, animals).
How to Contact/Writers: Accepting mss from agented or previously published writers only. Fiction/Nonfiction: Query or submit complete ms. Responds to queries in 1 month; mss in 6 months. Will consider simultaneous submissions. Mss returned with SASE. Queries must also have SASE.
Illustration: Works with 40 illustrators/year. Reviews ms/illustration packages from illustrators. Illustration only: Query with samples, résumé, portfolio. Responds only if interested. Samples returned with SASE; samples filed. Send attention: Art Deptartment.
Photography: Occasionally uses freelance photographers. Buys stock images. Uses mostly nature photos. Uses color prints, transparencies.
Terms: Pays authors royalty of 2-5% based on wholesale/retail price. Offers advance based on project. Pays illustrators by the project (range: 3,000-9,000), royalty of 2-4% based on retail price. Pays photographers by the project or per photo. Sends galleys to authors depending on project. Originals returned to artists at job's completion. Book catalogs available for 9×12 SASE with $3.20 postage.

Tips: "Prefer illustrators with book experience or a good deal of experience in illustration projects requiring consistency of characters and/or setting over several illustrations. Prefer manuscripts targeted to trade market plus crossover to educational market."

⊞ MOON MOUNTAIN PUBLISHING, 80 Peachtree Rd., North Kingstown RI 02852. (401)884-6703. Fax: (401)884-7076. E-mail: hello@moonmoutainpub.com. Website: www.moonmountainpub.com. Estab. 1999. Specializes in picture book fiction. **Manuscript Acquisitions:** Robert Holtzman. **Art Acquisitions:** Cate Monroe, publisher. Publishes 5 picture books/year. 50% of books by first-time authors. "We are a publisher of children's picture books. We are open to submissions of fiction manuscripts (including complete text/illustration packages) that lend themselves to picture book illustration and design. We publish books with positive, life-affirming themes. We strive to encourage the following qualities in children: kindness, honor, love, respect, courge, dedication, comfort, contentment, hope, intelligence, talent, creativity and imagination."
Fiction: Picture books: adventure, animal, concept, contemporary, fantasy, folktales, humor, multicultural, nature/environment. Average word length: picture books—200-2,000 words. Recently published *Hamlet & the Magnificent Sandcastle*, by Brian Lies (ages 5-8, picture book fiction); *Petronella*, by Jay Williams, illustrated by Margaret Oryan-Kean (age 8-12, picture book fiction); and *Hello Willow*, by Kimberly Poulton, illustrated by Jennifer O'Keefe (ages 0-5, picture book fiction).
How to Contact/Writers: Fiction: Submit complete ms. Responds to queries in 2 months; mss in 3 months. Publishes a book 1-3 years after acceptance. Will consider simultaneous submissions.
Illustration: Works with 9 illustrators/year. Uses color artwork only. Reviews ms/illustration packages from artists. Send ms with dummy or submit ms with 3-4 pieces of final art. Contact: Robert Holtzman, editor. Illustrations only: Query with samples; send promo sheet, portfolio and slides. Contact: Cate Monroe, publisher. Responds only if interested. Samples returned with SASE; samples filed.
Photography: Works on assignment only.
Terms: Pays authors royalty. Offers advances. Pays illustrators royalty and advance. Originals returned to artist at job's completion. Book catalog available for #10 SAE and 1 first-class stamp; ms guidelines available for SASE. Catalog available on website.

☑ MOREHOUSE PUBLISHING CO., 4775 Linglestown Rd., Harrisburg PA 17112. (717)541-8130. Fax: (717)541-8136. E-mail: dfarring@morehousegroup.com. Website: www.morehousegroup.com. Book publisher. Estab. 1884. **Manuscript Acquisitions:** Debra Farrington, editorial director. **Art Acquisitions:** Debbie Dortch, managing editor. Publishes 4-6 picture books/year. 25% of books by first-time authors.
Fiction: Picture Books: spirituality, religion. Wants to see new and creative approaches to theology for children. Recently published *Bless This Day*, by Anne E. Kitch, illustrated by Joni Oeltjenbruns.
Nonfiction: Picture Books: religion and prayers.
How to Contact/Writers: Fiction/nonfiction: Submit ms (1,500 word limit). Responds to mss in 2 months. Publishes a book 2 years after acceptance.
Illustration: Works with 2-3 illustrators/year. Reviews ms/illustration packages from artists. Submit résumé, tearsheets. Samples returned with SASE; samples filed.
Terms: Pays authors royalty based on net price. Offers modest advance payment. Pays illustrators royalty based on net price. Sends galleys to authors. Book catalog free on request if SASE ($2 postage) is supplied.
Tips: "Morehouse Publishing seeks books that wrestle with important theological questions in words and images that children can relate to and understand."

☑ MORGAN REYNOLDS PUBLISHING, 620 S. Elm St., Suite 223, Greensboro NC 27406. (336)275-1311. Fax: (336)275-1152. E-mail: editorial@morganreynolds.com. Website: www.morganreynolds.com. **Acquisitions:** Laura Shoemaker, editor. Book publisher. Publishes 18 young adult titles/year. 50% of books by first-time authors. Morgan Reynolds publishes nonfiction books for juvenile and young adult readers. We prefer lively, well-written biographies of interesting figures for our biography series. Subjects may be contemporary or historical. Books for our Great Events series should depict insightful and exciting looks at critical periods.
Nonfiction: Middle readers, young adults/teens: biography, history. Average word length: 17,000-20,000. Recently published *Dwight D. Eisenhower: Soldier and President*, by Jeff C. Young; and *Failure is Impossible: The Story of Susan B. Anthony*, by Lisa Frederiksen Bohannon.
How to Contact/Writers: Prefers to see entire ms. Query; submit outline/synopsis with 3 sample chapters. Responds to queries in 6 weeks; mss in 6 weeks. Publishes a book 1 year after acceptance. Will consider simultaneous submissions.
Terms: Pays authors negotiated price. Offers advances. Sends galleys to authors. Ms guidelines available for SASE. Visit website for complete catalog.
Tips: "Familiarize yourself with our titles before sending a query or submission. Visit our website."

⊞ MY CHAOTIC LIFE, Imprint of Walter Foster Publishing, 23062 La Cadena Dr., Laguna Hills CA 92653. (949)380-7510. Fax: (949)380-7575. Website: www.mychaoticlife.com. Estab. 2000. **Manuscript Acquisitions:** Sydney Sprague. **Art Acquisitions:** Shirley Dutchover-Kawabuchi, art direct/designer. Publishes 3-6 young readers; 7-10 young adult titles/year.

Nonfiction: Young readers, middle readers, young adults: activity books, concept, journals/memory books. Average word length: young readers—2,000-5,000 (depending on book format); young adults—3,000-5,000 (depending on book format). Recently published *A Kid's Travel Journal*, written by the creative staff, illustrated by Ali Douglass (age over 8, interactive memory journal—planner and memory book); *School Daze*, written by the creative staff, illustrated by Neryl Walker (age over 13, interactive memory journal—personal guided journal of high school years); and *What's Happening!*, written by the creative staff (age over 12, entertainment review journal).

How to Contact: Nonfiction: Query or submit outline/synopsis. Responds only if interested. Publishes a book 6-9 months after acceptance.

Illustration: Works with 6-12 illustrators/year. Uses color artwork only. Reviews ms/illustration packages from artists. Query with samples. Contact: Sydney Sprague, associate publisher. Illustrations only: Query with samples. Contact: Shirley Dutchover-Kawabuchi, art director. Responds only if interested. Samples not returned; samples filed.

Terms: Work purchased outright from authors. Pays illustrators by the project. Originals returned to artist at job's completion. Catalog available on website.

Tips: "It's important that our books have a broad appeal, so we're interested in common subjects. But we're also interested in qualities that distinguish our books from others on the market, including multicultural illustrations, fun activities, and text with a sassy/humorous edge. Please review the style and attitude of our publications before submitting your ideas, manuscripts, or illustrations."

N: NEW CANAAN PUBLISHING COMPANY INC., P.O. Box 752, New Canaan CT 06840. Phone/Fax: (203)966-3408. E-mail: djm@newcanaanpublishing.com. Website: www.newcanaanpublishing.com. Book publisher. Vice President: Kathy Mittelstadt. Publishes 2 picture books/year; 2 young readers/year; 2 middle readers/year; and 2 young adult titles/year. 50% of books by first-time authors. "We seek books with strong educational or traditional moral content and books with Christian themes."

Fiction: All levels: adventure, history, religion (Christianity), suspense/mystery. Picture books: phonics readers. "Stories about disfunctional families are not encouraged." Average word length: picture books—1,000-3,000; young readers—8,000-30,000; middle readers—8,000-40,000; young adults—15,000-50,000. Recently published *Journey to the Edge of Nowhere*, by Janet Baird; *Rainbows and Other Promises*, by Laurie Swinwood; *Olive, The Orphan Reindeer*, by Michael Christie, illustrated by Margeaux Lucas.

Nonfiction: All levels: geography, history, how-to, reference, religion (Christian only), textbooks. Average word length: picture books—1,000-3,000; young readers—8,000-30,000; middle readers—8,000-40,000; young adults—15,000-50,000.

How to Contact/Writers: Submit outline/synopsis or complete ms with biographical information and writing credentials. Responds to queries in 4-6 months; mss in 6 months. Publishes a book 12-18 months after acceptance. Will consider electronic submissions via disk or modem.

Illustration: Works with 3-5 illustrators/year. Reviews ms/illustration packages from artists. Query or send ms with dummy. Illustrations only: Query with samples; send résumé, promo sheet. Responds in 1-2 months. Samples returned with SASE.

Terms: Pays authors royalty of 7-12% based on wholesale price. Royalty may be shared with illustrator where relevant. Pays illustrators royalty of 4-6% as share of total royalties. Book catalog available for SAE; ms guidelines available for SASE.

Tips: "We are diligent but small, so please be patient."

N: NORTH LIGHT BOOKS, Imprint of F&W Publications, 1507 Dana Ave., Cincinnati OH 45207. (513)531-2690. Fax: (513)531-7107. E-mail: MaggieM@fwpubs.com. Website: www.artistsnetwork.com. Trade book publisher specializing in nonfiction. **Acquisitions Editor:** Maggie Moschell. Publishes 2 picture books/year; 2 young reader/year; 2 middle readers/year; and 2 young adult titles/year. 100% of books by first-time authors.

Nonfiction: All levels: Arts/Crafts. Average word length: nonfiction—7,500 words. Recently published: *Artistic Drawing*, by Kat Rakel-Ferguson (ages 6-9, fine art); *Creative Painting*, by Kat Rakel-Ferguson (ages 6-9, fine art); and *Painting on Rocks for Kids*, by Lin Welford.

How to Contact/Writers: Query with project/craft samples. Responds to queries/mss in 2 months. Will consider simultaneous submissions and electronic submissions via disk or modem. Book published 18 months after acceptance.

Terms: Authors paid flat fee or royalty; negotiable. Offers advance (average amount: $2,000). Original projects returned at job's completion. All company's imprints available in a single catalog.

VISIT OUR WEBSITES at www.writersmarket.com and www.writersdigest.com, for helpful articles, hot new markets, daily market updates, writers' guidelines and much more.

Tips: "If you submit arts or crafts ideas for kids, make sure they aren't cookie cutter crafts. Also, try to find new twists on old projects. We're looking for arts and crafts today's children will want to do without focusing on new, trendy materials."

⬛ NORTH WORD BOOKS FOR YOUNG READERS, North Word Press, 5900 Green Oak Dr., Minnetonka MN 55343. (952)936-4700. Specializes in mass market books, fiction, trade books, educational material, nonfiction. **Manuscript Acquisitions:** Aimee Jackson, executive editor. **Art Acquisitions:** Aimee Jackson, executive editor. Publishes 10-12 books/year—2-4 picture picture books (ages 5-8), 4-5 nonfiction (ages 5-8, 7-11, 8-10).
Fiction: Picture books, young readers: animal, nature/environment. Average word length: picture books—1,000; young readers—1,000-3,000. Recently published *The Family of Earth*, by Schim Schimmel (ages 4-7, picture book); *We are Wolves* and *We are Bears*, both written by Molly Grooms and illustrated by Lucia Guamotta (ages 4-7, picture books/natural history).
Nonfiction: Picture books, young readers, middle readers: activity books, animal, arts/crafts, cooking, hobbies, how-to, nature/environment. Recently published *My Cat and How to Have a Happy, Healthy Pet* and *My Dog*, by Lynn Cole (ages 6-10, nonfiction pet care books); *Rocks, Fossils, and Arrowheads*, by Laura Evert, illustrated by Linda Garrow (ages 7-10, interactive "field guide" book—nonfiction series).
How to Contact/Writers: Fiction: Submit complete ms. Query. Responds in 3 months. Publishes a book 1-2 years after acceptance. Will consider simultaneous submissions.
Illustration: Works with 5 illustrators/year. Uses color artwork only. Reviews ms/illustration packages from artists. Query. Contact: Aimee Jackson, executive editor. Illustrations only: Query with samples; send résumé and tearsheets. Responds in 3 months only if interested. Samples returned with SASE.
Photography: Buys stock images. Contact: Angela Hartwell, photo editor. Uses photos of animals *wildlife and natural history*. "Film must be labeled with species (common and Latin names) move information on photo better." Uses 35mm, 2¼×2¼, 4×5 transparencies. Submit cover letter, published samples, stock photo list.
Terms: Payment depends on project—most nonfiction series is flat fee if commissioned by us—some (fiction, usually) is advance against royalty (usually net). Sends galleys for review; dummies to illustrators. Originals returned to artist at job's completion. Book catalog available for SASE or call for catalog. Writer's, artist's and photographer's guidelines available for SASE.
Tips: "Always research house you are applying to. Make sure your work is appropriate for that house. Send to acquiring editor for manuscript, illustration and photography. And always allow *plenty* of time for review. *Do not* call editor to see if they "got your submissions." Include a return postcard to acknowledge receipt of work."

ℕ Ⓐ NORTH-SOUTH BOOKS, 11 E. 26th St., 17th Floor, New York NY 10010. (212)706-4545. Website: www.northsouth.com. **Acquisitions:** David Reuther, president and publisher; Andrea Spooner, editor-in-chief, Sea Star Books; Ellen Friedman, vice president and art director. U.S. office of Nord-Siid Verlag, Switzerland. Publishes 100 titles/year.
● North-South does not accept queries or unsolicited manuscripts.
Fiction: Picture books.
How to Contact/Writers: Only interested in agented material.
Illustration: Uses artists for picture book illustration.
Terms: Pays authors and illustrators advance and royalties.

⬛ THE OLIVER PRESS, INC., Charlotte Square, 5707 W. 36th St., Minneapolis MN 55416-2510. (952)926-8981. Fax: (952)926-8965. E-mail: queries@oliverpress.com. Website: www.oliverpress.com. Book publisher. **Acquisitions:** Denise Sterling, Jenna Anderson, Rachael Taaffe. Publishes 8 young adult titles/year. 10% of books by first-time authors. "We publish collective biographies of people who made an impact in one area of history, including science, government, archaeology, business and crime. Titles from The Oliver Press can connect young adult readers with their history to give them the confidence that only knowledge can provide. Such confidence will prepare them for the lifelong responsibilities of citizenship. Our books will introduce students to people who made important discoveries and great decisions."
Nonfiction: Middle reader, young adults: biography, history, multicultural, social issues, history of science and technology. "Authors should only suggest ideas that fit into one of our existing series. We would like to add to our Innovators series on the history of technology." Average word length: young adult—20,000 words. Recently published *Business Builders in Fast Food*, by Nathan Aaseng (ages 10 and up, collective biography); *Women with Wings*, by Jacqueline McLean (ages 10 and up, collective biography); *Weapons: Designing the Tools of War*, by Jason Richie (ages 10 and up, collective biography); and *Explorers, Missionaries and Trappers: Trailblazers of the West*, by Kieran Doherty (ages 10 and up, collective biography).
How to Contact/Writers: Nonfiction: Query with outline/synopsis. Responds in 6 months. Publishes a book approximately 1 year after acceptance.
Photography: Rarely buys photos from freelancers. Buys stock images. Looks primarily for photos of people in the news. Captions required. Uses 8×10 b&w prints. Submit cover letter, résumé and stock photo list.
Terms: Pays authors negotiable royalty. Work purchased outright from authors (fee negotiable). Pays photographers per photo (negotiable). Sends galleys to authors upon request. Book catalog and ms guidelines available for SASE.

Tips: "Authors should read some of the books we have already published before sending a query to The Oliver Press. Authors should propose collective biographies for one of our existing series."

ORCA BOOK PUBLISHERS, P.O. Box 5626 Station B, Victoria, British Columbia V8R 6S4 Canada. (604)380-1229. Fax: (604)380-1892. Book publisher. Estab. 1984. Publisher: R. Tyrrell. **Acquisitions:** Maggie deVries, children's book editor. Publishes 10 picture books/year; 4 middle readers/year; and 4 young adult titles/year. 25% of books by first-time authors. "We only consider authors who are Canadian or who live in Canada."
- Orca no longer considers nonfiction.

Fiction: Picture books: animals, contemporary, history, nature/environment. Middle readers: contemporary, history, nature/environment, problem novels. Young adults: adventure, contemporary, history, multicultural, nature/environment, problem novels, suspense/mystery. Average word length: picture books—500-2,000; middle readers—20,000-35,000; young adult—25,000-45,000. Published *Tall in the Saddle*, by Anne Carter, illustrated by David McPhail (ages 4-8, picture book); *Me and Mr. Mah*, by Andrea Spalding, illustrated by Janet Wilson (ages 5 and up, picture book); and *Alone at Ninety Foot*, by Katherine Holubitsky (young adult).

How to Contact/Writers: Fiction: Submit complete ms if picture book; submit outline/synopsis and 3 sample chapters. Nonfiction: Query with SASE. "All queries or unsolicited submissions should be accompanied by a SASE." Responds to queries in 2 months; mss in 3 months. Publishes a book 18-24 months after acceptance.

Illustration: Works with 8-10 illustrators/year. Reviews ms/illustration packages from artists. Submit ms with 3-4 pieces of final art. "Reproductions only, no original art please." Illustrations only: Query with samples; provide résumé, slides. Responds in 2 months. Samples returned with SASE; samples filed.

Terms: Pays authors royalty of 5% for picture books, 10% for novels, based on retail price. Offers advances (average amount: $2,000). Pays illustrators royalty of 5% minimum based on retail price and advance on royalty. Sends galleys to authors. Original artwork returned at job's completion if picture books. Book catalog available for legal or 8½×11 manila SAE and $2 first-class postage. Ms guidelines available for SASE. Art guidelines not available.

Tips: "American authors and illustrators should remember that the U.S. stamps on their reply envelopes cannot be posted in any country outside of the U.S."

ORCHARD BOOKS, 555 Broadway, New York NY 10012. (212)951-2600. Fax: (212)213-6435. Website: www.scholastic.com. Imprint of Scholastic, Inc. Book publisher. President and Publisher: Judy V. Wilson. **Manuscript Acquisitions:** Amy Griffin, senior editor. **Art Acquisitions:** Mina Greenstein, art director. "We publish approximately 25 books yearly including fiction, poetry, picture books, and some illustrated nonfiction." 10% of books by first-time authors.
- Orchard is not accepting unsolicited mss; query letters only. Their title *Momma, Where Are You From?*, by Marie Bradby, won a Golden Kite Honor Award for Picture Book Text in 2001.

Fiction: All levels: animal, contemporary, history, humor, multicultural, nature/environment, poetry. Recently published *Flora's Blanket*, by Deb Coliori; *Mouse in Love*, by Kraus and Aruego Dewey; *One Monday*, by Amy Huntington.

Nonfiction: "We rarely publish nonfiction." Recently published *A Dragon in the Sky*, by Pringle Marshall.

How to Contact/Writers: Query only with SASE. Responds in 3 months.

Illustration: Works with 15 illustrators/year. Art director reviews ms/illustration portfolios. Submit "tearsheets or photocopies or photostats of the work." Responds to art samples in 1 month. Samples returned with SASE. No disks or slides, please.

Terms: Most commonly an advance against list royalties. Sends galleys to authors; dummies to illustrators. Original artwork returned at job's completion. Book catalog free on request.

Tips: "Read some of our books to determine first whether your manuscript is suited to our list."

OTTENHEIMER PUBLISHERS, 5 Park Center Court, Suite 300, Owings Mills MD 21117-5001. (410)902-9100. Fax: (410)902-7210. E-mail: kputchinski@ottenheimerpub.com. Imprints: Dream House, Halo Press, Thurman House. Independent book producer/packager. Estab. 1896. **Acquisitions:** Kristin Putchinski. Publishes 2 picture books/year; 30 early readers/year. 20% of books by first-time authors. "We publish series; rarely single-title ideas. Early learning, religious, Beatrix Potter, activity books. We do lots of novelty formats and always want more ideas for inexpensive and creative packaging concepts. We are sticker book and pop-up book experts."

Nonfiction: Picture books: activity books, animal, concept, early learning novelty formats, geography, nature/environment, reference, religion. Recently published *My Bible Alphabet Block Pop-Up Book* (ages 3-6); *Wonders of Nature* (ages 3-6); and *Classic Christmas Sticker Books* (ages 3-6); *Legend of Rah and the Muggles*.

How to Contact/Writers: Query only. Currently not accepting unsolicited mss. Responds to queries/mss in 6-8 weeks. Publishes a book 6 months to 1 year after acceptance. Will consider simultaneous submissions; previously published work.

Illustration: Works with 8 illustrators/year. Reviews ms/illustration packages from artists. Query. Illustrations only: Send promo sheet and tearsheets to be kept on file. Responds only if interested. Samples returned with SASE; samples kept on file.

Photography: Buys stock images.

Terms: Pays authors royalty of 5-10% based on wholesale price or work purchased outright for $200-1,000. Offers advances. Pays illustrators by the project (range: $200-16,000). Sends galleys to authors. Originals returned to artist at job's completion. Ms guidelines for SASE.

Tips: "Don't submit single stories; we want series concepts for early learners, ages three to seven."

☑ **OUR CHILD PRESS**, P.O. Box 74, Wayne PA 19087-0074. (610)722-9937. Fax: (610)407-0943. E-mail: ocp98@aol.com. Website: www.ourchildpress.com. Book publisher. **Acquisitions:** Carol Hallenbeck, president. 90% of books by first-time authors.

Fiction/Nonfiction: All levels: adoption, multicultural, special needs. Published *Don't Call Me Marda*, written and illustrated by Sheila Kelly Welch; *Is That Your Sister?* by Catherine and Sherry Burin; and *Oliver: A Story About Adoption*, by Lois Wichstrom.

How to Contact/Writers: Fiction/Nonfiction: Query or submit complete ms. Responds to queries/mss in 6 months. Publishes a book 6-12 months after acceptance.

Illustration: Works with 1 illustrator/year. Reviews ms/illustration packages from artists. Ms/illustration packages and illustration only: Query first. Submit résumé, tearsheets and photocopies. Reports on art samples in 2 months. Samples returned with SASE; samples kept on file.

Terms: Pays authors in royalties of 5-10% based on wholesale price. Pays illustrators royalties of 5-10% based on wholesale price. Original artwork returned at job's completion. Book catalog for business-size SAE and 52¢ postage.

Tips: "Won't consider anything not related to adoption."

◖ **OUR SUNDAY VISITOR, INC.**, 200 Noll Plaza, Huntington IN 46750. (219)356-8400. Fax: (219)359-9117. E-mail: booksed@osv.com; jlindsey@osv.com; mdubruiel@osv.com; bmcnamara@osv.com. Website: www.osv.com. Book publisher. **Acquisitions:** Jacquelyn M. Lindsey, Michael Dubruiel, Beth McNamara. Art Director: Eric Schoenig. Publishes primarily religious, educational, parenting, reference and biographies. OSV is dedicated to providing books, periodicals and other products that serve the Catholic Church.

● Our Sunday Visitor, Inc., is publishing only those children's books that tie in to sacramental preparation. Contact the acquisitions editor for manuscript guidelines and a book catalog.

Nonfiction: Picture books, middle readers, young readers, young adults. Recently published *I Am Special*, by Joan and Paul Plum, illustrated by Andee Most (kindergarten program).

How to Contact/Writers: Query, submit complete ms, or submit outline/synopsis, and 2-3 sample chapters. Responds to queries in 2 months; mss in 2 months. Publishes a book 18-24 months after acceptance. Will consider simultaneous submissions, electronic submissions via disk or modem, previously published work.

Illustration: Reviews ms/illustration packages from artists. Illustration only: Query with samples. Contact: Aquisitions Editor. Responds only if interested. Samples returned with SASE; samples filed. Original artwork returned at job's completion.

Photography: Buys photos from freelancers. Contact: Acquisitions Editor.

Terms: Pays authors royalty of 10-12% net. Pays illustrators by the project (range: $200-1,500). Sends galleys to authors; dummies to illustrators. Book catalog available for SASE; ms guidelines available for SASE.

Tips: "Stay in accordance with our guidelines."

THE OVERMOUNTAIN PRESS, P.O. Box 1261, Johnson City TN 37605. (423)926-2691. Fax: (423)929-2464. E-mail: bethw@overmtn.com. Website: www.overmtn.com. Also www.silverdaggermysteries.com. Estab. 1970. Specializes in regional history trade books. **Manuscript Acquisitions:** Elizabeth L. Wright, senior editor. Publishes 3 picture books/year; 2 young readers/year; 2 middle readers/year. 50% of books by first-time authors. "We are primarily a publisher of southeastern regional history, and we have recently published several titles for children. We consider children's books about Southern Appalachia only!"

Fiction: Picture books: folktales, history. Young readers, middle readers: folktales, history, suspense/mystery. Average word length: picture books—800-1,000; young readers—5,000-10,000; middle readers—20-30,000. Recently published *Bloody Mary: The Mystery of Amanda's Magic Mirror*, by Patrick Bone (young, middle reader); *Zebordee's Miracle*, by Ann G. Cooper, illustrated by Adam Hickam (pre-elementary, picture book); and *Appalachian ABCs*, by Francie Hall, illustrated by Kent Oehm (pre-elementary, picture book).

Nonfiction: Picture books, young readers, middle readers: biography (regional), history (regional). Average word length: picture books—800-1,000; young readers—5,000-10,000; middle readers—20-30,000. Recently published *Ten Friends: A Child's Story About the Ten Commandments*, written and illustrated by Gayla Dowdy Seale (preschool-elementary, picture book).

How to Contact/Writers: Fiction/Nonfiction: Submit outline/synopsis and 2 sample chapters. Responds to queries in 2 months; mss in 6 months. Publishes book 1 year after acceptance. Will consider simultaneous submissions and previously published work.

Illustration: Works with 4 illustrators/year. Uses color artwork only. Reviews ms/illustration packages from artists. Send ms with dummy with at least 3 color copies of sample illustrations. Illustrations only: Send résumé. Responds only if interested. Samples not returned; samples filed.

Terms: Pays authors royalty of 5-15% based on wholesale price. Pays illustrators royalty of 5-10% based on wholesale price or by author/illustrator negotiations (author pays). Sends galleys to authors; dummies to illustrators. Originals sometimes returned to artist at job's completion. Book catalog available for 8½×11 SAE and 4 first-class stamps; ms guidelines available for SASE. All imprints included in a single catalog. Catalog available on website.

Tips: "Because we are fairly new in the children's market, we will not accept a manuscript without complete illustrations. We are compiling a database of freelance illustrators which is available to interested authors. Please call if you have questions regarding the submission process or to see if your product is of interest. The children's market is HUGE! If the author can find a good local publisher, he or she is more likely to get published. We are currently looking for authors to represent our list in the new millennium. At this point, we are accepting regional (Southern Appalachian) manuscripts only. *Please* call if you have a question regarding this policy."

RICHARD C. OWEN PUBLISHERS, INC., P.O. Box 585, Katonah NY 10536. (914)232-3903. Fax: (914)232-3977. Website: www.rcowen.com. Book publisher. **Acquisitions:** Janice Boland, children's books editor/art director. Publishes 20 picture story books/year. 90% of books by first-time authors. We publish "child-focused books, with inherent instructional value, about characters and situations with which five-, six-, and seven-year-old children can identify—books that can be read for meaning, entertainment, enjoyment and information. We include multicultural stories that present minorities in a positive and natural way. Our stories show the diversity in America."

Fiction: Picture books, young readers: adventure, animal, contemporary, folktales, hi-lo, humor, multicultural, nature/environment, poetry, science fiction, sports, suspense/mystery. Does not want to see holiday, religious themes, moral teaching stories. "No talking animals with personified human characteristics, jingles and rhymes, alphabet books, stories without plots, stories with nostalgic views of childhood, soft or sugar-coated tales. No stereotyping." Average word length: 40-200 words. Recently published *Digging to China*, by Katherine Goldsby, illustrated by Viki Woodworth; *The Red-Tailed Hawk*, by Lola Schaefer, illustrated by Stephen Taylor; and *Dogs at School*, by Suzanne Hardin, illustrated by Jo-Ann Friar.

Nonfiction: Picture books, young readers: animals, careers, hi-lo, history, how-to, music/dance, geography, multicultural, nature/environment, science, sports. Multicultural needs include: "Good stories respectful of all heritages, races, cultural—African-American, Hispanic, American Indian." Wants lively stories. No "encyclopedic" type of information stories. Average word length: 40-250 words. Recently published *New York City Buildings*, by Ann Mace, photos by Tim Holmstron.

How to Contact/Writers: Fiction/nonfiction: Submit complete ms. "*Must* request guidelines first with #10 SASE." Responds to mss in 18 months. Publishes a book 2-3 years after acceptance. Will consider simultaneous submissions.

Illustration: Works with 20 illustrators/year. Uses color artwork only. Illustration only: Send color copies/reproductions or photos of art or provide tearsheets; do not send slides. Must request guidelines first. Responds only if interested; samples filed.

Photography: Buys photos from freelancers. Contact: Janice Boland, art director. Wants photos that are child-oriented; candid shots; not interested in portraits. "Natural, bright, crisp and colorful—of children and of interesting subjects and compositions attractive to children. If photos are assigned, we buy outright—retain ownership and all rights to photos taken in the project." Sometimes interested in stock photos for special projects. Uses 35mm, 2¼×2¼, color transparencies.

Terms: Pays authors royalties of 5% based on wholesale price or outright purchase (range: $25-500). Offers no advances. Pays illustrators by the project (range: $100-2,500). Pays photographers by the project (range: $100-2,000) or per photo ($100-150). Original artwork returned 12-18 months after job's completion. Book brochure, ms/artists guidelines available for SASE.

Tips: Seeking "stories (both fiction and nonfiction) that have charm, magic, impact and appeal; that children living in today's society will want to read and reread; books with strong storylines, child-appealing language, action and interesting, vivid characters. Write for the ears and eyes and hearts of your readers—use an economy of words. Visit the children's room at the public library and immerse yourself in the best children's literature."

☑ PACIFIC PRESS, P.O. Box 5353. Nampa ID 83653-5353. (208)465-2500. Fax: (208)465-2531. E-mail: booksubmissions@pacificpress.com. Website: www.pacificpress.com. Estab. 1874. Specializes in Christian material. **Manuscript Acquisitions:** Tim Lale. **Art Acquisitions:** Randy Maxwell, creative director. Publishes 1 picture book/year; 1 young readers/year; 2 middle readers/year. 5% of books by first-time authors. Pacific Press brings the Bible and Christian lifestyle to children.

Fiction: Picture books, young readers, middle readers, young adults: Religion. Average word length: picture books—100; young readers—1,000; middle readers—15,000; young adults—40,000. Recently published *The Cat in the Cage and Other Great Stories*, by Jerry Thomas; *Detective Zack and the Secret of Blackloch Castle*, by Jerry Thomas; *Prince Prances Again*, by Heather Grovet.

Nonfiction: Picture books, young readers, middle readers, young adults: religion. Average word length: picture books—100; young readers—1,000; middle readers—15,000; young adults—40,000. Recently published *Before I Was a Kid*, by Rita Spears-Stewart; *God Spoke to a Girl*, by Dorothy Nelson; *My Talents for Jesus*, by Charles Mills; *My Very Best Friend*, by Linda Porter Carlyle; *Rescue From the River*, by Linda Porter Carlyle.

How to Contact/Writers: Fiction/Nonfiction: Query or submit outline/synopsis and 3 sample chapters. Responds to queries in 2 months; mss in 3 months. Publishes a book 6-9 months after acceptance. Will consider electronic submissions via disk or modem.

Written by Janice Boland, the acquisitions editor and art director of Richard C. Owen Publishers, Inc., *I Meowed* had tough visual standards. This publisher is internationally recognized for imaginative, charming depictions of childhood. Self-proclaimed lover of cats and illustrator Erin Mauterer was selected for the job. Discovered through mailings, full-time artist Mauterer continues to create calico cats, tabby cats, Himalayan cats, Siamese cats, . . .

Illustration: Works with 2 illustrators/year. Uses color artwork only. Query. Responds only if interested. Samples returned with SASE.

Photography: Buys stock and assigns work. Model/property releases required.

Terms: Pays author royalty of 6-15% based on wholesale price. Offers advances (Average amount: $1,500). Pays illustrators royalty of 6-15% based on wholesale price. Pays photographers royalty of 6-15% based on wholesale price. Sends galleys to authors. Originals returned to artist at job's completion. Book catalog available for 10×12 SAE and 5 first-class stamps; ms guidelines for SASE. All imprints included in a single catalog. Catalog available on website www.adventistbookcenter.com.

Tips: Pacific Press is owned by the Seventh-day Adventist Church. The Press rejects all material that is not Bible-based.

PACIFIC VIEW PRESS, P.O. Box 2657, Berkeley CA 94702. (510)849-4213. Fax: (510)843-5835. E-mail: PVP@sirius.com. Book publisher. **Acquisitions:** Pam Zumwalt, president. Publishes 1-2 picture books/year. 50% of books by first-time authors. "We publish unique, high-quality introductions to Asian cultures and history for children 8-12, for schools, libraries and families. Our children's books focus on hardcover illustrated nonfiction. We look for titles on aspects of the history and culture of the countries and peoples of the Pacific Rim, especially China, presented in an engaging, informative and respectful manner. We are interested in books that all children will enjoy reading and using, and that parents and teachers will want to buy."

Nonfiction: Young readers, middle readers: Asia-related multicultural only. Recently published *Kneeling Carabao and Dancing Giants: Celebrating Filipino Festivals*, by Rena Krasno, illustrated by Ileana C. Lee (ages 8-12, nonfiction on festivals and history of Philippines); and *Made in China: Ideas and Inventions from Ancient China*, by Suzanne Williams, illustrated by Andrea Fong (ages 10-12, nonfiction on history of China and Chinese inventions).

How to Contact/Writers: Query with outline and sample chapter. Responds in 3 months.

Illustration: Works with 2 illustrators/year. Responds only if interested. Samples returned with SASE.

Terms: Pays authors royalty of 8-12% based on wholesale price. Pays illustrators by the project (range: $2,000-5,000).

Tips: "We welcome proposals from persons with expertise, either academic or personal, in their area of interest. While we do accept proposals from previously unpublished authors, we would expect submitters to have considerable experience presenting their interests to children in classroom or other public settings and to have skill in writing for children."

PARENTING PRESS, INC., P.O. Box 75267, Seattle WA 98125. (206)364-2900. Fax: (206)364-0702. E-mail: office@parentingpress.com. Website: www.parentingpress.com. Book publisher. Estab. 1979. Publisher: Carolyn Threadgill. **Acquisitions:** Elizabeth Crary, (parenting) and Carolyn Threadgill (children and parenting). Publishes 4-5 books/year for parents or/and children and those who work with them. 40% of books by first-time authors. "Parenting Press publishes educational books for children in story format—no straight fiction. Our company publishes books that help build competence in parents and children. We are known for practical books that teach parents and can be used successfully by parent educators, teachers, and educators who work with parents. We are interested in books that help people feel good about themselves because they gain skills needed in dealing with others. We are particularly interested in material that provides 'options' rather than 'shoulds.'"

● Parenting Press's guidelines are available on their website.

Fiction: Picture books: concept. Publishes social skills books, problem-solving books, safety books, dealing-with-feelings books that use a "fictional" vehicle for the information. "We rarely publish straight fiction." Recently published *Heidi's Irresistible Hat, Willy's Noisy Sister, Amy's Disappearing Pickle*, by Elizabeth Crary, illustrated by Susan Avishai (ages 4-10); and *The Way I Feel*, written and illustrated by Janan Cain, a book that promotes emotional literacy.

Nonfiction: Picture books: health, social skills building. Young readers: health, social skills building books. Middle readers: health, social skills building. No books on "new baby; coping with a new sibling; cookbooks; manners; books about disabilities (which we don't publish at present); animal characters in anything; books that tell children what they should do, instead of giving options." Average word length: picture books—500-800; young readers—1,000-2,000; middle readers—up to 10,000. Published *Kids to the Rescue*, by Maribeth and Darwin Boelts (ages 4-12); *Bully on the Bus*, by Carl Bosch (ages 7-11).

How to Contact/Writers: Query. Responds to queries/mss in 3 months, "after requested." Publishes a book 18 months after acceptance. Will consider simultaneous submissions.

Illustrations: Works with 3-5 illustrators/year. Reviews ms/illustration packages from artists. "We do reserve the right to find our own illustrator, however." Query. Illustrations only: Submit "résumé, samples of art/drawings (no original art); photocopies or color photocopies okay." Responds only if interested. Samples returned with SASE; samples filed, if suitable.

Terms: Pays authors royalties of 3-8% based on wholesale price. Pays illustrators (for text) by the project; 3-5% royalty based on wholesale price. Pays illustrators by the project ($250-3,000). Sends galleys to authors; dummies to illustrators. Book catalog/ms/artist's guidelines for #10 SAE and 1 first-class stamp.

Tips: "Make sure you are familiar with the unique nature of our books. All are aimed at building certain 'people' skills in adults or children. Our publishing for children follows no trend that we find appropriate. Children need nonfiction social skill-building books that help them think through problems and make their own informed decisions." The traditional illustrated story book does not *usually* fit our requirements because it does all the thinking for the child.

PAULIST PRESS, 997 Macarthur Blvd., Mahwah NJ 07430. (201)825-7300. Fax: (201)825-8345. Website: www.paulistpress.com. Book publisher. Estab. 1865. **Acquisitions:** Susan Heyboer O'Keefe, editor. Publishes 2-4 picture books/year; 6-8 young reader titles/year; and 4-6 middle reader titles/year. 80% of books by first-time authors; 10% of books from agented writers. "Our goal is to produce books on Christian and Catholic themes."

Fiction: Picture books, young readers, middle readers and young adults: interested mainly in books providing an accessible introduction to basic religious and family values, but not preachy. Recently published *Child's Guide to the Mass*, by Sue Stanton; *Children's Book of Table*, by Ellen J. Kendig; *C.S. Lewis*, by Elaine Murray Stone; *Miracle of the Poinsettia (Milagro de la Flor de Nochebuena)*, by Brian Cavanaugh, T.O.R.

Nonfiction: All levels: biography, concept, multicultural, religion, self help, social issues.

How to Contact/Writers: Fiction/nonfiction: Submit complete ms. Responds to queries/mss in 3 months. Publishes a book 1-2 years after acceptance.

Illustration: Works with 6-10 illustrators/year. Editorial reviews all varieties of ms/illustration packages from artists. Submit complete ms with 1 piece of final art (photocopy only) remainder roughs. Illustrations only: Submit résumé, tearsheets. Reports on art samples in 6-8 months.

Photography: Buys photos from freelancers. Works on assignment only. Uses inspirational photos.

Terms: Pays authors royalty of 4-8% based on retail price. Offers average advance payment of $500. Pays illustrators by the project (range: $50-100) or royalty of 2-4% based on net price. Pays photographers by the project (range: $25-150; negotiable). Factors used to determine final payment: color art, b&w, number of illustrations, complexity of work. Pay for separate authors and illustrators: Author paid by royalty rate; illustrator paid by flat fee, sometimes by royalty. Sends galleys to authors; dummies to illustrators. Original artwork returned at job's completion, "if requested by illustrator."
Tips: "We cannot be responsible for unsolicited manuscripts. Please send copies, not originals. We try to respond to all manuscripts we receive—please understand if you have not received a response within six months the manuscript does not fit our current publishing plan. We look for authors who diligently promote their work."

PEACHTREE PUBLISHERS, LTD., 1700 Chattahoochee Ave., Atlanta GA 30318-2112. (404)876-8761. Fax: (404)875-2578. E-mail: hello@peachtree-online.com. Website: www.peachtree-online.com. Book publisher. Imprints: Peachtree Jr. and Freestone. Estab. 1977. **Acquisitions:** Helen Harriss. **Art Director:** Loraine Balcsik. Production Manager: Melanie McMahon. Publishes 20-24 titles/year.
Fiction: Picture books: adventure, animal, concept, history, nature/environment. Young readers: adventure, animal, concept, history, nature/environment. Middle readers: adventure, animal, history, nature/environment, sports. Young adults: fiction, mystery, adventure. Does not want to see science fiction, romance.
Nonfiction: Picture books: animal, history, nature/environment. Young readers, middle readers, young adults: animal, biography, nature/environment. Does not want to see religion.
How to Contact/Writers: Fiction/Nonfiction: Submit complete ms. Responds to queries in 3 months; mss in 4 months. Publishes a book 1-1½ years after acceptance. Will consider simultaneous and previously published submissions.
Illustration: Works with 8-10 illustrators/year. Illustrations only: Query production manager or art director with samples, résumé, slides, color copies to keep on file. Responds only if interested. Samples returned with SASE; samples filed.
Terms: Ms guidelines for SASE, or call for a recorded message.

PEEL PRODUCTIONS, P.O. Box 546, Columbus NC 28722. (828)894-8838. Fax: (801)365-9898. E-mail: editor@peelbooks.com. Book publisher. **Acquisitions:** Susan Dubosque, editor. Publishes 1 picture book/year; and 5 how-to-draw books/year.
Nonfiction: Young readers, middle readers: activity books (how to draw).
How to Contact/Writers: Fiction/Nonfiction: Submit outline/synopsis and 2 sample chapters. Responds to queries in 1 month; mss in 6 weeks. Publishes a book 1 year after acceptance. Will consider simultaneous submissions.
Terms: Pays authors royalty. Offers advances. Sends galleys to authors. Book catalog available for SAE and 2 first-class stamps. Ms guidelines available for SASE.

PELICAN PUBLISHING CO. INC., P.O. Box 3110, Gretna LA 70054-3110. (504)368-1175. Website: www.pelicanpub.com. Book publisher. Estab. 1926. **Manuscript Acquisitions:** Nina Kooij, editor-in-chief. **Art Acquisitions:** Tracey Clements, production manager. Publishes 18 young readers/year and 3 middle reader titles/year. 0% of books from agented writers. "Pelican publishes hardcover and trade paperback originals and reprints. Our children's books (illustrated and otherwise) include history, holiday, and regional."
Fiction: Young readers: history, holiday and regional. Middle readers: Louisiana history. Multicultural needs include stories about African-Americans, Irish-Americans, Jews, Asian-Americans, Cajuns and Hispanics. Does not want animal stories, general Christmas stories, "day at school" or "accept yourself" stories. Maximum word length: 1,100 young readers; middle readers—40,000. Recently published *The Warlord's Puzzle*, by Virginia Walton Pilegarde (ages 5-8, folktale).
Nonfiction: Young readers: biography, history. Middle readers: Louisiana history. Recently published *The Governors of Louisiana*, by Miriam G. Reeves (ages 8-12, biography).
How to Contact/Writers: Fiction/Nonfiction: Query. Responds to queries in 1 month; mss in 3 months. Publishes a book 9-18 months after acceptance.
Illustration: Works with 15 illustrators/year. Reviews ms/illustration packages from artists. Query first. Illustrations only: Query with samples (no originals). Responds only if interested. Samples returned with SASE; samples kept on file.
Terms: Pays authors in royalties; buys ms outright "rarely." Sends galleys to authors. Illustrators paid by "various arrangements." Book catalog and ms guidelines available for SASE.
Tips: "No anthropomorphic stories, pet stories (fiction or nonfiction), fantasy, poetry, science fiction or romance. Writers: Be as original as possible. Develop characters that lend themselves to series and always be thinking of new and interesting situations for those series. Give your story a strong hook—something that will appeal to a well-defined audience. There is a lot of competition out there for general themes. We look for stories with specific 'hooks' and audiences, and writers who actively promote their work."

PERFECTION LEARNING CORPORATION, Cover to Cover, 10520 New York, Des Moines IA 50322. (515)278-0133. Fax: (515)278-2980. E-mail: acquisitions@plconline.com. Website: www.perfectionlearni

ng.com. Book publisher, independent book producer/packager. **Manuscript Acquisitions:** S. Thies (K-12 books), Rebecca Christian (curriculum). **Art Acquisitions:** Randy Messer, art director. Publishes 20 early chapter books/year; 40-50 middle readers/year; 25 young adult titles/year.

• Perfection Learning Corp. publishes *all* hi-lo children's books on a variety of subjects.

Fiction: Grades 3-12, ages 8-18: adventure, animal, contemporary, fantasy, folktales, history, humor, multicultural, nature/environment, poetry, science fiction, special needs, sports, suspense/mystery. Average word length: early chapter books—4,000; middle readers—10,000-14,000; young adults: 10,000-30,000. Recently published *Holding the Yellow Rabbit*; and *Prairie Meeting*.

Nonfiction: All levels: animal, biography, careers, geography, health, history, hobbies, multicultural, nature/environment, science, social issues, special needs, sports. Multicultural needs include contemporary fiction by authors who are of the culture. Does not want to see ABC or picture books. Average word length: early chapter books—4,000; middle readers—10,000-14,000; young adults—10,000-14,000.

How to Contact/Writers: Fiction/Nonfiction: Submit a few sample chapters and synopsis. Responds to queries in 3 months; mss in 3 months. Publishes a book 18 months after acceptance.

Illustration: Works with 15-20 illustrators/year. Illustration only: Query with samples; send résumé, promo sheet, client list, tearsheets. Contact: Randy Messer, art director. Responds only if interested. Samples returned with SASE; samples filed.

Photography: Buys photos from freelancers. Contact: Randy Messer, art director. Buys stock and assigns work. Uses children. Uses color or up to 8×10 b&w glossy prints; $2\frac{1}{4} \times 2\frac{1}{4}$, 4×5 transparencies. Submit cover letter, client list, stock photo list, promo piece (color or b&w).

Terms: Pays authors "depending on going rate for industry." Offers advances. Pays illustrators by the project. Pays photographers by the project. Original artwork returned on a "case by case basis."

Tips: "Our materials are sold through schools for use in the classroom. Talk to a teacher about his/her needs."

PHILOMEL BOOKS, Penguin Putnam Inc., 345 Hudson St., New York NY 10014. (212)414-3610. Website: www.penguinputnam.com. Putnam Books. Book publisher. Estab. 1980. **Manuscript Acquisitions:** Patricia Gauch, editorial director; Emily Earle, assistant editor; Michael Green, senior editor. **Art Acquisitions:** Gina DiMassi, design assistant. Publishes 18 picture books/year; 2 middle-grade/year; 2 young readers/year; 4 young adult/year. 5% of books by first-time authors; 80% of books from agented writers. "We look for beautifully written, engaging manuscripts for children and young adults."

• Philomel Books is not accepting unsolicited manuscripts. Their title *So You Want to Be President?*, illustrated by David Small (text by Judith St. George), won the 2001 Caldecott Medal.

Fiction: All levels: adventure, animal, anthology, contemporary, fantasy, folktales, hi-lo, history, humor, poetry, sports, multicultural. Middle readers, young adults: problem novels, science fiction, suspense/mystery. No concept picture books, mass-market "character" books, or series. Average word length: 1,000 for picture books; 1,500 young readers; 14,000 middle readers; 20,000 young adult.

Nonfiction: Picture books, young readers, middle readers: hi-lo. "Creative nonfiction on any subject." Average word length: 2,000 for picture books; 3,000 young readers; 10,000 middle readers.

How to Contact/Writers: Not accepting unsolicited mss. Fiction: Submit outline/synopsis and first two chapters. Nonfiction: Query. Responds to queries in 3 months; mss in 4 months.

Illustration: Works with 20-25 illustrators/year. Reviews ms/illustration packages from artists. Query with art sample first. Illustrations only: Query with samples. Send résumé and tearsheets. Responds to on art samples in 1 month. Original artwork returned at job's completion. Samples returned with SASE or kept on file.

Terms: Pays authors in royalties. Average advance payment "varies." Illustrators paid by advance and in royalties. Sends galleys to authors; dummies to illustrators. Book catalog, ms guidelines free on request with SASE (9×12 envelope for catalog).

Tips: Wants "unique fiction or nonfiction with a strong voice and lasting quality. Discover your own voice and own story—and persevere." Looks for "something unusual, original, well-written. Fine art. The genre (fantasy, contemporary, or historical fiction) is not so important as the story itself and the spirited life the story allows its main character. We are also interested in receiving adolescent novels, particularly novels that contain regional spirit, such as a story about a young boy or girl written from a Southern, Southwestern or Northwestern perspective."

PHOENIX LEARNING RESOURCES, 12 W. 31st St., New York NY 10001-4415. (212)629-3887. (212)629-5648. E-mail: john@phoenixlr.com. Website: www.phoenixlr.com. Book publisher. Executive Vice President: John A. Rothermich. Publishes 20 textbooks/year. Publisher's goal is to provide proven skill building materials in reading, language, math and study skills for today's student, grades K-adult.

Nonfiction: Middle readers, young readers, young adults: hi-lo, textbooks. Recently published *Reading for Concepts*, Third Edition.

How to Contact/Writers: Nonfiction: Submit outline/synopsis. Responds to queries in 2 weeks; mss in 1 month. Will consider simultaneous submissions and previously published work.

Photography: Buys stock. Contact: John A. Rothermich, executive vice president. Uses color prints and 35mm, $2\frac{1}{4} \times 2\frac{1}{4}$, 4×5 transparencies. Submit cover letter.

Terms: Pays authors royalty based on wholesale price or work purchased outright. Pays illustrators and photographers by the project. Sends galleys to authors. Book catalog available for SASE.

Tips: "We look for classroom-tested and proven materials."

PIANO PRESS, P.O. Box 85, Del Mar CA 92014-0085. (858)481-5651. Fax: (858)755-1104. E-mail: PianoPress@aol.com. Website: www.pianopress.com. Estab. 1999. Specializes in fiction, educational material, multicultural material, nonfiction. **Manuscript Acquisitions:** Elizabeth C. Axford, M.A., editor. "We publish music-related books, either fiction or nonfiction, songbooks and poetry."
Fiction: Picture books, young readers, middle readers, young adults: folktales, multicultural, poetry, music. Average word length: picture books—1,500-2,000. Recently published *Shadows from the Clouds—A Collection of Poems*, by Elizabeth C. Axford.
Nonfiction: Picture books, young readers, middle readers, young adults: multicultural, music/dance. Average word length: picture books—1,500-2,000. Recently published *Merry Christmas Happy Hanukkah—A Multilingual Songbook & CD*, by Elizabeth C. Axford.
How to Contact/Writers: Fiction/Nonfiction: Query. Responds to queries in 2 months; mss in 6 months. Publishes a book 1 year after acceptance. Will consider simultaneous submissions, electronic submissions via disk or modem.
Illustration: Works with 1 or 2 illustrators/year. Reviews ms/illustration packages from artists. Query. Contact: Elizabeth C. Axford, editor. Illustrations only: Query with samples. Contact: Elizabeth C. Axford, editor. Responds in 2 months. Samples returned with SASE; samples filed.
Photography: Buys stock and assigns work. Contact: Elizabeth C. Axford, editor. Looking for seasonal, music-related, multicultural. Model/property releases required. Uses glossy or flat, color or b&w prints. Submit cover letter, résumé, client list, published samples, stock photo list.
Terms: Pays author royalty of 8-12% based on retail price. Pays illustrators royalty of 8-12% based on retail price. Pays photographers royalty of 8-12% based on retail price. Sends galleys to authors; dummies to illustrators. Originals returned to artist at job's completion. Book catalog available for #10 SAE and 2 first-class stamps. All imprints included in a single catalog. Catalog available on website.
Tips: "We are looking for music-related material only for any juvenile market. Query first before submitting anything."

PLAYERS PRESS, INC., P.O. Box 1132, Studio City CA 91614-0132. (818)789-4980. Book publisher. Imprints: Showcase Publishing; Gaslight Productions; Health Watch Books. Estab. 1965. Vice President/Editorial: Robert W. Gordon. **Manuscript Acquisitions:** Attention: Editor. **Art Acquisitions:** Attention: Art Director. Publishes 7-25 young readers dramatic plays and musicals/year; 2-10 middle readers dramatic plays and musicals/year; and 4-20 young adults dramatic plays and musicals/year. 35% of books by first-time authors; 1% of books from agented writers.
Fiction: Picture books, middle readers, young readers, young adults: history. Young adults: health, suspense/mystery. Recently published *Tower of London*, a play by William Hezlep; *Punch and Judy*, a play by William-Alan Landes; and *Silly Soup!*, by Carol Kerty (a collection of short plays with music and dance).
Nonfiction: Picture books, middle readers, young readers, young adults. "Any children's nonfiction pertaining to the entertainment industry, performing arts and how-to for the theatrical arts only." Needs include activity, arts/crafts, careers, history, how-to, music/dance, reference and textbook. Published *Stagecrafter's Handbook*, by I.E. Clark; and *New Monologues for Readers Theatre*, by Steven Porter. Recently published *Assignments in Musical Theatre Acting & Directing*, by Jacque Wheeler and Halle Laughlin (how-to on teaching or learning to a musical theater actor or director); and *Theatre for Children in the United States: A History*, by Nellie McCaslin (complete history of children's theater from the turn of the century through 1996).
How to Contact/Writers: Fiction/nonfiction: Submit plays or outline/synopsis and sample chapters of entertainment books. Responds to queries in 1 month; mss in 1 year. Publishes a book 10 months after acceptance. No simultaneous submissions.
Illustration: Works with 2-6 illustrators/year. Use primarily b&w artwork. Illustrations only: Submit résumé, tearsheets. Responds to art samples in 1 week only if interested. Samples returned with SASE; samples filed.
Terms: Pays authors royalties based on wholesale price. Pay illustrators by the project (range: $5-5,000). Pays photographers by the project (up to 1,000); royalty varies. Sends galleys to authors; dummies to illustrators. Book catalog and ms guidelines available for SASE.
Tips: Looks for "plays/musicals and books pertaining to the performing arts only. Illustrators: send samples that can be kept for our files."

PLAYHOUSE PUBLISHING, 1566 Akron-Peninsula Rd., Akron OH 44313. (330)926-1313. Fax: (330)926-1315. E-mail: info@playhousepublishing.com. Website: www.playhousepublishing.com. Specializes in mass market Christian and educational material. **Acquisitions:** Deborah D'Andrea, creative director. Imprints: Picture Me Books, Nibble Me Books. Publishes 10-15 picture books/year, 2-5 young readers/year. 50% of books by first-time authors. "Playhouse Publishing is dedicated to finding imaginative new ways to inspire young minds to read, learn and grow—one book at a time."
Fiction: Picture books: adventure, animal, concept, fantasy, folktales, humor, nature/environment, sports. Young readers: adventure, animal. Average word length: picture books—75; young readers—500. Recently published: *Picture Me as Mom's Little Helper*, illustrated by Wendy Rasmussen (age 2-7, board book); *Picture Me in the Circus*, by Heather Rhoades (age 1-5, board book); and *Cool School Story*, by Katina Jones, illustrated by Hoffman, Ottinger, Zaidan (age 4-8, picture book/early reader).

How to Contact/Writers: Fiction: Query or submit outline/synopsis. Reports on queries/mss in 2-4 months. Publishes a book 18 months after acceptance. Will consider simultaneous submissions and electronic submissions via disk or modem.

Illustration: Works with 7 illustrators/year. Uses color artwork only. Reviews ms/illustration packages. Query or submit ms with 1-2 pieces of final art. Illustrations only: Query with samples. Send résumé, promosheet and tearsheets. Contact: Deborah D'Andrea, creative director. Reports back in 1 month. Samples returned with SASE.

Photography: Works on assignment only. Model/property release required. Uses color prints.

Terms: Work purchased outright from authors. Illustrators and photographers paid by the project. Book catalog available for 9×12 SASE. All imprints included in single catalog. Catalog available online.

PLEASANT COMPANY PUBLICATIONS, 8400 Fairway Place, Middleton WI 53562-0998. (608)836-4848. Fax: (608)836-1999. Website: www.americangirl.com. Book publisher. Editorial Director: Judy Woodburn. **Manuscript Acquisitions:** Erin Falligant, submissions editor. Jodi Evert, editorial director fiction/picture books; Michelle Watkins, editorial director, American Girl Library. Andrea Weiss, contemporary fiction; Peg Ross, History mysteries. **Art Acquisitions:** Jane Varda, art director. Imprints: The American Girls Collection, American Girl Library, History Mysteries, AG Fiction. Publishes 30 middle readers/year. 10% of books by first-time authors. Publishes fiction and nonfiction for girls 7 and up. "Pleasant Company's mission is to educate and entertain girls with high-quality products and experiences that build self-esteem and reinforce positive social and moral values."

• Pleasant Company publishes *American Girl* magazine. See the listing for *American Girl* in the Magazines section.

Fiction: Middle readers: adventure, animal, contemporary, fantasy, history, suspense/mystery. Recently published *Meet Kit*, by Valerie Tripp, illustrated by Walter Rane (ages 7-12, historical fiction); *Smoke Screen*, by Amy Goldman Koss (ages 10 and up, contemporary fiction); *Trouble at Fort La Pointe*, by Kathleen Ernst (ages 10 an up, historical fiction/mystery).

Nonfiction: Middle readers: activity books, arts/crafts, cooking, history, hobbies, how-to, self help, sports. Recently published *Help! A Girl's Guide to Divorce and Stepfamilies*, by Nancy Holyoke, illustrated by Scott Nash (ages 8 and up; self-help); *Paper Punch Art*, by Laura Torres (ages 8 and up; craft); and *Quiz Book 2*, by Sarah Jane Brian, illustrated by Debbie Tilley (ages 8 and up; activity).

How to Contact/Writers: Fiction/nonfiction: Query or submit entire ms. Responds to queries/mss in 3 months. Will consider simultaneous submissions.

Illustration: Works with 10 illustrators/year. Reviews ms/illustration packages from artists. Illustrations only: Query with samples. Contact: Jane Varda, senior art director. Responds only if interested. Samples returned with SASE; copies of samples filed.

Photography: Buys stock and assigns work. Submit cover letter, published samples, promo piece.

Terms: Pays authors royalty or work purchased outright. Pays illustrators by the project. Pays photographers by the project. Sends galleys to authors; dummies to illustrators. Originals returned to artist at job's completion. Book catalog available for 8½×11 SAE and 4 first-class stamps. All imprints included in a single catalog.

✓ **POLYCHROME PUBLISHING CORPORATION**, 4509 N. Francisco, Chicago IL 60625. (773)478-4455. Fax: (773)478-0786. E-mail: polypub@earthlink.net. Website: http://home.earthlink.net/~polypub/. Book publisher. **Contact:** Editorial Board. **Art Director:** Brian Witkowski. Publishes 2-4 picture books/year; 1-2 middle readers/year; and 1-2 young adult titles/year. 50% of books are by first-time authors. Stories focus on children of Asian ancestry in the United States.

Fiction: All levels: adventure, contemporary, history, multicultural, problem novels, suspense/mystery. Middle readers, young adults: anthology. Multicultural needs include Asian American children's experiences. Not interested in animal stories, fables, fairy tales, folk tales. Published *Nene and the Horrible Math Monster*, by Marie Villanueva; *Stella: On the Edge of Popularity*, by Lauren Lee.

Nonfiction: All levels: multicultural. Multicultural needs include Asian-American themes.

How to Contact/Writers: Fiction/Nonfiction: Submit complete ms along with an author's bio regarding story background. Responds to queries in 4 months; mss in 6 months. Publishes a book 1-2 years after acceptance. Will consider simultaneous submissions.

Illustration: Works with 4-6 illustrators/year. Reviews ms/illustration packages from artists. Submit ms with bio of author, story background and photocopies of sample illustrations. Contact: Editorial Board. Illustrations only: Query with résumé and samples (can be photocopies) of drawings of multicultural children. Responds only if interested. Samples returned with SASE; samples filed "only if under consideration for future work."

Terms: Pays authors royalty of 2-10% based on wholesale price. Work purchased outright ($25 minimum). Pays illustrators 2-10% royalty based on wholesale price. Sends galleys to authors; dummies to illustrators. Book catalog available for #10 SAE and 34¢. Ms guidelines available for SASE.

Tips: Wants "stories about experiences that will ring true with Asian Americans, including tolerance and anti-bias that people of *ALL* colors can identify with."

✓ **PUFFIN BOOKS**, Penguin Putnam Inc., 345 Hudson St., New York NY 10014-3657. (212)366-2000. Website: www.penguinputnam.com. Imprint of Penguin Putnam Inc. **Acquisitions:** Sharyn November, senior editor; Joy Peskin, editor. Publishes trade paperback originals (very few) and reprints. Publishes 175-200 titles/

year. Receives 600 queries and mss/year. 1% of books by first-time authors; 5% from unagented writers. "Puffin Books publishes high-end trade paperbacks and paperback originals and reprints for preschool children, beginning and middle readers, and young adults."

Fiction: Picture books, young adult novels, middle grade and easy-to-read grades 1-3. "We publish mostly paperback reprints. We publish few original titles." Recently published *Go and Come Back*, by Joan Ablelove; *Speak*, by Laurie Halse Anderson.

Nonfiction: Biography, children's/juvenile, illustrated book, young children's concept books (counting, shapes, colors). Subjects include education (for teaching concepts and colors, not academic), women in history. " 'Women in history' books interest us." Reviews artwork/photos. Send color photocopies. Recently published *Rachel Carson: Pioneer of Ecology*, by "Fadlinski" (history); *Grandma Moses*, by O'Neill Ruff (history). Publishes the Alloy Books series.

How to Contact/Writers: Fiction: Submit complete picture book ms or 3 sample chapters with SASE. Nonfiction: Submit 5 pages of ms with SASE. "It could take up to 5 months to get response." Publishes book 1 year after acceptance. Will consider simultaneous submissions, if so noted.

Terms: Pays royalty. Offers advance (varies). Book catalog for 9×12 SASE with 7 first-class stamps; send request to Marketing Department.

G.P. PUTNAM'S SONS, Penguin Putnam Inc., 345 Hudson St., New York NY 10014. (212)366-2000. Website: www.penguinputnam.com. Book publisher. **Manuscript Acquisitions:** Kathy Dawson, senior editor; Susan Kochan, editor. **Art Acquisitions:** Cecilia Yung, art director, Putnam and Philomel. Publishes 20 picture books/year; 10 middle readers/year; and 2 young adult titles/year. 5% of books by first-time authors; 50% of books from agented authors.

● Putnam title *Hope Was Here*, by Joan Bauer, won a 2001 Newbery Honor Medal. Their *Miracle's Boys*, by Jacqueline Woodson, won the 2001 Coretta Scott King Author Award.

Fiction: Picture books: animal, concept, contemporary, humor, multicultural, special needs. Young readers: adventure, contemporary, history, humor, multicultural, special needs, suspense/mystery. Middle readers: adventure, contemporary, history, humor, multicultural, problem novels, special needs, sports, suspense/mystery. Young adults: contemporary, history, problem novels, special needs. "Multicultural books should reflect different cultures accurately but unobtrusively." Regarding special needs, "stories about physically or mentally challenged children should portray them accurately and without condescension." Does not want to see series, romances. Average word length: picture books—200-1,500; middle readers—10,000-30,000; young adults—40,000-50,000. Recently published *Car Wash*, by Susan Steen and Sandra Steen, illustrated by G. Brian Kaids (ages 2-5); and *Notes from a Liar and Her Dog*, by Gennifer Cholden Ko (ages 8-12).

Nonfiction: Picture books: animal, concept, nature/environment. Subject must have broad appeal but inventive approach. Average word length: picture books—200-1,500. Recently published *Wick Plays Baseball*, by Rachel Isadora, (ages 4-8, 32 pages).

How to Contact/Writers: Fiction/nonfiction: Query with outline/synopsis and 3 sample chapters. Unsolicited picture book mss only. Responds to queries in 2-3 weeks; mss in 4-10 weeks. Publishes a book 2 years after acceptance. Will consider simultaneous submissions on queries only.

Illustration: Works with 40 illustrators/year. Reviews ms/illustration packages from artists. Ms/illustration packages and illustration only: Query. Responds only if interested. Samples returned with SASE; samples filed.

Terms: Pays authors royalty based on retail price. Pays illustrators by the project or royalty based on retail price. Sends galleys to authors. Original artwork returned at job's completion. Books catalog and ms and artist's guidelines available for SASE.

Tips: "Study our catalogs and get a sense of the kind of books we publish, so that you know whether your project is likely to be right for us."

RAINBOW BOOKS, P.O. Box 261129, San Diego CA 92196. (858)271-7600. Book publisher. Estab. 1979. **Acquisitions:** Christy Allen, editor. Publishes 5 young readers/year; 5 middle readers/year; and 5 young adult titles/year. 50% of books by first-time authors. "Our mission is to publish Bible-based, Christ-centered materials that contribute to and inspire spiritual growth and development."

Nonfiction: Young readers, middle readers, young adult/teens: activity books, arts/crafts, how-to, reference, religion. Does not want to see traditional puzzles. Recently published *Worship Bulletins for Kids*, by Mary Rose Pearson and Jeanne Grieser (series of 2 books for ages 3-12).

How to Contact/Writers: Nonfiction: Submit outline/synopsis and 3-5 sample chapters. Responds to queries in 6 weeks; mss in 3 months. Publishes a book 18 months after acceptance. Will consider simultaneous submissions, submissions via disk and previously published work.

THE AGE-LEVEL INDEX, located in the back of this book, lists book publishers and magazines according to the age-groups for which they need material.

Illustration: Works with 2-5 illustrators/year. Reviews ms/illustration packages from artists. Submit ms with 2-5 pieces of final art. Illustrations only: Query with samples. Responds in 6 weeks. Samples returned with SASE; samples filed.

Terms: For authors work purchased outright (range: $500 and up). Pays illustrators by the project (range: $300 and up). Sends galleys to authors. Book catalog available for 10×13 SAE and 2 first-class stamps; ms guidelines available for SASE.

Tips: "Our Rainbow imprint carries reproducible books for teachers of children in Christian ministries, including crafts, activities, games and puzzles. Our Legacy imprint (new in '97) handles nonfiction titles for children and adults in the Christian realm, such as Bible story books, devotional books, and so on. Please write for guidelines and study the market before submitting material."

✓ ◻ RAINTREE STECK-VAUGHN, A Harcourt Company, 15 E. 26th St., New York NY 10010. (215)592-1000. Book publisher. **Art Director:** Richard Johnson. **Editorial Director:** Susan Hoffner. Publishes 30 young readers/year; 30 middle readers/year; 20 young adults/year.
- Raintree Steck-Vaughn publishes strictly nonfiction titles for schools and libraries. They have a new hi-lo imprint called Steadwell Books.

Nonfiction: Picture books, young readers, middle readers: animal, biography, geography, health, history, multicultural, nature/environment, science, sports. Young adults: biography, careers, geography, health, history, sports. Average page length: young readers—32; middle readers—48; young adults: 64-128. Recently published: *Indian Nation* series (Indian tribes); *Discovering Science* series (science); and *Making of America* series (American history).

How to Contact/Writers: Nonfiction: query with outline and sample chapters. Include SASE. Responds to queries/mss in 3-4 months.

Illustration: Contact Richard Johnson.

Photography: Contact Richard Johnson.

Terms: Pays authors royalty or flat fee. Offers advance. Sends galleys to authors. Book catalog available for 9×12 SAE and $3 first-class postage. Ms guidelines available for SASE.

Tips: "Request a catalog so you're not proposing books similar to those we've already done. Always include SASE."

✓ Ⓐ ☙ ◻ RANDOM HOUSE BOOKS FOR YOUNG READERS, 1540 Broadway, New York NY 10036. (212)782-9000. Random House, Inc. Book publisher. Estab. 1935. "Random House Books aims to create books that nurture the hearts and minds of children, providing and promoting quality books and a rich variety of media that entertain and educate readers from 6 months to 12 years." Vice President/Publishing Director: Kate Klimo. Vice President/Associate Publishing Director/Art Director: Cathy Goldsmith. **Acquisitions:** Easy-to-Read Books (step-into-reading and picture books): Heidi Kilgras, executive editor. Nonfiction: Alice Jonaitis, senior editor. Stepping Stones and middle grade fiction: Mallory Loehr, editor-in-chief. Fantasy & Science Fiction: Alice Alfonsi, executive editor. Baby & Toddler Books: Apple Jane Jordan. 100% of books published through agents; 2% of books by first-time authors.
- Random House accepts only agented material. Random House title *Only Passing Through: The Story of Sojourner Truth*, illustrated by R. Gregory Christie (text by Anne Rockwell), won a 2001 Coretta Scott King Illustrator Honor Award.

Fiction: Picture books: animal, easy-to-read, history, humor, sports. Young readers: adventure, animal, easy-to-read, history, sports, suspense/mystery. Middle readers: adventure, history, sports, suspense/mystery. Published works of Dr. Seuss, P.D. Eastman and the Berenstein Bears; *The Story of Babar*; the step into reading beginning reader series; the Junie B. Jones series; the Magic Tree house series; *The Protector of the Small Quartet*, by Tamora Pierce; and *The Phantom Tollbooth*, by Norman Juster; *Disney Books for Young Readers*, by Chris Angelilli; *Sesame Workshop*, by Naomi Kleinberg.

Nonfiction: Picture books: animal. Young readers: animal, biography, hobbies. Middle readers: biography, history, science, hobbies, sports.

How to Contact/Writers: Fiction/Nonfiction: Submit through agent only. Publishes a book 12-18 months after acceptance. Will consider simultaneous submissions.

Illustration: Reviews ms/illustration packages from artists through agent only.

Terms: Pays authors in royalties; sometimes buys mss outright. Sends galleys to authors. Book catalog free on request.

RED DEER PRESS, Rm 813, Mackimmie Library Tower, 2500 University Dr. NW, Calgary, Alberta T2N 1N4 Canada. (403)220-4334. Fax: (403)210-8191. E-mail: rdp@ucalgary.ca. Website: www.reddeerpress.com. Imprints: Northern Lights Books for Children, Northern Lights Young Novels. Book publisher. Estab. 1975. **Manuscript/Art Acquisitions:** Peter Carver, children's editor. Publishes 3 picture books/year; 4 young adult titles/year. 20% of books by first-time authors. Red Deer Press is known for their "high-quality international children's program that tackles risky and/or serious issues for kids."

Fiction: Picture books, young readers: adventure, contemporary, fantasy, folktales, history, humor, multicultural, nature/environment, poetry; middle readers, young adult/teens: adventure, contemporary, fantasy, folktales, hi-lo, history, humor, multicultural, nature/environment, problem novels, suspense/mystery. Recently published *The Game*, by Teresa Toten (over 14); *Waiting for the Sun*, by Alison Lohans, illustrated by Peter Ledwon and Marilyn Mets (ages 4-7, picture book); *The Dollmage*, by Martine Leavitt (over 12).

How to Contact/Writers: Fiction/Nonfiction: Query or submit outline/synopsis. Responds to queries in 6 months; ms in 8 months. Publishes a book 18 months after acceptance. Will consider simultaneous submissions.
Illustration: Works with 4-6 illustrators/year. Illustrations only: Query with samples. Responds only if interested. Samples not returned; samples filed for six months.
Photography: Buys stock and assigns work. Model/property releases required. Submit cover letter, résumé and color promo piece.
Terms: Pays authors royalty (negotiated). Occasionally offers advances (negotiated). Pays illustrators and photographers by the project or royalty (depends on the project). Sends galleys to authors. Originals returned to artist at job's completion. Guidelines not available.
Tips: "Red Deer Press is currently not accepting children's manuscripts unless the writer is an established Canadian children's writer with an original project that fits its publishing program. Writers, illustrators and photographers should familiarize themselves with RD Press's children's publishing program."

N **RENAISSANCE HOUSE**, Imprint of Laredo Publishing, 9400 Lloydcrest Dr., Beverly Hills CA 90210. (310)358-5288. Fax: (310)358-5282. E-mail: laredopub@cs.com. Website: www.renaissancehouse.net. Estab. 1991. Specializes in trade books, educational material, multicultural material. Independent book packager/producer. **Manuscript Acquisitions:** Raquel Benatar. **Art Acquisitions:** Sam Laredo. Publishes 5 picture books/year; 10 young readers/year; 10 middle readers/year; 5 young adult titles/year. 25% of books by first-time authors.
Fiction: Picture books: animal, folktales, multicultural. Young readers: animal, anthology, folktales, multicultural. Middle readers, young adult/teens: anthology, folktales, multicultural, nature/environment. Recently published *Isabel Allende, Memories for a Story* (English-Spanish, age 9-12, biography); *Stories of the Americas*, by several authors (ages 9-12, legend).
How to Contact/Writers: Submit outline/synopsis. Responds to queries/mss in 3 weeks. Publishes a book 1 year after acceptance. Will consider simultaneous submissions, electronic submissions via disk or modem.
Illustration: Works with 15 illustrators/year. Uses color artwork only. Reviews ms/illustration packages from artists. Send ms with dummy. Contact: Sam Laredo. Illustrations only: Send tearsheets. Contact: Raquel Benatar. Responds in 3 weeks. Samples not returned; samples filed.
Terms: Pays authors royalty of 5-10% based on retail price. Pays illustrators by the project. Sends galleys to authors; dummies to illustrators. Originals returned to artist at job's completion. Book catalog available for 9 × 12 SASE and $3 postage. All imprints included in a single catalog. Catalog available on website.

N **ROARING BROOK PRESS**, Imprint of The Millbrook Press, 2 Old New Milford Rd., Brookfield CT 06804. (203)740-2220. Fax: (203)775-5643. Estab. 2000. Specializes in fiction, trade books. **Manuscript Acquisitions:** Simon Boughton. Query only with SASE. **Art Acquisitions:** Simon Boughton. Publishes 20 picture books/year; 5 young readers/year; 10 middle readers/year; 10 young adult titles/year. 1% of books by first-time authors. This publisher's goal is "to publish distinctive high-quality children's literature for all ages. To be a great place for authors to be published. To provide personal attention and a focused and thoughtful publishing effort for every book and every author on the list."
Fiction: Picture books, young readers, middle readers, young adults: adventure, animal, contemporary, fantasy, history, humor, multicultural, nature/environment, poetry, religion, science fiction, sports, suspense/mystery. Recently published *Get to Work, Trucks*, by Don Carter (preschool, picture book); *Across a Dark, Wild Sea*, by Don Brown (grades 1-4, picture book); and *Objects in Mirror*, by Ronder Thomas Young (grades 6-9, young adult novel).
How to Contact/Writer: Primarily interested in agented material. Fiction: Submit outline/synopsis and 3 sample chapters. Responds to queries in 1 month; to agented mss in 1 month; to unsolicited queries in 3 months. Publishes a book 12-18 months after acceptance. Will consider simultaneous submissions.
Illustration: Primarily interested in agented material. Works with 25 illustrators/year. Reviews ms/illustration packages from artists or query with illustration samples. Contact: Simon Boughton, publisher. Illustrations only: Query with samples. Contact: Simon Boughton, publisher. Responds to agented queries/submissions in 1 month; unsolicited in 3 months. Samples returned with SASE.
Photography: Works on assignment only.
Terms: Pays authors royalty based on retail price. Offers advances. Pays illustrators royalty based on retail price. Sends galleys to authors; dummies to illustrators, if requested. Book catalog available spring 2002.
Tips: "You should find a reputable agent and have him/her submit your work."

RONSDALE PRESS, 3350 W. 21st Ave., Vancouver, British Columbia V6S 1G7 Canada. (604)738-4688. Fax: (604)731-4548. E-mail: ronhatch@pinc.com. Website: ronsdalepress.com. Book publisher. Estab. 1988. **Manuscript/Art Acquisitions:** Veronica Hatch, children's editor. Publishes 2 children's books/year. 80% of titles by first-time authors. "Ronsdale Press is a Canadian literary publishing house that publishes 8 to 10 books each year, two of which are children's titles. Of particular interest are books involving children exploring and discovering new aspects of Canadian history."

Fiction: Middle readers, young adults: Canadian historical novels. Average word length: for middle readers and young adults—40,000. Recently published *Tangled in Time*, by Lynne Fairbridge (ages 8-15); *The Keeper of the Trees*, by Beverley Brenna (ages 8-12); *Eyewitness*, by Margaret Thompson (ages 8-14); and *Hurricanes over London*, by Charles Reid (ages 8-14).

Nonfiction: Middle readers, young adults: animal, biography, history, multicultural, social issues. Average word length: young readers—90; middle readers—90.

How to Contact/Writers: Fiction/Nonfiction: Submit complete ms. Responds to queries in 2 weeks; ms in 2 months. Publishes a book 1 year after acceptance. Will consider simultaneous submissions.

Illustrations: Works with 2 illustrators/year. Reviews ms/illustration packages from artists. Requires only cover art. Responds in 2 weeks. Samples returned with SASE. Originals returned to artist at job's completion.

Terms: Pays authors royalty of 10% based on retail price. Pays illustrators by the project $800-1,200. Sends galleys to authors. Book catalog available for 8½×11 SAE and $1 postage; ms and art guidelines available for SASE.

Tips: "Ronsdale Press publishes well-written books that have a new slant on things or books that can take an age-old story and give it a new spin. We are particularly interested in novels for middle readers and young adults with a historical component that offers new insights into a part of Canada's history. We publish only Canadian authors."

THE ROSEN PUBLISHING GROUP INC., 29 E. 21st St., New York NY 10010. (212)777-3017. Fax: (212)777-0277. E-mail: rosened@erols.com. Website: www.rosenpublishing.com. **Art Acquisitions:** Cindy Reiman, photo manager. Imprints: Rosen (Young Adult) (Iris Rosoff, editorial director); Rosen Central (Iris Rosoff, editorial director); PowerKids Press (Kristin Eck, editorial director). Publishes 120 young adult books/year.

Nonfiction: Picture books: health, hi-lo, nature/environment, science, self-help, social issues, special needs, sports. Young readers: animal, biography, careers, cooking, geography, health, hi-lo, history, multicultural, nature/environment, religion, science, self-help, social issues, special needs. Middle readers: biography, careers, geography, health, history, hobbies, multicultural, nature/environment, religion, science, self-help, social issues, special needs, sports. Young adult: biography, careers, health, hi-lo, history, multicultural, nature/environment, reference, religion, science, self-help, social issues, special needs, sports. Average word length: young readers—800-950; middle readers—5,000-7,500; young adults—between 8,000 and 30,000. Recently published *Body Talk: A Girl's Guide to What's Happening to Your Body*.

How to Contact/Writers: Nonfiction: Query or submit outline/synopsis. Responds in 6 weeks. Publishes a book 1 year after acceptance.

Photography: Buys stock and assigns work. Contact: Cindy Reiman, photo manager.

Terms: Book catalog available—no SASE or postage necessary. Offers ms and photographer's guidelines with SASE or via website.

Tips: "Our list is specialized, and we publish only in series. Authors should familiarize themselves with our publishing program and policies before submitting."

ST. ANTHONY MESSENGER PRESS, 1615 Republic St., Cincinnati OH 45210-1298. (513)241-5615. Fax: (513)241-0399. E-mail: books@americancatholic.org. Website: www.AmericanCatholic.org. Book publisher. Managing Editor: Lisa Biedenbach. **Manuscript Acquisitions:** Katie Carroll. 25% of books by first-time authors. Imprints include Franciscan Communications (print and video) and Ikonographics (video). "Through print and electronic media marketed in North America and worldwide, we endeavor to evangelize, inspire and inform those who search for God and seek a richer Catholic, Christian, human life. We also look for books for parents and religious educators."

Fiction: Picture books, middle readers, young readers: religion.

Nonfiction: Picture books, young readers, middle readers, young adults: religion. "We like all our resources to include anecdotes, examples, etc., that appeal to a wide audience. All of our products try to reflect cultural and racial diversity." Recently published *Friend Jesus: Prayers for Children*, by Gaynell Bordes Cronin; *Growing Up a Friend of Jesus: A Guide to Discipleship for Children*, by Francoise Darcy-Berube and John Paul Berube (middle readers); *Can You Find Jesus? Introducing Your Child to the Gospel*, by Philip Gallery and Janet Harlow (ages 5-10); *God Is Calling* (family based catechetical program for ages 11-14 and under 10); and *Can You Find Bible Heroes? Introducing Your Child to the Old Testament*, by Philip Gallery and Janet Harlow (ages 5-10); *Can You Find Followers of Jesus? Introducing Your Child to Disciples*, by Philip Gallery and Janet Harlow (ages 5-10); *People of the Bible: Their Life and Customs*, by Claire Musatti (ages 5-10).

How to Contact/Writers: Query or submit outline/synopsis and sample chapters. Responds to queries in 1 month; mss in 2 months. Publishes a book 12-18 months after acceptance.

Illustration: Works with 2 illustrators/year. "We design all covers and do most illustrations in-house, unless illustrations are submitted with text." Reviews ms/illustration packages from artists. Query with samples, résumé. Contact: Jeanne Kortekamp, art director. Responds to queries in 1 month. Samples returned with SASE; samples filed. Originals returned at job's completion.

Photography: Purchases photos from freelancers. Contact: Jeanne Kortekamp, art director. Buys stock and assigns work.

Hurricanes over London

Charles Reid

A teenager's desire to learn about his grandfather's life during World War II in London may not be the ideal theme for an assignment-hungry illustrator to exemplify. However, since Canadian publisher Ronsdale Press has been especially pleased with Ljuba Levstek's depictions for several of their books before, there was no question about the artist's capabilities for the cover of *Hurricanes over London*. Ronsdale Press publishes two young adult historical novels yearly, and approximately 80% of their titles are by first-time authors.

Terms: Pays authors royalties of 10-12% based on net receipts. Offers average advance payment of $1,000. Pays illustrators by the project. Pays photographers by the project. Sends galleys to authors. Book catalog and ms guidelines free on request.

Tips: "Know our audience—Catholic. We seek popularly written manuscripts that include the best of current Catholic scholarship. Parents, especially baby boomers, want resources for teaching children about the Catholic faith for passing on values. We try to publish items that reflect strong Catholic Christian values."

SCHOLASTIC CANADA LTD., 175 Hillmount Rd., Markham, Ontario L6C 1Z7 Canada. (905)887-READ. Fax: (905)887-1131. Website: www.scholastic.ca; for ms/artist guidelines: www.scholastic.ca/guideline.ht ml. Imprints: North Winds Press; Les Éditions Scholastic. **Acquisitions**: Editor, children's books. Publishes hardcover and trade paperback originals. Publishes 30 titles/year; imprint publishes 4 titles/year. 3% of books from first-time authors; 50% from unagented writers. Canadian authors, theme or setting required.

Fiction: Children's/juvenile, young adult. Recently published *After the War*, by Carol Matas (novel).

Nonfiction: Animals, history, hobbies, nature, recreation, science, sports. Reviews artwork/photos as part of ms package. Send photocopies. Recently published *Whose Bright Idea Was It?*, by Larry Verstraete (about amazing inventions).

How to Contact/Writers: Query with synopsis, 3 sample chapters and SASE. Nonfiction: Query with outline, 1-2 sample chapters and SASE (IRC or Canadian stamps only). Responds in 3 months. Publishes book 1 year after acceptance.

Terms: Pays 5-10% royalty on retail price. Offers advance: $1,000-5,000 (Canadian). Book catalog for 8½ × 11 SAE with 2 first-class stamps (IRC or Canadian stamps only).

SCHOLASTIC INC., 555 Broadway, New York NY 10012. (212)343-6100. Website: www.scholastic.com. Estab. 1920. Senior Vice President and publisher: Jean Feiwel. **Manuscript Acquisitions:** Scholastic Press: Elizabeth Szabla, editorial director; Blue Sky Press: Bonnie Verburg, editorial director; Trade Paperback: Craig Walker, vice president and editorial director; Cartwheel Books: Bernette Ford, vice president and editorial director; Arthur A. Levine Books: Arthur Levine, editorial director; Orchard Books: Judy Wilson, publisher; Scholastic Reference: Kenneth Wright, editorial director. **Art Acquisitions:** David Saylor, creative director. "We are proud of the many fine, innovative materials we have created—such as classroom magazines, book clubs, book fairs, and our new literacy and technology programs. But we are most proud of our reputation as 'The Most Trusted Name in Learning.' "

● Scholastic is not interested in receiving ideas for more fiction paperback series. They do not accept unsolicited mss.

Illustration: Works with 50 illustrators/year. Does not review ms/illustration packages.Illustrations only: send promo sheet and tearsheets. Responds only if interested. Samples not returned. Original artwork returned at job's completion.

Terms: All contracts negotiated individually; pays royalty. Sends galleys to author; dummies to illustrators.

SCHOLASTIC PRESS, 555 Broadway, New York NY 10012. (212)343-6100. Website: www.scholastic.com. Book publisher. Imprint of Scholastic Inc. **Manuscript Acquisitions:** Dianne Hess, executive editor (picture book fiction/nonfiction); Lauren Thompson, senior editor (picture book fiction/nonfiction); Tracy Mack, executive editor (picture book, middle grade, YA). **Art Acquisitions:** David Saylor, Scholastic Press, Reference, Paperback; Edie Weinberg, Cartwheel Books. Publishes 60 titles/year. 1% of books by first-time authors.

Fiction: All levels: adventure, animal, anthology, concept, contemporary, fantasy, health, history, humor, multicultural, nature/environment, poetry, religion, science fiction, sports, suspense/mystery. Picture books, middle readers, young adults: all subjects. Multicultural needs include: strong fictional or nonfictional themes featuring non-white characters and cultures. Does not want to see mainstream religious, bibliotherapeutic, adult. Average word length: picture books—varies; young adults—150-200 pages. Recently published *Black Cat*, by Christopher Meyers.

Nonfiction: All levels: animal, biography, history, multicultural, music/dance, nature/environment, science, social issues, sports. Picture books: all subjects. Multicultural needs authenticity. Recently published *Blizzard!*, by Tim Murphy.

How to Contact/Writers: Fiction: "Send query with 1 sample chapter and synopsis. Don't call!" Nonfiction: young adult titles: query. Picture books: submit complete ms. Responds in 1-3 months.

Illustrations: Works with 30 illustrators/year. Uses both b&w and color artwork. Contact: Editorial Submissions. Illustration only: Query with samples; send tearsheets. Responds only if interested. Samples returned with SASE. Original artwork returned at job's completion.

Photography: Buys photos from freelancers. Contact: Photo Research Dept. Buys stock and assigns work. Uses photos to accompany nonfiction. Model/property releases required; captions required. Submit cover letter, résumé, client list, stock photo list.

Terms: Pays authors by varying royalty (usually standard trade roles) or outright purchase (rarely). Offers variable advance. Pays illustrators by the project (range: varies) or standard royalty based on retail price. Pays photographers by the project or royalty. Sends galleys to authors.

Tips: "Read *currently* published children's books. Revise, rewrite, rework and find your own voice, style and subject. We are looking for authors with a strong and unique voice who can tell a great story and have the ability to evoke genuine emotion. Children's publishers are becoming more selective, looking for irresistable talent and fairly broad appeal, yet still very willing to take risks, just to keep the game interesting."

SEEDLING PUBLICATIONS, INC., 4522 Indianola Ave., Columbus OH 43214-2246. (614)267-7333. Fax (614)267-4205. E-mail: Sales@SeedlingPub.com. Website: www.SeedlingPub.com. **Acquisitions:** Josie Stewart, vice president. 20% of books by first-time authors. Publishes books for the beginning reader in English. "Natural language and predictable text are requisite to our publications. Patterned text acceptable, but must have a unique storyline. Poetry, books in rhyme, full-length picture books or chapter books are not being accepted at this time. Illustrations are not necessary."
Fiction: Beginning reader books: adventure, animal, fantasy, hi-lo, humor, multicultural, nature/environment, special needs. Multicultural needs include stories which include children from many cultures and Hispanic-centered storylines. Does not want to see texts longer than 16 pages or over 150-200 words or stories in rhyme. Average word length: young readers—100. Recently published *Treasure in the Attic*, by Linda Kulp and *Before the Fridge*, by Heather Flanders (ages 3-7, paperback early reader).
Nonfiction: Beginning reader books: animal, concept, hi-lo, multicultural, music/dance, nature/environment, science, special needs, sports. Does not want to see texts longer than 16 pages or over 150-200 words. Average word length: young readers—100. Recently published *Zebras*, by Josie Stewart and Lynn Salem (ages 3-7, early reader).
How to Contact/Writers: Fiction/Nonfiction: Submit complete ms. Responds in 6 months. Publishes a book 1-2 years after acceptance. Will consider simultaneous submissions.
Illustration: Works with 4-5 illustrators/year. Uses color artwork only. Reviews ms/illustration packages from artists. Submit ms with dummy. Illustrations only: Send color copies. Responds only if interested. Samples returned with SASE only; samples filed if interested.
Photography: Buys photos from freelancers. Works on assignment only. Model/property releases required. Uses color prints and 35mm transparencies. Submit cover letter and color promo piece.
Terms: Pays authors royalty of 5% based on retail price or work purchased outright. Pays illustrators and photographers by the project. Original artwork is not returned at job's completion. Book catalog available for 2 first-class stamps.
Tips: "Follow our guidelines carefully and test your story with children and educators."

SILVER MOON PRESS, 160 Fifth Ave., New York NY 10010. (212)242-6499. Fax: (212)242-6799. E-mail: mail@silvermoonpress.com. Website: www.silvermoonpress.com. Publisher: David Katz. Managing Editor: Carmen McCain. **Marketing Coordinator:** Karin Lillebo. Book publisher. Publishes 2 books for grades 4-6. 25% of books by first-time authors; 10% books from agented authors. "We publish books of entertainment and educational value and develop books which fit neatly into curriculum for grades 4-6. Silver Moon Press publishes mainly American historical fiction with a strong focus on the Revolutionary War and Colonial times. History comes alive when children can read about other children who lived when history was being made!"
Fiction: Middle readers: historical, multicultural and mystery. Average word length: 14,000. Recently published *A Message for General Washington*, by Vivian Schurfranz; and *A Secret Party in Boston Harbor*, by Kris Hemphill (both historical fiction, ages 8-12); *Treason Stops at Oyster Bay*, by Anna Leah Sweetzer.
How to Contact/Writers: Fiction: Query. Send synopsis and/or a few chapters, along with a SASE. Responds to queries in 2-4 weeks; mss in 1-2 months. Publishes a book 1-2 years after acceptance. Will consider simultaneous submissions, or previously published work.
Illustration: Works with 2-3 illustrators/year. Reviews ms/illustration packages from artists. Query. Illustrations only: Query with samples, résumé, client list. Responds only if interested. Samples returned with SASE; samples filed. Original artwork returned at job's completion.
Photography: Buys photos from freelancers. Buys stock and assigns work. Uses archival, historical, sports photos. Captions required. Uses color, b&w prints; 35mm, 2¼×2¼, 4×5, 8×10 transparencies. Submit cover letter, résumé, published samples, client list, promo piece.
Terms: Pays authors royalty or work purchased outright. Pays illustrators by the project, no royalty. Pays photographers by the project, per photo, no royalty. Sends galleys to authors; dummies to illustrators. Book catalog available for 8½×11 SAE and 77¢ postage.

◤ SIMON & SCHUSTER BOOKS FOR YOUNG READERS, 1230 Avenue of the Americas, New York NY 10020. (212)698-7000. Fax: (212)698-2796. Website: www.simonsays.kids.com. Imprint of Simon & Schuster Children's Publishing Division. Vice President/Associate Publisher: Steve Geck. **Manuscript Acquisitions:** David Gale, editorial director; Kevin Lewis, senior editor; Amy Hampton-Knight, associate editor; Jessica Schulte, editor; Emily Thomas, editorial assistant. **Art Acquisitions:** Paul Zakris, art director. Publishes 75 books/year. "We publish high-quality fiction and nonfiction for a variety of age groups and a variety of markets. Above all we strive to publish books that will offer kids a fresh perspective on their world."
● Simon & Schuster Books for Young Readers does not accept unsolicited manuscripts. Simon & Schuster title *Click, Clack, Moo: Cows That Type*, illustrated by Betsy Lewin (text by Doreen Cronin), won a 2001 Caldecott Honor Medal. Their title *Virgie Goes to School with Us Boys*, illustrated by E.B. Lewis (text

by Elizabeth Fitzgerald Howard), won a 2001 Coretta Scott King Illustrator Honor Award. Their title *River Friendly, River Wild*, by Jane Kurtz, won the Golden Kite Award for Picture Book Text in 2001. See First Books to read about Simon & Schuster author Rachel Cohn and her book, *Gingerbread*. First Books Follow-up features Simon & Schuster author Sonya Sones.

Fiction: Picture books: animal, concept. Middle readers, young adult: adventure, suspense/mystery. All levels: anthology, contemporary, history, humor, poetry, nature/environment. Recently published *The School Story*, by Andrew Clements; and *When Kambia Elaine Flew in From Neptune*, by Lori Aurelia Williams.

Nonfiction: All levels: biography, history, nature/environment. Picture books: concept. "We're looking for picture book or middle grade nonfiction that has a retail potential. No photo essays." Recently published *Little Panda*, by Joanne Ryder.

How to Contact/Writers: Accepting query letters only. Responds to queries/mss in 1-2 months. Publishes a book 2-4 years after acceptance. Will consider simultaneous submissions.

Illustration: Works with 70 illustrators/year. Do not submit original artwork. Editorial reviews ms/illustration packages from artists. Submit query letter to Submissions Editor. Illustrations only: Query with samples; samples filed. Provide promo sheet, tearsheets. Responds only if interested. Originals returned at job's completion.

Terms: Pays authors royalty (varies) based on retail price. Pays illustrators or photographers by the project or royalty (varies) based on retail price. Original artwork returned at job's completion. Ms/artist's guidelines available via website or free on request (call (212)698-2707).

Tips: "We're looking for picture books centered on a strong, fully-developed protagonist who grows or changes during the course of the story; YA novels that are challenging and psychologically complex; also imaginative and humorous middle-grade fiction. And we want nonfiction that is as engaging as fiction. Our imprint's slogan is 'Reading You'll Remember.' We aim to publish books that are fresh, accessible and family-oriented; we want them to have an impact on the reader."

SOMERVILLE HOUSE INC., (formerly Somerville House Books Limited), 24 Dinnick Crescent, Toronto, Ontario M4N 1L5 Canada. (416)489-7769. Fax: (416)486-4458. E-mail: somer@sympatico.ca. Website: www.somervillehouse.com. Somerville publishes books and develops products. **Acquisitions:** Jane Somerville, publisher/president. Produces 20-30 titles/year in nonfiction and novelty formats.

- Somerville is currently accepting unsolicited mss in the areas of natural science, activities, sports and novelty formats.

Nonfiction: Young readers and middle readers: activity books, animal, arts/crafts, cooking, geography, history, hobbies, music/dance, nature/environment, science, sports. Recently published *The Hummingbird Book and Feeder*, by Neil Dawe; and *The Titantic Book and Submersible Model*, by Steve Santini.

How to Contact/Writers: Only interested in agented material. Responds to queries/mss in 2-3 months.

Illustration: Works with 20-30 illustrators/year. Responds only if interested. Samples not returned; samples filed.

SOUNDPRINTS, 353 Main Ave., Norwalk CT 06851-1552. (203)846-2274. Fax: (203)846-1776. E-mail: soundprints@soundprints.com. Website: www.soundprints.com. Estab. 1987. Specializes in trade books, educational material, multicultural material, fact-based fiction. **Manuscript Acquisitions:** Chelsea Shriver, assistant editor. **Art Acquisitions:** Marcin Pilchowski. Publishes 4 picture books/year; 8 young readers/year. Soundprints publishes children's books accompanied by plush toys and read-along cassettes that deal with wildlife, history and nature. All content must be accurate and realistic and is curated by experts for veracity. Soundprints will begin publishing early reader chapter books in the spring of 2002.

Fiction: Picture books: animal. Young readers: animal, multicultural, nature/environment. Middle readers: history, multicultural.

Nonfiction: Picture books: animals. Young readers: animal, multicultural, nataure/environment. Middle readers: history, multicultural. *Koala Country: Story of an Australian Eucalyptus Forest*, by Deborah Dennard, illustrated by James McKinnon (grades 1-4); *Box Turtle at Silver Pond*, by Susan Korman, illustrated by Stephen Mucclesi (grades ps-2); *Bear on His Own*, by Laura Gales Gatvin (ages 18 months to 3 years).

How to Contact/Writers: Fiction/Nonfiction: Query. Responds in 3 months. Publishes book 2 years after acceptance.

Illustration: Works with 12 illustrators/year. Uses color artwork only. Query. Contact: Chelsea Shriver, assistant editor. Query with samples. Samples not returned.

Photography: Works on assignment only.

**FOR EXPLANATIONS OF THESE SYMBOLS,
SEE THE INSIDE FRONT AND BACK COVERS OF THIS BOOK**

Terms: Work purchased outright from authors for $1,000-2,500. Pays illustrators by the project. Book catalog available for 8½×11 SASE; ms and art guidelines available for SASE. Catalog available on website.

SOURCEBOOKS, INC., 1935 Brookdale Rd., Suite 139, Naperville IL 60563-9245. (630)961-3900. Fax: (630)961-2168. Website: www.sourcebooks.com. Book publisher. **Manuscript Acquisitions:** Todd Stocke, editorial director; Hillel Black, agented manuscripts; Deborah Werksman, gift, humor, relationships. **Art Acquisitions:** Norma Underwood, director of production.
How to Contact/Writers: Fiction/Nonfiction: Query or submit outline/synopsis. Responds to queries/mss in 3 months. Publishes a book 1 year after acceptance. Will consider simultaneous submissions, electronic submissions via disk or modem and previously published work.
Illustration: Works with 10 illustrators/year. Reviews ms/illustration packages from artists. Query. Illustrations only: Query with samples. Samples returned with SASE; samples filed.
Photography: Buys stock.
Terms: Send galleys to authors. Originals returned to artist at job's completion. Book catalog for 9×12 SASE. All imprints included in a single catalog. Ms guidelines available for SASE or via website.

☑ **SOUTHWEST KIDS**, (formerly Rising Moon), P.O. Box 1389, Flagstaff AZ 86002-1389. (928)774-5251. Fax: (520)774-0592. E-mail: editorial@northlandpub.com. Website: www.northlandpub.com. Book publisher. **Manuscript Acquisitions:** Tammy Gates, editor. **Art Acquisitions:** Donna Boyd, art director. Publishes 10-12 picture books/year; 10% of books by first-time authors. "Southwest Kids is looking for original stories with Southwest flavor, fractured fairy tales and activity books."
Fiction: Picture books: humor, contemporary, multicultural, nature/environment, poetry. All levels: multicultural, bilingual. "Multicultural needs include stories with characters/plots that have to do with multicultural Hispanic aspects. No religion, science fiction, anthology. Average word length: picture books—300-1,500. Recently published *When Kangaroo Goes to School*, by Sonya Levitin, illustrated by Jeff Seaver (ages 4-7); *Clarence and the Great Surprise*, written and illustrated by Jean Ekman Adams (ages 5-8).
Nonfiction: Picture books: activity books, animal, nature/environment, sports. Young readers: activity books, board books, arts/crafts, nature/environment, sports.
How to Contact/Writers: We no longer accept unsolicited submissions. Accepts picture book ms from agented authors and previously published authors only.
Illustration: Works with 10-12 illustrators/year. Uses color artwork only. Reviews ms/illustration packages from artists. Submit ms with 3 pieces of final art (color copy). Illustrations only: Contact: art director with résumé, samples, promo sheet, slides, tearsheets. Samples returned with SASE; samples filed.
Terms: Pays authors royalty based on retail or wholesale price. Pays illustrators by the project or royalty based on retail or wholesale price. Sends galleys to authors; dummies to illustrators. Originals returned at job's completion. Catalog and writer's and artist's guidelines available for SASE.

◘ **THE SPEECH BIN, INC.**, 1965 25th Ave., Vero Beach FL 32960. (561)770-0007. Fax: (561)770-0006. Book publisher. Estab. 1984. **Acquisitions:** Jan J. Binney, senior editor. Publishes 10-12 books/year. 50% of books by first-time authors; less than 15% of books from agented writers. "Nearly all our books deal with treatment of children (as well as adults) who have communication disorders of speech or hearing or children who deal with family members who have such disorders (e.g., a grandparent with Alzheimer's disease or stroke)."
    ● The Speech Bin is currently overstocked with fiction.
Fiction: Picture books: animal, easy-to-read, health, special needs. Young readers, middle readers, young adult: health, special needs, communication disorders.
Nonfiction: Picture books, young readers, middle readers, young adults: activity books, health, textbooks, special needs, communication disorders.
How to Contact/Writers: Fiction/Nonfiction: Query. Responds to queries in 6 weeks; mss in 3 months. Publishes a book 10-12 months after acceptance. "Will consider simultaneous submissions *only* if notified; too many authors fail to let us know if manuscript is simultaneously submitted to other publishers! We *strongly* prefer sole submissions. No electronic or faxed submissions."
Illustration: Works with 4-5 illustrators/year ("usually in-house"). Reviews ms/illustration packages from artists. Ms/illustration packages and illustration only: "Query first!" Submit tearsheets (no original art). SASE required for reply or return of material. No electronic or faxed submissions without prior authorization.
Photography: Buys stock and assigns work. Looking for scenic shots. Model/property releases required. Uses glossy b&w prints, 35mm or 2¼×2¼ transparencies. Submit résumé, business card, promotional literature or tearsheets to be kept on file.
Terms: Pays authors in royalties based on selling price. Pay illustrators by the project. Photographers paid by the project or per photo. Sends galleys to authors. Original artwork returned at job's completion. Book catalog for $1.43 postage and 9×12 SAE; ms guidelines for #10 SASE.
Tips: "No calls, please. All submissions and inquiries must be in writing."

STANDARD PUBLISHING, 8121 Hamilton Ave., Cincinnati OH 45231. (513)931-4050. Fax: (513)931-0950. E-mail: customerservice@standardpub.com. Website: www.standardpub.com. Book publisher. Estab. 1866. Director, Children's Publishing: Diane Stortz. **Manuscript Acquisitions:** Lise Caldwell, children's editor, Ruth

Frederick, Church Resources. **Art Acquisitions:** Coleen Davis, art director. Imprints: Bean Sprouts™ Children's Books, Church Resources. Number and type of books varies yearly. Many projects are written in-house. No juvenile or young adult novels. 25-40% of books by first-time authors; 1% of books from agented writers. "We publish well-written, upbeat books with a Christian perspective. Books are fun with relevancy in Christian education."

 ● Standard publishes *Kidz Chat* and *Livewire*, both listed in Magazines. Also see listing for Standard Publishing in the Greeting Cards, Puzzles & Games section.

Fiction: Adventure, animal, contemporary, Bible stories. Average word length: board/picture books—400-1,000. Recent publications: *Noah! Noah!*, by Jennifer Stewart.

Nonfiction: Bible background, nature/environment, devotions. Average word length: 400-1,000. Recently published *Pattycake Devotions*, by Christine Tangiold, illustrated by Norma Garris (board books).

How to Contact/Writers: Responds in 6 weeks on queries, mss in 3 months.

Illustration: Works with 20 new illustrators/year. Illustrations only: Submit cover letter and photocopies. Responds to art samples only if interested. Samples returned with SASE; samples filed.

Terms: Pays authors royalties based on net price or work purchased outright (range varies by project). Pays illustrators (mostly) by project. Pays photographers by the photo. Sends galleys to authors on most projects. Book catalog available for $2 and 8½×11 SAE; ms guidelines for letter-size SASE.

Tips: "We look for manuscripts that help draw children into a relationship with Jesus Christ; help children develop insights about what the Bible teaches; make reading an appealing and pleasurable activity."

STEMMER HOUSE PUBLISHERS, INC., 2627 Caves Rd., Owings Mills MD 21117-9919. (410)363-3690. Fax: (410)363-8459. E-mail: stemmerhouse@home.com. Website: www.stemmer.com. Book publisher. Estab. 1975. **Acquisitions:** Barbara Holdridge, president. Publishes 1-3 picture books/year. "Sporadic" numbers of young reader, middle reader titles/year. 60% of books by first-time authors. "Stemmer House is best known for its commitment to fine illustrated books, excellently produced."

 ● Stemmer House is not currently accepting fiction.

Nonfiction: Picture books: animal, multicultural, nature. All level: animals, nature/environment. Multicultural needs include Native American, African. Recently published *Will You Sting Me? Will You Bite?*, by Sarah Swan Miller.

How to Contact/Writers: Fiction/Nonfiction: Query or submit outline/synopsis and sample chapters. Responds to queries/mss in 1 week. Publishes a book 18 months after acceptance. Will consider simultaneous submissions. No submissions via e-mail.

Illustration: Works with 2-3 illustrators/year. Uses color artwork only. Reviews ms/illustration packages from artists. Query first with several photocopied illustrations. Illustrations only: Submit tearsheets and/or slides (with SASE for return). Responds in 2 weeks. Samples returned with SASE; samples filed "if noteworthy."

Terms: Pays authors royalties of 4-10% based on net sales price. Offers average advance payment of $300. Pays illustrators royalty of 4-10% based on net sales price. Pays photographers 4-10% royalty based on net sales price. Sends galleys to authors. Original artwork returned at job's completion. Book catalog and ms guidelines for 9×12 SASE or via website.

Tips: Writers: "Simplicity, literary quality and originality are the keys." Illustrators: "We want to see ms/illustration packages—don't forget the SASE!"

SUPER MANAGEMENT, Smarty Pants A/V, 15104 Detroit, Suite 2, Lakewood OH 44107-3916. (216)221-5300. Fax: (216)221-5348. Estab. 1988. Specializes in mass market books, fiction, educational material, Christian material, audio with each book. **Acquisitions:** S. Tirk, CEO/President. Publishes 12 young readers/year. 5% of books by first-time authors. "We do mostly the classics or well known names such as Paddington Bear."

Fiction: Picture books: adventure, animal, folktales, multicultural, nature/environment, poetry. Average word length: young readers—24 pages. Recently published *The Best of Mother Goose*, from the "Real M.G."; *Beatrix Potter, Paddington Bear*.

Nonfiction: Picture books, young readers: activity books, animal, music/dance, nature/environment. Average word length: picture books—24 pages; middle readers—24 pages.

How to Contact/Writers: Fiction: Submit complete ms. Responds in 3 weeks. Publishes a book 6-12 months after acceptance. Will consider simultaneous submissions and previously published work.

Illustration: Only interested in agented material. Works with several illustrators/year. Uses color artwork only. Reviews ms/illustration packages from artists. Submit ms with dummy with return prepaid envelope. Contact: S. Tirk, CEO/President. Illustrations only: send promo sheet. Contact: S. Tirk, CEO/President. Responds in 3 weeks to queries. Samples returned with SASE.

Photography: Works on assignment only. Model/property releases required. Uses color prints. Submit color promo piece.

Terms: Pays author negotiable royalty. Buys artwork and photos outright. Manuscript and art guidelines available for SASE.

Tips: "We deal with mostly children's classics and well-known characters."

⬛ ⬜ **TEACHER IDEAS PRESS**, Libraries Unlimited, P.O. Box 6633, Englewood CO 80155-6633. (303)770-1220. Fax: (303)220-8843. E-mail: lu-books@lu.com. Website: www.lu.com/tip. Estab. 1965. Speciali zes in educational material, multicultural material. Independent book packager/producer.
Nonfiction: Young readers, middle readers, young adult: activity books, multicultural, reference, teacher resou rce books. Recently published *Science Through Children's Literature, 2002*, by Butzow (grades K-6, lit-based activity book); *More Novels & Plays: 30 Creative Teaching Guides for Grades 6-12*, by Worthington; and *Native American Today: Resources & Activities for Educators*, by Hirschfelder (grades 4-8).
How to Contact/Writers: Nonfiction: Query or submit outline/synopsis. Responds to queries in 6 weeks. Publishes a book 6-9 months after acceptance. Will consider simultaneous submission or electronic submissions via disk or modem.
Terms: Pays authors royalty of 10-15%. Send galleys to authors. Book catalog available for 9×12 SASE and t first-class stamps. Writer's guidelines available for SASE. Catalog and ms guidelines available online at www.lu.com.
Tips: "We encourage queries from writers with classroom experience as teachers, although we will consider others. Activity Books, annotated bios, story collections with supplemental materials, and books with many reproducibles are welcome for consideration."

TILBURY HOUSE, PUBLISHERS, 2 Mechanic St., #3, Gardiner ME 04345. (207)582-1899. Fax: (207)582-8227. E-mail: tilbury@tilburyhouse.com. Website: www.tilburyhouse.com. Book publisher. Publisher: Jennifer Elliott. Publishes 1-3 young readers/year.
Fiction: Picture books, young readers, middle readers: multicultural, nature/environment. Special needs include books that teach children about tolerance and honoring diversity. Recently published *Shy Mama's Halloween*, by Anne Broyles, illustrated by Leane Morin; and *Lucy's Family Tree*, by Karen Halversen Shreck, illustrated by Stephen Gassler.
Nonfiction: Picture books, young readers, middle readers: multicultural, nature/environment. Recently published *Sea Soup: Zooplankton*, by Mary Cerullo, with photography by Bill Curtsinger; and *Shelterwood*, by Susan Hand Shetterly, illustrated by Rebecca Haley McCall.
How to Contact/Writers: Fiction/Nonfiction: Submit outline/synopsis. Responds to queries/mss in 1 month. Publishes a book 1-2 years after acceptance. Will consider simultaneous submissions "with notification."
Illustration: Works with 2 illustrators/year. Illustrations only: Query with samples. Contact: J. Elliott, associate publisher. Responds in 1 month. Samples returned with SASE. Original artwork returned at job's completion.
Photography: Buys photos from freelancers. Contact: J. Elliott, publisher. Works on assignment only.
Terms: Pays authors royalty based on wholesale price. Pays illustrators/photographers by the project; royalty based on wholesale price. Sends galleys to authors. Book catalog available for 6×9 SAE and 55¢ postage.
Tips: "We are primarily interested in children's books that teach children about tolerance in a multicultural society and honoring diversity. We are also interested in books that teach children about environmental issues."

N **MEGAN TINGLEY BOOKS**, Imprint of Little, Brown and Company, Three Center Plaza, Boston MA 02143. (617)227-0730. Website: www.twbookmark.com. Estab. 2000. Specializes in trade books, nonfiction, fiction, multicultural material. **Manuscript Acquisitions:** Alvina Ling. **Art Acquisitions:** Ann-Marie Simundson, managing editor. Publishes 10 picture books/year; 1 middle readers/year; 1 young adult title/year. 2% of books by first-time authors.
• Megan Tingley Books accepts query letters and agented material only.
Fiction: Average word length: picture books—under 1,000 words. Recently published *You Read to Me, I'll Read to You: Very Short Stories to Read Together*, by Mary Ann Hoberman, illustrated by Michael Emberley (ages 4 and up, picture book); *It's Okay to be Different*, by Todd Parr (all ages, picture book); *Define Normal*, by Julie Peters.
Nonfiction: All levels: activity books, animal, arts/crafts, biography, concept, cooking, history, multicultural, music/dance, nature/environment, science, self help, social issues, special needs. Recently published *Twin Tales: The Magic & Mystery of Multiple Births*, by Donna Jackson (ages 10 and up, picture book); *Imaginative Inventions*, by Charise Harper (ages 4-8, picture book); *The Girls' Book of Friendship*, by Catherine Dee (ages 10 and up, middle reader).
How to Contact/Writers: Prefers agented material. Query. Responds to queries in 2 weeks; mss in 3 months. Publishes a book 2 years after acceptance. Will consider simultaneous submissions, electronic submissions via modem, previously published work.
Illustration: Works with 15 illustrators/year. Reviews ms/illustration packages from artists. Query. Contact: Alvina Ling, editorial assistant. Illustrations only: Query with samples. Contact: Alvina Ling, editorial assistant. Responds only if interested. Samples not returned; samples kept on file.
Photography: Buys stock images. Contact: Alvina Ling, editorial assistant. Submit cover letter, samples.
Terms: Pays authors royalty of 5% based on retail price or work purchased outright. Pays illustrators by the project, 5% royalty based on retail price. Pays photographers by the project, royalty 5% based on retail price. Sends galleys to authors. Originals returned to artist at job's completion. All imprints included in a single catalog. Book catalog and art guidelines available for SASE.

☑ **TOR BOOKS**, Forge, Orb, 175 Fifth Ave., New York NY 10010-7703. Fax: (212)388-0191. E-mail: juliet...leyba@tor.com. Website: www.tor.com. **Publisher, Middle Grade and Young Adult Division:** Kathleen Doherty. Children's, Young Adult Editor: Jonathan Schmidt. Educational Sales Coordinator: Benjamin Yots. Publishes 5-10 middle readers/year; 5-10 young adults/year.

Fiction: Middle readers, young adult titles: adventure, animal, anthology, concept, contemporary, fantasy, folktales, health, history, humor, multicultural, nature/environment, problem novel, science fiction, special needs, sports, suspense/mystery. "We are interested and open to books which tell stories from a wide range of perspectives. We are interested in materials that deal with a wide range of issues." Average word length: middle readers—10,000; young adults—30,000-60,000. Published *Mind Quakes: Stories to Shatter Your Brain* and *Scorpions Shards*, by Neal Shusterman (ages 8 and up); and *From One Experience to Another*, edited by Helen and Jerry Weiss (ages 10 and up).

Nonfiction: Middle readers and young adult: activity books, geography, history, how-to, multicultural, nature/environment, science, social issues. Does not want to see religion, cooking. Average word length: middle readers—10,000-15,000; young adults—40,000. Published *Strange Unsolved Mysteries*, by Phyllis Rabin Emert; *Stargazer's Guide* (to the Galaxy), by Q.L. Pearce (ages 8-12, guide to constellations, illustrated).

How to Contact/Writers: Fiction/Nonfiction: Submit outline/synopsis and 3 sample chapters or complete ms. Responds to queries in 3 weeks; mss in 6 months.

Illustration: Works with 40 illustrators/year. Reviews ms/illustration packages from artists. Query with samples. Contact: Jonathan Schmidt. Responds only if interested. Samples returned with SASE; samples kept on file.

Terms: Pays authors royalty. Offers advances. Pays illustrators by the project. Book catalog available for 9 × 12 SAE and 3 first-class stamps. Submission guidelines available with SASE.

Tips: "Know the house you are submitting to, familiarize yourself with the types of books they are publishing. Get an agent. Allow him/her to direct you to publishers who are most appropriate. It saves time and effort."

🔲 **TRADEWIND BOOKS**, 2216 Stephens St., Vancouver, British Columbia V6K 3W6 Canada.(604)730-0153. Fax: (604)730-0154. E-mail: tradewindbooks@eudoramail.com. Website: tradewindbooks.com. Estab. 1994. Trade book publisher. **Manuscript Acquisitions:** Michael Katz, publisher. **Art Acquisitions:** Carol Frank, art director. Publishes 3 picture books/year. 25% of books by first-time authors.

Fiction: Picture books: adventure, animal, multicultural, folktales. Average word length: 900 words. Recently published *Wherever Bears Be*; *The Girl Who Lost Her Smile*; and *Huevos Rancheros*.

Nonfiction: Picture books: animal and nature/environment.

How to Contact/Writers: Fiction: Submit complete ms. Will consider simultaneous submissions. Do not send query letter. Responds to mss in 6 weeks. Unsolicited submissions accepted only if authors have read at least 3 books published by Tradewind Books. Submissions must include a reference to these books.

Illustration: Works with 3-4 illustrators/year. Uses color artwork only. Reviews ms/illustration packages from artists. Send ms with dummy. Illustrations only: Query with samples. Responds only if interested. Samples returned with SASE; samples filed.

Photography: Works on assignment only. Uses color prints.

Terms: Royalties negotiable. Offers advances against royalties. Originals returned to artist at job's completion. Book catalog available for 3 × 5 SAE and 3 first-class stamps. Catalog available on website.

☑ **TRICYCLE PRESS**, Imprint of Ten Speed Press, P.O. Box 7123, Berkeley CA 94707. (510)559-1600. Fax: (510)559-1637. Website: www.tenspeed.com. Estab. 1993. **Acquisitions:** Nicole Geiger, publisher. Publishes 10 picture books/year; 3 activity books/year; 4 middle readers/year; 5 young adult/year. 25% of books by first-time authors. "Tricycle Press looks for something outside the mainstream; books that encourage children to look at the world from a different angle."

Fiction: Board books, picture books, middle reader: adventure, animal, contemporary, history, multicultural, nature/environment. Picture books, young readers: concept. Middle readers: anthology, novels, series fiction. Average word length: picture books—800. Recently published *Mother, Mother I Feel Sick, Send For The Doctor Quick Quick Quick*, by Remy Charlip (ages 4-7, picture book).

Nonfiction: Picture books, middle readers, young readers: activity books, animal, arts/crafts, concept, cooking, hobbies, how-to, nature/environment, science, self help, social issues. Young adult: hobbies. Recently published *Q is for Quark Science: An Alphabet Book*, by David M. Schwartz (ages 9 and up, picture book); *Honest Pretzels and 64 Other Amazing Recipes for Cooks Ages 8 & Up*, by Mollie Katzen (activity book); and *Smashed, Crashed, and Mashed: A Trip to Junkyard Heaven*, by Joyce Slayton Mitchell, photographs by Steven Borns (ages 7-10, nonfiction picture book).

How to Contact/Writers: Fiction: Submit complete ms for picture books. Submit outline/synopsis and 2-3 sample chapters for chapter book. "No queries!" Nonfiction: Submit complete ms. Responds to mss in 5 months. Publishes a book 1-2 years after acceptance. Welcomes simultaneous submissions and previously published work. Do not send original artwork; copies only, please. No electronic or faxed submissions.

Illustration: Works with 9 illustrators/year. Uses color and b&w. Reviews ms/illustration package from artists. Submit ms with dummy and/or 2-3 pieces of final art. Illustrations only: Query with samples, promo sheet, tearsheets. Contact: Nicole Geiger. Responds only if interested. Samples returned with SASE; samples filed. Original artwork returned at job's completion unless work for hire.

Photography: Works on assignment only. Contact: Nicole Geiger. Uses 35mm transparencies. Submit samples.

Terms: Pays authors royalty. Offers advances. Pays illustrators by the project or royalty. Pays photographers royalty and by the project. Sends galleys to authors. Book catalog for 9×12 SASE (3 first-class stamps). Ms guidelines for SASE (1 first-class stamp).
Tips: "We are looking for something a bit outside the mainstream and with lasting appeal (no one-shot-wonders). Lately we've noticed a sacrifice of quality writing for the sake of illustration."

TROPHY/TEMPEST PAPERBACKS, (formerly Trophy Books), 1350 Avenue of the Americas, New York NY 10019. (212)261-6500. Fax: (212)261-6668. Website: www.harpercollins.com. Subsidiary of HarperCollins Children's Books Group. Book publisher. Publishes 6-9 chapter books/year, 25-30 middle grade titles/year, 20 reprint picture books/year, 10-15 young adult titles/year.
● Tempest is primarily a teen paperback reprint imprint. They publish a limited number of hardback and paperback originals each year.
How to Contact/Writers: Writer's guidelines are available via website or with SASE.

TURTLE BOOKS, 866 United Nations Plaza, Suite 525, New York NY 10017. (212)644-2020. Website: www.turtlebooks.com. Book Publisher. Estab. 1997. **Acquisitions:** John Whitman. "Turtle Books publishes only picture books for young readers. Our goal is to publish a small, select list of quality children's books each spring and fall season. As often as possible, we will publish our books in both English and Spanish editions."
● Turtle does a small number of books and may be slow in responding to unsolicited manuscripts.
Fiction: Picture books: adventure, animal, concept, contemporary, fantasy, folktales, hi-lo, history, humor, multicultural, nature/environment, religion, sports, suspense/mystery. Recently published: *The Legend of Mexicatl*, by Jo Harper, illustrated by Robert Casilla (the story of Mexicatl and the origin of the Mexican people); *Vroom, Chugga, Vroom-Vroom*, by Anne Miranda, illustrated by David Murphy (a number identification book in the form of a race car story); *The Crab Man*, by Patricia VanWest, illustrated by Cedric Lucas (the story of a young Jamaican boy who must make the difficult decision between making an income and the ethical treatment of animals); *Prairie Dog Pioneers*, by Jo and Josephine Harper, illustrated by Craig Spearing (the story of a young girl who doesn't want to move, set in 1870s Texas); and *Keeper of the Swamp*, by Ann Garrett, illustrated by Karen Chandler (a dramatic coming-of-age story wherein a boy confronts his fears and learns from his ailing grandfather the secrets of the swamp); *The Lady in the Box*, by Ann McGovern, illustrated by Marni Backer (a modern story about a homeless woman named Dorrie told from the point of view of two children); and *Alphabet Fiesta*, by Anne Miranda, illustrated by young schoolchildren in Madrid, Spain (an English/Spanish alphabet story).
How to Contact/Writers: Send complete ms. "Queries are a waste of time." Response time varies.
Illustrators: Works with 6 illustrators/year. Responds to artist's queries/submissions only if interested. Samples returned with SASE only.
Terms: Pays royalty. Offers advances.

UAHC PRESS, 633 Third Ave., New York NY 10017. (212)650-4120. Fax: (212)650-4119. E-mail: press@uahc .org. Website: www.uahc.press.com. Book publisher. Estab. 1876. **Manuscript/Art Acquisitions:** Rabbi Hara Person, managing editor. Publishes 4 picture books/year; 2 young readers/year; 2 middle readers/year; 2 young adult titles and 4 textbooks/year. "The Union of American Hebrew Congregations Press publishes textbooks for the religious classroom, children's tradebooks and scholarly work of Jewish education import—no adult fiction and no YA fiction."
Fiction: Picture books, young readers, middle readers: religion. Average word length: picture books—150; young readers—500; middle readers—3,000. Recently published *A Tree Trunk Seder*, written and illustrated by Camille Kress (toddler's board book); *Solomon and the Trees*, by Matt Biers-Ariel, illustrated by Esti Silverberg-Kiss (ages 4-8, picture book); *Sophie and the Shofar*, written by Fran Manuskin and illustrated by Rosalind Charney Kaye (ages 3-7, Jewish fiction).
Nonfiction: Picture books, young readers, middle readers, young adult/teens: religion. Average word length: picture books—150; young readers—500; middle readers—3,000; young adult/teens—20,000. Recently published *My Jewish Holiday Fun Book*, written and illustrated by Ann Koffsky (ages 5-9, activity book); *Until the Messiah Comes*, by Kenneth Roseman (ages 10-13, do-it-yourself Jewish adventure); and *The Chocolate Chip Challah Activity Books*, written and illustrated by Lisa Rauchwerger (ages 5-10, activity book).
How to Contact/Writers: Fiction: Submit outline/synopsis and 2 sample chapters. Nonfiction: Submit complete ms. Responds to queries/ms in 4 months. Publishes a book 18 months-2 years after acceptance. Will consider simultaneous submissions.
Illustration: Works with 5 illustrators/year. Reviews ms/illustration packages from artists. Send ms with dummy. Illustrations only: Send portfolio to be kept on file. Responds in 2 months. Samples returned with SASE. Looking specifically for Jewish themes.
Photography: Buys stock and assigns work. Uses photos with Jewish content. Prefer modern settings. Submit cover letter and promo piece.
Terms: Offers advances. Pays photographers by the project (range: $200-3,000) or per photo (range:$20-100). Book catalog free; ms guidelines for SASE.
Tips: "Look at some of our books. Have an understanding of the Reform Jewish community. We sell mostly to Jewish congregations and day schools.' "

UNITY HOUSE, 1901 NW Blue Pkwy., Unity Village MO 64065-0001. (816)524-3550, ext. 3190. Fax: (816)251-3552. Website: www.unityworldhq.org. Book publisher. Estab. 1896. Publishes "spiritual, metaphysical, new thought publications." **Manuscript Acquisitions:** Raymond Teague. Other imprints: Wee Wisdom. Publishes 1 picture book every two years.

Fiction: All levels: religion. Recently published *I Turn to the Light*, by Connie Bowen (picture book); *Adventures of the Little Green Dragon*, by Mari Privette Ulmer, illustrated by Mary Maass (picture book anthology); and *The Sunbeam and the Wave*, by Harriet Hamilton, illustrated by Connie Bowen (picture book).

Nonfiction: All levels: religion.

How to Contact/Writers: Fiction/Nonfiction: Submit outline/synopsis and 1-3 sample chapters. Responds to queries/mss in up to 2 months. Publishes a book approximately 1 year after acceptance. Will consider simultaneous submission or previously self-published work. Writer's guidelines and catalog available upon request.

Illustration: Reviews ms/illustration packages from artists. Query. Contact: Raymond Teague, associate editor.

Terms: Pays authors royalty of 10-15% based on retail price or work purchased outright. Offers advances (Average amount: $1,500). Book catalog available.

Tips: "Read our Writer's Guidelines and study our catalog before submitting. All of our publications reflect Unity's spiritual teachings, but the presentations and applications of those teachings are wide open."

■ VIKING CHILDREN'S BOOKS, Penguin Putnam Inc., 345 Hudson St., New York NY 10014-3657. (212)366-2000. Website: www.penguinputnam.com. **Acquisitions:** Catherine Frank, assistant editor, picture books, middle grade and young adult fiction; Tracy Gates, executive editor, picture books, middle grade, and young adult fiction; Cathy Hennessy, editor, nonfiction, picture books, middle grade fiction/YA; Jill Davis, senior editor, nonfiction; Melanie Cecka, senior editor, easy-to-read and fiction. **Art Acquisitions:** Denise Cronin, Viking Children's Books. Publishes hardcover originals. Publishes 80 books/year. Receives 7500 queries/year. 25% of books from first-time authors; 33% from unagented writers. "Viking Children's Books is known for humorous, quirky picture books, in addition to more traditional fiction and publishes the highest quality trade books for children including fiction, nonfiction, and novelty books for pre-schoolers through young adults." Publishes book 1-2 years after acceptance of artwork. Hesitantly accepts simultaneous submissions.

● Viking title *The King & The Thieves*, illustrated by Kristen Balouch, won a Golden Kite Honor Award for Picture Book Illustration in 2001. See First Books to read about Viking author Dori Chacones and her book *On a Wintry Morning*.

Fiction: All levels: adventure, animal, anthology, contemporary, hi-lo, humor, multicultural, suspense/mystery, easy-to-read, history, poetry, religion, sports. Middle readers, young adults/teens: problem novels, fantasy, romance, science fiction. Recently published *Baloney, Henry P.*, by Jon Scieszka; *Dreamland*, by Sarah Dessen.

Nonfiction: Picture books: activity books, biography, concept. Young readers, middle readers, young adult: biography, history, reference, religion, science, sports. Middle readers: animal, biography, geography, hi-lo, history, hobbies, multicultural, music/dance, nature/environment, religion, science, social issues, sports. Young adult/teens: animal, biography, cooking, geography, hi-lo, history, multicultural, music/dance, nature/environment, reference, religion, science, social issues, sports.

Illustration: Works with 40 illustrators/year. Responds to artist's queries/submissions only if interested. Samples returned with SASE or samples filed. Originals returned at job's completion.

How to Contact/Writers: Picture books: submit entire ms and SASE. Novels: submit outline with 3 sample chapters and SASE. Nonfiction: query with outline, one sample chapter and SASE. Responds to queries/mss in 8 months.

Terms: Pays 2-10% royalty on retail price or flat fee. Advance negotiable.

Tips: Mistake often made is that "authors disguise nonfiction in a fictional format."

WALKER AND COMPANY, Books for Young Readers, 435 Hudson St., New York NY 10014. (212)727-8300. Fax: (212)727-0984. Website: www.walkerbooks.com. Division of Walker Publishing Co. Inc. Book publisher. Estab. 1959. **Manuscript Acquisitions:** Emily Easton, publisher; Timothy Travaglini, editor. Publishes 16 picture books/year; 4-6 middle readers/year; 2-4 young adult titles/year. 5% of books by first-time authors; 65% of books from agented writers.

Fiction: Picture books: animal, history, multicultural. Young readers: contemporary, history, humor, multicultural. Middle readers: animal, contemporary, history, multicultural, humor. Young adults: contemporary and historical fiction. Recently published *Stolen by the Sea*, by Anna Myers; *Trouble on the Tracks*, by Kathy Mallat; *The Lima Bean Monster*, by Dan Yaccarino.

Nonfiction: Young readers: biography, animals. Middle readers: animal, biography, health, history, multicultural, reference, social issues. Young adults: biography, health, history, multicultural, reference, social issues, sports. Published *The Sound That Jazz Makes*, by Carole Boston Weatherford, illustrated by Eric Velasquez; *The Great Ships*, by Patrick O'Brien; *5 Ways to Know About You*, by Karen Gravelle. Multicultural needs include "contemporary, literary fiction and historical fiction written in an authentic voice. Also high interest nonfiction with trade appeal."

How to Contact/Writers: Fiction/nonfiction: Submit outline/synopsis and sample chapters; query for novels. Responds to queries/mss in 3 months. Send SASE for writer's guidelines.

Illustration: Works with 10-12 illustrators/year. Uses color artwork only. Editorial department reviews ms/illustration packages from artists. Query or submit ms with 4-8 samples. Illustrations only: Tearsheets. "Please do not send original artwork." Responds to art samples only if interested. Samples returned with SASE.

Terms: Pays authors royalties of 5-10%; pays illustrators royalty or flat fee. Offers advance payment against royalties. Original artwork returned at job's completion. Sends galleys to authors. Book catalog available for 9×12 SASE; ms guidelines for SASE.

Tips: Writers: "Make sure you study our catalog before submitting. We are a small house with a tightly focused list. Illustrators: "Have a well-rounded portfolio with different styles." Does not want to see folktales, ABC books, paperback series, genre fiction. "Walker and Company is committed to introducing talented new authors and illustrators to the children's book field."

N WHAT'S INSIDE PRESS, P.O. Box 16965, Beverly Hills CA 90209. (800)269-7757. Fax: (800)856-2160. E-mail: whatsin@aol.com. Website: whatsinsidepress.com. Estab. 1998. Specializes in fiction. **Manuscript Acquisitions:** Shalen Williams. Publishes 5-10 picture books; 5-10 picture books. 50% of books by first-time authors. "The goal of What's Inside Press is to publish books that embrace the simple joys and journeys of childhood."

Fiction: Picture books: adventure, concept, contemporary, fantasy, humor. Young adults: contemporary, humor, problem novels. Recently published *The Tree in the Field of Mathingamy Theme*, by Walter Caldwell (picture book); and *Slam*, by Kinsley Foster (young adult novel, ages 11-17).

Illustration: Works with 4 illustrators/year. Uses color artwork only. Reviews ms/illustration packages from artists. Send postcard sample. Responds in 2 months only if interested. Samples not returned; samples filed.

Terms: Pays authors royalty 8-14% based on wholesale price. Offers advances (Average amount: $500). Pays illustrators by the project (range: $1,000-5,000). Book catalog available for catalog size SASE and 4 first-class stamps. Manuscript guidelines available for SASE. Catalog available on website.

Tips: "Be patient in receiving your reply. Send queries via regular mail only–no certified or express mail. Write to tell a story, not just to get published! Keep believing in your writing and don't give up! E-publishing will change children's publishing little if at all. The magic of books is here to stay!"

WHITECAP BOOKS, 351 Lynn Ave., North Vancouver, British Columbia V7J 2C4 Canada. (604)980-9852. E-mail: whitecap@whitecap.ca. Book publisher. **Acquisitions:** LeAnne McDonald, acquisitions editor. Publishes 4 young readers/year; and 2 middle readers/year.

Fiction: Picture books for children 3-7. Recently published *Pacific Alphabet*, by Margriet Ruurs (ages 4-7).

Nonfiction: Young readers, middle readers: animal, nature/environment. Does not want to see text that writes down to children. Recently published *Welcome to the World of Octopuses*, by Diane Swanson (ages 5-7); *Animals Eat the Weirdest Things*, by Diane Swanson (ages 8-11); *Whose Feet Are These*, by Wayne Lynch (ages 5-7).

How to Contact/Writers: Nonfiction: Query. Responds to queries in 1 month; ms in 3 months. Publishes a book 6 months after acceptance. Will consider simultaneous submissions. Please send international postal voucher if submission is from US.

Illustration: Works with 1-2 illustrators/year. Reviews ms/illustration packages from artists. Query. Illustrations only: Query with samples—"never send original art." Contact: Robin Rivers. Samples returned with SASE with international postal voucher for Canada if requested.

Photography: Buys stock. "We are always looking for outstanding wildlife photographs." Uses 35mm transparencies. Submit cover letter, client list, stock photo list.

Terms: Pays authors a negotiated royalty or purchases work outright. Offers advances. Pays illustrators by the project or royalty (depends on project). Pays photographers per photo (depends on project). Originals returned to artist at job's completion unless discussed in advance. Ms guidelines available for SASE with international postal voucher for Canada.

Tips: "Writers and illustrators should spend time researching what's already available on the market. Whitecap specializes in nonfiction for children and adults. Whitecap Fiction focuses on humorous events or extraordinary animals. Please review previous publications before submitting."

ALBERT WHITMAN & COMPANY, 6340 Oakton St., Morton Grove IL 60053-2723. (847)581-0033. Fax: (847)581-0039. Website: www.albertwhitman.com. Book publisher. Estab. 1919. **Manuscript Acquisitions:** Kathleen Tucker, editor-in-chief. **Art Acquisitions:** Scott Piehl, designer. Publishes 30 books/year. 15% of books by first-time authors; 15% of books from agented authors.

● See First Books on page 84 to read about Albert Whitman illustrator Theresa Smythe and her book *The Runaway Valentine*.

Fiction: Picture books, young readers, middle readers: adventure, animal, concept, contemporary, health, history, humor, multicultural, nature/environment, special needs. Middle readers: problem novels, suspense/mystery. "We are interested in contemporary multicultural stories—stories with holiday themes and exciting distinctive novels. We publish a wide variety of topics and are interested in stories that help children deal with their problems and concerns. Does not want to see "religion-oriented, ABCs, pop-up, romance, counting." Published *Pumpkin Jack*, by Will Hubbell; *Mabela the Clever*, by Margaret Read MacDonald, illustrated by Tim Coffey; *Girl, You're Amazing!*, by Virginina Kroll, illustrated by Melisande Potter.

Nonfiction: Picture books, young readers, middle readers: animal, biography, concept, geography, health, history, hobbies, multicultural, music/dance, nature/environment, special needs. Middle readers: biography, social issues. Does not want to see "religion, any books that have to be written in or fictionalized biographies." Recently published *Shelter Dogs*, by Peg Kehret; *I Have a Weird Brother Who Digested a Fly*, by Joan Hulub, illustrated by Patrick Girouard; and *The Riches of Oseola McCarty*, by Evelyn Coleman, illustrated by Daniel Minter.

How to Contact/Writers: Fiction/Nonfiction: Submit complete ms. Responds to queries in 6 weeks; mss in - 4 months. Publishes a book 18 months after acceptance. Will consider simultaneous submissions "but let us know if it is one."

Illustration: Works with 30 illustrators/year. Uses more color art than b&w. Reviews ms/illustration packages from artists. Illustrations only: Query with samples. Send slides or tearsheets. Samples returned with SASE; samples filed. Originals returned at job's completion. Responds in 2 months.

Photography: Publishes books illustrated with photos but not stock photos—desires photos all taken for project. "Our books are for children and cover many topics; photos must be taken to match text. Books often show a child in a particular situation (e.g., kids being home-schooled, a sister whose brother is born prematurely)." Photographers should query with samples; send unsolicited photos by mail.

Terms: Pays authors royalty. Offers advances. Pays illustrators and photographers royalty. Sends galleys to authors; dummies to illustrators. Original artwork returned at job's completion. Ms/artist's guidelines available for SASE, or on website. Book catalogs available with 9 × 12 SASE and $1.43 in postage.

Tips: "In both picture books and nonfiction, we are seeking stories showing life in other cultures and the variety of multicultural life in the U.S. We also want fiction and nonfiction about mentally or physically challenged children—some recent topics have been autism, stuttering, diabetes. Look up some of our books first, to be sure your submission is appropriate for Albert Whitman & Co."

JOHN WILEY & SONS, INC., 605 Third Ave., New York NY 10158. (212)850-6206. Fax: (212)850-6095. Website: www.wiley.com. Book publisher. **Acquisitions:** Kate Bradford, senior editor. Publishes 18 middle readers/year; 2 young adult titles/year. 10% of books by first-time authors. Publishes educational, nonfiction: primarily history, science, and other activities.

Nonfiction: Middle readers: activity books, animal, arts/crafts, biography, cooking, geography, health, history, hobbies, how-to, nature/environment, reference, science, self help. Young adults: activity books, arts/crafts, health, hobbies, how-to, nature/environment, reference, science, self help. Average word length middle readers—20,000-40,000. Recently published: *Teresa Weatherspoon's Basketball for Girls* (ages 8 and up, sports); *Civil War Days*, in the American Kids in History series (ages 8-12, history/activity).

How to Contact/Writers: Query. Submit outline/synopsis, 2 sample chapters and an author bio. Responds to queries in 1 month; mss in 3 months. Publishes a book 1 year after acceptance. Will consider simultaneous and previously published submissions.

Illustration: Works with 6 illustrators/year. Uses primarily black & white artwork. Reviews ms/illustration packages from artists. Query. Illustrations only: Query with samples, résumé, client list. Responds only if interested. Samples filed. Original artwork returned at job's completion. No portfolio reviews.

Photography: Buys photos from freelancers.

Terms: Pays authors royalty of 10-12% based on wholesale price, or by outright purchase. Offers advances. Pays illustrators by the project. Photographers' pay negotiable. Sends galleys to authors. Book catalog available for SASE.

Tips: "We're looking for topics and writers that can really engage kids' interest—plus we're always interested in a new twist on time-tested subjects."

WILLIAMSON PUBLISHING CO., Box 185, Charlotte VT 05445. (802)425-2102. Fax: (802)425-2199. E-mail: susan@williamsonbooks.com. Website: www.williamsonbooks.com. Book publisher. Estab. 1983. **Manuscript Acquisitions:** Susan Williamson, editorial director. **Art Acquisitions:** Jack Williamson, publisher. Publishes 12-15 young readers titles/year. 50% of books by first-time authors; 10% of books from agented authors. Publishes "very successful nonfiction series (Kids Can!® Series—3,000,000 sold) on subjects such as nature, creative play, arts/crafts, geography. Successfully launched *Little Hands*® series for ages 2-6, *Kaleidoscope Kids*® series (age 7 and up) and *Quick Startsfor Kids!*® series (ages 7 +). Our mission is to help every child fulfill his/her potential and experience personal growth.

Nonfiction: Hands-on activity books, arts/crafts, biography, careers, geography, health, hobbies, how-to, math, multicultural, music/dance, nature/environment, self-help, social issues. Does not want to see textbooks, picture books, poetry, fiction. "We are looking for books in which learning and doing are inseparable." Published *Gizmos and Gadgets*, by Jill Hauser, illustrated by Michael Kline (ages 6-12, exploring science); *Alphabet Art*, by Judy Press (ages 2-6, early learning skills); and *Ancient Greece!*, by Avery Hart and Paul Mantell, illustrated by Michael Kline (age 7 and up, learning history through activities and experience).

How to Contact/Writers: Query with outline/synopsis and 1 sample chapter. Responds to queries in 4 months; mss in 4 months. Publishes book, "depending on graphics, about 1 year" after acceptance. Writers may send a SASE for guidelines. Please do not query via e-mail.

Illustration: Works with 6 illustrator and 6 designers/year. "We're interested in expanding our illustrator and design freelancers." Uses primarily b&w artwork; some 2-color and 4-color. Responds only if interested. Samples returned with SASE; samples filed. Please do not send samples via e-mail.

Photography: Buys photos from freelancers; uses archival art and photos.

Terms: Pays authors royalty based on wholesale price or purchases outright. Pays illustrators by the project. Pays photographers per photo. Sends galleys to authors. Book catalog available for 8½×11 SAE and 4 first-class stamps; ms guidelines available for SASE.

Tips: "We're interested in interactive learning books with a creative approach packed with interesting information, written for young readers ages 2-6 and 4-10. In nonfiction children's publishing, we are looking for authors with a depth of knowledge shared with children through a warm, embracing style. Our publishing philosophy is based on the idea that all children can succeed and have positive learning experiences. Children's lasting learning experiences involve participation."

WINDSTORM CREATIVE LTD., 7419 Ebbert Dr. SE, Port Orchard WA 98367. Website: www.arabyfair. com. **Acquisitions:** Ms. Cris Newport, senior editor. Publishes trade paperback originals and reprints. Publishes 10 titles/year. 50% of books from first-time authors; 50% from unagented writers. WSC consists of the following imprints: Little Blue Works—Children's titles and young adult novels released in paper and on multimedia CD-ROM; WSC Lightning Rod Ltd: Internet & Episode Guides—Cutting-edge fiction. Publishes genre fiction and poetry primarily in paper and on multimedia CD-ROM; RAMPANT Gaming—Role-playing and other games for ages 14 and up; and Arts Ex Machine—Theatre, film and other arts. "WSC publishes work that is revolutionary in content. In order to understand what we mean by this, please read several of our books from the different imprints. We do not publish work that is racist, homophobic, sexist or graphically violent in content. All of our authors and artists should expect to be proactive in marketing their work. If you do not wish to read from and/ or sign your books and/or artwork, you should not submit work to us."

Fiction: All levels and categories. Published *Surprise for Ray*, by Ann Marie Stephens, illustrated by Michael Bolan; *Miss Panda Series*, by Ambika Mather Kamat/K. Michael Crawford (Multimedia CD-ROM); and *Tonight I Heard the Ghost Cat*, by Jennifer Anna, illustrated by Patrick Dengate.

Nonfiction: All levels and categories.

How to Contact/Writers: Read several of our titles in the genre you are writing in. Visit our website for guidelines.

Illustration: Works with 10 illustrators/year. Visit website for guidelines.

Photography: Buys photos from freelancers. Query first.

Terms: Pays 10-15% royalty based on wholesale price. Will consider simultaneous submissions. Artists and photographers are paid flat fee for covers only. All other work is paid on royalty basis. Royalty payment is 10% of gross monies received."

Tips: Be sure to request submission guidelines. "We reserve the right to destroy any submissions that deviate from our format."

WM KIDS, Imprint of White Mane Publishing Co., Inc., P.O. Box, 708, 63 W. Burd St., Shippensburg PA 17257. (717)532-2237. Fax: (717)532-6110. E-mail: marketing@whitemane.com. Book publisher. Estab. 1987. **Acquisitions:** Harold Collier. White Mane Books, Burd Street Press, White Mane Kids, Ragged Edge Press (Harold Collier, acquisitions editor). Publishes 10 middle readers/year. 50% of books are by first-time authors.

Fiction: Middle readers, young adults: history. Average word length: middle readers—30,000. Recently published *Freedom Calls: Journey of a Slave Girl*, by Ken Knapp Sawyer (grades 5 and up); *Young Heroes of History*, by Alan Kay (grades 5 and up).

Nonfiction: Middle readers, young adults: history. Average word length: middle readers—30,000.

How to Contact/Writers: Fiction: Query. Nonfiction: Submit outline/synopsis and 2-3 sample chapters. Responds to queries in 1 month; mss in 3 months. Publishes a book 1 year after acceptance. Will consider simultaneous submissions.

Illustration: Works with 3 illustrators/year. Reviews ms/illustration packages from artists. Submit ms with 3 pieces of final art. Contact: Harold Collier, acquisitions editor. Responds in 1 month. Samples returned with SASE.

Photography: Buys stock and assigns work. Submit cover letter and portfolio.

Terms: Pays authors royalty of 7-10%. Pays illustrators by the project. Pays photographers by the project. Sends galleys for review. Originals returned to artist at job's completion. Book catalog and writer's guidelines available for SASE. All imprints included in a single catalog.

WOMAN'S MISSIONARY UNION, P.O. Box 830010, Birmingham AL 35283-0010. (205)991-8100. Fax: (205)995-4841. Website: www.wmu.com. Imprint: New Hope. **Acquisitions:** Jan Turrentine. Publishes 2 picture books/year; 5 middle readers/year; 3 young adult titles/year. 50% of books from first-time authors.

Fiction: All levels: multicultural, religion. Multicultural fiction must be related to mission/ministry.

Nonfiction: All levels: multicultural, religion. Materials must teach missions concepts, evangelism or ministry and outreach to persons without Christ; materials published with this imprint are for Christian concepts.

How to Contact/Writers: Fiction/nonfiction: Submit complete ms. Responds to queries in 3 months. Publishes a book 2 years after acceptance. Will accept simultaneous submissions. We accept children's and ethnic mss also.

Illustration: Works with 2-3 illustrators/year. Reviews ms/illustration packages from artists. Send ms with dummy. Illustrations only: Query with samples (color copies). Responds only if interested. Samples filed.

Photography: Buys stock already on file. Model/property releases required.

Terms: Pays authors royalty of 7-10% (depends on length). Pays illustrators by the project. Sends galleys to authors. Originals returned to artist at job's completion. Book catalog available for 10×12 SAE and 3 first-class stamps. Ms guidelines available for SASE or via website.
Tips: "Obtain the catalog first to see the kinds of material we publish."

N □ WORLD BOOK, INC., 233 N. Michigan Ave., #2000, Chicago IL 60601. (312)729-5800. Fax: (312)729-5612. Website: www.worldbook.com. Book publisher. **Manuscript Acquisitions:** Paul A. Kobasa, product development executive director. **Art Acquisitions:** Roberta Dimmer, executive art director. World Book, Inc. (publisher of *The World Book Encyclopedia*), publishes reference sources and nonfiction series for children in the areas of science, mathematics, English-language skills, basic academic and social skills, social studies, history, and health and fitness. We publish print and nonprint material appropriate for children ages 3 to 14. WBT does not publish fiction, poetry, or wordless picture books."
Nonfiction: Young readers: animal, arts/crafts, careers, concept, geography, health, reference. Middle readers: animal, arts/crafts, careers, geography, health, history, hobbies, how-to, nature/environment, reference, science. Young adult: arts/crafts, careers, geography, health, history, hobbies, how-to, nature/environment, reference, science.
How to Contact/Writers: Nonfiction: Submit outline/synopsis only; no mss. Responds to queries/mss in 1-2 months. Unsolicited mss will not be returned. Publishes a book 18 months after acceptance. Will consider simultaneous submissions.
Illustration: Works with 10-30 illustrators/year. Illustrations only: Query with samples. Responds only if interested. Samples returned with SASE; samples filed "if extra copies and if interested."
Photography: Buys stock and assigns work. Needs broad spectrum; editorial concept, specific natural, physical and social science spectrum. Model/property releases required; captions required. Uses color 8×10 gloss and matte prints, 35mm, 2¼×2¼, 4×5, 8×10 transparencies. Submit cover letter, résumé, promo piece (color and b&w).
Terms: Payment negotiated on project-by-project basis. Sends galleys to authors. Book catalog available for 9×12 SASE. Ms and art guidelines for SASE.

✓ □ THE WRIGHT GROUP, 19201 120th Ave. NE, Suite 100, Bothell WA 98011. (800)523-2371. Fax: (800)543-7323. Website: www.wrightgroup.com. Specializes in fiction and nonfiction educational and multicultural material. **Manuscripts Acquisitions:** Judy Sommer, vice president marketing. **Art Acquisitions:** Vicky Tripp, director of design. Publishes 100+ young readers, 50+ middle readers/year. "The Wright Group is dedicated to improving literacy by providing outstanding tutorials for students and teachers."
Fiction: Picture books, young readers: adventure, animal, concept, contemporary, fantasy, folktales, hi-lo, history, humor, multicultural, nature/environment, poetry, sports, suspense/mystery. Middle readers: adventure, animal, contemporary, fantasy, folktales, hi-lo, history, humor, multicultural, nature/environment, poetry, problem novels. Average word length: young readers—50-5,000; middle readers—3,000-10,000. Recenty published: *Wild Crayons*, by Joy Cowley (young reader fantasy); *The Gold Dust Kids*, by Michell Dionetti (historical fiction chapter book for young readers); and *Watching Josh*, by Deborah Eaton (middle reader mystery).
Nonfiction: Picture books, young readers, middle readers: animal, biography, careers, concept, geography, health, hi-lo, history, how-to, multicultural, nature/environment, science, sports. Average word length: young readers 50-3,000. Recently published: *Iditarod*, by Joe Ramsey (young reader); and *The Amazing Ant*, by Sara Sams (young reader); and *Chameleons*, by Nic Bishop (young reader).
How to Contact/Writers: Fiction/Nonfiction: Submit complete manuscript or submit outline/synopsis and 3 sample chapters. Responds to queries in 1 month; mss in 5 months. Publishes a book 8 months after acceptance. Will consider previously published work.
Illustration Query with samples. Contact: Vicky Tripp. Responds only if interested. Samples kept on file.
Photography: Buys stock and assigns work. Contact: Vicky Tripp. Model/property release and captions required. Uses 8½×11 color prints. Submit published samples, promo pieces.
Terms: Work purchased outright from authors ($500-2,400). Illustrators paid by the project. Photographers paid by the project ($3,500-5,000) or per photo ($300-350). Book catalog available online.
Tips: "Much of our illustration assignments are being done by offsite developers, so our level of commission in this area is minimal."

Magazines

Children's magazines are a great place for unpublished writers and illustrators to break into the market. Illustrators, photographers and writers alike may find it easier to get book assignments if they have tearsheets from magazines. Having magazine work under your belt shows you're professional and have experience working with editors and art directors and meeting deadlines.

But magazines aren't merely a breaking-in point. Writing, illustration and photo assignments for magazines let you see your work in print quickly, and the magazine market can offer steady work and regular paychecks (a number of them pay on acceptance). Book authors and illustrators may have to wait a year or two before receiving royalties from a project. The magazine market is also a good place to use research material that didn't make it into a book project you're working on. You may even work on a magazine idea that blossoms into a book project.

TARGETING YOUR SUBMISSIONS

It's important to know the topics typically covered by different children's magazines. To help you match your work with the right publications, we've included several indexes in the back of this book. The **Subject Index** lists both book and magazine publishers by the fiction and nonfiction subjects they're seeking.

If you're a writer, use the Subject Index in conjunction with the **Age-Level Index** to narrow your list of markets. Targeting the correct age group with your submission is an important consideration. Most rejection slips are sent because a writer has not targeted a manuscript to the correct age. Few magazines are aimed at children of all ages, so you must be certain your manuscript is written for the audience level of the particular magazine you're submitting to. Magazines for children (just as magazines for adults) may also target a specific gender.

If you're a poet, refer to the **Poetry Index** to find which magazines publish poems.

Each magazine has a different editorial philosophy. Language usage also varies between periodicals, as does the length of feature articles and the use of artwork and photographs. Reading magazines *before* submitting is the best way to determine if your material is appropriate. Also, because magazines targeted to specific age groups have a natural turnover in readership every few years, old topics (with a new slant) can be recycled.

If you're a photographer, the **Photography Index** lists children's magazines that use photos from freelancers. Using it in combination with the subject index can narrow your search. For instance, if you photograph sports, compare the Magazine list in the Photography Index with the list under Sports in the Subject Index. Highlight the markets that appear on both lists, then read those listings to decide which magazines might be best for your work.

Since many kids' magazines sell subscriptions through direct mail or schools, you may not be able to find a particular publication at bookstores or newsstands. Check your local library, or send for copies of the magazines you're interested in. Most magazines in this section have sample copies available and will send them for a SASE or small fee.

Also, many magazines have submission guidelines and theme lists available for a SASE. (Visit www.writersdigest.com for a searchable database of more than 1,500 writers guidelines.) Check magazines' websites, too. Many offer excerpts of articles, submission guidelines and theme lists and will give you a feel for the editorial focus of the publication.

For insights into children's magazines from an experienced editor, turn to the Insider Report with *ASK* editor **Judy O'Malley** of the Cricket Magazine Group (page 208). For tips on breaking into magazines with craft projects, see the Insider Report with **Traci Sikkink** (page 226).

Information on magazines listed in the previous edition but not included in this edition of *Children's Writer's & Illustrator's Market* **may be found in the General Index.**

ADVOCATE, PKA'S PUBLICATION, PKA Publication, 301A Rolling Hills Park, Prattsville NY 12468. (518)299-3103. **Publisher**: Patricia Keller. Bimonthly tabloid. Estab. 1987. Circ. 12,000. "*Advocate* advocates good writers and quality writings. We publish art, fiction, photos and poetry. *Advocate*'s submitters are talented people of all ages who do not earn their livings as writers. We wish to promote the arts and to give those we publish the opportunity to be published through a for-profit means rather than in a not-for-profit way. We do this by selling advertising and offering reading entertainment."
● Gaited Horse Association newsletter is now included in our publication. Horse-oriented stories, poetry, art and photos are currently needed.
Fiction: Middle readers and young adults/teens: adventure, animal, contemporary, fantasy, folktales, health, humorous, nature/environment, problem-solving, romance, science fiction, sports, suspense/mystery. Looks for "well written, entertaining work, whether fiction or nonfiction." Buys approximately 42 mss/year. Average word length: 1,500. Byline given. Wants to see more humorous material, nature/environment and romantic comedy.
Nonfiction: Middle readers and young adults/teens: animal, arts/crafts, biography, careers, concept, cooking, fashion, games/puzzles, geography, history, hobbies, how-to, humorous, interview/profile, nature/environment, problem-solving, science, social issues, sports, travel. Buys 10 mss/year. Average word length: 1,500. Byline given.
Poetry: Reviews poetry any length.
How to Contact/Writers: Fiction/nonfiction: send complete ms. Responds to queries in 6 weeks/mss in 2 months. Publishes ms 2-18 months after acceptance.
Illustration: Uses b&w artwork only. Uses cartoons. Reviews ms/illustration packages from artists. Submit a photo print (b&w or color), an excellent copy of work (no larger than 8×10) or original. Illustrations only: "Send previous unpublished art with SASE, please." Responds in 2 months. Samples returned with SASE; samples not filed. Credit line given.
Photography: Buys photos from freelancers. Model/property releases required. Uses color and b&w prints. Send unsolicited photos by mail with SASE. Responds in 2 months. Wants nature, artistic and humorous photos.
Terms: Pays on publication with contributor's copies. Acquires first rights for mss, artwork and photographs. Pays in copies. Original work returned upon job's completion. Sample copies for $4. Writer's/illustrator/photo guidelines for SASE.
Tips: "Artists and photographers should keep in mind that we are a b&w paper."

AIM MAGAZINE, America's Intercultural Magazine, P.O. Box 1174, Maywood IL 60153-8174. **Contact:** Ruth Apilado (nonfiction), Mark Boone (fiction). **Photo Editor:** Betty Lewis. Quarterly magazine. Circ. 8,000. Readers are high school and college students, teachers, adults interested in helping, through the written word, to create a more equitable world. 15% of material aimed at juvenile audience.
Fiction: Young adults/teens: adventure, folktales, humorous, history, multicultural, "stories with social significance." Wants stories that teach children that people are more alike than they are different. Does not want to see religious fiction. Buys 20 mss/year. Average word length: 1,000-4,000. Byline given.
Nonfiction: Young adults/teens: biography, interview/profile, multicultural, "stuff with social significance." Does not want to see religious nonfiction. Buys 20 mss/year. Average word length: 500-2,000. Byline given.
How to Contact/Writers: Fiction: Send complete ms. Nonfiction: Query with published clips. Responds to queries in 2 weeks; mss in 6 weeks. Will consider simultaneous submissions.
Illustration: Buys 6 illustrations/issue. Preferred theme: Overcoming social injustices through nonviolent means. Reviews ms/illustration packages from artists. Query first. Illustrations only: Query with tearsheets. Responds to art samples only if interested. Samples returned with SASE or filed. Original artwork returned at job's completion "if desired." Credit line given.
Photography: Wants "photos of activists who are trying to contribute to social improvement."
Terms: Pays on acceptance. Buys first North American serial rights. Pays $15-25 for stories/articles. Pays in contributor copies if copies are requested. Pays $25 for b&w cover illustration. Photographers paid by the project. Sample copies for $5.
Tips: "We need material of social significance, stuff that will help promote racial harmony and peace and illustrate the stupidity of racism."

AMERICAN CAREERS, Career Communications, Inc., 6701 W. 64th St., Overland Park KS 66202. (913)362-7788. Fax: (913)362-4864. **Articles Editor:** Mary Pitchford. **Art Director:** Jerry Kanabel. Published 3 times/year. Estab. 1990. Circ. 400,000. Publishes career and education information for middle and high school students.
Nonfiction: Buys 20 mss/year. Average word length: 300-800. Byline given.

How to Contact/Writers: Nonfiction: Query with published clips. Responds to queries in 2 months. Publishes ms 6 months after acceptance. Will consider simultaneous submissions, electronic submissions.
Tips: Send a query in writing with résumé and clips.

AMERICAN CHEERLEADER, Lifestyle Ventures LLC, 250 W. 57th St., Suite 420, New York NY 10107. (212)265-8890. Fax: (212)265-8908. E-mail: editors@americancheerleader.com. Website: www.americancheerle ader.com. **Editorial Director:** Julie Davis. **Managing Editor:** Alyssa Roenigk. **Editor:** Sheila Noone. Bimonthly magazine. Estab. 1995. Circ. 200,000. Special interest teen magazine for kids who cheer.
Nonfiction: Young adults: biography, interview/profile (sports personalities), careers, fashion, beauty, health, how-to (cheering techniques, routines, pep songs, etc.), problem-solving, sports, cheerleading specific material. "We're looking for authors who know cheerleading." Buys 20 mss/year. Average word length: 750-2,000. Byline given.
How to Contact/Writers: Query with published clips. Responds to queries/mss in 3 months. Publishes ms 3 months after acceptance. Will consider electronic submission via disk or modem.
Illustration: Buys 6 illustrations/issue; 30-50 illustrations/year. Works on assignment only. Reviews ms/illustra tion packages from artists. Illustrations only: Query with samples; arrange portfolio review. Responds only if interested. Samples filed. Originals not returned at job's completion. Credit line given.
Photography: Buys photos from freelancers. Looking for cheerleading at different sports games, events, etc. Uses 35mm, 2¼×2¼ transparencies and 5x7 prints. Query with samples; provide résumé, business card, tear-sheets to be kept on file. "After sending query, we'll set up an interview." Responds only if interested.
Terms: Pays on publication. Buy all rights for mss, artwork and photographs. Pays $100-1,000 for stories. Pays illustrators $50-200 for b&w inside, $100-300 for color inside. Pays photographers by the project $300-750; per photo (range: $25-100). Sample copies for $5.
Tips: "Authors: We invite proposals from freelance writers who are involved in or have been involved in cheerleading—i.e. coaches, sponsors or cheerleaders. Our writing style is upbeat, and 'sporty' to catch and hold the attention of our teen readers. Articles should be broken down into lots of sidebars, bulleted lists, etc. Photogra phers and illustrators must have teen magazine experience or high profile experience."

N: AMERICAN CHEERLEADER JUNIOR, Lifestyle Ventures, 250 W. 57th St., #420, New York NY 10107. (212)265-8890. Fax: (212)265-8908. Website: www.americancheerleaderjunior.com. **Articles Editor:** Sheila Noone. **Art Director:** Kristin Fennell. Quarterly magazine. Estab. 2001. "We celebrate the young cheerleaders across the country and provide ways to improve their abilities, friendships and community service." 95% of publication aimed at juvenile market.
Fiction: Middle readers: sports. Byline given.
Nonfiction: Picture-oriented, young readers, middle readers: arts/crafts, games/puzzles, health, how-to, humor ous, sports. Average word length: 400. Byline given.
Poetry: Reviews poetry.
How to Contact/Writers: Fiction/nonfiction: Query with published clips. Responds in 1-2 months. Will consider electronic submission via disk or modem.
Illustration: Buys 2-4 illustrations/issue; 8-10 illustrations/year. Uses color artwork only. Works on assignment only. Reviews ms/illustration packages from artists. Contact: Kristin Fennell, art director. Illustrations only: query with samples, arrange portfolio review. Contact: Kristin Fennell. Responds only if interested. Samples not re turned; samples filed. Credit line given.
Photography: Looking for photos depicting action, cheer, friendship. Model/property release required. Uses color prints and 35mm transparencies. Query with samples; arrange a personal interview to show portfolio. Responds only if interested.
Terms: Pays on publication. Buys exclusive magazine rights or negotiates for rights. Buys first rights for artwork; all rights for photos. Additional payment for ms/illustration packages and for photos accompanying articles. Payment for illustrators varies. Payment for photographers varies. Samples copies free for SAE. Writer's guide lines free for SASE.
Tips: "We look for fun, wholesome illustrations aimed at athletic and energetic kids."

AMERICAN GIRL, Pleasant Company, 8400 Fairway Place, P.O. Box 620986, Middleton WI 53562-0984. (608)836-4848. E-mail: im_agmag_editor@pleasantco.com. Website: www.americangirl.com. **Editor:** Kristi Thom. **Managing Editor:** Barbara Stretchberry. **Contact:** Editorial Dept. Assistant. Bimonthly magazine. Estab. 1992. Circ. 750,000. "For girls ages 8-12. We run fiction and nonfiction, historical and contemporary."
Fiction: Middle readers: contemporary, historical, multicultural, suspense/mystery, good fiction about anything. No preachy, moralistic tales or stories with animals as protagonists. Only a girl or girls as characters—no boys. Buys approximately 6 mss/year. Average word length: 1,000-2,300. Byline given.
Nonfiction: Any articles aimed at girls ages 8-12. Buys 3-10 mss/year. Average word length: 600. Byline sometimes given.
How to Contact/Writers: Fiction: Send complete ms. Nonfiction: Query with published clips. Responds to queries/mss in 6-12 weeks. Will consider simultaneous submissions.
Illustration: Works on assignment only.

insider report

Experienced editor takes the helm of a new magazine

Judy O'Malley is an incurable children's book junkie. Defining the genre on her own terms as an editor for various magazines and books, O'Malley has inundated herself in children's and young adult literature. From polishing the sleek, modish pages of *Seventeen* and *Glamour* to forging some of the vivid, imaginative components of *ASK: Arts and Sciences for Kids*, this editing mogul has committed much of her life to enhancing children's awareness and education. Through the wide range of prominent positions she has held in the publishing world, O'Malley has become an authority on matters such as promoting literacy, cultivating academic tools for librarians and teachers, selecting promising manuscripts and, of course, editing. Currently the editor of a

Judy O'Malley

magazine and a line of books (both through Carus Publishing), O'Malley has gained eminent status in the land of talking animals, magical inventions and giggling stars.

In your publishing career, you've been most engrossed in the children's market. Why did you choose this medium to express your love for writing/reading?
Actually, children's literature chose me. My first several years in publishing were involved with trade fashion magazines. The emphasis was on fashion, beauty and lifestyle, not on books or reading. I had always intended to get into educational publishing, so when I made a change, I went to the College Board, where I was dealing with college prep books and *The College Handbook*. That experience led to a job as assistant editor at H.W. Wilson, where I expected to do reference books, only to find myself editing professional books for teachers and children's librarians. One of my very first books at Wilson was a revision of Anne Pellowski's *The World of Storytelling*. At the time we were working together, Anne was on the Hans Christian Andersen Award jury of IBBY (International Board on Books for Youth), so working with her was like taking a survey course of children's literature. I was thoroughly hooked on the power of advocating reading and good books by working with librarians, teachers and parents, so my next job as editor of *Book Links* at the American Library Association was a logical and delightful progression.

***Book Links* spotlights the importance of cultural roots, ethnic diversity, global harmony, for instance. As editor, did you see working for such a publication an avenue for your own activism?**
Editing *Book Links* was an exciting opportunity to respond to the needs and concerns of librarians and teachers who strive to share all kinds of books reflecting a variety of experiences with

From the publishers of Cricket and Smithsonian Magazine

Ask!

arts and sciences for kids

It's About Time!

Volume 1, Number 1   Premiere Issue   January 2002

Judy O'Malley edits *ASK*, the latest publication from the Cricket Magazine Group. "A strong visual design that conveys information through art, photographs, captions, and borders, as well as text, has been our aim while creating *ASK*," says O'Malley. The magazine for second- through fourth-graders "explores the world with the greatest inventors, artists, thinkers, and scientists of the past and present."

the children with whom they work. One of the exhilarating aspects of that job was that our readers were also our contributors. The very best articles came from the professionals working with kids and books and were based on their own success in teaching with books that break down boundaries and expand children's horizons.

The American Library Association receives over 650 complaints and calls for the removal of books each year. Did you deal with any of these instances, and how do you feel about censorship?
The Office of Intellectual Freedom at ALA works with librarians concerning challenges to the inclusion of books in library collections. At *Book Links*, we included books in bibliographies on the basis of their connections to a particular curriculum theme and to the children's lives and interests. Of course, appropriateness for various groups was a factor in a particular book's inclusion, but that call was usually made by library professionals on the basis of their experience in using the book. In some ways, we are constantly censoring, as we select what we read ourselves or recommend to others, of any age, based on our individual preferences, professional judgment and experience. I think using these criteria to expose children to a wide range of choices, and trusting young readers to select what they're ready to understand and deal with is a responsible and respectful approach.

How do you feel about television? What distinguishes an educational venue from a program that may not be considered "suitable" for kids?
I think television has enormous potential as another medium for introducing children to new ideas. Shows like PBS's *Between the Lions* promotes reading and the sharing of good stories in an entertaining format, and of course, educational programming like *Sesame Street* has given a whole generation of children a head start on learning. But, I think we're just beginning to discover how television and computer technology can promote literacy and the love of reading. We need more corporate and public support of such positive efforts.

Explain the conditions for working for a giant such as Condé Nast Publications in contrast to a smaller, more intimate environment.
It was a very stressful, highly competitive atmosphere at Conde Nast, with frequent turnover at all levels. But, it was also a very early stage in my publishing career, so I was not really aware that the frantic pace was particularly pronounced in trade magazine publishing. Later, when I was doing professional magazines and books, and now, doing both books and magazines for children, the pressures were and are still there, but relate more to the need to create high quality materials, and less to keeping up with trends.

At Carus, how is your time divided between editing a magazine and a line of books?
Start-up on a new publication is always time consuming, so my first months at Cricket were largely devoted to creating the mission and shape of *ASK* with Karen Kohn, the art director, and Marc Aronson, who assisted when he was the editorial director of both books and nonfiction magazines. *ASK* continues to represent about two-thirds of my time commitment. I am working with Marc on books as well, but the flow of projects is very organic, since many ideas that originate as articles for *ASK* have shown potential as nonfiction picture books. This integration of formats in getting materials to kids is just the reason I was and am excited about working at a company like Carus Publishing.

ASK **stimulates and challenges a particular age range. What are some important devices used to hold their attention?**

A strong visual design that conveys information through art, photographs, captions, and borders, as well as text, has been our aim while creating *ASK*. And, we constantly strive for an inquiring tone, rather than just a proscriptive one, imparting facts to be digested. Short articles that look at unusual aspects of such large ideas as conventions of time-keeping, or interactions between humans and animals in an environment are intended to pique children's curiosity, impel them to know more. Every issue of the magazine also has contests that challenge creativity and wacky crafts connected to the theme—just for fun.

What types of subjects/ideas stand out from the rest when you're plowing through an endless stack of queries?

Since I'm overseeing a nonfiction magazine for children ages 7-10 called *ASK*, and looking for books in all genres, fiction and nonfiction, that are also based on inquiry, I'm drawn by unusual approaches, unique perspectives on the world, innovative formats, engaging writing style, and when appropriate, humor.

Are you planning on presenting an online version of *ASK*?

No, we will not be presenting the magazine online, but we are offering Web activities and extensions of ideas presented in the print magazine. The Web can provide interactive opportunities and ways for children to share their ideas and their responses to our challenges to write, draw, invent and create their own works.

What would we find on your own bookshelves at home?

Most of my bookshelves are tightly packed with children's and young adult books because I truly enjoy children's literature and find it rewarding. I love poetry and have several collections by Nikki Giovanni, Naomi Shihab Nye, Paul Janesczko, Nikki Grimes, Liz Rosenberg, and Janet Wong. The picture books range from poetry to fiction and nonfiction and include works by Chris Raschka, Ed Young, and Javaka Steptoe. I enjoy both historical and contemporary novels. Among favorites are books by Sharon Creech, Karen Hesse, Virginia Euwer Wolff, Paul Fleischman, and Kyoko Mori. But, for a children's book junkie this is a question to which the answer just goes on and on and on and. . . .

—*Candi Lace*

Terms: Pays on acceptance. Buys first North American serial rights. Pays $500 minimum for stories; $300 minimum for articles. Sample copies for $3.95 and 9 × 12 SAE with $1.93 in postage (send to Editorial Department Assistant). Writer's guidelines free for SASE.
Tips: "Keep (stories and articles) simple but interesting. Kids are discriminating readers, too. They won't read a boring or pretentious story. We're looking for short (maximum 175 words) how-to stories and short profiles of girls for 'Girls Express' section, as well as word games, puzzles and mazes."

ANALOG SCIENCE FICTION AND FACT, Dell Magazines, 475 Park Ave., New York NY 10016. (212)686-7188. Fax: (212)686-7414. E-mail: analog@dellmagazines.com. Website: www.analogsf.com. **Articles Editor:** Stanley Schmidt. **Fiction Editor:** Stanley Schmidt. **Art Director:** Victoria Green. Magazine published 11 times/year (one double issue). Estab. 1930. Circ. 60,000. "We publish science fiction and science fact articles aimed at intelligent scientifically literate adults. Some bright teenagers read us, but we are *not* a children's magazine."
Fiction: Young adults: science fiction. Buys 70 mss/year. Average word length: 80,000 maximum. "We use very few stories between 20,000 and 40,000 words; longer ones are occassionally serialized." Byline given.

Nonfiction: Young adults: nature/environment, science. Buys 11 mss/year. Average word length: 3,000-5,000.
How to Contact/Writers: Fiction: Query for serials (over 20,000 words) only. Send complete ms if under 20,000 words. Responds to /mss in 1 month. Publishes ms 1 year after acceptance.
Illustration: Buys 4 illustrations/issue; 45 illustrations/year. Works on assignment only. Illustrations only: Query with samples. Send portfolio, slides. Contact: Victoria Green, art director. Responds only if interested. Samples returned with SASE.
Terms: Pays on acceptance. Buys first North American serial rights, nonexclusive foreign serial rights. Pays $20-4,000 for stories. Sample copies for $5. Writer's/illustrators guidelines for SASE; also available on website.
Tips: "Read the magazine to get a feel for what our readers like."

APPLESEEDS The Magazine for Young Readers, Cobblestone Publishing, A Division of Carus Publishing, 30 Grove St., Suite C, Peterborough NH 03458. E-mail: barbara_burt@posthavard.edu. Website: cobblestonepub. com/pages/writersAPPguides.html. **Editor:** Barbara Burt. Magazine published monthly except June, July and August. *AppleSeeds* is a theme-based social studies magazine from Cobblestone Publishing for ages 7-10. Published 9 times/year.
  • *AppleSeeds* is aimed toward readers ages 7-10. *Appleseed* themes for 2002 include Growing Up on the Erie Canal, The U.S. Capitol, Sacred Places, Exploring the Sahara, and Becoming An Artist.
How to Contact/Writers: Nonfiction: Query only. See website for submission guidelines and theme list.
Tips: "Submit queries specifically focused on the theme of an upcoming issue. We generally work 6 months ahead on themes. We look for unusual perspectives, original ideas, and excellent scholarship. We accept no unsolicited manuscripts. Writers should check our website at cobblestonepub.com/pages/writersAPPguides/html for current guidelines, topics, and query deadlines. We use very little fiction. Illustrators should not submit unsolicited art."

N ASK, Arts and Sciences for Kids, 332 S. Michigan Ave., Suite 1100, Chicago IL 60604. (312)939-1500, ext. 622. Fax: (312)939-8150. E-mail: askmagazine@caruspub.com. Website: www.caruspub.com. **Articles Editor:** Judy O'Malley. **AA Director:** Karen Kohn. Bimonthly magazine. Estab. 2002. "*ASK* encourages children between the ages of 7 and 10 to inquire about the world around them. Nonfiction articles, poetry, activities, and reprints from trade books will be considered for publication."
Fiction: Middle readers: adventure, animal, contemporary.
Nonfiction: Young readers, middle readers: animal, arts/crafts, biography, careers, games/puzzles, geography, health, history, humorous, interview/profile, math, multicultural, nature/environment, problem-solving, science, social issues, sports. Buys 30-40 mss/year. Average word length: 250-900. Byline given.
Poetry: Reviews poetry.
How to Contact/Writers: Nonfiction: Query. Responds to queries in 3 weeks; mss in 3 months. Will consider electronic submission via disk or modem, previously published work.
Illustration: Buys 10 illustrations/issue; 60 illustrations/year. Works on assignment only. Reviews ms/illustration packages from artists. Contact: Karen Kohn, art director. Illustrations only: Query with samples. Contact: Karen Kohn, art director.

BABYBUG, Carus Publishing Company, P.O. Box 300, Peru IL 61354. (815)224-6656. **Editor**: Paula Morrow. **Art Director:** Suzanne Beck. Published 10 times/year (monthly except for combined May/June and July/August issues). Estab. 1994. "A listening and looking magazine for infants and toddlers ages 6 to 24 months, *Babybug* is 6 ¼×7, 24 pages long, printed in large type (26-point) on high-quality cardboard stock with rounded corners and no staples."
Fiction: Looking for very simple and concrete stories, 4-6 short sentences maximum.
Nonfiction: Must use very basic words and concepts, 10 words maximum.
Poetry: Maximum length 8 lines. Looking for rhythmic, rhyming poems.
How to Contact/Writers: "Please do not query first." Send complete ms with SASE. "Submissions without SASE will be discarded." Responds in 3 months.
Illustration: Uses color artwork only. Works on assignment only. Reviews ms/illustration packages from artists. "The manuscripts will be evaluated for quality of concept and text before the art is considered." Contact: Suzanne Beck. Illustrations only: Send tearsheets or photo prints/photocopies with SASE. "Submissions without SASE will be discarded." Responds in 3 months. Samples filed.
Terms: Pays on publication for mss; after delivery of completed assignment for illustrators. Buys first rights with reprint option or (in some cases) all rights. Original artwork returned at job's completion. Rates vary ($25 minimum for mss; $250 minimum for art). Sample copy for $5. Guidelines free for SASE.
Tips: "*Babybug* would like to reach as many children's authors and artists as possible for original contributions, but our standards are very high, and we will accept only top-quality material. Before attempting to write for *Babybug*, be sure to familiarize yourself with this age child." (See listings for *Cricket*, *Cicada*, *Ladybug*, *Muse* and *Spider*.)

✓ BLABBER MOUTH, Deva Communications, P.O. Box 417, Mendon MA 01756. (508)579-2804. Fax: (508)529-6039. E-mail: submit@blabbermouthonline.com. Website: www.blabbermouthonline.com. **Articles Editor:** Amy Saunders. Bimonthly magazine published entirely online as of August 2001. Estab. 1999. *Blabber*

Mouth focuses on teenagers' interests and issues. We profile teens with hobbies and businesses; cover issues like preparing for college; and publish teen writing and artwork. Fiction, nonfiction, and art of various kinds is accepted. Most of our contributors are teenagers, but we don't exclude those older or younger. 100% of publication aimed at juvenile market.

Fiction: Young adults: adventure, animal, contemporary, fantasy, health, history, humorous, multicultural, nature/environment, problem-solving, science fiction, sports, suspense/mystery. Average word length: maximum 1,000 but will consider longer pieces.

Nonfiction: Young adults: animals, arts/crafts, biography, careers, cooking, games/puzzles, geography, health, history, hobbies, how-to, humorous, interview/profile, math, multicultural, nature/environment, problem-solving, science, social issues, sports, travel. Average word length: maximum 1,000 but will consider longer pieces. Byline given.

Poetry: Reviews poetry. All styles accepted. Maximum length: 50 lines. Unlimited poems per submission.

How to Contact/Writers: Fiction/nonfiction: Submit complete ms. Responds to queries in 1 month; mss in 3 months. Publishes ms 3 months after acceptance. Will consider simultaneous submissions, electronic submission via disk or modem, previously published work.

Illustration: Buys 1 illustration/issue; 6 illustrations/year. Reviews ms/illustration packages from artists. Query. Contact: Amy Saunders, editor. Illustrations only: Query with samples; send portfolio. Contact: Amy Saunders, editor. Responds only if interested. Samples returned with SASE; samples filed. Credit line given.

Photography: Looking for artistic, photojournalism type photos, though other types will be considered. Uses color and b&w prints. Query with samples. Responds only if interested.

Terms: Currently non-paying. Buys one-time rights for mss. Original artwork returned at job's completion. Pays with contributor's copies if the contributor requests a copy of the issue his/her work is published in. Sample copies for $2.25 US; $3 non-US. Writer's/illustrator's/photo guidelines for SASE.

Tips: Our audience and contributors are multicultural, coming from around the world. We particularly like personal experiences ranging from battling with a disease to how I learned to memorize facts in school. If you submit a pencil drawing, please darken the lines; otherwise it may not scan properly. Always have your name and complete address (including Zip code and country) on everything you submit.

BOYS' LIFE, Boy Scouts of America, 1325 W. Walnut Hill Lane, P.O. Box 152079, Irving TX 75015-2079. (214)580-2366. Website: www.bsa.scouting.org. **Editor-in-Chief:** J.D. Owen. **Managing Editor:** W.E. Butterworth, IV. **Senior Editor:** Michael Goldman. **Fiction Editor:** Rich Haddaway. **Director of Design:** Joseph P. Connolly. **Art Director:** Scott Feaster. Monthly magazine. Estab. 1911. Circ. 1,300,000. *Boys' Life* is "a 4-color general interest magazine for boys 8 to 18 who are members of the Cub Scouts, Boy Scouts or Venturers; a 4-color general interest magazine for all boys."

Fiction: Middle readers: adventure, animal, contemporary, fantasy, history, humor, problem-solving, science fiction, sports, spy/mystery. Does not want to see "talking animals and adult reminiscence." Buys only 12-16 mss/year. Average word length: 1,000-1,500. Byline given.

Nonfiction: "Subject matter is broad. We cover everything from professional sports to American history to how to pack a canoe. A look at a current list of the BSA's more than 100 merit badge pamphlets gives an idea of the wide range of subjects possible. Even better, look at a year's worth of recent issues. Column headings are science, nature, earth, health, sports, space and aviation, cars, computers, entertainment, pets, history, music and others." Average word length: 500-1,500. Columns 300-750 words. Byline given.

How to Contact/Writers: Fiction: Send complete ms with SASE. Nonfiction: query with SASE for response. Responds to queries/mss in 2 months.

Illustration: Buys 10-12 illustrations/issue; 100-125 illustrations/year. Works on assignment only. Reviews ms/illustration packages from artists. "Query first." Illustrations only: Send tearsheets. Responds to art samples only if interested. Samples returned with SASE. Original artwork returned at job's completion.

Terms: Pays on acceptance. Buys first rights. Pays $750-1,500 for fiction; $400-1,500 for major articles; $150-400 for columns; $250-300 for how-to features. Pays illustrators $1,500-3,000 for color cover; $100-1,500 color inside. Sample copies for $3 plus 9×12 SASE. Writer's/illustrator's/photo guidelines available for SASE.

Tips: "We strongly urge you to study at least a year's issues to better understand the type of material published. Articles for *Boys' Life* must interest and entertain boys ages 8 to 18. Write for a boy you know who is 12. Our readers demand crisp, punchy writing in relatively short, straightforward sentences. The editors demand well-reported articles that demonstrate high standards of journalism. We follow *The New York Times* manual of style and usage. All submissions must be accompanied by SASE with adequate postage."

BOYS' QUEST, The Bluffton News Publishing and Printing Co., 103 N. Main St., Bluffton OH 45817. (419)358-4610. Fax: (419)358-5027. **Articles Editor:** Marilyn Edwards. **Art Submissions:** Diane Winebar. Bimonthly magazine. Estab. 1995. "*Boys' Quest* is a magazine created for boys from 6 to 13 years, with youngsters 8, 9 and 10 the specific target age. Our point of view is that every young boy deserves the right to be a young boy for a number of years before he becomes a young adult. As a result, *Boys' Quest* looks for articles, fiction, nonfiction, and poetry that deal with timeless topics, such as pets, nature, hobbies, science, games, sports, careers, simple cooking, and anything else likely to interest a young boy."

Fiction: Young readers, middle readers: adventure, animal, history, humorous, nature/environment, problem-solving, sports, jokes, building, cooking, cartoons, riddles. Does not want to see violence, teenage themes. Buys 30 mss/year. Average word length: 200-500. Byline given.

Nonfiction: Young readers, middle readers: animal, arts/crafts, biography, cooking, games/puzzles, history, how-to, humorous, math, problem-solving, science. Prefer photo support with nonfiction. Buys 30 mss/year. Average word length: 200-500. Byline given.

Poetry: Reviews poetry. Maximum length: 21 lines. Limit submissions to 6 poems.

How to Contact/Writers: All writers should consult the theme list before sending in articles. To receive current theme list, send a SASE. Fiction/Nonfiction: Query or send complete ms (preferred). Send SASE with correct postage. No faxed material. Responds to queries in 2 weeks; mss in 3 weeks (if rejected); 4 months (if scheduled). Publishes ms 3 months-3 years after acceptance. Will consider simultaneous submissions and previously published work.

Illustration: Buys 6 illustrations/issue; 36-45 illustrations/year. Uses b&w artwork only. Works on assignment only. Reviews ms/illustration packages from artists. Send ms with dummy. Illustrations only: Query with samples, arrange portfolio review. Send portfolio, tearsheets. Responds in 2 weeks. Samples returned with SASE; samples filed. Credit line given.

Photography: Photos used for support of nonfiction. "Excellent photographs included with a nonfiction story is considered very seriously." Model/property releases required. Uses b&w, 5×7 or 3×5 prints. Query with samples; send unsolicited photos by mail. Responds in 3 weeks.

Terms: Pays on publication. Buys first North American serial rights for mss. Buys first rights for artwork. Pays 5¢/word for stories and articles. Additional payment for ms/illustration packages and for photos accompanying articles. Pays $150-200 for color cover. Pays photographers per photo (range: $5-10). "*Boys' Quest*, as a new publication, is aware that its rates of payment are modest at this time. But we pledge to increase those rewards in direct proportion to our success. Meanwhile, we will strive to treat our contributors and their work with respect and fairness. That treatment, incidentally, will include quick decision on all submissions." Originals returned to artist at job's completion. Sample copies for $4. Writer's/illustrator's/photo guidelines free for SASE.

Tips: "We are looking for lively writing, most of it from a young boy's point of view—with the boy or boys directly involved in an activity that is both wholesome and unusual. We need nonfiction with photos and fiction stories—around 500 words—puzzles, poems, cooking, carpentry projects, jokes and riddles. Nonfiction pieces that are accompanied by black and white photos are far more likely to be accepted than those that need illustrations. We will entertain simultaneous submissions as long as that fact is noted on the manuscript." (See listing for *Hopscotch*.)

BREAD FOR GOD'S CHILDREN, Bread Ministries, Inc., P.O. Box 1017, Arcadia FL 34265-1017. (863)494-6214. Fax: (863)993-0154. E-mail: bread@desoto.net. Website: www.breadministry.org. **Editor:** Judith M. Gibbs. Bimonthly magazine. Estab. 1972. Circ. 10,000 (US and Canada). "*Bread* is designed as a teaching tool for Christian families." 85% of publication aimed at juvenile market.

Fiction: Young readers, middle readers, young adult/teen: adventure, religious, problem-solving, sports. Looks for "teaching stories that portray Christian lifestyles without preaching." Buys approximately 20 mss/year. Average word length: 900-1,500 (for teens); 600-900 (for young children). Byline given.

Nonfiction: Young readers, middle readers: animal. All levels: how-to. "We do not want anything detrimental to solid family values. Most topics will fit if they are slanted to our basic needs." Buys 3-4 mss/year. Average word length: 500-800. Byline given.

Illustration: "The only illustrations we purchase are those occasional good ones coming with a story we accept."

How to Contact/Writers: Fiction/nonfiction: Send complete ms. Responds to mss in 3 weeks-6 months "if considered for use." Will consider simultaneous submissions and previously published work.

Terms: Pays on publication. Pays $10-50 for stories; $25 for articles. Sample copies free for 9×12 SAE and 5 first-class stamps (for 2 copies).

Tips: "We want stories or articles that illustrate overcoming by faith and living solid, Christian lives. Know our publication and what we have used in the past . . . know the readership . . . know the publisher's guidelines. Stories should teach the value of morality and honesty without preaching. Edit carefully for content and grammar."

CALLIOPE, Exploring World History, Cobblestone Publishing Company, 30 Grove St., Suite C, Peterborough NH 03458. (603)924-7209. Fax: (603)924-7380. Website: www.cobblestonepub.com. **Managing Editor:** Lou Waryncia. **Co-editors:** Rosalie Baker and Charles Baker. **Art Director:** Ann Dillon. Magazine published 9 times/year. "*Calliope* covers world history (East/West), and lively, original approaches to the subject are the primary concerns of the editors in choosing material."

- *Calliope* themes for 2002 include Leonardo DaVinci, The Roman Republic, The Gupta of India, and The Song Dynasty of China. For additional themes and time frames, visit the website.

Fiction: Middle readers and young adults: adventure, folktales, plays, history, biographical fiction. Material must relate to forthcoming themes. Word length: up to 800.

Nonfiction: Middle readers and young adults: arts/crafts, biography, cooking, games/puzzles, history. Material must relate to forthcoming themes. Word length: 300-800.

Poetry: Maximum line length: 100. Wants "clear, objective imagery. Serious and light verse considered."

How to Contact/Writers: "A query must consist of the following to be considered (please use nonerasable paper): a brief cover letter stating subject and word length of the proposed article; a detailed one-page outline explaining the information to be presented in the article; an extensive bibliography of materials the author intends to use in preparing the article; a self-addressed stamped envelope. Writers new to *Calliope* should send a writing sample with query. If you would like to know if your query has been received, please also include a stamped postcard that requests acknowledgment of receipt. In all correspondence, please include your complete address as well as a telephone number where you can be reached. A writer may send as many queries for one issue as he or she wishes, but each query must have a separate cover letter, outline, bibliography and SASE. Telephone queries are not accepted. Handwritten queries will not be considered. Queries may be submitted at any time, but queries sent well in advance of deadline *may not be answered for several months*. Go-aheads requesting material proposed in queries are usually sent five months prior to publication date. Unused queries will be returned approximately three to four months prior to publication date."
Illustration: Illustrations only: Send tearsheets, photocopies. Original work returned upon job's completion (upon written request).
Photography: Buys photos from freelancers. Wants photos pertaining to any forthcoming themes. Uses b&w/color prints, 35mm transparencies. Send unsolicited photos by mail (on speculation).
Terms: Buys all rights for mss and artwork. Pays 20-25¢/word for stories/articles. Pays on an individual basis for poetry, activities, games/puzzles. "Covers are assigned and paid on an individual basis." Pays photographers per photo ($15-100 for b&w; $25-100 for color). Sample copy for $4.95 and SAE with $2 postage. Writer's/illustrator's/photo guidelines for SASE. (See listings for *Apple Seesd*, *Cobblestone*, *Faces*, *Footsteps* and *Odyssey*.)

CAMPUS LIFE, Christianity Today, International, 465 Gundersen Dr., Carol Stream IL 60188. (630)260-6200. Fax: (630)260-0114. E-mail: clmag@campuslife.net. Website: www.campuslife.net. **Articles and Fiction Editor:** Chris Lutes. **Design Director:** Doug Johnson. Bimonthly magazine. Estab. 1944. Circ. 100,000. "Our purpose is to help Christian high school students navigate adolescence with their faith intact."
Fiction: Young adults: humorous, problem-solving. Buys 5-6 mss/year. Byline given.
Poetry: Reviews poetry.
How to Contact/Writers: Fiction/nonfiction: Query.
Illustration: Works on assignment only. Reviews illustration packages from artists. Contact: Doug Johnson, design director. Illustrations only: Query; send promo sheet. Contact: Doug Johnson, design director. Responds only if interested. Credit line given.
Photography: Looking for photos depicting lifestyle/authentic teen experience. Model/property release required. Uses 8×10 glossy prints and 35mm, 2¼×2¼, 4×5 transparencies. Query with samples. Responds only if interested.
Terms: Pays on acceptance. Original artwork returned at job's completion. Writer's/illustrator's/photo guidelines for SASE.

CAREER WORLD, General Learning Communications, 900 Skokie Blvd., Suite 200, Northbrook IL 60062-4028. (847)205-3000. Fax: (847)564-8197. **Articles Editor:** Carole Rubenstein. Monthly (school year) magazine. Estab. 1972. A guide to careers, for students grades 6-12.
Nonfiction: Young adults/teens: education, how-to, interview/profile, career awareness and development. Byline given.
How to Contact/Writers: Nonfiction: Query with published clips and résumé. "We do not want any unsolicited manuscripts." Responds to queries in 2 weeks.
Illustration: Buys 5-10 illustrations/year. Works on assignment only. Reviews ms/illustration packages from artists. Ms/illustration packages and illustration only: Query; send promo sheet and tearsheets. Credit line given.
Photography: Purchases photos from freelancers.
Terms: Pays on publication. Buys all rights for ms. Pays $150 and up for articles. Pays illustrators by the project. Writer's guidelines free, but only on assignment.

CAREERS & COLLEGES, E.M. Guild, 989 Avenue of the Americas, New York NY 10018. (212)563-4688. (212)967-2531. Website: www.careersandcolleges.com. **Editorial Director:** Don Rauf. Magazine published 4 times during school year (September, November, January, March). Circ. 750,000. "*Careers & Colleges* provides juniors and seniors in high school with useful, thought-provoking, and hopefully entertaining reading

---

"PICTURE-ORIENTED MATERIAL" is for preschoolers to 8-year-olds; "Young readers" are for 5- to 8-year-olds; "Middle readers" are for 9- to 11-year-olds; and "Young adults/teens" are for ages 12 and up. Age ranges may vary slightly from magazine to magazine.

on career choices, higher education and other topics that will help prepare them for life after high school. Each issue focuses on a specific single theme: How to Get Into College; How to Pay for College; Careers; and Life After High School."

- • *Careers & Colleges* won the 2001 Golden Lamp Award from the Association of Educational Publishers (Recognizing the "Best" of the Best).

Nonfiction: Young adults/teens: careers, college, health, how-to, humorous, interview/profile, personal development, problem-solving, social issues, sports, travel. Wants more celebrity profiles. Buys 20-30 mss/year. Average word length: 1,000-1,500. Byline given.

How to Contact/Writers: Nonfiction: Query. Responds to queries in 6 weeks. Will consider electronic submissions via disk or modem.

Illustration: Buys 8 illustrations/issue; buys 32 illustrations/year. Works on assignment only. Reviews ms/illustration packages from artists. Query first. Illustrations only: Send tearsheets, cards. Responds to art samples in 3 weeks if interested. Original artwork returned at job's completion. Credit line given.

Terms: Pays on acceptance plus 30 days. Buys first North American serial rights. Pays $100-600 for assigned/unsolicited articles. Additional payment for ms/illustration packages "must be negotiated." Pays $300-1,000 for color illustration; $200-700 for b&w/color inside illustration. Pays photographers by the project. Sample copy $5, writer's guidelines with SASE or via website.

Tips: "We look for articles with great quotes, good reporting, good writing. Articles must be rich with examples and anecdotes, and must tie in with our mandate to help our teenaged readers plan their futures. We are especially looking for the most current trends, policy changes and infomration regarding college admissions, financial aid, and career opportunities. Visit our website for a good sense of our magazine."

N: CAT FANCY, The Magazine for Responsible Cat Owners, Fancy Publications, P.O. Box 6050, Mission Viejo CA 92690. (949)855-8822. Fax: (949)855-3045. Website: www.catfancy.com. Monthly magazine. Estab. 1965. Circ. 300,000. "Our magazine is for cat owners who want to know more about how to care for their pets in a responsible manner. We want to see 500-750-word articles showing children relating to or learning about cats in a positive, responsible way. We'd love to see more craft projects for children." 3% of material aimed at juvenile audience.

Fiction: Middle readers, young adults/teens: animal (all cat-related). Does not want to see stories in which cats talk. Buys 2 mss/year. Average word length: 750-1,000. Byline given. Never wants to see work showing cats being treated abusively or irresponsibly or work that puts cats in a negative light. Never use mss written from cats' point of view. Query first.

Nonfiction: Middle readers, young adults/teens: careers, arts/crafts, puzzles, profiles of children who help cats (all cat-related). Buys 3-9 mss/year. Average word length: 450-1,000. Byline given. Would like to see more crafts and how-to pieces for children.

Poetry: Reviews short poems only. "No more than five poems per submission please."

How To Contact/Writers: Fiction/nonfiction: Send query only. Responds to queries in 1-2 months. Publishes ms (juvenile) 4-12 months after acceptance. Send SASE for writer's guidelines.

Illustration: Buys 2-10 illustrations/year. "Most of our illustrations are assigned or submitted with a story. We look for realistic images of cats done with pen and ink (no pencil)." Illustration only: "Submit photocopies of work; samples of spot art possibilities." Samples returned with SASE. Responds in 1-2 months. Credit line given.

Photography: "Cats only, in excellent focus and properly lit. Send SASE for photo needs and submit according to them."

Terms: Pays on publication. Buys first North American serial rights. Buys one-time rights for artwork and photos. Originals returned to artist at job's completion. Pays $50-200 for stories; $75-400 for articles; $35-50 for crafts or puzzles; $20 for poems. Pays illustrators $50-200 for color inside. Photographers paid per photo (range: $35-200). Writer's/artist's/photo guidelines free for #10 SAE and 1 first-class stamp.

Tips: "Perhaps the most important tip we can give is: consider what 9- to 14-year-olds want to know about cats and what they enjoy most about cats, and address that topic in a style appropriate for them. Writers, keep your writing concise, and don't be afraid to try again after a rejection. Illustrators, we use illustrations mainly as spot art; occasionally we make assignments to illustrators whose spot art we've used before."

CATHOLIC FORESTER, Catholic Order of Foresters, P.O. Box 3012, 355 Shuman Blvd., Naperville IL 60566-7012. (630)983-4900. Fax: (630)983-3384. **Articles Editor:** Patricia Baron. **Art Director:** Keith Halla. Bimonthly magazine. Estab. 1883. Circ. 100,000. Targets members of the Catholic Order of Foresters. In addition to the organization's news, it offers general interest pieces on health, finance, travel, family life. Also use inspirational and humorous fiction.

Fiction: Young readers, middle readers, young adults: humorous, nature/environment, religious. Buys 10-20 mss/year. Average word length: 500-1,500.

How to Contact/Writers: Fiction: Submit complete ms. Responds in 3-4 months. Will consider previously published work.

Illustration: Buys 8-12 illustrations/issue. Uses color artwork only. Works on assignment only.

Photography: Buys photos with accompanying ms only.

Terms: Pays on acceptance. Buys first North American serial rights, reprint rights, one-time rights. Sample copies for 9×12 SAE and 3 first-class stamps. Writer's guidelines free for SASE.

N: CELEBRATE, Word Action Publishing Co., Church of the Nazarene, 6401 The Paseo, Kansas City MO 64131. (816)333-7000, ext. 2358. Fax: (816)333-4439. E-mail: mhammer@nazarene.org. Website: www.wordacti on.com. **Editor:** Melissa Hammer. **Editorial Assistant**: Andrea Simms. Weekly publication. Estab. 2001. Circ. 30,000. "This weekly take-home paper connects Sunday School learning to life for preschoolers (age 3 and 4), kindergartners (age 5 and 6) and their families." 75% of publication aimed at juvenile market; 25% parents.
Nonfiction: Picture-oriented material: arts/crafts, cooking, poems, action rhymes, piggyback songs (theme based). 50% of mss nonfiction. Byline given.
Poetry: Reviews poetry. Maximum length: 4-8 lines. Unlimited submissions.
How to Contact/Writers: Nonfiction: query. Responds to queries in 1 month. Responds to mss in 6 weeks. Publishes ms 1 year after acceptance. Will accept electronic submission via e-mail.
Terms: Pays on acceptance. Buys all rights, multi-use rights. Pays a minimum of $2 for songs and rhymes; 25¢/ line for poetry; $15 for activities, crafts, recipes. Compensation includes 4 contributor copies. Sample copy for SASE.
Tips: "Please keep submissions simple, age-appropriate, and geared to the theme."

N: CHILD, G&N USA Pulishing, 375 Lexington Ave., New York NY 10017. (212)499-2000. Fax: (212)499-2038. E-mail: childmail@child.com. Website: www.child.com. **Articles Editor:** Jennifer Mackenzie. **Photo Editor:** Topaz LeTourneau. Monthly magazine. Estab. 1984. Circ. 1 million. "Child provides parents of children from birth to age 12 with the newest thinking, information, and advice they need to raise their families in a constantly changing, time-pressed world."
Nonfiction: Freelance writers are invited to submit query letters only, the topics of children's health, parenting and marital relationship issues, child behavior and developemtn, personal essays pertaining to family life. Buys 6 mss/year.
How to Contact/Writers: Responds to queries in 2 months.
Illustration: Only interested in agented material.
Terms: Pays on acceptance. Buys first rights. Sample copies for $3.95. Writer's guidelines for SASE.

✓ CHILD LIFE, Children's Better Health Institute, P.O. Box 567, Indianapolis IN 46206. Parcels and packages: please send to 1100 Waterway Blvd., 46202. (317)636-8881. Fax: (317)684-8094. Website: www.childlifemag .org. **Editor:** Susan Thompson. **Art Director:** Phyllis Lybarger. Magazine published 8 times/year. Estab. 1921. Circ. 80,000. Targeted toward kids ages 9-11. Focuses on health, sports, fitness, nutrition, safety, academic excellence, general interests, and the nostalgia of *Child Life's* early days. "We publish jokes, riddles and poems by children." Kids should include name, address, phone number (for office use) and school photo. "No mass duplicated, multiple submissions."
  • *Child Life* is no longer accepting manuscripts for publication. See listings for *Children's Playmate, Humpty Dumpty's Magazine, Jack And Jill, Turtle Magazine* and *U*S*Kids*.
Tips: "We use kids' submissions from our age range—9 to 11. Those older or younger should try one of our sister publications: *Children's Digest, Children's Playmate, Humpty Dumpty's Magazine, Jack And Jill, Turtle Magazine, U*S*Kids*."

CHILDREN'S BETTER HEALTH INSTITUTE, 1100 Waterway Blvd., P.O. Box 567, Indianapolis IN 46206. See listings for *Child Life, Children's Digest, Children's Playmate, Humpty Dumpty's Magazine, Jack and Jill, Turtle* and *U*S* Kids*.

✓ CHILDREN'S DIGEST, Children's Better Health Institute, 1100 Waterway Blvd., P.O. Box 567, Indianapolis IN 46206. (317)634-1100. Fax: (317)684-8094. Website: www.childrensdigestmag.org. Parcels and packages please send to 1100 Waterway Blvd., Indianapolis IN 46202. **Editor/Acting Art Director:** Penny Rasdall. Magazine published 8 times/year. Estab. 1950. Circ. 110,000. For preteens; focuses on health, sports, fitness, nutrition, safety, academic excellence, general interest, and the nostalgia of *Child's Life's* early days. "We publish jokes, riddles, and poems by children." Kids should include name, address, phone numbers (for office use), and school photo. no mass duplicated, multiple submissions.
  • *Children's Digest* is no longer accepting manuscripts for publication. See listings for *Children's Playmate, Humpty Dumpty's Magazine, Jack and Jill, Turtle Magazine, U*S* Kids*.
Tips: We use submissions from our age range—9-11. Those older or younger should try one of our sister publications—*Children's Playmate, Humpty Dumpty's Magazine, Jack and Jill, Turtle, U*S* Kids*.

CHILDREN'S PLAYMATE, Children's Better Health Institute, 1100 Waterway Blvd., Box 567, Indianapolis IN 46206. (317)636-8881. Website: www.childrensplaymatemag.org. **Editor:** Terry Harshman. **Art Director:** Chuck Horsman. Magazine published 8 times/year. Estab. 1929. Circ. 135,000. For children ages 6-8 years; approximately 50% of content is health-related.
Fiction: Average word length: 100-300. Byline given.
Nonfiction: Young readers: arts/crafts, easy recipes, games/puzzles, health, medicine, safety, science, sports. Buys 16-20 mss/year. Average word length: 300-500. Byline given.
Poetry: Maximum length: 20-25 lines.

How to Contact/Writers: Fiction/nonfiction: Send complete ms. Responds to mss in 3 months. Do not send queries.
Illustration: Works on assignment only. Reviews ms/illustration packages from artists. Query first.
Terms: Pays on publication for illustrators and writers. Buys all rights for mss and artwork. Pays 17¢/word for stories. Pays minimum $25 for poems. Pays $275 for color cover illustration; $90 for b&w inside; $70-155 for color inside. Sample copy $1.75. Writer's/illustrator's guidelines for SASE. (See listings for *Child Life*, *Children's Digest*, *Humpty Dumpty's Magazine*, *Jack and Jill*, *Turtle Magazine* and *U*S* Kids*.)

☑ **CHIRP**, The Owl Group, 49 Front St. E., 2nd Floor, Toronto, Ontario M5E 1B3 Canada. Fax: (416)340-9769. E-mail: owl@owl.on.ca. Website: www.owlkids.com. **Editor-in-chief:** Angela Keenlyside. **Creative Director:** Barb Kelly. Published monthly during school year. *Discovery* magazine for children ages 3-6. "*Chirp* aims to introduce preschool non-readers to reading for pleasure about the world around them."
Fiction: Picture-oriented material: nature/environment, adventure, animal, multicultural, problem-solving, sports. Word length: 250 maximum.
Nonfiction: Picture-oriented material: fun, easy craft ideas, animal, games/puzzles, how-to, multicultural, nature/environment, problem-solving.
Poetry: Wants rhymes and poetry. Maximum length: 8 lines.
How to Contact/Writers: Query. Responds to queries/mss in 3 months.
Illustration: Uses approximately 15 illustrations/issue; 135 illustrations/year. Samples returned with SASE. Originals returned at job's completion. Credit line given.
Terms: Pays on acceptance. Buys all rights. Pays on publication. Pays writers $250 (Canadian); illustrators $150-650 (Canadian); photographers paid per photo ($150-375 Canadian). Sample copies available for $4 (Canadian).
Tips: "Chirp editors prefer to read completed manuscripts of stories and articles, accompanied by photographs or suggestions of visual references where they are appropriate. All craft ideas should be based on materials that are found around the average household." (See listings for *Chickadee* and *OWL*.)

CICADA, Carus Publishing Company, P.O. Box 300, 315 Fifth St., Peru IL 61354. (815)224-6656. Fax: (815)224-6615. E-mail: CICADA@caruspub.com. Website: www.cicadamag.com. **Editor-in-Chief:** Marianne Carus. **Executive Editor:** Deborah Vetter. **Associate Editor:** Tracy C. Schoenle. **Senior Art Director:** Ron McCutchan. Bimonthly magazine. Estab. 1998. *Cicada* publishes fiction and poetry with a genuine teen sensibility, aimed at the high school and college-age market. The editors are looking for stories and poems that are thought-provoking but entertaining.
Fiction: Young adults: adventure, animal, contemporary, fantasy, history, humorous, multicultural, nature/environment, romance, science fiction, sports, suspense/mystery, stories that will adapt themselves to a sophisticated cartoon, or graphic novel format. Buys up to 60 mss/year. Average word length: about 5,000 words for short stories; up to 15,000 for novellas only—we run one novella per issue.
Nonfiction: Young adults: first-person, coming-of-age experiences that are relevant to teens and young adults (example-life in the Peace Corps). Buys 6 mss/year. Average word length: about 5,000 words. Byline given.
Poetry: Reviews serious, humorous, free verse, rhyming (if done well) poetry. Maximum length: up to 25 lines. Limit submissions to 5 poems.
How to Contact/Writers: Fiction/nonfiction: send complete ms. Responds to mss in 3 months. Publishes ms 1-2 years after acceptance. Will consider simultaneous submissions if author lets us know.
Illustration: Buys 20 illustrations/issue; 120 illustrations/year. Uses color artwork for cover; b&w for interior. Works on assignment only. Reviews ms/illustration packages from artists. Send ms with 1-2 sketches and samples of other finished art. Contact: Ron McCutchan, senior art director. Illustrations only: Query with samples. Contact: Ron McCutchan, senior art director. Responds in 6 weeks. Samples returned with SASE; samples filed. Credit line given.
Photography: Wants documentary photos (clear shots that illustrate specific artifacts, persons, locations, phenomena, etc., cited in the text) and "art" shots of teens in photo montage/lighting effects etc. Uses b&w 4×5 glossy prints. Submit portfolio for review. Responds in 6 weeks.
Terms: Pays on publication. Buys first rights for mss. Buys one-time, first publication rights for artwork and photographs. Pays up to 25¢/word for mss; up to $3/line for poetry. Pays illustrators $750 for color cover; $50-150 for b&w inside. Pays photographers per photo (range: $50-150). Sample copies for $8.50. Writer's/illustrator's/photo guidelines for SASE.
Tips: "Please don't write for a junior high audience. We're looking for good character development, strong plots, and thought-provoking themes for young people in high school and college. Don't forget humor!" (See listings for *Babybug*, *Click*, *Cricket*, *Ladybug*, *Muse* and *Spider*.)

◖ **CLASS ACT**, Class Act, Inc., P.O. Box 802, Henderson KY 42419-0802. E-mail: classact@henderson.net. Website: www.henderson.net/~classact. **Articles Editor:** Susan Thurman. Monthly, September-May. Newsletter. Estab. 1993. Circ. 300. "We are looking for practical, ready-to-use ideas for the English/language arts classroom (grades 6-12)."
Nonfiction: Young adults/teens: games/puzzles, how-to. Does not want to see esoteric material; no master's thesis; no poetry (except articles about how to write poetry). Buys 20 mss/year. Average word length: 200-2,000. Byline given.

How to Contact/Writers: Send complete ms. E-mail submissions (no attachments) and submissions on disk using Word encouraged. Responds to queries/mss in 1 month. Usually publishes ms 3-12 months after acceptance. Will consider simultaneous submissions. Must send SASE.

Terms: Pays on acceptance. Pays $10-40 per article. Buys all rights. Sample copy for $3 and SASE.

Tips: "We're only interested in language arts-related articles for teachers and students. Writers should realize teens often need humor in classroom assignments. In addition, we are looking for teacher-tested ideas that have already worked in the classroom. We currently have more puzzles than we need and are looking for prose rather than puzzles. Be clever. We've already seen a zillion articles on homonyms and haikus. If a SASE isn't sent, we'll assume you don't want a response."

COBBLESTONE: Discover American History, Cobblestone Publishing Co., 30 Grove St., Suite C, Peterborough NH 03458. (603)924-7209. Fax: (603)924-7380. Website: www.cobblestonepub.com. **Editor:** Meg Chorlian. **Art Director:** Ann Dillon. **Managing Editor:** Lou Waryncia. Magazine published 9 times/year. Circ. 33,000. "*Cobblestone* is theme-related. Writers should request editorial guidelines which explain procedure and list upcoming themes. Queries must relate to an upcoming theme. It is recommended that writers become familiar with the magazine (sample copies available)."
- *Cobblestone* themes through 2003 are available on website.

Nonfiction: Middle readers (school ages 8-14): activities, biography, games/puzzles (no word finds), history (world and American), interview/profile, science, travel. All articles must relate to the issue's theme. Buys 120 mss/year. Average word length: 600-800. Byline given.

Poetry: Up to 100 lines. "Clear, objective imagery. Serious and light verse considered." Pays on an individual basis. Must relate to theme.

How to Contact/Writers: Fiction/nonfiction: Query. "A query must consist of all of the following to be considered: a brief cover letter stating the subject and word length of the proposed article, a detailed one-page outline explaining the information to be presented in the article, an extensive bibliography of materials the author intends to use in preparing the article, a self-addressed stamped envelope. Writers new to *Cobblestone* should send a writing sample with query. If you would like to know if your query has been received, please also include a stamped postcard that requests acknowledgment of receipt. In all correspondence, please include your complete address as well as a telephone number where you can be reached. A writer may send as many queries for one issue as he or she wishes, but each query must have a separate cover letter, outline, bibliography and SASE. Telephone queries are not accepted. Handwritten queries will not be considered. Queries may be submitted at any time, but queries sent well in advance of deadline *may not be answered for several months*. Go-aheads requesting material proposed in queries are usually sent five months prior to publication date. Unused queries will be returned approximately three to four months prior to publication date."

Illustration: Buys 4 color illustrations/issue; 36 illustrations/year. Preferred theme or style: Material that is simple, clear and accurate but not too juvenile. Sophisticated sources are a must. Works on assignment only. Reviews ms/illustration packages from artists. Query. Illustrations only: Send photocopies, tearsheets, or other nonreturnable samples. "Illustrators should consult issues of *Cobblestone* to familiarize themselves with our needs." Responds to art samples in 2 weeks. Samples returned with SASE; samples not filed. Original artwork returned at job's completion (upon written request). Credit line given.

Photography: Photos must relate to upcoming themes. Send transparencies and/or color prints. Submit on speculation.

Terms: Pays on publication. Buys all rights to articles and artwork. Pays 20-25¢/word for articles/stories. Pays on an individual basis for poetry, activities, games/puzzles. Pays photographers per photo ($15-100 for b&w; $25-100 for color). Sample copy $4.95 with 7½×10½ SAE and 5 first-class stamps; writer's/illustrator's/photo guidelines free with SAE and 1 first-class stamp.

Tips: Writers: "Submit detailed queries which show attention to historical accuracy and which offer interesting and entertaining information. Study past issues to know what we look for. All feature articles, recipes, activities, fiction and supplemental nonfiction are freelance contributions." Illustrators: "Submit color samples, not too juvenile. Study past issues to know what we look for. The illustration we use is generally for stories, recipes and activities." (See listings for *AppleSeeds*, *Calliope*, *Dig*, *Faces*, *Footsteps* and *Odyssey*.)

☑ **COLLEGE BOUND MAGAZINE**, Ramholtz Publishing, Inc., 2071 Clove Rd., Staten Island NY 10304. (718)273-5700. Fax: (718)273-2539. E-mail: editorial@collegebound.net. Website: www.collegebound.net. **Articles Editor:** Gina LaGuardia. **Art Director:** Suzanne Vidal. Monthly magazine and website. Estab. 1987. Circ. 75,000 (regional); 750,000 (national). *College Bound Magazine* is written by college students for high school juniors and seniors. It is designed to provide an inside view of college life, with college students from around the country serving as correspondents. The magazine's editorial content offers its teen readership personal accounts on all aspects of college, from living with a roommate, choosing a major, and joining a fraternity or sorority, to college dating, interesting courses, beating the financial aid fuss, and other college-bound concerns. *College Bound Magazine* is published six times regionally throughout the tri-state area. Special issues include the Annual National Edition (published each February) and Spring California, Chicago, Texas and Florida issues. The magazine offers award-winning World Wide Web affiliates starting at *CollegeBound.NET*, at www.collegebound.net.

Nonfiction: Young adults: careers, college prep, fashion, health, how-to, interview/profile, problem-solving, social issues, college life. Buys 70 mss/year. Average word length: 400-1,100 words. Byline given.

How to Contact/Writers: Nonfiction: Query with published clips. Responds to queries in 5 weeks; mss in 6 weeks. Publishes ms 2-3 months after acceptance. Will consider electronic submission via disk or modem, previously published work (as long as not a competitor title).
Illustration: Buys 2-3 illustrations/issue. Uses color artwork only. Works on assignment only. Reviews ms/illustration packages from artists. Query. Contact: Suzanne Vidal, art director. Illustrations only: Query with samples. Responds in 2 months. Samples kept on file. Credit line given.
Terms: Pays on publication. Buys first North American serial rights, all rights or reprint rights for mss. Buys first rights for artwork. Originals returned if requested, with SASE. Pays $25-100 for articles 30 days upon publication. All contributors receive 2 issues with payment. Pays illustrators $25-125 for color inside. Sample copies free for #10 SASE and $3 postage. Writer's guidelines for SASE.
Tips: "Review the sample issue and get a good feel for the types of articles we accept and our tone and purpose."

CRICKET MAGAZINE, Carus Publishing, Company, P.O. Box 300, Peru IL 61354. (815)224-6656. Website: www.cricket.com. **Articles/Fiction Editor-in-Chief:** Marianne Carus. **Executive Editor:** Deborah Vetter. **Associate Editor:** Tracy Schoenle. **Associate Editor:** Julia M. Messina. **Art Director:** Ron McCutchan. Monthly magazine. Estab. 1973. Circ. 71,000. Children's literary magazine for ages 9-14.
Fiction: Middle readers, young adults/teens: adventure, animal, contemporary, fantasy, folk and fairy tales, history, humorous, multicultural, nature/environment, science fiction, sports, suspense/mystery. Buys 140 mss/year. Maximum word length: 2,000. Byline given.
Nonfiction: Middle readers, young adults/teens: animal, arts/crafts, biography, environment, experiments, games/puzzles, history, how-to, interview/profile, natural science, problem-solving, science and technology, space, sports, travel. Multicultural needs include articles on customs and cultures. Requests bibliography with submissions. Buys 40 mss/year. Average word length: 1,200. Byline given.
Poetry: Reviews poems, 1-page maximum length. Limit submissions to 5 poems or less.
How to Contact/Writers: Send complete ms. Do not query first. Responds to mss in 3 months. Does not like but will consider simultaneous submissions. SASE required for response.
Illustration: Buys 35 illustrations (14 separate commissions)/issue; 425 illustrations/year. Uses b&w and full-color work. Preferred theme or style: "strong realism; strong people, especially kids; good action illustration; no cartoons. All media, but prefer other than pencil." Reviews ms/illustration packages from artists "but reserves option to re-illustrate." Send complete ms with sample and query. Illustrations only: Provide tearsheets or good quality photocopies to be kept on file. SASE required for response/return of samples. Responds to art samples in 2 months.
Photography: Purchases photos with accompanying ms only. Model/property releases required. Uses color transparencies, b&w glossy prints.
Terms: Pays on publication. Buys first publication rights in the English language. Buys first publication rights plus promotional rights for artwork. Original artwork returned at job's completion. Pays up to 25¢/word for unsolicited articles; up to $3/line for poetry. Pays $750 for color cover; $75-150 for b&w, $150-250 for color inside. Pays $750 for color cover; $75-150 for b&w, $150-250 for color inside. Writer's/illustrator's guidelines for SASE.
Tips: Writers: "Read copies of back issues and current issues. Adhere to specified word limits. *Please* do not query." Illustrators: "Edit your samples. Send only your best work and be able to reproduce that quality in assignments. Put name and address on *all* samples. Know a publication before you submit—is your style appropriate?" (See listings for *Babybug, Cicada, Click, Ladybug, Muse* and *Spider*.)

CRUSADER, Calvinist Cadet Corps, P.O. Box 7259, Grand Rapids MI 49510. (616)241-5616. Website: www.calvinistcadets.org. **Editor:** G. Richard Broene. **Art Director:** Mary Broene. Magazine published 7 times/year. Circ. 12,000. "Our magazine is for members of the Calvinist Cadet Corps—boys aged 9-14. Our purpose is to show how God is at work in their lives and in the world around them. Our magazine offers nonfiction articles and fast-moving fiction—everything to appeal to interests and concerns of boys, teaching Christian values subtly."
Fiction: Middle readers, boys/early teens: adventure, humorous, multicultural, problem-solving, religious, sports. Buys 12 mss/year. Average word length: 900-1,500.
Nonfiction: Middle readers, boys/early teens: arts/crafts, games/puzzles, hobbies, how-to, humorous, interview/profile, problem-solving, science, sports. Buys 6 mss/year. Average word length: 400-900.
How to Contact/Writers: Fiction/nonfiction: Send complete ms. Responds to queries in 1 month; on mss in 1-2 months. Will consider simultaneous submissions.
Illustration: Buys 1 illustration/issue; buys 6 illustrations/year. Works on assignment only. Reviews ms/illustration packages from artists. Responds in 5 weeks. Samples returned with SASE. Originals returned to artist at job's completion. Credit line given.
Photography: Buys photos from freelancers. Wants nature photos and photos of boys.
Terms: Pays on acceptance. Buys first North American serial rights; reprint rights. Pays 4-5¢/word for stories/articles. Pays illustrators $50-200 for b&w/color cover or b&w inside. Sample copy free with 9×12 SAE and 4 first-class stamps.
Tips: "Our publication is mostly open to fiction; send SASE for a list of themes (available yearly in January). We use mostly fast-moving fiction that appeals to a boy's sense of adventure or sense of humor. Avoid preachiness;

avoid simplistic answers to complicated problems; avoid long dialogue with little action. Articles on sports, outdoor activities, bike riding, science, crafts, etc. should emphasize a Christian perspective but avoid simplistic moralisms."

THE CRYSTAL BALL, The Starwind Press, P.O. Box 98, Ripley OH 45167. (937)392-4549. E-mail: susannah @techgallery.com. Articles/Fiction Editor: Marlene Powell. **Assistant Editor:** Susannah C. West. Quarterly magazine. Estab. 1997. Circ. 1,000. Publishes science fiction and fantasy for young adults.
Fiction: Young adults: fantasy, folktale, science fiction. Buys 8-12 mss/year. Average word length: 1,500-5,000. Byline given.
Nonfiction: Young adults: biography, how-to, interview/profile, science. Buys 8-12 mss/year. Average word length: 1,000-3,000.
Poetry: Only publishes poetry by kids.
How to Contact/Writers: Fiction: send complete ms. Nonfiction: query. Responds to queries and mss in 4 months. Publishes ms 6-12 months after acceptance. Will consider previously published work if published in noncompeting market.
Illustration: Buys 6-8 illustrations/issue; 24-32 illustrations/year. Uses b&w camera ready artwork only. Works on assignment only. Reviews ms/illustration packages from artists. Send ms with dummy. Contact: Marlene Powell, editor. Illustrations only: query with samples. Contact: Marlene Powell, editor. Responds in 4 months if SASE enclosed. Samples kept on file. Credit line given.
Photography: Looking for photos to illustrate nonfiction pieces. Uses b&w, line shots or already screened. Responds in 3 months.
Terms: Pays on acceptance. Buys first North American serial rights for mss, artwork and photos. Original artwork returned at job's completion if requested. Pays $5-20 for stories and articles. Additional payment for photos accompanying article. Pays illustrators $5-20 for b&w inside and cover. Pays photographers per photo (range: $5-20). Sample copies for $3. Writer's/illustrator's guidelines for SASE.
Tips: Be familiar with the science fiction/fantasy genre.

N: DANCE MAGAZINE, 111 Myrtle St., Suite 203, Oakland CA 94607. (510)839-6060. Fax: (510)839-6066. Website: www.dancemagazine.com. **Articles Editor:** KC Patrick. **Art Director:** James Lambertus. Monthly magazine. Estab. 1927. Circ. 35,000. Covers "all things dance—features, news, reviews, calendar. We have a Young Dancer section." Byline given.
How to Contact: Fiction: Query with published clips.
Photography: Uses dance photos.
Terms: Pays on publication. Buys first rights. Additional payment for ms/illustration packages and for photos accompanying articles. Pays photographers per photo. Sample copies for $6.50.
Tips: "Study the magazine for style."

☑ DIG, (formerly *Archaeology's Dig*), Cobblestone Publishing, 30 Grove St., Suite C, Peterburough NH 03450. (603)924-7209. Fax: (603)924-7380. E-mail: cfbakeriii@meganet.net. Website: www.digonsite.com. **Editor:** Rosalie Baker. **Editorial Director:** Lou Waryncia. **Art Director:** Ann Rillon. Bimonthly magazine. Estab. 1999. Circ. 60,000. An archaeology magazine for kids ages 8-14. Publishes entertaining and educational stories about discoveries, dinosaurs, etc.
    • *Dig* was purchased by Cobblestone Publishing.
Nonfiction: Middle readers, young adults: biography, games/puzzles, history, science, archaeology. Buys 50 mss/year. Average word length: 400-800. Byline given.
How to Contact/Writers: Fiction/nonfiction: Query. "A query must consist of all of the following to be considered: a brief cover letter stating the subject and word length of the proposed article, a detailed one-page outline explaining the information to be presented in the article, an extensive bibliography of materials the author intends to use in preparing the article, and a SASE. Writers new to *Dig* should send a writing sample with query. If you would like to know if query has been received, include a stamped postcard that requests acknowledgement of receipt." Multiple queries accepted (include separate cover letter, outline, bibliography, SASE)—may not be answered for many months. Go-aheads requesting material proposed in queries are usually sent 5 months prior to publication date. Unused queries will be returned approximately 3-4 months prior to publication date.
Illustration: Buys 10-15 illustrations/issue; 60-75 illustrations/year. Uses color artwork only. Works on assignment only. Reviews ms/illustration packages from artists. Query. Contact: Ken Feisel, art director. Illustrations only: Query with samples. Arrange portfolio review. Send tearsheets. Contact: Ken Feisel, art director. Responds in 2 months only if interested. Samples not returned; samples filed. Credit line given.
Photography: Uses anything related to archaeology, history, artifacts, dinosaurs and current archaeological events that relate to kids. Uses color prints and 35mm transparencies. Provide résumé, business card, promotional literature or tearsheets to be kept on file. Responds only if interested.
Terms: Pays on publication. Buys all rights for mss. Buys first North American rights for artwork and photos. Original artwork returned at job's completion. Pays 50¢/word. Additional payment for ms/illustration packages and for photos accompanying articles. Pays illustrators $1,000 and up for color cover; $150-2,000 for color inside. Pays photographers by the project (range: $500-1,000). Pays per photo (range: $100-500).

Tips: "We are looking for writers who can communicate archaeological and paleontological concepts in a conversational style for kids. Writers should have some idea where photography can be located to support their work."

DISCOVERIES, Children's Ministries, 6401 The Paseo, Kansas City MO 64131. (816)333-7000. Fax: (816)333-4439. E-mail: vfolsom@nazarene.org. **Editor**: Virginia Folsom. **Executive Editor**: Randy Cloud. **Editorial Assistant:** Kathy Hendrixson. Weekly tabloid. "*Discoveries* is a leisure-reading piece for third and fourth graders. It is published weekly by WordAction Publishing. The major purpose of the magazine is to provide a leisure-reading piece which will build Christian behavior and values and provide reinforcement for Biblical concepts taught in the Sunday School curriculum. The focus of the reinforcement will be life-related, with some historical appreciation. *Discoveries'* target audience is children ages eight to ten in grades three and four. The readability goal is third to fourth grade."
Fiction: Middle readers: adventure, contemporary, humorous, religious. "Fiction—stories should vividly portray definite Christian emphasis or character-building values, without being preachy. The setting, plot and action should be realistic." 500-word maximum. Byline given.
Nonfiction: Game/puzzles, history (all Bible-related) and Bible "trivia."
How to Contact/Writers: Fiction: Send complete ms. Responds to queries/mss in 1 month.
Terms: Pays "approximately one year before the date of issue." Buys multi-use rights. Pays 5¢/word. Contributor receives 4 complimentary copies of publication. Sample copy free for #10 SASE with 1 first-class stamp. Writer's/artist's guidelines free with #10 SAE.
Tips: "*Discoveries* is committed to reinforcement of the Biblical concepts taught in the Sunday School curriculum. Because of this, the themes needed are mainly as follows: faith in God, obedience to God, putting God first, choosing to please God, accepting Jesus as Savior, finding God's will, choosing to do right, trusting God in hard times, prayer, trusting God to answer, importance of Bible memorization, appreciation of Bible as God's Word to man, Christians working together, showing kindness to others, witnessing." (See listing for *Passport.*)

DISCOVERY, John Milton Society for the Blind, 475 Riverside Dr., Room 455, New York NY 10115. (212)870-3335. Fax: (212)870-3229. E-mail: ipeck@jmsblind.org. Website: www.jmsblind.org. **Assistant Editor**: Ingrid Peck. **Executive Director & Editor**: Darcy Quigley. Quarterly braille magazine. Estab. 1935. Circ. 2,000. "*Discovery* is a free Christian braille magazine for blind and visually impaired youth ages 8-18. 95% of material is stories, poems, quizzes and educational articles, reprinted from 20 Christian and other magazines for youth. Original pieces from individual authors must be ready to print with little or no editing involved. We cannot offer reprint fees. Christian focus."
Fiction: Young readers, middle readers, young adults/teens: all categories and issues pertaining to blind; adventure, animal, contemporary, fantasy, folktales, health, history, humorous, multicultural, nature/environment, problem solving, religious. Does not want stories in which blindness is described as a novelty. It should be part of a story with a larger focus. Buys less than 10 mss/year. Average word length: 1,500 words (maximum). Byline given.
Nonfiction: Young readers, middle readers, young adults/teens: animal, biography, careers, concept, cooking, games/puzzles, geography, health, history, hobbies, how-to, humorous, interview/profile, multicultural, nature/environment, problem solving, religion, science, social issues. Also want inspirational stories involving visually impaired. Buys less than 10 mss/year. Average word length: 1,500 words (maximum). Byline given.
Poetry: Reviews poetry. Maximum length: 500 words.
How to Contact/Writers: Fiction/nonfiction: Send complete ms. Responds to queries/mss in 6-8 weeks. Publishes ms 3-12 months after acceptance. Will consider simultaneous submissions, previously published work.
Terms: Acquires reprint rights. Authors do not receive payment, only sample copy. Sample copies free with SASE.
Tips: "95% of the material in *Discovery* is reprinted from Christian and other periodicals for youth. Previously unpublished material must therefore be ready to print with little or no editing involved. Please send complete manuscripts or request our 'Writers' Guidelines' which includes a list of periodicals we reprint from."

☑ **DISCOVERY TRAILS**, Gospel Publishing House, 1445 N. Boonville Ave., Springfield MO 65802-1894. (417)862-2781. E-mail: rl-discoverytrails@gph.org. Website: www.radiantlife.org. **Articles Editor:** Sinda S. Zinn. **Art Director:** Diane Lamb. Quarterly take-home paper. Circ. 20,000. "*Discovery Trails* provides fiction stories that promote Christian living through application of biblical principles. Puzzles and activities are fun ways to learn more about God's Word and "bytes" of information are provided to inspire readers to be in awe of God's wonderful creation."
Fiction: Middle readers: adventure, animal, contemporary, humorous, nature/environment, problem-solving, religious, suspense/mystery. Buys 100 or less mss/year.
Nonfiction: Middle readers: animal, arts/crafts, how-to, humorous, nature/environment, problem-solving, religion. Buys 50-100 mss/year. Average word length: 200-500. Byline given.
Poetry: Reviews poetry. Limit submissions, at one time, to 2 poems.
How to Contact/Writers: Fiction/nonfiction: Send complete ms. Responds in 1 month. Publishes ms 15-24 months after acceptance. Will consider simultaneous submissions or previously published work. Please indicate such.

Illustration: Buys 1 illlustration issue; 50-60 illustrations/year from assigned freelancers. Uses color artwork only. Works on assignment only. Send promo sheet, portfolio. Contact: Diane Lamb, art coordinator. Responds only if interested. Samples returned with SASE; samples filed. Credit line given.

Terms: Pays on acceptance. Pays authors 7-10¢ per word. Buys first rights or reprint rights for mss. Buys reprint rights for artwork. Original artwork returned at job's completion. Sample copies for 6×9 SAE and 2 first-class stamps. Writer's guidelines for SASE.

DOLPHIN LOG, The Cousteau Society, 870 Greenbriar Circle, Suite 402, Chesapeake VA 23320. (800)441-4395. Website: www.dolphin.org. **Editor:** Lisa Rao. Bimonthly magazine for children ages 7-13. Circ. 80,000. Entirely nonfiction subject matter encompasses all areas of science, natural history, marine biology, ecology and the environment as they relate to our global water system. The philosophy of the magazine is to delight, instruct and instill an environmental ethic and understanding of the interconnectedness of living organisms, including people. Of special interest are articles on ocean- or water-related themes which develop reading and comprehension skills.

Nonfiction: Middle readers, young adult: animal, games/puzzles, geography, interview/profile, nature/environment, science, ocean. Multicultural needs include indigenous peoples, lifestyles of ancient people, etc. Does not want to see talking animals. No dark or religious themes. Buys 10 mss/year. Average word length: 500-700. Byline given.

How to Contact/Writers: Nonfiction: Query first. Responds to queries in 3 months; mss in 6 months.

Illustration: Buys 1 illustration/issue; buys 6 illustrations/year. Preferred theme: Biological illustration. Reviews ms/illustration packages from artists. Illustrations only: Query; send résumé, promo sheet, slides. Reports on art samples in 8 weeks only if interested. Credit line given to illustrators.

Photography: Wants "sharp, colorful pictures of sea creatures. The more unusual the creature, the better." Submit duplicate slides only.

Terms: Pays on publication. Buys first North American serial rights; reprint rights. Pays $75-250 for articles. Pays $100-400 for illustrations. Pays $75-200/color photos. Sample copy $2.50 with 9×12 SAE and 3 first-class stamps. Writer's/illustrator's guidelines free with #10 SASE.

Tips: Writers: "Write simply and clearly and don't anthropomorphize." Illustrators: "Be scientifically accurate and don't anthropomorphize. Some background in biology is helpful, as our needs range from simple line drawings to scientific illustrations which must be researched for biological and technical accuracy."

✓ **DRAMATICS**, Educational Theatre Association, 2343 Auburn Ave., Cincinnati OH 45219. (513)421-3900. E-mail: dcorathers@edta.org. Website: www.etassoc.org. **Articles Editor:** Don Corathers. **Art Director:** William Johnston. Published monthly September-May. Estab. 1929. Circ. 35,000. "Dramatics is for students (mainly high school age) and teachers of theater. Mix includes how-to (tech theater, acting, directing, etc.), informational, interview, photo feature, humorous, profile, technical. "We want our student readers to become a more discerning and appreciative audience. Material is directed to both theater students and their teachers, with strong student slant."

Fiction: Young adults: drama (one-act and full-length plays.) Does not want to see plays that show no understanding of the conventions of the theater. No plays for children, no Christmas or didactic "message" plays. "We prefer unpublished scripts that have been produced at least once." Buys 5-9 plays/year. Emerging playwrights have better chances with short plays, 10 minute or one-act.

Nonfiction: Young adults: arts/crafts, careers, how-to, interview/profile, multicultural (all theater-related). "We try to portray the theater community in all its diversity." Does not want to see academic treatises. Buys 50 mss/year. Average word length: 750-3,000. Byline given.

How to Contact/Writers: Send complete ms. Responds in 3 months (longer for plays). Published ms 3 months after acceptance. Will consider simultaneous submissions and previously published work occasionally.

Illustration: Buys 0-2 illustrations/year. Works on assignment only. Arrange portfolio review; send résumé, promo sheets and tearsheets. Responds only if interested. Samples returned with SASE; sample not filed. Credit line given.

Photography: Buys photos with accompanying ms only. Looking for "good-quality production or candid photography to accompany article. We very occasionally publish photo essays." Model/property release and captions required. Uses 5×7 or 8×10 b&w glossy prints and 35mm transparencies. Query with résumé of credits. Responds only if interested.

Terms: Pays on acceptance. Buys one-time rights, occasionally reprint rights. Buys one-time rights for artwork and photos. Original artwork returned at job's completion. Pays $100-400 for plays; $50-300 for articles; up to $100 for illustrations. Pays photographers by the project or per photo. Sometimes offers additional payment for ms/illustration packages and photos accompanying a ms. Sample copy available for $2.50 and 9×12 SAE. Writer's and photo guidelines available for SASE or via website.

VISIT OUR WEBSITES at www.writersmarket.com and www.writersdigest.com, for helpful articles, hot new markets, daily market updates, writers' guidelines and much more.

Tips: "Obtain our writer's guidelines and look at recent back issues. The best way to break in is to know our audience—drama students, teachers and others interested in theater—and write for them. Writers who have some practical experience in theater, especially in technical areas, have an advantage, but we'll work with anybody who has a good idea. Some freelancers have become regular contributors."

✓ **DYNAMATH**, Scholastic Inc., 555 Broadway, New York NY 10012-3999. (212)343-6458. Fax: (212)343-6333. E-mail: dynamath@scholastic.com. Website: www.scholastic.com/dynamath. **Editor:** Matt Friedman. **Art Director:** James Sarfati. Monthly magazine. Estab. 1981. Circ. 225,000. Purpose is "to make learning math fun, challenging and uncomplicated for young minds in a very complex world."
Nonfiction: Middle readers: animal, arts/crafts, cooking, fashion, games/puzzles, health, history, hobbies, how-to, humorous, math, multicultural, nature/environment, problem-solving, science, social issues, sports—all must relate to math and science topics.
How to Contact/Writers: Nonfiction: Query with published clips, send ms. Responds to queries in 1 month; mss in 6 weeks. Publishes ms 4 months after acceptance. Will consider simultaneous submissions.
Illustration: Buys 4 illustrations/issue. Illustration only: Query first; send résumé and tearsheets. Responds on submissions only if interested. Credit line given.
Terms: Pays on acceptance. Buys all rights for mss, artwork, photographs. Originals returned to artist at job's completion. Pays $50-450 for stories. Pays artists $800-1,000 for color cover illustration; $100-800 for color inside illustration. Pays photographers $300-1,000 per project.
Tips: See listings for *Junior Scholastic, Scholastic Math Magazine, Science World* and *Superscience*.

✓ **FACES, People, Places & Cultures**, Cobblestone Publishing, Inc., 30 Grove St., Peterborough NH 03458. (603)924-7209. Fax: (603)924-7380. E-mail: facesmag@yahoo.com. Website: www.cobblestonepub.com. **Editor**: Elizabeth Crooker Carpentiere. **Managing Editor**: Lou Warnycia. **Art Director**: Ann Dillon. Magazine published 9 times/year (September-May). Circ. 15,000. *Faces* is a theme-related magazine; writers should send for theme list before submitting ideas/queries. Each month a different world culture is featured through the use of feature articles, activities and photographs and illustrations.
• *Faces* themes for 2002 include World Refugees, Chile, Poland, Palestinians, Prairie Provinces of Canada.
Fiction: Middle readers, young adults/teens: adventure, folktales, history, multicultural, plays, religious, travel. Does not want to see material that does not relate to a specific upcoming theme. Buys 9 mss/year. Maximum word length: 800. Byline given.
Nonfiction: Middle readers and young adults/teens: animal, anthropology, arts/crafts, biography, cooking, fashion, games/puzzles, geography, history, how-to, humorous, interview/profile, nature/environment, religious, social issues, sports, travel. Does not want to see material not related to a specific upcoming theme. Buys 63 mss/year. Average word length: 300-800. Byline given.
Poetry: Clear, objective imagery; up to 100 lines. Must relate to theme.
How to Contact/Writers: Fiction/nonfiction: Query with published clips and 2-3 line biographical sketch. "Ideas should be submitted six to nine months prior to the publication date. Responses to ideas are usually sent approximately four months before the publication date."
Illustration: Buys 3 illustrations/issue; buys 27 illustrations/year. Preferred theme or style: Material that is meticulously researched (most articles are written by professional anthropologists); simple, direct style preferred, but not too juvenile. Works on assignment only. Roughs required. Reviews ms/illustration packages from artists. Illustrations only: Send samples of b&w work. "Illustrators should consult issues of *Faces* to familiarize themselves with our needs." Reports on art samples only if interested. Samples returned with SASE. Original artwork returned at job's completion (upon written request). Credit line given.
Photography: Wants photos relating to forthcoming themes.
Terms: Pays on publication. Buys all rights for mss and artwork. Pays 20-25¢/word for articles/stories. Pays on an individual basis for poetry. Covers are assigned and paid on an individual basis. Pays illustrators $50-300 for color inside. Pays photographers per photo ($25-100 for color). Sample copy $4.95 with 7½×10½ SAE and 5 first-class stamps. Writer's/illustrator's/photo guidelines via website or free with SAE and 1 first-class stamp.
Tips: "Writers are encouraged to study past issues of the magazine to become familiar with our style and content. Writers with anthropological and/or travel experience are particularly encouraged; *Faces* is about world cultures. All feature articles, recipes and activities are freelance contributions." Illustrators: "Submit b&w samples, not too juvenile. Study past issues to know what we look for. The illustration we use is generally for retold legends, recipes and activities." (See listing for *AppleSeeds, Calliope, Cobblestone, Footsteps* and *Odyssey*.)

✓ **FAITH & FAMILY**, (formerly *Catholic Faith & Family*), Circle Media, 432 Washington Ave., North Haven CT 06472. (203)230-3800. Fax: (203)230-3838. E-mail: editor@twincircle.com. **Editor:** Duncan Anderson. **Art Director:** Tom Brophy. Bimonthly tabzine. Estab. 1965. Circ. 18,000.
Nonfiction: Buys hundreds of mss/year. Average word length: 450-2,000. Byline given.
How to Contact/Writers: Nonfiction: Send complete ms. Responds to queries in 2 months; mss in 6 months. Will consider electronic submission via disk or modem.
Illustration: Uses color artwork only. Reviews ms/illustration packages from artists. Query; send ms with dummy. Illustrations only: Query with samples. Contact: Duncan Anderson, editor. Responds in 3 months. Samples returned with SASE. Credit line given.

Photography: Needs photos depicting family-oriented activities. Uses color glossy prints and 35mm, $2\frac{1}{4} \times 2\frac{1}{4}$, 4×5 or 8×10 transparencies. Query with samples; call. Responds in 3 months.
Terms: Pays on publication. Buys first North American rights. Buys one-time rights for artwork. Original artwork returned at job's completion. Pays $75-300 for articles. Pays illustrators $75-100 for color cover; $25-50 for color inside. Pays photographers per photo. Sample copies for SASE. Writer's/illustrator's/photo guidelines for SASE.
Tips: "We need photos of families—parents, kids, grandparents and combos for our publication. They should be showing a variety of emotions and activities."

Focus on the Family CLUBHOUSE; Focus on the Family CLUBHOUSE JR., Focus on the Family, 8605 Explorer Dr., Colorado Springs CO 80920. (719)531-3400. Fax: (719)531-3499. Website: www.clubhousemagazine.org. **Editor:** Jesse Florea *Clubhouse*; Annette Bourland, editor *Clubhouse Jr.* **Art Director:** Timothy Jones. Monthly magazine. Estab. 1987. Combined circulation is 210,000. "*Focus on the Family Clubhouse* is a 24-page Christian magazine, published monthly, for children ages 8-12. Similarly, *Focus on the Family Clubhouse Jr.* is published for children ages 4-8. We want fresh, exciting literature that promotes biblical thinking, values and behavior in every area of life."
Fiction: Young readers, middle readers: adventure, contemporary, multicultural, nature/environment, religious. Middle readers: history, sports, science fiction. Multicultural needs include: "interesting, informative, accurate information about other cultures to teach children appreciation for the world around them." Buys approximately 6-10 mss/year. Average word length: *Clubhouse*, 500-1,400; *Clubhouse Jr.*, 250-1,100. Byline given on all fiction and puzzles.
Nonfiction: Young readers, middle readers: arts/crafts, cooking, games/puzzles, how-to, multicultural, nature/environment, religion, science. Young readers: animal. Middle readers, young adult/teen: interview/profile. Middle readers: sports. Buys 3-5 mss/year. Average word length: 200-1,000. Byline given.
Poetry: Wants to see "humorous or biblical" poetry for 4-8 year olds. Maximum length: 250 words.
How to Contact/Writers: Fiction/nonfiction: send complete ms. Responds to queries/mss in 6 weeks.
Illustration: Buys 8 illustrations/issue. Uses color artwork only. Works on assignment only. Reviews ms/illustration packages from artists. Submit ms with rough sketches. Contact: Tim Jones, art director. Illustrations only: Query with samples, arrange portfolio review or send tearsheets. Contact: Tim Jones, art director. Responds in 3 months. Samples returned with SASE; samples kept on file. Credit line given.
Photography: Buys photos from freelancers. Uses 35mm transparencies. Photographers should query with samples; provide résumé and promotional literature or tearsheets. Responds in 2 months.
Terms: Pays on acceptance. Buys first North American serial rights for mss. Buys first rights or reprint rights for artwork and photographs. Original artwork returned at job's completion. Additional payment for ms/illustration packages. Pays writers $150-300 for stories; $50-150 for articles. Pays illustrators $300-700 for color cover; $200-700 for color inside. Pays photographers by the project or per photo. Sample copies for 9×12 SAE and 3 first-class stamps. Writer's/illustrators/photo guidelines for SASE.
Tips: "Test your writing on children. The best stories avoid moralizing or preachiness and are not written *down* to children. They are the products of writers who share in the adventure with their readers, exploring the characters they have created without knowing for certain where the story will lead. And they are not always explicitly Christian, but are built upon a Christian foundation (and, at the very least, do not contradict biblical views or values)."

FOOTSTEPS, The Magazine of African American History, Cobblestone Publishing Co., 30 Grove St., Suite C, Peterborough NH 03458. (603)924-7204 or (800)821-0115. Fax: (608)924-7380. Website: www.cobblestonepub.com. **Editor:** Charles F. Baker. Magazine on African American history for readers ages 8-14.
  • *Footsteps* won a 2000 Parent's Choice Gold Award and Ed Press's One Theme Issue Award for 2000.
  Footsteps is theme based—please view the website for upcoming topics.
Fiction: Middle readers: adventure, history, multicultural. Word length: up to 700 words.
Nonfiction: Middle readers: history, interviews/profile. Word length: 300-750 words.
Terms: Writer's guidelines available on website.
Tips: "We are looking for articles that are lively, age-appropriate, and exhibit an original approach to the theme of the issue. Cultural sensitivity and historical accuracy are extremely important."

FOR SENIORS ONLY, Campus Communications, Inc., 339 N. Main St., New City NY 10956. (845)638-0333. **Publisher:** Darryl Elberg. **Articles/Fiction Editor:** Judi Oliff. **Art Director:** David Miller. Semiannual magazine. Estab. 1971. Circ. 350,000. Publishes career-oriented articles for high school students, college-related articles, and feature articles on travel, etc.
Fiction: Young adults: health, humorous, sports, travel. Byline given.
Nonfiction: Young adults: careers, games/puzzles, health, how-to, humorous, interview/profile, social issues, sports, travel. Buys 4-6 mss/year. Average word length: 1,000-2,500. Byline given.
How to Contact/Writers: Fiction/nonfiction: Send complete ms. Publishes ms 2-4 months after acceptance. Will consider simultaneous submissions, electronic submissions via disk or modem and previously published work.

insider report

A crafty way to break into children's writing

It seemed whenever Traci Sikkink discussed her passion for writing children's books with friends and acquaintances, she'd get "the look." "You know the look," says Sikkink, "the look that says, 'You're kidding me, right?' " Not allowing negativity to influence her, she has been writing stories non-stop ever since the inspiration to be a children's author hit her. Excitedly, she'd show her stories to publishers, agents and friends only to hear, "You're not ready yet." Those "no's" hit really hard. "I put away my stories, determined not to try again until I was more prepared."

Traci Sikkink

With a passion for children, Sikkink then threw herself into a childhood goal of becoming a teacher. She soon found herself in a South Central L.A. classroom teaching English as a Second Language (ESL) to a room full of Spanish-speaking third-graders. "It was right after the passing of Proposition 227 which abolished bilingual education. The schools were unprepared for such a drastic and sudden change. There were no textbooks to adhere to this new policy." Sikkink had no choice but to create most of the curriculum herself. She discovered right away the importance of visuals in instruction, especially for second language learners. Maybe craft projects would be just what they needed, she thought.

Sikkink has always been drawn to craft projects herself. "When other kids were off playing sports or socializing, I was tucked away somewhere with crayons, scissors, and paper." Later, as an adult, she realized the power of origami as a teaching tool when a presenter at a math conference brought a geometry lesson to life by folding eight square pieces of paper into an origami star. Sikkink wondered not only if this ancient art form could excite and motivate her ESL students, but how the origami star could be integrated into a craft that her students could then take home. (See what she came up with in the *Clubhouse* feature "Tree-ific Ornaments") Sikkink soon found great success teaching origami to her students. "Origami brought out their curiosity, compassion to assist others, and desire to learn." Successfully teaching through visuals all of her students were reading, writing and speaking in English by the end of the year.

Sikkink's new-found success as a teacher boosted her confidence. Maybe she *could* be a children's author after all. "My students' enthusiasm and enjoyment of the crafts I taught them gave me confidence in their publishability," she says. But it wasn't until she flipped through the Magazines section of *Children's Writer's & Illustrator's Market* that she noticed many of the magazines were interested in nonfiction how-to features. "I knew then that I had a great opportunity to break into publishing with how-to craft articles." She decided it was now or never—she'd either start taking actions toward her writing goals or give up the dream entirely.

Sikkink bought the 2000 edition of *Children's Writer's & Illustrator's Market* and did not put it down for an entire week.

"Children don't understand symbols," says Tracy Sikkink. "They do understand, and are not intimidated by, letters of the alphabet. That is why I write my instructions using alphabet letters, directing them to fold point A to point B." Since children also learn through associations, Sikkink might point out how a preliminary fold for the final product resembles a house or other familiar shape. "As soon as I make reference to something children know, such as a house, then the connection is made and I can move forward with the directions."

She studied every query letter closely hoping to discover the formula. How could she write a query letter that was as professional and appealing as the examples in the book? Was she strong enough, now, to handle rejection? Maybe not just yet! Sikkink decided the best way to deal with her fear of rejection was to begin with "how-to" craft projects for children's magazines instead of with her stories. After all, she reasoned, psychologically, if a how-to piece gets rejected, she wouldn't take it as personally. "I love arts 'n' crafts, but I'm not as emotionally invested in them as I am with my characters. Besides, I know firsthand how much my students have enjoyed making and creating what I have taught them. That gives me tremendous encouragement that other children will enjoy them too."

The hours Sikkink invested studying other writers' successful query letters paid off. She wrote one query letter and tailored it to the various magazines she targeted. Two weeks later, she got a call from *Guideposts for Kids*. Soon after, a letter from *Clubhouse* magazine arrived. The *Clubhouse* assignment led to a project with *Clubhouse Jr.* Lastly, as a direct result of that first mailing, Sikkink received a request from *Skipping Stones*, a multicultural magazine, to submit additional crafts that would appeal to a diversity of cultures and religions.

For the rest of the summer and fall, Sikkink aggressively pursued the how-to market in children's magazines. "I discovered there is a need for how-to craft articles and editors are buying them. It's also a great way to break-in, become familiar with the publishing process, build your résumé, and prove to yourself and editors that you are a professional."

Whenever Sikkink finds a craft she likes, she asks herself three questions—first, How can I write children-friendly instructions for this craft? Second, How can I create an educational lesson from this craft? And three, How can I integrate this craft into a theme/holiday?"

Always send along the finished product with your query letter," advises Sikkink. "It may take additional time and expense to get an item ready for submission but it is well worth it. Pictures don't do justice to certain crafts. They just aren't enticing enough. If you want your craft to stand out then you must send the completed item. The craft will then speak for itself."

To date Sikkink has sold over 20 craft articles to magazines. That success has fueled her courage to try integrating her fictional characters within the how-to articles. One of her characters (Miss Heart, a character with hair made out of origami hearts) was featured in the table of contents for *Guideposts for Kids*. It was the first time Sikkink had seen one of her characters in print. "I had to sit down for that one. I think my screams woke up the entire neighborhood. It was definitely a moment I will never forget."

Sikkink has a busy full-time position with UCLA as a coordinator, instructor and writer of math professional development institutes for elementary school teachers. She is also busy developing her own website, www.CreateWithYourChild.com, a website featuring how-to crafts for children and their parents. She has mastered not only the query letter, but the book proposal as well, completing a manuscript called *Miss Heart's Welcome to Origamiville. . . An A—Z Encyclopedia of Origami Animals* to submit to book publishers. She's dreaming big these days: a line of stationery products featuring children's coloring books, stickers, notepads, journals, pencils, erasers—all of the things she loved as a child. She no longer fears rejection and is sending her characters out into the world. "This may sound kind of corny, but I believe characters are given to us as gifts. Gifts given to us by whatever higher power or destiny you believe in. It is then up to the recipient of the gift to nurture it, believe in it, and watch it grow." Sikkink's biggest dream of all is to see Miss Heart in an animated feature some day—maybe even a holiday classic.

—*Mary Cox*

May 7, 2000

Jesse Florea, Editor
Focus on the Family CLUBHOUSE
8605 Explorer Dr.
Colorado Springs, CO 80920

Dear Mr. Florea:

Article Proposal
"ORIGAMI WREATHS AND ORNAMENTS FOR THE HOLIDAYS"

This season create handmade holiday wreaths and ornaments for the holidays through the art of origami. The octagon star, an origami-based activity, is magical in its ability to transform from an eight sided figure to—a few pushes and slides later—a STAR. The fascination this transformation elicits from all who encounter it is nothing less than a HIT! But this activity is more than just a geometrical phenomena, it also provides an educational, festive, fun way to create handmade seasonal décor.

As a third grade teacher in South Central L.A. this activity provided me with an inexpensive, yet instruction-rich, opportunity to celebrate the season with my students. We made ornaments and wreaths to give as gifts, to hang on doors and place on trees. We decorated our school's main hallway with a "Happy Holidays" bulletin of wreaths and our classroom tree with ornaments backed with school photographs. It was definitely an origami holiday!

Last year I was the recipient of an excellence in art instruction award, and currently I present origami-based activities for the UCLA math project at conferences for elementary school teachers. I will receive my masters in Education this fall and am a member of SCBWI.

I hope you enjoy the origami wreath and ornaments I've enclosed as well as photographs of our classroom tree and other holiday creations. I've enclosed a SASE for your convenience.

I appreciate your consideration, and look forward to "folding" for you sometime soon.

Sincerely,

Traci Sikkink
808 Crafty Lane, #1
Los Angeles CA 90000
323-555-2000
origamiqueen@fold.net

Enclosures:
Handmade origami ornaments and wreath
School photographs
SASE

Using this same basic query letter, Traci Sikkink sold craft projects to several children's magazines including *Skipping Stones* and *Clubhouse Jr.* To date she's sold 20 projects to magazines. This letter to *Clubhouse* not only led to a sale, but her craft was also featured on the magazine's cover.

Illustration: Reviews ms/illustration packages from artists. Query; submit complete package with final art; submit ms with rough sketches. Illustrations only: Query; send slides. Responds only if interested. Samples not returned; samples kept on file. Original work returned upon job's completion. Credit line given.
Photography: Model/property release required. Uses $5\frac{1}{2} \times 8\frac{1}{2}$ and $4\frac{7}{8} \times 7\frac{3}{8}$ color prints; 35mm and 8×10 transparencies. Query with samples; send unsolicited photos by mail. Responds only if interested.
Terms: Pays on publication. Buys exclusive magazine rights. Payment is byline credit. Writer's/illustrator's/photo guidelines for SASE. Unsolicited ms will *not* be returned; responds **only** if interested.

✓ FOX KIDS MAGAZINE, Peter Green Design/Fox Kids Network, 127 S. Brand Blvd., Suite 330, Glendale CA 91204. (818)546-3200. Fax: (818)546-3260. E-mail: bananadog@aol.com. Website: www.foxkids.com. **Articles Editor:** Scott Russell. **Art Director:** Tim Sims. Quarterly magazine. Estab. 1990. Circ. 4 million. Features "fun and hip articles, games and activities for Fox Kids Club members ages 6-13, promoting Fox Kids shows."
Nonfiction: Young readers, middle readers, young adults/teens: animals, arts/crafts, concept, games/puzzles, how-to, humorous, science, nature/environment, sports. Middle readers, young adult: interview/profile, hobbies. Any material tied in to a Fox Kids Network show or one of our other features (no religious material). Buys 16 mss/year. Average word length: 100-300.
How to Contact/Writers: Nonfiction only: Query with published clips. Responds to queries/mss in 2-3 months. Publishes mss 2-6 months after acceptance. Will consider simultaneous submissions and electronic submissions via disk or modem.
Illustration: Buys 5 illustrations/issue. Uses color artwork only. Works on assignment only. Prefers "cartoon character work, must be *on model*." Reviews ms/illustration packages from artists. Query. Illustrations only: Send résumé, promo sheet, tearsheets. Responds only if interested. Samples returned with SASE; samples filed. Original work returned at job's completion. Credit line given.
Photography: Buys photos from freelancers. Uses a variety of subjects, depending on articles. Model/property release required. Uses color prints and 4×5 or 35mm transparencies. Query with résumé, business card, tearsheets. Responds only if interested.
Terms: Pays 30 days from acceptance. Buys all rights. Pays $100-400 for stories/articles. Additional payment for ms/illustration packages and for photos accompanying articles. Sample writer's guidelines for SASE.
Tips: "Practice. Read. Come up with some new and creative ideas. Our articles are almost always humorous. We try to give kids cutting-edge information. All of our articles are tied into Fox Kids shows."

THE FRIEND MAGAZINE, The Church of Jesus Christ of Latter-day Saints, 50 E. North Temple, Salt Lake City UT 84150-3226. (801)240-2210. **Editor:** Vivian Paulsen. **Art Director:** Mark Robison. Monthly magazine for 3-11 year olds. Estab. 1971. Circ. 350,000.
Needs: Children's/true stories—adventure, ethnic, some historical, humor, mainstream, religious/inspirational, nature. Length: 1,000 words maximum. Publishes short stories length 250 words.
Poetry: Reviews poetry. Maximum length: 20 lines.
How to Contact/Writers: Send complete ms. Responds to mss in 2 months.
Illustration: Illustrations only: Query with samples; arrange personal interview to show portfolio; provide résumé and tearsheets for files.
Terms: Pays on acceptance. Buys all rights for mss. Pays 9-11¢/word for unsolicited fiction articles; $25 and up for poems; $10 for recipes, activities and games. Contributors are encouraged to send for sample copy for $1.50, 9×11 envelope and four 34¢ stamps. Free writer's guidelines.
Tips: "*The Friend* is published by The Church of Jesus Christ of Latter-day Saints for boys and girls up to twelve years of age. All submissions are carefully read by the *Friend* staff, and those not accepted are returned within two months when a self-addressed, stamped envelope is enclosed. Submit seasonal material at least eight months in advance. Query letters and simultaneous submissions are not encouraged. Authors may request rights to have their work reprinted after their manuscript is published."

Ｎ FUN FOR KIDZ, P.O. Box 227, Bluffton OH 45817-0027. (419)358-4610. **Articles Editor:** Marilyn Edwards. Bimonthly magazine. Estab. 2002. "*Fun for Kidz* is a magazine created for boys and girls ages 6-13, with youngsters 8, 9, and 10 the specific target age. The magazine is designed as an activity publication to be enjoyed by both boys and girls on the alternative months of *Hopscotch* and *Boys' Quest* magazine."
- *Fun for Kidz* is theme-oriented. Upcoming themes include: Helping Others, Pets, Gardening, Camping, Winter Wonder and Indoor Fun, among others. Send SASE for theme list.
Fiction: Picture-oriented material, young readers, middle readers: adventure, animal, humorous, nature/environment, sports. Average word length: 300-700.
Nonfiction: Picture-oriented material, young readers, middle readers: animal, arts/crafts, cooking, games/puzzles, nature/environment, sports, carpentry projects. Average word length: 300-700. Byline given.
Poetry: Reviews poetry.
How to Contact/Writers: Fiction/nonfiction: Send complete ms. Will consider simultaneous submissions.
Illustration: Works on assignment mostly. "We are anxious to find artists capable of illustrating stories and features. Our inside art is pen & ink." Query with samples. Samples kept on file.
Photography: "We use a number of back & white photos inside the magazine; most support the articles used."

Terms: Pays on publication. Buys first American serial rights. Buys first American serial rights and photos for artwork. Pays 5¢/word; $10/poem or puzzle; $35 for art (full page); $25 for art (partial page). Pays illustrators $5-10 for b&w photos.
Tips: "Our point of view is that every child deserves the right to be a child for a number of years before he or she becomes a young adult. As a result, *Fun for Kidz* looks for activities that deal with timeless topics, such as pets, nature, hobbies, science, games, sports, careers, simple cooking, and anything else likely to interest a child."

GIRLS' LIFE, Monarch, 4517 Harford Rd., Baltimore MD 21214. (410)426-9600. Fax: (410)254-0991. Website: www.girlslife.com. **Executive Editor**: Kelly White. **Creative Director**: Chun Kim. Bimonthly magazine. Estab. 1994. General interest magazine for girls, ages 9-15.
Nonfiction: Interview/profile, multicultural, nature/environment, new products, party ideas, skin care, social issues, sports, travel, health, hobbies, humorous. Buys appoximately 25 mss/year. Word length varies. Byline given. "No fiction!"
How to Contact/Writers: Nonfiction: Query with published clips or send complete ms on spec only. Responds in 2 weeks. Publishes ms 3 months after acceptance. Will consider simultaneous submissions. No phone calls. No e-mail.
Illustration: Buys 4 illustrations/issue. Uses color artwork only. Works on assignment only. Reviews ms/illustration packages from artists. Send ms with dummy. Illustration only: Query with samples; send tearsheets. Contact: Chun Kim, creative director. Responds only if interested. Samples returned with SASE; samples filed. Credit line given.
Photography: Buys photos from freelancers. Uses 35mm transparencies. Provide samples. Responds only if interested.
Terms: Pays on publication. Original artwork returned at job's completion. Pays $500-800 for features; $150-350 for departments. Sample copies available for $5. Writer's guidelines for SASE or via website.
Tips: "Don't call with queries. Make query short and punchy."

GO-GIRL.COM, The Collegebound Network, 1200 South Ave., Suite 202, Staten Island NY 10312. (718)273-5700. Fax: (718)273-2539. E-mail: editorial@collegebound.net. Website: www.go-girl.com. **Articles Editor:** Gina LaGuardia. Weekly online magazine. Estab. 1997. "The CollegeBound Network and its affiliate of websites are devoted entirely to college-bound teenagers. Student surfers have access to real people who guide them through their college and career choices. Our content is highly interactive—students can enter challenging contests, win scholarships and prizes, meet other students, and discover valuable information on the college application process."
Nonfiction: Young adults: biography, careers, fashion, health, how-to, interview/profile, social issues, travel, celebrity education. Buys 50 mss/year. Average word length: 100-900. Byline given.
How to Contact/Writer: Nonfiction: Query. Responds to queries in 6 weeks; mss in 7 weeks. Publishes ms 2-3 months after acceptance. Will consider simultaneous submissions, electronic submission via disk or modem (upon acceptance).
Terms: Pays on publication. Buys first rights. Pays $50-100 for articles. Writer's guidelines for SASE.

GUIDE MAGAZINE, Review and Herald Publishing Association, 55 W. Oak Ridge Dr., Hagerstown MD 21740. (301)393-4038. Fax: (301)393-4055. E-mail: guide@rhpa.org. Website: www.guidemagazine.org. **Articles Editor**: Randy Fishell. **Designer**: Brandon Reese. Weekly magazine. Estab. 1953. Circ. 32,000. "Ours is a weekly Christian journal written for middle readers and young adults (ages 10-14), presenting true stories relevant to the needs of today's young person, emphasizing positive aspects of Christian living."
Nonfiction: Middle readers, young adults/teens: adventure, animal, character-building, contemporary, games/puzzles, humorous, multicultural, problem-solving, religious. "We need true, or based on true, happenings, not merely true-to-life. Our stories and puzzles must have a spiritual emphasis." No violence. No articles. "We always need humorous adventure stories." Buys 150 mss/year. Average word length: 500-600 minimum, 1,000-1,200 maximum. Byline given.
How to Contact/Writers: Nonfiction: Send complete ms. Responds in 1 month. Will consider simultaneous submissions. "We can only pay half of the regular amount for simultaneous submissions." Responds to queries/mss in 6 weeks. Credit line given.
Terms: Pays on acceptance. Buys first North American serial rights; first rights; one-time rights; second serial (reprint rights); simultaneous rights. Pays 6-12¢/word for stories and articles. "Writer receives several complimentary copies of issue in which work appears." Sample copy free with 6×9 SAE and 2 first-class stamps. Writer's guidelines for SASE.
Tips: "Children's magazines want mystery, action, discovery, suspense and humor—no matter what the topic. For us, truth is stronger than fiction."

GUIDEPOSTS FOR KIDS, 1050 Broadway, Suite 6, Chesterton IN 46304. Fax: (219)926-3839. E-mail: gp4k@guideposts.org. Website: www.gp4k.com. **Editor-in-Chief**: Mary Lou Carney. **Managing Editor:** Rosanne Tolin. **Assistant Editor:** Allison Payne. **Art Director**: Mike Lyons. **Art Coordinator**: Rose Pomeroy. Electronic magazine. Estab. 1998. 36,000 plus unique visitors/month. "*Guideposts for Kids* online by Guideposts for kids 6-11 years old (emphasis on upper end of that age bracket). It is a value-centered, electronic magazine that is *fun* to visit. The site hosts a long list of interactive and editorial features including games, puzzles, how-tos, stories, poems, and facts and trivia.

• *Guideposts for Kids* is no longer available in a print version; online only.

Fiction: Middle readers: adventure, animal, contemporary, fantasy, folktales, historical, humorous, multicultural, nature/environment, problem-solving, science fiction, sports, suspense/mystery. Multicultural needs include: Kids in other cultures—school, sports, families. Does not want to see preachy fiction. "We want real stories about real kids doing real things—conflicts our readers will respect; resolutions our readers will accept. Problematic. Tight. Filled with realistic dialogue and sharp imagery. No stories about 'good' children always making the right decision. If present at all, adults are minor characters and *do not* solve kids' problems for them." Buys approximately 10 mss/year. Average word length: 500-1,200. Byline given.

Nonfiction: Middle readers: animal, current events, games/puzzles, history, how-to, humorous, interview/profile, multicultural, nature/environment, problem-solving, profiles of kids, science, seasonal, social issues, sports. "Make nonfiction issue-oriented, controversial, thought-provoking. Something kids not only *need* to know but *want* to know as well." Buys 20 mss/year. Average word length: 200-1,300. Byline usually given.

How to Contact/Writers: Fiction: Send complete ms. Nonfiction: Query or send ms. Responds to queries/mss in 6 weeks.

Photography: Looks for "spontaneous, *real* kids in action shots."

Terms: Pays on acceptance. Buys electronic and nonexclusive print rights. "Features range in payment from $50-300; fiction from $150-350. We pay higher rates for stories exceptionally well-written or well-researched. Regular contributors get bigger bucks, too." Writer's guidelines free for SASE.

Tips: "Make your manuscript good, relevant and playful. No preachy stories about Bible-toting children. *Guideposts for Kids* is not a beginner's market. Study our e-zine magazine. (Sure, you've heard that before—but it's *necessary*!) Neatness *does* count. So do creativity and professionalism. SASE essential." (See listings for *Guideposts for Teens*.)

☑ **GUIDEPOSTS FOR TEENS**, 1050 Broadway, Suite 6, Chesterton IN 46304. (219)929-4429. Fax: (219)926-3839. E-mail: gp4t@guideposts.org. Website: www.gp4teens.com. **Editor-in-Chief:** Mary Lou Carney. **Art Director:** Michael Lyons. **Art Coordinator:** Rose Pomeroy. Bimonthly magazine. Estab. 1998. "We are a value-centered magazine that offers teens advice, humor and true stories—lots of true stories. These first-person (ghostwritten) stories feature teen protagonists and are filled with action, adventure, overcoming adversity and growth—set against the backdrop of God at work in everyday life."

Nonfiction: Young adults: how-to, humorous, interview/profile, social issues, sports, true stories. Average word length: 300-1,500. Byline sometimes given.

How to Contact/Writers: Nonfiction: Query. Responds to queries/mss in 6 weeks. Will consider simultaneous submissions or electronic submission via disk or modem. Send SASE for writer's guidelines.

Illustration: Uses color artwork only. Works on assignment only. Reviews ms/illustration packages from artists. Query. Contact: Michael Lyons, art director. Illustrations only: Query with samples. Responds only if interested. Samples kept on file. Credit line given.

Photography: Buys photos separately. Wants location photography and stock; digital OK. Uses color prints and 35mm, 2¼×2¼, 4×5 or 8×10 transparencies. Query with samples; provide web address. Responds only if interested.

Terms: Pays on acceptance. Buys all rights for mss. Buys one-time rights for artwork. Original artwork returned at job's completion. Pays $300-500 for true stories; $100-300 for articles. Additional payment for photos accompanying articles. Pays illustrators $125-1,500 for color inside (depends on size). Pays photographers by the project (range: $100-1,000). Sample copies for $4.50 from: Guideposts, 39 Seminary Hill Rd., Carmel NY 10512. Attn: Special Handling.

Tips: "Language and subject matter should be current and teen-friendly. No preaching, please! For illustrators: We get illustrators from two basic sources: submissions by mail and submissions by Internet. We also consult major illustrator reference books. We prefer color illustrations, "on-the-edge" style. We accept art in almost any digital or reflective format."

ℕ HIGH ADVENTURE, Assemblies of God, 1445 Boonville Ave., Springfield MO 65802. (417)862-2781, Ext. 4177. Fax: (417)831-8230. E-mail: rangers@ag.org. Website: royalranger.ag.org. **Editor:** Jerry Parks. Quarterly magazine. Circ. 86,000. Estab. 1971. Magazine is designed to provide boys ages 5-18 with worthwhile, enjoyable, leisure reading; to challenge them in narrative form to higher ideals and greater spiritual dedication; and to perpetuate the spirit of Royal Rangers through stories, ideas and illustrations. 75% of material aimed at juvenile audience.

Fiction: Buys 100 mss/year; adventure, humorous, problem solving, religious, sports, travel. Maximum word length: 1,000. Byline given.

Nonfiction: Articles: Christian living, devotional, Holy Spirit, salvation, self-help; biography; missionary stories; news items; testimonies, inspirational stories based on true-life experiences; arts/crafts, games/puzzles, geography, health, hobbies, how-to, humorous, nature/environment, problem solving, sports, travel.

How to Contact/Writers: Fiction/nonfiction: Send complete ms. Responds to queries in 6-8 weeks. Will consider simultaneous submissions. Samples returned with SASE. Prefer hardcopy and media (3.5, Zip or Jaz).

Terms: Pays on publication. Buys first or all rights. Pays 6¢/word for articles ($30-35 for one page; 60-65 for two pages); $25-30 for cartoons; $15 for puzzles, $5 for jokes. Sample copy free with 9 × 12 SASE. Free writer's/illustrator's guidelines with SASE.
Tips: Obtain writer's guidelines and themes list.

☑ **HIGHLIGHTS FOR CHILDREN**, 803 Church St., Honesdale PA 18431. (570)253-1080. E-mail: emberge r@highlights-corp.com. **Contact:** Manuscript Coordinator. Senior Editor: Carolyn Yoder. Senior Editor: Marileta Robinson. Associated Editor: Judy Burke. **Art Director:** Janet Moir McCaffrey. Monthly magazine. Estab. 1946. Circ. 2.8 million. "Our motto is 'Fun With a Purpose.' We are looking for quality fiction and nonfiction that appeals to children, encourages them to read, and reinforces positive values. All art is done on assignment."
Fiction: Picture-oriented material, young readers, middle readers: adventure, animal, contemporary, fantasy, folktales, history, humorous, multicultural, problem-solving, sports. Multicultural needs include first person accounts of children from other cultures and first-person accounts of children from other countries. Does not want to see war, crime, violence. "We see too many stories with overt morals." Would like to see more suspense/stories/articles with world culture settings, sports pieces, action/adventure and stories with children in contemporary settings. Buys 150 mss/year. Average word length: 400-800. Byline given.
Nonfiction: Picture-oriented material, young readers, middle readers: animal, arts/crafts, biography, careers, games/puzzles, geography, health, history, hobbies, how-to, interview/profile, multicultural, nature/environment, problem solving, science, sports. Multicultural needs include articles set in a country *about* the people of the country. "We have plenty of articles with Asian and Spanish settings." Does not want to see trendy topics, fads, personalities who would not be good role models for children, guns, war, crime, violence. "We'd like to see more nonfiction for younger readers—maximum of 600 words. We still need older-reader material, too—600-900 words." Buys 200 mss/year. Maximum word length: 900. Byline given.
How to Contact/Writers: Send complete ms. Responds to queries in 1 month; mss in 6 weeks.
Illustration: Buys 25-30 illustrations/issue. Preferred theme or style: Realistic, some stylization, cartoon style acceptable. Works on assignment only. Reviews ms/illustration packages from artists. Illustrations only: photocopies, promo sheet, tearsheets, or slides. Résumé optional. Portfolio only if requested. Contact: Janet Moir McCaffrey, art director. Responds to art samples in 6 weeks. Samples returned with SASE; samples filed. Credit line given.
Terms: Pays on acceptance. Buys all rights for mss. Pays $100 and up for unsolicited articles. Pays illustrators $1,000 for color cover; $25-200 for b&w inside, $100-500 for color inside. Sample copies $3.95 and 9 × 11 SASE with 4 first-class stamps. Writer's/illustrator's guidelines free with SASE.
Tips: "Know the magazine's style before submitting. Send for guidelines and sample issue if necessary." Writers: "At *Highlights* we're paying closer attention to acquiring more nonfiction for young readers than we have in the past." Illustrators: "Fresh, imaginative work encouraged. Flexibility in working relationships a plus. Illustrators presenting their work need not confine themselves to just children's illustrations as long as work can translate to our needs. We also use animal illustrations, real and imaginary. We need party plans, crafts and puzzles—any activity that will stimulate children mentally and creatively. We are always looking for imaginative cover subjects. Know our publication's standards and content by reading sample issues, not just the guidelines. Avoid tired themes, or put a fresh twist on an old theme so that its style is fun and lively. We'd like to see stories with subtle messages, but the fun of the story should come first. Write what inspires you, not what you think the market needs.''

☑ **HOLIDAYS & SEASONAL CELEBRATIONS**, Teaching & Learning Company, 1204 Buchanan, P.O. Box 10, Carthage IL 62321. (217)357-2591. Fax: (217)357-6789. E-mail: donnabor@interl.net. Website: www.tea chinglearning.com. **Contact:** Articles Editor or Art Director. Quarterly magazine. Estab. 1995. "Every submission must be seasonal or holiday-related. Materials need to be educational and consistent with grades pre-K through 3 development and curriculum."
Fiction: Young readers: health, multicultural, nature/environment; must be holiday or seasonal-related. Buys 8 mss/year. Byline given.
Nonfiction: Young readers: arts/crafts, cooking, games/puzzles, geography, how-to, math, multicultural, nature/environment, science. "We need holiday and seasonally related ideas from all cultures that can be used in the classroom." Buys 150 mss/year. Byline given.
Poetry: Reviews holiday or seasonal poetry.
How to Contact/Writers: Fiction: Query. Nonfiction: Send complete ms. Responds to queries in 2 months; mss in 3 months. Publishes ms 4-12 months after acceptance. Will consider electronic submissions via disk or modem.
Illustration: Buys 70 illustrations/issue; 300 illustrations/year. Uses b&w and color artwork. Works on assignment only. "Prefers school settings with lots of children; b&w sketches at this time." Reviews ms/illustration packages from artists. Submit ms with rough sketches. Illustrations only: submit résumé, promo sheet, tearsheets, sketches of children. Responds in 1 month. Samples returned with SASE; samples filed. Credit line sometimes given.
Terms: Pays on publication. Buys all rights. Pays $20-75 for stories; $10-125 for articles. Additional payment for ms/illustration packages. Pays illustrators $150-300 for color cover; $15-18 for b&w inside. Pays photographers per photo. Sample copy available for $4.95. Writer's/illustrator's guidelines for SASE.

Tips: "95% of our magazine is written by freelancers. Writers must know that this magazine goes to teachers for use in the classroom, grades pre-K through 3. Also 90% of our magazine is illustrated by freelancers. We need illustrators who can provide us with 'cute' kids grades pre-K through 3. Representation of ethnic children is a must. Because our magazine is seasonal, it is essential that we receive manuscripts approximately 8-12 months prior to the publication of that magazine. Too often we receive a holiday-related article way past the deadline."

N HOME SCHOOLING TODAY, P.O. Box 1608, Ft. Collins CO 80522. (970)493-2716. Fax; (970)493-8781. Website: www.homeschooltoday.com. Bimonthly magazine. Publishes lessons and how-to articles for home schoolers.
Nonfiction: All levels: animal, arts/crafts, biography, geography, history, how-to, interview/profile, math, religion, science. Buys 6 mss/year. Average word length: 500-2,000. Byline given.
How to Contact/Writers: Nonfiction: send complete ms. Responds in 3 months. Publishes ms 6-12 months after acceptance. Will consider simultaneous submissions, electronic submission via disk or modem.
Terms: Pays on publication. Buys all rights. Pays 8¢/word.

HOPSCOTCH, The Magazine for Girls, The Bluffton News Publishing and Printing Company, 103 N. Main St., Bluffton OH 45817. (419)358-4610. **Editor:** Marilyn Edwards. **Contact:** Diane Winebar, editorial assistant. Bimonthly magazine. Estab. 1989. Circ. 14,000. For girls from ages 6-12, featuring traditional subjects—pets, games, hobbies, nature, science, sports, etc.—with an emphasis on articles that show girls actively involved in unusual and/or worthwhile activities."
Fiction: Picture-oriented material, young readers, middle readers: adventure, animal, history, humorous, nature/environment, science fiction, sports, suspense/mystery. Does not want to see stories dealing with dating, sex, fashion, hard rock music. Buys 30 mss/year. Average word length: 300-700. Byline given.
Nonfiction: Picture-oriented material, young readers, middle readers: animal, arts/crafts, biography, cooking, games/puzzles, geography, hobbies, how-to, humorous, math, nature/environment, science. Does not want to see pieces dealing with dating, sex, fashion, hard rock music. "Need more nonfiction with quality photos about a *Hopscotch*-age girl involved in a worthwhile activity." Buys 46 mss/year. Average word length: 400-700. Byline given.
Poetry: Reviews traditional, wholesome, humorous poems. Maximum word length: 300; maximum line length: 20. Will accept 6 submissions/author.
How to Contact/Writers: All writers should consult the theme list before sending in articles. To receive a current theme list, send a SASE. Fiction: Send complete ms. Nonfiction: Query, send complete ms. Responds to queries in 2 weeks; on mss in 2 months. Will consider simultaneous submissions.
Illustration: Buys illustrations for 6-8 articles/issue; buys 50-60 articles/year. "Generally, the illustrations are assigned after we have purchased a piece (usually fiction). Occasionally, we will use a painting—in any given medium—for the cover, and these are usually seasonal." Uses b&w artwork only for inside; color for cover. Review ms/illustration packages from artists. Query first or send complete ms with final art. Illustrations only: Send résumé, portfolio, client list and tearsheets. Responds to art samples with SASE in 2 weeks. Credit line given.
Photography: Purchases photos separately (cover only) and with accompanying ms only. Looking for photos to accompany article. Model/property releases required. Uses 5×7, b&w prints; 35mm transparencies. Black & white photos should go with ms. Should show girl or girls ages 6-12.
Terms: For mss: pays a few months ahead of publication. For mss, artwork and photos, buys first North American serial rights; second serial (reprint rights). Original artwork returned at job's completion. Pays 5¢/word and $5-10/photo. "We always send a copy of the issue to the writer or illustrator." Text and art are treated separately. Pays $150-200 for color cover. Photographers paid per photo (range: $5-15). Sample copy for $4. Writer's/illustrator's/photo guidelines free for #10 SASE.
Tips: "Remember we publish only six issues a year, which means our editorial needs are extremely limited. Please look at our guidelines and our magazine . . . and remember, we use far more nonfiction than fiction. If decent photos accompany the piece, it stands an even better chance of being accepted. We believe it is the responsibility of the contributor to come up with photos. Please remember, our readers are 6-12 years—most are 7-10—and your text should reflect that. Many magazines try to entertain first and educate second. We try to do the reverse of that. Our magazine is more simplistic, like a book to be read from cover to cover. We are looking for wholesome, non-dated material." (See listing for *Boys' Quest*.)

HUMPTY DUMPTY'S MAGAZINE, Children's Better Health Institute, 1100 Waterway Blvd., P.O. Box 567, Indianapolis IN 46206. (317)636-8881. Fax: (317)684-8094. Website: www.humptydumptymag.org. **Editor:** Nancy S. Axelrad. **Art Director:** Brad Turner. Magazine published 8 times/year—Jan/Feb; Mar; April/May; June; July/Aug; Sept; Oct/Nov; Dec. *HDM* is edited for children ages 4-6. It includes fiction (easy-to-reads; read alouds; rhyming stories; rebus stories), nonfiction articles (some with photo illustrations), poems, crafts, recipes, and puzzles. Content encourages development of better health habits.
● *Humpty Dumpty's* publishes material promoting health and fitness with emphasis on simple activities, poems and fiction.

Fiction: Picture-oriented stories: adventure, animal, contemporary, fantasy, folktales, health, humorous, multicultural, nature/environment, problem-solving, science fiction, sports. Does not want to see "bunny-rabbits-with-carrot-pies stories! Also, talking inanimate objects are very difficult to do well. Beginners (and maybe everyone) should avoid these." Buys 8-10 mss/year. Maximum word length: 300. Byline given.

Nonfiction: Picture-oriented articles: animal, arts/crafts, concept, games/puzzles, health, how-to, humorous, nature/environment, no-cook recipes, science, social issues, sports. Buys 6-10 mss/year. Prefers very short nonfiction pieces—200 words maximum. Byline given.

How to Contact/Writers: Send complete ms. Nonfiction: Send complete ms with bibliography if applicable. "No queries, please!" Responds to mss in 3 months. Send seasonal material at least 8 months in advance.

Illustration: Buys 13-16 illustrations/issue; 90-120 illustrations/year. Preferred theme or style: Realistic or cartoon. Works on assignment only. Illustrations only. Query with slides, printed pieces or photocopies. Contact: Brad Turner, art director. Samples are not returned; samples filed. Responds to art samples only if interested. Credit line given.

Terms: Writers: Pays on publication. Artists: Pays within 1-2 months. Buys all rights. "One-time book rights may be returned if author can provide name of interested book publisher and tentative date of publication." Pays up to 22¢/word for stories/articles; payment varies for poems and activities. 10 complimentary issues are provided to author with check. Pays $275 for color cover illustration; $35-90 per page b&w inside; $70-155 for color inside. Sample copies for $1.75. Writer's/illustrator's guidelines free with SASE.

Tips: Writers: "Study current issues and guidelines. Observe word lengths and adhere to requirements. Submit what you do best. Don't send your first, second, or even third drafts. Polish your piece until it's as perfect as you can make it." Illustrators: "Please study the magazine before contacting us. Your art must have appeal to three-to seven-year-olds." (See listings for *Child Life, Children's Digest, Children's Playmate, Jack and Jill, Turtle Magazine* and *U*S* Kids*.)

✓ I.D., Cook Communications Ministries, 4050 Lee Vance View, Colorado Springs CO 80918. Fax: (719)536-3296. Website: www.cookministries.org. **Editor:** Gail Rohlfing. **Design Manager:** Paul Segsworgh. **Designer:** Joe Matisek. Weekly magazine. Estab. 1991. Circ. 100,000. "*I.D.* is a class-and-home paper for senior high Sunday school students. Stories relate to Bible study."

Nonfiction: Young adults/teens: animal, arts/crafts, biography, careers, concept, geography, health, history, how-to, humorous, interview/profile, multicultural, nature/environment, problem solving, religion, science, social issues, sports. "Sometimes material sent to us is too 'preachy.' " Buys 25 mss/year. Average word length: 600-1,000. Byline sometimes given if written in the first person.

How to Contact/Writers: Send complete ms. Responds in 6 months. Publishes ms 15 months after acceptance. Will consider simultaneous submissions.

Illustrations: Buys 5 illustrations/year. Uses b&w and color artwork. Reviews ms/illustration packages from artists. Submit ms with rough sketches. Illustrations only: Query. Works on assignment only. Responds only if interested.

Terms: Pays on acceptance. Pays $50-300 for stories and articles.

INSIGHT, Teens Meeting Christ, 55 W. Oak Ridge Dr., Hagerstown MD 21740. (301)393-4038. Fax: (301)393-4055. E-mail: insight@rhpa.org. Website: http://insightmagazine.org. **Articles Editor:** Lori Peckham. **Art Director:** Sebastian Bruce. **Photo Editor:** Sebastian Bruce. Weekly magazine. Estab. 1970. Circ. 20,000. "Our readers crave true stories written by teens or written about teens that convey a strong spiritual or portray a spiritual truth." 100% of publication aimed at teen and college-age market.

Nonfiction: Young adults: animal, biography, fashion, health, humorous, interview/profile, multicultural, nature/environment, problem-solving, social issues, sports, travel: first-person accounts preferred. Buys 200 mss/year. Average word length: 500-1,500. Byline given.

Poetry: Reviews poetry. Publishes poems written by teens. Maximum length: 250-500 words.

How to Contact/Writers: Nonfiction: Send complete ms. Responds to queries in 1-2 months. Publishes ms 6-12 months after acceptance. Will consider simultaneous submissions, electronic submission via disk or modem, previously published work.

Illustration: Works on assignment only. Reviews ms/illustration packages from artists. Query. Contact: Sebastian Bruce, design. Illustrations only: Query with samples. Contact: Sebastian Bruce, designer. Samples kept on file. Credit line given.

Photography: Looking for photos that will catch a young person's eye with unique elements such as juxtaposition. Model/property release required; captions not required but helpful. Uses color prints and 35mm, 2¼×2¼, 4×5, 8×10 transparencies. Query with samples; provide business card, promotional literature or tearsheets to be kept on file. Responds only if interested.

Terms: Pays on acceptance. Buys first North American serial rights for mss. Buys one-time rights for artwork and photos. Original artwork returned at job's completion. Pays $10-100 for stories; $10-100 for articles. Pays illustrators $100-300 for b&w (cover); $100-300 for color cover; $100-300 for b&w (inside), $100-300 for color inside. Pays photographers by the project. Sample copies for 9×14 SAE and 4 first-class stamps.

Tips: "Do your best to make your work look 'hip,' 'cool' appealing to young people."

INTEEN, Urban Ministries, Inc., 1551 Regency Ct., Calumet City IL 60409. (708)868-7100, ext. 239. Fax: (708)868-7105. E-mail: umil551@aol.com. **Editor:** Katara A. Washington. **Art Acquisitions:** Larry Taylor. Quarterly magazine. Estab. 1970. "We publish Sunday school lessons for urban teens and features for the same group."
   • Contact *Inteen* for guidelines. They work on assignment only—do not submit work.
Nonfiction: Young adults/teens: careers, games/puzzles, how-to, interview/profile, religion. "We make 40 assignments/year."
Terms: Pays $75-150 for stories.

☑ **JACK AND JILL**, Children's Better Health Institute, 1100 Waterway Blvd., P.O. Box 567, Indianapolis IN 46206. (317)636-8881. Website: www.jackandjillmag.org. **Editor:** Daniel Lee. **Art Director:** Emilie Frazier. Magazine published 8 times/year. Estab. 1938. Circ. 360,000. "Write entertaining and imaginative stories *for* kids, not just *about* them. Writers should understand what is funny to kids, what's important to them, what excites them. Don't write from an adult 'kids are so cute' perspective. We're also looking for health and healthful lifestyle stories and articles, but don't be preachy."
Fiction: Young readers and middle readers: adventure, contemporary, folktales, health, history, humorous, nature, sports. Buys 30-35 mss/year. Average word length: 700. Byline given.
Nonfiction: Young readers, middle readers: animal, arts/crafts, cooking, games/puzzles, history, hobbies, how-to, humorous, interview/profile, nature, science, sports. Buys 8-10 mss/year. Average word length: 500. Byline given.
Poetry: Reviews poetry.
How to Contact/Writers: Fiction/nonfiction: Send complete ms. Responds to mss in 3 months. Guidelines by request with a #10 SASE.
Illustration: Buys 15 illustrations/issue; 120 illustrations/year. Responds only if interested. Samples not returned; samples filed. Credit line given.
Terms: Pays on publication; minimum 17¢/word. Pays illustrators $275 for color cover; $35-90 for b&w, $70-155 for color inside. Pays photographers negotiated rate. Sample copies $1.25. Buys all rights.
Tips: See listings for *Child Life*, *Children's Digest*, *Children's Playmate*, *Humpty Dumpty's Magazine*, *Turtle Magazine* and *U*S* Kids*. Publishes writing/art/photos by children.

N THE KIDS HALL OF FAME NEWS, The Kids Hall of Fame, 3 Ibsen Court, Dix Hills NY 11746. (631)242-9105. Fax: (631)242-8101. E-mail: VictoriaNesnick@TheKidsHallofFame.com. Website: www.TheKid sHallofFame.com. **Editor:** Victoria Nesnick. **Art/Photo Editor:** Amy Gilvary. Quarterly magazine. Estab. 1998. "We spotlight and archive extraordinary positive achievements of contemporary and historical kids internationally under age 20. Their inspirational stories are meant to provide positive peer role models and empower kids to say, 'If that kids can do it, so can I,' or 'I can do better.' Our magazine is the prelude to the Kids Hall of Fame set of books (one volume per year) and museum."
How to Contact/Writers: Query with published clips or send complete manuscripts with SASE for response. Go to website for nomination form for The Kids Hall of Fame.
Tips: "Nomination stories must be positive and inspirational. See sample stores and nomination form on our website. Request writers' guidelines and list of suggested nominees. Evening telephone queries acceptable."

N KIDS' HIGHWAY, Oo! what a ride!, G. S. & S., P.O. Box 6275, Bryan TX 77805-6275. E-mail: kidshigh way@earthlink.net. Website: http://home.earthlink.net/~kidshighway/index.html. **Articles Editor:** Miranda Garza. **Fiction Editor:** Hector Cole Garza. Magazine published 5 times/year. "We are a family magazine with kids at the wheel. We publish anything fun. Fun things to do, go, smell, touch, cook, make, read, etc. whether poetry, fiction or nonfiction." 90% of publication aimed at juvenile market.
Fiction: Young readers, middle readers, young adults: adventure, animal, contemporary, history, humorous, multicultural, nature/environment, science fiction, sports, suspense/mystery, anything fun. "No horror, magic, holiday material, or that which addresses social or poltical issues." Buys 30-40 mss/year. Average word length: 200-1,500.
Nonfiction: Young readers, middle readers, young adults: animal, arts/crafts, biography, careers, cooking, games/puzzles, geography, history, hobbies, how-to, humorous, interview/profile, math, multicultural, nature/environment, science, sports, travel. "Nonfiction can be about something fun to do, see, visit, etc. The *Career Watch* series consists of articles written by adults for kids. These articles should tell what's exciting about a career, what

---

MARKET CONDITIONS are constantly changing! If you're still using this book and it is 2003 or later, buy the newest edition of *Children's Writer's & Illustrator's Market* at your favorite bookstore or order directly from Writer's Digest Books.

doors it opens, an experience or two, and further research references. Adults must be experienced in the field they write about. We also publish book and video reviews, short shorts and fillers." Buys 25-30 mss/year. Average word length: 200-500. Byline given.

Poetry: Reviews poetry. Maximum length: 20 lines. Limit submissions to 5 poems.

How to Contact/Writers: Fiction/nonfiction: Submit complete ms. Responds to queries in 3 weeks; mss in 3 months. Publishes ms 1-3 months after acceptance. Will consider simultaneous submissions, electronic submission via e-mail—no attachments, previously published work.

Terms: Pays on publication "most of the time, but at times we've paid on acceptance." Buys reprint rights, one-time rights, non exclusive electronic rights. Pays ¼-½¢ for stories; ¼-½¢ for articles. Additional payment for ms/illustration packages. Sample copies for $6 and 9×12 SASE with 3 ounce postage.

Tips: "Be enthusiastic. We love it showing through the cover letter and piece. Please read guidelines. About 50% of our rejections are pieces inappropriate for *Kids' Highway*. We publish that which leaves our readers with a smile, any kind of smile: humor, warmth, satisfaction, or 'hey, yeah, I can do this.' Remember *fun*. If you have fun writing the piece, we'll probably have fun reading it.. And *that's* what we publish."

KIDZ CHAT, Standard Publishing, 8121 Hamilton Ave., Cincinnati OH 45231. (513)931-4050. **Editor:** Elaina Meyers. Weekly magazine. Circ. 55,000.
- *Kidz Chat®* has decided to reuse much of the material that was a part of the first publication cycle. They will not be sending out theme lists or accepting any unsolicited material because of this policy.

Tips: See listings for *Encounter* and *Live Wire*.

LADYBUG, The Magazine for Young Children, Carus Publishing Company, P.O. Box 300, Peru IL 61354. (815)224-6656. **Editor-in-Chief**: Marianne Carus. **Editor:** Paula Morrow. **Art Director:** Suzanne Beck. Monthly magazine. Estab. 1990. Circ. 130,000. Literary magazine for children 2-6, with stories, poems, activities, songs and picture stories.

Fiction: Picture-oriented material: adventure, animal, fantasy, folktales, humorous, multicultural, nature/environment, problem-solving, science fiction, sports, suspense/mystery. "Open to any easy fiction stories." Buys 50 mss/year. Average word length 300-850 words. Byline given.

Nonfiction: Picture-oriented material: activities, animal, arts/crafts, concept, cooking, humorous, math, nature/environment, problem-solving, science. Buys 35 mss/year.

Poetry: Reviews poems, 20-line maximum length; limit submissions to 5 poems. Uses lyrical, humorous, simple language.

How to Contact/Writers: Fiction/nonfiction: Send complete ms. Queries not accepted. Responds to mss in 3 months. Publishes ms up to 2 years after acceptance. Will consider simultaneous submissions if informed. Submissions without SASE will be discarded.

Illustration: Buys 12 illustrations/issue; 145 illustrations/year. Prefers "bright colors; all media, but use watercolor and acrylics most often; same size as magazine is preferred but not required." To be considered for future assignments: Submit promo sheet, slides, tearsheets, color and b&w photocopies. Responds to art samples in 3 months. Submissions without SASE will be discarded.

Terms: Pays on publication for mss; after delivery of completed assignment for illustrators. For mss, buys first publication rights; second serial (reprint). Buys first publication rights plus promotional rights for artwork. Original artwork returned at job's completion. Pays 25¢/word for prose; $3/line for poetry. Pays $750 for color (cover) illustration, $50-100 for b&w (inside) illustration, $250/page for color (inside). Sample copy for $5. Writer's/illustrator's guidelines free for SASE.

Tips: Writers: "Get to know several young children on an individual basis. Respect your audience. We want less cute, condescending or 'preachy-teachy' material. Less gratuitous anthropomorphism. More rich, evocative language, sense of joy or wonder. Keep in mind that people come in all colors, sizes, physical conditions. Be inclusive in creating characters. Set your manuscript aside for at least a month, then reread critically." Illustrators: "Include examples, where possible, of children, animals, and—most important—action and narrative (i.e., several scenes from a story, showing continuity and an ability to maintain interest)." (See listings for *Babybug*, *Cicada*, *Cricket*, *Muse* and *Spider*.)

LISTEN, Drug-Free Possibilities for Teens, The Health Connection, 55 West Oak Ridge Dr., Hagerstown MD 21740. (301)393-4019. Fax: (301)393-4055. E-mail: listen@healthconnection.org. **Editor:** Larry Becker. Monthly magazine, 9 issues. Estab. 1948. Circ. 50,000. "*Listen* offers positive alternatives to drug use for its teenage readers. Helps them have a happy and productive life by making the right choices."

Fiction: Young adults: health, humorous, problem-solving peer pressure. Buys 50 mss/year. Average word length: 1,000-1,200. Byline given.

Nonfiction: Young adults: biography, games/puzzles, hobbies, how-to, health, humorous, problem solving, social issues, drug-free living. Wants to see more factual articles on drug abuse. Buys 50 mss/year. Average word length: 1,000-1,200. Byline given.

How to Contact/Writers: Fiction/nonfiction: Query. Responds to queries in 6 weeks; mss in 2 months. Will consider simultaneous submissions, electronic submission via disk or e-mail and previously published work.

Illustration: Buys 8-10 illustrations/issue; 72 illustrators/year. Reviews ms/illustration packages from artists. Ms/illustration packages and illustration only: Query. Contact: Doug Bendall, designer. Responds only if interested. Originals returned at job's completion. Samples returned with SASE. Credit line given.

Photography: Purchases photos from freelancers. Photos purchased with accompanying ms only. Uses color and b&w photos; 35mm, 2¼×2¼. Query with samples. Looks for "youth oriented—action (sports, outdoors), personality photos."

Terms: Pays on acceptance. Buys exclusive magazine rights for ms. Buys one-time rights for artwork and photographs. Pays $50-200 for stories/articles. Pay illustrators $500 for color cover; $75-225 for b&w inside; $135-450 for color inside. Pays photographers by the project (range: $125-500); pays per photo (range: $125-500). Additional payment for ms/illustration packages and photos accompanying articles. Sample copy for $1 and 9×12 SASE and 2 first class stamps. Writer's guidelines free with SASE.

Tips: "*Listen* is a magazine for teenagers. It encourages development of good habits and high ideals of physical, social and mental health. It bases its editorial philosophy of primary drug prevention on total abstinence from tobacco, alcohol, and other drugs. Because it is used extensively in public high school classes, it does not accept articles and stories with overt religious emphasis. Four specific purposes guide the editors in selecting materials for *Listen*: (1) To portray a positive lifestyle and to foster skills and values that will help teenagers deal with contemporary problems, including smoking, drinking, and using drugs. This is *Listen*'s primary purpose. (2) To offer positive alternatives to a lifestyle of drug use of any kind. (3) To present scientifically accurate information about the nature and effects of tobacco, alcohol, and other drugs. (4) To report medical research, community programs, and educational efforts which are solving problems connected with smoking, alcohol, and other drugs. Articles should offer their readers activities that increase one's sense of self-worth through achievement and/or involvement in helping others. They are often categorized by three kinds of focus: (1) Hobbies. (2) Recreation. (3) Community Service.

☑ **LIVE WIRE**, Standard Publishing Co., 8121 Hamilton Ave., Cincinnati OH 45231. (513)931-4050. Fax: (513)931-0950. E-mail: redford@standardpub.com. Website: www.standardpub.com. **Editor:** Margie Redford. Newspaper published quarterly in weekly parts. Estab. 1997. Circ. 40,000. "*Live Wire* is a weekly publication geared to preteens (10-12 year olds). 'who want to connect to Christ.' Articles are in a news brief format that feature current events and profiles. We publish true stories about kids, puzzles, activities, interviews."

Nonfiction: Middle readers: animal, arts/crafts, biography, religion, Bible, geography, health, history, how-to, interview/profile, multicultural, nature/environment, science, sports. Buys 50-70 mss/year. Average word length: 250-350. Byline given.

Poetry: Reviews poetry from preteens only. Limit submissions to 5 poems.

How to Contact/Writers: Nonfiction: Send complete ms. Responds to queries in 1-2 weeks; mss in 2-3 months. Ms published 1 year after acceptance. Accepts simultaneous submissions and previously published work.

Illustration: Buys 4 illustrations/issue; 200 illustrations/year. Uses color artwork only. Works on assignment only. Reviews ms/illustration packages from artists. Ms/illustration packages: query first.

Terms: Pays on acceptance. Buys first rights or reprint rights for mss. Buys full rights for artwork; one-time use for photos. Pays 6-8¢/word for articles. Additional payment for photos accompanying articles. Pays illustrators $100-200 for color cover, $25-125 for color inside. Pays photographers per photo (range: $100-150). Writer's guidelines, theme list for SASE.

Tips: "We want articles about preteens who have done something significant for their church or community. Submit articles closely related to themes; articles must be interesting news briefs." (See listings for *Encounter* and *Kidz Chat*).

🅽 **THE MAGAZINE OF FANTASY & SCIENCE FICTION**, Spilogale, Inc., P.O. Box 3447, Hoboken NJ 07030. Phone/fax: (201)876-2551. E-mail: FandSF@aol.com. Website: www.fsfmag.com. **Articles Editor:** Gordon Van Gelder. **Fiction Editor:** Gordon Van Gelder. Estab. 1949. Circ. 50,000. "We are one of the longest-running magazines devoted to fantasy and science fiction."

Fiction: Young adults: fantasy, science fiction. "We have no formula for fiction. We are looking for stories that will appeal to science fiction and fantasy readers. The SF element may be slight, but it should be present. We prefer character-oriented stories. We receive a lot of fantasy fiction, but never enough science fiction or humor." Buys 80-120 mss/year. Average word length: 25,000 maximum. Byline given.

Nonfiction: Buys 0-1 ms/year. Byline given.

How to Contact/Writers: Fiction: Send complete ms. Responds to mss in up to 2 months. Publishes ms 9 months after acceptance. Will consider previously published work.

Illustration: Buys 1 illustration/issue; 11 illustrations/year. Uses color artwork only. Works on assignment only. Responds only if interested.

Terms: Pays on acceptance. Buys first North American serial rights. Original artwork returned at job's completion. Pays 5-8¢/word. Sample copies for $5. Writer's guidelines for SASE.

Tips: "We are not aimed primarily at young readers, but we value our young readers and we have published many works that have become classics for youngsters (such as Daniel Keyes's 'Flowers for Algernon' and 'The Brave Little Toaster', by Thomas M. Disch). Read a sample issue before submitting."

N: MH-18, Rodale Inc., 33 E. Miner St., Emmaus PA 18098. (610)967-5171. E-mail: MH-18editors@rodale.c om. Website: www.MH-18.com. **Articles Editor:** Jenny Everett. Bimonthly. "We provide irreverant, useful information to 13- to 18-year-old guys. Focusing on fitness, sports, girls, gear and life."
Nonfiction: Young adults: careers, fashion, health, hobbies, how-to, interview/profile, social issues, sports. Byline sometimes given.
How to Contact/Writers: Nonfiction: Query with published clips. Responds to queries in 1 month; mss in 2 months. Publishes ms 4 months after acceptance. Will consider simultaneous submissions, electronic submissions via disk or modem.
Illustration: Query with samples. Credit line given.

☑ MUSE, Carus Publishing, 332 S. Michigan Ave, Suite 1100, Chicago IL 60604. (312)939-1500. Fax: (312)939-8150. E-mail: muse@caruspub.com. Website: www.musemag.com **Editor:** Diana Lutz. **Art Director:** Karen Kohn. **Photo Editor:** Carol Parden. Estab. 1996. Circ. 60,000. "The goal of *Muse* is to give as many children as possible access to the most important ideas and concepts underlying the principal areas of human knowledge. It will take children seriously as developing intellects by assuming that, if explained clearly, the ideas and concepts of an article will be of interest to them. Articles should meet the highest possible standards of clarity and transparency aided, wherever possible, by a tone of skepticism, humor, and irreverence."
  • *Muse* is published in cooperation of the Cricket Magazine Group and *Smithsonian* magazine.
Nonfiction: Middle readers, young adult: animal, biography, history, interview/profile, math, multicultural, nature/environment, problem-solving, science, social issues. Buys 60-75 mss/year. Length: 500-1,500 words. Work on commision only. "Each article must be about a topic that children can understand. The topic must be a 'large' one that somehow connects with a fundamental tennet of some discipline or area of practical knowledge. The topic and presentation must lead to further questioning and exploration; it must be open-ended rather than closed. The treatment of the topic must be of the competence one would expect of an expert in the field in which the topic resides. It must be interesting and hold the reader's attention, not because of the way it is written, but because of the compelling presentation of the ideas it describes."
How to Contact/Writers: Nonfiction: Query with résumé, writing samples, published clips, detailed story ideas and SASE. Will consider simultaneous submissions, electronic submissions via disk or modem or previously published work.
Illustration: Buys 6 illustrations/issue; 40 illustrations/year. Uses color artwork only. Works on assignment only. Reviews ms/illustration packages. Send ms with dummy. Illustrations only: Query with samples. Send résumé, promo sheet and tearsheets. Responds only if interested. Samples returned with SASE. Credit line given.
Photography: Needs vary. Query with samples. Responds only if interested.
Terms: Pays within 60 days of acceptance. Buys first publications rights; all rights for feature articles. Pays 50¢/word for assigned articles; 25¢/word for unsolicited manuscripts. Writer's guidelines and sample copy available for $5.
Tips: "*Muse* may on occasion publish unsolicited manuscripts, but the easiest way to be printed in *Muse* is to send a query. However, manuscripts may be submitted to the Cricket Magazine Group for review, and any that are considered suitable for *Muse* will be forwarded. Such manuscripts will also be considered for publication in *Cricket*, *Spider* or *Ladybug*." (See listing for *ASK*, *Babybug*, *Click*, *Cricket*, *Ladybug* and *Spider*.)

N: MY FRIEND, The Catholic Magazine for Kids, Pauline Books & Media, 50 St. Paul's Ave., Jamaica Plain, Boston MA 02130-3491. (617)522-8911. Fax: (617)541-9805. E-mail: myfriend@pauline.org. Website: www.myfriendmagazine.com. **Articles/Fiction Editor:** Sr. Kathryn James, FSP. **Art Director:** Sister Helen Rifa, FSP. Monthly magazine. Estab. 1979. Circ. 12,000. "*My Friend* is a 32-page monthly Catholic magazine for boys and girls. Its' goal is to celebrate the Catholic Faith—as it is lived by today's children and as it has been lived for centuries. Its pages are packed with fun, learning, new experiences, information, crafts, global awareness, friendships and inspiration. Together with it's web-page KidStuff. *My Friend* provides kids and their families a wealth of information and contacts on every aspect of the Faith."
Fiction: Young readers, middle readers: adventure, Christmas, contemporary, humorous, multicultural, nature/ environment, problem-solving, religious, sports, science fiction. Does not want to see poetry, animals as main characters in religious stories, stories whose basic thrust would be incompatible with Catholic values. Buys 50 mss/year. Average word length: 750-1,100. Byline given.
Nonfiction: Young readers, middle readers: games/puzzles, humorous, interview/profile, media literacy, nature/ environment, problem-solving, religious, multicultural, social issues. Does not want to see material that is not compatible with Catholic values; no "New Age" material. Buys 10 mss/year. Average word length: 450-750. Byline given.
How to Contact/Writers: Fiction/nonfiction: Send complete ms. Responds to queries/mss in 2 months.
Illustration: Buys 8 illustrations/issue; buys 60-80 illustrations/year. Preferred theme or style: realistic depictions of children, but open to variety!
Terms: Pays on acceptance for mss. Buys first rights for mss; variable for artwork. Original artwork returned at job's completion. Pays $60-150 for stories/articles. Pays illustrators $250/color (cover); $50-150/b&w (inside); $75-175/color (inside). Pays photographers $15-250/photo. Sample copy $2.75 with 9 × 12 SAE and 4 first-class stamps. Writer's guidelines free with SAE and 1 first-class stamp.

Tips: Writers: "We are looking for fresh perspectives into a child's world that are imaginative, unique, challenging, informative, current and fun. We prefer articles that are visual, not necessarily text-based—articles written in 'windows' style with multiple points entry. Illustrators: Please contact us! For the most part, we need illustrations for fiction stories."

☑ **NATIONAL GEOGRAPHIC WORLD**, National Geographic Society, 1145 17th St. NW, Washington DC 20036-4688. (202)857-7000. Fax: (202)775-6112. Website: www.nationalgeographic.com/world. **Editor:** Melina Bellows. **Art Director:** Ursula Vosseler. **Photo Editor:** Chuck Herron. Monthly magazine. Estab. 1975. Circ. 870,000.
Nonfiction: Young readers, middle readers, young adult/teens: animal, arts/crafts, biography, cooking, games/puzzles, geography, history, hobbies, how-to, interview/profile, multicultural, nature/environment, science, sports, travel. Middle readers, young adult/teens: social issues. "We do not review or buy unsolicited manuscripts, but do use freelance writers."
Illustration: Buys 100% of illustrations from freelancers. Works on assignment only. Query. Illustrations only: Query with samples. Responds in 2 months. Samples returned with SASE; samples filed. Credit line given.
Photography: Buys photos separately. Looking for active shots, funny, strange animal close-ups. Uses 35mm transparencies. Query with samples. Responds in 2 months. Photo guidelines are available on website or with SASE.
Terms: Pays on acceptance. Buys all rights for mss and artwork. Originals returned to artist at job's completion. Writers get 3 copies of issue their work appears in. Pays photographers by the project. Sample copies for 9×12 SAE and 2 first-class stamps; photo guidelines available free for SASE.
Tips: "Most story ideas are generated in-house and assigned to freelance writers. Query with cover letter and samples of your writing for children or young adults. Keep in mind that *World* is a visual magazine. A story will work best if it has a very tight focus and if the photos show children interacting with their surroundings as well as with each other."

☑ **NATURE FRIEND MAGAZINE**, 2673 TR421, Sugarcreek OH 44681. (330)852-1900. Fax: (330)852-3285. **Articles Editor:** Marvin Wengerd. Monthly magazine. Estab. 1983. Circ. 10,000.
Fiction: Picture-oriented material, conversational, no talking animal stories.
Nonfiction: Picture-oriented material, animal, how-to, nature. No talking animal stories. No evolutionary material. Buys 100 mss/year. Average word length: 500. Byline given.
How to Contact/Writers: Nonfiction: Send complete ms. Responds to mss in 4 months. Will consider but must note simultaneous submissions.
Illustration: Buys approximately 8 illustrations/issue from freelancers; 96 illustrations/year. Reports on artist's submissions in 1 month. Works on assignment only. Credit line given.
Terms: Pays on publication. Buys one-time rights. Pays $15-75. Payment for illustrations: $15-80/b&w, $50-100/color inside. Two sample copies and writer's guidelines for $5 with 9×12 SAE and $2 postage. Writer's/illustrator's guidelines for $2.50.
Tips: Looks for "main articles, puzzles and simple nature and science projects. Needs conversationally-written stories about unique animals or nature phenomena. Please examine samples and writer's guide before submitting." Current needs: science and nature experiments.

NEW MOON: The Magazine For Girls & Their Dreams, New Moon Publishing, Inc., P.O. Box 3620, Duluth MN 55803-3620. (218)728-5507. Fax: (218)728-0314. E-mail: girl@newmoon.org. Website: www.newmoon.org. **Managing Editors:** Deb Mylin. Bimonthly magazine. Estab. 1992. Circ. 25,000. *New Moon* is for every girl who wants her voice heard and her dreams taken seriously. *New Moon* portrays strong female role models of all ages, backgrounds and cultures now and in the past. 100% of publication aimed at juvenile market.
Fiction: Middle readers, young adults: adventure, animal, contemporary, fantasy, folktales, history, humorous, multicultural, nature/environment, problem-solving, religious, science fiction, sports, suspense/mystery, travel. Buys 3 mss/year from adults and 3 mss/year from girls. Average word length: 900-1,200. Byline given.
Nonfiction: Middle readers, young adults: animal, arts/crafts, biography, careers, cooking, games/puzzles, health, history, hobbies, humorous, interview/profile, math, multicultural, nature/environment, problem-solving, science, social issues, sports, travel, stories about real girls. Does not want to see how-to stories. Wants more stories about real girls doing real things written by girls. Buys 6-12 adult-written mss/year. 30 girl-written mss/year. Average word length: 600. Byline given.
How to Contact/Writers: Fiction/Nonfiction: Does not return or acknowledge unsolicited mss. Send only copies. Responds only if interested. Will consider simultaneous submissions and electronic submission e-mail.
Illustration: Buys 6-12 illustrations/year from freelancers. *New Moon* seeks 4-color cover illustrations as well as b&w illustrations for inside. Reviews ms/illustrations packages from artists. Query. Submit ms with rough sketches. Illustration only: Query; send portfolio and tearsheets. Samples not returned; samples filed. Responds in 6 months only if interested. Credit line given.
Terms: Pays on publication. Buys all rights for mss. Buys one-time rights, reprint rights, for artwork. Original artwork returned at job's completion. Pays 6-12¢/word for stories; 6-12¢/word for articles. Pays in contributor's copies. Pays illustrators $400 for color cover; $50-300 for b&w inside. Sample copies for $6.50. Writer's/cover art guidelines for SASE or available on website.

Tips: "Please refer to a copy of *New Moon* to understand the style and philosophy of the magazine. Writers and artists who understand our goals have the best chance of publication. We're looking for stories about real girls; women's careers, and historical profiles. We publish girl's and women's writing only." Publishes writing/art/photos by girls.

■ **NICK JR. MAGAZINE**, Nickelodeon Magazines, Inc., 1633 Broadway, 7th Floor, New York NY 10019. (212)654-6389. Fax: (212)654-4840. Website: www.nickjr.com. **Articles Editor:** Wendy Smolen, deputy editor. **Art Director:** Josh Klenert. **Director:** Don Morris. Bimonthly magazine. Estab. 1999. Circ. 500,000. A magazine where kids play to learn and parents learn to play. 50% of publication aimed at juvenile market.
Fiction: Picture-oriented material: adventure, animal, contemporary, humorous, multicultural, nature/environment, problem-solving, sports. Byline sometimes given.
Nonfiction: Picture-oriented material: animal, arts/crafts, concept, cooking, games/puzzles, hobbies, how-to, humorous, math, multicultural, nature/environment, problem-solving, science, social issues, sports. Byline sometimes given.
How to Contact/Writers: Only interested in agented material. Fiction/nonfiction: Query or submit complete ms. Responds to queries/mss in 3-12 weeks. Will consider simultaneous submissions.
Illustration: Only interested in agented material. Works on assignment only. Reviews ms/illustration packages from artists. Query or send ms with dummy. Contact: Wendy Smolen, deputy editor. Illustrations only: arrange portfolio review; send résumé, promo sheet and portfolio. Contact: Josh Klenert, art director. Responds only if interested. Samples not returned; samples kept on file. Credit line sometimes given.
Photography: Looking for photos of children. Model/property release required.
Query with résumé of credits; provide résumé, business card, promotional literature or tearsheets. Responds only if interested.
Terms: Writer's guidelines for SASE.

■ **ODYSSEY, Adventures in Science**, Cobblestone Publishing Company, 30 Grove St., Suite C, Peterborough NH 03458. (603)924-7209. Fax: (603)924-7380. E-mail: odyssey@cobblestonepub.com. Website: www.odysseymagazine.com. (Also see www.cobblestonepub.com.) **Editor:** Elizabeth E. Lindstrom. **Managing Editor:** Lou Waryncia. **Art Director**: Ann Dillon. Magazine published 9 times/year. Estab. 1979. Circ. 22,000. Magazine covers earth, general science and technology, astronomy and space exploration for children ages 10-16. All material must relate to the theme of a specific upcoming issue in order to be considered.
• *Odyssey* won 2000 Parents'Choice Silver Award. *Odyssey* themes for 2002 include Sleep and Dreams, Why We Love Music, Planets X, and The Magic in Math.
Fiction: Middle readers and young adults/teens: science fiction, science, astronomy. Does not want to see anything not theme-related. Average word length: 900-1,200 words.
Nonfiction: Middle readers and young adults/teens: interiors, activities. Don't send anything not theme-related. Average word length: 200-750, depending on section article is used in.
How to Contact/Writers: "A query must consist of all of the following to be considered (please use nonerasable paper): a brief cover letter stating the subject and word length of the proposed article; a detailed one-page outline explaining the information to be presented in the article; an extensive bibliography of materials the author intends to use in preparing the article; a SASE. Writers new to *Odyssey* should send a writing sample with query. If you would like to know if your query has been received, please also include a stamped postcard that requests acknowledgment of receipt. In all correspondence, please include your complete address as well as a telephone number and e-mail address where you can be reached. A writer may send as many queries for one issue as he or she wishes, but each query must have a separate cover letter, outline, bibliography, and SASE. Telephone queries are not accepted. Handwritten queries will not be considered. Queries may be submitted at any time, but queries sent well in advance of deadline *may not be answered for several months*. Go-aheads requesting material proposed in queries are usually sent four months prior to publication date. Unused queries will be returned approximately three to four months prior to publication date."
Illustration: Buys 3 illustrations/issue; 27 illustrations/year. Works on assignment only. Reviews ms/illustration packages from artists. Query. Contact: Beth Lindstrom, editor. Illustration only: Query with samples. Send tearsheets, photocopies. Responds in 2 weeks. Samples returned with SASE; samples not filed. Original artwork returned upon job's completion (upon written request).
Photography: Wants photos pertaining to any of our forthcoming themes. Uses b&w and color prints; 35mm transparencies. Photographers should send unsolicited photos by mail on speculation.
Terms: Pays on publication. Buys all rights for mss and artwork. Pays 20-25¢/word for stories/articles. Covers are assigned and paid on an individual basis. Pays photographers per photo ($15-100 for b&w; $25-100 for color). Sample copy for $4.95 and SASE with $2 postage. Writer's/illustrator's/photo guidelines for SASE. (See listings for *Apple Seeds, Calliope, Cobblestone, Dig, Faces* and *Footsteps*.)

■ **ON COURSE, A Magazine for Teens**, General Council of the Assemblies of God, 1445 Boonville Ave., Springfield MO 65802-1894. (417)862-2781. Fax: (417)862-1693. E-mail: oncourse@ag.org. **Editor:** Melinda Booze. **Art Director:** Jared Van Bruaene. Bimonthly magazine. Estab. 1991. Circ. 190,000. *On Course* is a magazine to empower students to grow in a real-life relationship with Christ.

Fiction: Young adults: Christian discipleship, contemporary, humorous, multicultural, problem-solving, sports. Average word length: 1,000. Byline given.

Nonfiction: Young adults: careers, interview/profile, multicultural, religion, social issues, college life, Christian discipleship.

How to Contact/Writers: Works on assignment basis only. Résumés and writing samples will be considered for inclusion in Writer's File to receive story assignments.

Illustration: Buys 4 illustrations/issue; 16 illustrations/year. Uses color artwork only. Reviews ms/illustration packages from artists. Query. Illustration only: Query with samples or send résumé, promo sheet, slides, client list and tearsheets. Contact Melinda Booze, editor. Responds only if interested. Originals not returned at job's completion. Credit line given.

Photography: Buys photos from freelancers. "Teen life, church life, college life; unposed; often used for illustrative purposes." Model/property releases required. Uses color glossy prints and 35mm or 2¼×2¼ transparencies. Query with samples; send business card, promotional literature, tearsheets or catalog. Responds only if interested.

Terms: Pays on acceptance. Buys first or reprint rights for mss. Buys one-time rights for photographs. Pays 10¢/word for stories/articles. Pays illustrators and photographers "as negotiated." Sample copies free for 9×11 SAE. Writer's guidelines for SASE.

ON THE LINE, Mennonite Publishing House, 616 Walnut Ave., Scottdale PA 15683. (724)887-8500. Fax: (724)887-3111. E-mail: otl@mph.org. **Editor:** Mary Clemens Meyer. Magazine published monthly. Estab. 1970. Circ. 5,500. "*On The Line* is a children's magazine for ages 9-14, emphasizing self-esteem and Christian values. Also emphasizes multicultural awareness, care of the earth and accepting others with differences."

Fiction: Middle readers, young adults: contemporary, history, humorous, nature/environment, problem-solving, religious, science fiction, sports. "No fantasy or fiction with animal characters." Buys 45 mss/year. Average word length: 1,000-1,800. Byline given.

Nonfiction: Middle readers, young adults: arts/crafts, biography, cooking, games/puzzles, health, history, hobbies, how-to, humorous, sports. Does not want to see articles written from an adult perspective. Average word length: 200-600. Byline given.

Poetry: Wants to see light verse, humorous poetry.

How to Contact/Writers: Fiction/nonfiction: Send complete ms. "No queries, please." Responds to mss in 1 month. Will consider simultaneous submissions. Prefers no e-mail submissions.

Illustration: Buys 5-6 illustrations/issue; buys 60 illustrations/year. "Inside illustrations are done on assignment only to accompany our stories and articles—our need for new artists is limited." Looking for new artists for cover illustrations—full-color work. Illustrations only: "Prefer samples they do not want returned; these stay in our files." Responds to art samples only if interested.

Terms: Pays on acceptance. For mss buys one-time rights; second serial (reprint rights). Buys one-time rights for artwork and photos. Pays 3-5¢/word for assigned/unsolicited articles. Pays $50 for full-color inside illustration; $150 for full-color cover illustration. Photographers are paid per photo, $25-50. Original artwork returned at job's completion. Sample copy free with 7×10 SAE. Free writer's guidelines.

Tips: "We focus on the age 12-13 group of our age 9-14 audience."

OWL, The Discovery Magazine for Children, Bayard Press, 49 Front St. E, Toronto, Ontario M5E 1B3 Canada. (416)340-2700. Fax: (416)340-9769. E-mail: owl@owl.on.ca. Website: www.owlkids.com. **Editor:** Marybeth Leatherdale. **Creative Director:** Barb Kelly. **Photo Editor:** Kim Gillingham. Monthly magazine. Circ. 75,000. "*OWL* helps children over eight discover and enjoy the world of science, nature and technology. We look for articles that are fun to read, that inform from a child's perspective, and that motivate hands-on interaction. *OWL* explores the reader's many interests in the natural world in a scientific, but always entertaining, way."

Nonfiction: Middle readers: animal, biology, games/puzzles, high-tech, humor, nature/environment, science, social issues, sports, travel. Especially interested in puzzles and game ideas: logic, math, visual puzzles. Does not want to see religious topics, anthropomorphizing. Buys 6 mss/year. Average word length: 500-1,500. Byline given.

How to Contact/Writers: Nonfiction: Query with published clips. Responds to queries/mss in 3-4 months.

Illustration: Buys 3-5 illustrations/issue; 40-50 illustrations/year. Uses color artwork only. Preferred theme or style: lively, involving, fun, with emotional impact and appeal. "We use a range of styles." Works on assignment only. Illustrations only: Send tearsheets and slides. Reports on art samples only if interested. Original artwork returned at job's completion.

Photography: Looking for shots of animals and nature. "Label the photos." Uses 2¼×2¼ and 35mm transparencies. Photographers should query with samples.

Terms: Pays on publication. Buys first North American and world rights for mss, artwork and photos. Pays $200-500 (Canadian) for assigned/unsolicited articles. Pays up to $650 (Canadian) for illustrations. Photographers are paid per photo. Sample copies for $4.28. Writer's guidelines for SAE (large envelope if requesting sample copy) and money order for $1 postage (no stamps please).

Tips: Writers: "*OWL* is dedicated to entertaining kids with contemporary and accurate information about the world around them. *OWL* is intellectually challenging but is never preachy. Ideas should be original and convey a spirit of humor and liveliness." (See listings for *Chickadee* and *Chirp*.)

N PARENTING NEW HAMPSHIRE, Telegraph Publishing Co., P.O. Box 1291, Nashua NH 03061. (603)594-6434. Fax: (603)594-6565. E-mail: news@parentingnh.com. Website: www.parentingnh.com. **Articles Editor:** Beth Quarm Todgham. Purpose is "to provide news, information and resources to New Hampshire parents."
Nonfiction: Buys 10-12 mss/year. Average word length: 900-1,800. Byline given.
How to Contact/Writers: Nonfiction: Send complete ms. Responds to queries/mss in 6 months. Publishes ms 30 days after acceptance. Will consider simultaneous submissions, electronic submissions via disk or modem, previously pubished work.
Photography: Looks for photos related to children and families—primarily use as cover artwork. Uses color prints and 35mm, 2¼×2¼, 4× or 8×10 transparencies. Provide résumé, business card, promotional literature or tearsheets to be kept on file. Resopnds only if interested.
Terms: Pays on publication. Buys reprint rights, one-time rights, web rights for up to 1 year. Original artwork returned at job's completion. Pays $25-125 for stories. Additional payment for ms/illustration packages and for photos accompanying articles. Sample copies for $1. Writer's guidelines for SASE.

☑ PASSPORT, (formerly *Power and Light*). Sunday School Curriculum, 6401 The Paseo, Kansas City MO 64131-1284. (816)333-7000. Fax: (816)333-4439. Website: www.nazarene.org. **Editor**: Emily Freeburg. Weekly story paper. "*Passport* looks for a casual, witty approach to Christian themes. We want hot topics relevant to preteens."
Nonfiction: Middle readers, young adults: archaeological, biography, history, games/puzzles, how-to, interview/profile, problem-solving, multicultural, religion, social issues, travel. Multicultural needs include: ethnics and cultures—other world areas especially English-speaking.
How to Contact/Writers: Send complete ms. Responds to queries/mss in 2 months. Publishes ms 2 years after acceptance.
Terms: Pays on publication. "Payment is made approximately one year before the date of issue." Buys multiple use rights for mss. Purchases all rights for artwork and first/one-time rights for photographs. Pays $15-30/word for stories/articles. Writer's guidelines for SASE.
Tips: Writers: "Themes and outcomes should conform to the theology and practices of the Church of the Nazarene, Evangelical Friends, Free Methodist, Wesleyan and other Bible-believing Evangelical churches." We look for bright, colorful illustrations; concise, short articles and stories. Keep it realistic and contemporary. Request guidelines first!" (See listing for *Discoveries*.)

POCKETS, Devotional Magazine for Children, The Upper Room, 1908 Grand, P.O. Box 34004, Nashville TN 37203-0004. (615)340-7333. Fax: (615)340-7267. E-mail: pockets@upperroom.org. Website: www.upperroom.org/pockets. **Articles/Fiction Editor:** Lynn W. Gilliam. **Art Director**: Chris Schechner, Suite 207, 3100 Carlisle Plaza, Dallas TX 75204. Magazine published 11 times/year. Estab. 1981. Circ. 96,000. "*Pockets* is a Christian devotional magazine for children ages 6-12. Stories should help children experience a Christian lifestyle that is not always a neatly wrapped moral package but is open to the continuing revelation of God's will."
Fiction: Picture-oriented, young readers, middle readers: adventure, contemporary, folktales, multicultural, nature/environment, problem-solving, religious. Does not want to see violence or talking animal stories. Buys 40-45 mss/year. Average word length: 800-1,400. Byline given.
Nonfiction: Picture-oriented, young readers, middle readers: cooking, games/puzzles, interview/profile, religion. Does not want to see how-to articles. "Our nonfiction reads like a story." Multicultural needs include: stories that feature children of various racial/ethnic groups and do so in a way that is true to those depicted. Buys 10 mss/year. Average word length: 800-1,600. Byline given.
How to Contact/Writers: Fiction/nonfiction: Send complete ms. "Prefer not to deal with queries." Responds to mss in 6 weeks. Will consider simultaneous submissions.
Illustration: Buys 40-50 illustrations/issue. Preferred theme or style: varied; both 4-color and 2-color. Works on assignment only. Illustrations only: Send promo sheet, tearsheets.

RANGER RICK, National Wildlife Federation, 11100 Wildlife Center Dr., Reston VA 20190. (703)438-6000. Website: www.nwf.org.
 ● Ranger Rick is no longer accepting unsolicited queries or mss.

READ, Weekly Reader Corporation, 200 First Stamford Place, P.O. Box 120023, Stamford CT 06912-0023. Fax: (203)705-1661. E-mail: sbarchers@weeklyreader.com. Website: www.weeklyreader.com. **Managing Editor:** Suzanne Barchers. Magazine published 18 times during the school year. Language arts periodical for use in classrooms for students ages 12-16; motivates students to read and teaches skills in listening, comprehension, speaking, writing and critical thinking.
Fiction: Wants short stories, narratives and plays to be used for classroom reading and discussions. Middle readers, young adult/teens: adventure, animal, contemporary, fantasy, folktales, history, humorous, multicultural, nature/environment, sports. Average word length: 1,000-2,500.
Nonfiction: Middle readers, young adult/teen: animal, games/puzzles, history, humorous, problem solving, social issues.
How to Contact: Responds to queries/mss in 6 weeks.

Children's Writer's & Illustrator's Market goofed! In our 2001 edition, we showed a cover of *READ* magazine featuring what we said was an illustration by Suzanne Hankins. Unfortunately, we printed the wrong illustration, mistakenly showcasing a piece by another artist. We apologize for the error. Here is Hankins's illustration, a watercolor used to illustrate a piece in *READ* titled "The Sea Dragon of Fife," written by Jane Yolen. Hankins's elegant, fun, fantastical style perfectly fit the mood and theme of Yolen's story.

Illustration: Buys 2-3 illustrations/issue; 20-25 illustration jobs/year. Responds only if interested. Samples returned with SASE. Credit line given.

Terms: Pays on publication. Rights purchased varies. Pays writers $100-800 for stories/articles. Pays illustrators $650-850 for color cover; $125-750 for b&w and color inside. Pays photographers by the project (range: $450-650); per photo (range: $125-650). Samples copies free for digest-sized SAE and 3 first-class stamps.

Tips: "We especially like plot twists and surprise endings. Stories should be relevant to teens and contain realistic conflicts and dialogue. Plays should have at least 12 speaking parts for classroom reading. Avoid formula plots, trite themes, underage material, stilted or profane language, and sexual suggestion. Get to know the style of our magazine as well as our teen audience. They are very demanding and require an engaging and engrossing read. Grab their attention, keep the pace and action lively, build to a great climax, and make the ending satisfying and/or surprising. Make sure characters and dialogue are realistic. Do not use cliché, but make the writing fresh—simple, yet original. Obtain guidelines and planned editorial calendar first. Be sure submissions are relevant."

☑ **SCHOOL MATES, USCF's Magazine for Beginning Chess Players**, United States Chess Federation, 3054 Rt. 9W, New Windsor NY 12553. (845)562-8350. Fax: (845)561-CHES. E-mail: magazines@uschess.org. Website: www.uschess.org. **Editor:** Peter Kurzdorfer. **Graphic Designer:** Jami Anson. Quarterly magazine. Estab. 1987. Circ. 37,000. Magazine for beginning and scholastic chess players. Offers instructional articles, features on famous players, scholastic chess coverage, games, puzzles, occasional fiction, listing of chess tournaments.

Nonfiction: Young readers, middle readers, young adults: games/puzzles, chess. Middle readers, young adults: interview/profile (chess-related). "No *Mad Magazine* type humor. No sex, no drugs, no alcohol, no tobacco. No stereotypes. We want to see chess presented as a wholesome, non-nerdy activity that's fun for all. Good sportsmanship, fair play, and 'thinking ahead' are extremely desirable in chess articles. Also, celebrities who play chess."

Poetry: Infrequently published. Must be chess related.

How to Contact/Writers: Send complete ms. Responds to queries/mss in 5 weeks.

Illustration: Buys 10-25 illustrations/year. Prefers b&w and ink; cartoons OK. Illustration only: Query first. Responds only if interested. Credit line sometimes given. "Typically, a cover is credited while an illustration inside gets only the artist's signature in the work itself."

Photography: Purchases photos from freelancers. Wants "action shots of chess games (at tournament competitions), well-done portraits of popular chess players."

Terms: Pays on publication. Buys one-time rights for mss, artwork and photos. For stories/articles, pays $20-100. Pays illustrators $50-75 for b&w cover; $20-50 for b&w inside. Pays photographers per photo (range: $25-75). Sample copies free for 9×12 SAE and 2 first-class stamps. Writer's guidelines free on request.

Tips: Writers: "Lively prose that grabs and sustains kids' attention is desirable. Don't talk down to kids or over their heads. Don't be overly 'cute.' " Illustration/photography: "Whimsical shots are often desirable."

☑ **SCIENCE WEEKLY**, Science Weekly Inc., P.O. Box 70638, Chevy Chase MD 20813. (301)680-8804. Fax: (301)680-9240. E-mail: sciencew@erols.com. Website: www.scienceweekly.com. **Editor:** Deborah Lazar. Magazine published 16 times/year. Estab. 1984. Circ. 200,000.
  • *Science Weekly* uses freelance writers to develop and write an entire issue on a single science topic. Send résumé only, not submissions. Authors must be within the greater DC, Virginia, Maryland area. *Science Weekly* works on assignment only.

Nonfiction: Young readers, middle readers, (K-8th grade): science/math education, education, problem-solving.

Terms: Pays on publication. Prefers people with education, science and children's writing background. *Send résumé only.* Samples copies free with SAE and 2 first-class stamps.

Ⓝ **SCIENCE WORLD**, Scholastic Inc., 557 Broadway, New York NY 10012-3999. (212)343-6299. Fax: (212)343-6333. E-mail: scienceworld@scholastic.com. **Editor:** Mark Bregman. **Art Director:** Susan Kass. Magazine published biweekly during the school year. Estab. 1959. Circ. 400,000. Publishes articles in Life Science/Health, Physical Science/Technology, Earth Science/Environment/Astronomy for students in grades 7-10. The goal is to make science relevant for teens.
  • *Science World* publishes a separate teacher's edition with lesson plans and skills pages to accompany feature articles.

Nonfiction: Young adults/teens: animal, concept, geography, health, nature/environment, science. Multicultural needs include: minority scientists as role models. Does not want to see stories without a clear news hook. Buys 20 mss/year. Average word length: 500-1,000. Byline given. Currently does not accept unsolicited mss.

How to Contact/Writers: Nonfiction: Query with published clips and/or brief summaries of article ideas. Responds to queries in 3 months.

Illustration: Buys 2 illustrations/issue; 28 illustrations/year. Works on assignment only. Illustration only: Query with samples, tearsheets. Contact: Susan Kass, art director. Responds only if interested. Samples returned with SASE; samples filed "if we use them." Credit line given.

Photography: Model/property releases required; captions required including background information. Provide résumé, business card, promotional literature or tearsheets to be kept on file. Responds only if interested.

Terms: Pays on acceptance. Buys all right for mss/artwork. Originals returned to artist at job's completion. For stories/articles, pays $200. Pays photographers per photo.

☑ **SEVENTEEN MAGAZINE**, Primedia, 850 Third Ave., New York NY 10022. (212)407-9700. Fax: (212)407-9899. Website: http://seventeen.com. **Editor-in-Chief:** Patrice G. Adcroft. **Editor:** Claudia Boutote, fiction. **Deputy Editor:** Tamara Glenny. **Art Director:** Carol Pagliuco. Monthly magazine. Estab. 1944. Circ. 2.5 million. "*Seventeen* is a young woman's first fashion and beauty magazine."

• *Seventeen* ranked number 1 on *Writer's Digest*'s 1999 Fiction 50, the magazine's annual list of "50 best places to publish your short stories."

Fiction: "We consider all good literary short fiction." Buys 6-12 mss/year. Average word length: 800-4,000. Byline given.

Nonfiction: Young adults: animal, beauty, entertainment, fashion, careers, health, hobbies, how-to, humorous, interview/profile, multicultural, relationships, religion, social issues, sports. Buys 150 mss/year. Word length: Varies from 800-1,000 words for short features and monthly columns to 800-2,500 words for major articles. Byline given.

How to Contact/Writers: Fiction: Send complete ms. Nonfiction: Query with published clips or send complete ms. "Do not call." Responds to queries/mss in 3 months. Will consider simultaneous submissions.

Terms: Pays on acceptance. Strongly recommends requesting writers guidelines with SASE and reading recent issues of the magazine.

SHARING THE VICTORY, Fellowship of Christian Athletes, 8701 Leeds, Kansas City MO 64129. (816)921-0909. Fax: (816)921-8755. Website: www.fca.org. **Articles/Photo Editors:** David Smale, Allen Palmeri. **Art Director:** Frank Grey. Magazine published 9 times a year. Estab. 1982. Circ. 80,000. "Purpose is to present to coaches and athletes, and all whom they influence, the challenge and adventure of receiving Jesus Christ as Savior and Lord."

Nonfiction: Young adults/teens: interview/profile, sports. Buys 30 mss/year. Average word length: 700-1,200. Byline given.

Poetry: Reviews poetry. Maximum length: 50-75 words.

How to Contact/Writers: Nonfiction: Query with published clips. Responds in 3 weeks. Publishes ms 3 months after acceptance. Will consider simultaneous submissions, electronic submissions via disk or modem and previously published work. Writer's guidelines available on website.

Photography: Purchases photos separately. Looking for photos of sports action. Uses color, b&w prints and 35mm transparencies.

Terms: Pays on publication. Buys first rights and second serial (reprint) rights. Pays $50-200 for assigned and unsolicited articles. Photographers paid per photo (range: $50-100). Sample copies for 9×12 SASE and $1. Writer's/photo guidelines for SASE.

Tips: "Be specific—write short. Take quality, sharp photos that are useable." Wants interviews and features, articles on athletes with a solid Christian base; be sure to include their faith and testimony. Interested in colorful sports photos.

☑ **SHINE brightly**, (formerly *Touch*), GEMS Girls' Clubs, Box 7259, Grand Rapids MI 49510. (616)241-5616. Fax: (616)241-5558. E-mail: sara@gemsgc.org. Website: www.gospelcom.net/gems. **Editor:** Jan Boone. **Managing Editor:** Sara Lynne Hilton. Monthly (with combined May/June/July/August summer issue) magazine. Circ. 16,000. "*Shine brightly* is designed to help girls ages 9-14 see how God is at work in their lives and in the world around them."

Fiction: Middle readers: adventure, animal, contemporary, health, history, humorous, multicultural, nature/environment, problem-solving, religious, sports. Does not want to see unrealistic stories and those with trite, easy endings. Buys 30 mss/year. Average word length: 400-1,000. Byline given.

Nonfiction: Middle readers: animal, arts/crafts, careers, cooking, fashion, games/puzzles, health, hobbies, how-to, humorous, nature/environment, multicultural, problem-solving, religious, social issues, sports, travel. Buys 9 mss/year. Average word length: 200-800. Byline given.

How to Contact/Writers: Send for annual update for publication themes. Fiction/nonfiction: Send complete ms. Responds to mss in 1 month. Will consider simultaneous submissions.

Illustration: Buys 3 illustrations/year. Prefers ms/illustration packages. Works on assignment only. Responds to submissions in 1 month. Samples returned with SASE. Credit line given.

Terms: Pays on publication. Buys first North American serial rights, first rights, second serial (reprint rights) or simultaneous rights. Original artwork not returned at job's completion. Pays $5-30 for stories; $5-30 for assigned articles; $5-30 for unsolicited articles. "We send complimentary copies in addition to pay." Pays $25-75 for color cover illustration; $25-50 for color inside illustration. Pays photographers by the project ($25-75 per photo). Writer's guidelines for SASE.

Tips: Writers: "The stories should be current, deal with adolescent problems and joys, and help girls see God at work in their lives through humor as well as problem-solving."

Ⓝ **SKATING**, U.S. Figure Skating Association, 20 First St., Colorado Springs CO 80906. (719)635-5200. Fax: (719)635-9548. **Articles Editor:** Laura Fawcett. Magazine published 10 times/year. Estab. 1923. Circ. 45,000. "The mission of *SKATING* is to communicate information about the sport (figure skating) to the USFSA membership and figure skating fans, promoting USFSA programs, personalities, events and trends that affect the sport."

Nonfiction: Middle readers, young adults: biography, health, interview/profile, sports. Buys 20 mss/year. Average word length: 750-2,000. Byline given.

How to Contact/Writers: Nonfiction: Query with published clips. Responds to queries/mss in 2 months. Publishes ms 2 months after acceptance. Will consider electronic submissions via disk or modem.

Illustration: Buys 1 illustration/year. Works on assignment only. Reviews ms/illustration packages from artists. Query. Contact: Laura Fawcett, editor. Illustrations only: Query with samples. Contact: Laura Fawcett, editor. Responds only if interested. Samples returned with SASE; or filed. Credit line given.

Photography: Uses photos of kids learning to skate on ice. Model/property release required; captions required. Uses color most sizes matte or glossy prints, 35mm transparencies. Contact by e-mail if interested in submitting. Responds only if interested.

Terms: Pays on publication. Buys first rights for mss, artwork and photos. Original artwork returned at job's completion. Pays $75-150 for stories and articles. Additional payment if photos are used. Pays photographers per photo (range: $15-35). Sample copies for SAE. Writer's/photo guidelines for SASE.

Tips: "*SKATING* covers Olympic-eligible skating, primarily focusing on the U.S. We do *not* cover professional skating. We would like more skating how-to articles and informative technical tips."

SKIPPING STONES, A Multicultural Children's Magazine, P.O. Box 3939, Eugene OR 97403. (541)342-4956. E-mail: skipping@efn.org. Website: www.efn.org/~skipping. **Articles/Photo/Fiction Editor:** Arun N. Toké. Bimonthly magazine. Estab. 1988. Circ. 2,500. "*Skipping Stones* is a multicultural, nonprofit children's magazine designed to encourage cooperation, creativity and celebration of cultural and ecological richness. We encourage submissions by minorities and under-represented populations."

- Send SASE for *Skipping Stones* guidelines and theme list for detailed descriptions of the topics they're looking for.

Fiction: Middle readers, young adult/teens: contemporary, meaningful, humorous. All levels: folktales, multicultural, nature/environment. Multicultural needs include: bilingual or multilingual pieces; use of words from other languages; settings in other countries, cultures or multi-ethnic communities.

Nonfiction: All levels: animal, biography, cooking, games/puzzles, history, humorous, interview/profile, multicultural, nature/environment, creative problem-solving, religion and cultural celebrations, sports, travel, social and international awareness. Does not want to see preaching or abusive language; no poems by authors over 18 years old; no suspense or romance stories for the sake of the same. Average word length: 500-750. Byline given.

How to Contact/Writers: Fiction: Query. Nonfiction: Send complete ms. Responds to queries in 1 month; mss in 4 months. Will consider simultaneous submissions; reviews artwork for future assignments. Please include your name on each page.

Illustration: Prefers color and/or b&w drawings, especially by teenagers and young adults. Will consider all illustration packages. Ms/illustration packages: Query; submit complete ms with final art; submit tearsheets. Responds in 4 months. Credit line given.

Photography: Black & white photos preferred, but color photos with good contrast are welcome. Needs: youth 7-17, international, nature, celebration.

Terms: Acquires first or reprint rights for mss and artwork; reprint rights for photographs. Pays in copies for authors, photographers and illustrators. Sample copies for $5 with SAE and 4 first-class stamps. Writer's/illustrator's guidelines for 4×9 SASE.

Tips: "We want material meant for children and young adults/teenagers with multicultural or ecological awareness themes. Think, live and write as if you were a child—naturally, uninhibited." Wants "material that gives insight on cultural celebrations, lifestyle, custom and tradition, glimpse of daily life in other countries and cultures. Photos, songs, artwork are most welcome if they illustrate/highlight the points. Translations are invited if your submission is in a language other than English. Upcoming themes will include cultural celebrations, living abroad, disability, hospitality customs of various cultures, cross-cultural communications, African, Asian and Latin American cultures, humor, international, and turning points in life, caring for the earth, the Internet's Impact on Multicutural Awareness."

SOCCER JR., The Soccer Magazine for Kids, Scholastic Inc., 27 Unquowa Rd., Fairfield CT 06430-5015. (203)259-5766. Fax: (203)256-1119. E-mail: jschoff@soccerjr.com. Website: www.soccerjr.com. **Articles/Fiction Editor:** Jill Schoff. Bimonthly magazine. Estab. 1992. Circ. 100,000. *Soccer Jr.* is for soccer players 8-14 years old. "The editorial focus of *Soccer Jr.* is on the fun and challenge of the sport. Every issue contains star interviews, how-to tips, lively graphics, action photos, comics, games, puzzles and contests. Fair play and teamwork are emphasized in a format that provides an off-the-field way for kids to enjoy the sport."

Fiction: Middle readers, young adults/teens: sports (soccer). Does not want to see "cute," preachy or "moralizing" stories. Buys 3-4 mss/year. Average word length: 1,000-1,500. Byline given.

Nonfiction: Young readers, middle readers, young adults/teens: sports (soccer). Buys 10-12 mss/year.

How to Contact/Writers: Fiction: Send complete ms. Nonfiction: Send query letter. Responds to mss in 6 weeks. Publishes ms 2 months after acceptance. Will consider simultaneous submissions.

Illustration: Buys 2 illustrations/issue; 20 illustrations/year. Works on assignment only. Illustrations only: Send samples to be filed. Samples not returned; samples kept on file. "We have a small pool of artists we work from but look for new freelancers occasionally, and accept samples for consideration." Credit line given.

Terms: Pays on acceptance. Buys first rights for mss. Pays $50-600 for stories. Pays illustrators $300-750 for color cover; $50-200 for b&w inside; $75-300 for color inside. Pays photographers per photo (range: $75-300). Sample copies for 9×12 SAE and 5 first-class stamps.
Tips: "We ask all potential writers to understand *Soccer Jr.*'s voice. We write to kids, not to adults. We request a query for any feature ideas, but any fiction pieces can be sent complete. All submissions, unless specifically requested, are on a speculative basis. Please indicate if a manuscript has been submitted elsewhere or previously published. Please give us a brief personal bio, including your involvement in soccer, if any, and a listing of any work you've had published. We prefer manuscripts in Microsoft Word, along with an attached hard copy." The magazine also accepts stories written by children.

SPELLBOUND MAGAZINE, Eggplant Productions, P.O. Box 2248, Schiller Park IL 60176. (847)928-9925. Fax: (801)720-0706. E-mail: spellbound@eggplant-productions.com. Website: www.eggplantproductions.com/spellbound. **Articles Editor:** Raechel Henderson Moon. Quarterly magazine. Estab. 1999. Circ. 300. "*Spellbound Magazine*'s goal is to introduce new readers to the fantasy genre in all its wonderful forms. We publish intelligent fiction, nonfiction and poetry to excite kids. We like artwork that is fun."
• *Spellbound* only accepts e-mail submissions. All postal submissions are returned unread.
Fiction: Middle readers, young adults: fantasy, folktale, multicultural. Buys 20 mss/year. Average word length: 500-2,500. Byline given.
Nonfiction: Middle readers, young adults: myths/legends. Buys 1-2 mss/year. Average word length: 500-1,000. Byline given.
Poetry: Reviews free verse, traditional, rhyming poetry. Maximum length: 36 lines. Limit submissions to 5 poems.
How to Contact/Writers: Fiction: Send complete ms. Nonfiction: Query. Responds to queries in 2 weeks; mss in 1 month. Publishes ms 6 months after acceptance. Will consider simultaneous submissions; only considers electronic submission via modem.
Illustration: Buys 3-4 illustrations/issue; 12-16 illustrations/year. Uses b&w artwork only. Reviews ms/illustration packages from artists. Submit through e-mail to spellbound@eggplant-productions.com. Contact: Raechel Henderson Moon, editor. Illustrations only: Query with samples. Contact: Raechel Henderson Moon, editor. Responds in 2 weeks. Samples kept on file. Credit line given.
Terms: Pays on publication. Buys first world English-language rights for mss. Buys one-time rights for art. Pays $1.50 stories; $1.50 for articles. Artists are paid 2 contributor copies and $1.50 per interior art; 3 contributor copies and $5 for cover art. Sample copies for $5.
Tips: "Keep in mind that this is a market for children, but don't let that limit your work. We see too much that preaches or talks down to readers or that relies on old plot lines. Write the kind of story or poem that you would like to have read when you were 11. Then send it our way."

SPIDER, The Magazine for Children, Carus Publishing Company, P.O. Box 300, Peru IL 61354. (815)224-6656. Website: www.cricketmag.com. **Editor-in-Chief:** Marianne Carus. **Assistant Editor:** Heather Delabre. **Art Director**: Tony Jacobson. Monthly magazine. Estab. 1994. Circ. 73,000. *Spider* publishes high-quality literature for beginning readers, primarily ages 6-9.
Fiction: Young readers: adventure, animal, contemporary, fantasy, folktales, history, humorous, multicultural, nature/environment, problem-solving, science fiction, sports, suspense/mystery. "Authentic, well-researched stories from all cultures are welcome. No didactic, religious, or violent stories, or anything that talks down to children." Average word length: 300-900. Byline given.
Nonfiction: Young readers: animal, arts/crafts, cooking, games/puzzles, geography, history, math, multicultural, nature/environment, problem-solving, science. "Well-researched articles on all cultures are welcome. Would like to see more games, puzzles and activities, especially ones adaptable to *Spider*'s takeout pages. No encyclopedic or overtly educational articles." Average word length: 300-800. Byline given.
Poetry: Serious, humorous, nonsense rhymes. Maximum length: 20 lines.
How to Contact/Writers: Fiction/nonfiction: Send complete ms. Responds to mss in 3 months. Publishes ms 2-3 years after acceptance. Will consider simultaneous submissions and previously published work.
Illustration: Buys 20 illustrations/issue; 240 illustrations/year. Uses color artwork only. "Any medium—preferably one that can wrap on a laser scanner—no larger than 20×24. We use more realism than cartoon-style art." Works on assignment only. Reviews ms/illustration packages from artists. Submit ms with rough sketches. Illustrations only: Send promo sheet and tearsheets. Responds in 6 weeks. Samples returned with SASE; samples filed. Credit line given.
Photography: Buys photos from freelancers. Buys photos with accompanying ms only. Model/property releases required; captions required. Uses 35mm or $2\frac{1}{4} \times 2\frac{1}{4}$ transparencies. Send unsolicited photos by mail; provide résumé and tearsheets. Responds in 6 weeks.
Terms: Pays on publication for text; within 45 days from acceptance for art. Buys first, one-time or reprint rights for mss. Buys first and promotional rights for artwork; one-time rights for photographs. Original artwork returned at job's completion. Pays 25¢/word for previously unpublished stories/articles. Authors also receive 2 complimentary copies of the issue in which work appears. Additional payment for ms/illustration packages and for photos accompanying articles. Pays illustrators $750 for color cover; $200-300 for color inside. Pays photographers per photo (range: $25-75). Sample copies for $5. Writer's/illustrator's guidelines for SASE.

Tips: Writers: "Read back issues before submitting." (See listings for *Babybug*, *Cicada*, *Cricket*, *Click*, *Muse* and *Ladybug*.)

☑ SPORTS ILLUSTRATED FOR KIDS, 135 W. 50th St., New York NY 10020-1393. (212)522-1212. Fax: (212)522-0120. Website: www.sikids.com. **Managing Editor:** Neil Cohen. **Art Director:** Beth Bugler. **Photo Editor:** Andrew McCloskey. Monthly magazine. Estab. 1989. Circ. 950,000. Each month *SI Kids* brings the excitement, joy, and challenge of sports to life for boys and girls ages 8-14 via: action photos, dynamic designs, interactive stories; a spectrum of sports: professional, extreme, amateur, women's and kids; profiles, puzzles, playing tips, sports cards; posters, plus drawings and writing by kids. 100% of publication aimed at juvenile market.

Nonfiction: Middle readers, young adults: biography, games/puzzles, interview/profile, sports. Buys less than 20 mss/year. Average word length: 500-700. Byline given.

How to Contact/Writers: Nonfiction: Query. Responds in 4-6 weeks. Will consider simultaneous submissions. **Illustration: Only interested in agented material.** Buys 50 illustrations/year. Works on assignment only. Reviews ms/illustration packages from artists. Submit ms/illustration package with SASE. Contact: Beth Bugler, art director. Illustrations only: Send promo sheet and samples. Contact: Beth Bugler, art director. Responds in 1 month. Samples kept on file. Credit line given.

Photography: Looking for action sports photography. Uses color prints and 35mm transparencies. Submit portfolio for review. Responds in 1 month.

Terms: Pays 25% on acceptance 75% on publication. Buys all rights for mss. Buys all rights for artwork. Buys all rights for photos. Original artwork returned at job's completion. Pays $500 for 500-600 word articles. by the project—$400; $500/day; per photo (range: $75-1,000). Sample copies free for 9×12 SASE. Writer's guidelines for SASE or via website.

STORY FRIENDS, Mennonite Publishing House, 616 Walnut Ave., Scottdale PA 15683. (724)887-8500. Fax: (724)887-3111. E-mail: RSTUTZ@mph.org. **Editor:** Rose Mary Stutzman. **Art Director:** Jim Butti. Estab. 1905. Circ. 6,000. Monthly magazine that reinforces Christian values for children ages 4-9.

Fiction: Picture-oriented material: contemporary, humorous, multicultural, nature/environment, problem-solving, religious, relationships. Multicultural needs include fiction or nonfiction pieces which help children be aware of cultural diversity and celebrate differences while recognizing similarities. Buys 45 mss/year. Average word length: 300-800. Byline given.

Nonfiction: Picture-oriented: animal, humorous, interview/profile, multicultural, nature/environment. Buys 10 mss/year. Average word length: 300-800. Byline given.

Poetry: Average length: 4-12 lines.

How to Contact/Writers: Fiction/nonfiction: Send complete ms. Responds to mss in 10 weeks. Will consider simultaneous submissions.

Illustration: Works on assignment only. Send tearsheets with SASE. Responds in 2 months. Samples returned with SASE; samples filed. Credit line given.

Photography: Occasionally buys photos from freelancers. Wants photos of children ages 4-8.

Terms: Pays on acceptance. Buys one-time rights or reprint rights for mss and artwork. Original artwork returned at job's completion. Pays 3-5¢/word for stories and articles. Pays photographers $15-30 per photo. Writer's guidelines free with SAE and 2 first-class stamps.

Tips: "Become immersed in high quality children's literature."

TODAY'S CHRISTIAN TEEN, Marketing Partners Inc., P.O. Box 100, Morgantown PA 19543. (610)372-1111. Fax: (610)372-8227. E-mail: tcpubs@mkpt.com. **Articles Editor:** Elaine Williams. Publishes issues of interest to teenagers from a conservative biblical view.

Nonfiction: Young adults: health, religion, social issues. Buys 10 mss/year. Average word length: 800-1,100. Byline given.

How to Contact/Writers: Nonfiction: send complete ms. Responds to queries in 2 weeks; mss in 3 months. Publishes ms 1 year after acceptance. Will consider simultaneous submissions, electronic submissions via disk or modem and previously published work.

Terms: Pays on publication. Pays $75-150 for articles. Sample copies free for 9×12 SAE with 4 first-class stamps. Writer's guidelines for SASE.

Tips: "Make articles applicable to conservative teens with a biblical perspective—something they can use, not just entertainment."

☑ TURTLE MAGAZINE, For Preschool Kids, Children's Better Health Institute, 1100 Waterway Blvd., P.O. Box 567, Indianapolis IN 46206. (317)636-8881. Fax: (317)684-8094. Website: www.turtlemag.org. **Editor:** Terry Harshman. **Art Director:** Bart Rivers. Monthly/bimonthly magazine published 8 times/year. Circ. 300,000. *Turtle* uses read-aloud stories, especially suitable for bedtime or naptime reading, for children ages 2-5. Also uses poems, simple science experiments, easy recipes and health-related articles.

Fiction: Picture-oriented material: adventure, contemporary, fantasy, health-related, history, holiday themes, humorous, multicultural, nature/environment, problem-solving, sports, suspense/mystery. "We need very simple experiments illustrating basic science concepts. Also needs action rhymes to foster creative movement. Avoid stories in which the characters indulge in unhealthy activities. Buys 30 mss/year. Average word length: 100-300. Byline given. Currently accepting submissions for Rebus stories only.

Nonfiction: Picture-oriented material: animal, arts/crafts, cooking, games/puzzles, geography, health, multicultural, nature/environment, science, sports. Buys 24 mss/year. Average word length: 100-300. Byline given.

Poetry: "We're especially looking for short poems (4-8 lines) and slightly longer action rhymes to foster creative movement in preschoolers. We also use short verse on our back cover."

How to Contact/Writers: Fiction/nonfiction: "Prefer complete manuscript to queries." Responds to mss in 3 months.

Photography: Buys photos from freelancers with accompanying ms only.

Terms: Pays on publication. Buys all rights for mss/artwork; one-time rights for photographs. Pays up to 22¢/word for stories and articles (depending upon length and quality) and 10 complimentary copies. Pays $25 minimum for poems. Pays $30-70 for b&w inside. Sample copy $1.75. Writer's guidelines free with SASE.

Tips: "Our need for health-related material, especially features that encourage fitness, is ongoing. Health subjects must be age-appropriate. When writing about them, think creatively and lighten up! Always keep in mind that in order for a story or article to educate preschoolers, it first must be entertaining—warm and engaging, exciting, or genuinely funny. Here the trend is toward leaner, lighter writing. There will be a growing need for interactive activities. Writers might want to consider developing an activity to accompany their concise manuscripts." (See listings for *Child Life, Children's Digest, Children's Playmate, Humpty Dumpty's Magazine, Jack and Jill* and *U*S* Kids.*)

☑ **U*S* KIDS**, Children's Better Health Institute, 1100 Waterway Blvd., P.O. Box 567, Indianapolis IN 46206. (317)636-8881. Website: www.uskidsmag.org. **Editor:** Daniel Lee. **Art Director:** Tim LaBelle. Magazine published 8 times a year. Estab. 1987. Circ. 230,000.

Fiction: Young readers: adventure, animal, contemporary, health, history, humorous, multicultural, nature/environment, problem-solving, sports, suspense/mystery. Buys limited number of stories/year. Query first. Average word length: 500-800. Byline given.

Nonfiction: Young readers: animal, arts/crafts, cooking, games/puzzles, health, history, hobbies, how-to, humorous, interview/profile, multicultural, nature/environment, science, social issues, sports, travel. Wants to see interviews with kids ages 5-10, who have done something unusual or different. Buys 30-40 mss/year. Average word length: 400. Byline given.

Poetry: Maximum length: 8-24 lines.

How to Contact/Writers: Fiction: Send complete ms. Responds to queries and mss in 2-3 months.

Illustration: Buys 8 illustrations/issue; 70 illustrations/year. Color artwork only. Works on assignment only. Reviews ms/illustration packages from artists. Query. Illustrations only: Send résumé and tearsheets. Responds only if interested. Samples returned with SASE; samples kept on file. Does not return originals. Credit line given.

Photography: Purchases photography from freelancers. Looking for photos that pertain to children ages 5-10. Model/property release required. Uses color and b&w prints; 35mm, 2¼×2¼, 4×5 and 8×10 transparencies. Photographers should provide résumé, business card, promotional literature or tearsheets to be kept on file. Responds only if interested.

Terms: Pays on publication. Buys all rights for mss. Purchases all rights for artwork. Purchases one-time rights for photographs. Pays 25¢/word minimum. Additional payment for ms/illustration packages. Pays illustrators $155/page for color inside. Photographers paid by the project or per photo (negotiable). Sample copies for $2.95. Writer's/illustrator/photo guidelines for #10 SASE.

Tips: "Write clearly and concisely without preaching or being obvious." (See listings for *Child Life, Children's Digest, Children's Playmate, Humpty Dumpty's Magazine, Jack and Jill* and *Turtle Magazine.*)

☑ **W.O.W. (Wild Outdoor World®)**, Suites 16-20, P.O. Box 1329, Helena MT 59624. (406)449-1335. Fax: (406)449-9197. E-mail: wowgirl@quest.net. **Editorial Director:** Carolyn Zieg Cunningham. **Executive Editor:** Kay Morton Ellerhoff. **Design Editor:** Bryan Knaff. Publishes 5 issues/year. Estab. 1993. Circ. 200,000. "A magazine for young conservationists (age 8-12)." W.O.W. is distributed in fourth grade classrooms throughout the US and Canada.

Nonfiction: Middle readers: adventure (outdoor), animal, nature/environment, sports (outdoor recreation), travel (to parks, wildlife refuges, etc.). Average word length: 800 maximum. Byline given.

How to Contact/Writers: Nonfiction: Query. Responds in 6 months.

Illustration: Buys 2 illustrations/issue; 12-15 illustrations/year. Prefers work on assignment. Reviews ms/illustration packages from artists. Illustrations only: Query; send slides, tearsheets. Responds in 2 months. Samples returned with SASE; samples sometimes filed. Credit line given.

Photography: *Must* be submitted in 20-slide sheets and individual protectors, such as KYMAC. Looks for "children outdoors—camping, fishing, doing 'nature' projects." Model/property releases required. Photo captions required. Uses 35mm transparencies. Does not accept unsolicited photography. Contact: Theresa Morrow Rush, photo editor. Responds in 2 months.

Terms: Pays 30-60 days after publication. Buys one-time and electronic rights for mss and photographs. Original work returned at job's completion. Pays $100-300 for articles; $50 for fillers. Pays illustrators variable rate for b&w inside; $250 color cover; $35-100 color inside. Pays photographers $150 for full inside; per photo (range: $125-300); $375 for cover photo. Sample copies for $3.95 and 8½×11 SAE. Writer's/illustrator's/photo guidelines for SASE.

Tips: "We are seriously overloaded with manuscripts and do not plan to buy very much new material in the next year."

[N] [□] WEE ONES E-MAGAZINE, 1321 Ridge Rd., Baltimore MD 21228. E-mail: info@weeonesmag.com. Website: www.weeonesmag.com. **Editor:** Jennifer Reed. Monthly online magazine. Estab. 2001. "We are an online children's magazine for children ages 3-8. Our mission is to use the Internet to encourage kids to read. We promote literacy and family unity." 50% of publication aimed at juvenile market.

Fiction: Picture-oriented material: adventure, contemporary, health, history, humorous, multicultural, nature/environment, problem solving, sports, rebus with illustrations. Buys 60 mss/year. Average word length: up to 500. Byline given.

Nonfiction: Picture-oriented material: animal, arts/crafts, biography, concept, cooking, games/puzzles, geography, health, history, hobbies, how-to, humorous, multicultural, nature/environment, problem-solving, science, sports, travel. Buys 30 mss/year. Average word length: up to 500. Byline given.

Poetry: Uses rhyming poetry. Limit submissions to 3 poems.

How to Contact/Writers: Fiction/nonfiction: Send complete ms via e-mail. Responds to mss in 1 month. Publishes ms 6-12 months after acceptance. Will consider simultaneous submissions, electronic submissions via modem.

Illustration: Buys 6 illustrations/issue. Works on assignment only. Reviews ms/illustration packages from artists. Query. Contact: Jeff Reed, art editor. Illustrations only: Query with samples. Contact: Jeff Reed, art editor. Responds only if interested. Samples returned with SASE, kept on file. Credit line given.

Photography: Uses photos of children in various activities. Uses color b&w 4×6 prints. Responds only if interested.

Terms: Pays on publication. Buys one time electronic rights for mss, artwork and photos. Pays 3¢/word for stories and articles. Additional payment for ms/illustration packages and for photos accompanying articles. Pays $5-20 for b&w and color inside. Pays photographers per photo (range: $3). Writer's/illustrator's/photo guidelines for SASE.

Tips: "*Wee Ones* is the first online children's magazine. We are not in print! Study our magazine before submitting. Our guidelines are located on our site. Your chances on getting accepted depend widely only how well you follow our guidelines and submit *only* through e-mail."

[✓] WEEKLY READER, Weekly Reader Corporation, 200 First Stamford Place, Stampford CT 06912-0023. (203)705-3500. Website: www.weeklyreader.com. **Managing Editor:** Bill Walter (grades 2-4). **Group Art Director:** Rick Ruthman. Weekly magazine. Estab. 1902. Circ. 8 million. Classroom periodicals bring news to kids from pre-K to high school in 17 grade-specific periodicals. Publication aimed at juvenile market.

Illustration: Uses color artwork only. Works on assignment only. Illustrations only: Query with samples or send tearsheets. Contact: Rick Ruthman, group art director. Responds only if interested. Samples returned with SASE; samples filed. Credit line given.

Photography: Uses color prints. Query with samples, Provide tearsheets. Responds only if interested.

Terms: Pays 30 days after submission of invoice. Buys all rights for mss. Buys one-time usage for artwork. Buys one-time usage for photos. Original artwork returned at job's completion. Pays illustrators $400-800 for color cover.

Tips: Please do not call to see if samples were received, as many arrive daily.

[▲] WHAT MAGAZINE, (formerly *What! A Magazine*), What! Publishers Inc. 108-93 Lombard Ave., Winnipeg, Manitoba R3B 3B1 Canada. (204)985-8160. Fax: (204)957-5638. E-mail: l.malkin@m2ci.mb.ca. **Articles Editor:** Leslie Malkin. **Art Director:** Brian Kauste. Magazine published 6 times/year. Estab. 1987. Circ. 250,000. "Informative and entertaining teen magazine for both genders. Articles deal with issues and ideas of relevance to Canadian teens. The magazine is distributed through schools so we aim to be cool and responsible at the same time."

Nonfiction: Young adults (3 and up): biography, careers, concept, health, how-to, humorous, interview/profile, nature/environment, science, social issues, sports. "No cliché teen stuff. Also, we're getting too many heavy pitches lately on teen pregnancy, AIDS, etc." Buys 8 mss/year. Average word length: 675-2,100. Byline given.

How to Contact/Writers: Nonfiction: Query with published clips. Responds to queries/mss in 2 months. Publishes ms 2 months after acceptance.

Terms: Pays on publication plus 30 days. Buys first rights for mss. Pays $100-500 (Canadian) for articles. Sample copies when available for 9×12 and $1.45 (Canadian). Writer's guidelines free for SASE.

Tips: "Teens are smarter today than ever before. Respect that intelligence in queries and articles. Aim for the older end of our age-range (14-19) and avoid cliché. Humor works for us almost all the time."

WINNER, The Health Connection, 55 W. OakRidge Dr., Hagerstown MD 21740. (301)393-4010. Fax: (301)393-4055. E-mail: Winner@healthconnection.org. **Articles Editor:** Anita Jacobs. **Art Director:** Tina Ivaney. Monthly magazine (September-May). (4) Estab. 1958. Publishes articles that will promote choosing a positive lifestyle for children in grades 4-6.

Fiction: Young readers, middle readers: contemporary, health, nature/environment, problem-solving, anti-tobacco, alcohol, and drugs. Byline sometimes given.

Nonfiction: Young readers, middle readers: biography, games/puzzles, health, hobbies, how-to, problem-solving, social issues. Buys 20 mss/year. Average word length: 600-700. Byline sometimes given.

How to Contact/Writers: Fiction/nonfiction: Query. Responds in 6 weeks. Publishes ms 6-12 months after acceptance. Will consider simultaneous submissions, electronic submission via disk or e-mail.

Illustration: Buys 3 illustrations/issue; 30 illustrations/year. Uses color artwork only. Works on assignment only. Reviews ms/illustration packages from artists. Send ms with dummy. Contact: Tina Ivaney, art director. Responds only if interested. Samples returned with SASE.

Terms: Pays on acceptance. Buys first rights for mss. Original artwork returned at job's completion. Additional payment for ms/illustration packages. Sometimes additional payment when photos accompany articles. Pays $200-400 for color inside. Writer's and illustrator's guidelines free for SASE. Sample magazine $1.00; include 9x12 envelope with 2 first-class stamps.

Tips: Keep material upbeat and positive for elementary age children.

WITH, The Magazine for Radical Christian Youth, Faith & Life Resources, 722 Main, P.O. Box 347, Newton KS 67114. (316)283-5100. Fax: (316)283-0454. E-mail: deliag@gcmc.org. **Editor:** Carol Duerksen. Published 6 times a year. Circ. 5,800. Magazine published for Christian teenagers, ages 15-18. "We deal with issues affecting teens and try to help them make choices reflecting a radical Christian faith."

Fiction: Young adults/teens: contemporary, fantasy, humorous, multicultural, problem-solving, religious, romance. Multicultural needs include race relations, first-person stories featuring teens of ethnic minorities. Buys 15 mss/year. Average word length: 1,000-2,000. Byline given.

Nonfiction: Young adults/teens: first-person teen personal experience (as-told-to), how-to, humorous, multicultural, problem-solving, religion, social issues. Buys 15-20 mss/year. Average word length: 1,000-2,000. Byline given.

Poetry: Wants to see religious, humorous, nature. "Buys 1-2 poems/year." Maximum length: 50 lines.

How to Contact/Writers: Send complete ms. Query on first-person teen personal experience stories and how-to articles. (Detailed guidelines for first-person stories, how-tos, and fiction available for SASE.) Responds to queries in 3 weeks; mss in 6 weeks. Will consider simultaneous submissions.

Illustration: Buys 6-8 assigned illustrations/issue; buys 64 assigned illustrations/year. Uses b&w and 2-color artwork only. Preferred theme or style: candids/interracial. Reviews ms/illustration packages from artists. Query first. Illustrations only: Query with portfolio (photocopies only) or tearsheets. Responds only if interested. Credit line given.

Photography: Buys photos from freelancers. Looking for candid photos of teens (ages 15-18), especially ethnic minorities. Uses 8×10 b&w glossy prints. Photographers should send unsolicited photos by mail.

Terms: Pays on acceptance. For mss buys first rights, one-time rights; second serial (reprint rights). Buys one-time rights for artwork and photos. Original artwork returned at job's completion upon request. Pays 6¢/word for unpublished manuscripts; 4¢/word for reprints. Will pay more for assigned as-told-to stories. Pays $10-25 for poetry. Pays $50-60 for b&w cover illustration and b&w inside illustration. Pays photographers per project (range: $120-180). Sample copy for 9×12 SAE and 4 first-class stamps. Writer's/illustrator's guidelines for SASE.

Tips: "We want stories, fiction or nonfiction, in which high-school-age youth of various cultures/ethnic groups are the protaganists. Stories may or may not focus on cross-cultural relationships. We're hungry for stuff that makes teens laugh—fiction, nonfiction and cartoons. It doesn't have to be religious, but must be wholesome. Most of our stories would not be accepted by other Christian youth magazines. They would be considered too gritty, too controversial, or too painful. Our regular writers are on the *With* wavelength. Most writers for Christian youth magazines aren't." For writers: "Fiction and humor are the best places to break in. Send SASE and request guidelines." For photographers: "If you're willing to line up models and shoot to illustrate specific story scenes, send us a letter of introduction and some samples of your work."

WONDER TIME, WordAction Publications, 6401 The Paseo, Kansas City MO 64131. (816)333-7000. Fax: (816)333-4439. E-mail: psmits@nazarene.org. **Editor:** Pamela Smits. Weekly magazine. Circ. 45,000. "*Wonder Time* is a full-color story paper for first and second graders. It is designed to connect Sunday School learning with daily living experiences of the primary child. *Wonder Time*'s target audience is children ages six to eight. The readability goal should be at beginning readers level. The intent of *Wonder Time* is to: Provide a life-related paper enabling Christian values, encourage good choices and provide reinforcement for biblical concepts taught in WordAction Sunday School curriculum."

Fiction: Contemporary. "We need ethnic balance—stories and illustrations from a variety of experiences." Buys 52 mss/year. Average word length: 100-150. Byline given.

How to Contact/Writers: Fiction: Send complete ms. Responds to queries/mss in 6 weeks. Send SASE for themes and guidelines.

Terms: Pays on acceptance. Pays $25 per story for all rights.
Tips: "Basic themes reappear regularly. Please write for a theme list. Ask for guidelines, sample copies, theme list *before* submitting. Send SASE."

WRITER'S INTL. FORUM, "For Those Who Write to Sell," Bristol Services Intl., P.O. Box 2109, Sequim WA 98382. E-mail: services@bristolservicesintl.com. Website: www.bristolservicesintl.com. **Editor:** Sandra E. Haven. Estab. 1990. "Periodic writing competitions held exclusively at our website." Up to 25% aimed at writers of juvenile literature. "We have published past winning short stories and essays along with a professional critique. Website includes writing lessons and information."
Fiction: Middle readers, young readers, young adults/teens: adventure, contemporary, fantasy, humorous, nature/environment, problem-solving, religious, romance, science fiction, suspense/mystery. "No experimental formats; no poetry." Byline and bio information printed.
How to Contact/Writers: Send SASE or see website to determine if a contest is currently open. Only send a manuscript if a contest is open.
Terms: See details at website.

YES MAG, Canada's Science Magazine for Kids, Peter Piper Publishing Inc., 3968 Long Gun Place, Victoria, British Columbia V8N 3A9 Canada. Phone/fax: (250)477-5543. E-mail: shannon@yesmag.ca. Website: www.yesmag.ca. **Articles Editor:** Shannon Hunt. **Art/Photo Director:** David Garrison. Quarterly magazine. Estab. 1996. Circ. 15,000. "*YES Mag* is designed to make science accessible, interesting, exciting, and FUN. Written for children ages 8 to 14, *YES Mag* covers a range of topics including science and technology news, environmental updates, do-at-home projects and articles about Canadian students and scientists."
Nonfiction: Middle readers: animal, health, math, nature/environment, science. Buys 70 mss/year. Average word length: 250-1,250. Byline given.
How to Contact/Writers: Nonfiction: Query with published clips or send complete ms (on spec only). Responds to queries/mss in 3 weeks. Publishes ms 3 months after acceptance. Will consider simultaneous submissions, electronic submission via disk or modem, previously published work.
Illustration: Buys 2 illustrations/issue; 10 illustrations/year. Uses color artwork only. Works on assignment only. Reviews ms/illustration packages from artists. Query. Contact: David Garrison, art director. Illustration only: Query with samples. Contact: David Garrison, art director. Responds in 3 weeks. Samples filed. Credit line given.
Photography: "Looking for science, technology, nature/environment photos based on current editorial needs." Photo captions required. Uses color prints. Provide résumé, business card, promotional literature, tearsheets if possible. Responds in 3 weeks.
Terms: Pays on publication. Buys one-time rights for mss. Buys one-time rights for artwork/photos. Original artwork returned at job's completion. Pays $25-125 for stories and articles. Sample copies for $3.50. Writer's guidelines for SASE.
Tips: "We do not publish fiction or science fiction. Visit our website for more information, sample articles and writers guidelines. We accept queries via e-mail. Articles relating to the physical sciences and mathematics are encouraged."

YM, 15 E. 26th St., New York NY 10010. (646)758-0493. Fax: (646)758-0808. E-mail: annemarie@ym.com. **Editor-in-Chief:** Annemarie Iverson. **Executive Editor:** Christina Kelly. "*YM* is a national magazine for girls ages 12-24 to help guide them through the joys and challenges of young adulthood."
Nonfiction: "*YM* covers dating, psychology, entertainment, friendship, self-esteem, human interest and news trends. All articles should be lively and empowering and include quotes from experts and real teens. We do not publish fiction or poetry." Word length: 800-2,000 words.
How to Contact/Writers: Nonfiction: Query with SASE. (Write "query"on envelope.) Responds to queries in 4-6 weeks; mss in 1-2 months.
Terms: Pays on acceptance. Rates vary. Sample copies available for $2.99 with 8½×11 SASE.

YOUNG & ALIVE, Christian Record Services, P.O. Box 6097, Lincoln NE 68506. (402)488-0981. Fax: (402)488-7582. E-mail: editorial@christianrecord.org. Website: www.christianrecord.org. **Articles Editor:** Ms. Gaylena Gibson. Quarterly magazine. Estab. 1976. Circ. 28,000. "We seek to provide wholesome, entertaining material for teens and others through age 25."
Nonfiction: Young adult/teen: animal, biography, careers, games/puzzles, health, history, humorous, interview/profile, multicultural, nature/environment, problem-solving, religion ("practical Christianity"), sports, travel. Buys 40-50 mss/year from freelancers. Word length: 700-1,400. Byline given.
How to Contact/Writers: Send complete ms. Responds to queries in 2 months; mss in 5 months. Published a ms "at least 2 years" after acceptance. Considers simultaneous submissions and previously published work. "Please don't send the work as a previously published piece; send a clean copy."
Illustration: Works on assignment only. Reviews ms/illustration packages from artists. Send ms with dummy. Contact Gaylena Gibson, editor.
Photography: Buys photos with accompanying ms only. Model/property release required; captions required. Uses color or b&w 3×5 or 8×10 prints.

Terms: Pays on acceptance. Buys one-time rights for ms and photos. Original artwork returned at job's completion. Pays 4-5¢/word for stories/article. Pays $25-40 for b&w inside illustration. Pays photographers by the project ($25-75). Sample copies available for 8×10 SASE and 5 first-class stamps. Writers guidelines available for SASE.

N; YOUNG RIDER, The Magazine for Horse and Pony Lovers, Fancy Publications, P.O. Box 8237, Lexington KY 40533. (859)260-9800. Fax: (859)260-9812. Website: www.youngrider.com. **Editor:** Lesley Ward. Bimonthly magazine. Estab. 1994. "*Young Rider* magazine teaches young people, in an easy-to-read and entertaining way, how to look after their horses properly, and how to improve their riding skills safely."
Fiction: Young adults: adventure, animal, horses, horse celebrities, famous equestrians. Buys 10 mss/year. Average word length: 1,500 maximum. Byline given.
Nonfiction: Young adults: animal, careers, health (horse), sports, riding. Buys 8-10 mss/year. Average word length: 1,000 maximum. Byline given.
How to Contact/Writers: Fiction/nonfiction: Query with published clips. Responds to queries in 2 weeks. Publishes ms 6-12 months after acceptance. Will consider simultaneous submissions, electronic submissions via disk or modem, previously published work.
Illustration: Buys 2 illustrations/issue; 10 illustrations/year. Works on assignment only. Reviews ms/illustration packages from artists. Query. Contact: Lesley Ward, editor. Illustrations only: Query with samples. Contact: Lesley Ward, editor. Responds in 2 weeks. Samples returned with SASE. Credit line given.
Photography: Buys photos with accompanying ms only. Uses color, slides, photos—in focus, good light. Model/property release required; captions required. Uses color 4×6 prints, 35mm transparencies. Query with samples. Responds in 2 weeks.
Terms: Pays on publication. Buys first North American serial rights for mss, artwork, photos. Original artwork returned at job's completion. Pays $150 maximum for stories; $250 maximum for articles. Additional payment for ms/illustration packages and for photos accompanying articles. Pays $70-140 for color inside. Pays photographers per photo (range: $65-155). Sample copies for $3.50. Writer's/illustrator's/photo guidelines for SASE.
Tips: "Fiction must be in third person. Read magazine before sending in a query. No 'true story from when I was a youngster.' No moralistic stories. Fiction must be up-to-date and humorous, teen-oriented. Need horsey interest or celebrity rider features. No practical or how-to articles—all done in-house."

YOUTH UPDATE, St. Anthony Messenger Press, 1615 Republic St., Cincinnati OH 45210. (513)241-5615. E-mail: carolann@americancatholic.org. Website: www.AmericanCatholic.org. **Articles Editor:** Carol Ann Morrow. **Art Director:** June Pfaff Daley. Monthly newsletter. Estab. 1982. Circ. 23,000. "Each issue focuses on one topic only. *Youth Update* addresses the faith and Christian life questions of young people and is designed to attract, instruct, guide and challenge its audience by applying the gospel to modern problems and situations. The students who read *Youth Update* vary in their religious education and reading ability. Write for average high school students. These students are 15-year-olds with a C+ average. Assume that they have paid attention to religious instruction and remember a little of what 'sister' said. Aim more toward 'table talk' than 'teacher talk.'"
Nonfiction: Young adults/teens: religion. Buys 12 mss/year. Average word length: 2,200-2,300. Byline given.
How to Contact/Writers: Nonfiction: Query. Responds to queries/mss in 3 months. Will consider computer printout and electronic submissions via disk, after query approval.
Photography: Buys photos from freelancers. Uses photos of teens (high-school age) with attention to racial diversity and with emotion.
Terms: Pays on acceptance. Buys first North American serial rights for mss. Buys one-time rights for photographs. Pays $350-500 for articles. Pays photographers per photo ($50-75 minimum). Sample copy free with #10 SASE. Writer's guidelines free on request.
Tips: "Read the newsletter yourself—3 issues at least. In the past, our publication has dealt with a variety of topics including: dating, Lent, teenage pregnancy, baptism, loneliness, violence, confirmation and the Bible. When writing, use the *New American Bible* as translation. Interested in church-related topics."

Greeting Cards, Puzzles & Games

In this section you'll find companies that produce puzzles, games, greeting cards and other items (like coloring books, stickers and giftwrap) especially for kids. These are items you'll find in children's sections of bookstores, toy stores, department stores and card shops.

Because these markets create an array of products, their needs vary greatly. Some may need the service of freelance writers for greeting card copy or slogans for buttons and stickers. Others are in need of illustrators for coloring books or photographers for puzzles. Artists should send copies of their work that art directors can keep on file—never originals. Carefully read through the listings to find companies' needs, and send for guidelines and catalogs if they're available, just as you would for book or magazine publishers.

If you'd like to find out more about the greeting card industry beyond the market for children, there are a number of resources to help you. The Greeting Card Association is a national trade organization for the industry. For membership information, contact the GCA at 1030 15th NW, Suite 870, Washington DC 20005, (202)393-1778, www.greetingcard.org. *Greetings Etc.* (Edgel Communications), a quarterly trade magazine covering the greeting card industry, is the official publication of the Greeting Card Association. For information call (973)895-3300. Illustrators should check out *Greeting Card Designs*, by Joanne Fink. For a complete list of companies, consult the latest edition of *Artist's & Graphic Designer's Market* (Writer's Digest Books). Writers should see *You Can Write Greeting Cards*, by Karen Ann Moore and *How to Write & Sell Greeting Cards, Bumper Stickers, T-shirts and Other Fun Stuff*, by Molly Wigand (both Writer's Digest Books).

Information on greeting card, puzzle and game companies listed in the previous edition but not included in this edition of *Children's Writer's & Illustrator's Market* may be found in the General Index.

AMCAL, INC., 2500 Bisso Lane, #500, Concord CA 94520. (925)689-9930. Fax: (925)689-0108. Website: www.amcalart.com. Vice President/Creative Development: Judy Robertson. Estab. 1975. Cards, calendars, desk diaries, boxed Christmas cards, journals, mugs, and other high quality gift and stationery products.
Illustration: Receives over 150 submissions/year. "AMCAL publishes high quality full color, narrative and decorative art for a wide market from traditional to contemporary. "Currently we are seeking updated interpretations of classic subjects such as florals and animals, strong decorative icons that are popular in the market place as well as in country folk art and decorative styles. Know the trends and the market. Juvenile illustration should have some adult appeal. We don't publish cartoon, humorous or gag art, or bold graphics. We sell to mostly small, exclusive gift retailers. Submissions are always accepted for future lines." To contact, send samples, photocopies, slides and SASE for return of submission. Responds in approximately 1 month. Pays on publication. Pay negotiable/usually advance on royalty. Rights purchased negotiable. Guideline sheets for #10 SASE and 1 first-class stamp.
Tips: To learn more about AMCAL and our products, please visit our website at: www.amcalart.com.

ARISTOPLAY, LTD., 8122 Main St., Dexter MI 48130. (734)424-0123. Fax: (734)424-0124. Website: www.aristoplay.com. Art Director: Doreen Consiglio. Estab. 1979. Produces educational board games and card decks, activity kits—all educational subjects. 100% of products are made for kids or have kids' themes.
Illustration: Needs freelance illustration and graphic designers (including art directors) for games, card decks and activity kits. Makes 2-4 illustration assignments/year. To contact, send cover letter, résumé, published samples or color photocopies. Responds back in 1 month if interested. For artwork, pays by the project, $500-5,000. Pays on acceptance (½-sketch, ½-final). Buys all rights. Credit line given.
Photography: Buys photography from freelancers. Wants realistic, factual photos.

Tips: "Creating board games requires a lot of back and forth in terms of design, illustration, editorial and child testing; the more flexible you are, the better. Also, factual accuracy is important." Target age group 4-14. "We are an educational game company. Writers and illustrators working for us must be willing to research the subject and period of focus."

✔ **AVANTI PRESS, INC.**, 155 W. Congress, Suite 200, Detroit MI 48226. (313)961-0022. Submit images to this address: Avanti, 6 W. 18th St., 12the Floor, New York NY 10011. (212)414-1025. Fax: (212)414-1055. Website: www.avantipress.com. **Photo Editors**: Bridget Hoyle and Judith Rosenbaum. Estab. 1979. Greeting card company. Publishes photographic greeting cards—nonseasonal and seasonal.
Photography: Purchases photography from freelancers. Buys stock and assigns work. Buys approximately 150 stock images/year. Makes approximately 150 assignments/year. Wants "narrative, storytelling images, graphically strong and colorful!" Accepts only photographs. Uses b&w/color prints; any size or format. Pays either a flat fee or a royalty which is discussed at time of purchase." Pays on acceptance. Buys exclusive product rights (world-wide card rights). Credit line given. Photographer's guidelines for SASE or via website.
Tips: At least 75% of products have kids' and pets themes. Submit seasonal material 9 months-1 year in advance. "All images submitted should express some kind of sentiment which either fits an occasion or can be versed and sent to the recipient to convey some feeling."

◤◢ **AVONLEA TRADITIONS, INC.**, 17075 Leslie St., Units 12-15, Newmarket, Ontario L3Y-8E1 Canada. (905)853-1777. Fax: (905)853-1763. Website: www.avonlea-traditions.com. President: Kathryn Morton. Estab. 1988. Giftware importer and distributor. Designs, imports and distributes products related to Canada's most famous storybook, *Anne of Green Gables*, and other Canadian themes. Publishes greeting cards (blank), novelties, website.
Illustration: Needs freelance illustration for stationery and packaging for giftware. Makes 2-3 illustration assignments/month; 24/year. Prefers romantic, Victorian, storybook artwork. To contact, send color photocopies and promo pieces. Responds only if interested. Materials not returned; materials filed. For other artwork, pays by the hour (range: $10-25). Pays on publication. Buys all rights. Credit line sometimes given.
Photography: Works on assignment only. Wants product photos. Prefers digital format. To contact, send portfolio and promo piece. Responds only if interested. Materials not returned; material filed. Pays on usage. Buys all rights. Credit line sometimes given.
Tips: "We strongly prefer artists/writers who are Canadian. Also give preference to those located in the Toronto area. Submit seasonal material 6 months in advance."

THE BEISTLE COMPANY, P.O. Box 10, Shippensburg PA 17257. (717)532-2131. Fax: (717)532-7789. E-mail: beistle@mail.cvn.net. Website: www.beistle.com. **Product Manager**: C. Michelle Luhrs-Wiest. Estab. 1900. Paper products company. Produces decorations and party goods, posters—baby, baptism, birthday, holidays, educational, wedding/anniversary, graduation, ethnic themes, and New Year parties. 50% of products are made for kids or have kids' themes.
Illustration: Needs freelance illustration for decorations, party goods, school supplies, point-of-purchase display materials and gift wrap. Makes 100 illustration assignments/year. Prefers fanciful style, cute 4- to 5-color illustration in gouache and/or computer illustration. To contact, send cover letter, résumé, client list, promo piece. To query with specific ideas, phone, write or fax. Responds only if interested. Materials returned with SASE; materials filed. Pays by the project or by contractual agreement; price varies according to type of project. Pays on acceptance. Buys all rights. Artist's guidelines available for SASE.
Tips: Submit seasonal material 6 months in advance.

CARDMAKERS, P.O. Box 236, 66 High Bridge Rd., Lyme NH 03768-0236. (603)795-4422. Fax: (603)795-4222. E-mail: info@cardmakers.com. Website: cardmakers.com. Owner: Peter Diebold. Estab. 1978. "We publish whimsical greeting cards with an emphahsis on Christmas and business-to-business."
Writing: To contact, send cover letter and writing samples with SASE. Responds in 3 months. Returns materials if accompanied by SASE. Pays on acceptance. Buys all rights. Credit line given. Writer's guidelines available for SASE.
Illustration: Needs freelance illustration for greeting cards. Makes 30-50 illustration assignments/year. Looking for happy holidays, "activity" themes—nothing with an "edge." To contact, send cover letter, published samples, color photocopies, promo pieces and SASE. Query with specific ideas, keep it simple. Responds in 3 months. Materials returned with SASE. For greeting cards, pays flat fee of $100-400. Pays on acceptance. Credit line given. Artist's guidelines available for SASE.
Photography: Buys stock images. Wants humor. To contact, send cover letter, published samples, SASE. Responds in 3 months. Returns material with SASE. Pays per photo (range: $100-400 for b&w, $100-400 for color). Pays on acceptance. Buys exclusive product rights. Credit line given. Guidelines available for SASE.
Tips: Submit seasonal material 9 months in advance. "Be brief. Be polite. We look at all our mail. No calls, no fax, no e-mails. Worst times to submit—September-December. The best submissions we see are simple, right to the point, color samples with a 'check-off' stamped, return postcard eliciting comments/expression of interest."

As a nonprofit greeting card company for children and adults with disabilities, *Courage Cards* strives to provide clever, jubilant products for their long list of "patrons and friends." Expressing a world peace message, illustrator Pam Peltier designed this holiday card for $350. Peltier says she wanted to include as many countries as she could to reflect her desire for universal compassion and happiness.

☑ **COURAGE CARDS**, 3915 Golden Valley Rd., Golden Valley MN 55422. (763)520-0211. Fax: (763)520-0299. E-mail: artsearch@courage.org. Website: www.courage.cards.org. **Art and Production:** Laura Brooks. Estab. 1959. Nonprofit greeting card company. Courage Cards helps support Courage Center, a nonprofit provider of rehabilitation services for children and adults with disabilities. Published holiday/seasonal greeting cards. 10% of products are made for kids or have kid's themes.
Illustration: Needs freelance illustration for children's greeting cards. Makes 40 illustration assignments/year. Prefers colorful holiday, peace, ethnic, diversity art. Uses color artwork only. To contact, request guidelines and application—send art with submission. Responds in 3 months. Returns materials if accompanied by SASE. For greeting cards, pays flat fee of $350. Pays on publication. Buys reprint rights. Artist photo and profile on the back of every card; credit line given.
Tips: "Please contact us for specific guidelines for the annual art search."

🅐 **CREATE-A-CRAFT**, P.O. Box 941293, Plano TX 75094-1293. **Contact:** Editor. Estab. 1967. Greeting card company. Produces greeting cards (create-a-card), giftwrap, games (create-a-puzzle), coloring books, calendars (create-a-calendar), posters, stationery and paper tableware products for all ages.
Writing: Needs freelance writing for children's greeting cards and other children's products. Makes 5 writing assignments/year. For greeting cards, accepts both rhymed and unrhymed verse ideas. Other needs for freelance writing include rhymed and unrhymed verse ideas on all products. To contact, send via recognized agent only. Responds only if interested. Material not returned. For greeting cards pay depends on complexity of project. Pays on publication. Buys all rights. Writer's guidelines available for SASE and $2.50—includes sample cards.
Illustration: Works with 3 freelance artists/year. Buys 3-5 designs/illustrations/year. Primary age concentration is 4-8 year old market. Prefers artists with experience in cartooning. Works on assignment only. Buys freelance designs/illustrations mainly for greetings cards and T-shirts. Also uses freelance artists for calligraphy, P-O-P displays, paste-up and mechanicals. Considers pen & ink, watercolor, acrylics and colored pencil. Prefers humorous and "cartoons that will appeal to families. Must be cute, appealing, etc. No religious, sexual implications or off-beat humor." Produces material for all holidays and seasons. Contact only through artist's agent. Some samples are filed; samples not filed are not returned. Responds only if interested. Write for appointment to show portfolio of original/final art, final reproduction/product, slides, tearsheets, color and b&w. Original artwork is

not returned. "Payment depends upon the assignment, amount of work involved, production costs, etc. involved in the project." Pays after all sales are tallied. Buys all rights. For guidelines and sample cards, send $2.50 and #10 SASE.

Tips: Submit 6 months in advance. "Demonstrate an ability to follow directions exactly. Too many submit artwork that has no relationship to what we produce. No phone calls accepted. Follow directions given. Do not ignore them. We do not work with anyone who does not follow them."

☑ **CREATIF LICENSING CORP.**, 31 Old Town Crossing, Mt. Kisco NY 10549. (914)241-6211. E-mail: creatif@usa.net. Website: www.creatifysa.com. **President:** Paul Cohen. Estab. 1975. Gift industry licensing agency. Publishes greeting cards, puzzles, posters, calendars, fabrics, home furnishings, all gifts. 50% of products are made for kids or have kids' themes.

Illustration: Needs freelance illustration for children's greeting cards, all gift and home furnishings. Makes many illustration assignments/month. To contact, send cover letter, résumé, client list, published samples, photocopies, portfolio, promo piece and SASE. Responds in 1 month. Materials returned with SASE; materials filed. For greeting cards, pays royalty and advance. For other artwork, pays royalty and advance. Pays on acceptance or publication. Artists and submission guidelines are available on website. Does not accept images via e-mail.

Tips: Submit seasonal material 8-12 months in advance.

DESIGN DESIGN INC., P.O. Box 2266, Grand Rapids MI 49501. (616)774-2448. Fax: (616)774-4020. President: Don Kallil. Creative Director: Tom Vituj. Estab. 1986. Greeting card company. 5% of products are made for kids or have kids themes.

Writing: Needs freelance writing for children's greeting cards. Prefers both rhymed and unrhymed verse ideas. To contact, send cover letter and writing samples. Materials returned with SASE; materials not filed. For greeting cards, pays flat fee. Buys all rights or exclusive product rights; negotiable. No credit line given. Writer's guidelines for SASE.

Illustration: Needs freelance illustration for children's greeting cards and related products. To contact, send cover letter, published samples, color or b&w photocopies, color or b&w promo pieces or portfolio. Returns materials with SASE. Pays by royalty. Buys all rights or exclusive product rights; negotiable. Artist's guidelines available for SASE. Do not send original art.

Photography: Buys stock and assigns work. Looking for the following subject matter: babies, animals, dog, cats, humorous situations. Uses 4×5 transparencies or high quality 35mm slides. To contact, send cover letter with slides, stock photo list, color copies, published samples and promo piece. Materials returned with SASE; materials not filed. Pays royalties. Buys all rights or exclusive product rights; negotiable. Photographer's guidelines for SASE. Do not send original photography.

Tips: Seasonal material must be submitted 1 year in advance.

☑ **FAX-PAX USA, INC.**, 37 Jerome Ave., Bloomfield CT 06002. (860)242-3333. Fax: (860)242-7102. **Editor:** Stacey L. Savin. Estab. 1990. Buys 1 freelance project/year. Publishes art and history flash cards. Needs include US history, natural history.

Writing/Illustration: Buys all rights. Pays on publication. Cannot return material.

Tips: "We need concise, interesting, well-written 'mini-lessons' on various subjects including U.S. and natural history."

☑ **GALLERY GRAPHICS, INC.**, 2400 S. Hwy. 59, P.O. Box 502, Noel MO 64854-0502. (417)475-6191. Fax: (417)475-6494. E-mail: badgerow@gallerygraphics.com. Website: www.gallerygraphics.com. **Marketing Director**: Mimi Badgerow. Estab. 1979. Greeting card, paper products company. Specializes in products including prints, cards, calendars, stationery, magnets, framed items, books, flue covers and sachets. We market towards all age groups. Publishes reproductions of children's books from the 1800's. 10% of products are made for kids or have kid's themes.

Illustration: Needs freelance illustration for children's greeting cards, other children's products. Makes 8 illustration assignments/year. Prefers children, angels, animals in any medium. Uses color artwork only. To contact, send cover letter, published samples, photocopies (prefer color), promo pieces. Responds in 3 weeks. "We'll return materials at our cost. If artist can send something we can file, that would be ideal. I'll usually make copies." For greeting cards, pays flat fee of $100-700, or royalty of 5-7% for life of card. Pays on sales. Buys exclusive product rights. Credit line sometimes given.

Tips: "We've significantly increased our licensing over the last year. Most of these are set up on a 5% royalty basis. Submit various art subjects."

GREAT AMERICAN PUZZLE FACTORY, INC., 16 S. Main St., S. Norwalk CT 06854. (203)838-4240. Fax: (203)866-9601. E-mail: Frankd@greatamericanpuzzle.com. Website: www.greatamericanpuzzle.com. **Art Director:** Frank DeStefano. Estab. 1976. Produces puzzles. 70% of products are made for kids or have kids' themes.

Illustration: Needs freelance illustration for puzzles. Makes over 20 freelance assignments/year. To contact, send cover letter, color photocopies and color promo pieces (no slides or original art) with SASE. Responds in 1 month. Artists guidelines available for SASE. Rights purchased vary. Buys all rights to puzzles. Pays on publication. Pay varies.

Photography: Needs local cityscapes for regional puzzles. "Photos that we have used have been of wildlife. We do occasionally use city skylines. These are only for custom jobs, though, and must be 4 × 5 or larger format."

Tips: Targets ages 4-12 and adult. "Go to a toy store and look at puzzles. See what is appropriate. No slides. Send color copies (3-4) for style. Looking for whimsical, fantasy and animal themes with a bright, contemporary style. Not too washy or cute. No people, babies, abstracts, landscapes or still life. We often buy reprint rights to existing work. Graphic, children's-book style work is ideal for puzzles." Submit seasonal material 1 year in advance.

INTERCONTINENTAL GREETINGS LTD., 176 Madison Ave., New York NY 10016. (212)683-5830. Fax: (212)779-8564. Art Director: Thea Groene. Estab. 1964. 100% of material freelance written and illustrated. Intended for greeting cards, scholastic products (notebook covers, pencil cases), novelties (gift bags, mugs), tin gift boxes, shower and bedding curtains. 30-40% of products are made for kids or have kids' themes.

Illustration: Needs children's greeting cards, notebook cover, photo albums, gift products. Makes 3 illustration assignments/month. Prefers primarily greeting card subjects, suitable for gift industry. To contact, send cover letter, résumé, client list, published samples, photocopies, slides and promo piece with SASE. Responds in 6 weeks. For greeting cards pays 20% royalty for life. For other artwork pays 20% royalty for life. Pays on publication. Buys exclusive product rights for contract period of 2 years. Credit line sometimes given.

Photography: Needs stylized and interesting still lifes, studio florals, all themed toward the paper and gift industry. Guidelines available for SASE.

Tips: Target group for juvenile cards: ages 1-10. Illustrators: "Use clean colors, not muddy or dark. Send a neat, concise sampling of your work. Include some color examples, a SASE to issue return of your samples if wanted."

INTERNATIONAL PLAYTHINGS, INC., 75D Lackawanna Ave., Parsippany NJ 07054-1712. (973)316-2500. Fax: (973)316-5883. E-mail: lindag@intplay.com. Website: www.intplay.com. Product Manager: Linda Golowko. Estab. 1968. Toy/game company. Distributes and markets children's toys, games and puzzles in specialty toy markets. 100% of products are made for kids or have kids' themes.

Illustration: Needs freelance illustration for children's puzzles and games. Makes 10-20 illustration assignments/year. Prefers fine-quality, original illustration for children's puzzles. Uses color artwork only. To contact, send published samples, slides, portfolio, or color photocopies or promo pieces. Responds in 1 month only if interested. Materials filed. For artwork, pays by the project (range: $500-2,000). Pays on publication. Buys one-time rights, negotiable.

Tips: "Mail correspondence only, please. No phone calls. Send child-themed art, not cartoon-y. Use up-to-date themes and colors."

✔ **JILLSON & ROBERTS GIFT WRAPPINGS,** 3300 W. Castor St., Santa Ana CA 92704-3908. (714)424-0111. Fax: (714)424-0054. Website: www.jillsonroberts.com. Art Director: Josh Neufeld. Estab. 1973. Paper products company. Makes gift wrap/gift bags. 20% of products are made for kids or have kids' themes.

Illustration: Needs freelance illustration for children's gift wrap. Makes 6-12 illustration assignments/year. Wants children/baby/juvenile themes. To contact, send cover letter. Responds in 1 month. Returns material with SASE; materials filed. For wrap and bag designs, pays flat fee (varies). Pays on publication. Rights negotiable. Artist's guidelines for SASE.

Tips: Seasonal material should be submitted up to 3½ months in advance. "We produce two lines of gift wrap per year: one everyday line and one Christmas line. The closing date for everyday is July 1 and Christmas is September 1."

J.T. MURPHY COMPANY, 200 W. Fisher Ave., Philadelphia PA 19120. Greeting card company. Publishes greeting cards. 30% of products are made for kids or have kids' themes.

Writing: To contact, send writing samples. Materials returned with SASE. Pays on acceptance.

Illustration: Needs freelance illustration for children's greeting cards.

✔ **NOVO CARD PUBLISHERS, INC.,** 3630 W. Pratt Ave., Lincolnwood IL 60712. (847)763-0077. Fax: (847)763-0020. E-mail: novo@novocards.com. Website: www.novocard.net. **Contact:** Art Production. Estab. 1926. Greeting card company. Company publishes greeting cards, note/invitation packs and gift envelopes for middle market. Publishes greeting cards (Novo Card/Cloud-9). 20% of products are made for kids or have kids' themes.

Writing: Needs freelance writing for children's greeting cards. Makes 400 writing assignments/year. Other needs for freelance writing include invitation notes. To contact send writing samples. To query with specific ideas, write to request disclosure form first. Responds in approximately 1 month only if interested. Materials returned only with SASE. For greeting cards, pays flat fee of $2/line. Pays on acceptance. Buys all rights.No royalties. Credit line sometimes given. Writer's guidelines available for SASE.

Illustration: Needs freelance illustration for children's greeting cards. Makes 1,000 illustration assignments/year. Prefers just about all types: traditional, humor, contemporary, etc. To contact, send published samples, slides and color photocopies. To query with specific ideas write to request disclosure form first. Responds in approximately 1 month if interested. Materials returned with SASE. For greeting cards, pay negotiable. Pays on acceptance. Buys all greeting card and stationary rights. Credit line sometimes given. Artist's guidelines available for SASE.

Photography: Buys stock and assigns work. Buys more than 100 stock images/year. Wants all types. Uses color and b&w prints; 35mm transparencies. To contact, send slides, stock photo list, published samples, paper copies acceptable. Responds in approximately 1 month. Materials returned with SASE. Pays negotiable rate. Pays on acceptance. Buys all greeting card and stationary rights. Credit line sometimes given. Guidelines for SASE.

Tips: Submit seasonal material 10-12 months in advance. "Novo has extensive lines of greeting cards: everyday, seasonal (all) and alternative lives (over 24 separate lines of note card packs and gift enclosures). Our lines encompass all types of styles and images."

NRN DESIGNS, 5142 Argosy Ave., Long Beach CA 92649. (714)898-6363. Fax: (714)898-0015. Website: nrndesigns.com. Art Director: Linda Braun. Estab. 1984. Paper products company. Publishes imprintables. 25% of products are made for kids or have kid's themes.

Illustration: Needs freelance illustration for children's imprintables. Uses color artwork only. To contact, send published samples. Materials filed.

Tips: Submit seasonal material anytime.

P.S. GREETINGS/FANTUS PAPER PRODUCTS, 5730 North Tripp Ave., Chicago IL 60646. (773)267-6069 or (800)334-2141. Fax: (773)267-6055. Website: www.psg-fpp.com. **Art Director:** Jennifer Dodson. Estab. 1950. Greeting card company. Publishes boxed and individual counter greeting cards. Seasons include: Christmas, every major holiday and everyday. 30% of products are made for kids or have kid's themes. No phone calls please.

Writing: Needs freelance writing for children's greeting cards. Makes 10-20 writing assignments/year. To contact, send writing samples. Responds in 1 month. Material returned only if accompanied with SASE. For greeting cards, pays flat fee/line. Pays on acceptance. Buys greeting card rights. Credit line given. Writer's guidelines free with SASE.

Illustration: Needs freelance illustration for children's greeting cards. Makes about 10-20 illustration assignments/year. Open to all mediums, all themes. To contact, send published samples, color promo pieces and color photocopies only. Responds in 1 month. Returns materials with SASE. Pays flat fee upon acceptance. Buys greeting card rights. Credit line given. Artist's guidelines free with SASE.

Photography: Buys photography from freelancers. Buys and assigns work. Buys 5-10 stock images/year. Makes 5-10 assignments/year. Wants florals, animals, seasonal (Christmas, Easter, valentines, etc.). Uses 35mm transparencies. To contact, send slides. Responds in 6 weeks. Materials returned with SASE; materials filed. Pays flat fee upon acceptance. Buys greeting card rights. Credit line given. Photographer's guidelines free with SASE.

Tips: Seasonal material should be submitted 8 months in advance.

N PANDA INK, P.O. Box 5129, West Hills CA 91308-5129. (818)340-8061. Fax: (818)883-6193. **Owner, Art/Creative Director:** Ruth Ann Epstein. Estab. 1981. Greeting card company and producer of clocks, magnets, bookmarks. Produces Judaica—whimsical, metaphysical, general, everyday. Publishes greeting cards. 15% of products are made for kids or have kids' themes.

Writing: Needs freelance writing for children's greeting cards. Makes 1-2 writing assignments/year. For greeting cards, accepts both rhymed and unrhymed verse ideas. Looks for greeting card writing which is Judaica or metaphysical. To contact, send cover letter and SASE. To query with specific ideas, write to request disclosure form first. Responds in 1 month. Materials returned with SASE; materials filed. For greeting cards, pays flat fee of $3-20. Pays on acceptance. Rights negotiable. Credit line sometimes given.

Illustration: Needs freelance illustration for children's greeting cards, magnets, bookmarks. Makes 1 illustration assignment/year. Needs Judaica (Hebrew wording), metaphysical themes. Uses color artwork only. To contact, send cover letter. Query with specific ideas. Responds in 2 months. Materials returned with SASE; materials filed. Payment is negotiable. Pays on acceptance. Rights negotiable. Credit line sometimes given.

Tips: Submit seasonal material 1 year in advance. "Always send SASE."

N PEACEABLE KINGDOM PRESS, 950 Gilman, Suite 200, Berkeley CA 94710. (510)588-2051. Fax: (510)558-2052. E-mail: pkp@pkpress.com. Website: www.pkpress.com. **Editor, Creative Development:** Helen Ring. **Creative Director:** Suellen Ehnebuske. Estab. 1983. Produces posters, greeting cards, bookmarks and related products. Uses children's book illustrators exclusively, but not necessarily targeted only to children. 98% of products are made for kids or have kids' themes.

Writing: Needs freelance writing for children's greeting cards. Makes approximately 300 writing assignments/year. To contact, send cover letter, client list, writing samples. Responds in 6-8 weeks. Materials not returned; materials filed. For greeting cards, pays a flat fee of $50.

Illustration: Needs freelance illustration for children's greeting cards and posters. Makes 50 illustration assignments/year. "For specific occasions—Christmas, Valentine's Day, Mother's and Father's Days, etc., we look for

visually sophisticated work with a narrative element." To contact, send cover letter, slides, promo pieces, published books or f&g's. and color photocopies. To query with specific ideas, submit 5×7 of same dimensions enlarged, vertical, plus ⅛, if full bleed color. Materials returned with SASE; materials not filed. Contact Helen Ring. Responds in 2 months. Pays on publication with advance and royalties. Buys first rights and reprint rights; negotiable for greeting cards. Buys rights to distribution worldwide. Artist's guidelines available for SASE.
Tips: "We only choose from illustrations that are from published children's book illustrators, or commissioned art by established children's book illustrators. Submit seasonal and everyday greeting cards one year in advance."

PLUM GRAPHICS INC., P.O. Box 136, Prince St. Station, New York NY 10012. (212)337-0999. Fax: (212)633-9910. E-mail: plumgraphi@aol.com. **Owner:** Yvette Cohen. Estab. 1983. Greeting card company. Produces die-cut greeting cards for ages 5-105. Publishes greeting cards, message boards and journals.
Writing: Needs freelance writing for greeting cards. Makes 2 writing assignments/year. Looks for "greeting card writing which is fun." To contact, send SASE for guidelines. Contact: Michelle Reynoso. Responds in 3 months. Materials returned with SASE; materials filed. For greeting cards, pays flat fee of $40. Pays on publication. Buys all rights. Writer's guidelines available for SASE.
Illustration: Needs freelance illustration for greeting cards. Makes 10 freelance illustration assignments/year. Prefers very tight artwork that is fun and realistic. Uses color artwork only. To contact, send b&w photocopies. Contact: Yvette Cohen. Responds only if interested. Materials returned with SASE; materials filed. For greeting cards, pays flat fee of $350-450 "plus $50 each time we reprint." Pays on publication. Buys exclusive product rights. Credit line given.
Tips: "Go to a store and look at our cards and style before submitting work."

☑ **RESOURCE GAMES,** P.O. Box 151, Redmond WA 98052. (425)883-3143. Fax: (425)883-3136. Website: www.resourcegames.com. Owner: John Jaquet. Estab. 1987. Educational game manufacturer. Resource Games manufactures a line of high-quality geography theme board and card games for ages 6 and up. Publishes games. 100% of products made for kids or have kids' themes.
Tips: "We are always on the lookout for innovative educational games for the classroom and the home. If accepted, we enter into royalty agreements ranging from 5-10%."

☑ **SHULSINGER JUDAICA, LTD.,** (formerly Shulsinger Sales, Inc.), 799 Hinsdale St., Brooklyn NY 11207. (718)345-3300. Fax: (718)345-1540. **Merchandiser:** Raizy Lasker. Estab. 1979. Greeting card, novelties and paper products company. "We are a Judaica company, distributing products such as greeting cards, books, paperware, puzzles, games, novelty items—all with a Jewish theme." Publishes greeting cards, novelties, coloring books, children's books, giftwrap, tableware and puzzles. 60% of products are made for kids or have kids' themes to party stories, temples, bookstores, supermarkets and chain stores.
Writing: Looks for greeting card writing which can be sent by children to adults and sent by adults to children (of all ages). Makes 10-20 freelance writing assignments/year. To contact, send cover letter. To query with specific ideas, write to request disclosure form first. Responds in 2 weeks. Materials returned with SASE; materials filed. For greeting cards, pays flat fee (this includes artwork). Pays on acceptance. Buys exclusive product rights.
Illustration: Needs freelance illustration for children's greeting cards, books, novelties, games. Makes 10-20 illustration assignments/year. "The only requirement is a Jewish theme." To contact, send cover letter and photocopies, color if possible. To query with specific ideas, write to request disclosure form first. Responds in 2 weeks. Returns materials with SASE; materials filed. For children's greeting cards, pays flat fee (this includes writing). For other artwork, pays by the project. Pays on acceptance. Buys exclusive product rights. Credit line sometimes given. Artist's guidelines not available.
Tips: Seasonal material should be submitted 6 months in advance. "An artist may submit an idea for any item that is related to our product line. Generally, there is an initial submission of a portfolio of the artist's work, which will be returned at the artist's expense. If the art is appropriate to our specialized subject matter, then further discussion will ensue regarding particular subject matter. We request a sampling of at least 10 pieces of work, in the form of tearsheets, or printed samples, or high quality color copies that can be reviewed and then kept on file if accepted. If art is accepted and published, then original art will be returned to artist. Shulsinger Judaica, Ltd. maintains the right to re-publish a product for a mutually agreed upon time period. We pay an agreed upon fee per project."

☑ **STANDARD PUBLISHING,** 8121 Hamilton Ave., Cincinnati OH 45231. (513)931-4050. Fax: (513)931-0950. E-mail: tneunschwander@standardpub.com. Website: www.standardpub.com. **Directors:** Diane Stortz (children's series) and Ruth Frederick (children's resources). **Art Directors:** Coleen Davis and Rob Glover. Estab. 1866. Publishes children's books and teacher helps for the religious market. 75% of products are made for kids or have kids' themes.
• Standard also has a listing in Book Publishers.
Writing: Considers Christian puzzle books, activity books and games. Responds in 3 months. Payment method varies. Credit line given.
Illustration: Needs freelance illustration for puzzle, activity books, teacher guides. Makes 6-10 illustration assignments/year. To contact, send cover letter and photocopies. Responds in 3 months if interested. Payment method varies. Credit line given.

Photography: Buys a limited amount of photos from freelancers. Wants mature, scenic and Christian themes. **Tips** "Many of our projects are developed in-house and assigned. Study our catalog and products; visit Christian bookstores. We are currently looking for Bible-based word puzzles and activities."

■ **TALICOR, INC.**, 14175 Telephone Ave., Suite A, Chino CA 91710. (909)517-1962. Fax: (909)517-1962. E-mail: webmaster@talicor.com. Website: www.talicor.com. **President:** Lew Herndon. Estab. 1971. Game and puzzle manufacturer. Publishes games and puzzles (adults' and children's). 70% of products are made for kids or have kids' themes.

Writing: Makes 1 writing assignment/month.

Illustration: Needs freelance illustration for games and puzzles. Makes 12 illustration assignments/year. To contact, send promo piece. Responds in 6 months. Materials returned with SASE; materials filed. For artwork, pays by the hour, by the project or negotiable royalty. Pays on acceptance. Buys negotiable rights.

Photography: Buys stock and assigns work. Buys 6 stock images/year. Wants photos with wholesome family subjects. Makes 6 assignments/year. Uses 4×5 transparencies. To contact, send color promo piece. Responds only if interested. Materials returned with SASE; materials filed. Pays per photo, by the hour, by the day or by the project (negotiable rates). Pays on acceptance. Buys negotiable rights.

Tips: Submit seasonal material 6 months in advance.

Play Publishers & Producers

Writing plays for children and family audiences is a special challenge. Whether creating an original work or adapting a classic, plays for children must hold the attention of audiences that often include children and adults. Using rhythm, repetition and dramatic action are effective ways of holding the attention of kids. Pick subjects children can relate to, and never talk down to them.

Theater companies often have limited budgets so plays with elaborate staging and costumes often can't be produced. Touring companies want simple sets that can be moved easily. Keep in mind that they may have as few as three actors, so roles may have to be doubled up.

Many of the companies listed here produce plays with roles for adults and children, so check the percentage of plays written for adult and children's roles. Most importantly, study the types of plays a theater wants and doesn't want. Many name plays they've recently published or produced, and some have additional guidelines or information available. For more listings of theaters open to submissions of children's and adult material and information on contests and organizations for playwrights, consult *Dramatists Sourcebook* (Theatre Communications Group, Inc.).

Information on play publishers listed in the previous edition but not included in this edition of *Children's Writer's & Illustrator's Market* may be found in the General Index.

■ **A.D. PLAYERS**, 2710 W. Alabama, Houston TX 77098. (713)526-2721. Fax: (713)522-5475. E-mail: adplayer@hearn.org. Website: www.adplayers.org. Estab. 1967. Produces 4-5 children's plays/year in new Children's Theatre Series; 5 musicals/year. Produces children's plays for professional productions.
- A.D. Players has received the Dove family approval stamp; an award from the Columbia International Film & Video Festival; and a Silver Angel Award.

Needs: 99-100% of plays/musicals written for adult roles; 0-1% for juvenile roles. "Cast must utilize no more than five actors. Need minimal, portable sets for proscenium or arena stage with no fly space and no wing space." Does not want to see large cast or set requirements or New Age themes. Recently produced plays: *Samson: The Hair Off His Head*, by William Shryoch (courage and obedience for preK-grade 6); *The Wizard of Oz*, by Danny Siebert (new adaptation for preK-grade 6).

How to Contact: Send script with SASE. No tapes or pictures. Will consider simultaneous submissions and previously performed work. Responds in 9 months.

Terms: Buys some residual rights. Pay negotiated. Submissions returned with SASE.

Tips: "Children's musicals tend to be large in casting requirements. For those theaters with smaller production capabilities, this can be a liability for a script. Try to keep it small and simple, especially if writing for theaters where adults are performing for children. We are interested in material that reflects family values, emphasizes the importance of responsibility in making choices, encourages faith in God and projects the joy and fun of telling a story."

ALABAMA SHAKESPEARE FESTIVAL, #1 Festival Dr., Montgomery AL 36117. (334)271-5300. Fax: (334)271-5348. E-mail: asf@asf.net. Website: www.asf.net. **Artistic Director:** Kent Thompson. Estab. 1972. Produces 1 children's play/year.

Needs: Produces children's plays for professional LORT (League of Regional Theaters) theatre. 90% of plays/musicals written for adult roles; 10% for juvenile roles. Must have moderate sized casts (2-10 characters); have two stages (750 seat house/250 seat house). Interested in works for the Southern Writers' Project (contact ASF for information). Does not want to see plays exclusively for child actors. Recently produced plays: *Wiley and the Hairy Man*, by Susan Zeder (southern folk tale for elementary ages); *Androcles and the Lion*, by Aurand Harris (folktale for elementary ages).

How to Contact: Plays: Query first with synopsis, character breakdown and set description; scripts which meet/address the focus of the Southern Writers' Project. Musicals: Query with synopsis, character breakdown and set description; scripts which meet/address the focus of the Southern Writers' Project. Will consider simultaneous submissions and previously performed work. Responds in 1 year. Send submissions to Literary Manager.

Terms: Submissions returned with SASE.

Tips: "Created in 1991 by Artistic Director Kent Thompson, the Alabama Shakespeare Festival's Southern Writers' Project is an exploration and celebration of its rich Southern cultural heritage. In an attempt to reach this goal the project seeks: to provide for the growth of a 'new' voice for Southern writers and artists; to encourage new works dealing with Southern issues and topics including those that emphasize African American experiences; to create theatre that speaks in a special way to ASF's unique and racially diverse audiences. In this way the Southern Writers' Project strives to become a window to the complexities and beauty found in this celebrated region of our country, the South."

AMERICAN STAGE, P.O. Box 1560, St. Petersburg FL 33731. (727)823-1600. Website: www.americanstage.o rg. **Artistic Director:** Ken Mitchell. **Managing Director:** Lee Manwaring Lowry. Estab. 1977. Produces 3 children's plays/year. Produces children's plays for professional children's theater program, mainstage, school tour, performing arts halls.

Needs: Limited by budget and performance venue. Subject matter: classics and original work for children (ages K-12) and families. Recently produced plays: *Schoolhouse Rock Live!*, by Lynn Ahrens and Bob Borough (5-adult); *The Gifts of the Magi*, by Mark St. Germain and Randy Courts (6-adults). Does not want to see plays that look down on children. Approach must be that of the child or fictional beings or animals.

How to Contact: Query with synopsis, character breakdown and set description. Will consider simultaneous submissions and previously performed work.

Terms: Purchases "professional rights." Pays writers in royalties (6-8%); $25-35/performance. SASE for return of submission.

Tips: Sees a move in plays toward basic human values, relationships and multicultural communities.

ANCHORAGE PRESS, INC., P.O. Box 2901, Louisville KY 40201-2901. (502)583-2288. Fax: (502)583-2281. E-mail: applays@bellsouth.net. Website: www.applays.com. **Publisher:** Merilee Miller. Estab. 1935. Publishes 6-8 children's plays/year; 2-3 children's musicals/year.

Needs: "There is no genre, subject of preferred interest. We want plays of high literary/theatrical quality. Like music, such material—by nature of the stage—will appeal to any age capable of following a story. Obviously some appeal more to primary ages, some secondary." Does not want send-ups—cutesies—jargon-laden—pendantic/subject specific. "Plays—like ice cream—work only if they are superb. Teaching is not the purpose of theatre—entertainment is, and that may include serious subjects fascinatingly explored." Recently produced plays: *The Orphan Train*, by Aurand Harris (play about lives of 10 children who rode "orphan" trains of 1914, for ages 7-18); *Tokoloshe*, by Pieter Scholtz (Zulu tale of a water-sprite and a modern little Zulu girl seeking her father, for ages 5-9).

How to Contact: Query for guidelines first. Will consider simultaneous submissions and previously performed work "essential to be proven." Reports 1-2 months.

Terms: Buys all stage rights. Pays royalty (varies extensively from 50% minimum to 80%). Submissions returned with SASE.

Tips: "Obtain guidelines, have proof of three distinct productions and get a catalog first. SASE essential."

APPLE TREE THEATRE, 595 Elm Place, Suite 210, Highland Park IL 60035. (847)432-8223. Fax: (847)432-5214. Produces 3 children's plays/year.

Needs: Produces professional, daytime and educational outreach programs for grades 4-9. 98% of plays written for adult roles; 2% for juvenile roles. Uses a unit set and limited to 9 actors. No musicals. Straight plays only. Does not want to see: "children's theater," i.e. . . . Peter Rabbit, Snow White. Material *must* be based in social issues. Recently produced plays: *Devil's Arithmetic*, adapted from the novel by Jane Yolen (about the Holocaust, ages 10-up); *Roll of Thunder, Hear My Cry*, adapted from the novel by Mildred Taylor (about Civil rights, racial discrimination in Mississippi in 1930s, ages 10-up).

How to Contact: Query first. Query with synopsis, character breakdown and set description. Will consider simultaneous submissions and previously performed work. Responds in 2 months.

Terms: Pay negotiated per contract. Submissions returned with SASE.

Tips: "Never send an unsolicited manuscript. Include reply postcard for queries."

BAKER'S PLAYS, P.O. Box 699222, Quincy MA 02269-9222. (617)745-0805. Fax: (617)745-9891. E-mail: info@bakersplays.com. Website: www.bakersplays.com. **Associate Editor:** Kurt Gombar. Estab. 1845. Publishes 20 plays/year; 2 musicals/year.

Needs: Adaptations of both popular and lesser known folktales. Subject matter: full lengths for family audience and full lengths and one act plays for teens." Recently published plays: *An Incredible Journey to Chauyan*, by Zanne Hall; *More Aesop's (oh so slightly) Updated Fables*, by Kim Esop-Wylie.

How to Contact: Submit complete ms, score and tape of songs. Responds in 6-8 months.

Terms: Obtains worldwide rights. Pays writers in production royalties (amount varies) and book royalties.

Tips: "Know the audience you're writing for before you submit your play anywhere. 90% of the plays we reject are not written for our market. When writing for children, never be afraid to experiment with language, characters or story. They are fertile soil for fresh, new ideas."

BARTER THEATRE EDUCATION WING, P.O. Box 867, Abingdon VA 24212. (540)628-2281, ext. 318. Fax: (540)619-3335. E-mail: education@bartertheatre.com. Website: www.bartertheatre.com. **Artistic Director:** Richard Rose. Education Director: Jeremy Baker. Estab. 1933. Produces 2-4 children's plays and 1 children's musical/year.

Needs: "We produce 'By Kids for Kids' productions as well as professional and semi-professional children's productions. 5-10% of plays/musicals written for adult roles; 90% written for juvenile roles. Recently produced plays: *Sleeping Beauty* (fairytale for all ages); and *Winnie the Pooh* (classic for all ages).

How to Contact: Query with synopsis, character breakdown and set description. Will consider simultaneous submissions and previously performed work. Reports back only if interested.

Terms: Pays for performance ($20-60). Submissions returned with SASE.

Tips: "Find creative, interesting material for children K-12. Don't talk below the audience."

☑ **BILINGUAL FOUNDATION OF THE ARTS**, 421 N. Avenue 19th, Los Angeles CA 90031. (323)225-4044. Fax: (323)225-1250. E-mail: bfateatro@aol.com. Website: www.bfateatro.org. Artistic Director: Margarita Galban. **Contact:** Agustín Coppola, dramaturg. Estab. 1973. Produces 6 children's plays/year; 4 children's musicals/year.

Needs: Produces children's plays for professional productions. 60% of plays/musicals written for adult roles; 40% for juvenile roles. No larger than 8 member cast. Recently produced plays: *Second Chance*, by A. Cardona and A. Weinstein (play about hopes and fears in every teenager for teenagers); *Choices*, by Gannon Daniels (violence prevention, teens); *Fool 4 Kool*, by Leane Schirmer and Guillermo Reyes.

How to Contact: Plays: Query with synopsis, character breakdown and set description and submit complete ms. Musicals: Query with synopsis, character breakdown and set description and submit complete ms with score. Will consider simultaneous submissions and previously performed work. Responds in 6 months.

Terms: Pays royalty; per performance; buys material outright; "different with each play."

Tips: "The plays should reflect the Hispanic experience in the U.S."

BIRMINGHAM CHILDREN'S THEATRE, P.O. Box 1362, Birmingham AL 35201-1362. (205)458-8181. Fax: (205)458-8895. E-mail: bertb@bct123.org. Website: www.bct123.org. **Managing Director:** Bert Brosowsky. Estab. 1947. Produces 8-10 children's plays/year; some children's musicals/year.

Needs: "BCT is an adult professional theater performing for youth and family audiences September-May." 99% of plays/musicals written for adult roles; 1% for juvenile roles. "Our 'Wee Folks' Series is limited to 4-5 cast members and should be written with preschool-grade 1 in mind. We prefer interactive plays for this age group. We commission plays for our 'Wee Folks' Series (preschool-grade 1), our Children's Series (K-6) and our Young Adult Series (6-12)." Recently produced plays: *To Kill a Mockingbird*, dramatized by Christopher Sergel (YA series); *Young King Arthur*, by Michael Price Nelson (children's series); *Three Billy Goats Gruff*, by Jean Pierce (Wee Folks' Series). No adult language. Will consider musicals, interactive theater for Wee Folks Series. Prefer children's series and young adult series limited to 4-7 cast members.

How to Contact: Query first, query with synopsis, character breakdown and set description. Responds in 4 months.

Terms: Buys negotiable rights. Submissions returned with SASE.

Tips: "We would like our commissioned scripts to teach as well as entertain. Keep in mind the age groups (defined by each series) that our audience is composed of. Send submissions to the attention of Bert Brosowsky, managing director."

CALIFORNIA THEATRE CENTER, P.O. Box 2007, Sunnyvale CA 94087. (408)245-2979. Fax: (408)245-0235. E-mail: ctc@ctcinc.org. Website: www.ctcinc.org. **General Director:** Gayle Cornelison. Estab. 1975. Produces 15 children's plays and 1 musical for professional productions.

Needs: 75% of plays/musicals written for adult roles; 20% for juvenile roles. Prefers material suitable for professional tours and repertory performance; one-hour time limit, limited technical facilities. Recently produced *Most Valuable Player*, by Mary Hall Surface (U.S. history for grades 3 and up); *Sleeping Beauty*, by Gayle Cornelison (fairy tale for ages K-5).

How to Contact: Query with synopsis, character breakdown and set description. Send to: Will Huddleston. Will consider previously performed work. Responds in 6 months.

Terms: Rights negotiable. Pays writers royalties; pays $35-50/performance. Submissions returned with SASE.

Tips: "We sell to schools, so the title and material must appeal to teachers who look for things familiar to them. We look for good themes, universality. Avoid the cute. We also do a summer conservatory that requires large cast plays."

CHILDREN'S STORY SCRIPTS, Baymax Productions, PMB 130, 2219 W. Olive Ave., Burbank CA 91506-2648. (818)787-5584. E-mail: baymax@earthlink.net. **Editor:** Deedra Bebout. Estab. 1990. Produces 1-10 children's scripts/year.

Needs: "Except for small movements and occasionally standing up, children remain seated in Readers Theatre fashion." Publishes scripts sold primarily to schools or wherever there's a program to teach or entertain children. "All roles read by children except K-2 scripts, where kids have easy lines, leader helps read the narration. Prefer multiple cast members, no props or sets." Subject matter: scripts on all subjects that dovetail with classroom subjects. Targeted age range—K-8th grade, 5-13 years old. Recently published plays: *A Clever Fox*, by Mary Ellen Holmes (about using one's wits, grades 2-4); *Memories of the Pony Express*, by Sharon Gill Askelson (grades 5-8). No stories that preach a point, no stories about catastrophic disease or other terribly heavy topics, no theatrical scripts without narrative prose to move the story along, no monologues or 1-character stories.

How to Contact: Submit complete ms. Will consider simultaneous submissions and previously performed work (if rights are available). Responds in 2 weeks.

Terms: Purchases all rights; authors retain copyrights. "We add support material and copyright the whole package." Pays writers in royalties (10-15% on sliding scale, based on number of copies sold). SASE for reply and return of submission.

Tips: "We're only looking for stories related to classroom studies—educational topics with a freshness to them. Our scripts mix prose narration with character dialogue—we do not publish traditional, all-dialogue plays." Writer's guidelines packet available for business-sized SASE with 2 first-class stamps. Guidelines explain what Children's Story Scripts are, give 4-page examples from 2 different scripts, give list of suggested topics for scripts.

CIRCA '21 DINNER THEATRE, P.O. Box 3784, Rock Island IL 61204-3784. (309)786-2667. Fax: (309)786-4119. Website: circa21.com. **Producer:** Dennis Hitchcock. Estab. 1977. Produces 3 children's musicals/year.

Needs: Produces children's plays for professional productions. 95% of musicals written for adult roles; 5% written for juvenile roles. "Prefer a cast of four to eight—no larger than ten. Plays are produced on mainstage sets." Recently produced plays: *Winnie the Pooh*, by Bill Theisen (ages 4-10), *The Christmas Wish*, by John Fogerty (ages 4-16).

How to Contact: Send complete script with audiotape of music. Responds in 3 months.

Terms: Payment negotiable.

I.E. CLARK PUBLICATIONS, P.O. Box 246, Schulenburg TX 78956-0246. (979)743-3232. Fax: (979)743-4765. E-mail: ieclark@cvtv.net. **General Manager:** Donna Cozzaglio. Estab. 1956. Publishes 3 or more children's plays/year; 1 or 2 children's musicals/year.

Needs: Publishes plays for all ages. Published plays: *Little Women*, by Thomas Hischak (dramatization of the Alcott novel for family audiences); *Heidi*, by Ann Pugh, music by Betty Utter (revision of our popular musical dramatization of the Johanna Spyri novel). Does not want to see plays that have not been produced.

How to Contact: Submit complete ms and audio or video tape. Will consider simultaneous submissions and previously performed work. Responds in 4 months.

Terms: Pays writers in negotiable royalties. SASE for return of submission.

Tips: "We publish only high-quality literary works. Request a copy of our writer's guidelines before submitting. Please send only one manuscript at a time and be sure to include videos and audiotapes."

COLUMBIA ENTERTAINMENT COMPANY, % Betsy Phillips, 309 Parkade, Columbia MO 65202-1447. (573)874-5628. **Content Director:** Betsy Phillips. Estab. 1988. Produces 0-2 children's plays/year; 0-1 children's musicals/year.

Needs: "We produce children's theatre plays. Our theatre school students act all the roles. We cast adult and children roles with children from theatre school. Each season we have 5 plays done by adults (kid parts possible)—3 theatre school productions. We need large cast plays-20+, as plays are produced by theater school classes (ages 12-14). Any set changes are completed by students in the play." Musical needs: Musicals must have songs written in ranges children can sing. Recently produced: *Musical! The Bard is Back*, by Stephen Murray.

How to Contact: Plays: Submit complete ms; use SASE to get form. Musicals: Submit complete ms and score; tape of music must be included, use SASE to get entry form. Will consider simultaneous submissions and previously performed work. Responds in 2-6 months. All scripts are read by a minimum of 3 readers. The authors will receive a written evaluation of the strengths and weaknesses of the play.

Terms: Buys production (sans royalties) rights on mss. "We have production rights sans royalties for one production. Production rights remain with author." Pays $250 1st prize. Submissions returned with SASE.

Tips: "Please write a play/musical that appeals to all ages. We always need lots of parts, especially for girls."

☑ **CONNECTICUT STRATFORD SHAKESPEARE FESTIVAL THEATRE**, 1850 Elm St., Stratford CT 06615. (203)378-1200. Fax: (203)385-5018. E-mail: joeywish@hotmail.com or /dpict@aol.com. Website: www.stratfordfesct.com. **Artistic Director:** Louis S. Burke. Re-estab. 2000. Planning to produce 2-3 children's plays/year; at least 1 children's musical/year.

Needs: Produces children's plays for professional productions. 80% of plays/musicals written for adult roles; 20% for juvenile roles. Musical needs: Prefers musicals with name recognition—classic stories, or well-known modern children's tales.

How to Contact: Plays: Query with synopsis, character breakdown and set description; and a few pages to assess the writing (dialog sample). Musicals: Query with synopsis, character breakdosn and set description; some dialog pages and a sample of at least 2 songs on cassette or CD. Will consider simultaneous submissions, electronic submissions via disk/modem, previously performed work. Responds in 6-8 weeks.

Terms: Rights negotiable Lort B contract.

CONTEMPORARY DRAMA SERVICE, Division of Meriwether Publishing Ltd., 885 Elkton Dr., Colorado Springs CO 80907-3557. (719)594-4422. Fax: (719)594-9916. E-mail: merpcds@aol.com. Website: www.meriwe therpublishing.com. **Executive Editor:** Arthur L. Zapel. Estab. 1979. Publishes 60 children's plays/year; 15 children's musicals/year.
Needs: Prefer shows with a large cast. 50% of plays/musicals written for adult roles; 50% for juvenile roles. Recently published plays: *Is There A Doctor in the House*, by Tim Kelly (a musical); *Princess*, by Judy Wickland (a fairy tale spoof); *'Twas the Night Before*, by Rachel Olson (a Christmas musical for children). "We publish church plays for elementary level for Christmas and Easter. Most of our secular plays are for teens or college level." Does not want to see "full-length, three-act plays unless they are adaptations of classic works or have unique comedy appeal."
How to Contact: Query with synopsis, character breakdown and set description; "query first if a musical." Will consider simultaneous submissions or previously performed work. Responds in 1 month.
Terms: Purchases first rights. Pays writers royalty (10%) or buys material outright for $200-1,000. SASE for return of submission.
Tips: "If the writer is submitting a musical play, an audiocassette of the music should be sent. We prefer plays with humorous action. We like comedies, spoofs, satires and parodies of known works. A writer should provide credentials of plays published and produced. Writers should not submit items for the elementary age level."

DALLAS CHILDREN'S THEATER, 2215 Cedar Springs, Dallas TX 75201. Website: www.dct.org. **Artistic Director:** Robyn Flatt. Estab. 1984. Produces 10 children's plays/year.
Needs: Produces children's plays for professional theater. 80% of plays/musicals written for adult roles; 20% for juvenile roles. Prefer cast size between 8-12. Musical needs: "We do produce musical works, but prefer non-musical. Availability of music tracks is a plus." Does not want to see: anything not appropriate for a youth/family audience. Recently produced plays: *Bless Cricket, Crest Toothpaste, and Tommy Tune*, by Linda Daugherty (explores a young girl's relationship with her older brother who has Down Syndrome); *Island of the Blue Dolphins*, by Burgess Clark based on book by Scott O'Dell (survival story of a young Indian girl living alone for 18 years on a deserted island. Based on popular youth novel.)
How to Contact: Plays: Query with synopsis, character breakdown and set description. Musicals: Query with synopsis, character breakdown and set description. Will consider previously performed work. Responds only if interested.
Terms: Rights are negotiable. Pay is negotiable. Submissions returned with SASE. All scripts should be sent to the attention of Artie Olaisen.
Tips: "We are most interested in substantive works for a student/youth/family audience. Material which enlightens aspects of the global community, diverse customs and perspectives, adaptations of classical and popular literature, myth, and folk tale. Topics which focus on the contemporary concerns of youth, families, and our diverse communities are also of great interest. Full-length works are preferred rather than one-acts or classroom pieces."

DRAMATIC PUBLISHING, INC., 311 Washington St., Woodstock IL 60098. (815)338-7170. Fax: (815)338-8981. E-mail: plays@dramaticpublishing.com. Website: www.dramaticpublishing.com. **Acquisitions Editor:** Linda Habjan. Estab. 1885. Publishes 10-15 children's plays/year; 4-6 children's musicals.
Needs: Recently published: *The Cay*, by Dr. Gayle Cornelison and Robert Taylor; *The Dream Thief*, by Robert Schenkkan (fantasy classic by Pulitzer-prize-winning author); and *Alexander and the Terrible, Horrible, No Good, Very Bad Day*, book lyrics by Judith Viorst and Shelly Markham (for family audiences); *Anastasia Krupnik*, by Meryl Friedman, based on the book by Lois Lowry.
How to Contact: Submit complete ms/score and cassette/video tape (if a musical); include SASE if materials are to be returned. Responds in 6 months. Pays writers in royalties.
Tips: "Scripts should be from ½ to 1½ hours long and not didactic or condescending. Original plays dealing with hopes, joys and fears of today's children are preferred to adaptations of old classics. No more adapted fairytales."

☑ DRAMATICS MAGAZINE, 2343 Auburn Ave., Cincinnati OH 45219-2815. (513)421-3900. Fax: (513)421-7077. Website: www.edta.org. **Associate Editor:** Laura C. Kelley. Estab. 1929. Publishes 6 young adult plays/year.
Needs: Most of plays written for high school actors. 14-18 years old (grades 9-12) appropriate for high school production and study.
How to Contact: Plays: Submit complete ms. Musicals: Not accepted. Will consider simultaneous submissions, electronic submissions via disk/modem, previously performed work. Responds in 3-6 months.

VISIT THE WRITER'S DIGEST WEBSITE at www.writersdigest.com for hot new markets, daily market updates, writers' guidelines and much more.

Terms: Buys one-time publication rights. Payment varies. Submissions returned with SASE.
Tips: Consider our readers, who are savvy high school theater students and teachers.

EARLY STAGES CHILDREN'S THEATRE @ STAGES REPERTORY THEATRE, 3201 Allen Parkway, Suite 101, Houston TX 77019. (713)527-0220. Fax: (713)527-8669. E-mail: chesleyk@stagestheatre.com. Website: www.stagestheatre.com. **Artistic Director:** Chesley Krohn. Early Stages Director: Chesley Krohn. Estab. 1978. Produces 5 children's plays/year; 1-2 children's musicals/year.
Needs: In-house professional children's theatre. 100% of plays/musicals written for adult roles. Cast size must be 8 or less. Performances are in 2 theaters—Arena has 230 seats; Thrust has 180 seats. Musical needs: Shows that can be recorded for performance; no live musicians. Recently produced plays: *Cinderella*, by Sidney Berger, music by Rob Landes, *The Courage of Mandy Kate Brown*, by Kate Pogue (a tale of the Underground Railroad).
How to Contact: Plays/musicals: Query with synopsis, character breakdown and set description. Will consider simultaneous submissions and previously performed work. Responds only if interested.
Terms: Mss optioned exclusively. Pays 3-8% royalties. Submissions returned with SASE.
Tips: "Select pieces that are intelligent, as well as entertaining, and that speak to a child's potential for understanding. We are interested in plays/musicals that are imaginative and open to full theatrical production."

EL CENTRO SU TEATRO, 4725 High, Denver CO 80216. (303)296-0219. Fax: (303)296-4614. E-mail: elcentro@suteatro.org. Website: www.suteatro.org. **Artistic Director:** Anthony J. Garcia. Estab. 1971. Produces 2 children's plays/year.
Needs: "We are interested in plays by Chicanos or Latinos that speak to that experience. We do not produce standard musicals. We are a culturally specific company." Recently produced *Joaquim's Christmas*, by Anthony J. Garcia (children's Christmas play for ages 7-15); and *The Dragonslayer*, by Silviana Woods (young boy's relationship with grandfather for ages 7-15); *And Now Miguel*, by Jim Krungold. Does not want to see "cutesy stuff."
How to Contact: Query with synopsis, character breakdown and set description. Will consider simultaneous submissions and previously performed work. Responds in 6 months. Buys regional rights.
Terms: Pays writers per performance: $35 1st night, $25 subsequent. Submissions returned with SASE.
Tips: "People should write within their realm of experience but yet push their own boundaries. Writers should approach social issues within the human experience of their character."

ELDRIDGE PUBLISHING CO. INC., P.O. Box 1595, Venice FL 34284-1595. (941)496-4679. Fax: (941)493-9680. E-mail: info@histage.com. Website: www.histage.com or www.95church.com. **Editor:** Nancy Vorhis. Estab. 1906. Publishes approximately 25 children's plays/year; 4-5 children's musicals/year.
Needs: Prefers simple staging; flexible cast size. "We publish for junior and high school, community theater and children's theater (adults performing for children), all genres, also religious plays." Recently published plays: *Oliver T*, by Craig Sodaro ("Oliver Twist" reset behind 1950s TV for ages 12-14); *teensomething*, book, music, lyrics by Michael Mish (a revue of teen life for ages 12-19). Prefers work which has been performed or at least had a staged reading.
How to Contact: Submit complete ms, score and tape of songs (if a musical). Will consider simultaneous submissions if noted. Responds in 3 months.
Terms: Purchases all dramatic rights. Pays writers royalties of 50%; 10% copy sales; buys material outright for religious market.
Tips: "Try to have your work performed, if at all possible, before submitting. We're always on the lookout for comedies which provide a lot of fun for our customers. But other more serious topics which concern teens, as well as intriguing mysteries and children's theater programs are of interest to us as well. We know there are many new talented playwrights out there, and we look forward to reading their fresh scripts."

ENCORE PERFORMANCE PUBLISHING, P.O. Box 692, Orem UT 84059. (801)225-0605. Fax: (807)765-0489. E-mail: encoreplay@aol.com. Website: www.Encoreplay.com. **Contact:** Mike Perry. Estab. 1978. Publishes 20-30 children's plays/year; 10-20 children's musicals/year.
Needs: Prefers close to equal male/female ratio if possible. Adaptations for K-12 and older. 60% of plays written for adult roles; 40% for juvenile roles. Recently published plays: *Boy Who Knew No Fear*, by G. Riley Mills/Mark Levenson (adaptation of fairy tale, ages 8-16); *Two Chains*, by Paul Burton (about drug abuse, ages 11-18).
How to Contact: Query first with synopsis, character breakdown, set description and production history. Will only consider previously performed work. Responds in 2 months.
Terms: Purchases all publication and production rights. Author retains copyright. Pays writers in royalties (50%). SASE for return of submission.
Tips: "Give us issue and substance, be controversial without offense. Use a laser printer! Don't send an old manuscript. Make yours look the most professional."

FLORIDA STUDIO THEATRE, 1241 N. Palm Ave., Sarasota FL 34236. (941)366-9017. Fax: (941)955-4137. E-mail: james@fst2000.org. Website: www.fst2000.org. **Artistic Director:** Richard Hopkins. **Coordinator:** James Ashford. Estab. 1973. Produces 3 children's plays/year; 1-3 children's musicals/year.

Needs: Produces children's plays for professional productions. 50% of plays/musicals written for adult roles; 50% for juvenile roles. "Prefer small cast plays that use imagination more than heavy scenery." Will consider simultaneous submissions and previously performed work.
How to Contact: Query with synopsis, character breakdown, 5 pages of sample dialogue, and set description. Responds in 3 months. Rights negotiable. Pay negotiable. Submissions returned with SASE.
Tips: "Children are a tremendously sophisticated audience. The material should respect this."

THE FOOTHILL THEATRE COMPANY, P.O. Box 1812, Nevada City CA 95959-1812. (530)265-9320. Fax: (530)265-9325. E-mail: ftc@foothilltheatre.org. Website: www.foothilltheatre.org. **Literary Manager:** Gary Wright. Estab. 1977. Produces 0-2 children's plays/year; 0-1 children's musicals/year. Professional nonprofit theater.
Needs: 95% of plays/musicals written for adult roles; 5% for juvenile roles. "Small is better, but will consider anything." Produced *Peter Pan*, by J.M. Barrie (kids vs. grownups, for all ages); *Six Impossible Things Before Breakfast*, by Lee Potts & Marilyn Hetzel (adapted from works of Lewis Carroll, for all ages). Does not want to see traditional fairy tales.
How to Contact: Query with synopsis, character breakdown and set description. Will consider simultaneous submissions and previously performed work. Responds in 6 months.
Terms: Buys negotiable rights. Payment method varies. Submissions returned with SASE.
Tips: "Trends in children's theater include cultural diversity, real life issues (drug use, AIDS, etc.), mythological themes with contemporary resonance. Don't talk down to or underestimate children. Don't be preachy or didactic—humor is an excellent teaching tool."

SAMUEL FRENCH, INC., 45 W. 25th St., New York NY 10010. (212)206-8990. Fax: (212)206-1429. **Senior Editor:** Lawrence Harbison. Estab. 1830. Publishes 2 or 3 children's plays/year; "variable number of musicals."
Needs: Subject matter: "all genres, all ages. No puppet plays. No adaptations of any of those old 'fairy tales.' No 'Once upon a time, long ago and far away.' No kings, princesses, fairies, trolls, etc."
How to Contact: Submit complete ms and demo tape (if a musical). Responds in 8 months.
Terms: Purchases "publication rights, amateur and professional production rights, option to publish next 3 plays." Pays writers "book royalty of 10%; variable royalty for professional and amateur productions. SASE for return of submissions.
Tips: "Children's theater is a very tiny market, as most groups perform plays they have created themselves or have commissioned."

HAYES SCHOOL PUBLISHING CO. INC., 321 Pennwood Ave., Wilkinsburg PA 15221. (412)371-2373. Fax: (412)371-6408. Website: www.hayespub.com. Estab. 1940.
Needs: Wants to see supplementary teaching aids for grades K-12. Interested in all subject areas, especially music, foreign language (French, Spanish, Latin), early childhood education.
How to Contact: Query first with table of contents, sample page of activities. Will consider simultaneous and electronic submissions. Responds in 6 weeks.
Terms: Purchases all rights. Work purchased outright. SASE for return of submissions.

HEUER PUBLISHING COMPANY, P.O. Box 248, Cedar Rapids IA 52406. (319)364-6311. Fax: (319)364-1771. E-mail: editor@hitplays.com. Website: www.hitplays.com. **Associate Editor:** Geri Albrecht. Estab. 1928. Publishes 10-15 plays/year for young audiences and community theaters; 5 musicals/year.
Needs: "We publish plays and musicals for schools and community theatres (amateur)." 100% for juvenile roles. Single sets preferred. Props should be easy to find and costumes, other than modern dress, should be simple and easy to improvise. Stage effects requiring complex lighting and/or mechanical features should be avoided. Musical needs: "We need musicals with large, predominantly female casts. We publish plays and musicals for middle, junior and senior high schools." Recently published plays: *Pirate Island*, by Martin Follose (popular for all producing groups); *Virgil's Wedding*, by Eddie McPherson (delightful characters and non-stop laughter).
How to Contact: Plays: Query with synopsis. Musicals: Query with synopsis. Will consider simultaneous submissions and previously performed work. Responds in 2 months.
Terms: Buys amateur rights. Pays royalty or purchases work outright. Submissions returned with SASE.
Tips: "We sell almost exclusively to junior and smaller senior high schools so the subject matter and language should be appropriate for schools and young audiences."

LAGUNA PLAYHOUSE YOUTH THEATRE, P.O. Box 1747, Laguna Beach CA 92652. (949)497-2787. Fax: (949)376-8185. E-mail: jlauderdale@lagunaplayhouse.com. **Artistic Director:** Joe Lauderdale. Estab. 1986. Produces 4 mainstage (1 musical) and 2-4 touring shows/year.
Needs: The Laguna Playhouse is an L.R.C theatre company with an amateur youth theatre. 40% of plays/musicals written for adult roles; 60% for juvenile roles. "We especially look for small touring shows based on existing children's literature." Musical needs: Small combos of 4-7 people with some doubling of instruments possible. Recently produced plays: *James and the Giant Peach*, by Richard R. George and *And Then They Came for Me*, by James Still.

How to Contact: Submit letter of intent and synopsis. Musicals should also submit recording. Responds in 6 months.

Terms: Pays 5-8% royalties.

Tips: "Although the majority of our work is literary based and for younger audiences, we produce at least one original work that is targeted for junior high and high school. This piece for older audiences should be educational, enlightening and entertaining."

MERRY-GO-ROUND YOUTH THEATRE, P.O. Box 506, Auburn NY 13021. (315)255-1305. Fax: (315)252-3815. E-mail: youthmgr@dreamscape.com. Website: www.merry-go-round.com. **Producing Director:** Ed Sayles. Estab. 1958. Produces 10 children's plays/year; 3 children's musicals/year.

Needs: 100% of plays/musicals written for adult roles. Cast maximum, 4-5 and staging must be tourable. Recently produced plays: *Seagirl*, by Francis Elitzig (Chinese folktale); *There Once Was a Longhouse, Where Now There is Your House*, (Native Americans of New York state).

How to Contact: Plays/musicals: query with synopsis, character breakdown and set description; submit complete ms and score. Will consider simultaneous submissions, electronic submissions via disk/modem and previously performed work. Responds in 2 months.

Terms: "Realize that our program is grade/curriculum specific. And understanding of the NYS Learning Standards may help a writer to focus on a point of curriculum that we would like to cover."

NEBRASKA THEATRE CARAVAN, 6915 Cass St., Omaha Ne 68132. (402)553-4890, ext. 154. Fax: (402)553-6288. E-mail: caravan@omahaplayhouse.com. Website: www.omahaplayhouse.com. **Director:** Richard L. Scott. Estab. 1976. Produces 2 children's plays/year; 1-2 children's musicals/year.

Needs: Produces children's plays for professional productions with a company of 5-6 actors touring. 100% of plays/musicals written for adult roles; setting must be adaptable for easy touring. 75 minute show for grades 7-12; 60 minutes for elementary. Musical need: 1 piano or keyboard accompaniment. Recently produced plays: *A Thousand Cranes*, by Kathryn Schultz Miller (Sadako Susaki, for ages K-8).

How to Contact: Plays: query with synopsis, character breakdown and set description. Musicals: query first. Will consider simultaneous submissions and previously performed work. Responds in 3 months.

Terms: Pays $35-40/performance; pays commission—option 1—own outright, option 2—have right to produce at any later date—playwright has right to publish and produce. Submissions returned with SASE.

Tips: "Be sure to follow guidelines."

THE NEW CONSERVATORY THEATRE CENTER, 25 Van Ness Ave., San Francisco CA 94102-6033. (415)861-4914. Fax: (415)861-6988. E-mail: nctcsf@yahoo.com. Website: www.nctcsf.org. **Executive Director:** Ed Decker. Estab. 1981. Produces 6 children's plays/year; 1 children's musical/year.

Needs: Limited budget and small casts only. Produces children's plays as part of "a professional theater arts training program for youths ages 4-19 during the school year and 2 summer sessions. The New Conservatory also produces educational plays for its touring company. We do not want to see any preachy or didactic material." Recently produced plays: *Aesop's Funky Fables*, adapted by Dyan McBride (fables, for ages 4-9); *A Little Princess*, by Frances Hodgson Burnett, adapted by June Walker Rogers (classic story of a young girl, for ages 5-10).

How to Contact: Query with synopsis, character breakdown and set description, or submit complete ms and score. Responds in 3 months.

Terms: Rights purchased negotiable. Pays writers in royalties. SASE for return of submission.

Tips: "Wants plays with name recognition, i.e., *The Lion, the Witch and the Wardrobe* as well as socially relevant issues. Plays should be under 50 minutes in length."

NEW PLAYS INCORPORATED, P.O. Box 5074, Charlottesville VA 22905-0074. (804)979-2777. Fax: (804)984-2230. E-mail: patwhitton@aol.com. Website: www.newplaysforchildren.com. **Publisher:** Patricia Whitton Forrest. Estab. 1964. Publishes 3-4 plays/year; 1 or 2 children's musicals/year.

Needs: Publishes "generally material for kindergarten through junior high." Recently published: *On The Line*, audience participation play, by Carol Koty (woolen mill strikes in Lawrence, MA); *Dye Frye* and *Wicked John and the Devil*, Appalachian Folk Plays, by Loren Crawford.

How to Contact: Submit complete ms and score. Will consider simultaneous submissions and previously performed work. Responds in 2 months (usually).

Terms: Purchases exclusive rights to sell acting scripts. Pays writers in royalties (50% of production royalties; 10% of script sales). SASE for return of submission.

Tips: "Write the play you really want to write (not what you think will be saleable) and find a director to put it on."

NEW YORK STATE THEATRE INSTITUTE, 37 First St., Troy NY 12180. (518)274-3200. Fax: (518)274-3815. E-mail: nysti@capital.net. Website: www.nysti.org. **Artistic Director:** Patricia B. Snyder. **Associate Artistic Director:** Ed Lange. Estab. 1976. Produces 5 children's plays/year; 1-2 children's musicals/year.

Needs: Produces family plays for professional theater. 90% of plays/musicals are written for adult roles; 10% for juvenile roles. Does not want to see plays for children only. Produced plays: *A Tale of Cinderella*, by Will Severin, W.A. Frankonis and George David Weiss (all ages); *Miracle On 34th Street*, by Valentine Davies.
How to Contact: Query with synopsis, character breakdown and set description; submit tape of songs (if a musical). Will consider simultaneous submissions and previously performed work. Responds in 1 month for queries. SASE for return of submission.
Tips: Writers should be mindful of "audience *sophistication*. We do not wish to see material that is childish. Writers should submit work that is respectful of young people's intelligence and perception—work that is appropriate for families, but that is also challenging and provocative."

THE OPEN EYE THEATER, P.O. Box 959, Margaretville NY 12455. Phone/fax: (914)586-1660. E-mail: openeye@catskill.net. Website: www.theopeneye.org. **Producing Artistic Director:** Amie Brockway. Estab. 1972 (theater). Produces 3 plays/year for a family audience. Most productions are with music but are not musicals.
Needs: "Casts of various sizes. Technical requirements are kept to a minimum for touring purposes." Produces professional productions combining professional artists and artists-in-training (actors of all ages). Recently produced plays: *The Weaver and the Sea*, by Julia Steiny, music by Dennis Livingston (myth, family); *Hoax*, by Pamela Monk (the Cardiff Giant, family); *Sundiata*, by Edward Mast (myth, family).
How to Contact: "No videos or cassettes. Letter of inquiry only." Will consider previously performed work. Responds in 6 months.
Terms: Rights agreement negotiated with author. Pays writers one-time fee or royalty negotiated with publisher. SASE for return of submission.
Tips: "Send letter of inquiry only. We are interested in plays for a multigenerational audience (8-adult)."

PHOENIX THEATRE'S COOKIE COMPANY, 100E. McDowell, Phoenix AZ 85004. (602)258-1974. Fax: (602)253-3626. E-mail: phoenixtheatre@yahoo.com. Website: phoenixtheatre.net. **Artistic Director:** Alan J. Prewitt. Estab. 1980. Produces 4 children's plays/year.
Needs: Produces theater with professional adult actors performing for family audiences. 95% of plays/musicals written for adult roles; 5% for juvenile roles. Requires small casts (4-7), small stage, mostly 1 set, flexible set or ingenious sets for a small space. "We're just starting to do plays with music—no musicals per se." Does not want to see larger casts, multiple sets, 2 hour epics. Recently produced *Holidays on the Prairie*, by Alan J. Prewitt (a single mother with children faces the Santa Fe Trail, for ages 4-12); *The Sleeping Beauty*, by Alan J. Prewitt (classic tale gets "truthful parent" twist, for ages 4-12)).
How to Contact: Plays/musicals: Query with synopsis, character breakdown and set description. Will consider simultaneous submissions. Responds only if interested within 1 month.
Terms: Submissions returned with SASE.
Tips: "Only submit innovative, imaginative work that stimulates imagination and empowers the child. We specialize in producing original scripts based on classic children's literature."

PIONEER DRAMA SERVICE, P.O. Box 4267, Englewood CO 80155-4267. (303)779-4035. Fax: (303)779-4315. E-mail: editors@pioneerdrama.com. Website: www.pioneerdrama.com. **Submissions Editor:** Beth Somers. Publisher: Steven Fendrich. Estab. 1960. Publishes more than 10 new plays and musicals/year.
Needs: "We are looking for plays up to 90 minutes long, large casts and simple sets." Publishes plays for ages middle school-12th grade and community theatre. Recently published plays/musicals: *Let Your Hair Down Rapunzel*, by Karen Boettcher-Tate, music and lyrics by Scott DeTurk; *The Frog Princess*, by Cathy Howard. Wants to see "script, scores, tapes, pics and reviews."
How to Contact: Query with synopsis, character breakdown, running time and set description. Submit complete ms and score (if a musical) with SASE. Will consider simultaneous submissions, CAD electronic submissions via disk or modem, previously performed work. Contact: Beth Somers, submissions editor. Responds in 4 months. Send for writer's guidelines.
Terms: Purchases all rights. Pays writers in royalties (10% on sales, 50% royalties on productions). Research Pioneer through catalog and website.
Tips: "Research the company. Include a cover letter and a SASE."

PLAYERS PRESS, INC., P.O. Box 1132, Studio City CA 91614-0132. (818)789-4980. **Vice President:** R. W. Gordon. Estab. 1965. Publishes 10-20 children's plays/year; 3-12 children's musicals/year.
Needs: Subject matter: "We publish for all age groups." Recently published: *African Folk Tales*, by Carol Korty (for ages 10-14).
How to Contact: Query with synopsis, character breakdown and set description; include #10 SASE with query. Considers previously performed work only. Responds to query in 1 month; submissions in 1 year.
Terms: Purchases stage, screen, TV rights. Payment varies; work purchased possibly outright upon written request. Submissions returned with SASE.
Tips: "Submit as requested—query first and send only previously produced material. Entertainment quality is on the upswing and needs to be directed at the world, no longer just the U.S. Please submit with two #10 SASEs plus ms-size SASE. Please do not call."

PLAYS, The Drama Magazine for Young People, P.O. Box 600160, Newton MA 02460. E-mail: lpreston@p laysmag.com. Website: www.playsmag.com. **Editor:** Elizabeth Preston. Estab. 1941. Publishes 70-75 children's plays/year.

Needs: "Props and staging should not be overly elaborate or costly. There is little call among our subscribers for plays with only a few characters; ten or more (to allow all students in a class to participate, for instance) is preferred. Our plays are performed by children in school from lower elementary grades through junior-senior high." 100% of plays written for juvenile roles. Subject matter: Audience is lower grades through junior/senior high. Recently published plays: *Boxes*, by Joanna L. Evans (One-time football hero comes home to confront tense family relationship); *The Knight of the Honest Heart Returns*, by Christina Hamlett (Wedding day wisdom, sometime in the Middle Ages); *Confusion at the Castle*, by Pamela Love (Reporter's nose for news—and unusual birthmark—help solve mystery of the long lost princess): *The Search for the Notorious Teo Teo*, by Elizabeth Boike Burdich (A large-cast play celebrating the importance of community). "Send nothing downbeat—no plays about drugs, sex or other 'heavy' topics."

How to Contact: Query first on adaptations of folk tales and classics; otherwise submit complete ms. Responds in 3 weeks.

Terms: Purchases all rights. Pay rates vary. Guidelines available; send SASE. Sample copy $4.

Tips: "Get your play underway quickly. Keep it wholesome and entertaining. No preachiness, heavy moral or educational message. Any 'lesson' should be imparted through the actions of the characters, not through unbelievable dialogue. Use realistic situations and settings without getting into downbeat, depressing topics. No sex, drugs, violence, alcohol."

RIVERSIDE CHILDREN'S THEATRE, 3280 Riverside Park Dr., Vero Beach FL 32963. (561)234-8052. Fax: (561)234-4407. E-mail: ret@riversidetheatre.com. Website: www.riversidetheatre.com. **Education Director:** Linda Downey. Estab. 1980. Produces 4 children's plays/year; 2 children's musicals/year.

Needs: Produces amateur youth productions. 100% of plays/musicals written for juvenile roles. Musical needs: For children ages 6-18. Produced plays: *The Beloved Dently*, by Dory Cooney (pet bereavement, general); *Taming of the Shrew*, by Shakespeare (general).

How to Contact: Plays/musicals: Query with synopsis, character breakdown and set description. Will consider simultaneous submissions, electronic submissions via disk/modem and previously performed work. Responds only if interested.

Terms: Pays royalty or $40-60 per performance. Submissions returned with SASE.

Tips: "Interested in youth theatre for children ages 6-18 to perform."

STAGE ONE: THE LOUISVILLE CHILDREN'S THEATRE, 501 W. Main, Louisville KY 40202-2957. (502)589-5946. Fax: (502)588-5910. E-mail: stageone@stageone.org. Website: www.stageone.org. **Producing Director:** Moses Goldberg. Estab. 1946. Produces 6-8 children's plays/year; 1-4 children's musicals/year.

Needs: Stage One is an Equity company producing children's plays for professional productions. 100% of plays/ musicals written for adult roles. "Sometimes we do use students in selected productions." Produced plays: *Pinocchio*, by Moses Goldberg, music by Scott Kasbaum (ages 8-12); and *John Lennon & Me*, by Cherie Bennett (about cystic fibrosis; peer acceptance for ages 11-17). Does not want to see "camp or condescension."

How to Contact: Submit complete ms, score and tape of songs (if a musical); include the author's résumé if desired. Will consider simultaneous submissions, electronic submissions via disk or modem and previously performed work. Responds in 4 months.

Terms: Pays writers in royalties (5-6%) or $25-75/performance.

Tips: Looking for "stageworthy and respectful dramatizations of the classic tales of childhood, both ancient and modern; plays relevant to the lives of young people and their families; and plays directly related to the school curriculum."

TADA!, 120 W. 28th St., New York NY 10001-6109. (212)627-1732. Fax: (212)243-6736. E-mail: tada@tad atheater.com. Website: www.tadatheater.com. **Artistic Director:** Janine Nina Trevens. Estab. 1984. Produces 5 staged readings of children's plays and musicals/year; 0-5 children's plays/year; 2-3 children's musicals/year.

Needs: "All actors are children, ages 8-17." Produces children's plays for professional, year-round theater. 100% of plays/musicals written for juvenile roles. Recently produced musicals: *Sleepover*, by Phillip Freedman and James Belloff (peer acceptance, for ages 3 and up); *The Little House of Cookies*, by Janine Nina Trevens and Joel Gelpe (international communication and friendship). Does not want to see fairy tales or material that talks down to children.

How to Contact: Query with synopsis, character breakdown and set description; submit complete ms, score and tape of songs (if a musical). Responds in 1 year "or in October following the August deadline for our Annual Playwriting Competition. (Send two copies of manuscript if for competition)."

Terms: Rights purchased "depend on the piece." Pays writers in royalties of 1-6% and/or pays commissioning fee. SASE a must for return of submissions.

Tips: "For plays for our Annual Playwriting Competition, submit between January and August 15. We're looking for plays with current topics that specific age ranges can identify with, with a small cast of children and one or two adults. Our company is multi-racial and city-oriented. We are not interested in fairy tales. We like to produce material that kids relate to and that touches their lives today."

THEATREWORKS/USA, 151 W. 26th, 7th Floor, New York NY 10001. (212)647-1100. Fax: (212)924-5377. E-mail: info@theatreworksusa.org. Website: www.theatreworks.org. **Artistic Director:** Barbara Pasternack. **Assistant Artistic Director:** Michael Alltop. Estab. 1960. Produces 3-4 children's plays and musicals/year.

Needs: Cast of 5 or 6 actors. Play should be 1 hour long, tourable. Professional children's theatre comprised of adult equity actors. 100% of shows are written for adult roles. Produced plays: *The Mystery of King Tut*, by Mindi Dickstein and Daniel Messé (Ancient Egypt); *Ferdinand the Bull*, by Robert Lopez, Jeff Marx and Rob Barron (adaptation, K-3).

How to Contact: Query first with synopsis, character breakdown and sample songs. Will consider previously performed work. Responds in 3 months.

Terms: Pays writers royalties of 6%. SASE for return of submission.

Tips: "Plays should be not only entertaining, but 'about something.' They should touch the heart and the mind. They should not condescend to children. We accept full scripts, with the thought that we're looking for good playwrights, not necessarily plays to produce."

Young Writer's & Illustrator's Markets

The listings in this section are special because they publish work of young writers and artists (under age 18). Some of the magazines listed exclusively feature the work of young people. Others are adult magazines with special sections for the work of young writers. There are also a few book publishers listed that exclusively publish the work of young writers and artists. Many of the magazines and publishers listed here pay only in copies, meaning authors and illustrators receive one or more free copies of the magazine or book to which they contributed.

As with adult markets, markets for children expect writers to be familiar with their editorial needs before submitting. Many of the markets listed will send guidelines to writers stating exactly what they need and how to submit it. You can often get these by sending a request with a self-addressed, stamped envelope (SASE) to the magazine or publisher, or by checking a publication's website (a number of listings include web addresses). In addition to obtaining guidelines, read through a few copies of any magazines you'd like to submit to—this is the best way to determine if your work is right for them.

A number of kids' magazines are available on newsstands or in libraries. Others are distributed only through schools, churches or home subscriptions. If you can't find a magazine you'd like to see, most editors will send sample copies for a small fee.

Before you submit your material to editors, take a few minutes to read Before Your First Sale on page 8 for more information on proper submission procedures. You may also want to check out two other sections—Contests & Awards and Conferences & Workshops. Some listings in these sections are open to students (some exclusively)—look for the phrase **open to students** in bold. Additional opportunities for writers can be found in *The Young Writers Guide to Getting Published* (Writer's Digest Books) and *A Teen's Guide to Getting Published: the only writer's guide written by teens for teens*, by Danielle and Jessica Dunn (Prufrock Press). More information on these books are given in the Helpful Resources section in the back of this book.

Information on companies listed in the previous edition but not included in this edition of *Children's Writer's & Illustrator's Market* may be found in the General Index.

THE ACORN, 1530 Seventh St., Rock Island IL 61201. (309)788-3980. Newsletter. Estab. 1989. **Editor:** Betty Mowery. Audience consists of "kindergarten-12th grade students, parents, teachers and other adults. Purpose in publishing works for children: "to expose children's manuscripts to others and provide a format for those who might not have one. We want to showcase young authors who may not have their work published elsewhere and present wholesome writing material that will entertain and educate—audience grades K-12." Children must be K-12 (put name, address, grade on manuscripts). Guidelines available for SASE.
Magazines: 100% of magazine written by children. Uses 6 fiction pieces (500 words); 20 pieces of poetry (32 lines). No payment; purchase of a copy isn't necessary to be printed. Sample copy $3. Subscription $10 for 4 issues. Submit mss to Betty Mowery, editor. Send complete ms. Will accept typewritten, legibly handwritten and/or computer printout. Include SASE. Responds in 1 week. Will not respond without SASE.
Artwork: Publishes artwork by children. Looks for "all types; size 4×5. Use black ink in artwork." No payment. Submit artwork either with ms or separately to Betty Mowery. Include SASE. Responds in 1 week.
Tips: "My biggest problem is not having names on the manuscripts. If the manuscript gets separated from the cover letter, there is no way to know whom to respond to. Always put name, age or grade and address on manuscripts, and if you want your material returned, enclose a SASE. Don't send material with killing of humans or animals, or lost love poems or stories."

AMELIA MAGAZINE, 329 "E" St., Bakersfield CA 93304-2031. (805)323-4064. Magazine. Published quarterly. Strives to offer the best of all genres. Purpose in publishing works for children: wants to offer first opportunities to budding writers. Also offers the annual Amelia Student Scholarship ($500) for high school students. Submissions from young writers must be signed by parent, teacher or guardian verifying originality. Guidelines are not specifically for young writers; they cover the entire gamut of publication needs. For sample of past winner send $3 and SASE.

Magazines: 3% of magazine written by children. Uses primarily poetry, often generated by teachers in creative writing classes. Uses 1 story in any fiction genre (1,500 words); 4 pieces of poetry, usually haiku (3 lines). Would like to receive more general poetry from young writers. Pays in copies for haiku; $2-10 for general poetry. Regular $35 rate for fiction or nonfiction. Submit mss to Frederick A. Raborg, editor. Submit complete ms (teachers frequently submit student's work). Will accept handwritten ms. Include SASE. Responds in 3 weeks.

Artwork: Publishes artwork and photography by children. Looks for photos no smaller than 5×7; artwork in any medium; also cartoons. Pays $5-20 on publication. Submit well-protected artwork with SASE. Submit artwork/photos to Frederick A. Raborg, Jr., editor. Include SASE. Responds in 3 weeks. Sample issue: $10.95.

Tips: "Be neat and thorough. Photos should have captions. Cartoon gaglines ought to be funny; try them out on someone before submitting. We want to encourage young writers because the seeds of literary creativity are sown quite young with strong desires to read and admiration for the authors of those early readings."

AMERICAN GIRL, 8400 Fairway Place, Middleton WI 53562. (608)836-4848. Fax: (608)831-7089. Website: www.americangirl. **Contact:** Magazine Department Assistant. Bimonthly magazine. Audience consists of girls ages 8-12 who are joyful about being girls. Purpose in publishing works by young people: "self-esteem boost and entertainment for readers. *American Girl* values girls' opinions and ideas. By publishing their work in the magazine, girls can share their thoughts with other girls! Young writers should be 8-12 years old. We don't have writer's guidelines for children's submissions. Instruction for specific solicitations appears in the magazine."

Magazines: 5% of magazine written by young people. "A few pages of each issue feature articles that include children's answers to questions or requests that have appeared in a previous issue of *American Girl*." Pays in copies. Submit to address listed in magazine. Will accept legibly handwritten ms. Include SASE. Responds in 3 months.

Tips: "Please, no stories, poems, etc. about American Girls Collection Characters (Felicity, Samantha, Molly, Kirsten, Addy or Josefina). Inside *American Girl*, there are several departments that call for submissions. Read the magazine carefully and submit your ideas based on what we ask for."

BEYOND WORDS PUBLISHING, INC., 20827 NW Cornell Rd., Suite 500, Hillsboro OR 97124-9808. (503)531-8700. Fax: (503)531-8773. E-mail: barbara@beyondword.com. Website:www.beyondword.com. Book publisher. **Managing Editor of Children's Department:** Barbara Mann. Publishes 2-3 books by children/year. Looks for "books that inspire integrity in children ages 5-15 and encourage creativity and an appreciation of nature." Wants to "encourage children to write, create, dream and believe that it is possible to be published. The books must be unique, be of national interest, and the child author must be personable and promotable." Writer's guidelines available with SASE.

Books: Holds yearly writing contests for activity/advice books written by and for children/teens. Also publishes nonfiction advice books for and by children, such as joke books or guides for kids about pertinent concerns. Submit mss to Michelle Roehm McCann, Director of Children's Division. Responds in 6 months.

Artwork/Photography: Publishes artwork by children. Submit artwork to Barbara Mann, managing editor.

Tips: "Write about issues that affect your life. Trust your own instincts. You know best!"

N: BLUE JEAN MAGAZINE, 1115 E. Main St., Box 60, Rochester NY 14609. (716)288-6980. E-mail: editors@bluejeanonline.com. Bimonthly national magazine. "*Blue Jean Magazine, Blue Jean Online* and Blue Jean Press showcase the writing, artwork and creativity of young women around the world. Our cover stories profile interesting and exciting teen girls and young women in action. You will find no supermodels, tips on dieting or fashion spreads on our pages. We publish teen-produced poetry, artwork, photography, fiction and much more!" Audience is girls ages 12-19. Purpose in showcasing work by young women: "to stay true to what really matters, which is publishing what young women are thinking, saying and doing." Writer's guidelines available on request for SASE.

Magazine: 90% of magazine written by young people. Uses 1 fiction story; 8-14 nonfiction stories (250-3,000 words); 1-3 poems. Pays adult freelancers $75 per Body and Mind article, After High School article. Payment will be sent with 2 complimentary issues within 30 days of publication. Submit complete mss per submission guidelines. Will accept typewritten mss. Include SASE. Responds in 3-4 months at most. "Many times within two months."

Artwork: Publishes artwork and photography by teens. Will consider a variety of styles! Artwork must be submitted by a teen artist (ages 12-19). Submit art between 2 pieces of paperboard or cardboard. Include SASE with enough postage for return. Responds in 3-4 months.

Tips: "Submissions may be sent via mail or e-mail. Do not inquire about your work by calling. Replies guaranteed when material sent through mail with SASE."

CHICKADEE MAGAZINE, 49 Front St. Toronto, Ontario M5E 1B3 Canada. (416)340-2700. Fax: (416)340-9769. E-mail: owl@owl.on.ca. Website: www.outkids.com. **Editor:** Hilary Bain. Magazine published 9 times/year. "*Chickadee* is for children ages 6-9. Its purpose is to entertain and educate children about science, nature and the world around them. We publish children's drawings to give readers the chance to express themselves. Drawings must relate to the topics that are given in the 'All Your Own' section of each issue."
Artwork: Publishes artwork by children. No payment given. Mail submissions with name, age and return address for thank you note. Submit to Mitch Butler, All Your Own Editor. Responds in 4 months.

CHILDREN WRITING FOR CHILDREN NONPROFIT (CWC), 7142 Dustin Rd., Galena OH 43021-7959. (800)759-7171. Website: www.cwcbooks.org. **Executive Director:** Susan Schmidt. Purpose of organization: A non-profit corporation established to educate the public at large about children's issues through literary works created by children and to celebrate and share the talents of children as authors. Books must be written and/or illustrated by children and young adults. "We look for kids to write about personal experiences that educate and reveal solutions to problems." Open submissions are accepted. Books published to date include those dealing with cancer, child abuse, cerebral palsy, Tourette's syndrome and avoiding teen violence.
Books: Publishing focus is on nonfiction writings about children's issues such as peer pressure, illness, and special challenges or opportunities. Stories with educational value are preferred. Writer's guidelines available with SASE. Pays royalties, but no advances. Will accept typewritten, legibly handwritten and computer-printed ms. Include SASE for ms return and/or comments. Responds in 6 months.
Artwork/Photography: Publishes books with artwork and/or photography accompanying nonfiction stories written and illustrated by children. Please submit photocopies of art—no originals please.
Tips: Write about personal experiences in challenging situations, painting a word picture of the people involved, the story, how you resolved or responded to the situation and what you learned or gained from the experience.

CICADA, Carus Publishing Company, P.O. Box 300, Peru IL 61354. (815)224-6656. Fax: (815)224-6615. E-mail: cicada@caruspub.com. Website: www.cicadamag.com. **Editor-in-Chief:** Marianne Carus. Editor: Deborah Vetter. Senior Art Director: Ron McCutchan.
  • *Cicada* publishes work of writers and artists of high-school age (must be at least 14 years old). See the *Cicada* listing in the magazines section for more information, or check their website or copies of the magazine.

THE CLAREMONT REVIEW, 4980 Wesley Rd., Victoria, British Columbia Canada V8Y 1Y9. (604)658-5221. Fax: (250)658-5387. E-mail: aurora@home.com. Website: www.members.home.net/review. Magazine. Publishes 2 books/year by young adults. Publishes poetry and fiction with literary value by students aged 13-19 anywhere in English-speaking world. Purpose in publishing work by young people: to provide a literary venue. Sponsors annual poetry contest.
Magazines: Uses 10-12 fiction stories (200-2,500 words); 30-40 poems. Pays in copies. Submit mss to editors. Submit complete ms. Will accept typewritten mss. SASE. Responds in 6 weeks (except during the summer).
Artwork: Publishes artwork by young adults. Looks for b&w copies of imaginative art. Pays in copies. Send picture for review. Negative may be requested. Submit art and photographs to editors. SASE. Responds in 6 weeks.
Tips: "Read us first—it saves disappointment. Know who we are and what we publish. We're closed July and August. SASE a must. American students send I.R.C.'s as American stamps *do not* work in Canada."

CREATIVE KIDS, P.O. Box 8813, Waco TX 76714-8813. (800)998-2208. Fax: (254)756-3339. E-mail: creative_kids@prufrock.com. Website: www.prufrock.com. **Editor:** Libby Lindsey. Magazine published 4 times/year. Estab. 1979. "All material is by children, for children." Purpose in publishing works by children: "to create a product that provides children with an authentic experience and to offer an opportunity for children to see their work in print. *Creative Kids* contains the best stories, poetry, opinion, artwork, games and photography by kids ages 8-14." Writers ages 8-14 must have statement by teacher or parent verifying originality. Writer's guidelines available on request with SASE.
Magazines: Uses "about 6" fiction and nonfiction stories (800-900 words); poetry, plays, ideas to share (200-750 words) per issue. Pays "free magazine." Submit mss to submissions editor. Will accept typewritten mss. Include SASE. Responds in 1 month.
Artwork/Photography: Publishes artwork and photos by children. Looks for "any kind of drawing, cartoon, or painting." Pays "free magazine." Send original or a photo of the work to submissions editor. Include SASE. Responds in 1 month.
Tips: "*Creative Kids* is a magazine by kids, for kids. The work represents children's ideas, questions, fears, concerns and pleasures. The material never contains racist, sexist or violent expression. The purpose is to provide children with an authentic experience. A person may submit one piece of work per envelope. Each piece must be labeled with the student's name, birth date, grade, school, home address and school address. Include a photograph, if possible. Recent school pictures are best. Material submitted to *Creative Kids* must not be under consideration by any other publication. Items should be carefully prepared, proofread and double checked (perhaps also by a parent or teacher). All activities requiring solutions must be accompanied by the correct answers. Young writers and artists should always write for guidelines and then follow them."

CREATIVE WITH WORDS, Thematic anthologies, Creative with Words Publications, P.O. Box 223226, Carmel CA 93922. Fax: (831)655-8627. E-mail: cwwpub@usa.net. Website: members.tripod.com/CreativeWith Words. **Editor:** Brigitta Geltrich. Nature Editor: Bert Hower. Publishes 14 anthologies/year. Estab. 1975. "We publish the creative writing of children (4 anthologies written by children; 4 anthologies written by adults; 4-6 anthologies written by all ages)." Audience consists of children, families, schools, libraries, adults, reading programs. Purpose in publishing works by children: to offer them an opportunity to get started in publishing. "Work must be of quality, typed, original, unedited, and not published before; age must be given (up to 19 years old) and home address." SASE must be enclosed with all correspondence and mss. Writer's guidelines and theme list available on request with SASE, via e-mail or on website.
Books: Considers all categories except those dealing with sensationalism, death, violence, pornography and overly religious. Uses fairy tales, folklore items (up to 1,500 words) and poetry (not to exceed 20 lines, 46 characters across). Published *Nature Series: Seasons, Nature, School, Love* and *Relationships* (all children and adults). Pays 20% discount on each copy of publication in which fiction or poetry by children appears. Best of the month is published on website, and author receives one free copy of issue. Submit mss to Brigitta Geltrich, editor. Query; child, teacher or parent can submit; teacher and/or parents must verify originality of writing. Will accept typewritten and/or legibly handwritten mss. SASE. "Will not go through agents or overly protective 'stage mothers'." Responds in 1 month after deadline of any theme.
Artwork/Photography: Publishes b&w artwork, b&w photos and computer artwork created by children (language art work). Pays 20% discount on every copy of publication in which work by children appears. Submit artwork to Brigitta Geltrich, editor, and request info on payment.
Tips: "Enjoy the English language, life and the world around you. Look at everything from a different perspective. Look at the greatness inside all of us. Be less descriptive and use words wisely. Let the reader experience a story through a viewpoint character, don't be overly dramatic. Match illustrations to the meaning of the story or poem."

GREEN KNEES, Imprint of Azro Press, PMB 342, 1704 Llano St. B, Santa Fe NM 87505. (505)989-3272. Fax: (505)989-3832. E-mail: books@azropress.com. Website: www.greenknees.com. Book. Publishes 3 books/year by children. "Green Knees is primarily interested in picture books and easy readers written and illustrated by children who are 13 years old or younger." The book must have been written by a child under 13 and illustrations done by the author or children in the same grade or school. Writer's guidelines available on request.
Books: Publishes picture books and young readers; interested in animal stories and humor. Length: 1,000 words for fiction. Submit mss to Jaenet Guggenheim. Query or submit complete ms or synopsis and sample illustration (if longer than 40 pages). Send a copy of the ms, do not send original material. Will accept typewritten or electronically (disk or e-mail). Include SASE. Responds in 2 months.
Artwork/Photography: Publishes artwork by children. "We only accept manuscripts that have already been illustrated. You need to send only a few pictures."

HIGH SCHOOL WRITER, P.O. Box 718, Grand Rapids MN 55744-0718. (218)326-8025. Fax: (218)326-8025. E-mail: writer@mx3.com. Editor: Barbara Eiesland. Magazine published monthly during the school year. "The *High School Writer* is a magazine written *by* students *for* students. All submissions must exceed contemporary standards of decency." Purpose in publishing works by young people: to provide a real audience for student writers—and text for study. Submissions by junior high and middle school students accepted for our junior edition. Senior high students' works are accepted for our senior high edition. Students attending schools that subscribe to our publication are eligible to submit their work." Writer's guidelines available on request.
Magazines: Uses fiction, nonfiction (2,000 words maximum) and poetry. Submit mss to Barbara Eiesland, editor. Submit complete ms (teacher must submit). Will accept typewritten, computer-generated (good quality) mss.
Tips: "Submissions should not be sent without first obtaining a copy of our guidelines (see page 2 of every issue). Also, submissions will not be considered unless student's school subscribes."

KIDS' WORLD, The Magazine That's All Kids!, 1300 Kicker Rd., Tuscaloosa AL 35404. (205)553-2284. E-mail: dragontea@earthlink.net. Magazine. Published 4 times a year. Audience consists of young children up to age 10. "I'm creating a fun magazine for kids to read and a good place for young writers to get a start." Purpose in publishing works by young people: "So that my magazine will be unique—edited by a kid, for kids, by kids (all kids!). Authors must be under 18—no horror or romance." Writer's guidelines available on request.
Magazines: 100% of magazine written by young people. Uses 4-10 short stories; 1-2 essays about favorite things, etc.; 4-10 poems and art. Pays one free copy per ms or artwork. Submit mss to Lillian Kopaska-Merkel, editor. Submit complete mss. Will accept typewritten and legibly handwritten mss. Include SASE. Responds in 2-6 months.
Artwork/Photography: Publishes artwork and photography by children. Looks for "children/babies and things of interest to them (food, toys, animals . . .)." Must be b&w in pen. Pays one free copy per artwork. Send the artwork, plus a note and SASE. Responds in 2-4 weeks.
Tips: "Have an adult check spelling, punctuation and grammar. I get a lot of submissions, so I can only publish the really good ones, within reason for a child's age."

KWIL KIDS PUBLISHING, The Little Publishing Company That Kwil Built, Kwilville, P.O. Box 29556, Maple Ridge, British Columbia V2X 2V0 Canada. Phone/fax: (604)465-9101. E-mail: kwil@telus.net.

Website: www.members.home.com/kwilkids/. Publishes greeting cards, newspaper column, newsletter and web page. Publishes weekly column in local paper, four quarterly newsletters. "*Kwil Kids* come in all ages, shapes and sizes—from 4-64 and a whole lot more! Kwil does not pay for the creative work of children but provides opportunity/encouragement. We promote literacy, creativity and written 'connections' through written and artistic expression and publish autobiographical, inspirational, fantastical, humorous stories of gentleness, compassion, truth and beauty. Our purpose is to foster a sense of pride and enthusiasm in young writers and artists, to celebrate the voice of youth and encourage growth through joy-filled practice and cheerleading, not criticism." Must include name, age, school, address and parent signature (if a minor). Will send guideline upon request and an application to join "The Kwil Club."

Books: Publishes autobiographical, inspirational, creative stories (alliterative, rhyming refrains, juicy words) fiction; short rhyming and non-rhyming poems (creative, fun, original, expressive, poetry). Length: 1,000 words for fiction; 8-16 lines for poetry. No payment—self-published and sold "at cost" only (1 free copy). Submit mss to Kwil publisher. Submit complete ms; send copy only—expect a reply but will not return ms. Will accept typewritten and legibly handwritten mss and e-mail. Include SASE. Publishes greeting cards with poems, short stories and original artwork. Pays 5¢ royalty on each card sold (rounded to the nearest dollar and paid once per year) as a fundraiser. Responds in April, August and December.

Newsletter: 95% of newsletter written by young people. Uses 15 short stories, poems, jokes (20-100 words). No payment—free newsletters only. Submit complete ms. Will accept typewritten and legibly handwritten mss and e-mail. Kwil answers every letter in verse. Responds in April, August and December.

Artwork: Publishes artwork and photography by children with writing. Looks for black ink sketches to go with writing and photos to go with writing. Submit by postal mail only; white background for sketches. Submit artwork/photos to Kwil publisher. Include SASE. Responds in 3 months.

Tips: "We love stories that teach a lesson or encourage peace, love and a fresh, new understanding. Just be who you are and do what you do. Then all of life's treasures will come to you."

NATIONAL GEOGRAPHIC WORLD, 1145 17th St. NW, Washington DC 20036-4688. (202)857-7000. Fax: (202)775-6112. Website: www.nationalgeographic.com.world. Magazine published monthly. Picture magazine for ages 8-14. Purpose in publishing work by young people: to encourage in young readers a curiosity about the world around them.

• *National Geographic World* does not accept unsolicited manuscripts.

Tips: Publishes art, letters, poems, games, riddles, jokes and craft ideas by children in mailbag section only. No payment given. Send by mail to: Submissions Committee. "Sorry, but *World* cannot acknowledge or return your contributions."

NEW MOON: The Magazine For Girls & Their Dreams, New Moon Publishing, Inc., P.O. Box 3620, Duluth MN 55803-3620. (218)728-5507. Fax: (218)728-0314. E-mail: girl@newmoon.org. Website: www.newmoon.org. **Managing Editor:** Deb Mylin. Magazine. Published bimonthly. *New Moon*'s primary audience is girls ages 8-14. "We publish a magazine that listens to girls." More than 70% of *New Moon* is written by girls. Purpose in publishing work by children/teens: "We want girls' voices to be heard. *New Moon* wants girls to see that their opinions, dreams, thoughts and ideas count." Writer's guidelines available for SASE or online.

Magazine: 75% of magazine written by young people. Buys 3 fiction mss/year (900-1,200 words); 30 nonfiction mss/year (600 words). Submit to Deb Mylin, managing editor. Submit query, complete mss for fiction and nonfiction. Will accept typewritten, legibly handwritten mss and disk (IBM compatible). "We do not return or acknowledge unsolicited material. Do not send originals—we will not return any materials." Responds in 6 months if interested.

Artwork/Photography: Publishes artwork and photography by children. Looks for cover and inside illustrations. Pay negotiated. Submit art and photographs to Deb Mylin, managing editor. "We do not return unsolicited material."

Tips: "Read *New Moon* to completely understand our needs."

POTLUCK CHILDREN'S LITERARY MAGAZINE, P.O. Box 546, Deerfield IL 60015-0546. Fax: (847)317-9492. E-mail: nappic@aol.com. Website: www.potluckmagazine.com. Quarterly magazine. "We look for works with imagery and human truths. Occasionally we will work with young authors on editing their work. We are available to the writer for questions and comments. The purpose of *Potluck* is to encourage creative expression and to supply young writers with a forum in which they can be heard. We also provide informative articles to help them become better writers and to prepare them for the adult markets. For example, recent articles dealt with work presentation, tracking submissions and rights." Writer's guidelines available on request with a SASE or online.

Magazines: 99% of magazine written by young people. Uses fiction (300-400 words); nonfiction (300-400 words); poetry (30 lines); book reviews (150 words). Pays with copy of issue published. Submit mss to Susan Napoli Picchietti, editor. Submit complete ms; teacher may send group submissions, which have different guidelines and payment schedules. Will accept typewritten and e-mailed mss (no attachments work within body of e-mail). Include SASE. Responds 6 weeks after deadline.

Artwork/Photography: Publishes artwork by young artists. Looks for all types of artwork—no textured works. Must be 8½ × 11 only. Pays in copies. Do not fold submissions. If you want your work returned, you must include proper postage and envelope. Color photo copy accepted. Submit artwork to Susan Napoli Picchietti, editor. Include SASE. Responds in 6 weeks.

Tips: "Relax—observe and acknowledge all that is around you. Life gives us a lot to draw on. Don't get carried away with style—let your words speak for themselves. If you want to be taken seriously as a writer, you must take yourself seriously. The rest will follow. Enjoy yourself and take pride in every piece, even the bad—they keep you humble."

SKIPPING STONES, Multicultural Children's Magazine, P.O. Box 3939, Eugene OR 97403. (541)342-4956. E-mail: skipping@efn.org. Website: www.efn.org/~skipping. **Articles/Poems/Fiction Editor:** Arun N. Toké. 5 issues a year. Estab. 1988. Circulation 2,500. "*Skipping Stones* is a multicultural, nonprofit, children's magazine to encourage cooperation, creativity and celebration of cultural and environmental richness. It offers itself as a creative forum for communication among children from different lands and backgrounds. We prefer work by children under 18 years old. International, minorities and under-represented populations receive priority, multilingual submissions are encouraged."

● *Skipping Stones*' theme for the 2002 Youth Honor Awards is the Internet's impact on multicultural issues. Send SASE for guidelines and more information on the awards.

Magazines: 50% written by children and teenagers. Uses 5-10 fiction short stories and plays (500-750 words); 5-10 nonfiction articles, interviews, letters, history, descriptions of celebrations (500-750 words); 15-20 poems, jokes, riddles, proverbs (250 words or less) per issue. Pays in contributor's copies. Submit mss to Mr. Arun Toké, editor. Submit complete ms for fiction or nonfiction work; teacher and parents can also submit their contributions. Submissions should include "cover letter with name, age, address, school, cultural background, inspiration piece, dreams for future." Will accept typewritten, legibly handwritten and computer/word processor mss. Include SASE. Responds in 4 months. Accepts simultaneous submissions.

Artwork/Photography: Publishes artwork and photography for children. Will review all varieties of ms/illustration packages. Wants comics, cartoons, b&w photos, paintings, drawings (preferably ink & pen or pencil), 8 × 10, color photos OK. Subjects include children, people, celebrations, nature, ecology, multicultural. Pays in contributor's copies.

Terms: "*Skipping Stones* is a labor of love. You'll receive complimentary contributor's (up to four) copies depending on the length of your contribution and illustrations." Responds to artists in 4 months. Sample copy for $5 and 4 first-class stamps.

Tips: "Let the 'inner child' within you speak out—naturally, uninhibited." Wants "material that gives insight on cultural celebrations, lifestyle, custom and tradition, glimpse of daily life in other countries and cultures. Please, no mystery for the sake of mystery! Photos, songs, artwork are most welcome if they illustrate/highlight the points. Upcoming features: Living abroad, turning points, inspirations and outstanding moments in life, cultural celebrations around the world, consciousness, caring for the earth, current events, and the Internet's impact."

SKYLARK, Purdue University Calumet, 2200 169th St., Hammond IN 46323-2094. (219)989-2273. Fax: (219)989-2165. **Editor:** Pamela Hunter. **Young Writers' Editor:** Shirley Jo Moritz. Annual magazine. Circ. 1,000. 20% of material written by juvenile authors. Presently accepting material by children. "*Skylark* wishes to provide a vehicle for creative writing of all kinds (with emphasis on an attractive synthesis of text and layout), especially by writers ages 5-18, who live in the Illinois/Indiana area and who have not ordinarily been provided with such an outlet. Children need a place to see their work published alongside that of adults." Proof of originality is required from parents or teachers for all authors. Age or grade of submitter must be provided, too. "We feel that creativity should be nurtured as soon as possible in an individual. By publishing young, promising authors and illustrators in the same magazine which also features work by adults, perhaps we will provide the impetus for a young person to keep at his/her craft." Writer's guidelines available upon request with a SASE.

Magazines: 20% of magazine written by young people. In previous issues, *Skylark* has published mysteries, fantasy, humor, good narrative fiction stories (400-800 words), personal essays, brief character sketches, nonfiction stories (400-650 words), poetry (no more than 20 lines). Does not want to see material that is obviously religious or sexual. Pays in contributor's copies. Two copies per prose published (one copy for each poem by the same author). Submit ms to Shirley Jo Moritz, Young Writers' editor. Submit complete ms. Prefers typewritten ms. Must include SASE for response or return of material. Responds in 3 months. Byline given.

Artwork/Photography: Publishes artwork and photographs by children. Looks for "photos of animals, landscapes and sports, and for artwork to go along with text." Pays in contributor's copies. One copy per each piece of artwork published. Artwork and photos may be b&w or color. Use unlined paper. Do not use pencil and no copyrighted characters. Markers are advised for best reproduction. Include name and address on the back of each piece. Also, provide age or grade of artist. Package properly to avoid damage. Submit artwork/photos to Pamela Hunter, editor-in-chief. Include SASE. Responds in 5 months.

Tips: "We're looking for literary work. Follow your feelings, be as original as you can and don't be afraid to be different. You are submitting to a publication that accepts work by adults and young people alike. Be responsible. Abide by our guidelines, especially the one concerning an SASE for return of your work or notification of

Circulated to over 20,000 readers under the age of 13, *Stone Soup* has a solid reputation to uphold. Underscoring scientific, historical and cultural themes, the bimonthly magazine publishes imagery and writing based on a child's "close observation of the world." For this illustration of "Honesty," a story written by Zhang He, nine-year-old Natalie Chin simply drew from her experiences as a Chinese-American.

acceptance. Check your manuscript for correct grammar and spelling. If the editor receives two manuscripts that have equally promising content, that editor will always select the work that requires less proofreading corrections."

SPRING TIDES, 824 Stillwood Dr., Savannah GA 31419. (912)925-8800. Annual magazine. Audience consists of children 5-12 years old. Purpose in publishing works by young people: to promote and encourage writing. Requirements to be met before work is published: must be 5-12 years old. Writers guidelines available on request. **Magazines:** 100% of magazine written by young people. Uses 5-6 fiction stories (1,200 words maximum); autobiographical experiences (1,200 words maximum); 15-20 poems (20 lines maximum) per issue. Writers are not paid. Submit complete ms or teacher may submit. Will accept typewritten mss. SASE. Responds in 2 months. **Artwork:** Publishes artwork by children. "We have so far used only local children's artwork because of the complications of keeping and returning pieces."

STONE SOUP, The Magazine by Young Writers and Artists, Children's Art Foundation, P.O. Box 83, Santa Cruz CA 95063. (831)426-5557. Fax: (831)426-1161. E-mail: editor@stonesoup.com. Website: www.stone soup.com. **Articles/Fiction Editor, Art Director:** Ms. Gerry Mandel. Magazine published 6 times/year. Circ. 20,000. "We publish fiction, poetry and artwork by children through age 13. Our preference is for work based on personal experiences and close observation of the world. Our audience is young people through age 13, as well as parents, teachers, librarians." Purpose in publishing works by young people: to encourage children to read and to express themselves through writing and art. Writer's guidelines available upon request with a SASE. **Magazines:** Uses animal, contemporary, fantasy, history, problem-solving, science fiction, sports, spy/mystery/ adventure fiction stories. Uses 5-10 fiction stories (100-2,500 words); 5-10 nonfiction stories (100-2,500 words); 2-4 poems per issue. Does not want to see classroom assignments and formula writing. Buys 65 mss/year. Byline given. Pays on publication. Buys all rights. Pays $30 each for stories and poems, $30 for book reviews. Contributors also receive 2 copies. Sample copy $4. Free writer's guidelines. "We don't publish straight nonfiction, but we do publish stories based on real events and experiences." Send complete ms to Ms. Gerry Mandel, editor. Will accept typewritten and legibly handwritten mss. Include SASE. Responds in 1 month. **Artwork/Photography:** Publishes any type, size or color artwork/photos by children. Pays $20 for b&w or color illustrations. Contributors receive 2 copies. Sample copy $4. Free illustrator's guidelines. Send originals if possible. Send submissions to Ms. Gerry Mandel, editor. Include SASE. Responds in 1 month. Original artwork returned at job's completion. All artwork must be by children through age 13. **Tips:** "Be sure to enclose a SASE. Only work by young people through age 13 is considered. Whether your work is about imaginary situations or real ones, use your own experiences and observations to give your work depth and a sense of reality. Read a few issues of our magazine to get an idea of what we like."

VIRGINIA WRITING, Longwood College, 201 High St., Farmville VA 23909-1839. (804)395-2160. Fax: (804)392-6441. E-mail: tdean@longwood.lwc.com. Website: www.lwc.edu/vawriting. Submit entries to: Billy C. Clark, editor. Magazine published twice yearly. "*Virginia Writing* publishes prose, poetry, fiction, nonfiction, art, photography, music and drama from Virginia high school students and teachers. The purpose of the journal is to give "promising writers, artists and photographers, the talented young people of Virginia, an opportunity to have their works published. Our audience is mainly Virginia high schools, Virginia public libraries, Department of Education offices, and private citizens. The magazine is also used as a supplementary text in many of Virginia's high school classrooms. The children must be attending a Virginia high school, preferably in no less than 9th grade (though some work has been accepted from 8th graders). Originality is strongly encouraged. The guidelines are in the front of our magazine or available with SASE." No profanity or racism accepted.
 • *Virginia Writing* is the recipient of 16 national awards, including the 1997 Golden Shoestring Honor Award, eight Distinguished Achievement Awards for Excellence in Educational Journalism and the Golden Lamp Honor Award as one of the top four educational magazines in the U.S. and Canada.
Magazines: 85% of magazine written by children. Uses approximately 7 fiction and nonfiction short stories and essays, 56 poems per issue. Submit complete ms. Will accept only typewritten mss. All works (writings, art, and photography) must be titled. Responds in 4 months, "but must include SASE to receive a reply in the event manuscript is not accepted." **Artwork/Photography:** Publishes artwork by children. Considers all types of artwork, including that done on computer. Color slides or prints of artwork are acceptable. All original work is returned upon publication in a non-bendable, well protected package. Responds as soon as possible. **Tips:** "All works should be submitted with a cover letter describing student's age, grade and high school currently attending. Submit as often as you like and in any quantity. We cannot accept a work if it features profanity or racism."

WHOLE NOTES, P.O. Box 1374, Las Cruces NM 88004-1374. (505)541-5744. E-mail: rnhastings@zianet.c om. **Editor:** Nancy Peters Hastings. Magazine published twice yearly. "We encourage interest in contemporary poetry by showcasing outstanding creative writing. We look for original, fresh perceptions in poems that demonstrate skill in using language effectively, with carefully chosen images and clear ideas. Our audience (general) loves poetry. We try to recognize excellence in creative writing by children as a way to encourage and promote imaginative thinking." Writer's guidelines available for SASE.

Highlighting multicultural and nature awareness issues intimately, 13-year-old Sophia Sansone presented this drawing and an essay to *Skipping Stones'* popular annual youth Honor Awards program last year. Established in 1988, *Skipping Stones* promotes creativity and communication for young minorities and under-represented populations. Their annual contest results in hundreds of submissions from youth writers and artists around the world.

Magazines: Every fourth issue is 100% by children. Writers should be 21 years old or younger. Uses 30 poems/issue (length open). Pays complimentary copy. Submit mss to Nancy Peters Hastings, editor. Submit complete ms. "No multiple submissions, please." Will accept typewritten and legibly handwritten mss. SASE. Responds in 2 months.

Artwork/Photography: Publishes artwork and photographs by children. Looks for b&w line drawings which can easily be reproduced; b&w photos. Pays complimentary copy. Send clear photocopies. Submit artwork to Nancy Peters Hastings, editor. SASE. Responds in 2 months.

Tips: Sample issue is $3. "We welcome translations. Send your best work. Don't send your only copy of your poem. Keep a photocopy."

WORD DANCE, Playful Productions, Inc., P.O. Box 10804, Wilmington DE 19850-0804. (302)894-1950. Fax: (302)894-1957. E-mail: playful@worddance.com. Website: www.worddance.com. **Director:** Stuart Unger. Magazine. Published quarterly. "We're a magazine of creative writing and art that is for *and* by children in kindergarten through grade eight. We give children a voice."

Magazines: Uses adventure, fantasy, humorous, etc. (fiction); travel stories, poems and stories based on real life experiences (nonfiction). Publishes 250 total pieces of writing/year; maximum length: 3 pages. Submit mss to Stuart Ungar, articles editor. Sample copy $3. Free writer's guidelines and submissions form. SASE. Responds in 9 months.

Artwork: Illustrations accepted from young people in kindergarten through grade 8. Accepts illustrations of specific stories or poems and other general artwork. Must be high contrast. Query. Submit complete package with final art to art director. SASE. Responds in 8 months.

Tips: "Submit writing that falls into one of our specific on-going departments. General creative writing submissions are much more competitive."

THE WRITERS' SLATE, (The Writing Conference, Inc.), P.O. Box 27288, Overland Park KS 66225-7288. (913)681-8894. Fax: (913)681-8894. E-mail: jbushman@writingconference.com. Website: www.writingconference.com. Magazine. Publishes 3 issues/year. *The Writers' Slate* accepts original poetry and prose from students enrolled in kindergarten-12th grade. The audience is students, teachers and librarians. Purpose in publishing works by young people: to give students the opportunity to publish and to give students the opportunity *to read* quality literature written by other students. Writer's guidelines available on request.

Magazines: 90% of magazine written by young people. Uses 10-15 fiction, 1-2 nonfiction, 10-15 other mss per issue. Submit mss to Dr. F. Todd Goodson, editor, Kansas State University, 364 Bluemont Hall, Manhattan KS 66506-5300. Submit complete ms. Will accept typewritten mss. Responds in 1 month. Include SASE with ms if reply is desired.

Artwork: Publishes artwork by young people. Bold, b&w, student artwork may accompany a piece of writing. Submit to Dr. F. Todd Goodson, editor. Responds in 1 month.

Tips: "Always accompany submission with a letter indicating name, home address, school, grade level and teacher's name. If you want a reply, submit a SASE."

Resources
Agents & Art Reps

This section features listings of literary agents and art reps who either specialize in or represent a good percentage of children's writers or illustrators. While there are a number of children's publishers who are open to nonagented material, using the services of an agent or rep can be beneficial to a writer or artist. Agents and reps can get your work seen by editors and art directors more quickly. They are familiar with the market and have insights into which editors and art directors would be most interested in your work. Also, they negotiate contracts and will likely be able to get you a better deal than you could get on your own.

Agents and reps make their income by taking a percentage of what writers and illustrators receive from publishers. The standard percentage for agents is 10-15 percent; art reps generally take 25-30 percent. We have not included any agencies in this section that charge reading fees.

WHAT TO SEND

When putting together a package for an agent or rep, follow the guidelines given in their listings. Most agents open to submissions prefer initially to receive a query letter describing your work. For novels and longer works, some agents ask for an outline and a number of sample chapters, but you should send these only if you're asked to do so. Never fax or e-mail a query letter or sample chapters to agents without their permission. Just as with publishers, agents receive a large volume of submissions. It may take them a long time to reply, so you may want to query several agents at one time. It's best, however, to have a complete manuscript considered by only one agent at a time. Always include a self-addressed, stamped envelope (SASE).

For initial contact with art reps, send a brief query letter and self-promo pieces. Again, follow the guidelines given in the listings. If you don't have a flier or brochure, send photocopies. (For tips on creating promotional material see Self-Promotion for Illustrators on page 27.) Always include a SASE.

An Organization for Agents

In some listings of agents you'll see references to AAR (The Association of Authors' Representatives). This organization requires its members to meet an established list of professional standards and code of ethics.

The objectives of AAR include keeping agents informed about conditions in publishing and related fields; encouraging cooperation among literary organizations; and assisting agents in representing their author-clients' interests. Officially, members are prohibited from directly or indirectly charging reading fees. They offer writers a list of member agents on their website or through the mail (for $7 plus 55¢ postage). They also offer a list of recommended questions an author should ask an agent. They can be contacted at AAR, P.O. Box 237201, Ansonia Station NY 10003. Website: www.aar-online.org.

For those who both write and illustrate, some agents listed will consider the work of author/ illustrators. Read through the listings for details.

As you consider approaching agents and reps with your work, keep in mind that they are very choosy about who they take on to represent. Your work must be high quality and presented professionally to make an impression on them. For insights from an art rep on what impresses him in a submission, read the Insider Report with **Barry Goldblatt** on page 288. For more listings of agents and more information and tips see *Guide to Literary Agents*; for additional listing of art reps see *Artist's & Graphic Designer's Market* (both Writer's Digest Books).

Information on agents and art reps listed in the previous edition but not included in this edition of *Children's Writer's & Illustrator's Market* may be found in the General Index.

AGENTS

ALLRED & ALLRED, 7834 Alabama Ave., Canoga Park CA 91304-4905. (818)346-4313. **Contact:** Robert Allred and Kim Allred. Seeking both new and established writers. Estab. 1991. Represents 8 clients. 75% of clients are new/previously unpublished writers. 25% of material handled is books for young readers. Staff includes Robert Allred, Kim Allred.
Represents: Considers fiction, nonfiction, middle grade, young adult. Handles all and any material except picture books.
How to Contact: Send outline and first 2 sample chapters. Considers simultaneous queries and submissions. Responds in 1 month to queries; 2 months to mss. Returns material only with SASE. Obtains clients through queries/solicitations.
Recent Sales: Sold 2 books for young readers in the last year. *Diamond in the Rough*, by Richard Blacke (Wiede Western); *Red Rose, White Rose*, by Betty Stuart (Sunset).
Terms: Agent receives 10% on domestic sales; 20% on foreign sales. Offers written contract, binding for 1 year. 1-month notice must be given to terminate contract.

BOOKS & SUCH, 4799 Carissa Ave., Santa Rosa CA 95405. (707)538-4184. Fax: (626)398-0246. E-mail: jkgbooks@aol.com. **Contact:** Janet Kobobel Grant. Estab. 1996. Associate member of CBA. Represents 35 clients. 12% of clients are new/unpublished writers. Specializes in "the Christian booksellers market but is expanding into the ABA market with children's and young adult projects."
• Before becoming an agent, Ms. Grant was an editor for Zondervan and managing editor for *Focus on the Family*.
Represents: 25% juvenile books. Considers: nonfiction, fiction, picture books, young adult.
How to Contact: Query with SASE. Considers simultaneous queries. Responds in 1 month on queries; 6 weeks on mss. Returns material only with SASE.
Recent Sales: *The Roadrunner Reader* series (Cook Communications).
Needs: Actively seeking "material appropriate to the Christian market or that would crossover to the ABA market as well." Obtains new clients through recommendations and conferences.
Terms: Agent receives 15% commission on domestic and foreign sales. Offers written contract. 2 months notice must be given to terminate contract. Charges for postage, photocopying, fax and express mail.
Tips: "The heart of my motivation is to develop relationships with the authors I serve, to do what I can to shine the light of success on them, and to help be a caretaker of their gifts and time."

ANDREA BROWN LITERARY AGENCY, INC., P.O. Box 371027, Montara CA 94037-1027. (650)728-1783. E-mail: ablitag@pacbell.net. **President:** Andrea Brown. Estab. 1981. Member of SCBWI and WNBA. 10% of clients are new/previously unpublished writers. Specializes in "all kinds of children's books—illustrators and authors."
• Prior to opening her agency, Brown served as an editorial assistant at Random House and Dell Publishing and as an editor with Alfred A. Knopf.
Member Agents: Andrea Brown; Laura Rennert, associate agent.
Represents: 98% juvenile books. Considers: nonfiction (animals, anthropology/archaeology, art/architecture/ design, biography/autobiography, current affairs, ethnic/cultural interests, history, how-to, nature/environment, photography, popular culture, science/technology, sociology, sports); fiction (historical, science fiction); picture books, young adult.
How to Contact: Query. Responds in 1 month on queries; 3 months on mss. E-mail queries only.
Needs: Mostly obtains new clients through recommendations, editors, clients and agents.
Terms: Agent receives 15% commission on domestic sales; 20% on foreign sales. Written contract.

Tips: Query first. "Taking on very few picture books. Must be unique—no rhyme, no anthropomorphism. Do not call, or fax queries or manuscripts." Agents at Andrea Brown Literary Agency attend Austin Writers League; SCBWI, Columbus Writers Conference, Willamette Writers Conference, Orange County Conferences; Mills College Childrens Literature Conference (Oakland CA); Asilomar (Pacific Grove CA); Maui Writers Conference, Southwest Writers Conference; San Diego State University Writer's Conference; Big Sur Children's Writing Workshop. Recent sales include *All About The 50 States*, by Bill Gutman (Random House); *Music Teacher from the Black Lagoon*, by Mike Thaler (Scholastic); *Jill Tater and Seti*, by Ellen Jackson (Houghton-Mifflin); *Christmas John*, by Marget Raven (Farrar, Staus & Giroux).

☑ PEMA BROWNE LTD., HCR Box 104B, 71 Pine Rd., Neversink NY 12765-9603. (845)985-2936. Website: www.geocities.com/pemabrowneltd. **Contact:** Perry Browne or Pema Browne ("Pema rhymes with Emma"). Estab. 1966. Member of SCBWI. Represents 30 clients. Handles selected commercial fiction, nonfiction, romance, business, new age, reference, pop culture, juvenile and children's picture books.
  • Prior to opening their agency, Perry Browne was a radio and TV performer; Pema Browne was a fine artist and art buyer.
Member Agents: Pema Browne (children's fiction and nonfiction, adult nonfiction); Perry Browne (adult fiction and nonfiction).
Represents: 35% juvenile books. Considers: nonfiction, fiction, picture books, young adult.
How to Contact: Query with SASE. No fax queries. No e-mail queries. Responds in 3 weeks on queries; within 6 weeks on mss. Prefers to be the only reader. "We do not review manuscripts that have been sent out to publishers."Returns materials only with SASE.
Needs: Actively seeking nonfiction, juvenile, middle grade, some young adult, picture books. Obtains new clients through "editors, authors, *LMP*, *Guide to Literary Agents* and as a result of longevity!"
Terms: Agent receives 15% commission on domestic sales; 20% on foreign sales.
Tips: "In nonfiction, one must have credentials to lend credence to a proposal. Make sure of margins, double-space and use clean, dark type." This agency sold 20 books in the last year.

Ⓝ RUTH COHEN, INC. LITERARY AGENCY, P.O. Box 2244, LaJolla CA 92038-2244. (858)456-5805. **Contact:** Ruth Cohen. Estab. 1982. Member of AAR, Authors Guild, Sisters in Crime, Romance Writers of America, SCBWI. Represents 45 clients. 15% of clients are new/previously unpublished writers. Specializes in "quality writing in contemporary fiction; women's fiction; mysteries; thrillers and juvenile fiction."
  • Prior to opening her agency, Cohen served as directing editor at Scott Foresman & Company (now HarperCollins).
Represents: 35% juvenile. Considers: nonfiction, fiction, picture books, young adult.
How to Contact: *No unsolicited mss.* Send outline plus 2 sample chapters. "Please indicate your phone number or e-mail address." *Must include SASE.* Responds in 3 weeks on queries.
Needs: Obtains new clients through recommendations from others and through submissions.
Terms: Agent receives 15% commission on domestic sales; 20% on foreign sales, "if a foreign agent is involved." Offers written contract, binding for 1 year "continuing to next." Charges for foreign postage, phone calls, photocopying submissions and overnight delivery of mss when appropriate.
Tips: "As the publishing world merges and changes, there seem to be fewer opportunities for new writers to succeed in the work that they love. We urge you to develop the patience, persistence and perseverance that have made this agency so successful. Prepare a well-written and well-crafted manuscript, and our combined best efforts can help advance both our careers."

Ⓝ THE CONTENT COMPANY INC., 5111 JFK Blvd. E, West New York NJ 07093. (201)558-0323. Fax: (201)558-0307. E-mail: info@theliteraryagency.com. Website: www.theliteraryagency.com, therightsagency.com. **Contact:** Lauren Mactas. Estab. 1979. Represents 20 clients. 5% of clients are new/previously unpublished writers. 30% of material handled is books for young readers.
  • Prior to starting an agency, Peter Elek worked as an art director/ production director for book and magazine publishing.
Member Agents: Lauren Mactas; Peter Elek (illustration/picture books).
Represents: Considers nonfiction/picture books. "Our strength is based on proven success combining text and imagery—interpreting author's vision." Actively seeking fresh, original, nonderivative ideas—proving the author/illustrator identifies with a child's psyche. Not looking for "issues" and "causes" books, nor single stories featuring a character that can be made into a series, nor ideas that envision licensed product to make them palatable! Books that "would make a great animated TV series" are discouraged as well.
How to Contact: Query with SASE or send outline and 2 sample chapters for longer works. Accepts queries by e-mail. Prefers to read material exclusively. Responds in 3 weeks to queries; 2 months to mss. Returns material only with SASE. Obtains clients through recommendations from others.
Recent Sales: Sold 6 books for young readers in the last year. *Attack on Pearl Harbor* (Hyperion); *Princess*, by Hugh Brewster (HarperCollins); *My Mommy Hung the Moon*, by Laura Cornell (Jamie Lee Curtis) (Joanna Cotler Books/HarperCollins); *Ice Age Mammoths* (Crown Books for Young Readers); *Before You Were Big*, by Laura Cornell (Jennifer Davis) (Workman).

Terms: Agent receives 15% commission on domestic sales; 20% on foreign sales. Offers written contract. 1-month notice must be given to terminate contract (with surviving terms).
Writing Conferences: Will attend LIBF in London March 2002; Bologna in Bologna Italy April 2002; Book Expo in New York May 2002.
Tips: "We are not editorially driven, but after 25 years we recognize good writing. We are a market driven company that provides emotional and professional support to our clients. We enhance and mediate the author/illustrator-publisher/editor relationship but don't feel the need to interpose our will on that relationship."

DWYER & O'GRADY, INC., P.O. Box 239, Lempster NH 03605-0239. (603)863-9347. Fax: (603)863-9346. **Contact:** Elizabeth O'Grady. Estab. 1990. Member of SCBWI. Represents 20 clients. Represents only writers and illustrators of children's books.
• Dwyer & O'Grady is currently not accepting new clients.
Member Agents: Elizabeth O'Grady (children's books); Jeff Dwyer (children's books).
Represents: 100% juvenile books. Considers: nonfiction, fiction, picture books, young adult.
Recent Sales: *Moon Over Blind Eye*, by N. Tarpley/E.B. Lewis (Knopf Byr); *Louisa May & Mr. Thoreau's Flute*, by J. Duhlar/M.Azarian (Dial Byr); *Gleam & Glow*, by E. Bunting/P. Sylvada (Harcourt).
Needs: Obtains new clients through referrals or direct approach from agent to writer whose work they've read. Does not accept unsolicited mss.
Terms: Agent receives 15% commission on domestic sales; 20% on foreign sales. Offers written contract. Thirty days notice must be given to terminate contract. Charges for "photocopying of longer manuscripts or mutually agreed upon marketing expenses."
Tips: Agents from Dwyer & O'Grady attend Book Expo; American Library Association; Society of Children's Book Writers & Illustrators conferences. Clients include: Kim Ablon, Tom Bodett, Odds Bodkin, Donna Clair, Leonard Jenkins, Rebecca Rule, Steve Schuch, Virginia Stroud, Natasha Tarpley, Zong-Zhou Wang, Rashida Watson, Peter Sylvada, Mary Azarian, and E.B. Lewis.

ETHAN ELLENBERG LITERARY AGENCY, 548 Broadway, #5-E, New York NY 10012. (212)431-4554. Fax: (212)941-4652. E-mail: eellenberg@aol.com. Website: http://EthanEllenberg.com. **Contact:** Ethan Ellenberg. Estab. 1983. Represents 70 clients. 10% of clients are new/previously unpublished writers. Children's books are an important area for us.
• Prior to opening his agency, Ellenberg was contracts manager of Berkley/Jove and associate contracts manager for Bantam.
Represents: "We do a lot of children's books." Considers: nonfiction, fiction, picture books, young adult.
How to Contact: Children's submissions—send full ms. Young adults—send outline plus 3 sample chapters. Accepts queries by e-mail; does not accept attachments to e-mail queries or fax queries. Considers simultaneous queries and submissions. Responds in 10 days on queries; 3-4 weeks on mss. Returns materials only with SASE.
Terms: Agent receives 15% on domestic sales; 10% on foreign sales. Offers written contract, "flexible." Charges for "direct expenses only: photocopying, postage."
Tips: "We do consider new material from unsolicited authors. Write a good clear letter with a succinct description of your book. We prefer the first three chapters when we consider fiction, but for children's book submissions, we prefer the full manuscript. For all submissions you must include SASE for return or the material is discarded. It's always hard to break in, but talent will find a home. We continue to seek natural storytellers and nonfiction writers with important books." This agency sold over 100 titles in the last year, including *The Invisible Enemy*, by Martha Jocelyn.

N GEM LITERARY, 4717 Poe Rd., Medina OH 44256. (330)725-8807. E-mail: gemlit@earthlink.net. Website: www.gembooks.com. **Contact:** Darla Pfenniger. Seeking both new and established writers. Estab. 1996. Member of ABA, Sisters in Crime. Represents 50 clients. 90% of clients are new/previously unpublished writers. 15% of material handled is books for young readers. Charges writers "generally between $125-175—all expenses that are incurred in marketing their manuscripts." Writers are reimbursed fees after sale of ms.
Tips: "We are hands on and will make suggestions as needed. Relationships vary with the author and length of time we've worked together. We use the editor's knowledge to steer books to the most likely prospects."

N BARRY GOLDBLATT LITERARY AGENCY, PMB 266/320 7th Ave., Brooklyn NY. (718)832-8787. Fax: (718)832-5558. E-mail: bgliterary@earthlink.net. **Contact:** Barry Goldblatt. Estab. 2000. Member of SCBWI. Represents 15 clients. 40% of clients are new/previously unpublished writers. 100% of material handled is books for young readers.
Staff includes Barry Goldblatt (picture books, middle grade and young adult novels).
Represents: Considers picture books, fiction, middle grade, young adult.
How to Contact: Send entire manuscript for picture books; outline and 3 sample chapters for fiction. Prefers to read material exclusively. Reports in 3 weeks on queries; 2 months on manuscripts. Returns material only with SASE. Obtains clients through recommendations from others.
Recent Sales: Sold 10 books for young readers in the last year.
Terms: Agent receives 15% commission on domestic sales; 20% on foreign sales.

insider report

New agent seeks strong voice and great characters

"Children's publishing was pretty much an accidental career for me," says Barry Goldblatt, founder of Barry Goldblatt Literary Agency. Goldblatt first arrived in New York with dreams of acquiring an editorial position for a science fiction magazine. After several dead ends in the sci-fi field, he began exploring the possibility of a career in subsidiary rights. Eventually, he ended up at Dutton Children's Books with a job as rights assistant, where he first discovered his love for the world of children's publishing.

When he first met with Donne Forrest at Dutton Children's books, Goldblatt recalls, "I didn't think I knew the first thing about children's books, but she handed me copies of *Winnie-the-Pooh* and William Sleator's *Interstellar Pig*, and I think a Rosemary Wells picture book, and I suddenly felt a connection. It helped

Barry Goldblatt

that Donne really gave me lots of opportunities to grow and learn the business, and within three months I was hooked." Goldblatt was drawn into the arena of children's publishing so much that he later turned down a job in science fiction publishing. After years of working in subsidiary rights at Dutton, The Putnam & Grosset Group, and finally, as Rights and Contracts Director at Orchard Books, Goldblatt took what to him was "the natural next step" in his career and opened his own literary agency in September 2000.

The skills Goldblatt gained working as rights director have proven quite beneficial to him as an agent. "My primary focus is negotiating deals with publishers, which is what I did as a rights director. Now I just have the added (and incredibly challenging) task of finding books and authors to represent." In addition to the similarities in job description, Goldblatt centers his agency around a familiar subject matter as well. His agency specializes in young adult and middle grade novels, and thus the contacts Goldblatt made in the world of children's publishing as rights director serve him well in agenting. And working with children's books over the years has developed in him some rather specific literary preferences on which he focuses his agency.

Goldblatt suggests that his predilection towards children's books echoes his "sense of the importance of children's literature. These books are the first exposure most people will have to the power of the written word and the world of art, to the marvelous way reading can transport you anywhere in the universe." And with novels, he recognizes whether or not a manuscript will work almost right away. "When I read a novel, I'm confident I'll recognize something special: a terrific character, a fascinating plot, an emotional resonance." Although picture books prove to be a greater challenge for an agent, especially with only a manuscript, Barry Goldblatt Literary Agency also represents many picture book authors and illustrators. "It's certainly much easier to sell an entire picture book, art and text, because then the whole thing is there in front of you, but sometimes, you know you've got a great text and you just have to find the right editor who can match it to a dynamite artist."

Goldblatt finds the market for children's books, especially those for young adults and teenagers, to be an ever-changing and expanding one, and that children's books, in themselves, are becoming more and more accepted as a "literary art form." In young adult novels, "there are no holds barred, no real taboos anymore. Fiction for teens can be as powerful and liberating as any adult book on the market, and much to my delight, can often even reach an adult audience, which only helps to bring young adult literature more well-deserved attention."

As far as finding new authors and books goes, Goldblatt knows what he likes when he sees it. He describes his ideal submission simply as a manuscript that blows him away. "I need to find myself laughing hysterically or weeping my eyes out, or I need to be marveling at the intricate details of a plot or fascinated by an extraordinary voice." And his opinion of the book usually depends on his opinion of the characters. For Goldblatt the heart of the story lies in characterization and voice—if either of these is lacking, the story as a whole fails to work effectively. "Plotlines can be fixed, style and structure can be tinkered with, but if the voice isn't there, that almost indefinable something that makes a book come alive, then I'm just not interested."

An agent's personal taste often aids in the decision of whether or not to represent an author. Goldblatt has a personal fondness for "wacky humor," and he always wants to receive stories with "an edge, a bite, something unusual, unexpected and unique." First and foremost, Goldblatt requires that a manuscript bring out something in him; he has to like it. "If I'm not passionate about something, it's going to be much more challenging to be passionate in how I sell it, and that's not fair to the author, or, ultimately, to myself."

While appealing to an agent's personal tastes is somewhat out of an author's control, certain aspects of a submission make it more appealing no matter how emotionally engaged an agent feels by the manuscript. One of the consistent problems with submissions, Goldblatt says, is that authors do not put enough time and effort into their cover letters. A bad cover letter is "the kiss of death for me," he says. "I often won't even read the manuscript if the letter is full of typos and bad grammar. The ideal cover letter for me says, 'Here's my manuscript. Hope you like it.' That's it, short, sweet and to the point."

Although he has no set standards for the agent-client relationship, Goldblatt maintains that whether an author depends on him as an agent for editorial guidance or not, he expects at least one thing in return: honesty. "Nothing will contaminate this kind of relationship faster and more destructively than hiding feelings or, worse, lying about them. If one of my clients is unhappy with something I've done, I need to know, or how else can I possibly work to solve the problem?" And it goes both ways—he has to be able to tell clients when they fail to hold up their end of the bargain. "Talking with each other is the only way problems can be resolved, compromises reached, whatever it is sorted out. It's key."

Goldblatt sums up his job description as an agent, saying, "I'm passionate and hungry, and I'll do all I can to make sure each and every one of my clients has a stupendous career . . . hopefully all agents want that for their clients." He advises authors who are considering choosing an agent to "do research, ask lots of questions, and never settle for someone just because they're available. An agent is a big factor in your career; they're going to be involved with you financially, and, since writing is such a personal career, they're also going to be very much a part of your life, so you don't want just anyone. Make sure it's someone with whom you have simpatico, a common sense of where to go and how to get there."

—*Stefanie Hayner*

Tips: "I structure my relationship with each client differently, according to their wants and needs. I'm mostly hands-on, but some want more editorial input, others less. I'm pretty aggressive selling work, but I'm fairly laid back in how I deal with clients. I'd say I'm quite friendly with most of my clients, and I like it that way. To me this is more than just a simple busines relationship."

BARBARA S. KOUTS, LITERARY AGENT, P.O. Box 560, Bellport NY 11713. (631)286-1278. **Contact:** Barbara Kouts. Estab. 1980. Member of AAR. Represent 50 clients. 10% of clients are new/previously unpublished writers. Specializes in adult fiction and nonfiction and children's books.
Represents: 60% juvenile books. Considers: nonfiction, fiction, picture books, young adult.
How to Contact: Query. Responds in 3 days on queries; 6 weeks on mss.
Needs: Obtains new clients through recommendations from others, solicitation, at conferences, etc.
Terms: Agent receives 15% commission on domestic sales; 20% on foreign sales. Charges for photocopying.
Tips: "Write, do not call. Be professional in your writing." Recent sales of this agency include *Dancing on the Edge*, by Han Nolan (Harcourt Brace); *Cendrillon*, by Robert San Souci (Simon & Schuster).

RAY LINCOLN LITERARY AGENCY, Elkins Park House, Suite 107-B, 7900 Old York Rd., Elkins Park PA 19027. (215)635-0827. Fax: (215)782-8882. **Contact:** Mrs. Ray Lincoln. Estab. 1974. Represents 30 clients. 35% of clients are new/previously unpublished writers. Specializes in biography, nature, the sciences, fiction in both adult and children's categories.
Member Agents: Jerome A. Lincoln.
Represents: 20% juvenile books. Considers nonfiction, fiction, young adult, chapter and picture books.
How to Contact: Query first, then on request send outline, 2 sample chapters and SASE. "I send for balance of manuscript if it is a likely project." Responds in 2 weeks on queries; 1 month on mss.
Needs: Obtains new clients usually from recommendations.
Terms: Agent receives 15% commission on domestic sales; 20% on foreign sales. Offers written contract, binding "but with notice, may be cancelled." Charges only for overseas telephone calls. "I request authors to do manuscript photocopying themselves. Postage or shipping charge on manuscripts accepted for representation by agency."
Tips: "I always look for polished writing style, fresh points of view and professional attitudes." Recent sales of this agency include *The Best Halloween Ever*, by Barbara Robinson; *The Loser*, by Jerry Spinelli; *Moe McTooth*, by Eileen Spinelli (Houghton Mifflin); and *Towanda and Me*, by Susan Katz (Orchard Books).

GINA MACCOBY LITERARY AGENCY, P.O. Box 60, Chappaqua NY 10514. (914)238-5630. **Contact:** Gina Maccoby. Estab. 1986. Represents 35 clients. Represents writers and illustrators of children's books.
Represents: 33% juvenile books. Considers: nonfiction, fiction, young adult.
How to Contact: Query with SASE. "Please, no unsolicited mss." Considers simultaneous queries and submisssions. Responds in 2 months. Returns materials only with SASE.
Needs: Usually obtains new clients through recommendations from own clients.
Terms: Agent receives 15% commission on domestic sales; 25% on foreign sales. Charges for photocopying. May recover certain costs such as airmail postage to Europe or Japan or legal fees.
Tips: This agency sold 18 titles last year including *All Kinds of Families*, by Mary Ann Hoberman.

N: BARBARA MARKOWITZ LITERARY AGENCY, 117 H. Mansfield Ave., Los Angeles CA 90036-3020. (323)939-5927. **Contact:** Barbara Markowitz. Seeking both new and established writers. Estab. 1980. Member of SCBWI. Represents 12 clients. 80% of clients are new/previously unpublished writers. 50% of material handled is books for 8-11 year old, mid-level readers. Staff includes Judith Rosenthal (young adult, historical fiction); Barbara Markowitz (mid-level and young adult, contemporary fiction).
   ● Prior to opening her agency, Markowitz owned Barbara Bookstores in Chicago.
Represents: Considers fiction, middle grade, young adult (11-15 year olds) historical fiction. Actively seeking contemporary and historical fiction no more than 35,000 words for 8-11 year olds and 11-15 year olds. Not looking for fable, fantasy, fairytales; no illustrated; no science fiction; no books about dogs, cats, pigs.
How to Contact: Query with SASE or send outline and 3 sample chapters. Considers simultaneous queries and submissions. Responds in 1 week to queries; 6 weeks to mss. Returns material only with SASE. "If no SASE provided, I discard." Obtains new clients through recommendations from others, queries/solicitations.
Recent Sales: Sold 4 books for young readers in the last year. *The Red Rose Box*, by Brenda Wood (Putnam); *Just Jane*, by William Lavender (Harcourt); *Fame & Glory*, by Barbara O'Connor (FSG/Frances Foster).
Terms: Agent receives 15% commission on domestic sales; 15% on foreign sales. Offers written contract, binding for 1 year. 1-month notice must be given to terminate contract.
Fees; Charges clients for postage only.
Tips: Markowitz agenting style is "very hands on. Yes, I read, critique, light edit, make/request revisions. It's a very personal small agency."

THE NORMA-LEWIS AGENCY, 311 W. 43rd St., Suite 602, New York NY 10036. (212)664-0807. **Contact:** Norma Liebert. Estab. 1980. 50% of clients are new/previously unpublished writers. Specializes in juvenile books (pre-school to high school).

Represents: 60% juvenile books. Considers: nonfiction, fiction, picture books, middle grade young adult.
How to Contact: Prefers to be only reader. Responds in 6 weeks. Returns materials only with SASE.
Terms: Agent receives 15% commission on domestic sales; 20% on foreign sales.

STERNIG & BYRNE LITERARY AGENCY, 3209 S. 55th St., Milwaukee WI 53219-4433. (414)328-8034. Fax: (414)328-8034. E-mail: jackbyrne@aol.com. **Contact:** Jack Byrne. Estab. 1950s. Member of SFWA and MWA. Represents 30 clients. 10% of clients are new/unpublished writers. Sold 12 titles in the last year. "We have a small, friendly, personal, hands-on teamwork approach to marketing."
Member Agents: Jack Byrne.
Represents: 20% juvenile books. Considers: nonfiction, fiction, young adult.
How to Contact: Query. Considers simultaneous queries; no simultaneous submissions. Responds in 3 weeks on queries; 3 months on mss. Returns materials only with SASE. "No SASE equals no return." Currently taking on a few new clients.
Needs: Actively seeking science fiction/fantasy. Does not want to receive romance, poetry, textbooks, highly specialized nonfiction, picture books.
Terms: Agent receives 15% commission on domestic sales; 20% on foreign sales. Offers written contract, open/ non binding. 60 days notice must be given to terminate contract.
Tips: "Don't send first drafts; have a professional presentation . . . including cover letter; know your field (read what's been done . . . good and bad)." Reads *Publishers Weekly*, etc. to find new clients."

SCOTT TREIMEL NY, 434 Lafayette St., New York NY 10003. (212)505-8353. Fax: (212)505-0664. E-mail: mescottyt@earthlink.net. **Contact:** Scott Treimel. Estab. 1995. Represents 19 clients. 15% of clients are new/ unpublished writers. Specializes in children's books, all genres: tightly focused segments of the trade and, to a lesser extent, educational markets. Member AAR.
● Prior to opening his agency, Treimel was an assistant to Marilyn E. Marlow of Curtis Brown; a rights agent for Scholastic, Inc.; a book packager and rights agent for United Feature Syndicate; the founding director of Warner Bros. Worldwide Publishing, a freelance editor; and a rights consultant for HarperCollins Children's Books.
Represents: 100% juvenile books. Considers all juvenile fiction and most nonfiction areas. No religious books.
How to Contact: Query with SASE. For picture books, send entire ms (no more than 2). Does not accept queries by fax or e-mail. No multiple submissions. Requires "30-day exclusivity on requested manuscripts." Replies to materials only with SASE, otherwise discards.
Needs: Interested in seeing picture book author-illustrators, first chapter books, middle-grade fiction and teen fiction. Obtains most clients through recommendations.
Terms: Agent receives 15-20% commission on domestic sales; 20-25% on foreign sales. Offers verbal or written contract, binding on a "contract-by-contract basis." Charges for photocopying, overnight/express postage, messengers and book orders.
Tips: Attends Society of Children's Book Writers & Illustrators Conferences (Los Angeles, August). Sold 20 titles in the last year. Do not pitch: let your work speak for itself. Offers editorial guidance selectively, if extensive charges higher commission.

WECKSLER-INCOMCO, 170 West End Ave., New York NY 10023. (212)787-2239. Fax: (212)496-7035. **Contact:** Sally Wecksler. Estab. 1971. Represents 25 clients. 50% of clients are new/previously unpublished writers. "However, I prefer writers who have had something in print." Specializes in nonfiction with illustrations (photos and art).
● Prior to becoming an agent, Wecksler was an editor at *Publishers Weekly*; publisher with the international department of R.R. Bowker; and international director at Baker & Taylor.
Member Agents: Joann Amparan (general, children's books), Sally Wecksler (general, foreign rights/co-editions, fiction, illustrated books, children's books).
Represents: 25% juvenile books. Considers: nonfiction, fiction, picture books.
How to Contact: Query with outline plus 3 sample chapters. Include brief bio. Responds in 1 month on queries; 2 months on mss.
Needs: Actively seeking "illustrated books for adults or children with beautiful photos or artwork." Does not want to receive "science fiction or books with violence." Obtains new clients through recommendations from others and solicitations.
Terms: Agent receives 15% commission on domestic sales; 20% on foreign sales. Offers written contract, binding for 3 years.
Tips: "Make sure a SASE is enclosed. Send three chapters and outline, clearly typed or word processed manuscript, double-spaced, written with punctuation and grammar in approved style. *We do not like to receive presentations by fax.*"

KATHERINE J. WERNER, 2177 Fairmount Ave., St. Paul MN 55105. (651)690-2419. Fax: (651)690-1427. E-mail: kjwerner2177@earthlink.net. Seeking both new and established writers. Estab. 2000. Member of SCBWI. Represents 12 clients. 40% of clients are new/previously unpublished writers. 100% of material handled is books for young readers.

● Prior to opening her agency, Werner worked in book publishing since 1982 for 5 different publishers in sales/marketing capacities.

Represents: Fiction, nonfiction, picture books, middle grade, young adult, illustrators. "I created this agency to combine my passion for children's literature with 20 years in book publishing sales. My goal is to find the right home for writers and illustrators and to achieve 'win-win' situations for all parties, ultimately creating good books for children." Actively seeking all formats and all ages. Not looking for science fiction, horror, comic/graphic, fantasy novels.

How to Contact: Query with SASE of send outline and 2-3 sample chapters. If picture book, send entire ms. Considers simultaneous queries and submissions. Responds in 2 weeks to queries; 1 month to mss. Returns material only with SASE. Obtains clients through recommendations from others, queries/solicitations, conferences, professional listings, advertisement.

Terms: Agent receives 15% commission on domestic sales. Offers written contract. Offers a letter of agreement on a book-by-book basis. 1-month notice must be given to terminate contract.

Fees: Charges the client for postage, photocopying or any other direct expenses incurred towards the submission of their material. Does not charge marketing fees or pass along other office overhead such as telephone calls.

Writers' Conferences: SCBWI Regional Conference in St. Paul MN March 2001.

Tips: "My goal is to create and build long-term relationships between my clients as well as the editors and publishers. I tend to be 'medium aggressive.' Bye representing only children's writers and illustrators, I believe I can offer more focus and dedicated service to all parties."

WRITERS HOUSE, 21 W. 26th St., New York NY 10010. (212)685-2400. Fax: (212)685-1781. Estab. 1974. Member of AAR. Represents 280 clients. 50% of clients were new/unpublished writers. Specializes in all types of popular fiction and nonfiction. No scholarly, professional, poetry or screenplays.

Member Agents: Amy Berkower (major juvenile authors); Merrilee Heifetz (quality children's fiction); Susan Cohen, Jodi Reamer (juvenile and young adult fiction and nonfiction); Susan Ginsberg; Fran Lebowitz (juvenile and young adult); Robin Rue (YA fiction).

Represents: 35% juvenile books. Considers: nonfiction, fiction, picture books, young adult.

How to Contact: Query. Responds in 1 month on queries.

Needs: Obtains new clients through recommendations from others.

Terms: Agent receives 15% commission on domestic sales; 20% on foreign sales. Offers written contract, binding for 1 year.

Tips: "Do not send manuscripts. Write a compelling letter. If you do, we'll ask to see your work."

N WRITERS HOUSE, (West Coast Office), 3368 Governor Dr., #224F, San Diego CA 92122. (858)678-8767. Fax: (858)678-8530. **Contact:** Steven Malk.

● See Writers House listing above for more information.

Represents: Nonfiction, fiction, picture books, young adult.

ART REPS

ARTCO/GAIL THURM, 232 Madison Ave., Suite 512, New York NY 10016. (212)889-8777. Fax: (212)447-1475. E-mail: artco1@mindspring.com. Website: www.artcorep.com. **Contact:** Gail Thurm. Commercial illustration representative. Estab. 1980. Member of Graphic Artists Guild & Society of Illustrators. Represents 43 illustrators. Approximately 15% of artwork handled is children's book illustration. Staff includes Gail Thurm, Jeff Palmer. Currently open to illustrators seeking representation. Open to both new and established illustrators.

Handles: Illustration.

Recent Sales: *Follow the Moon*, illustrated by Suzanne Duranceau (HarperCollins/Laura Geringer); *Whitefish Will Rides Again*, by Mort Drucker (HarperCollins/Michael di Capua); *Tomatoes From Mars*, by Mort Drucker (HarperCollins di Capua). Represents Sue Hughes, Sally Vitsky, Tim Barnes, Mort Drucker, Inkwell Studios, Suzanne Duranceau.

Terms: Offers written contract. Advertising costs are split: approximately 70% paid by illustrators; 30% paid by rep. Requires portfolio and tearsheets for promotional purposes. Advertises in *Picturebook, American Showcase, The Creative Black Book, The Workbook, Directory of Illustration*.

How to Contact: For first contact, send any of the following: photostats, SASE (required for return of materials), slides, direct mail flier/brochure, photographs, tearsheets, photocopies. Responds only if interested. Portfolio should include tearsheets, slides and photocopies. Finds illustrators through recommendations from other, queries/solicitations, conferences or e-mail with jpg's.

ARTISTS INTERNATIONAL, 17 Wheaton Rd., Marbledale CT 06791. (860)868-1011. Fax: (860)868-6655. E-mail: artsintl@javanet.com. Website: www.artsintl.com. **Contact:** Michael Brodie. Commercial illustration representative. Estab. 1970. Represents 20 illustrators. Specializes in children's books. Markets include: design firms; editorial/magazines; licensing.

Handles: Illustration.

Terms: Rep receives 30% commission. No geographic restrictions. Advertising costs are split: 70% paid by talent; 30% paid by representative.
How to Contact: For first contact, send slides, photocopies and SASE. Reports in 1 week.
Tips: Obtains new talent through recommendations from others, solicitation, conferences, *Literary Market Place*, etc. "SAE with example of your work; no résumés please."

ASCIUTTO ART REPS., INC., 1712 E. Butler Circle, Chandler AZ 85225. (480)899-0600. Fax: (480)899-3636. **Contact:** Mary Anne Asciutto. Children's illustration representative. Estab. 1980. Member of SPAR, Society of Illustrators. Represents 12 illustrators. Specializes in children's illustration for books, magazines, posters, packaging, etc. Markets include: publishing/packaging/advertising.
• Asciutto is now representing children's book writers as well as illustrators.
Handles: Stories and illustration for children only.
Terms: Rep receives 25% commission. No geographic restrictions. Advertising costs are split: 75% paid by talent; 25% paid by representative. For promotional purposes, talent should provide "prints (color) or originals within an $8\frac{1}{2} \times 11$ size format."
How to Contact: Send printed materials, tearsheets, photocopies and/or ms in a SASE. Responds in 2 weeks. After initial contact, send appropriate materials if requested. Portfolio should include original art on paper, tearsheets, photocopies or color prints of most recent work. If accepted, materials will remain for assembly.
Tips: In obtaining representation "be sure to connect with an agent who handles the kind of accounts you (the artist/writer) *want*."

CAROL BANCROFT & FRIENDS, 121 Dodgingtown Rd., P.O. Box 266, Bethel CT 06801. (203)748-4823 or (800)720-7020. Fax: (203)748-4581. E-mail: artists@carolbancroft.com. Website: www.carolbancroft.com. **Owner:** Carol Bancroft. Illustration representative for children's publishing. Estab. 1972. Member of SPAR, Society of Illustrators, Graphic Artists Guild. Represents 40 illustrators. Specializes in illustration for children's publishing—text and trade; any children's-related material. Clients include Scholastic, Houghton Mifflin, Harper-Collins, Dutton, Harcourt Brace.
Handles: Illustration for children of all ages. Seeking multicultural and fine artists.
Terms: Rep receives 25-30% commission. Advertising costs are split: 75% paid by talent; 25% paid by representative. For promotional purposes, talent must provide "laser copies (not slides), tearsheets, promo pieces, good color photocopies, etc.; 6 pieces or more is best; narrative scenes and children interacting." Advertises in *RSVP*, *Picturebook*.
How to Contact: Send samples and SASE."
Tips: "We're looking for artists who can draw animals and people with energy and, above all, imagination. They need to show characters in an engaging way with action in situational settings. Must be able to take a character through a story."

N: SHERYL BERANBAUM, 75 Scenic Dr., Warwick RI 02886. (401)737-8591. Fax: (401)739-5189. E-mail: sheryl@beranbaum.com. Website: www.beranbaum.com. Commercial illustration representative. Estab. 1985. Member of Graphic Artists Guild. Represents 15 illustrators. 75% of artwork handled is children's book illustration. Currently open to illustrators seeking representation. Open to both new and established illustrators. Submission guidelines available by phone.
Handles: Illustration.
Recent Sales: Books by Albert Molnar (Harcourt, Simon & Schuster); Beth Buffington (Harcourt, Houghton Mifflin); John Kastner (Harcourt). "My illustrators are diversified and their work comes from a variety of the industry's audiences."
Terms: Receives 30% commission. Charges marketing plan fee or web only fee. Offers written contract. Advertising costs are split: 75% paid by illustrators; 25% paid by rep. Requires Itoya portfolio; postcards only for promotion. Advertises in *The Black Book*.
How to Contact: For first contact, send direct mail flier/brochure, tearsheets, photocopies. Responds only if interested. Portfolio should include photocopies.

SAM BRODY, ARTISTS & PHOTOGRAPHERS REPRESENTATIVE & CONSULTANT, 77 Winfield St., Apt. 4, E. Norwalk CT 06855-2138. Phone/fax: (203)854-0805 (for fax, add 999). E-mail: sambrody@bigplan et.com. **Contact:** Sam Brody. Commercial illustration and photography representative and broker. Estab. 1948. Member of SPAR. Represents 4 illustrators, 3 photographers, 2 designers. Markets include: advertising agencies; corporations/client direct; design firms; editorial/magazines; publishing/books; sales/promotion firms.
Handles: Consultant.
Terms: Agent receives 30% commission. Exclusive area representation is required. For promotional purposes, talent must provide back-up advertising material, i.e., cards (reprints—*The Workbook*, etc.) and self-promos.
How to Contact: For first contact, send bio, direct mail flier/brochure, tearsheets. Reports in 3 days or within 1 day if interested. After initial contact, call for appointment or drop off or mail in appropriate materials for review. Portfolio should include tearsheets, slides, photographs. Obtains new talent through recommendations from others, solicitation.
Tips: Considers "past performance for clients that I check with and whether I like the work performed."

☑ **PEMA BROWNE LTD.**, HCR Box 104B, 71 Pine Rd., Neversink NY 12765. (845)985-2936 or (845)985-2062. Fax: (914)985-7635. **Contact:** Pema Browne or Perry Browne. Estab. 1966. Represents 10 illustrators. Specializes in general commercial. Markets include: all publishing areas; children's picture books; collector plates and dolls; advertising agencies. Clients include HarperCollins, Thomas Nelson, Bantam Doubleday Dell, Nelson/Word, Hyperion, Putnam. Client list available upon request.
Handles: Illustration. Looking for "professional and unique" talent.
Terms: Rep receives 30% commission. Exclusive area representation is required. For promotional purposes, talent must provide color mailers to distribute. Representative pays mailing costs on promotion mailings.
How to Contact: For first contact, send query letter, direct mail flier/brochure and SASE. If interested will ask to mail appropriate materials for review. Portfolios should include tearsheets and transparencies or good color photocopies, plus SASE. Obtains new talent through recommendations and interviews (portfolio review).
Tips: "We are doing more publishing—all types—less advertising." Looks for "continuity of illustration and dedication to work."

N **CATUGEAU: ARTIST AGENT**, 110 Rising Ridge Rd., Ridgefield CT 06877. (203)438-7307. Fax: (203)984-1993. E-mail: catartrep@aol.com. Website: www.CATugeau.com. **Owner:** Chris Tugeau. Children's publishing rep—trade, mass market, educational. Estab. 1994. Member of SPAR, SCBWI, Graphic Artists Guild. Represents 35 illustrators. 100% of artwork handled is children's book illustration. Staff includes Chris Tugeau, owner and rep.
Handles: Illustration.
Terms: Receives 25% commission. "Artists responsible for providing samples for portfolios, promotional books and mailings." Exclusive representation required. Offers written contract. Advertises in *Picturebook*, *RSVP*, *Directory of Illustration*.
How to Contact: For first contact, send SASE, direct mail flier/brochure, photocopies. Responds ASAP. Portfolio should include original art, tearsheets, photocopies. Finds illustrators through recommendations from others, conferences, personal search. Do not e-mail samples. No CDs!
Tips: "Do research, look at artists' websites, talk to other artists—make sure you're comfortable with personality of rep. Be professional yourself . . . know what you do best and be prepared to give rep what they need to present you!"

CORNELL & MCCARTHY, LLC, 2-D Cross Hwy., Westport CT 06880. (203)454-4210. Fax: (203)454-4258. E-mail: cmartreps@aol.com. Website: http://cornellandmccarthy.com. **Contact:** Merial Cornell. Children's book illustration representative. Estab. 1989. Member of SCBWI and Graphic Artists Guild. Represents 30 illustrators. Specializes in children's books: trade, mass market, educational.
Handles: Illustration.
Terms: Agent receives 25% commission. Advertising costs are split: 75% paid by talent; 25% paid by representative. For promotional purposes, talent must provide 10-12 strong portfolio pieces relating to children's publishing.
How to Contact: For first contact, send query letter, direct mail flier/brochure, tearsheets, photocopies and SASE. Responds in 1 month. Obtains new talent through recommendations, solicitation, conferences.
Tips: "Work hard on your portfolio."

CREATIVE FREELANCERS, INC., (formerly Creative Freelancers Management, Inc.), 99 Park Ave., #210A, New York NY 10016. (800)398-9544. Fax: (203)532-2927. Website: www.freelancers.com. **Contact:** Marilyn Howard. Commercial illustration representative. Estab. 1988. Represents 30 illustrators. "Our staff members have art direction, art buying or illustration backgrounds." Specializes in children's books, advertising, architectural, conceptual. Markets include: advertising agencies; corporations/client direct; design firms; editorial/magazines; paper products/greeting cards; publishing/books; sales/promotion firms.
Handles: Illustration. Artists must have published work.
Terms: Rep receives 30% commission. Exclusive area representation is preferred. Advertising costs are split: 75% paid by talent; 25% paid by representative. For promotional purposes, talent must provide "printed pages to leave with clients. Co-op advertising with our firm could also provide this. Transparency portfolio preferred if we take you on, but we are flexible." Advertises in *American Showcase*, *Workbook*.
How to Contact: For first contact, send tearsheets or "whatever best shows work." Responds back only if interested.
Tips: Looks for experience, professionalism and consistency of style. Obtains new talent through "word of mouth and website."

DWYER & O'GRADY, INC., P.O. Box 239, Lempster NH 03605. (603)863-9347. Fax: (603)863-9346. **Contact:** Elizabeth O'Grady. Agents for children's picture book artists and writers. Estab. 1990. Member of Society of Illustrators, SCBWI, ABA. Represents 12 illustrators and 6 writers. Staff includes Elizabeth O'Grady, Jeffrey Dwyer. Specializes in children's picture books (middle grade and young adult). Markets include: publishing/books, audio/film.
● Dwyer & O'Grady is currently not accepting new clients.
Handles: Illustrators and writers of children's books.

Terms: Receives 15% commission domestic, 20% foreign. Additional fees are negotiable. Exclusive representation is required (world rights). Advertising costs are paid by representative. For promotional purposes, talent must provide both color slides and prints of at least 20 sample illustrations depicting the figure with facial expression.

HANNAH REPRESENTS, 14431 Ventura Blvd., #108, Sherman Oaks CA 91423. (818)378-1644. E-mail: hannahrepresents@yahoo.com. **Contact:** Hannah Robinson. Literary representative for illustrators. Estab. 1997. Represents 8 illustrators. 100% of artwork handled is children's book illustration. Looking for established illustrators only.
Handles: Manuscript/illustration packates. Looking for illustrators with book already under contract.
Terms: Receives 15% commission. Offers written contract. Advertises in *Picturebook*.
How to Contact: For first contact, send SASE and tearsheets. Responds only if interested. Call to schedule an appointment. Portfolio should include photocopies. Finds illustrators through recommendations from other, conferences, queries/solicitations, international.
Tips: Present a carefully developed range of characterization illustrations that are world-class enough to equal those in the best children's books.

[N] HERMAN AGENCY, 350 Central Park West, New York NY 10025. (212)749-4907. Fax: (212)662-5151. E-mail: HermanAgen@aol.com. Website: www.HermanAgencyInc.com. **Contact:** Ronnie Ann Herman. Commercial illustration representative. Estab. 1999. Member of SCBWI. Represents 24 illustrators. 100% of artwork handled is children's book illustration. Staff includes Ronnie Ann Herman. Currently open to illustrators seeking representation. Looking for established illustrators only.
Handles: Illustration, illustration/manuscript packages.
Recent Sales: Four book contract (one is *Imaginary Safari*) photographer, Tom Arma (Harry Abrams); two book contract/Barnaby is the character, written and illustrated by Wendy Rouillard (Scholastic); four one-word readers, written and illustrated by Michael Rex (Scholastic); and Brian Jacqués new picture book to be illustrated by Alexi Natchev. Represents Joy Allen, Dawn Apperly, Tom Arma, Mary Bono, Rebecca Dickinson, Doreen Gay-Kassel, Barry Gott, Steve Haskamp, Aleksey Ivonov, Gideon Kendall, Scott McDougall, Bob McMahon, Alexi Natchev, Jill Newton, John Nez, Betina Ogden, Tamara Petrosino, Lynn Rowe Reed, Michael Rex, Ken Robbins, Wendy Rouillard, David Sheldon, Mark Weber, Nick Zarin-Ackerman.
Terms: Receives 25% commission. Artists pay 75% of costs for promotional material—about $300 a year. Exclusive representation usually required. Offers written contract. Advertising costs are split: 75% paid by illustrator; 25% paid by rep. Advertises in *Picturebook*, *Directory of Illustration*.
How to Contact: For first contact, send samples, SASE, direct mail flier/brochure, tearsheets, photocopies. Responds in 1 month or less. "I will contact you if I like your samples." Portfolio should include tearsheets, photocopies, books, dummies. Finds illustrators through recommendations from others, conferences, queries/solicitations.

HK PORTFOLIO, 666 Greenwich St., New York NY 10014. (212)675-5719. E-mail: harriet@hkportfolio.com. Website: www.hkportfolio.com. **Contact:** Harriet Kasak or Mela Bolinao. Commercial illustration representative. Estab. 1986. Member of SPAR, Society of Illustrators and Graphic Artists Guild. Represents 50 illustrators. Specializes in illustration for juvenile markets. "Sub-agent for Peters, Fraser & Dunlop (London)." Markets include: advertising agencies; editorial/magazines; publishing/books.
Handles: Illustration.
Recent Sales: *The Book of Bad Ideas*, by Laura Huliska-Beith (Little, Brown); *Marsupial Sue*, by Jack E. Davis; and *Who Was Born This Special Day*, by Leonid Gore.
Terms: Rep receives 25% commission. No geographic restrictions. Advertising costs are split: 75% paid by talent; 25% paid by representative. Advertises in *Picturebook* and *The Workbook*.
How to Contact: No geographic restrictions. For first contact, send query letter, direct mail flier/brochure, tearsheets, slides, photographs, photostats and SASE. Responds in 1 week. After initial contact, drop off or mail in appropriate materials for review. Portfolio should include tearsheets, slides, photographs, photostats, photocopies.
Tips: Leans toward highly individual personal styles.

KIRCHOFF/WOHLBERG, ARTISTS' REPRESENTATION DIVISION, 866 United Nations Plaza, #525, New York NY 10017. (212)644-2020. Fax: (212)223-4387. **Director of Operations:** John R. Whitman. Estab. 1930. Member of SPAR, Society of Illustrators, AIGA, Association of American Publishers, Bookbuilders of Boston, New York Bookbinders' Guild. Represents over 50 illustrators. Artist's Representative: Elizabeth Ford. Specializes in juvenile and young adult trade books and textbooks. Markets include: publishing/books.
Handles: Illustration and photography (juvenile and young adult).
Terms: Rep receives 25% commission. Exclusive representation to book publishers is usually required. Advertising costs paid by representative ("for all Kirchoff/Wohlberg advertisements only"). "We will make transparencies from portfolio samples; keep some original work on file." Advertises in *American Showcase*, *Art Directors' Index*, *Society of Illustrators Annual*, children's book issues of *Publishers Weekly*.

How to Contact: Please send all correspondence to the attention of Elizabeth Ford. For first contact, send query letter, "any materials artists feel are appropriate." Responds in 6 weeks. "We will contact you for additional materials." Portfolios should include "whatever artists feel best represents their work. We like to see children's illustration in any style."

LINDGREN & SMITH, 250 W. 57th St., #521, New York NY 10107. (212)397-7330. Fax: (212)397-7334. E-mail: pat@lindgrensmith.com. Website: www.lindgrensmith.com. **President:** Pat Lindgren. Illustration representative. Estab. 1984. Member of SPAR, GAG, SCBWI. Markets include children's books, advertising agencies; corporations; design firms; editorial; publishing.
Handles: Illustration.
Recent Sales: *Wolf Who Cried Boy*, by Steven Salerno, illustrator (Dutton); Steven Salerno; *The Christmas Treasury*, by Valerie Sokolova illustrator (Golden).
Terms: Exclusive representation is required. Advertises in *American Showcase*, *The Workbook*, *The Black Book* and *Picturebook*.
How to Contact: For first contact, send direct mail flier, photocopies or postcard. "We will respond by mail or phone—if interested. For response include SASE."
Tips: "Check to see if your work seems appropriate for the group. We only represent experienced artists who have been professionals for some time."

N̪ MARLENA AGENCY, INC., 145 Witherspoon St., Princeton NJ 08542. (609)252-9405. Fax: (609)252-1949. E-mail: marzena@bellatlantic.net. Website: www.marlenaagency.com. Commercial illustration representative. Estab. 1990. Member of Society of Illustrators. Represents 25 illustrators. Staff includes Marlena Torzecka, Greta T'Jonck, Ella Lupo. Currently open to illustrators seeking representation. Open to both new and established illustrators. Submission guidelines available for #10 SASE.
Handles: Illustration.
Recent Sales: *Pebble Soup*, by Marc Mongeau (Rigby); *Sees Behind Trees*, by Linda Helton (Harcourt Brace & Company); *New Orleans Band*, by Marc Mongeau (Scott Foresman); and *My Cat*, by Linda Helton (Scholastic). Represents Marc Mongeau, Gerard Dubois, Linda Helton, George Black, Cyril Cabry, Normand Cousineau, Martin Jarrie, Serge Bloch, and Ferrucio Sardella.
Terms: Receives 30% commission. Exclusive representation required. Offers written contract. Advertising costs are split: 70% paid by illustrator; 30% paid by rep. Requires printed portfolios, transparencies, direct mail piece (such as postcards) printed samples. Advertises in *Picturebook*, *American Showcase*, *The Black Book*, *The Workbook*.
How to Contact: For first contact, send tearsheets, photocopies. Responds only if interested. Drop off or mail portfolio, photocopies. Portfolio should include tearsheets, photocopies. Finds illustrators through queries/solicitations, magazines and graphic design.
Tips: "Be creative and persistent."

☑ NACHREINER BOIE ART FACTORY, 925 Elm Grove Rd., Elm Grove WI 53122. (262)785-1940. Fax: (262)785-1611. E-mail: nbart@execpc.com. Website: www.expecpc.com/artfactory. **Contact:** Tom Stocki. Commercial illustration representative. Estab. 1978. Represents 9 illustrators. 10% of artwork handled is children's book illustration. Currently open to illustrators seeking representation. Open to both new and established illustrators.
Handles: Illustration.
Recent Sales: Represents Tom Buchs, Tom Nachreiner, Todd Dakins, Linda Godfrey, Larry Mikec, Bill Scott, Amanda Aquino, Gary Shea.
Terms: Receives 25-30% commission. Offers written contract. Advertising costs are split: 75% paid by illustrators; 25% paid by rep. "We try to mail samples of all our illustrators at one time and we try to update our website; so we ask the illustrators to keep up with new samples." Advertises in *Picturebook*, *The Workbook*.
How to Contact: For first contact, send query letter, tearsheets. Responds only if interested. Call to schedule an appointment. Portfolio should include tearsheets. Finds illustrators through queries/solicitations.
Tips: "Have a unique style."

☑ WANDA NOWAK/CREATIVE ILLUSTRATION AGENCY, 231 E. 76th St., 5D, New York NY 10021. (212)535-0438. Fax: (212)535-1629. E-mail: wandanowak@aol.com. Website: www.wandanow.com. **Contact:** Wanda Nowak. Commercial illustration representative. Estab. 1996. Member of Graphic Artists Guild. Represents 16 illustrators. 25% of artwork handled is children's book illustration. Staff includes Wanda Nowak. Open to both new and established illustrators.
Handles: Illustration. Looking for "unique, individual style."
Recent Sales: Represents Martin Matje, Emilie Chollat, Herve Blondon, Thea Kliros, Pierre Pratt, Frederique Bertrand, Ilja Bereznickas, Boris Kulikov, Yayo, Charlene Potts, Donald Saaf, Beatriz Vidal, Christiana Sun.
Terms: Receives 30% commission. Exclusive representation required. Offers written contract. Advertising costs are split: 70% paid by illustrators; 30% paid by rep. Advertises in *Picturebook*, *The Workbook*, *The Alternative Pick*.

How to Contact: For first contact, send SASE. Responds only if interested. Drop off portfolio. Portfolio should include tearsheets. Finds illustrators through recommendations from other, sourcebooks like *CA Picture Book*, *The Black Book*, exhibitions.

Tips: Develop your own style, send a little illustrated story, which will prove you can carry a character in different situations with facial expressions etc.

N: RENAISSANCE HOUSE, 9400 Lloydcrest Dr., Beverly Hills CA 90210. (310)358-5288. Fax: (310)358-5282. E-mail: laredopub@cs.com. Website: www.renaissancehouse.net. **Contact:** Raquel Benatar. Children's, multicultural, educational, commercial and advertising rep. Estab. 1991. Represents 40 illustrators. 95% of artwork handled is children's book illustration. Currently open to illustrators seeking representation. Open to both new and established illustrators.

Handles: Illustration, photography.

Recent Sales: Vivi Escriva (Houghton Mifflin); Pablo Torrecilla (Grolier); Ana Lopez (Scholastic); Ruth Araceli (Renaissance House). Represents Vivi Escriva, Ruth Araceli, Pablo Torrecilla, Adrian Rubio, Ana Lopez, etc.

Terms: Receives 40% commission. Exclusive representation required. Offers written contract. Illustrators must provide scans of illustrations. Advertises in *Picturebook*, *Directory of Illustration*, own website and catalog of illustrators.

How to Contact: For first contact send tearsheets. Responds in 2 weeks. Call to schedule an appointment or e-mail. Portfolio should include tearsheets. Finds illustrators through recommendations from other illustrators, conferences, international shows.

S.I. INTERNATIONAL, 43 E. 19th St., New York NY 10003. (212)254-4996. Fax: (212)995-0911. E-mail: info@si-i.com. Website: www.si-i.com. Commercial illustration representative. Estab. 1983. Member of SPAR, Graphic Artists Guild. Represents 50 illustrators. Specializes in license characters, educational publishing and children's illustration, digital art and design, mass market paperbacks. Markets include design firms; publishing/books; sales/promotion firms; licensing firms; digital art and design firms.

Handles: Illustration. Looking for artists "who have the ability to do children's illustration and to do license characters either digitally or reflexively."

Terms: Rep receives 25-30% commission. Advertising costs are split: 70% paid by talent; 30% paid by representative. "Contact agency for details. Must have mailer." Advertises in *Picturebook*.

How to Contact: For first contact, send query letter, tearsheets. Reports in 3 weeks. After initial contact, write for appointment to show portfolio of tearsheets, slides.

LIZ SANDERS AGENCY, 16 Phaedra, Laguna Niguel CA 92677. (949)495-3664. Fax: (949)495-0229. E-mail: liz@lizsanders.com. Website: www.lizsanders.com. Commercial illustration representative. Estab. 1985. Represents 15 illustrators. Currently open to illustrators seeking representation. Open to both new and established illustrators.

Handles: Illustration. Markets include publishing, packaging, advertising.

Recent Sales: Represents Amy Ning, Tom Pansini, Chris Lensch, Barbara Johansen-Newman, Bachrun Lomele, Judy Pedersen, Susan Synarski, Kari Kroll and more.

Terms: Receives 30% commission. Offers written contract. Advertises in *Picturebook*, *American Showcase*, *The Workbook*, *Directory of Illustration*. No geographic restrictions.

How to Contact: For first contact, send tearsheets, direct mail flier/brochure, color copies, —nonreturnables. Responds only if interested. After initial contact, drop off or mail portfolio. Portfolio should include tearsheets, photocopies.

Tips: Obtains new talent through recommendations from others, conferences and queries/solicitations, *Literary Market Place*.

N: GWEN WALTERS ARTIST REPRESENTATIVE, 50 Fuller Brook Rd., Wellesley MA 02482. (781)235-8658. Fax: (781)235-8635. E-mail: artincgw@aol. Website: www.gwenWaltersartrep.com. Commercial illustration representative. Estab. 1976. Represents 18 illustrators. 90% of artwork handled is children's book illustration. Currently open to illustrators seeking representation. Looking for established illustrators only.

Handles: Illustration.

Recent Sales: Sells to "All major book publishers."

Terms: Receives 30% commission. Artist needs to supply all promo material. Offers written contract. Advertising costs are split: 70% paid by illustrator; 30% paid by rep. Advertises in *Picturebook*, *RSVP*, *Directory of Illustration*.

How to Contact: For first contact, send tearsheets. Responds only if interested. Finds illustrators through recommendations from others.

Tips: "Go out and get some first-hand experience. Learn to tell yourself to understand the way the market works."

Clubs & Organizations

Contacts made through organizations such as the ones listed in this section can be quite beneficial for children's writers and illustrators. Professional organizations provide numerous educational, business and legal services in the form of newsletters, workshops or seminars. Organizations can provide tips about how to be a more successful writer or artist, as well as what types of business records to keep, health and life insurance coverage to carry and competitions to consider.

An added benefit of belonging to an organization is the opportunity to network with those who have similar interests, creating a support system. As in any business, knowing the right people can often help your career, and important contacts can be made through your peers. Membership in a writer's or artist's organization also shows publishers you're serious about your craft. This provides no guarantee your work will be published, but it gives you an added dimension of credibility and professionalism.

Some of the organizations listed here welcome anyone with an interest, while others are only open to published writers and professional artists. Organizations such as the Society of Children's Book Writers and Illustrators (SCBWI, www.scbwi.org)) have varying levels of membership. SCBWI offers associate membership to those with no publishing credits, and full membership to those who have had work for children published. Many national organizations such as SCBWI also have regional chapters throughout the country. Write or call for more information regarding any group that sounds interesting, or check the websites of the many organizations that list them. Be sure to get information about local chapters, membership qualifications and services offered.

Information on organizations listed in the previous edition but not included in this edition of *Children's Writer's & Illustrator's Market* may be found in the General Index.

AMERICAN ALLIANCE FOR THEATRE & EDUCATION, Theatre Department, Arizona State University, Box 872002, Tempe AZ 85287-2002. (480)965-6064. Fax: (480)965-5351. E-mail: aate.info@asu.edu. Website: www.aate.com. **Administrative Director:** Christy M. Taylor. Purpose of organization: to promote standards of excellence in theatre and drama education by providing the artist and educator with a network of resources and support, a base for advocacy, and access to programs and projects that focus on the importance of drama in the human experience. Membership cost: $98 annually for individual in US and Canada, $131 annually for organization, $60 annually for students, $71 annually for retired people; add $20 outside Canada and US. Annual conference. Newsletter published quarterly (on website only). Contests held for unpublished play reading project and annual awards for best play. Awards plaque and stickers for published playbooks. Publishes list of unpublished plays deemed worthy of performance in newsletter and press release and staged readings at conference.
How to Contact/Writers: Manuscripts should be 8-10 pages, or 2,000 words. Manuscripts may include lesson plans, interviews, Coda Essays, and reviews of computer software, books, and plays (as scripts or in performance). A three-sentence biographical statement should also be included with a SASE.

N: AMERICAN SOCIETY OF JOURNALISTS AND AUTHORS, 1501 Broadway, New York NY 10036. E-mail: staff@asja.org. Website: www.asja.org. **Executive Director:** Brett Harvey. Qualifications for membership: "Need to be a professional nonfiction writer who's published a minimum of 6 full-length, bylined articles in general circulation publications." Membership cost: Application fee—$25; annual dues—$195. Group sponsors national conferences; monthly workshops in New York City. Workshops/conferences open to nonmembers. Publishes a newsletter for members that provides confidential information for nonfiction writers.

ARIZONA AUTHORS ASSOCIATION, P.O. Box 87857, Phoenix AZ 85080-7857. Fax: (623)780-0468. E-mail: info@azauthors.com. Website: www.azauthors.com. **President:** Vijaya Schartz. Purpose of organization: to offer professional, educational and social opportunities to writers and authors, and serve as a network. Members must be authors, writers working toward publication, agents, publishers, publicists, printers, illustrators, etc. Membership cost: $45/year writers; $30/year students; $60/year other professionals in publishing industry. Holds regular workshops and meetings. Publishes bimonthly newsletter and Arizona Literary Magazine. Sponsors

Annual Literary Contest in poetry, essays, short stories, novels, and published books with cash prizes and awards bestowed at a public banquet in Phoenix. Winning entries are also published or advertised in the *Arizona Literary Magazine*. Send SASE or view website for guidelines.

ASSITEJ/USA, % Steve Bianchi, 724 Second Ave. S., Nashville TN 37210. (615)254-5719. Fax: (615)254-3255. E-mail: usassitej@aol.com. Website: www.assitej-usa.org. Purpose of organization: to promote theater for children and young people by linking professional theaters and artists together; sponsoring national, international and regional conferences and providing publications and information. Also serves as US Center for International Association of Theatre for Children and Young People. Different levels of membership include: organizations, individuals, students, retirees, libraries. *TYA Today* includes original articles, reviews and works of criticism and theory, all of interest to theater practitioners (included with membership). Publishes journal that focuses on information on field in US and abroad.

☑ **THE AUTHORS GUILD**, 31 E. 28th St., 10th Floor, New York NY 10016. (212)563-5904. Fax: (212)564-8363. E-mail: staff@authorsguild.org. Website: www.authorsguild.org. **Executive Director:** Paul Aiken. Purpose of organization: to offer services and materials intended to help authors with the business and legal aspects of their work, including contract problems, copyright matters, freedom of expression and taxation. Guild has 8,000 members. Qualifications for membership: Must be book author published by an established American publisher within 7 years or any author who has had 3 works (fiction or nonfiction) published by a magazine or magazines of general circulation in the last 18 months. Associate membership also available. Annual dues: $90. Different levels of membership include: associate membership with all rights except voting available to an author who has a firm contract offer or is currently negotiating a royalty contract from an established American publisher. "The Guild offers free contract reviews to its members. The Guild conducts several symposia each year at which experts provide information, offer advice and answer questions on subjects of interest and concern to authors. Typical subjects have been the rights of privacy and publicity, libel, wills and estates, taxation, copyright, editors and editing, the art of interviewing, standards of criticism and book reviewing. Transcripts of these symposia are published and circulated to members. The *Authors Guild Bulletin*, a quarterly journal, contains articles on matters of interest to writers, reports of Guild activities, contract surveys, advice on problem clauses in contracts, transcripts of Guild and League symposia and information on a variety of professional topics. Subscription included in the cost of the annual dues."

☒ **LEWIS CARROLL SOCIETY OF NORTH AMERICA**, P.O. Box 204, Napa CA 94559. E-mail: hedgehog@napanet.net. Website: www.lewiscarroll.org/lcsna.html. **Secretary:** Cindy Watter. "We are an organization of Carroll admirers of all ages and interests and a center for Carroll studies." Qualifications for membership: "An interest in Lewis Carroll and a simple love for Alice (or even the Snark)." Membership cost: $20/year. There is also a contributing membership of $50. Publishes a quarterly newsletter.

☑ **THE CHILDREN'S BOOK COUNCIL, INC.**, 12 W. 37th St., 2nd Floor, New York NY 10018. (212)966-1990. Fax: (212)966-2073. E-mail: info@cbcbooks.org. Website: www.cbcbooks.org. **President:** Paula Quint. Purpose of organization: "A nonprofit trade association of children's and young adult publishers and packagers, CBC promotes the enjoyment of books for children and young adults and works with national and international organizations to that end. The CBC has sponsored National Children's Book Week since 1945 and Young People's Poetry Week since 1999." Qualifications for membership: US trade publishers and packagers of children's and young adult books and related literary materials are eligible for membership. Publishers wishing to join should e-mail membership@cbcbooks.org or contact the CBC for dues information." Sponsors workshops and seminars. Publishes a newsletter with articles about children's books and publishing and listings of free or inexpensive materials available from member publishers. Individuals wishing to receive mailings from the CBC (semi-annual newsletter *CBC Features* with articles of interest to people working with children and books and materials brochures) may be placed on CBC's mailing list for a one-time-only fee of $60. Sells reading encouragement graphics and informational materials suitable for libraries, teachers, booksellers, parents, and others working with children.

FLORIDA FREELANCE WRITERS ASSOCIATION, Cassell Network of Writers, P.O. Box A, North Stratford NH 03590. (603)922-8338. Fax: (603)922-8339. E-mail: danakcnw@ncia.net. Website: www.writers-editors.com. **Executive Director:** Dana K. Cassell. Purpose of organization: To act as a link between Florida writers and buyers of the written word; to help writers run more effective communications businesses. Qualifications for membership: "None—we provide a variety of services and information, some for beginners and some for established pros." Membership cost: $90/year. Publishes a newsletter focusing on market news, business news, how-to tips for the serious writer. Non-member subscription: $39—does not include Florida section—includes national edition only. Annual *Directory of Florida Markets* included in FFWA newsletter section and on disk. Publishes annual *Guide to CNW/Florida Writers*, which is distributed to editors around the country. Sponsors contest: annual deadline March 15. Guidelines available fall of each year and on website. Categories: juvenile, adult nonfiction, adult fiction and poetry. Awards include cash for top prizes, certificate for others. Contest open to nonmembers.

GRAPHIC ARTISTS GUILD, 90 John St., Suite 403, New York NY 10038. (800)500-2672. E-mail: membership@gag.org. Website: www.gag.org. **Executive Director:** Steven Schubert, CAE. Purpose of organization: "to promote and protect the economic interests of member artists. It is committed to improving conditions for all creators of graphic arts and raising standards for the entire industry." Qualification for full membership: 50% of income derived from artwork. Associate members include those in allied fields, students and retirees. Initiation fee: $25. Full memberships $120, $165, $215, $270; student membership $55/year. Associate membership $115/year. Publishes *Graphic Artists Guild Handbook, Pricing and Ethical Guidelines* (free to members, $34.95 retail) and bimonthly *Guild News* (free to members, $12 to non-members). "The Guild UAW Local 3030 is a national union that embraces all creators of graphic arts intended for presentation as originals or reproductions at all levels of skill and expertise. The long-range goals of the Guild are: to educate graphic artists and their clients about ethical and fair business practices; to educate graphic artists about emerging trends and technologies impacting the industry; to offer programs and services that anticipate and respond to the needs of our members, helping them prosper and enhancing their health and security, to advocate for the interests of our members in the legislative, judicial and regulatory arenas; to assure that our members are recognized financially and professionally for the value they provide; to be responsible stewards for our members by building an organization that works efficiently on their behalf."

HORROR WRITERS ASSOCIATION, P.O. Box 50577, Palo Alto CA 94303. E-mail: hwa@horror.org. Website: www.horror.org. **Office Manager:** Nancy Etchemendy. Purpose of organization: To encourage pubic interest in horror and dark fantasy and to provide networking and career tools for members. Qualifications for membership: Anyone who can demonstrate a serious interest in horror may join as an affiliate. Any non-writing professional in the horror field may join as an associate. (Booksellers, editors, agents, librarians, etc.) To qualify for full active membership, you must be a published, professional writer of horror. **Open to students** as affiliates, if unpublished in professional venues. Membership cost: $55 annually in North America; $65 annually elsewhere. Holds annual Stoker Awards Weekend and HWA Business Meeting. Publishes monthly newsletter focusing on market news, industry news, HWA business for members. Sponsors awards. We give the Bram Stoker Awards for superior achievement in horror annually. Awards include a handmade Stoker trophy designed by sculptor Stephen Kirk. Awards open to non-members.

INTERNATIONAL READING ASSOCIATION, 800 Barksdale Rd., Newark DE 19714-8139. (302)731-1600 ext. 293. Fax: (302)731-1057. E-mail: jbutler@reading.org. Website: www.reading.org. **Public Information Associate:** Janet Butler. Purpose of organization: "Formed in 1956, the International Reading Association seeks to promote high levels of literacy for all by improving the quality of reading instruction through studying the reading process and teaching techniques; serving as a clearinghouse for the dissemination of reading research through conferences, journals, and other publications; and actively encouraging the lifetime reading habit. Its goals include professional development; enhance and improve professional development, advocacy, partnerships, research and global literacy development. **Open to students.** Basic membership: $30. Sponsors annual convention. Publishes a newsletter called "Reading Today." Sponsors a number of awards and fellowships. Visit the IRA website for more information on membership, conventions and awards.

THE INTERNATIONAL WOMEN'S WRITING GUILD, P.O. Box 810, Gracie Station, New York NY 10028. (212)737-7536. **Executive Director and Founder:** Hannelore Hahn. IWWG is "a network for the personal and professional empowerment of women through writing." Qualifications: open to any woman connected to the written word regardless of professional portfolio. Membership cost: $45 annually. "IWWG sponsors several annual conferences a year in all areas of the US. The major conference is held in August of each year at Skidmore College in Saratoga Springs NY. It is a week-long conference attracting over 500 women internationally." Also publishes a 32-page newsletter, *Network*, 6 times/year; offers health insurance at group rates, referrals to literary agents.

LEAGUE OF CANADIAN POETS, 54 Wolseley St., 3rd Floor, Toronto, Ontario M5T 1A5 Canada. (416)504-1657. Fax: (416)504-0096. **Executive Director:** Edita Petrauskaite. President: Alice Major. Inquiries to Program Manager: Sandra Drzewiecki. The L.C.P. is a national organization of published Canadian poets. Our constitutional objectives are to advance poetry in Canada and to promote the professional interests of the members. Qualifications for membership: full—publication of at least 1 book of poetry by a professional publisher; associate membership—an active interest in poetry, demonstrated by several magazine/periodical publication credits, stu-

FOR EXPLANATIONS OF THESE SYMBOLS, SEE THE INSIDE FRONT AND BACK COVERS OF THIS BOOK

dent—an active interest in poetry, 12 sample poems required; supporting—any friend of poetry. Membership fees: full—$175/year, associate—$60, student—$30, supporting—$100. Holds an Annual General Meeting every spring; some events open to nonmembers. "We also organize reading programs in schools and public venues. We publish a newsletter which includes information on poetry/poetics in Canada and beyond. Also publish the books *Poetry Markets for Canadians*; *Who's Who in the League of Canadian Poets*; *Poets in the Classroom* (teaching guide) plus a series of cassettes. The Gerald Lampert Memorial Award for the best first book of poetry published in Canada in the preceding year and The Pat Lowther Memorial Award for the best book of poetry by a Canadian woman published in the preceding year. Deadline for awards December 31. Send SASE for more details. Sponsors youth poetry competition. Deadline November 1 of each year. Send SASE for details.

THE NATIONAL LEAGUE OF AMERICAN PEN WOMEN, 1300 17th St. N.W., Washington D.C. 20036-1973. (202)785-1997. Fax: (202)452-6868. E-mail: nlapw1@juno.com. Website: members.aol.com/penwomen/pen.htm. **President:** Wanda Rider. Purpose of organization: to promote professional work in art, letters, and music since 1897. Qualifications for membership: An applicant must show "proof of sale" in each chosen category—art, letters, and music. Membership cost: $40 ($10 processing fee and $30 National dues); Annual fees—$30 plus Branch/State dues. Different levels of membership include: Active, Associate, International Affiliate, Members-at-Large, Honorary Members (in one or more of the following classifications: Art, Letters, and Music). Holds workshops/conferences. Publishes magazine 6 times a year titled *The Pen Woman*. Nonmember subscription $18 per year. Sponsors various contests in areas of Art, Letters, and Music. Awards made at Biennial Convention. Biannual scholarships awarded to non-Pen Women for mature women. Awards include cash prizes— up to $1,000. Specialized contests open to non-members.

NATIONAL WRITERS ASSOCIATION, 3140 S. Peoria St., #295PMB, Aurora CO 80014. (303)841-0246. Fax: (303)751-8593. E-mail: ExecDirSandyWhelchel@nationalwriters.com. Website: www.nationalwriters .com. **Executive Director:** Sandy Whelchel. Purpose of organization: association for freelance writers. Qualifications for membership: associate membership—must be serious about writing; professional membership—must be published and paid writer (cite credentials). Membership cost: $65-associate; $85-professional; $35-student. Sponsors workshops/conferences: TV/screenwriting workshops, NWA Annual Conferences, Literary Clearinghouse, editing and critiquing services, local chapters, National Writer's School. Open to non-members. Publishes industry news of interest to freelance writers; how-to articles; market information; member news and networking opportunities. Nonmember subscription $20. Sponsors poetry contest; short story contest; article contest; novel contest. Awards cash for top 3 winners; books and/or certificates for other winners; honorable mention certificate places 11-20. Contests open to nonmembers.

PEN AMERICAN CENTER, 568 Broadway, New York NY 10012. (212)334-1660. Fax: (212)334-2181. E-mail: jm@pen.org. Purpose of organization: "To foster understanding among men and women of letters in all countries. International PEN is the only worldwide organization of writers and the chief voice of the literary community. Members of PEN work for freedom of expression wherever it has been endangered." Qualifications for membership: "The standard qualification for a writer to join PEN is that he or she must have published, in the United States, two or more books of a literary character, or one book generally acclaimed to be of exceptional distinction. Editors who have demonstrated commitment to excellence in their profession (generally construed as five years' service in book editing), translators who have published at least two book-length literary translations, and playwrights whose works have been professionally produced, are eligible for membership." An application form is available upon request from PEN Headquarters in New York. Candidates for membership should be nominated by 2 current members of PEN. Inquiries about membership should be directed to the PEN Membership Committee. Friends of PEN is also open to writers who may not yet meet the general PEN membership requirements. PEN sponsors public events at PEN Headquarters in New York, and at the branch offices in Boston, Chicago, New Orleans, San Francisco and Portland, Oregon. They include tributes by contemporary writers to classic American writers, dialogues with visiting foreign writers, symposia that bring public attention to problems of censorship and that address current issues of writing in the United States, and readings that introduce beginning writers to the public. PEN's wide variety of literary programming reflects current literary interests and provides informal occasions for writers to meet each other and to welcome those with an interest in literature. Events are all open to the public and are usually free of charge. The Children's Book Authors' Committee sponsors biannual public events focusing on the art of writing for children and young adults and on the diversity of literature for juvenile readers. The PEN/Norma Klein Award was established in 1991 to honor an emerging children's book author. The PEN/Phyllis Naylor Working Writer Fellowship was established in 2001 to assist a North American author of fiction for children or young adults. Pamphlets and brochures all free upon request. Sponsors several competitions per year. Monetary awards range from $2,000-20,000.

PUPPETEERS OF AMERICA, INC., P.O. Box 29417, Parma OH 44129-0417. (888)568-6235. Fax: (440)843-7867. E-mail: pofajoin@aol.com. Website: www.puppeteers.org. **Membership Officer:** Joyce and Chuck Berty. Purpose of organization: to promote the art of puppetry as a means of communications and as a performing art. Qualifications for membership: interest in the art form. Membership cost: single adult, $40; youth member, $20 (6-17 years of age); full-time college student, $25; retiree, $25 (65 years of age); family, $60; couple, $50. Membership includes a bimonthly newsletter (*Playboard*). Discounts for workshops/conferences, access to the Audio Visual Library & Consultants in many areas of Puppetry. *The Puppetry Journal* provides news about puppeteers, puppet theaters, exhibitions, touring companies, technical tips, new products, new books, films, television, and events sponsored by the Chartered Guilds in each of the 8 P of A regions. Subscription: $35 (libraries only). The Puppeteers of America sponsors an annual National Day of Puppetry the last Saturday in April.

N SCIENCE-FICTION AND FANTASY WRITERS OF AMERICA, INC., P.O. Box 877, Chestertown MD 21620. E-mail: execdir@sfwa.org. Website: www.sfwa.org. **Executive Director:** Jane Jewell. Purpose of organization: to encourage public interest in science fiction literature and provide organization format for writers/ editors/artists within the genre. Qualifications for membership: at least 1 professional sale or other professional involvement within the field. Membership cost: annual active dues—$50; affiliate—$35; one-time installation fee of $10; dues year begins July 1. Different levels of membership include: active—requires 3 professional short stories or 1 novel published; affiliate—requires 1 professional sale or professional involvement. Workshops/ conferences: annual awards banquet, usually in April or May. Open to nonmembers. Publishes newsletter, *The Bulletin*. Nonmember subscription: $18/year in US. Sponsors SFWA Nebula® Awards for best published science fiction in the categories of novel, novella, novelette and short story. Awards trophy.

SOCIETY OF CHILDREN'S BOOK WRITERS AND ILLUSTRATORS, 8271 Beverly Blvd., Los Angeles CA 90048. (323)782-1010. E-mail: info@scbwi.org (autoresponse). Website: www.scbwi.org. **President:** Stephen Mooser. **Executive Director:** Lin Oliver. Chairperson, Board of Directors: Sue Alexander. Purpose of organization: to assist writers and illustrators working or interested in the field. Qualifications for membership: an interest in children's literature and illustration. Membership cost: $50/year. Plus one time $10 initiation fee. Different levels of membership include: full membership—published authors/illustrators; associate membership—unpublished writers/illustrators. Holds 100 events (workshops/conferences) around the country each year. Open to nonmembers. Publishes a newsletter focusing on writing and illustrating children's books. Sponsors grants for writers and illustrators who are members.

SOCIETY OF ILLUSTRATORS, 128 E. 63rd St., New York NY 10021-7303. (212)838-2560. Fax: (212)838-2561. Website: www.societyillustrators.org. **Director:** Terrence Brown. Purpose of organization: to promote interest in the art of illustration for working professional illustrators and those in associated fields. Membership cost: Initiation fee—$250. Annual dues for non-resident members (those living more than 125 air miles from SI's headquarters) are $287. Dues for Resident Artist Members are $475 per year; Resident Associate Members $552. Different levels of membership: *Artist Members* "shall include those who make illustration their profession" and through which they earn at least 60% of their income. *Associate Members* are "those who earn their living in the arts or who have made a substantial contribution to the art of illustration." This includes art directors, art buyers, creative supervisors, instructors, publishers and like categories. The candidate must complete and sign the application form which requires a brief biography, a listing of schools attended, other training and a résumé of his or her professional career." Candidates for *Artist* membership, in addition to the above requirements, must submit examples of their work. Sponsors "The Annual of American Illustration." Awards include gold and silver medals. Open to nonmembers. Deadline: October 1. Sponsors "The Original Art: The Best of Children's Book Illustration." Deadline: mid-August. Call for details.

N SOCIETY OF MIDLAND AUTHORS, % SMA, P.O. 10419, Chicago IL 60610-0419. E-mail: DCWN66 @aol.com. Website: www.midlandauthors.com. **Membership Secretary:** David Cowan. Purpose of organization: create closer association among writers of the Middle West; stimulate creative literary effort; maintain collection of members' works; encourage interest in reading and literature by cooperating with other educational and cultural agencies. Qualifications for membership: author or co-author of a book demonstrating literary style and published by a recognized publisher and be identified through residence with Illinois, Indiana, Iowa, Kansas, Michigan, Minnesota, Missouri, Nebraska, North Dakota, Ohio, South Dakota or Wisconsin. Membership cost: $35/year dues. Different levels of membership include: regular—published book authors; associate, nonvoting—not published as above but having some connection with literature, such as librarians, teachers, publishers and editors. Program meetings at Cliff Dwellers, 200 S. Michigan Ave., Borg-Warner Bldg. Chicago, held 5 times a year, featuring authors, publishers, editors or the like individually or on panels. Usually second Tuesday of October, November, February, March and April. Also holds annual awards dinner at Cliff Dwellers, 200 S. Michigan Ave., Chicago, in May. Publishes a newsletter focusing on news of members and general items of interest to writers. Non-member subscription: $5. Sponsors contests. "Annual awards in six categories, given at annual dinner in May. Monetary awards for books published which premiered professionally in previous calendar year. Send SASE to contact person for details." Categories include adult fiction, adult nonfiction, juvenile fiction, juvenile nonfiction, poetry, biography. No picture books. Contest open to non-members. Deadline for contest: January 30.

N SOCIETY OF SOUTHWESTERN AUTHORS, P.O. Box 30355, Tucson AZ 85751-0355. Fax: (520)296-5562. E-mail: wporter202@aol.com. Website: www.azstarnet.com/nonprofit/ssa. **President:** Penny Porter. Purpose of organization: to promote fellowship among members of the writing profession, to recognize members' achievements, to stimulate further achievement, and to assist persons seeking to become professional writers. Qualifications for membership: proof of publication of a book, articles, TV screenplay, etc. Membership cost: $25 initiation plus $20/year dues. The Society of Southwestern Authors has annual Writers' Conference, traditionally held the last Saturday of January (write for more information). Publishes a newsletter, *The Write Word*, about members' activities and news of interest to members. Each spring a short story contest is sponsored. Contest open to non-members. Applications are available in September. Send SASE to the P.O. Box, Attn: Contest.

TEXT AND ACADEMIC AUTHORS ASSOCIATION, University of South Florida, St. Petersburg FL 33701. (813)553-1195. E-mail: taa@bayflash.stpt.usf.edu. Website: http://taa.winona.msus.edu/taa. **President:** Peggy Stanfield. Purpose of organization: to address the professional concerns of text and academic authors, to protect the interests of creators of intellectual property at all levels, and support efforts to enforce copyright protection. Qualifications for membership: all authors and prospective authors are welcome. Membership cost: $30 first year; $60 per year following years. Workshops/conferences: June each year. Newsletter focuses on all areas of interest to text authors.

N VOLUNTEER LAWYERS FOR THE ARTS, 1 E. 53rd St., 6th Floor, New York NY 10022-4201. (212)319-2787 ext. 10 (administration); ext.9 (the Art Law Line). Fax: (212)752-6575. E-mail: askvla@vlany.org. Website: www.vlany.org. **Executive Director:** Amy Schwartzman. Purpose of organization: Volunteer Lawyers for the Arts is dedicated to providing free arts-related legal assistance to low-income artists and not-for-profit arts organizations in all creative fields. Over 800 attorneys in the New York area donate their time through VLA to artists and arts organizations unable to afford legal counsel. There is no membership required for our services. Everyone is welcome to use VLA's Art Law Line, a legal hotline for any artist or arts organization needing quick answers to arts-related questions. VLA also provides clinics, seminars and publications designed to educate artists on legal issues which affect their careers. Membership is through donations and is not required to use our services. Members receive discounts on publications and seminars as well as other benefits. Some of the many publications we carry are *All You Need to Know About the Music Business*; *Business and Legal Forms for Fine Artists, Photographers & Authors & Self-Publishers*; *Contracts for the Film & TV Industry*, plus many more. Please call Steven Malmberg, publications coordinator at ext. 10 to order. VLA's Seminars include "Not-for-Profit Incorporation and Tax Exemption Seminar" and "Copyright Basics for all Seminars."

WESTERN WRITERS OF AMERICA, INC., 1012 Fair St., Franklin TN 37064-2718. (615)791-1444. Fax: (615)791-1444. E-mail: candywwa@aol.com or tncrutch@aol.com. Website: www.westernwriters.org. **Secretary/Treasurer:** James A. Crutchfield. **Open to students.** Purpose of organization: to further all types of literature that pertains to the American West. Membership requirements: must be a *published* author of Western material. Membership cost: $75/year ($90 foreign). Different levels of membership include: Active and Associate—the two vary upon number of books published. Holds annual conference. The 2002 conference will be held in Wichita, KS. Publishes bimonthly magazine focusing on market trends, book reviews, news of members, etc. Non-members may subscribe for $30 ($50 foreign). Sponsors contests. Spur awards given annually for a variety of types of writing. Awards include plaque, certificate, publicity. Contest open to nonmembers.

Conferences & Workshops

Writers and illustrators eager to expand their knowledge of the children's publishing industry should consider attending one of the many conferences and workshops held each year. Whether you're a novice or seasoned professional, conferences and workshops are great places to pick up information on a variety of topics and network with experts in the publishing industry, as well as your peers.

Listings in this section provide details about what conference and workshop courses are offered, where and when they are held, and the costs. Some of the national writing and art organizations also offer regional workshops throughout the year. Write or call for information.

Writers can find listings of more than 1,000 conferences (searchable by type, location and date) at The Writer's Digest/Shaw Guides Directory to Writers' Conferences, Seminars and Workshops—www.writersdigest.com/conferences.

Members of the Society of Children's Book Writers and Illustrators can find information on conferences in national and local SCBWI newsletters. Nonmembers may attend SCBWI events as well. SCBWI conferences are listed in the beginning of this section under a separate subheading. For information on SCBWI's annual national conferences, contact them at (323)782-1010 or check their website for a complete calendar of national and regional events (www.scbwi.org).

Information on conferences listed in the previous edition but not this edition of *Children's Writer's & Illustrator's Market* may be found in the General Index.

SCBWI CONFERENCES
The Society of Children's Book Writers and Illustrators (SCBWI) is an international organization with about 12,000 members. SCBWI offers an array of regional events that can be attended by both members and nonmembers. Listings of regional events follow. For more information, contact the conference coordinators listed or visit SCBWI's website, www.scbwi.org for a complete calendar of events. SCBWI members will also find event information listed in the bimonthly SCBWI *Bulletin*, free with membership. In addition to the regional events, SCBWI offers two naitonal conferences—one in August in Los Angeles, the other in February in New York City. For information about conferences or membership in SCBWI, check www.scbwi.or or contact the SCBWI offices: 8271 Beverly Blvd., Los Angeles CA 90048, (323)782-1010.

SCBWI; NATIONAL CONFERENCE ON WRITING AND ILLUSTRATING FOR CHILDREN, (for merly Annual Writers & Illustrators Conference in Children's Literature), 8271 Beverly Blvd., Los Angeles CA 90048. (323)782-1010. Fax: (323)782-1892. E-mail: scbwi@scbwi.org. Website: www.scbwi,org, **Conference Director:** Lin Oliver. Writer and illustrator workshops geared toward all levels. **Open to students.** Covers all aspects of children's book and magazine publishing—the novel, illustration techniques, marketing, etc. Annual conference held on February 16-17 in Manhattan. Cost of conference: approximately $350; includes all 4 days and one banquet meal. Write for more information or visit our website.

SCBWI—CANADA; ANNUAL CONFERENCE, 130 Wren St., Dunrobin, Ontario K0A 1T0 Canada. E-mail: lflatt@muskoka.com or portage@compmore.net. **Contact:** Lizanne Flatt or Noreen Violetta. Writer and illustrator conference geared toward all levels. Offers speakers forums, book sale, portfolio displays, one-on-one critiques and a silent auction. Annual conference held in May 11, 2002 just outside of Ottawa, Ontario at Sam Jakes Inn, Merrickville. Write above address for brochure or e-mail for more information.

■ **SCBWI—CAROLINAS; ANNUAL FALL CONFERENCE**. Fax: (919)929-6643. **Contact:** Frances A. Davis, regional advisor at (919)967-2549. E-mail: eld573@earthlink.net. Conference will be held on October 13 in Chapel Hill, NC, and geared toward picture books, writing for middle grade, and young adults. Speakers include Richard Peck and Jane O'Conner. Fee: $60 for SCBWI members, $65 for NCWN and SCWN members, and $70 for nonmembers. Critiques for writers, illustration portfolios displayed. Conference open to adult students.

SCBWI—FLORIDA CONFERENCE, 2158 Portland Ave., Wellington FL 33414. (561)798-4824. E-mail: barcafer@aol.com. **Florida Regional Advisor:** Barbara Casey. Writer and illustrator workshops geared toward beginner, intermediate, advanced and professional levels. Subjects to be announced. Workshop. Workshop dates and location to be announced. Registration limited to 100/class. Cost of workshop: $60 for members, $65 for non-members. Special rates are offered through the West Palm Beach Airport Hilton Hotel for those attending the conference who wish to spend the night. Write or e-mail for more information.

SCBWI—HOFSTRA UNIVERSITY CHILDREN'S LITERATURE CONFERENCE, (formerly Children's Literature Conference), 250 Hofstra University, U.C.C.E., Hempstead NY 11549. (516)463-5016. Fax: (516)463-4833. E-mail: kenneth.a.henwood@hofstra.edu. Website: www.hofstra.edu (under "Academics/Continuing Education"). **Writers/Illustrators Contact:** Kenneth Henwood, director, Liberal Arts Studies. Writer and illustrator workshops geared toward all levels. Emphasizes: fiction, nonfiction, poetry, submission procedures, picture books. Workshops will be held April 20, 2002. Length of each session: 1 hour. Cost of workshop: approximately $75; includes 2 workshops, reception, lunch, 2 general sessions, and panel discussion with guest speakers and a critiquing of randomly selected first-manuscript pages submitted by registrants. Write for more information. Co-sponsored by Society of Children's Book Writers & Illustrators.

SCBWI—HOUSTON CONFERENCE, 7730 Highland Farms, Houston TX 77095. (281)855-9561. E-mail: phoebe5@pdq.net. Website: www.scbwi-houston.org. **Conference Chair:** Melanie Chrismer. Writer and illustrator workshops geared toward all levels. **Open to students.** Annual conference. Conference covers picture books, text and illustration, middle grade novels and nonfiction. Editors' Open House held February 10, 2002. Conference held November 3, 2002. Cost of workshop: $85; includes lunch; critiques $25 extra. Contact Mary Wade for more information.

SCBWI—ILLINOIS; SPRING RETREAT—THE WRITE CONNECTION: 3 ACQUIRING EDITORS, 2408 Elmwood, Wilmette IL 60091. E-mail: esthersh@aol.com. **Regional Advisor, SCBWI-Illinois:** Esther Hershenhorn. The workshop is held in Woodstock, Illinois. Next scheduled retreat April 5-7, 2002. Enrollment limited to 55. Writer workshops geared toward intermediate, advanced and professional levels. Offers teaching sessions; open mic; ms critiques; panel discussions; editor presentations. Biannual workshop.

SCBWI—INDIANA; SPRING & FALL WRITERS' AND ILLUSTRATORS' CONFERENCE, 934 Fayette St., Indianapolis IN 46202. E-mail: s_murray@iquest.net. **Conference Director:** Sara Murray-Plumer. Writer and illustrator workshops geared toward all levels. Three conferences in April (Crowne Point, Indiana), June (Indianapolis Children's Museum), and September (Terre Haute, Indiana). Speakers include: Frannie Billingsley, author of children's literature, and Ann Rider, editor at Houghton Mifflin. Cost of workshop includes meal and workshops. Write or e-mail for more information.

SCBWI—LOS ANGELES COUNTY (CALIFORNIA); ILLUSTRATOR'S DAY, P.O. Box 1728, Pacific Palisades CA 90272. (310)573-7318. **Co-regional Advisors:** Claudia Harrington (claudiascbwi@earthlink.net) and Collyn Justus (collynscbwi@aol.com). Website: www.scbwisocal.org. A one-day conference for children's book illustrators, usually includes a featured editor, presentations by published illustrators, workshops, a general portfolio display, and optional paid portfolio review. This is an annual event held late September/early October. Conference fee $80, includes entire day of speakers and lunch. Individual portfolio review fee $10-15.

SCBWI—LOS ANGELES COUNTY (CALIFORNIA); WORKING WRITER'S RETREAT, P.O. Box 1728, Pacific Palisades CA 90272. (310)573-7318. **Co-regional Advisors:** Claudia Harrington (claudiascbwi@earthlink.net) and Collyn Justus (collynscbwi@aol.com). A three-day, two-night retreat in Encino, California, usually featuring a children's book editor, presentations by published authors, creativity workshops, and numerous critiquing sessions facilitated by staff. Conference held on November 15-17, 2002. Attendance is limited. Event fees $300; covers all events, lodgings and meals.

SCBWI—LOS ANGELES COUNTY (CALIFORNIA); WRITER'S DAY, P.O. Box 1728, Pacific Palisades CA 90272. (310)573-7318. **Co-regional Advisors:** Claudia Harrington (claudiascbwi@earthlink.net) and Collyn Justus (collynscbwi@aol.com). A one-day conference for children's book writers geared toward all levels. Emphasizes fiction and nonfiction writing for children from picture books through young adult. Conference includes presentations by a children's book editor and children's book authors. Annual conference, next held April 21, 2002. Cost of conference: $80; includes entire day of speakers, lunch and a Writer's Day Contest.

SCBWI—METRO NEW YORK; PROFESSIONAL SERIES, 440 E. 20th St., #4H, New York NY 10009-8208. (718)937-6810. E-mail: ndlewis@inx.net. Website: www.scbwi.org/regions/nymetro. **Regional Advisors:** Nancy Lewis and Vicky Shiefman. Writer and illustrator workshops geared toward all levels. **Open to**

students. The Metro New York Professional Series meets the second Tuesday of each month, from October to June, 7-9 p.m., at Teachers and Writers Collaborative, 5 Union Square West (14/15 streets), 7th floor. Cost of workshop: $10 for SCBWI members; $12 for nonmembers. "We feature an informal, almost intimate evening with coffee, cookies, and top editors, art directors, agents, publicity and marketing people, librarians, reviewers and more."

☑ **SCBWI—MICHIGAN; ANNUAL RETREAT**, E-mail: lannrhugh@provide.net. Website: www.kidsboo klink.org. **Event Chair:** Lisa Wroble. Writer and illustrator workshops geared toward intermediate and advanced levels. Program focus: the craft of writing. Features peer facilitated critique groups, creativity, motivation and professional issues. Retreat held October 4-6, 2002 in Gull Lake (near Battle Creek and Kalamazoo). Registration limited. Cost of retreat: approximately $199 for members, $219 for nonmembers; includes meals, lodging, linens and tuition. Write or e-mail for additional information.

SCBWI—MICHIGAN; FINDING YOUR VOICE, 7989 Fernwood Dr., Augusta MI 49012. E-mail: buffysilv er@yahoo.com. Website: www.Kidsbooklink.org. **Event Chairs:** Buffy Silverman, Paula Payton, Karen Bjork.. Location TBA. One-day workshop for writers and illustrators focusing on craft. Speakers will include published authors and an editor from a major publishing house. Registration fee TBA, but approximately $85, including lunch.

SCBWI—MIDSOUTH CONFERENCE, P.O. Box 120061, Nashville TN 37212. (615)297-1667. E-mail: scbwi.midsouth@juno.com. **Regional Advisor:** Tracy Barrett. Writer workshops geared toward all levels. Illustrator workshops geared toward beginner and intermediate levels. **Open to Students.** Previous workshop topics have included Promoting Yourself, A Beginner's Guide to Getting Published, Writing for the Older Child, Stone Soup: The Making of a Picture Book, Introduction to Magazine Illustration. There are also opportunities for ms and portfolio critiques, which may be formed at the conference. Conference held April 20, 2002. Speakers include working authors, illustrators, editors, and others. Cost of conference: $65 SCBWI members; $70 nonmembers; ms critiques extra. Manuscripts for critique must be typed, double-spaced, and submitted in advance with payment. Portfolios are brought to the conference, but reservations for critique time and payment must be made in advance.

SCBWI—MISSOURI; CHILDREN'S WRITER'S CONFERENCE, (formerly Children's Writer's Conference), St. Charles County Community College, P.O. Box 76975, 103 CEAC, St. Peters MO 63376-0975. (314)213-8000 ext. 4108. E-mail: suebe@cyberedge.net. **SCBWI MO Regional Advisor:** Sue Bradford Edwards. Writer and illustrator conference geared toward all levels. **Open to students.** Speakers include editors, writers and other professionals, mainly from the Midwest. Topics vary from year to year, but each conference offers sessions for both writers and illustrators as well as for newcomers and published writers. Previous topics included: "What Happens When Your Manuscript is Accepted" by Dawn Weinstock, editor; "Writing—Hobby or Vocation?" by Chris Kelleher; "Mother Time Gives Advice: Perspectives from a 25 Year Veteran" by Judith Mathews, editor; "Don't Be a Starving Writer" by Vicki Berger Erwin, author; and "Words & Pictures: History in the Making," by author-illustrator Cheryl Harness. Annual conference held in early November. For exact date, see SCBWI website: www.SCBWI.org. Registration limited to 50-70. Cost of conference: $50-70; includes one day workshop (8 a.m. to 5 p.m.) plus lunch. Write for more information.

SCBWI—NEW MEXICO; FALL RETREAT. E-mail: Kelitchman@yahoo.com. Retreat held third weekend in October at Hummingbird Music Camp in the Jemez Mountains of New Mexico. E-mail for more information or check calendar on SCBWI's website (www.scbwi.org).

☑ **SCBWI—NEW YORK; CONFERENCE FOR CHILDREN'S BOOK ILLUSTRATORS & AUTHOR/ILLUSTRATORS**, Society of Illustrators, 32 Hillside Ave., Monsey NY 10952. (845)356-7273. **Conference Chair:** Frieda Gates. Held May 6, 2002. Held at the Society of Illustrators in New York City. Registration limited to 80 portfolios shown out of 125 conferees. Portfolios are not judged—first come—first served. Cost of conference: with portfolio—$95, members, $100 others; without portfolio—$60 members, $70 others; $50 additional for 30-minute portfolio evaluation; $25 additional for 15-minute book dummy evaluation. Call Frieda Gates (845)356-7273 to receive a flier. "In addition to an exciting program of speakers, this conference provides a unique opportunity for illustrators and author/illustrators to have their portfolios reviewed by scores of art buyers and agents from the publishing and allied industries. One-on-one consultations with illustrator agents and/or editors are also available. Art buyers admitted free. Our reputation for exhibiting high-quality work of both new and established children's book illustrators, plus the ease of examining such an abundance of portfolios, has resulted in a large number of productive contacts between buyers and illustrators."

SCBWI—NEW YORK STATE, NORTH COUNTRY (WATERTOWN); GROWING AS AUTHORS AND ILLUSTRATORS, P.O. Box 710, Black River NY 13612. (315)773-5847. E-mail: amarston@twcny.rr.c om. **Contact:** Hope Irvin Marston. Writer and illustrator workshops geared toward all levels. Keynote speaker: Harold Underdown, ipicturebooks. Additional presenters include authors Mary Jane Auch, Margery Facklam, Pat Hermes, Robin Puver; illustrator Nick Catalano; author/editor Deborah Noyes Wayshak, Candlewick Press; and editor Judith Whipple, Marshall Cavendish Books. Breakout sessions will be conducted by local published authors and illustrators. Annual workshop held April 27, 2002. Cost of workshop: $50 for members; $60 for nonmembers; includes coffee, lunch and conference packet. Limited number of individual critique sessions with the agents are available for an additional fee of $35. Send SASE for registration form after February 1, 2002.

SCBWI—NORCAL (SAN FRANCISCO/SOUTH); RETREAT AT ASILOMAR. Website: www.scbwino rcal.com. **Regional Advisor:** Jim Averbeck. While we welcome "not-yet-published" writers and illustrators, lectures and workshops are geared toward professionals and those striving to become professional. Program topics cover aspects of writing or illustrating picture books to young adult novels. Past speakers include editors, art directors, published authors and illustrators. Annual conference, generally held last weekend in February; Friday evening through Sunday lunch. Registration limited to 100. Most rooms shared with one other person. Additional charge for single when available. Desks available in most rooms. All rooms have private baths. Conference center is set in wooded campus on Asilomar Beach in Pacific Grove, California. Cost: $265 for SCBWI members, $315 for nonmembers, includes shared room, 6 meals, ice breaker party and all conference activities. Vegetarian meals available. One full scholarship is available to SCBWI members. Registration opens at the end of September and the conference sells out very quickly. A waiting list is formed. "Coming together for shared meals and activities builds a strong feeling of community among the speakers and conferees. For more information, visit our website."

SCBWI—NORTH CENTRAL CALIFORNIA; MARCH IN MODESTO, 8931 Montezuma Rd., Jamestown CA 95327. (209)984-5556. Fax: (209)984-0636. E-mail: trigar@mlode.com. **SCBWI North Central CA Regional Advisor:** Tekla White. **Conference Coordinator:** Tricia Gardella. Writer and illustrator workshops geared toward all levels. **Open to students.** Offers talks on different genres, illustration evaluations and afternoon question breakout sessions. Annual conference. Conference held March 23, 2002. Cost of conference: $55; $60 for nonmembers. Write for more information.

SCBWI—OREGON CONFERENCES, P.O. Box 336, Noti OR 97461. E-mail: robink@rio.com. Website: www.rio.com/~robink/scbwi.html. **Regional Advisor:** Robin Koontz. Writer and illustrator workshops and presentations geared toward all levels. "We invite editors, agents, authors, illustrators and others in the business of writing and illustrating for children. They present lectures, workshops and critiques." Annual retreat and conference. Two events per year: Working Writers and Illustrators Retreat: Retreat held in September (3-5 days). Cost of retreat: $200-350 (depending on length); includes double occupancy and all meals; Spring Conference: Held in Tualatin, Oregon (1-day event in May); cost: about $60, includes continental breakfast and lunch. Registration limited to 100 for the conference and 50 for the retreat.

N: SCBWI—ROCKY MOUNTAIN; 2002 EVENTS. Website: rmc.scbwi.org/events.html. **Regional Advisor:** Phyllis Cahill. SCBWI Rocky Mountain chapter will offer these events in 2002: Spring Workshop, April 6, Golden, Colorado; Summer Retreat, July 19-21, Colorado Springs, Colorado; Fall Conference, September 21-22, Golden, Colorado. For more information check website.

N: SCBWI—SAN DIEGO; WORKSHOP AND CONFERENCE, San Diego—SCBWI, 16048 Lofty Trail Dr., San Diego CA 92127. Chapter voice mail: (619)230-9342. E-mail: ra-sd@sandiego-scbwi.org. Website: www.sandiego-scbwi.org. **Regional Advisor:** Arlene Bartle. Writer and illustrator meetings and workshops geared toward all levels. Topics vary but emphasize writing and illustrating for children. Annual workshop; conference held every other year January 12, 2002; workshop features Richard Peck. Cost $35-55 (check website). Write or e-mail for more information. "The San Diego chapter holds meetings the second Saturday of each month from September-May at the University of San Diego's Manchester Hall, usually 2-4 p.m.; cost $6-8. Chapter newsletter subscription cost $16/year and includes market updates."

N: SCBWI—SAN FRANCISCO EAST/NORTH BAY; WRITER'S DAY. E-mail: ebnorcara@aol.com. Website: www.scbwinorca.org. **Regional Advisor:** Susan Hart Lindquist. Writers' Day held May 18, 2002 in Walnut Creek, California. See website for specifics and registration information.

SCBWI—SOUTHERN BREEZE; SPRINGMINGLE '02, P.O. Box 26282, Birmingham AL 35260. E-mail: joanbroerman@home.com. Website: members.home.net/southernbreeze. **Regional Advisor:** Joan Broerman. Writer and illustrator workshops geared toward intermediate, advanced and professional levels. **Open to college students.** All sessions pertain specifically to the production and support of quality children's literature. Annual conference held in one of the three states comprising the Southern Breeze region. Registration limited to 60. Cost of conference: $100 for members; $110 for nonmembers; includes Saturday lunch and Saturday banquet. Breakfast is complimentary for hotel guests. Pre-registration is necessary. Write to Southern Breeze, P.O. Box 26282, Birmingham AL 35260 for more information or visit our website: members.home.net/southernbreeze. "Springmingle will be held in Gulf Shores, Alabama, February 22-24. Speakers include author Larry Dave Brimner, illustrator Karen Stormer Brooks, Paula Morrow (*Ladybug*, *Baby Bug*), Alison Keehn, (Barefoot Books)."

SCBWI—SOUTHERN BREEZE; WRITING AND ILLUSTRATING FOR KIDS, P.O. Box 26282, Birmingham AL 35260. E-mail: joanbroerman@home.com. Website: members.home.net/southernbreeze/. Regional Advisor: Joan Broerman. Writer and illustrator workshops geared toward all levels. **Open to college students.** All sessions pertain specifically to the production and support of quality children's literature. This one-day conference offers 30 workshops on craft and the business of writing. Picture books, chapter books, novels covered. Entry and professional level topics addressed by published writers and illustrators, editors and agents. Annual conference. Fall conference is held in October. All workshops are limited to 20 or fewer people. Pre-registration is necessary. Some workshops fill quickly. This is a metropolitan area with many museums in a short driving distance. Also—universities and colleges. Cost of conference: $60 for members, $75 for nonmembers; includes program—key note and luncheon speaker, wrap-up panel, 4 workshops (selected from 30). Does not include lunch (about $6 or registrant can brown bag) or individual consultations (mss must be sent early). Registration is by mail ahead of time. Manuscript and portfolio reviews must be pre-paid and scheduled. Write to: Southern Breeze, P.O. Box 26282, Birmingham AL 35260 or visit webpage: members.home.net/southernbreeze/. "Fall conference is always held in Birmingham, Alabama. Room block at a hotel near conference site (usually a school) is by individual reservation and offers a conference rate. Keynote speaker will be Lin Oliver and we will be celebrating the 10th anniversay of the founding of Southern Breeze."

N: SCBWI—SOUTHERN CALIFORNIA; SPRING AND FALL EVENTS. (909)860-8536. E-mail: Region6@aol.com. **Regional Advisor:** Francesca Rusackas. Assistant Regional Advisor: Q.L. Pearce, (909)621-9694, qlpearce@earthlink.net. Illustrator Coordination: Priscilla Burris, (714)543-1248, burrisdraw@aol.com. Writers and Illustrators workshops geared towards all levels, various topics throughout the year. Annual Palm Springs Retreat held last weekend in March. Cost of retreat: $75 members, $80 nonmembers (breakfast and reception included, lodging not). Annual Fall Conference held first Saturday in October. Cost of conference: $65 members, $75 nonmembers (continental breakfast and lunch included). Illustrators field trip held first Saturday in November $20 members, $25 nonmembers (lunch included). Spaces limited for all events. E-mail for more information. Beginning writers and illustrators are welcome.

SCBWI—VENTURA/SANTA BARBARA; FALL CONFERENCE, P.O. Box 941389, Simi Valley CA 93094-1389. (805)581-1906. E-mail: alexisinca@aol.com. Website: www.scbwisocal.org/calendar.htm. **Regional Advisor:** Alexis O'Neill. Writers conference geared toward all levels. "We invite editors, authors and author/illustrators and agents. We have had speakers on the picture book, middle grade, YA, magazine and photo essay books. Both fiction and nonfiction are covered." Conference held October 26, 2002. Scheduled at California Lutheran University in Thousand Oaks, California in cooperation with the School of Education. Cost of conference $65; includes all sessions and lunch. Write for more information.

SCBWI—WASHINGTON STATE/NORTHERN IDAHO, 14816 205th Ave., SE, Renton WA 98059-8926. (425)235-0566. E-mail: scbwiwa@oz.net. Website: www.scbwi-washington.org. **Regional Advisor:** S. Ford. Writer workshops geared toward all levels. **Open to students.** All aspects of writing and illustrating children's books are covered from picture books to YA novels, from contracts to promotion. Editors, an art director, an agent and published authors and illustrators serve as conference faculty. Annual conference and workshop. Conference held April 13, 2002. Registration limited to about 250. Cost of conference: $60-90; includes registration, morning snack and lunch. The conference is a one-day event held at Seattle Pacific University. Hour sessions run back-to-back so attendees have 4 or 5 choices. "In this way we can meet the needs of both entry-level and those more advanced."

☑ SCBWI—WISCONSIN; FALL RETREAT FOR WORKING WRITERS, 15255 Turnberry Dr., Brookfield WI 53005. (262)783-4890. E-mail: aangel@aol.com. **Co-Regional Advisor:** Ann Angel. Writer and illustrator conference geared toward all levels. All our sessions pertain to children's writing/illustration. Faculty addresses writing/illustrating/publishing. Annual conference held October 18-20, 2002 in Burlington, WI. Registration limited to 70. Bedrooms have desks/conference center has small rooms—can be used to draw/write. Program has free time scheduled in. Cost of conference: $255; includes program, meals, lodging. Write for more information. "We usually offer individual critique of manuscripts with faculty—$40 extra."

OTHER CONFERENCES

Many conferences and workshops included here focus on children's writing or illustrating and related business issues. Others appeal to a broader bse of writers or artists, but still provide information that can be useful in creating material for children. Illustrators may be interested in painting and drawing workshops, for example, while writers can learn about techniques and meet editors and agents at general writing conferences. For more informtion visit the websites listed or contact conference coordinator.

AMERICAN CHRISTIAN WRITERS CONFERENCE, P.O. Box 110390, Nashville TN 37222-0390. 1(800)21-WRITE or (615)834-0450. Fax: (615)834-7736. E-mail: regaforder@aol.com. Website: www.acwriters.

com. **Director:** Reg Forder. Writer and illustrator workshops geared toward beginner, intermediate and advanced levels. Classes offered include: fiction, nonfiction, poetry, photography, music, etc. Workshops held in 3 dozen US cities. Call or write for a complete schedule of conferences. 75 minutes. Maximum class size: 30 (approximate). Cost of conference: $99, 1-day session; $169, 2-day session (discount given if paid 30 days in advance) includes tuition only.

ANNUAL SPRING POETRY FESTIVAL, City College, 138th St. at Convent Ave., New York NY 10031. (212)650-6343. E-mail: barrywal23@aol.com. **Director, Poetry Outreach Center:** Barry Wallenstein. Writer workshops geared to all levels. **Open to students.** Annual poetry festival. Festival held Friday, May 17, 2002. Registration limited to 325. Cost of workshops and festival: free. Write for more information.

N: HARRIETTE AUSTIN WRITERS CONFERENCE, G-9 Aderhold, University of Georgia, Athens GA 30602. (706)542-3876. Fax: (706)542-0360. E-mail: hawc@coe.uga.edu. Website: www.coe.uga.edu/torrance/ hawc. **Program Director:** Dr. Charles Connor. Writer workshops geared toward beginner, intermediate, advanced, professional. **Open to students.** Sessions offered include Finding the Story in your Story, Writing Across Genres, Developing the Story Idea in Science Fiction, What is Southern, Anyway?, Characters That Get Noticed, Breaking into Hollywood's Asylum, Building Your Characters and Revealing Their Substance, What Writers Can Write About Other People, How to Write the Juvenile Mystery, Research and Writing: Knowing What You Write About. Annual conference. Workshop held July 20-21, 2002. No limitation on registration; 30 workshop sessions, 3 general sessions; average attendance is over 400. Cost of workshop: $155, plus optional meals and hotel; includes attendance at the Friday evening reception and entertainment, all general and concurrent sessions, Saturday lunch, refreshment breaks, and the authors' book signing. There is an additional charge of $20 for the optional Saturday evening dinner. Manuscript evaluations and a one-on-one meeting with an editor, agent or writing instructor are available. Participants wishing to have an evaluation must submit a two-page ms synopsis and up to 15 double-spaced, typed sample pages. Must be received no later than 1 month prior to the conference. There is a $30 fee for each evaluation/interview. Write for more information. "The goal of the Harriette Austin Writers Conference is to bring writers, agents, editors and special experts together in a supportive environment for a productive and memorable experience. We make every effort to extend the best in professionalism and Southern hospitality. Our reputation is best expressed by those who have been here and those who choose to come back again and again. Complete information about us can be found on our website at www.coe.uga.edu/torrance/hawc/. Come visit us in Georgia."

☑ BUTLER UNIVERSITY CHILDREN'S LITERATURE CONFERENCE, 4600 Sunset Drive, Indianapolis IN 46208. (317)940-9861. Fax: (317)940-9644. E-mail: sdaniell@butler.edu. **Contact:** Shirley Daniell. Writer and illustrator conference geared toward intermediate level. Open to college students. Annual conference held January 26, 2002. Includes sessions such as Creating the Children's Picture Book, and Nuts and Bolts for Beginning Writers. Registration limited to 350. Cost of conference: $85; includes meals, registration, 3 plenary addresses, 2 workshops, book signing, reception and conference bookstore. Write for more information. "The conference is geared toward three groups: teachers, librarians and writers/illustrators."

CAT WRITERS ASSOCIATION ANNUAL WRITERS CONFERENCE, 22841 Orchid Creek Lane, Lake Forest CA 92630. (949)454-1368. Fax: (949)454-0134. E-mail: kthornton@home.com. Website: www.catwr iters.org. **President:** Amy D. Shojai. Writer workshops geared toward beginner, intermediate, advanced and professional levels. Illustrator workshops geared toward intermediate, advanced and professional levels. **Open to students.** Annual workshop. Workshop held in November. Cost of workshop: approximately $90; includes 9-10 seminars, 2 receptions, 1 banquet, 1 breakfast, press pass to other events, interviews with editors and book signing/art sale event. Conference information becomes available in June/July prior to event, and is posted on the website (including registration material). Seminars held/co-sponsored with the Dog Writers Association (We often receive queries from publishers seeking illustrators or writers for particular book/article projects—these are passed on to CWA members).

CELEBRATION OF CHILDREN'S LITERATURE, Montgomery College, 51 Mannakee St., Workforce Development and Continuing Education, Room 220, Rockville MD 20850. (301)251-7914. Fax: (301)251-7937. E-mail: ssonner@mc.cc.md.us. **Senior Program Director:** Sandra Sonner. Writer and illustrator workshops geared toward all levels. **Open to students.** Past topics included The Publisher's Perspective, Successful Picture Book Design, The Oral Tradition in Children's Literature, The Best and Worst Children's Books, Websites for Children, The Pleasures of Nonfiction and The Book as Art. Annual workshop. Will be held in April. Registration limited to 200. Art display facilities, continuing education classrooms and large auditorium. Cost of workshop: approximately $75; includes workshops, box lunch and coffee. Contact Montgomery College for more information.

CHATTANOOGA CONFERENCE ON SOUTHERN LITERATURE, P.O. Box 4203, Chattanooga TN 37405-0203. (423)267-1218. Fax: (423)267-1018. E-mail: srobinson@artsedcouncil.org. Website: www.artsedco uncil.org. **Executive Director:** Susan Robinson. **Open to students.** Conference is geared toward readers. No workshops are held. Biennial conference. Conference held April 2002. Registration limited to first 1,000 people. Cost of conference: $50. Write for more information. "The Chattanooga Conference on Southern Literature is a conference that celebrates literature of the South. Panel discussions, readings, music, food and art are featured."

CHILDREN'S BOOK ILLUSTRATION WITH DEBORAH NOURSE LATTIMORE, 108 Civic Plaza Dr., Taos NM 87571. (505)758-2793. E-mail: tia@taosnet.com. Website: www.tiataos.com. **Curriculum Director:** Susan Miholic. Illustrator workshop geared toward beginner, intermediate and advanced levels. **Open to students over 18.** Workshops take place March-October 2002—check website for dates. Registration limited to 12. All classroom needs are accommodated, but students buy/bring materials, computers, etc. Cost: $395 plus $40 registration fee.

CHILDREN'S BOOK WRITING WITH DONNA W. GUTHRIE, 108 Civic Plaza Dr., Taos NM 87571. (505)758-2793. E-mail: tia@taosnet.com. Website: www.tiataos.com. **Curriculum Director:** Susan Miholic. Writer workshop geared toward beginner, intermediate and advanced levels. **Open to students over 18.** Workshops take place March-October 2002—check website for dates. Registration limited to 12. All classroom needs are accommodated, but students buy/bring materials, computers, etc. Cost: $395 plus $40 registration fee.

CHRISTIAN WRITERS' CONFERENCE, P.O. Box 42429, Santa Barbara CA 93140. (805)647-9162. E-mail: h.coganptl@aol.com. **Coordinator:** Opal Dailey. Writer conference geared toward beginner, intermediate and advanced levels. **Open to students.** Sessions at 2000 conference included one with Ellen Kelly—"Writing for Children: How to make your story garden grow." (writing and marketing). We always have children writing instruction. Annual conference. Conference held October 6, 2002. Registration limited to 100. Cost of conference: approximately $59; includes lunch and refreshment breaks. Write for more information.

COLLEGE OF NEW JERSEY WRITERS CONFERENCE, Dept. of English, The College of New Jersey, P.O. Box 7718, Ewing NJ 08628-0718. (609)771-3254. Fax: (609)637-5112. E-mail: write@tcnj.edu. **Director:** Jean Hollander. Writer and illustrator workshop geared toward all levels. **Open to students.** Sessions at 2000 workshop included "Literature for the Young," taught by Nancy Hinkel, assistant editor, Knopf and Crown Books for Young Readers. Annual conference held in April. Cost: $40-70 ($20 and up for students); includes admission to all talks, panels and readings. Workshops are $10 each.

THE COLUMBUS WRITERS CONFERENCE, P.O. Box 20548, Columbus OH 43220-0176. (614)451-3075. Fax: (614)451-0174. E-mail: angelapl28@aol.com. Website: www.creativevista.com. **Director:** Angela Palazzolo. Writer workshops geared toward all levels. "The conference offers a wide variety of topics including writing in the following markets: children's, young adult, screenwriting, historical fiction, humor, suspense, science fiction/fantasy, travel, educational and greeting card. Other topics have included writing the novel, the short story, the nonfiction book; playwriting; finding and working with an agent; independent publishing; book reviewing; technical writing; and time management for writers. Specific sessions that have pertained to children: children's writing, children's markets, writing and publishing children's poetry and stories. Annual conference. Conference held in September. Cost of full conference: $169 for early registration (includes a day-and-a-half of sessions, Friday night dinner program, open mic sessions, Saturday continental breakfast, lunch and refreshments); $189 regular registration. Saturday only: $119 for early registration; $139 regular registration. Friday night dinner program is $38; $60 early registration for Friday afternoon sessions, $75 for regular registration. Call, e-mail or write for more information.

CONFERENCE FOR WRITERS & ILLUSTRATORS OF CHILDREN'S BOOKS, 51 Tamal Vista Blvd., Corte Madera CA 94925. (415)927-0960, ext. 229. Fax: (415)927-3069. E-mail: conferences@bookpassage.com. Website: www.bookpassage.com. **Conference Coordinator:** Sarah Wingfield. Writer and illustrator conference geared toward beginner, intermediate and advanced levels. Sessions cover such topics as the nuts and bolts of writing and illustrating, publisher's spotlight, market trends, developing characters/finding voice in your writing. Conference held June 21-23, 2002. Registration limited to 80. Cost: $465, includes 3 lunches and a gala opening reception and dinner.

A CRITIQUE RETREAT FOR WRITING WOMEN, P.O. Box 14282, Pittsburgh PA 15239. (724)325-4964. Fax: (724)387-1438. Website: www.geocities.com/jmjwriter/index.html. **Co-director:** MaryJo Rulnick. Writer workshop geared toward beginner, intermediate and advanced levels. The weekend includes five critiquing sessions for attendees. Group leaders include published authors, screenplay writers and freelance writers, editors and columnists. Networking and advice discussions. Annual workshop held twice a year. Annual workshop held June and fall. Registration limited to under 100. Attendees have their own rooms which is included in the price along with meals. Cost of workshop: $225; includes five critiquing sessions, five meals, two nights' accommodations and writer's information packet. Write for more information. The retreat is held at St. Joseph's Center in Greensburg, PA (30 minutes outside Pittsburgh).

PETER DAVIDSON'S HOW TO WRITE A CHILDREN'S PICTURE BOOK SEMINAR, 982 S. Emerald Hills Dr., P.O. Box 497, Arnolds Park IA 51331-0497. Fax: (712)362-8363. **Seminar Presenter:** Peter

Davidson. "This seminar is for anyone interested in writing and/or illustrating children's picture books. Beginners and experienced writers alike are welcome." **Open to students.** *How to Write a Children's Picture Book* is a one-day seminar devoted to principles and techniques of writing and illustrating children's picture books. Topics include Definition of a Picture Book, Picture Book Sizes, Developing an Idea, Plotting the Book, Writing the Book, Illustrating the Book, Typing the Manuscript, Copyrighting Your Work, Marketing Your Manuscript and Contract Terms. Seminars are presented year-round at community colleges. Even-numbered years, presents seminars in Minnesota, Iowa, Nebraska, Kansas, Colorado and Wyoming. Odd-numbered years, presents seminars in Illinois, Minnesota, Iowa, South Dakota, Missouri, Arkansas and Tennessee (write for a schedule). One day, 9 a.m.-4 p.m. Cost of workshop: varies from $40-59, depending on location; includes approximately 35 pages of handouts. Write for more information.

N: FIRST NOVEL FEST, P.O. Box 18612, Milwaukee WI 53218-0612. (414)463-2301. Fax: (414)463-5032. E-mail: books@gardeniapress.com. Website: www.gardeniapress.com. **Senior Editor:** Bob Collins. **President:** Elizabeth Collins. Writer workshops geared toward beginner. **Open to students.** Emphasizes story writing of book-length work for children of all ages, including young adult. Annual conference. Workshop held October. Cost of workshop: changes depending on location of conference. Cost includes agent appointments, contest consultation, banquet and more.

FLORIDA CHRISTIAN WRITERS CONFERENCE, 2344 Armour Ct., Titusville FL 32780. (321)269-5831. Fax: (321)264-0037. E-mail: dwilson@digital.net. Website: www.flwriters.org. **Conference Director:** Billie Wilson. Writer workshops geared toward all levels. **Open to students.** "We offer 50 one-hour workshops and 6 six-hour classes. Approximately 24 of these are for the children's genre: Seeing Through the Eyes of an Artist; Characters . . . Inside and Out; Seeing Through the Eyes of a Child; Picture Book Toolbox; and CD-ROM & Interactive Books for Children. Annual workshop held each February. We have 30 publishers and publications represented by editors teaching workshops and reading manuscripts from the conferees. The conference is limited to 200 people. Usually workshops are limited to 25-30. Advanced or professional workshops are by invitation only via submitted application." Cost of conference: $500; includes food, lodging, tuition and manuscript critiques and editor review of your manuscript. Write for more information.

✔ GLORIETA CHRISTIAN WRITERS' CONFERENCE, P.O. Box 8, Glorieta NM 87535-0008. ((800)797-4222. Fax: (505)797-6149. E-mail: bdaniel@lifeway.com. Website: www.bssb.com/glorieta. **Events Director:** Brian Daniel. Writer conference geared toward all levels. **Open to students.** Sessions include children's writing, screenwriting, poetry, public speaking, novel, magazine writing, drama, nonfiction books, . . . etc. Annual conference held in October. Lines for modems in all hotel rooms and classrooms. Cost of conference: $500-600; includes tuition, double or single hotel room for 4 nights, 12 all-you-can-eat meals. Write or check out the website for additional information.

N: ✔ GOD USES INK CONFERENCE, M.I.P. Box 3745, Markham, Ontario L3R 0Y4 Canada. (905)479-5885. Fax: (905)479-4742. E-mail: ft@efc-canada.com. Website: www.faithtoday.ca. Writer workshops geared toward beginner, intermediate. **Open to Students.** Our conference is for writers who are Christians. A 1.5 hour workshop on writing for children is usually one of a variety of options that we offer. Our 2001 workshop was about writing and marketing ficiton for children. Annual conference. Workshop held June 13-15, 2002; similar weekend in following years. Cost of workshop: $300 Canadian ($215 U.S.; includes food and accommodations, all workshops).

HIGHLAND SUMMER CONFERENCE, Box 7014, Radford University, Radford VA 24142-7014. (540)831-5366. Fax: (540)831-5004. E-mail: jasbury@radford.edu. Website: www.radford.edu/~arsc. **Director:** Grace Toney Edwards. **Assistant to the Director:** Jo Ann Asbury. **Open to students.** Writer workshops geared toward beginner, intermediate and advanced levels. Emphasizes Appalachian literature, culture and heritage. Annual workshop. Workshop held last 2 weeks in June annually. Registration limited to 20. Writing facilities available: computer center. Cost of workshop: Regular tuition (housing/meals extra). Must be registered student or special status student. E-mail, fax or call for more information. Past visiting authors include: Wilma Dykeman, Sue Ellen Bridgers, George Ella Lyon, Lou Kassem.

HIGHLIGHTS FOUNDATION WRITERS WORKSHOP AT CHAUTAUQUA, Dept. CWL, 814 Court St., Honesdale PA 18431. (570)253-1192. Fax: (570)253-0179. E-mail: maewain@highlightsfoundation.org. **Contact:** Maggie Ewain. Writer workshops geared toward those interested in writing for children; beginner, intermediate and advanced levels. Classes offered include: Children's Poetry; Book Promotion; Autobiographical Writing. Annual workshop. Workshops held July 2002, at Chautauqua Institution, Chautauqua, NY. Registration limited to 100/class. Cost of workshop: $1,485; includes tuition, meals, conference supplies. Cost does not include housing. Call for availability and pricing. Scholarships are available for first-time attendees. Write for more information.

HOFSTRA UNIVERSITY SUMMER WRITERS' CONFERENCE, 250 Hofstra University, UCCE, Hempstead NY 11549. (516)463-5016. Fax: (516)463-4833. E-mail: uccelibarts@hofstra.edu. Director, **Liberal Arts**

Studies: Kenneth Henwood. Writer workshops geared toward all levels. Classes offered include fiction, nonfiction, poetry, children's literature, stage/screenwriting and other genres. Children's writing faculty has included Pam Conrad, Johanna Hurwitz, Tor Seidler and Jane Zalben, with Maurice Sendak once appearing as guest speaker. Annual workshop. Workshops held for 2 weeks July 8-19, 2002. Each workshop meets for 2½ hours daily for a total of 25 hours. Students can register for 2 workshops, schedule an individual conference with the writer/instructor and submit a short ms (less than 10 pages) for critique. Enrollees may register as certificate students or credit students. Cost of workshop: noncredit students' enrollment fee is approximately $425; 2-credit student enrollment fee is approximately $1,100/workshop undergraduate and graduate (2 credits); $2,100 undergraduate and graduate (4 credits). On-campus accommodations for the sessions are available for approximately $350/person for the 2-week conference. Students may attend any of the ancillary activities, a private conference, special programs and social events.

✅ **INSPIRATIONAL WRITERS ALIVE!**, 6038 Greenmont, Houston TX 77092. (713)686-7209. E-mail: martharexrogers@aol.com. **State President:** Martha Rogers. Annual conference held 1st Saturday in August. **Open to students** and adults. Registration usually 60-75 conferees. First Baptist Church, Christian Life Center, Houston TX. Cost of conference: member $65; nonmember $75; seniors $60; at the door: members $85; nonmembers $100. Write for more information. "Annual IWA Contest presented. Manuscripts critiqued along with one-on-one 15 minute sessions with speaker(s). (Extra ms. if there is room.)" For more information send for brochure: Attn: Martha Rogers, Board President, 6038 Greenmont, Houston TX 77092, (713)686-7209 or Maxine Holder, (903)795-3986 or Pat Vance, (713)477-4968.

✅ **INTERNATIONAL CREATIVE WRITING CAMP**, 1725 11th St. SW, Minot ND 58701. (701)838-8472. Fax: (701)838-8472. E-mail: info@internationalmusiccamp.com. Website: internationalmusiccamp.com. **Camp Director:** Joseph T. Alme. Writer and illustrator workshops geared toward beginner, intermediate and advanced levels. **Open to students.** Sessions offered include those covering poems, plays, mystery stories, essays. Annual workshop held the last week in July of each summer. Registration limited to 20. The summer camp location at the International Peace Garden on the Border between Manitoba and North Dakota is an ideal site for generating creative thinking. Excellent food, housing and recreation facilities are available. Cost of workshop: $200. Write for more information.

🆕 **INTERNATIONAL WOMEN'S WRITING GUILD "REMEMBER THE MAGIC" ANNUAL SUMMER CONFERENCE**, P.O. Box 810, Gracie Station, New York NY 10028. (212)737-7536. **Executive Director:** Hannelore Hahn. Writer and illustrator workshops geared toward all levels. Offers 65 different workshops—some are for children's book writers and illustrators. Also sponsors 13 other events throughout the US. Annual workshops. Workshops held 2nd or 3rd week in August. Length of each session: 1 hour-15 minutes; sessions take place for an entire week. Registration limited to 500. Cost of workshop: $375 (plus $375 room and board). Write for more information. "This workshop always takes place at Skidmore College in Saratoga Springs NY."

🆕 **JOURNEY CONFERENCE**, Author's Venue, 9720 Tapatio Dr., NW, Albuequerque NM 87114. (505)898-5048. Fax: (505)890-8673. Website: www.authorsvenue.com. **Director of Events:** Stephanie Dooley. Writer workshops geared toward intermediate level. **Open to students.** Sessions offered include appointments with editors and agents, "Problems with Contracts," "What's New in Publishing." Annual conference. Conference held May 9-11, 2002 at Hilton in Mesa, AZ. Cost of conference: $350-500; includes all sessions of conference and keynote banquet. Pre-conference sessions are extra as well as excursions, if any. Write for more information. We also do writing for children seminars during the year all over the country.

KENTUCKY WOMEN WRITERS CONFERENCE, 251 W. Second St., Lexington KY 40507. (859)254-4175. Fax: (859)281-1151. E-mail: kywwc@hotmail.com. Website: www.carnegieliteracy.org. **Contact:** Jan Isenhour. Writer workshops geared toward beginner, intermediate and advanced levels. **Open to students.** Past sessions have included "writing for young adults" with Gloria Velasquez, author of *Tommy Stands Alone*; a variety of workshops with children's writer George Ella Lyon, Anne Shelby and other women writers such as Maya Angelou, Alice Walker, Joy Harjo, Barbara Kingsolver, Lee Smith and a host of others. Annual conference. Cost of conference: $80-150; includes all conference registration, some meals, some performances. Write for more information.

🆕 **LEAGUE OF UTAH WRITERS' ROUNDUP**, 4621 W. Harman Dr., West Valley City, Utah Valley City UT 84120. Phone/fax: (801)964-0861. E-mail: Crofts@numucom.com. Website: http://luwrite.tripod.com/. **Membership & Contest Chair:** Dorothy Crofts. Writer workshops geared toward beginner, intermediate, advanced. Illustrator workshops geared toward beginner. **Open to students.** "One of our main guest speakers is Jennifer Wingertzahn, a children's book editor from Random House. This year for the first time ever, we have included an 'Illustrations' category in our annual contest."

Annual workshop. Workshop held 3rd weekend of September 2002. Registration limited to approximately 400. Our conference is held at the Hilton Hotel. Cost of workshop: $100 for members/$150 for nonmembers; includes 4 meals, all workshops, all general sessions, a syllabus of all handout materials and a conference packet. "When requesting information, please provide an e-mail address and/or fax number."

LIFEWAY WORKSHOP, 127 Ninth Ave. N., Nashville TN 37234-0148. (615)251-2828. Fax: (615)251-5067. E-mail: jwoolridge@lifeway.com. **Workshop Director:** Judy Woolridge. Writer workshops geared toward beginner and intermediate levels. **Open to students.** Bible study curriculum, devotional materials, leisure-reading materials, magazine articles for parents and leaders. Annual workshop held July 29-August 1, 2002. Registration limited to 100. Cost of workshop: $90 (early bird) or $110; includes participation in all workshop presentations and conferences, folio of workshop materials and handouts, banquet, breaks with editors, free evaluation of a writing sample. Write for more information.

LIGONIER VALLEY WRITERS CONFERENCE, P.O. Box B, Ligonier PA 15658-1602. (724)537-3341. Fax: (724)537-0482. **Contact:** Sally Shirey. Writer programs geared toward all levels. Annual conference features fiction, nonfiction, poetry and other genres. Conference held July 12-14, 2002. Write or call for more information.

☑ **MANHATTANVILLE WRITERS' WEEK**, Manhattanville College, 2900 Purchase St., Purchase NY 10577-2103. (914)694-3425. Fax: (914)694-3488. E-mail: rdowd@mville.edu. Website: www.gps.mville.edu. **Dean, School of Graduate & Professional Studies:** Ruth Dowd. Writer workshops geared toward beginner, intermediate and advanced levels. **Open to students.** Writers' week offers a special workshop for writers interested in children's/young adult writing. We have featured such workshop leaders as: Patricia Gauch, Richard Peck, Elizabeth Winthrop and Janet Lisle. Annual workshop held last week in June. Length of each session: one week. Cost of workshop: $560 (non-credit); includes a full week of writing activities, 5-day workshop on children's literature, lectures, readings, sessions with editors and agents, etc. Workshop may be taken for 2 graduate credits. Write for more information.

MARITIME WRITERS' WORKSHOP, Department Extension & Summer Session, P.O. Box 4400, University of New Brunswick, Fredericton, New Brunswick E3B 5A3 Canada. Phone/fax: (506)474-1144. E-mail: k4jc@unb.ca. Website: unb.ca/coned/writers/writers.htm. **Coordinator:** Rhona Sawlor. Week-long workshop on writing for children, general approach, dealing with submitted material, geared to all levels and held in July. Annual workshop. 3 hours/day. Group workshop plus individual conferences, public readings, etc. Registration limited to 10/class. Cost of workshop: $350 tuition; meals and accommodations extra. Room and board on campus is approximately $280 for meals and a single room for the week. 10-20 ms pages due before conference (deadline announced). Scholarships available.

☒ **MAUI WRITERS CONFERENCE**, P.O. Box 1118, Kihei HI 96753. (888)974-8373 or (808)879-0061. Fax: (808)879-6233. E-mail: writers@maui.net. Website: www.mauiwriters.com. **Director:** Shannon Tullius. Writer workshops geared toward beginner, intermediate, advanced. **Open to students.** "We offer a small children's writing section covering picture books, middle grade and young adult. We invite one *New York Times* Bestselling Author and agents and editors, who give consultations." Annual workshop. Workshop held Labor Day weekend. Cost includes admittance to all conference sessions and classes only—no airfare, food, or consultations.

☑ **MIDLAND WRITERS CONFERENCE**, Grace A. Dow Memorial Library, 1710 W. St. Andrews, Midland MI 48640-2698. (517)837-3435. Fax: (517)837-3468. E-mail: ajarvis@midland-mi.org. Website: www.midland-mi.org/gracedowlibrary. **Conference Chair:** Ann Jarvis. **Open to students.** Writer and illustrator workshops geared toward all levels. "Each year, we offer a topic of interest to writers of children's literature. Last year, Brenda Shannon Yee "Writing for Children—Hearing the Voice" was the agenda. Classes offered include: how to write poetry, writing for youth, your literary agent/what to expect. Annual workshop. Workshops held usually second Saturday in June. Length of each session: concurrently, 4 1-hour sessions repeated in the afternoon. Maximum class size: 50. "We are a public library." Cost of workshop: $60; $50 seniors and students; includes choice of workshops and the keynote speech given by a prominent author (last year Jerri Nielsen). Write for more information.

MIDWEST WRITERS WORKSHOP, Department of Journalism, Ball State University, Muncie IN 47306. (765)285-5587. Fax: (765)285-7997. **Director:** Earl L. Conn. Writer workshops geared toward intermediate level. Topics include most genres. Past workshop presenters include Joyce Carol Oates, James Alexander Thom, Bill Brashler and Richard Lederer. Workshop also includes ms evaluation and a writing contest. Annual workshop. Workshop will be held July 25-27, 2002. Registration tentatively limited to 125. Cost of workshop: $195; includes everything but room. Most meals included. Offers scholarships. Write for more information.

MISSISSIPPI VALLEY WRITERS CONFERENCE, 3403 45th St., Moline IL 61265. E-mail: kimseuss@aol.com. **Conference Director:** David R. Collins. Writer workshops geared toward all levels. Conference open to adults. Weeklong workshops in Basics for Beginners, Poetry, Juvenile Writing, Nonfiction, Basics of the Novel, Novel Manuscript Seminar, Short Story, Photography, Writing to Sell. Annual workshop. Workshops held June

3-7, 2002; usually it is the second week in June each year. Length of each session: Monday-Friday, 1 hour each day. Registration limited to 20 participants/workshop. Writing facilities available: college library. Cost of workshop: $25 registration; $50 to participate in 1 workshop, $90 in 2, $40 for each additional; $25 to audit a workshop. Write for more information.

N. MISSOURI WRITERS' GUILD 86th STATE CONVENTION, P.O. Box 22506, Kansas City MO 64113-0506. (816)361-1281. E-mail: eblivingsfun@hotmail.com. **State President:** Jane Simmons. Writer and illustrator workshops geared to all levels. **Open to students.** Annual workshop. Workshop held late April or early May each year. Cost of workshop: $56.

MONTROSE CHRISTIAN WRITER'S CONFERENCE, 5 Locust St., Montrose PA 18801-1112. (570)278-1001. Fax: (570)278-3061. E-mail: mbc@montrosebible.org. Website: www.montrosebible.org. **Executive Director:** Jim Fahringer. **Secretary-Registrar:** Donna Kosik. **Open to adults and students.** Writer workshops geared toward beginner, intermediate and advanced levels. Annual workshop. Workshop held in July. Cost of workshop: $120 tuition. Write for more information.

☑ MOUNT HERMON CHRISTIAN WRITERS CONFERENCE, Mount Hermon Christian Conference Center, P.O. Box 413, Mount Hermon CA 95041-0413. (831)335-4466. Fax: (831)335-9413. E-mail: slist@mhca mps.org. Website: www.mounthermon.org. **Director of Adult Ministries:** David R. Talbott. Writer workshops geared toward all levels. Open to students over 16 years. Emphasizes religious writing for children via books, articles; Sunday school curriculum; marketing. Classes offered include: Suitable Style for Children; Everything You Need to Know to Write and Market Your Children's Book; Take-Home Papers for Children. Workshops held annually over Palm Sunday weekend: March 22-26, 2002 and April 6-10, 2002. Length of each session: 5-day residential conferences held annually. Registration limited 45/class, but most are 10-15. Conference center with hotel-style accommodations. Cost of workshop: $565-800 variable; includes tuition, resource notebook, refreshment breaks, full room and board for 13 meals and 4 nights. Write or e-mail for more information.

THE NATIONAL WRITERS ASSOCIATION FOUNDATION CONFERENCE, (formerly The National Writers Association Conference), 3140 S. Peoria #295, Aurora CO 80014. (303)841-0246. **Executive Director:** Sandy Whelchel. Writer workshops geared toward all levels. Classes offered include marketing, agenting, "What's Hot in the Market." Annual workshop. In 2002 the workshop will be held in Denver, Colorado, June 7-9. Write for more information or check our website: www.nationalwriters.com.

N. NEW JERSEY SOCIETY OF CHRISTIAN WRITERS FALL SEMINAR, P.O. Box 405, Millville NJ 08332-0405. (856)327-1231. Fax: (856)327-0291. E-mail: daystar405@aol.com. Website: www.daystarministries .com/njscw. **Founder/Director:** Dr. Mary Ann Diorio. Writer workshops geared toward beginner, intermediate. **Open to students.** Annual workshop. Workshop held first Saturday in November. Cost of workshop: $75 includes lunch; $65 does not include lunch. Write for more information. "We have one guest speaker per conference—usually 30-50 attendees."

OF DARK AND STORMY NIGHTS, P.O. Box 1944, Muncie IN 47308-1944. (765)288-7402. E-mail: spurge onmwa@juno.com. **Director:** W.W. Spurgeon. Writer workshops geared toward beginner, intermediate, advanced and professional. **Open to adults and students.** Topics include mystery and true crime writing for all ages. Annual workshop. Location: Rolling Meadows, IL (suburban Chicago). Workshop held June 8, 2002. Registration limited to 175. "This is a concentrated one-day program with panels and speakers." Cost of workshop: $165; includes all sessions, continental breakfast and full luncheon. Mss critiques available for an extra charge. Write for more information.

OHIO KENTUCKY INDIANA CHILDREN'S LITERATURE CONFERENCE, % Greater Cincinnati Library Consortium (GCLC), 2181 Victory Parkway, Suite 214, Cincinnati OH 45206-2855. (513)751-4422. Fax: (513)751-0463. E-mail: gclc@gclc-lib.org. Website: www.gclc-lib.org. **Staff Development Coordinator:** Judy Malone. Writer and illustrator conference geared toward all levels. **Open to students.** Annual conference. Emphasizes multicultural literature for children and young adults. Conference held annually in November. Contact GCLC for more information. Registration limited to 250. Cost of conference: $40; includes registration/attendance at all workshop sessions, continental breakfast, lunch, author/illustrator signings. Write for more information.

OUTDOOR WRITERS ASSOCIATION OF AMERICA ANNUAL CONFERENCE, 158 Lower Georges Valley Rd., Spring Mills PA 16875. (814)364-9557. Fax: (814)364-9558. E-mail: eking4owaa@cs.com. **Meeting Planner:** Eileen King. Writer workshops geared toward all levels. Annual workshop. Workshop held in June. Cost of workshop: $175; includes attendance at all workshops and most meals. Attendees must have prior approval from Executive Director before attendance is permitted. Write for more information.

PERSPECTIVES IN CHILDREN'S LITERATURE CONFERENCE, School of Education, 226 Furcolo Hall, University of Massachusetts, Amherst MA 01003-3035. (413)545-4325 or (413)545-1116. Fax: (413)545-2879. E-mail: childlit@educ.umass.edu. Website: www.unix.oit.umass.edu/~childlit. **Coordinator of Confer-**

ence: Jane Kelley Pierce. Writer and illustrator workshops geared to all levels. Conference 2002 will feature Eric Carle and Joseph Bruchac as keynote speakers. Additional presenters include Jane Yolen and Norton Juster. Presenters talk about what inspires them, how they bring their stories to life and what their visions are for the future. Next conference will be held on Saturday, April 6, 2002, at the University of Massachusetts. For more information contact Jane Kelley Pierce by phone, fax or e-mail."

☑ **PHOTOGRAPHY: A DIVERSE FOCUS**, 610 W. Poplar St., #4, Zionsville IN 46077-1220. Phone/fax: (317)873-0738. E-mail: charlenefaris@hotmail.com. **Director:** Charlene Faris. Writer and illustrator workshops geared to beginners. "Conferences focus primarily on children's photography; also literature and illustration. Annual conferences are held very often throughout year." Registration is not limited, but "sessions are generally small." Cost of conference: $200 (2 days), $100 (1 day). "Inquiries with a SASE only will receive information on seminars."

ROBERT QUACKENBUSH'S CHILDREN'S BOOK WRITING AND ILLUSTRATING WORK-SHOP, 460 E. 79th St., New York NY 10021-1443. Phone/fax: (212)861-2761. E-mail: rqstudios@aol.com. (E-mail inquirers please include mailing address). Website: www.rquackenbush.com. **Contact:** Robert Quackenbush. Writer and illustrator workshops geared toward all levels. **Open to students.** Five-day extensive workshop on writing and illustrating books for children, emphasizes picture books from start to finish. Also covered is writing fiction and nonfiction for middle grades and young adults, if that is the attendees' interest. Current trends in illustration are also covered. This July workshop is a full 5-day (9 a.m.-4 p.m) extensive course. Next workshop July 8-12, 2002. Registration limited to 10/class. Writing and/or art facilities available; work on the premises; art supply store nearby. Cost of workshop: $650 for instruction. Cost of workshop includes instruction in preparation of a ms and/or book dummy ready to submit to publishers. Class limited to 10 members. Attendees are responsible for arranging their own hotel and meals, although suggestions are given on request for places to stay and eat. "This unique workshop, held annually since 1982, provides the opportunity to work with Robert Quackenbush, a prolific author and illustrator of children's books with more than 170 fiction and nonfiction books for young readers to his credit, including mysteries, biographies and song-books. The workshop attracts both professional and beginning writers and artists of different ages from all over the world." Recommended by Foder's *Great American Learning Vacations*.

📰 **ROCKY MOUNTAIN RETREATS FOR WRITERS & ARTISTS**, 81 Cree Court, Lyons CO 80540. (303)823-0530. E-mail: deborah@indra.com. Website: www.expressionretreats.com. **Director:** Deborah DeBord. Writers and illustrator workshops geared to all levels. **Open to students.** Include information on releasing creative energy, identifying strengths and interests, balancing busy lives, marketing creative works. Monthly conference. Registration limited to 4 per session. Writing studio, weaving studio, private facilities available. Cost of workshop: $1,066/week; includes room, meals, materials, instruction. "Treat yourself to a week of mountain air, sun, and personal expression. Flourish with the opportunity for sustained work punctuated by structured experiences designed to release the artist's creative energies. Relax over candlelit gourmet meals followed by fireside discussions of the day's efforts. Discover the rhythm of filling the artistic well and drawing on its abundant resources."

SAGE HILL WRITING EXPERIENCE, Writing Children's & Young Adult Fiction Workshop, Box 1731, Saskatoon, Saskatchewan S7K 3S1 Canada. Phone/fax: (306)652-7395. E-mail: sage.hill@sk.sympatico.ca Website: www.lights.com/sagehill. . **Executive Director:** Steven Ross Smith. Writer conference geared toward intermediate level. **Open to students.** This program occurs every 2 or 3 years, but the Sage Hill Conference is annual. Conference held July 25-August 5. Registration limited to 6 participants. Cost of conference: $675; includes instruction, meals, accommodation. Require ms samples prior to registration. Write for more information.

SAN DIEGO STATE UNIVERSITY WRITERS' CONFERENCE, The College of Extended Studies, San Diego CA 92182-1920. (619)594-2517. Fax: (619)594-8566. E-mail: ppierce@mail.sdsu.edu. Website: www.ces.sdsu.edu. **Conference Facilitator:** Paula Pierce. Writer workshops geared toward beginner, intermediate and advanced levels. Emphasizes nonfiction, fiction, screenwriting, advanced novel writing; includes sessions specific to writing and illustrating for children. Workshops offered by children's editors, agents and writers. Workshops held third weekend in January each year. Registration limited. Cost of workshop: approximately $280. Write for more information or see our home page at the above website.

SANDHILLS WRITERS CONFERENCE, Augusta State University, 2500 Walton Way, Augusta GA 30904. (706)737-1500. Fax: (706)667-4770. E-mail: akellman@aug.edu. Website: www.aug.edu//Langlitcom/sand_hills_conference. **Conference Director:** Anthony Kellman. Writer and illustrator workshops geared toward beginner and intermediate levels. "Each year we have a children's literature author on our staff who speaks on various aspects of the craft of this genre." Annual conference held March 21-23, 2002. Registration limited to 150. "We have free word processing and Internet access through our Reese Library." Cost of conference: $156; includes 1 ms consultation, 2 luncheons, attendence at all events, one ms submission. Participants should submit mms samples usually by the second week of February. The professional staffer critiques these prior to registration and meets with the authors of the scripts in one-on-one conferences during the conference. Awards are given.

☑ **THE WILLIAM SAROYAN WRITER'S CONFERENCE**, P.O. Box 5331, Fresno CA 93755-5331. Phone/fax: (559)224-2516. E-mail: law@pacbell.net. **President:** Linda West. **Conference Chair:** Stephen Mette. Writer and illustrator workshops geared toward advanced level. **Open to Students.** Past sessions have featured Barbara Kuroff, editor of Writer's Digest Books and Andrea Brown, agent for children's book authors and illustrators. Annual conference. Conference held April, 2002 at Piccadilly Inn-airport. Registration limited to 185. Cost of conference: $300. Friday noon to Sunday noon workshops (35 to choose from) most meals, critique groups, one-on-ones with agents, editors. Write for more information. "We try to cover a wide variety of writing. Children's books would be one topic of many."

☑ **SEATTLE CHRISTIAN WRITERS CONFERENCE**, sponsored by Writers Information Network, P.O. Box 11337, Bainbridge Island WA 98110. (206)842-9103. Fax: (206)842-0536. E-mail: writersinfonetwork@juno .com. Website: www.bluejaypub.com/win. **Director:** Elaine Wright Colvin. Writer workshops geared toward all levels. Conference open to students. Past conferences have featured subjects such as 'Making It to the Top as a Children's Book Author,' featuring Debbie Trafton O'Neal. Quarterly workshop (4 times/year). Workshop dates to be announced. Cost of workshop: $25. Write for more information and to be added to mailing list.

🎒 **SOUTH COAST WRITERS CONFERENCE**, P.O. Box 590, 29392 Ellensburg Ave., Gold Beach OR 97444. (541)247-2741. Fax: (541-247-6247. E-mail: scwc@southwestern.cc.or.us. **Coordinator:** Janet Pretti. Writer workshops geared toward beginner, intermediate levels. **Open to students.** Include fiction, nonfiction, nuts and bolts, poetry, feature writing, children's writing, publishing. From 2001—Archetypes & Ideas in Children's Writing, How I Sold My Babies into Bondage for Fun & Profit (Making a living as a children's writer); from 1999—Children Have Language . . . Listen, Writing & Selling a Children's Book. Annual workshop. Workshop held February 15-16, 2002, Friday and Saturday of President's day weekend in February. Registration limited to 25-30 students/workshop. Cost of workshop: $45 before January 31, $55 after; includes Friday night author's reading and book signing, Saturday conference, choice of 4 workshop sessions, Saturday evening writers' circle (networking and critique). Write for more information. "We also have two six-hour workshops that Friday, offering more intensive writing exercises. The cost is an additional $25."

STATE OF MAINE WRITERS' CONFERENCE, 18 Hill Rd., Belmont MA 02478. (617)489-1548. **Chairs:** June Knowles and Mary Pitts. Writers' workshops geared toward beginner, intermediate, advanced levels. **Open to students and adults.** Emphasizes poetry, prose, mysteries, editors, publishers, etc. Conference held August 21-24, 2002. Cost of workshop: $100; includes all sessions and supper, snacks, poetry booklet. Send SASE for more information.

☑ **STEAMBOAT SPRINGS WRITERS CONFERENCE**, P.O. Box 774284, Steamboat Springs CO 80477. (970)879-8079. E-mail: MsHFreiberger@cs.com. **Conference Director:** Harriet Freiberger. Writers' workshops geared toward intermediate levels. **Open to students.** Some years offer topics specific to children's writing. Annual conference since 1982. Workshops held July 22, 2002; conference will be July 21. Registration limited to 30. Cost of workshop: $45; includes 4 seminars and luncheon. Write or e-mail for more information.

☑ **TAOS SUMMER WRITERS' CONFERENCE**, University of New Mexico, Humanities 255, Albuquerque NM 87131. (505)277.6248. Fax: (505)277-5573. E-mail: swarner@unm.edu. Website: www.unm.edu/~taosco nf. **Director:** Sharon Oard Warner. Writer workshops geared toward all levels. **Open to students.** Must be 18 years old. "Our conference offers both week-long and weekend conferences, not only in children's writing, but also adult fiction (novel, short story), creative nonfiction, poetry and screenwriting." Annual conference held July 13-July 19, 2002—(usually 3rd week of July). Maximum of 12 people per workshop. Usually 5 weekend workshops and 8- or 10-week-long workshops. "We provide an on-site computer room." Cost of conference: approximately $475/weeklong; $225/weekend; includes tuition, opening and closing night dinner, all the readings by instructors, Wednesday night entertainment. Lodging and meals extra but we offer a reduced rate at the Sagebrush Inn in Taos, Comfort Suites; breakfast included. Write for more information.

THE 21ST CENTURY WRITER'S GET-A-WAY, 625 Schuring, Suite B, Portage MI 49024-5106. (616)232-2100. Fax: (509)694-1153. E-mail: ishaeefaw@aol.com. Website: justfriendspublishing.com. **Public Relations Manager:** John Williams. Writer and illustrator workshops geared toward all levels. Sessions offered include "Marketing Strategies For The 21st Century." **Open to students.** In this workshop our workshop facilitator brings the latest information on software for graphic arts design and/or recommended art workshops. Workshop held twice a year, April 20-22 and August 10-12, 2002. This event will be held at Michigan State University Kellogg Biological Station. All workshops include writing, and one workshop will demo structure book cover designs. Cost of workshop: $200. $150 covers 5 meals, notebook and materials plus registration fee. $50 covers lodging. Write for more information.

🎒 **UNIVERSITY OF THE NATIONS SCHOOL OF WRITING AND WRITERS WORKSHOPS**, P.O. Box 1380 YWAM Woodcrest Lindale TX 75771-1380. (903)882-WOOD [9663]. Fax: (903)882-1161. E-mail: info@ywamwoodcrest.com. Website: www.ywamwoodcrest.com. **Director of Training:** Pamela Warren. Writer workshops geared toward beginner, intermediate, advanced levels. **Open to students.** Workshops held

September 26 to December 17, 2002. Workshops held various weeks during that time. Cost for workshop: $50 registration fee (nonrefundable) plus $225 tuition per week plus $125/week if staying on our campus. (Call for cost of 12-week school of writing.) $225 tuition/week covers lectures, critique groups, hands-on-training. $215 if staying at our campus includes food and housing. Otherwise student must make own arrangements for lodging and meals. If you want college credit for the workshop or are taking the entire 12-week school of writing, you must have completed the University of the Nations Discipleship Training School first. Otherwise no requirements for workshop students. Write for more information. Although we are associated with the Youth with A Mission missionary group we welcome inquiries from all interested parties–not just missionaries.

VANCOUVER INTERNATIONAL WRITERS FESTIVAL, 1398 Cartwright St., Vancouver, British Columbia V6H 3R8 Canada. (604)681-6330. Fax: (604)681-8400. E-mail: viwf@writersfest.bc.ca. Website: www.writersfest.bc.ca. **Artistic Director:** Alma Lee. Annual literary festival. The Vancouver International Writers Festival strives to encourage an appreciation of literature and to promote literacy by providing a forum where writers and readers can interact. This is accomplished by the production of special events and an annual Festival which feature writers from a variety of countries whose work is compelling and diverse. The Festival attracts over 11,000 people and presents approximately 40 events in four venues during five days on Granville Island, located in the heart of Vancouver. The first 3 days of the festival are programmed for elementary and secondary school students. Held third week in October (5-day festival). All writers who participate are invited by the A.D. The events are open to anyone who wishes to purchase tickets. Cost of events ranges from $10-25.

THE VICTORIA SCHOOL OF WRITING, P.O. Box 8152, Victoria, British Columbia V8W 3R8 Canada. (250)598-5300. E-mail: vicwrite@islandnet.com. Website: www.islandnet.com/vicwrite. **Director:** Ruth Slavin. Writer conference geared toward intermediate level. In the 2002 conference there may be 1 workshop on writing for children and young adults. Annual conference. Workshop third week of July. Registration limited to 100. Conference includes close mentoring from established writers. Cost of conference: $575 (Canada); includes tuition and some meals. To attend, submit 3-10 pages of writing samples. Write for more information.

WESLEYAN WRITERS CONFERENCE, Wesleyan University, Middletown CT 06459. (860)685-3604. Fax: (860)685-2441. E-mail: agreene@wesleyan.edu. Website: www.wesleyan.edu/writing/conferen.html. **Director:** Anne Greene. Writer workshops geared toward all levels. "This conference is useful for writers interested in how to structure a story, poem or nonfiction piece. Although we don't always offer classes in writing for children, the advice about structuring a piece is useful for writers of any sort, no matter who their audience is." Classes in the novel, short story, fiction techniques, poetry, journalism and literary nonfiction. Guest speakers and panels offer discussion of fiction, poetry, reviewing, editing and publishing. Individual ms consultations available. Conference held annually the last week in June. Length of each session: 6 days. "Usually, there are 100 participants at the Conference." Classrooms, meals, lodging and word processing facilities available on campus. Cost of workshop: tuition—$530, room—$120, meals (required of all participants)—$190. "Anyone may register; people who want financial aid must submit their work and be selected by scholarship judges." Call for a brochure or look on the Web at address above.

WHIDBEY ISLAND WRITERS' CONFERENCE, P.O. Box 1289, Langley WA 98260. (360)331-6714. E-mail: writers@whidbey.com. Website: www.whidbey.com/writers. Director: Celeste Mergens. Writer and illustrator workshops geared toward beginner, intermediate and advanced levels. **Open to students**. Topics include "Writing for Children," "Writing in a Bunny Eat Bunny World," "The Art of Revision." Annual conference in March. Registration limited to 275. Cost of conference: $308; includes all workshops and events, 2 receptions, activities and daily luncheons. "For writing consultations participants pay $35 for 20 minutes to submit the first five pages of a chapter book, youth novel or entire picture book idea with a written 1-page synopsis." Write, e-mail or check website for more information. "This is a uniquely personable weekend that is designed to be highly interactive."

WILLAMETTE WRITERS ANNUAL WRITERS CONFERENCE, 9045 SW Barbur Blvd., Suite 5A, Portland OR 97219. (503)452-1592. Fax: (503)452-0372. E-mail: wilwrite@teleport.com. Website: www.willamettewriters.com. **Office Manager:** Bill Johnson. Writer workshops geared toward all levels. Emphasizes all areas of writing, including children's and young adult. Opportunities to meet one-on-one with leading literary agents and editors. Workshops held in August. Cost of conference: $246; includes membership.

TENNESSEE WILLIAMS/NEW ORLEANS LITERARY FESTIVAL, 938 Lafayette St., Suite 300, New Orleans LA 70113. (504)581-1144. Fax: (504)523-3680. E-mail: info@tennessee@williams.net. Website: www.tennesseewilliams.net. **Executive Director:** Lou Ann Morehause. Writer workshops geared toward beginner, intermediate levels. **Open to students.** Annual workshop. Workshop held March 20-24, 2002. Master classes are limited in size to 100—all other panels offered have no cap. Cost of workshop: prices range from $15-45. Write for more information. "We are a literary festival and may occasionally offer panels/classes on children's writing and/or illustration, but this is not done every year."

WISCONSIN REGIONAL WRITER'S ASSOCIATION, INC., Spring and Fall Conferences, 510 W. Sunset Ave., Appleton WI 54911-1139. (920)734-3724. E-mail: wrwa@lakefield.net. Website: www.inkwells.net/wrwa. **Contact:** Donna Potrykus, vice president. Estab. 1948. Annual. Conferences held in May and September are dedictated to self-improvement through speakers, workshops and presentations. Topics and speakers vary with each event. Average attendance: 100-150. We honor all genres of writing. Spring conference is a one-day event that features speakers and awards for two contests (humor writing and feature article writing). Fall conference is a two-day event featuring the Jade Ring Banquet and awards for six genre categories. Spring 2002: Holiday Inn—Manitowoc, WI. Agents and editors participate in each conference. Cost of workshop: $40-75. Provides a list of area hotels or lodging options. "We negotiate special rates at each facility. A block of rooms is set aside for a specific time period." Award winners receive a certificate and a cash prize. First Place winners of the Jade Ring contest receive a jade ring. Must be a member to enter all contests. For brochure call, write, e-mail or visit our website.

WRITE ON THE SOUND WRITERS CONFERENCE, 700 Main St., Edmonds WA 98020-3032. (425)771-0228. Fax: (425)771-0253. E-mail: wots@ci.edmonds.wa.us. Website: www.ci.edmonds.wa.us. **Cultural Resources Coordinator:** Frances Chapin. Writer workshops geared toward beginner, intermediate, advanced and professional levels with some sessions on writing for children. Annual conference held the first weekend in October with 2 full days of a variety of lectures and workshops." Registration limited to 200. Cost of workshop: approximately $50/day, or $85 for the weekend, includes 4 workshops daily plus one ticket to keynote lecture. Writing contest for conference participants. Brochures are mailed in August. Attendees must preregister. Write, e-mail or call for brochure.

✔ **WRITERS' LEAGUE OF TEXAS WORKSHOP SERIES**, (formerly Austin Writers' League Conference Workshop Series), 1501 W. Fifth St., Suite E-2, Austin TX 78703. (512)499-8914. Fax: (512)499-0441. E-mail: awl@writersleague.org. Website: www.writersleague.org. **Executive Director:** Jim Bob McMillan. Writer and illustrator workshops and conferences geared toward all levels for children and adults. Annual conferences. Classes are held during the week, and workshops are held on Saturdays during March, April, May, September, October and November. Annual Teddy Children's Book Award of $1,000 presented each fall to book published in specified time period. Write for more information. The Austin Writers' League has available audiotapes of past workshop programs.

✔ **WRITE-TO-PUBLISH CONFERENCE**, 9731 N. Fox Glen Dr., #6F, Niles IL 60714-4222. (847)296-3964. Fax: (847)296-0754. E-mail: lin@wtpublish.com. Website: www.WTPublish.com. **Director:** Lin Johnson. Writer workshops geared toward all levels. **Open to students.** Conference is focused for the Christian market and includes a class on writing for children. Annual conference held June 5-8, 2002. Cost of conference: $340; includes conference and banquet. For information, call (847)299-4755 or e-mail brochure@wtpublish.com. Conference takes place at Wheaton College in the Chicago area.

N: WRITING FOR CHILDREN: A Conference for Teachers, Parents, Writers & Illustrators, 933 Hamlet St., Columbus OH 43201-3595. (614)291-8644. E-mail: jmmengel@yahoo.com. Website: www.sjms.net/conf. **Development Director:** Jim Mengel. Writer and illustrator workshops geared toward beginner, intermediate and advanced levels. **Open to students.** Annual workshop. Workshop held Saturday, April 27, 2002. Registration limited to 140. Cost of workshop: $95; $45 full-time college students; $40 additional charge for ms or portfolio evaluations; includes attendance, lunch, continental breakfast, snacks. Manuscript and portfolio evaluation require pre-registration (call Jim Mengel). Manuscripts and/or portfolios to be evaluated must be submitted (to evaluator directly) by March 15, 2002. "Event will be at the Crowne Plaze in downtown Columbus, OH and will be an all-day affair with three keynote speakers—Shonto Begay, Sharon Mills Draper and Linda Sue Park."

N: WRITING FOR YOUNG READERS WORKSHOP, 348 HCEB, Provo UT 84602-1532. (801)378-2568. Fax: (801)378-8165. Website: http://ce.byu.edu/cw/writing. **Coordinator:** Susan Overstreet. Writer workshops geared toward all levels. **Open to students.** Offers workshops on picture books, chapter books, middle grade novels, YA novels, and a special beginners workshop. Annual workshop. Workshop held July 15-18, 2002. Registration limited to 125 people. Computer lab, library, conference rooms available. Cost of workshop: $369 early; $385 regular; includes workshop fees, concluding banquet, access to facilities. "Workshoppers are expected to bring a manuscript." Write for more information.

✔ **WRITING TODAY**, Birmingham-Southern College, Box 549003, Birmingham AL 35254. (205)226-4921. Fax: (205)226-3072. E-mail: dcwilson@bsc.com. Website: www.bsc.edu. **Director of Special Events:** Annie Green. Writer's workshop geared toward all levels. **Open to students.** "The Writing Today Conference brings together writers, editors, publishers, playwrights, poets and other literary professionals from around the country for two days of workshops and lectures on the literary arts, as well as practical information necessary to the craft of writing. Programs explore poetry, playwriting, children's books, novels, short stories, etc." Major speakers have included Eudora Walty, Edward Albee, James Dickey, Erskine Caldwell, Ray Bradbury, Pat Conroy, John Barth, Ernest Gaines and Galway Kinnell. Annual Conference. Conference held April 12-13, 2002. Registration limited to 500. Cost of Conference: $120; includes all workshop sessions, continental breakfast and lunch both days and a Friday and Saturday reception. Individual mss critiques available for an additional fee. Write for more information.

N̲ WWG WRITER'S CONFERENCE & WRITING COMPETITION, P.O. Box 132451, Spring TX 77393-2451. Website: www.woodlandsonline.com/wwg. **Conference Coordinator:** Mary-Ann Ball. Writer and illustrator workshops geared to beginner level. **Open to students.** Annual workshop. Workshop held September 2002. Registration limited to 125. Cost of workshop: $80 nonmembers, $60 members. Write for more information.

Contests, Awards & Grants

Publication is not the only way to get your work recognized. Contests and awards can also be great ways to gain recognition in the industry. Grants, offered by organizations like SCBWI, offer monetary recognition to writers, giving them more financial freedom as they work on projects.

When considering contests or applying for grants, be sure to study guidelines and requirements. Regard entry deadlines as gospel and follow the rules to the letter.

Note that some contests require nominations. For published authors and illustrators, competitions provide an excellent way to promote your work. Your publisher may not be aware of local competitions such as state-sponsored awards—if your book is eligible, have the appropriate person at your publishing company nominate or enter your work for consideration.

To select potential contests and grants, read through the listings that interest you, then send for more information about the types of written or illustrated material considered and other important details. A number of contests offer information through websites given in their listings.

If you are interested in knowing who has received certain awards in the past, check your local library or bookstores or consult *Children's Books: Awards & Prizes*, compiled and edited by the Children's Book Council (www.cbcbooks.org). Many bookstores have special sections for books that are Caldecott and Newbery Medal winners. Visit these websites for more information on award-winning children's books: The Caldecott—www.ala.org/alsc/caldecott.html; The Newbery—www.ala.org/alsc/newbery.html; The Coretta Scott King Award—www.ala.org/srrt/csking; The Michael L. Printz Award—www.ala.org/yalsa/printz; The Boston Globe-Horn Book Award—www.hbook.com/bghb.html; The Golden Kite Award—www.scbwi.org/goldkite.htm.

For insight into successfully applying for a grant, read the Insider Report with **Carla McClaffery**, recipient of a SCBWI Work-in-Progress Grant (page 336).

Information on contests listed in the previous edition but not included in this edition of *Children's Writer's & Illustrator's Market* **may be found in the General Index.**

N. JANE ADDAMS CHILDREN'S BOOK AWARDS, Jane Addams Peace Association, Inc./Women's International League for Peace and Freedom. 777 United Nations Plaza, New York NY 10017. (212)682-8830. Fax: (212)286-8211. E-mail: japa@igc.apc.org. Website: www.educationwisc.edu/ccbc/public/jaddams.htm. **Award Director:** Ginny Moore Kruse. Submit entries to: Ginny Moore Kruse. "Two copies of published books (in previous year only)" Address: 1708 Regent St. Madison WI 53705. Annual award. Estab. 1953. Previously published submissions only. Submissions made by author, author's agent, a person or group, submitted by the publisher. Must be published January 1-December 31 of preceding year. Deadline for entries: January 1 each year. SASE for contest rules and entry forms but better to check website. Awards cash and certificate $1,000 to winners (awards are for longer book, shorter book) and $500 each to Honor Book winners—(split between author and illustrator, if necessary). Judging by national committee from various N.S. regions (all are members of W.I.L.P.F.).

N. AESOP PRIZE AND AESOP ACCOLADES PRIZE, American Folklore Society, 23 Rosewood Court, San Rafael CA 94901. (415)459-4572. E-mail: cplevin@aol.com. **Contest/Award Director:** Cherry P. Levin. **Open to students.** Annual contest. Estab. 1993. Purpose of contest: To promote and award quality children's literature that use some form of folklore as their basis. Submissions must be current for the year. Submissions made by author or by author's agent. Must be published 2001-2002. Deadline for entries: September 30, 2001-September 30, 2002. SASE for contest rules and entry forms. An award seal embossed stickers recognition in the *AFS Journal* and other children's publications such as *The Horn Book*, *Parent's Magazine*, etc. Aesop Committee of the Annual Folklore Society, Children's Section. In nominated books, folklore should be central to the book's content and, if appropriate, to the illustrations; the folklore presented in the book should accurately reflect the culture and worldview of the people whose folklore is the focus of the book; the reader's understanding of folklore should be enhanced by the book, as should the book be enhanced by the presence of folklore; the book should reflect the high artistic standards of the best of children's literature and should have strong appeal to the child reader; folklore sources must be fully acknowledged and annotations referenced within the bound contents of the publication.

AIM Magazine Short Story Contest, P.O. Box 1174, Maywood IL 60153-8174. (773)874-6184. **Contest Directors:** Ruth Apilado, Mark Boone. Annual contest. **Open to students.** Estab. 1983. Purpose of contest: "We solicit stories with social significance. Youngsters can be made aware of social problems through the written word, and hopefully they will try solving them." Unpublished submissions only. Deadline for entries: August 15. SASE for contest rules and entry forms. SASE for return of work. No entry fee. Awards $100. Judging by editors. Contest open to everyone. Winning entry published in fall issue of *AIM*. Subscription rate $12/year. Single copy $4.50.

✔ ⬛ **ALCUIN CITATION AWARD**, The Alcuin Society, P.O. Box 3216, Vancouver, British Columbia V6B 3X8 Canada. (604)888-9049. Fax: (604)888-9052. E-mail: deeddy@attglobal.net. Website: www.alcuinsoci ety.com. **Secretary:** Doreen E. Eddy. Annual award. Estab. 1983. **Open to students.** Purpose of contest: Alcuin Citations are awarded annually for excellence in Canadian book design. Previously published submissions only, "in the year prior to the Awards Invitation to enter; i.e., 1996 awards went to books published in 1995." Submissions made by the author, publishers and designers. Deadline for entries: March 15. SASE. Entry fee is $10 per book. Awards certificate. Judging by professionals and those experienced in the field of book design. Requirements for entrants: Winners are selected from books designed and published in Canada. Awards are presented annually at the Annual General Meeting of the Alcuin Society held in late May or early June each year.

AMERICA & ME ESSAY CONTEST, Farm Bureau Insurance, Box 30400, 7373 W. Saginaw, Lansing MI 48909-7900. (517)323-7000. Fax: (517)323-6615. E-mail: lfedewa@fbinsmi.com. Website: farmbureauinsura nce-mi.co. **Contest Coordinator:** Lisa Fedewa. Annual contest. **Open to students.** Estab. 1968. Purpose of the contest: to give Michigan 8th graders the opportunity to express their thoughts/feelings on America and their roles in America. Unpublished submissions only. Deadline for entries: mid-November. SASE for contest rules and entry forms. "We have a school mailing list. Any school located in Michigan is eligible to participate." Entries not returned. No entry fee. Awards savings bonds and plaques for state top ten ($500-1,000), certificates and plaques for top 3 winners from each school. Each school may submit up to 10 essays for judging. Judging by home office employee volunteers. Requirements for entrants: "Participants must work through their schools or our agents' sponsoring schools. No individual submissions will be accepted. Top ten essays and excerpts from other essays are published in booklet form following the contest. State capitol/schools receive copies."

✔ **AMERICAN ASSOCIATION OF UNIVERSITY WOMEN, NORTH CAROLINA DIVISION, AWARD IN JUVENILE LITERATURE**, North Carolina Literary and Historical Association, 4610 Mail Service Center, Raleigh NC 27699-4610. (919)733-9375. Fax: (919)733-8807. **Award Coordinator:** Mr. Michael Hill. Annual award. Purpose of award: to reward the creative activity involved in writing juvenile literature and to stimulate in North Carolina an interest in worthwhile literature written on the juvenile level. Book must be published during the year ending June 30 of the year of publication. Submissions made by author, author's agent or publisher. Deadline for entries: July 15. SASE for contest rules. Awards a cup to the winner and winner's name inscribed on a plaque displayed within the North Carolina Division of Archives and History. Judging by Board of Award selected by sponsoring organization. Requirements for entrants: Author must have maintained either legal residence or actual physical residence, or a combination of both, in the State of North Carolina for three years immediately preceding the close of the contest period.

AMERICAS AWARD, Consortium of Latin American Studies Programs (CLASP), CLASP Committee on Teaching and Outreach, % Center for Latin American and Caribbean Studies, University of Wisconsin-Milwaukee, P.O. Box 413, Milwaukee WI 53201. (414)229-5986. Fax: (414)229-2879. E-mail: jkline@uwm.edu. Website: www.uwm.edu/Dept/CLA/outreach_americas.html. **Coordinator:** Julie Kline. Annual award. Estab. 1993. Purpose of contest: "Up to two awards are given each spring in recognition of U.S. published works (from the previous year) of fiction, poetry, folklore or selected nonfiction (from picture books to works for young adults) in English or Spanish which authentically and engagingly relate to Latin America, the Caribbean, or to Latinos in the United States. By combining both and linking the "Americas," the intent is to reach beyond geographic borders, as well as multicultural-international boundaries, focusing instead upon cultural heritages within the hemisphere." Previously published submissions only. Submissions open to anyone with an interest in the theme of the award. Deadline for entries: January 15. SASE for contest rules and any committee changes. Awards $200 cash prize, plaque and a formal presentation at the Library of Congress, Washington DC. Judging by a review committee consisting of individuals in teaching, library work, outreach and children's literature specialists.

AMHA LITERARY CONTEST, American Morgan Horse Association Youth, P.O. Box 960, Shelburne VT 05482. (802)985-4944. E-mail: info@morganhorse.com. Website: www.morganhorse.com. **Contest Director:** Pat Kent. Annual contest. Open to students under 21. Purpose of contest: "to award youth creativity." The contest includes categories for both poetry and essays. Unpublished submissions only. Submissions made by author. Deadline for entries: October 1. SASE for contest rules and entry forms. No entry fee. Awards $25 cash and ribbons to up to 5th place. "Winning entry will be published in *AMHA News and Morgan Sales Network*, a monthly publication."

N. HANS CHRISTIAN ANDERSEN AWARD, IBBY International Board on Books for Young People, Nonnenweg 12, Postfach, CH-4003 Basel Switzerland. Phone: (004161)272 29 17. Fax: (004161)272 27 57. E-mail: lbby@eye.ch. Website: www.ibby.org. **Executive Assistant:** Liz Page. Award offered every two years. Purpose of award: A Hans Christian Andersen Medal shall be awarded every two years by the International Board on Books for Young People (IBBY) to an author and to an illustrator, living at the time of the nomination, who by the outstanding value of their work are judged to have made a lasting contribution to literature for children and young people. The complete works of the author and of the illustrator will be taken into consideration in awarding the medal, which will be accompanied by a diploma. Previously published titles only. Submissions are nominated by National Sections of IBBY in good standing. The National Sections select the candidates. The Hans Christian Andersen Award, named after Denmark's famous storyteller, is the highest international recognition given to an author and an illustrator of children's books. The Author's Award has been given since 1956, the Illustrator's Award since 1966. The Andersen Award is often called the "Little Nobel Prize." Her Majesty Queen Margrethe of Denmark is the Patron of the Hans Christian Andersen Awards. The Hans Christian Andersen Jury judges the books submitted for medals according to literary and artistic criteria. The awards are presented at the biennial congresses of IBBY.

N. ASPCA CHILDREN'S ESSAY CONTEST, American Society for the Prevention of Cruelty to Animals, 424 E. 92nd St., New York NY 10028-6804. (212)876-7700. Fax: (212)860-3435. E-mail: education@aspca.org. Website: www.aspca.org. **Contest Manager:** Miriam Ramos. Submit entries to: Miriam Ramos, manager, education programs, humane education. **Open to students.** Annual contest. Estab. 1990. An essay contest for students in grades 1-6. Unpublished submissions only. Submissions made by author, parent, teacher. Deadline for entries: November 1, 2002. SASE for contest rules and entry forms. Prizes vary, could include books, magazine subscriptions, T-shirts. Judging by ASPCA staff. Requirements for entrants: Open to all students in grades 1-6, must be student's own writing. Prizes are given for winning individuals and their classrooms. Judging in 2 categories, Grades 1-3 and Grades 4-6.

N. THE ASPCA HENRY BERGH CHILDREN'S BOOK AWARD, The American Society For the Prevention of Cruelty to Animals, 424 E. 92nd St., New York NY 10128-6804. (212)876-7700, ext. 4409. Fax: (212)860-3435. E-mail: education@aspca.org. Website: www.aspca.org. . **Award Manager:** Miriam Ramos. Submit entries to: Miriam Ramos, manager of education programs, humane education. Competition open to adults. Annual award. Estab. 2000. Purpose of contest: To honor outstanding children's literature that fosters empathy and compassion for all living things. Awards presented to authors. Previously published submissions only. Submissions made by author or author's agent. Must be published January 2002-December 2002. Deadline for entries: October 31, 2002. SASE for contest rules and entry forms. Awards foil award seals, plaque, certificate. Judging by professionals in animal welfare and children's literature. Requirements for entrants: Open to children's literature about animals and/or the environment published in 2002. Includes fiction, nonfiction and poetry in 3 categories: Companion Animals, Ecology and Environment and Humane Heroes.

BAKER'S PLAYS HIGH SCHOOL PLAYWRITING CONTEST, Baker's Plays, P.O. Box 6992222, Quincy MA 02269-9222. Fax: (617)745-9891. E-mail: help@bakersplays.com. Website: www.bakersplays.com. **Contest Director:** Kurt Gombar. Annual contest. Estab. 1990. Purpose of the contest: to acknowledge playwrights at the high school level and to insure the future of American theater. Unpublished submissions only. Postmark deadline: January 30, 2002. Notification: May. SASE for contest rules and entry forms. No entry fee. Awards $500 to the first place playwright and Baker's Plays will publish the play; $250 to the second place playwright with an honorable mention; and $100 to the third place playwright with an honorable mention in the series. Judged anonymously. **Open to any high school student.** Plays must be accompanied by the signature of a sponsoring high school drama or English teacher, and it is recommended that the play receive a production or a public reading prior to the submission. "Please include a SASE." Teachers must not submit student's work. The first place playwright will have their play published in an acting edition the September following the contest. The work will be described in the Baker's Plays Catalogue, which is distributed to 50,000 prospective producing organizations.

JOHN AND PATRICIA BEATTY AWARD, California Library Association, 717 20th Street, Suite 200, Sacramento CA 95814. (916)447-8541. Fax: (916)447-8394. E-mail: info@cla-net.org. Website: www.cla-net.org. **Executive Director:** Susan Negreen. Annual award. Estab. 1987. Purpose of award: "The purpose of the John and Patricia Beatty Award is to encourage the writing of quality children's books highlighting California, its culture, heritage and/or future." Previously published submissions only. Submissions made by the author, author's agent or review copies sent by publisher. The award is given to the author of a children's book published the preceding year. Deadline for entries: Submissions may be made January-December. Contact CLA Executive Director who will liaison with Beatty Award Committee. Awards cash prize of $500 and an engraved plaque.

Judging by a 5-member selection committee appointed by the president of the California Library Association. Requirements for entrants: "Any children's or young adult book set in California and published in the U.S. during the calendar year preceding the presentation of the award is eligible for consideration. This includes works of fiction as well as nonfiction for children and young people of all ages. Reprints and compilations are not eligible. The California setting must be depicted authentically and must serve as an integral focus for the book." Winning selection is announced through press release during National Library Week in April. Author is presented with award at annual California Library Association Conference in November.

THE IRMA S. AND JAMES H. BLACK BOOK AWARD, Bank Street College of Education, 610 W. 112th St., New York NY 10025-1898. (212)875-4450. Fax: (212)875-4558. E-mail: lindag@bnkst.edu. Website: http://streetcat.bnkst.edu/html/isb.html. **Contact:** Linda Greengrass. Annual award. Estab. 1972. Purpose of award: "The award is given each spring for a book for young children, published in the previous year, for excellence of both text and illustrations." Entries must have been published during the previous calendar year (between January '01 and December '01 for 2001 award). Deadline for entries: December 15th. "Publishers submit books to us by sending them here to me at the Bank Street Library. Authors may ask their publishers to submit their books. Out of these, three to five books are chosen by a committee of older children and children's literature professionals. These books are then presented to children in selected second, third and fourth grade classes here and at a few other cooperating schools on the East Coast. These children are the final judges who pick the actual award. A scroll (one each for the author and illustrator, if they're different) with the recipient's name and a gold seal designed by Maurice Sendak are awarded in May."

BOOK OF THE YEAR FOR CHILDREN, Canadian Library Association, 328 Frank St., Ottawa, Ontario K2P 0X8 Canada. (613)232-9625. Fax: (613)563-9895. Websiter: www.cla.ca. **Contact:** Chairperson, Canadian Association of Children's Librarians. Annual award. Estab. 1947. "The main purpose of the award is to encourage writing and publishing in Canada of good books for children up to and including age 14. If, in any year, no book is deemed to be of award calibre, the award shall not be made that year. To merit consideration, the book must have been published in Canada and its author must be a Canadian citizen or a permanent resident of Canada." Previously published submissions only; must be published between January 1 and December 1 of the previous year. Deadline for entries: January 1. SASE for award rules. Entries not returned. No entry fee. Awards a medal. Judging by committee of members of the Canadian Association of Children's Librarians. Requirements for entrants: Contest open only to Canadian authors or residents of Canada. Winning books are on display at CLA headquarters.

BOOK PUBLISHERS OF TEXAS, Children's/Young People's Award, The Texas Institute of Letters, % Center for the Study of the Southwest, P.O. Box 298300, Ft. Worth TX 76129. (512)245-2232. Fax: (512)245-7462. E-mail: mbl3@swt.edu. Website: www.English.swt.edu/css/TIL/rules.htm. **Contact:** Mark Busby. Send SASE to above address for list of judges to whom entries should be submitted. Annual award. Purpose of the award: "to recognize notable achievement by a Texas writer of books for children or young people or by a writer whose work deals with a Texas subject. The award goes to the author of the winning book, a work published during the calendar year before the award is given. Judges list available each July. Submissions go directly to judges, so current list of judges is necessary. Write to above address. Deadline is first postally operative day of January." Previously published submissions only. SASE for award rules and entry forms. No entry fee. Awards $250. Judging by a panel of 3 judges selected by the TIL Council. Requirements for entrants: The writer must have lived in Texas for 2 consecutive years at some time, or the work must have a Texas theme.

THE BOSTON GLOBE-HORN BOOK AWARDS, The Boston Globe & The Horn Book, Inc., The Horn Book, 56 Roland St., Suite 200, Boston MA 02129. (617)628-0225. Fax: (617)628-0882. E-mail: info@hbook.com. Website: www.hbook.com/bghb.shtml. Annual award. Estab. 1967. Purpose of award: "to reward literary excellence in children's and young adult books. Awards are for picture books, nonfiction and fiction. Up to two honor books may be chosen for each category." Books must be published between June 1, 2001 and May 31, 2002. Deadline for entries: May 15. "Publishers usually submit books. Award winners receive $500 and silver engraved bowl, honor book winners receive a silver plate." Judging by 3 judges involved in children's book field. "*The Horn Book Magazine* publishes speeches given at awards ceremonies. The book must have been published in the U.S."

ANN ARLYS BOWLER POETRY CONTEST, *Read* Magazine, 200 First Stamford Place, P.O. Box 120023, Stamford CT 06912-0023. (203)705-3406. Fax: (203)705-1661. E-mail: jkroll@weeklyreader.com. Website: www.weeklyreader.com/read.html. **Contest Director:** Jennifer Kroll. Annual contest. Estab. 1988. Purpose of the contest: to reward young-adult poets (grades 6-12). Unpublished submissions only. Submissions made by the author or nominated by a person or group of people. Entry form must include signature of teacher, parent or guardian, and student verifying originality. Maximum number of submissions per student: three poems. Deadline for entries: January 15. SASE for contest rules and entry forms. No entry fee. Awards 6 winners $100 each, medal of honor and publication in *Read*. Semifinalists receive $50 each. Judging by *Read* and *Weekly Reader* editors and teachers. Requirements for entrants: the material must be original. Winning entries will be published in a spring issue of *Read*.

⟦N⟧ BRANT POINT PRIZE, What's Inside Press, P.O. Box 18203, Beverly Hills CA 90209. (800)269-7757. Fax: (800)856-2160. E-mail: bpp@whatsinsidepress.com. Website: www.whatsinsidepress.com. and www.brantp ointprize.com. Submit entries to: Brant Point Prize. **Open to students.** Annual contest. Estab. 1999. Purpose of contest: To recognize excellence in unpublished children's writing and provide opportunities to get published. Unpublished submissions only. Submissions made by author. Deadline for entries: August. SASE for contest rules and entry forms. Entry fee is $10 fully tax-deductible donation to children's charity. Awards publishing contract. Other prizes include Tiffany & Co. pens, money, T-shirts. Judging panel changes every year. Includes previous year's winner. Rights to winning material acquired. Contest is open to everyone.

⟦N⟧ ⟦▪⟧ ANN CONNOR BRIMER AWARD, Nova Scotia Library Association, P.O. Box 36036, Halifax, Nova Scotia B3J 3S9 Canada. (902)490-5875. Fax: (902)490-5893. **Award Director:** Heather MacKenzie. Annual award. Estab. 1991. Purpose of the contest: to recognize excellence in writing. Given to an author of a children's book who resides in Atlantic Canada. Previously published submissions only. Submissions made by the author's agent or nominated by a person or group of people. Must be published in previous year. Deadline for entries: January 31. SASE for contest rules and entry forms. No entry fee. Awards $1,000. Judging by a selection committee. Requirements for entrants: Book must be intended for children up to age 15; in print and readily available; fiction or nonfiction except textbooks.

BUCKEYE CHILDREN'S BOOK AWARD, Ada Kent c/o Ohio School for the Deaf, 500 Morse Rd., Columbus OH 43214. (614)728-1414. E-mail: akent@freenet.columbus.oh.us. Website: www.wpl.lib.oh.us/buckeyeb ook/. **Chairperson:** Nancy Smith. Correspondence should be sent to Ruth A. Metcalf at the above address. **Open to students.** Award offered every two years. Estab. 1981. Purpose of the award: "The Buckeye Children's Book Award Program was designed to encourage children to read literature critically, to promote teacher and librarian involvement in children's literature programs, and to commend authors of such literature, as well as to promote the use of libraries. Awards are presented in the following three categories: grades K-2, grades 3-5 and grades 6-8." Previously published submissions only. Deadline for entries: February 1. "The nominees are submitted by this date during the even year and the votes are submitted by this date during the odd year. This award is nominated and voted upon by children in Ohio. It is based upon criteria established in our bylaws. The winning authors are awarded a special plaque honoring them at a banquet given by one of the sponsoring organizations. The BCBA Board oversees the tallying of the votes and announces the winners in March of the voting year in a special news release and in a number of national journals. The book must have been written by an author, a citizen of the United States and originally copyrighted in the U.S. within the last three years preceding the nomination year. The award-winning books are displayed in a historical display housed at the Columbus Metropolitan Library in Columbus, Ohio."

BYLINE MAGAZINE CONTESTS, P.O. Box 130596, Edmond OK 73013-0001. E-mail: mpreston@bylinem ag.com. Website: www.bylinemag.com. **Contest Director:** Marcia Preston. **Open to adults.** Purpose of contest: *ByLine* runs 4 contests a month on many topics to encourage and motivate writers. Past topics include first chapter of a novel, children's fiction, children's poem, nonfiction for children, personal essay, general short stories, valentine or love poem, etc. Send SASE for contest flier with topic list. Unpublished submissions only. Submissions made by the author. "We do not publish the contests' winning entries, just the names of the winners." SASE for contest rules. Entry fee is $3-4. Awards cash prizes for first, second and third place. Amounts vary. Judging by qualified writers or editors. List of winners will appear in magazine.

BYLINE MAGAZINE STUDENT PAGE, P.O. Box 130596, Edmond OK 73013-0001. (405)348-5591. Website: www.bylinemag.com. **Contest Director:** Marcia Preston, publisher. Estab. 1981. "We offer writing contests for students in grades 1-12 on a monthly basis, September through May, with cash prizes and publication of top entries." Previously unpublished submissions only. "This is not a market for illustration." Deadline for entries varies. "Entry fee usually $1." Awards cash and publication. Judging by qualified editors and writers. "We publish top entries in student contests. Winners' list published in magazine dated 2 months past deadline." Send SASE for details.

RANDOLPH CALDECOTT MEDAL, Association for Library Service to Children, Division of the American Library Association, 50 E. Huron, Chicago IL 60611. (312)280-2163. Website: www.ala.org/alsc/caldecott.html. **Interim Executive Director:** Stephanie Anton. Annual award. Estab. 1938. Purpose of the award: to honor the artist of the most distinguished picture book for children published in the US (Illustrator must be US citizen or resident.) Must be published year preceding award. Deadline for entries: December. SASE for award rules. Entries not returned. No entry fee. "Medal given at ALA Annual Conference during the Newbery/Caldecott Banquet."

CALIFORNIA YOUNG PLAYWRIGHTS CONTEST, Playwrights Project, 450 B St., Suite 1020, San Diego CA 92101. (619)239-8222. Fax: (619)239-8225. E-mail: write@playwrightsproject.com. Website: www.pl aywrightsproject.com. **Director:** Deborah Salzer. **Open to Californians under age 19.** Annual contest. Estab. 1985. "Our organization and the contest is designed to nurture promising young writers. We hope to develop playwrights and audiences for live theater. We also teach playwriting." Submissions required to be unpublished and not produced professionally. Submissions made by the author. Deadline for entries: April 1. SASE for contest rules and entry form. No entry fee. Award is professional productions of 3-5 short plays each year, participation of the writers in the entire production process, with a royalty awarded. Judging by professionals in the theater community, a committee of 5-7; changes somewhat each year. Works performed in San Diego at the Cassius Carter Centre Stage of the Globe Theatres. Writers submitting scripts of 10 or more pages receive a detailed script evaluation letter.

CALLIOPE FICTION CONTEST, Writers' Specialized Interest Group (SIG) of American Mensa, Ltd., P.O. Box 466, Moraga CA 94556-0466. E-mail: cynthia@theriver.com. **Fiction Editor:** Sandy Raschke. **Open to students.** Annual contest. Estab. 1991. Purpose of contest: To promote good writing and opportunities for getting published. To give our member/subscribers and others an entertaining and fun exercise in writing. Unpublished submissions only (all genres, no violence, profanity or extreme horror). Submissions made by author. Deadline for entries: changes annually but usually around September 15. Entry fee is $2 for non-subscribers; subscribers get first entry fee. Awards small amount of cash (up to $25 for 1st place, to $5 for 3rd), certificates, full or mini-subscriptions to *Calliope* and various premiums and books, depending on donations. All winners are published in subsequent issues of *Calliope*. Judging by fiction editor, with concurrence of other editors, if needed. Requirements for entrants: one-time rights. Open to all writers. No special considerations—other than following the guidelines. Contest theme, due dates and sometimes entry fees change annually. Always send SASE for complete rules; available after April 15 each year. Sample copies with prior winners are available for $3 and large SAE envelope with 3 first-class stamps.

REBECCA CAUDILL YOUNG READERS' BOOK AWARD, Illinois Reading Council, Illinois School Library Media Association, Illinois Association of Teachers of English, P.O. Box 6536, Naperville IL 60567-6536. (630)420-6378. Fax: (630)420-3241. **Award Director** Bonita Slovinski. Annual award. Estab. 1988. Purpose of contest: to award the Children's Choice Award for grades 4-8 in Illinois. Submissions nominated by students. Must be published within the last 5 years. Awards honorarium, plaque. Judging by children, grades 4-8.

CHILDREN'S BOOK AWARD, Federation of Children's Book Groups. The Old Malt House, Aldbourne Marlborough, Wiltshire SN8 2DW England. 01672 540629. Fax: 01672 541280. E-mail: marianneadey@cs.com. **Coordinator:** Marianne Adey. Purpose of the award: "The C.B.A. is an annual prize for the best children's book of the year judged by the children themselves." Categories: (I) picture books, (II) short novels, (III) longer novels. Estab. 1980. Previously unpublished submissions only. Deadline for entries: December 31. SASE for rules and entry forms. Entries not returned. Awards "a magnificent silver and oak trophy worth over $6,000 and a portfolio of children's work." Silver dishes to each category winner. Judging by children. Requirements for entrants: Work must be fiction and published in the UK during the current year (poetry is ineligible). Work will be published in current "Pick of the Year" publication.

CHILDREN'S WRITER WRITING CONTESTS, 93 Long Ridge Rd., West Redding CT 06896-1124. (203)792-8600. Fax: (203)792-8406. Contest offered twice per year by *Children's Writer*, the monthly newsletter of writing and publishing trends. Purpose of the award: To promote higher quality children's literature. "Each contest has its own theme. Our 2002 contest will include a history article for ages 7 to 10 (650 words) and a pre-k story for ages 1 to 4 (350 words). Any original unpublished piece, not accepted by any publisher at the time of submission, is eligible." Submissions made by the author. Deadline for entries: Last weekday in February and October. "We charge a $10 entry fee for nonsubscribers only, which is applicable against a subscription to *Children's Writer*." Awards 1st place—$250 or $500, a certificate and publication in *Children's Writer*; 2nd place—$100 or $250, and certificate; 3rd-5th places—$50 or $100 and certificates. To obtain the rules and theme for the current contest send a SASE to *Children's Writer* at the above address. Put "Contest Request" in the lower left of your envelope. Judging by a panel of 4 selected from the staff of the Institute of Children's Literature. "We acquire First North American Serial Rights (to print the winner in *Children's Writer*), after which all rights revert to author." Open to any writer. Entries are judged on age targeting, originality, quality of writing and, for nonfiction, how well the information is conveyed and accuracy. "Submit clear photocopies only, not originals; submission will *not* be returned. Manuscripts should be typed double-spaced. No pieces containing violence or derogatory, racist or sexist language or situations will be accepted, at the sole discretion of the judges."

☑ **CHILDREN'S WRITERS FICTION CONTEST**, Stepping Stones, P.O. Box 8863, Springfield MO 65801-8863. (417)863-7369. Fax: (417)864-4745. E-mail: verwil@alumni.pace.edu. **Coordinator:** V.R. Williams. Annual contest. Estab. 1993. Purpose of contest: to promote writing for children by giving children's writers an opportunity to submit work in competition. Unpublished submissions only. Submissions made by the author. Deadline for entries: July 31. SASE for contest rules and entry forms. Entry fee is $8. Awards cash prize, certificate and publication in chapbook; certificates for Honorable Mention. Judging by Goodin, Williams and Goodwin. First rights to winning material acquired or purchased. Requirements for entrants: Work must be suitable for children and no longer than 2,000 words. "Send SASE for list of winners."

MR. CHRISTIE'S BOOK AWARD® PROGRAM, Christie Brown & Co., Division of Nabisco Ltd, 95 Moatfield Dr., Toronto, Ontario M3B 3L6 Canada. (416)441-5238. Fax: (416)441-5328. E-mail: pamela.singh@kraft.com. **Coordinator:** Pamela Singh. Competition is open to Canadian citizens, landed immigrants and students.

Books must be published in Canada in 2001. Annual award. Estab. 1989. Purpose of award: to honor Canadian authors and illustrators of the best English/French published children's books. Contest includes three categories: Best Book for 7 and under; 8-11; and 12 and up. Submissions are made by the author, made by the author's agent, publishers. Deadline for entries: January 31. SASE for contest rules and entry forms. No entry fee. Awards a total of $45,000. Judging by a panel consisting of people in the literary/teaching community across Canada. Requirements for entrants: must have published children's literature in English or French.

✓ **THE CHRISTOPHER AWARDS**, The Christophers, 12 E. 48th St., New York NY 10017. (212)759-4050. E-mail: awards@christophers.org, Website: www.christophers.org. **Christopher Awards Program Manager:** Judith Trojan. **Children's Book Coordinator:** Virginia Armstrong. Annual award. Estab. 1969 (for young people; books for adults honored since 1949). "Christopher Awards are presented annually to films, TV broadcast and cable network programs, books for adults and books for children that affirm the highest values of the human spirit. Christopher Award winners remind readers (in this case), of any faith and of no particular faith, of their worth, individuality and power to make a difference and positively impact and shape our world. In a nutshell, Christopher Award winners celebrate the humanity of people in a positive way." Published submissions only; must be published between January 1 and December 31 of the current calendar year. Two calls for entry deadlines: June 1 and November 1 per year, but books may be submitted throughout year of release/publication.. Two copies should be sent to Judith Trojan, 12 E. 48th St., New York NY 10017 and two copies to Virginia Armstrong, 22 Forest Ave., Old Tappan NJ 07675." Also send promo materials with the books (press releases, press kits and/or catalog copy with books to both individuals above). Entries not returned. No entry fee. Awards a bronze medallion. Books are judged by reading and subject specialists and young people. Requirements for entrants: "only published works are eligible and must be submitted during the calendar year in which they are first published."

COLORADO BOOK AWARDS, Colorado Center for the Book, 2123 Downing St., Denver CO 80205. (303)839-8320. Fax: (303)839-8319. E-mail: ccftb@compuserve.com. Website: www.coloradobook.org. **Award Director:** Christiane Citron. Award open to adults. Annual award. Estab. 1993. Previously published submissions only. Submissions are made by the author, author's agent, nominated by a person or group of people. Requires Colorado residency by authors. Deadline for entries: January 15, 2002. SASE for contest rules and entry forms. Entry fee is $40. Awards $350 and plaque. Judging by a panel of literary agents, booksellers and librarians. Please note, we *also* have an annual competition for illustrators to design a poster and associated graphics for our Book Festival. The date varies. Inquiries are welcomed.

THE COMMONWEALTH CLUB'S BOOK AWARDS CONTEST, The Commonwealth Club of California, 595 Market St., San Francisco CA 94105. (415)597-4846. Fax: (415)597-6729. E-mail: blane@commonwealthclub.org. Website: www.commonwealthclub.org/bookawards. **Attn:** Barbara Blane. Chief Executive Officer: Gloria Duffy. Annual contest. Estab. 1932. Purpose of contest: the encouragement and production of literature in California. Juvenile category included. Previously published submission; must be published from January 1 to December 31, previous to contest year. Deadline for entries: January 31. SASE for contest rules and entry forms. No entry fee. Awards gold and silver medals. Judging by the Book Awards Jury. The contest is only open to California writers/illustrators (must have been resident of California when ms was accepted for publication). "The award winners will be honored at the Annual Book Awards Program." Winning entries are displayed at awards program and advertised in newsletter.

CRICKET LEAGUE, *Cricket Magazine*, P.O. Box 300, 315 Fifth St., Peru IL 61354. (815)224-6633. Website: www.cricketmag.com. Address entries to: Cricket League. Monthly. Estab. 1973. "The purpose of Cricket League contests is to encourage creativity and give young people an opportunity to express themselves in writing, drawing, painting or photography. There is a contest each month. Possible categories include story, poetry, art or photography. Each contest relates to a *specific theme* described in each *Cricket* issue's Cricket League page. Signature verifying originality, age and address of entrant required and permission to publish. Entries which do not relate to the current month's theme cannot be considered." Unpublished submissions only. Deadline for entries: the 25th of each month. Cricket League rules, contest theme, and submission deadline information can be found in the current issue of *Cricket* and via website. "We prefer that children who enter the contests subscribe to the magazine or that they read *Cricket* in their school or library." No entry fee. Awards certificate suitable for framing and children's books or art/writing supplies. Judging by *Cricket* editors. Obtains right to print prizewinning entries in magazine. Refer to contest rules in current *Cricket* issue. Winning entries are published on the Cricket League pages in the *Cricket* magazine 3 months subsequent to the issue in which the contest was announced. Current theme, rules, and prizewinning entries also posted on the website.

MARGUERITE DE ANGELI PRIZE, Delacorte Press, Random House Books for Young Readers, 1540 Broadway, New York NY 10036. Estab. 1992. Fax: (212)782-9452 (note re: Marguerite De Angeli Prize). Website: www.randomhouse.com. Annual award. Purpose of the award: to encourage the writing of fiction for children aged 7-10, either contemporary or historical; to encourage unpublished writers in the field of middle grade fiction. Unpublished submissions only. No simultaneous submissions. Length: between 40-144 pages. Submissions made by author or author's agent. Entries should be postmarked between April 1st and June 30th. SASE for award rules. No entry fee. Awards a $1,500 cash prize plus a hardcover and paperback book contract with a $3,500 advance against a royalty to be negotiated. Judging by Delacorte Press editorial staff. Open to US and Canadian writers who have not previously published a novel for middle-grade readers (ages 7-10). Works published in an upcoming Bantam Doubleday Dell Books for Young Readers list.

DELACORTE PRESS PRIZE FOR A FIRST YOUNG ADULT NOVEL, Delacorte Press, Books for Young Readers Department, 1540 Broadway, New York NY 10036. (212)782-9000. Fax: (212)302-7985. Website: www.randomhouse.com/kids/submit. Annual award. Estab. 1982. Purpose of award: to encourage the writing of contemporary young adult fiction. Previously unpublished submissions only. Mss sent to Delacorte Press may not be submitted to other publishers while under consideration for the prize. "Entries must be submitted between October 1 and New Year's Day. The real deadline is a December 31 postmark. Early entries are appreciated." SASE for award rules. No entry fee. Awards a $1,500 cash prize and a $6,000 advance against royalties for world rights on a hardcover and paperback book contract. Contest results will be announced in April, 2002. Works published in an upcoming Delacorte Press, an imprint of Random House, Inc., Books for Young Readers list. Judged by the editors of the Books for Young Readers Department of Delacorte Press. Requirements for entrants: The writer must be American or Canadian and must *not* have previously published a young adult novel but may have published anything else. Foreign-language mss and translations and mss submitted to a previous Delacorte Press are not eligible. Send SASE for new guidelines. Guidelines are also available on our website: www.randomhouse.com/kids/submit.

MARGARET A. EDWARDS AWARD, American Library Association, 50 East Huron St., Chicago IL 60611-2795. (312)944-6780 or (800)545-2433. Fax: (312)664-7459. E-mail: yalsa@ala.org. Website: www.ala.org/yalsa. Annual award administered by the Young Adult Library Services Association (YALSA) of the American Library Association (ALA) and sponsored by *School Library Journal* magazine. Purpose of award: "ALA's Young Adult Library Services Association (YALSA), on behalf of librarians who work with young adults in all types of libraries, will give recognition to those authors whose book or books have provided young adults with a window through which they can view their world and which will help them to grow and to understand themselves and their role in relationships, society and the world." Previously published submissions only. Submissions are nominated by young adult librarians and teenagers. Must be published five years before date of award. SASE for award rules and entry forms. No entry fee. Judging by members of the Young Adult Library Services Association. Deadline for entry: June 1. "The award will be given annually to an author whose book or books, over a period of time, have been accepted by young adults as an authentic voice that continues to illuminate their experiences and emotions, giving insight into their lives. The book or books should enable them to understand themselves, the world in which they live, and their relationship with others and with society. The book or books must be in print at the time of the nomination."

ARTHUR ELLIS AWARD, Crime Writers of Canada, 3007 Kingston Rd., Box 113, Scarborough, Ontario M1M 1P1 Canada. (416)461-9826. Fax: (416)461-4489. E-mail: ap113@torfree.net.on.ca. Submit entries to: Secretary/Treasurer. Annual contest. Estab. 1984. Purpose of contest: to honor the best juvenile writing with a theme of crime, detective, espionage, mystery, suspense and thriller, fictional or factual accounts of criminal doings. Includes novels with a criminous theme. Previously published submissions only. Submissions made by author or by author's agent or publisher. Must be published during year previous to award. Deadline for entries: January 31. SASE for contest rules and entry forms. Awards a statuette of a hanged man—with jumping jack limbs. Judging by 2 nonmembers and one member per category. Can be any publication, regardless of language, by a writer, regardless of nationality, resident in Canada or a Canadian writer resident abroad.

DOROTHY CANFIELD FISHER CHILDREN'S BOOK AWARD, Vermont Department of Libraries, % Northeast Regional Library, 23 Tilton Rd., St. Johnsbury VT 05819. (802)828-3261. Fax: (802)828-2199. E-mail: ggreene@dol.state.vt.us. Website: www.dol.state.vt.us. **Chairman:** Joanna Rudge Long. Annual award. Estab. 1957. Purpose of the award: to encourage Vermont children to become enthusiastic and discriminating readers by providing them with books of good quality by living American authors published in the current year. Deadline for entries: December of year book was published. SASE for award rules and entry forms. No entry fee. Awards a scroll presented to the winning author at an award ceremony. Judging is by the children grades 4-8. They vote for their favorite book. Requirements for entrants: "Titles must be original work, published in the United States, and be appropriate to children in grades 4 through 8. The book must be copyrighted in the current year. It must be written by an American author living in the U.S."

FLICKER TALE CHILDREN'S BOOK AWARD, Flicker Tale Award Committee, North Dakota Library Association, Bismarck Public Library, 515 N. Fifth St., Bismarck ND 58501. (701)222-6412. Fax: (701)221-6854. **Contact:** Marvia Boettcher. Estab. 1979. Purpose of award: to give children across the state of North Dakota a chance to vote for their book of choice from a nominated list of 10: 5 in the picture book category; 5 in the juvenile category. Also, to promote awareness of quality literature for children. Previously published submissions only. Submissions nominated by librarians and teachers across the state of North Dakota. Awards a plaque from North Dakota Library Association and banquet dinner. Judging by children in North Dakota. Entry deadline in June.

FLORIDA STATE WRITING COMPETITION, Florida Freelance Writers Association, P.O. Box A, North Stratford NH 03590. (603)922-8338. Fax: (603)922-8339. E-mail: danakcnw@ncia.net. Website: www.writers-editors.com. **Executive Director:** Dana K. Cassell. Annual contest. Estab. 1984. Categories include children's literature (length appropriate to age category). Entry fee is $5 (members), $10 (nonmembers). Awards $100 first prize, $75 second prize, $50 third prize, certificates for honorable mentions. Judging by teachers, editors and published authors. Judging criteria: interest and readability within age group, writing style and mechanics, originality, salability. Deadline: March 15. For copy of official entry form, send #10 SASE or go to www.writers-editors.com. List of 2001 winners on website.

DON FREEMAN MEMORIAL GRANT-IN-AID, Society of Children's Book Writers and Illustrators, 8271 Beverly Blvd., Los Angeles CA 90048. E-mail: scbwi@juno.com. Website: www.scbwi.org. Estab. 1974. Purpose of award: to "enable picture book artists to further their understanding, training and work in the picture book genre." Applications and prepared materials will be accepted between January 15 and February 15. Grant awarded and announced on June 15. SASE for award rules and entry forms. SASE for return of entries. No entry fee. Annually awards one grant of $1,500 and one runner-up grant of $500. "The grant-in-aid is available to both full and associate members of the SCBWI who, as artists, seriously intend to make picture books their chief contribution to the field of children's literature."

AMELIA FRANCES HOWARD GIBBON AWARD FOR ILLUSTRATION, Canadian Library Association, 328 Frank St., Ottawa, Ontario K2P 0X8 Canada. (613)232-9625. Website: www.cla.ca. **Contact:** Chairperson, Canadian Association of Children's Librarians. Annual award. Estab. 1971. Purpose of the award: "to honor excellence in the illustration of children's book(s) in Canada. To merit consideration the book must have been published in Canada and its illustrator must be a Canadian citizen or a permanent resident of Canada." Previously published submissions only; must be published between January 1 and December 31 of the previous year. Deadline for entries: January 1. SASE for award rules. Entries not returned. No entry fee. Awards a medal. Judging by selection committee of members of Canadian Association of Children's Librarians. Requirements for entrants: illustrator must be Canadian or Canadian resident. Winning books are on display at CLA Headquarters.

GOLD MEDALLION BOOK AWARDS, Evangelical Christian Publishers Association, 1969 East Broadway Rd., Suite Two, Tempe AZ 85282. (480)966-3998. Fax: (480)966-1944. E-mail: dross@ecpa.org. Website: www.ecpa.org. **President:** Doug Ross. Annual award. Estab. 1978. Categories include Preschool Children's Books, Elementary Children's Books, Youth Books. "All entries must be evangelical in nature and cannot be contrary to ECPA's Statement of Faith (stated in official rules)." Deadlines for entries: December 1. SASE for award rules and entry form. "The work must be submitted by the publisher." Entry fee is $300 for nonmembers. Awards a Gold Medallion plaque.

GOLDEN KITE AWARDS, Society of Children's Book Writers and Illustrators, 8271 Beverly Blvd., Los Angeles CA 90048. (323)782-1010. E-mail: scbwi@scbwi.org. Website: www.scbwi.org. **Coordinators:** Ruby Guerrero and Mercedes Coats. Annual award. Estab. 1973. "The works chosen will be those that the judges feel exhibit excellence in writing, and in the case of the picture-illustrated books—in illustration, and genuinely appeal to the interests and concerns of children. For the fiction and nonfiction awards, original works and single-author collections of stories or poems of which at least half are new and never before published in book form are eligible—anthologies and translations are not. For the picture-illustration awards, the art or photographs must be original works (the texts—which may be fiction or nonfiction—may be original, public domain or previously published). Deadline for entries: December 15. SASE for award rules. No entry fee. Awards statuettes and plaques. The panel of judges will consist of professional authors, illustrators, editors or agents." Requirements for entrants: "must be a member of SCBWI." Winning books will be displayed at national conference in August. Books to be entered, as well as further inquiries, should be submitted to: The Society of Children's Book Writers and Illustrators, above address.

HIGHLIGHTS FOR CHILDREN FICTION CONTEST, 803 Church St., Honesdale PA 18431-2030. (570)253-1080. Fax: (570)251-7487. Mss should be addressed to **Fiction Contest. Editor:** Kent L. Brown Jr. Annual contest. Estab. 1980. Purpose of the contest: to stimulate interest in writing for children and reward and recognize excellence. Unpublished submissions only. Deadline for entries: February 28; entries accepted after January 1 only. SASE for contest rules and return of entries. No entry fee. Awards 3 prizes of $1,000 each in cash and a pewter bowl (or, at the winner's election, attendance at the Highlights Foundation Writers Workshop at Chautauqua). Judging by *Highlights* editors. Winning pieces are purchased for the cash prize of $1,000 and

MARKET CONDITIONS are constantly changing! If you're still using this book and it is 2003 or later, buy the newest edition of *Children's Writer's & Illustrator's Market* at your favorite bookstore or order directly from Writer's Digest Books.

published in *Highlights*; other entries are considered for purchase. Requirements for entrants: open to any writer. Winners announced in June. Length up to 900 words. Stories for beginning readers should not exceed 500 words. Stories should be consistent with *Highlights* editorial requirements. No violence, crime or derogatory humor. Send SASE for guidelines. 2002 theme: "Stories About Today's Kids."

HRC'S ANNUAL PLAYWRITING CONTEST, Hudson River Classics, Inc., P.O. Box 940, Hudson NY 12534. (518)828-0175. Fax: (518)828-1480. **President:** Jan M. Grice. Annual contest. Estab. 1992. Hudson River Classics is a not-for-profit professional theater company dedicated to the advancement of performing in the Hudson River Valley area through reading of plays and providing opportunities for new playwrights. Unpublished submissions only. Submissions made by author and by the author's agent. Deadlines for entries: May 1st. SASE for contest rules and entry forms. Entry fee is $5. Awards $500 cash plus concert reading by professional actors. Judging by panel selected by Board of Directors. Requirements for entrants: Entrants must live in the northeastern US.

INFORMATION BOOK AWARD, Children's Literature Roundtables of Canada, Dept. of Language Education, University of British Columbia, 2125 Main Mall, Vancouver, British Columbia V6T 1Z4 Canada. (604)822-5788. Fax: (604)922-1666. E-mail: aprilg@direct.ca. Website: www.library.ubc.ca/edlib/rdtable.html. **Award Directors:** April Gill and Dr. Ron Jobe. Annual contest. Estab. 1987. Purpose of contest: The Information Book Award recognizes excellence in the writing of information books for young people from 5 to 15 years. It is awarded to the book that arouses interest, stimulates curiosity, captures the imagination, and fosters concern for the world around us. The award's aim is to recognize excellence in Canadian publishing of nonfiction for children. Previously published submissions only. Submissions nominated by a person or group of people. Work must have been published the calendar year previous to the award being given. Send SASE for contest rules. Certificates are awarded to the author and illustrator, and they share a cash prize of $500 (Canadian). Judging by members of the children's literature roundtables of Canada. In consultation with children's bookstores across Canada, a national committee based in Vancouver sends out a selective list of over 20 titles representing the best of the information books from the preceding year. The Roundtables consider this preliminary list and send back their recommendations, resulting in 5-7 finalists. The Roundtables make time at their Fall meetings to discuss the finalists and vote on their choices, which are collated into one vote per Roundtable (the winner is announced in November for Canada's Book Week). The award is granted at the Serendipity Children's Literature Conference held in February in Vancouver British Columbia.

INSIGHT WRITING CONTEST, *Insight Magazine*, 55 W. Oak Ridge Dr., Hagerstown MD 21740-7390. E-mail: insight@rhpa.org. Website: www.insightmagazine.org. **Open to students.** Annual contest. Unpublished submissions only. Submissions made by author. Deadline for entries: June 1, 2002. SASE for contest rules and entry forms. Awards First prizes, $100-250; second prizes, $75-200; third prizes, $50-150. Winning entries will be published in *Insight*. Contest includes three catagories: Student Short Story, General Short Story and Student Poetry. You must be age 21 or under to enter the student catagories. Entries must include cover sheet form available with SASE or on website.

INSPIRATIONAL WRITERS ALIVE! OPEN WRITERS COMPETITION, Texas Christian Writer's Forum, 6038 Greenmont, Houston TX 77092-2332. Fax: (713)686-7209. E-mail: martharexrogers@aol.com or patav@aol.com. **Contact:** Contest Director. Annual contest. Estab. 1990. Purpose of contest: to help aspiring writers in the inspirational/religion markets and to encourage writers in their efforts to write for possible future publication. Our critique sheets give valuable information to our participants. Unpublished submissions only. Submissions made by author. Deadline: May 1. SASE for contest rules. Entry fee is $10 (devotional, short story or article); $10 (3 poems). Awards certificate of merit for 1st, 2nd and 3rd place; plus a small monetary award of $25 1st, $15 2nd, $10 3rd. Requirements for entrants: Cannot enter published material. "We want to aid especially new and aspiring writers." Contest has 5 categories—to include short story (adult), short story (for children and teens) article, daily devotions, and poetry and book proposal. Request complete guidelines from M. Rogers. Entry forms and info available after January 1, 2002. "*Must* include a cover sheet with every category."

IRA CHILDREN'S BOOK AWARDS, International Reading Association, 800 Barksdale Rd., P.O. Box 8139, Newark DE 19714-8139. (302)731-1600. Fax: (302)731-1057. E-mail: exec@reading.org. Website: www.reading.org. Open to adults. Annual award. Awards are given for an author's first or second published book for fiction and nonfiction in three categories: primary (ages preschool-8), intermediate (ages 9-13, and young adult (ages 14-17). This award is intended for newly published authors who show unusual promise in the children's book field. Deadline for entries: November 1, 2001. Awards $500. For guidelines write or e-mail exec@reading.org.

JOSEPH HENRY JACKSON AND JAMES D. PHELAN LITERARY AWARDS, sponsored by The San Francisco Foundation. Administered by Intersection for the Arts. 446 Valencia St., San Francisco CA 94103. (415)626-2787. Fax: (415)626-1636. E-mail: info@theintersection.org. Submit entries to Awards Coordinator. **Open to Students**. Annual award. Estab. 1937. Purpose of award: to encourage young writers for and unpublished manuscript-in-progress. Submissions must be unpublished. Submissions made by author. Deadline for entry: January 31. SASE for contest rules and entry forms. Judging by established peers. All applicants must be 20-35 years of age. Applicants for the Henry Jackson Award must be residents of northern California or Nevada for 3 consecutive years immediately prior to the January 31 deadline. Applicants for the James D. Phelan awards must have been born in California but need not be current residents.

THE EZRA JACK KEATS NEW WRITER AWARD, Ezra Jack Keats Foundation/Administered by the New York Public Library Early Childhood Resource and Information Center, 66 Leroy St., New York NY 10014. (212)929-0815. Fax: (212)242-8242. E-mail: rpayne@nypl.org. **Program Coordinator:** Rachel Payne. **Open to students.** Annual award. Purpose of the award: "The award will be given to a promising new writer of picture books for children. Selection criteria include books for children (ages nine and under) that reflect the tradition of Ezra Jack Keats. These books portray: the universal qualities of childhood, strong and supportive family and adult relationships, the multicultural nature of our world." Submissions made by the author, by the author's agent or nominated by a person or group of people. Must be published in the preceding year. Deadline for entries: December 15, 2001. SASE for contest rules and entry forms. No entry fee. Awards $1,000 coupled with Ezra Jack Keats Silver Medal. Judging by a panel of experts. "The author should have published no more than five books. Entries are judged on the outstanding features of the text, complemented by illustrations. Candidates need not be both author and illustrator. Entries should carry a 2001 copyright (for the 2002 award)." Winning books and authors to be presented at reception at The New York Public Library.

KENTUCKY BLUEGRASS AWARD, Northern Kentucky University & Kentucky Reading Association, % Jennifer Smith, Steely Library, Northern Kentucky University, Highland Heights KY 41099. (859)572-6620. Fax: (859)572-5390. E-mail: smithjen@nku.edu. **Award Directors:** Jennifer Smith. Submit entries to: Jennifer Smith. Annual award. Estab. 1983. Purpose of award: to promote readership among young children and young adolescents. Also to recognize exceptional creative efforts of authors and illustrators. Previously published submissions only. Submissions made by author, made by author's agent, nominated by teachers or librarians. Must be published between 1998 and 2001. Deadline for entries: March 15. SASE for contest rules and entry forms. No entry fee. Awards a framed certificate and invitation to be recognized at the annual luncheon of the Kentucky Bluegrass Award. Judging by children who participate through their schools or libraries. "Books are reviewed by a panel of teachers and librarians before they are placed on a Master List for the year. These books must have been published within a three year period prior to the review. Winners are chosen from this list of pre-selected books. Books are divided into four divisions, K-2, 3-5, 6-8, 9-12 grades. Winners are chosen by children who either read the books or have the books read to them. Children from the entire state of Kentucky are involved in the selection of the annual winners for each of the divisions."

KERLAN AWARD, University of Minnesota, 113 Elmer L. Andersen Library, 222-21st Ave. S, Minneapolis MN 55455. (612)624-4576. Website: http://special.lib.umn.edu/clrc. **Curator:** Karen Nelson Hoyle. Annual award. Estab. 1975. "Given in recognition of singular attainments in the creation of children's literature and in appreciation for generous donation of unique resources to the Kerlan Collection." Previously published submissions only. Deadline for entries: October 16. Anyone can send nominations for the award, directed to the Kerlan Collection. No materials are submitted other than the person's name. Requirements for entrants: open to all who are nominated. "For serious consideration, entrant must be a published author and/or illustrator of children's books (including young adult fiction) and have donated original materials to the Kerlan Collection."

ANNE SPENCER LINDBERGH PRIZE IN CHILDREN'S LITERATURE, The Charles A. and Anne Morrow Lindbergh Foundation, % Lindbergh Foundation, 2150 Third Ave., Suite 310, Anoka MN 55303. (763)576-1596. Fax: (763)576-1664. E-mail: info@lindberghfoundation.org. Website: www.lindberghfoundation. org. Competition open to adults. Contest is offered every 2 years. Estab. 1996. Purpose of contest: To recognize the children's fantasy novel judged to be the best published in the English language during the 2-year period. Prize program honors Anne Spencer Lindbergh, author of a number of acclaimed juvenile fantasies, who died in late 1993 at the age of 53. Previously published submissions only. Submissions made by author, author's agent or publishers. Must be published between January 1 of odd numbered years and December 31 of even numbered years. Deadline for entries: November 1 of even numbered years. Entry fee is $25. Awards $5,000 to author of winning book. Judging by panel drawn from writers, editors, librarians and teachers prominent in the field of children's literature. Requirements for entrants: Open to all authors of children's fantasy novels published during the 2-year period. Entries must include 4 copies of books submitted. Winner announced in January.

LONGMEADOW JOURNAL LITERARY COMPETITION, % Rita and Robert Morton, 6750 N. Longmeadow, Lincolnwood IL 60712. (312)726-9789. Fax: (312)726-9772. **Contest Directors:** Rita and Robert Morton. Competition open to students (anyone age 10-19). Held annually and published every year. Estab. 1986. Purpose of contest: to encourage the young to write. Submissions are made by the author, made by the author's agent, nominated by a person or group of people, by teachers, librarians or parents. Deadline for entries: June 30. SASE. No entry fee. Awards first place, $175; second place, $100; and five prizes of $50. Judging by Rita Morton and Robert Morton. Works are published every year and are distributed to teachers and librarians and interested parties at no charge.

MAGAZINE MERIT AWARDS, Society of Children's Book Writers and Illustrators, 8271 Beverly Blvd., Los Angeles CA 90048. Fax: (323)782-1010. Website: www.scbwi.org. **Award Coordinator:** Dorothy Leon. Annual award. Estab. 1988. Purpose of the award: "to recognize outstanding original magazine work for young people published during that year and having been written or illustrated by members of SCBWI." Previously published submissions only. Entries must be submitted between January 31 and December 15 of the year of publication. For brochure (rules) write Award Coordinator. No entry fee. Must be a SCBWI member. Awards plaques and honor certificates for each of the 3 categories (fiction, nonfiction, illustration). Judging by a magazine editor and two "full" SCBWI members. "All magazine work for young people by an SCBWI member—writer, artist or photographer—is eligible during the year of original publication. In the case of co-authored work, both authors must be SCBWI members. Members must submit their own work." Requirements for entrants: 4 copies each of the published work and proof of publication (may be contents page) showing the name of the magazine and the date of issue. The SCBWI is a professional organization of writers and illustrators and others interested in children's literature. Membership is open to the general public at large.

MILKWEED PRIZE FOR CHILDREN'S LITERATURE, Milkweed Editions, 1011 Washington Ave. S., Suite 300, Minneapolis MN 55415-1246. (612)332-3192. Fax: (612)215-2550. E-mail: editor@milkweed.org. Website: www.milkweed.org. **Award Director:** Emilie Buchwald, publisher/editor. Annual award. Estab. 1993. Purpose of the award: to find an outstanding literary novel for readers ages 8-13 and encourage writers to turn their attention to readers in this age group. Unpublished submissions only "in book form." Must send SASE for award guidelines. The prize is awarded to the best work for children ages 8-13 that Milkweed agrees to publish in a calendar year by a writer not previously published by Milkweed. The Prize consists of a $10,000 advance against royalties agreed to at the time of acceptance. Submissions must follow our usual children's guidelines.

N: MINNESOTA BOOK AWARDS, Minnesota Center for the Book, 987 E. Ivy Ave., St. Paul MN 55106-2046. (651)774-0105, ext. 111. Fax: (651)774-0205. E-mail: lisab@thinkmhc.org. Website: www.mnbooks.org. **Award Director:** Lisa Brienzo. Submit entries to: Lisa Brienzo, director. Annual award. Estab. 1988. Purpose of contest: To recognize and honor Minnesota authors and books. Previously published submissions only. Submissions made by author, nominated by a person or group, author's agent. Work must hold 2002 copyright. Deadline for entries: December 15, 2002. Awards certificate; winners announced at a public ceremony in April 2003. Judging bymembers of Minnesota's book community: booksellers, librarians, teachers and scholars, writers, reviewers. Requirements for entrants: Primary book creator must be a Minnesotan. The Minnesota Book Awards includes 10 standing award categories. Two of these categories are Children and Youth Literature.

N: MYTHOPOEIC FANTASY AWARD FOR CHILDREN'S LITERATURE, The Mythopoeic Society, P.O. Box 320486. San Francisco CA 94132-0486. E-mail: emfarrell@earthlink.net. Website: www.mythsoc.org. **Award Director:** Eleanor M. Farrell. Annual award. Estab. 1992 (previous to 1992, a single Mythopoeic Fantasy Award was given to either adult or children's books). Previously published submissions only. Submissions nominated. Must be published previous calendar year. Deadline for entries: February 28. Awards statuette. Judging by committee members of Mythopoeic Society. Requirements for entrants: books only; nominations are made by Mythopoeic Society members.

THE NATIONAL CHAPTER OF CANADA IODE VIOLET DOWNEY BOOK AWARD, Suite 254, 40 Orchard View Blvd., Toronto, Ontario M5R 1B9 Canada. (416)487-4416. Fax: (416)487-4417. Website: www.iodecanada.ca. **Award Director:** Sandra Connery. Annual award. Estab. 1985. Purpose of the award: to honor the best children's English language book by a Canadian, published in Canada for ages 5-13, over 500 words. Fairy tales, anthologies and books adapted from another source are not eligible. Previously published submissions only. Books must have been published in Canada in previous calendar year. Submissions made by author, author's agent; anyone may submit. Three copies of each entry are required. Must have been published during previous calendar year. Deadline for entries: December 31, 2001. SASE for award rules and entry forms. No entry fee. Awards $3,000 for the year 2001 for books published in 2002. Judging by a panel of 6, 4 IODE members and 2 professionals.

NATIONAL CHILDREN'S THEATRE FESTIVAL, Actor's Playhouse at the Miracle Theatre, 280 Miracle Mile, Coral Gables FL 33134. (305)444-9293. Fax: (305)444-4181. Website: www.actorsplayhouse.org. **Director:** Earl Maulding. **Open to Students**. Annual contest. Estab. 1994. Purpose of contest: to encourage new, top quality musicals for young audiences. Submissions must be unpublished. Submissions are made by author or author's agent. Deadline for entries: August 1, 2002. SASE for contest rules and entry forms or online at www.actorsplayhouse.org. Entry fee is $10. Awards: first prize of $500 plus production. Final judges are of national reputation. Past judges include Joseph Robinette, Moses Goldberg and Luis Santeiro.

NATIONAL PEACE ESSAY CONTEST, United States Institute of Peace, 1200 17th St. NW, Washington DC 20036. (202)429-3854. Fax: (202)429-6063. E-mail: essay_contest@usip.org. Website: www.usip.org. Annual contest. Estab. 1987. "The contest gives students the opportunity to do valuable research, writing and thinking on a topic of importance to international peace and conflict resolution. Teaching guides are available for teachers who allow the contest to be used as a classroom assignment." Deadline for entries is January 23, 2002. "Interested students, teachers and others may write or call to receive free contest kits. Please do not include SASE." No entry fee. State Level Awards are $1000 college scholarships. National winners are selected from among the 1st place state winners. National winners receive scholarships in the following amounts: first place $10,000; second $5,000; third $2,500. Judging is conducted by education professionals from across the country and by the Board of Directors of the United States Institute of Peace. "All submissions become property of the U.S. Institute of Peace to use at its discretion and without royalty or any limitation. Students grades 9-12 in the U.S., its territories and overseas schools may submit essays for review by completing the application process. U.S. citizenship required for students attending overseas schools. National winning essays will be published by the U.S. Institute of Peace."

NATIONAL WRITERS ASSOCIATION NONFICTION CONTEST, 3140 S. Peoria, Suite 295, Aurora CO 80014. (303)841-0246. **Executive Director:** Sandy Whelchel. Annual contest. Estab. 1971. Purpose of contest: "to encourage writers in this creative form and to recognize those who excel in nonfiction writing." Submissions made by author. Deadline for entries: December 31. SASE for contest rules and entry forms. Entry fee is $18. Awards three cash prizes; choice of books; Honorable Mention Certificate. "Two people read each entry; third party picks three top winners from top five." Judging sheets sent if entry accompanied by SASE. Condensed version of 1st place published in *Authorship*.

NATIONAL WRITERS ASSOCIATION SHORT STORY CONTEST, 3140 S. Peoria, Suite 295, Aurora CO 80014. (303)841-0246. **Executive Director:** Sandy Whelchel. Annual contest. Estab. 1971. Purpose of contest: "To encourage writers in this creative form and to recognize those who excel in fiction writing." Submissions made by the author. Deadline for entries: July 1. SASE for contest rules and entry forms. Entry fee is $15. Awards 3 cash prizes, choice of books and certificates for Honorable Mentions. Judging by "two people read each entry; third person picks top three winners." Judging sheet copies available for SASE. First place published in *Authorship* Magazine.

THE NENE AWARD, Hawaii State Library, 478 S. King St., Honolulu HI 96813. (808)586-3510. Fax: (808)586-3584. E-mail: hslear@netra.lib.state.hi.us. Estab. 1964. "The Nene Award was designed to help the children of Hawaii become acquainted with the best contemporary writers of fiction, become aware of the qualities that make a good book and choose the best rather than the mediocre." Previously published submissions only. Books must have been copyrighted not more than 6 years prior to presentation of award. Work is nominated. Ballots are usually due around the beginning of March. Awards Koa plaque. Judging by the children of Hawaii in grades 4-6. Requirements for entrants: books must be fiction, written by a living author, copyrighted not more than 6 years ago and suitable for children in grades 4, 5 and 6. Current and past winners are displayed in all participating school and public libraries. The award winner is announced in April.

NEW ENGLAND BOOK AWARDS, New England Booksellers Association, 1770 Massachusetts Ave., Suite 332, Cambridge MA 02140. (617)576-3070. Fax: (617)576-3091. E-mail: neba@neba.org. Website: newenglandbooks.org. **Award Director:** Mayre Plunkett. Annual award. Estab. 1990. Purpose of award: "to promote New England authors who have produced a body of work that stands as a significant contribution to New England's culture and is deserving of wider recognition." Previously published submissions only. Submissions made by New England booksellers; publishers. "Award given to authors 'body of work' not a specific book." Entries must be still in print and available. SASE for contest rules and entry forms. No entry fee. Judging by NEBA membership. Requirements for entrants: Author/illustrator must live in New England. Submit written nominations only; actual books should not be sent. Member bookstores receive materials to display winners' books.

NEW VOICES AWARD, Lee & Low Books, 95 Madison Ave., New York NY 10016. (212)779-4400. Fax: (212)683-1894. E-mail: info@leeandlow.com. Website: www.leeandlow.com. **Executive Editor:** Louise May. **Open to students and adults.** Annual award. Estab. 2000. Purpose of contest: Lee & Low Books is one of the few publishing companies owned by people of color. We have published over 50 first-time writers and illustrators. Titles include *In Daddy's Arms I Am Tall: African Americans Celebrating Fathers*, winner of the 1998 Coretta Scott King Illustrator Award; *Passage to Freedom: The Sugihara Story*, an American Library Association Notable Book; and *Crazy Horse's Vision*, a Bank Street College Children's Book of the Year. Submissions made by author. Deadline for entries: September 30. SASE for contest rules. No entry fee. Awards New Voices Award—$1,000 prize and a publication contract along with an advance on royalties; New Voices Honor Award—$500 prize. Judging by Lee & Low editors. Restrictions of media for illustrators: The author must be a writer of color who is a resident of the US and who has not previously published a children's picture book. For additional information, send SASE, call for entries or visit Lee & Low's website.

JOHN NEWBERY MEDAL AWARD, Association for Library Service to Children, Division of the American Library Association, 50 E. Huron, Chicago IL 60611. E-mail: alsc@ala.org. Website: www.ala.org/alsc/newbery.html. (312)280-2163. **Executive Director, ALSC:** Malore Brown. Annual award. Estab. 1922. Purpose of award: to recognize the most distinguished contribution to American children's literature published in the US. Previously published submissions only; must be published prior to year award is given. Deadline for entries: December 31. SASE for award rules. Entries not returned. No entry fee. Medal awarded at Caldecott/Newbery banquet during annual conference. Judging by Newbery Award Selection Committee.

✔ **NORTH AMERICAN INTERNATIONAL AUTO SHOW SHORT STORY AND HIGH SCHOOL POSTER CONTEST**, Detroit Auto Dealers Association, 1900 W. Big Beaver Rd., Troy MI 48084-3531. (248)643-0250. Fax: (248)283-5160. E-mail: sherp@dada.org. Website: naias.com. **Contact:** Sandy Herp. **Open to students.** Annual contest. Submissions made by the author and illustrator. Contact DADA for contest rules and entry forms. No entry fee. Five winners of the short story contest will each receive $500. Entries will be judged by an independent panel comprised of knowledgeable persons engaged in the literary field in some capacity. Entrants must be Michigan residents, including high school students enrolled in grades 9-12. Junior high school students in 9th grade are also eligible. Awards in the High School Poster Contest are as follows: Best Theme, Best Use of Color, Best Use of Graphics & Most Creative. A winner will be chosen in each category from grades 9, 10, 11 and 12. Each winner in each grade from each category will win $250. The winner of the Chairman's Award will receive $1,000. Entries will be judged by an independent panel of recognized representatives of the art community. Entrants must be Michigan high school students enrolled in grades 9-12. Junior high students in 9th grade are also eligible. Winners will be announced during the North American International Auto Show in January and may be published in the *Auto Show Program* at the sole discretion of the D.A.D.A. "No shared work please."

THE SCOTT O'DELL AWARD FOR HISTORICAL FICTION, 1700 E. 56th St., Suite 3907, Chicago IL 60637-1936. **Award Director:** Mrs. Zena Sutherland. Annual award. Estab. 1981. Purpose of the award: "To promote the writing of historical fiction of good quality for children and young adults." Previously published submissions only; must be published between January 1 and December 31 previous to deadline. Deadline for entries: December 31. "Publishers send books, although occasionally a writer sends a note or a book." SASE for award rules. No entry fee. There is only 1 book chosen each year. Award: $5,000. Judging by a committee of 3. Requirements for entrants: "Must be published by a U.S. publisher in the preceding year; must be written by an American citizen; must be set in North or South America; must be historical fiction."

✔ **OHIOANA BOOK AWARDS**, Ohioana Library Association, 274 E. First Ave., Suite 300, Columbus OH 43201. (614)466-3831. Fax: (614)728-6974. E-mail: ohioana@sloma.state.oh.us. Website: www.oplin.lib.oh.us/OHIOANA/. **Director:** Linda R. Hengst. Annual award. "The Ohioana Book Awards are given to books of outstanding literary quality. Purpose of contest: to provide recognition and encouragement to Ohio writers and to promote the work of Ohio writers. Up to six are given each year. Awards may be given in the following categories: fiction, nonfiction, children's literature, poetry and books about Ohio or an Ohioan. Books must be received by the Ohioana Library during the calendar year prior to the year the award is given and must have a copyright date within the last two calendar years." Deadline for entries: December 31. SASE for award rules and entry forms. No entry fee. Winners receive citation and glass sculpture. "Any book that has been written or edited by a person born in Ohio or who has lived in Ohio for at least five years" is eligible. The Ohioana Library Association also awards the "Ohioana Book Award in the category of juvenile books." Send SASE for more information.

OKLAHOMA BOOK AWARDS, Oklahoma Center for the Book, 200 NE 18th, Oklahoma City OK 73105. (405)521-2502. Fax: (405)525-7804. E-mail: gcarlile@oltn.odl.state.ok.us. Website: www.odl.state.ok.us/ocb. **Executive Director:** Glenda Carlile. Annual award. **Open to students.** Estab. 1989. Purpose of award: "to honor Oklahoma writers and books about our state." Previously published submissions only. Submissions made by the author, author's agent, or entered by a person or group of people, including the publisher. Must be published during the calendar year preceding the award. Awards are presented to best books in fiction, nonfiction, children's, design and illustration, and poetry books about Oklahoma or books written by an author who was born, is living or has lived in Oklahoma. Deadline for entries: early January. SASE for award rules and entry forms. No entry fee. Awards a medal—no cash prize. Judging by a panel of 5 people for each category—a librarian, a working writer in the genre, booksellers, editors, etc. Requirements for entrants: author must be an Oklahoma native, resident, former resident or have written a book with Oklahoma theme. Winner will be announced at banquet in Oklahoma City. The Arrell Gibson Lifetime Achievement Award is also presented each year to an Oklahoma author for a body of work.

ONCE UPON A WORLD BOOK AWARD, Simon Wiesenthal Center's Museum of Tolerance, 1399 S. Roxbury Dr., Los Angeles CA 90035-4709. (310)772-7605. Fax: (310)277-6568. E-mail: library@wiesenthal.net or aklein@wiesenthal.net. **Award Director:** Adaire J. Klein. Submit entries to: Adaire J. Klein, Director of Library and Archival Services. Annual award. Estab. 1996. Previously published submissions only. Submissions made by publishers, author or by author's agent. Must be published January-December of previous year. Deadline for entries: March 31, 2002. SASE for contest rules and entry forms. Awards $1,000 and plaque. Judging by 3 independent judges familiar with children's literature. Award open to any writer with work in English language on subject of tolerance, diversity, and social justice for children 6-10 years old. Award is presented in October. Book Seal available from the library. 2000 winner: Ruby Bridges, *Through My Eyes* (NY: Scholastic Press, 1999).

ORBIS PICTUS AWARD FOR OUTSTANDING NONFICTION FOR CHILDREN, The National Council of Teachers of English, 1111 W. Kenyon Rd., Urbana IL 61801-1096. (217)328-3870, ext. 3603. **Co-Chairs, NCTE Committee on the Orbis Pictus Award for Outstanding Nonfiction for Children:** Karen P. Smith, Queens College, New York and Richard Kerper, Millersville University, Pennsylvania. Annual award. Estab. 1989. Purpose of award: to honor outstanding nonfiction works for children. Previously published submissions only. Submissions made by author, author's agent, by a person or group of people. Must be published January 1-December 31 of contest year. Deadline for entries: November 30. Call for award information. No entry fee. Awards a plaque given at the NCTE Elementary Section Luncheon at the NCTE Annual Convention in November. Judging by a committee.

THE ORIGINAL ART, Society of Illustrators, 128 E. 63rd St., New York NY 10021-7303. (212)838-2560. Fax: (212)838-2561. E-mail: si1901@aol.com. Website: www.societyillustrators.org. Annual contest. Estab. 1981. Purpose of contest: to celebrate the fine art of children's book illustration. Previously published submissions only. Deadline for entries: August 20. Request "call for entries" to receive contest rules and entry forms. Entry fee is $20/book. Judging by seven professional artists and editors. Works will be displayed at the Society of Illustrators Museum of American Illustration in New York City October-November annually. Medals awarded.

HELEN KEATING OTT AWARD FOR OUTSTANDING CONTRIBUTION TO CHILDREN'S LITERATURE, Church and Synagogue Library Association, P.O. Box 19357, Portland OR 97280-0357. (503)244-6919. Fax: (503)977-3734. E-mail: csla@worldaccessnet.com. Website: www.worldaccessnet.com/~csla. **Chair of Committee:** Barbara Messner. Annual award. Estab. 1980. "This award is given to a person or organization that has made a significant contribution to promoting high moral and ethical values through children's literature." Deadline for entries: April 1. "Recipient is honored in July during the conference." Awards certificate of recognition and a conference package consisting of all meals, day of awards banquet, two nights' housing and a complimentary 1 year membership. "A nomination for an award may be made by anyone. It should include the name, address and telephone number of the nominee, plus the church or synagogue relationship where appropriate. Nominations of an organization should include the name of a contact person. A detailed description of the reasons for the nomination should be given, accompanied by documentary evidence of accomplishment. The person(s) making the nomination should give his/her name, address and telephone number and a brief explanation of his/her knowledge of the nominee's accomplishments. Elements of creativity and innovation will be given high priority by the judges."

◼ OWL MAGAZINE CONTESTS, Writing Contest, Photo Contest, Poetry Contest, *OWL Magazine*, 49 Front St., E., 2nd Floor, Toronto, Ontario M5E 1B3 Canada. (416)340-2700. Fax: (416)340-9769. E-mail: owl@owlkids.com. Website: www.owlkids.com. **Contact:** Hoot Editor. Annual contests. Purpose of contests: "to encourage children to contribute and participate in the magazine." Unpublished submissions only. Deadlines change yearly. Prizes/awards "change every year. Often we give books as prizes." Winning entries published in the magazine. Judging by art and editorial staff. Entries become the property of Bayard Press. "The contests and awards are open to children up to 14 years of age. Check the Hoot section of *OWL* for information and updates. Contests have specific themes, so children should not send unsolicited poetry and fiction until they have checked contest details."

PATERSON PRIZE FOR BOOKS FOR YOUNG PEOPLE, Poetry Center at Passaic County Community College, One College Blvd., Paterson NJ 07505-1179. (973)684-6555. Fax: (973)684-5843. E-mail: mgillan@pcc c.cc.nj.us. Website: www.pccc.cc.nj.us/poetry. **Director:** Maria Mazziotti Gillan. **Open to students.** Estab. 1996. Poetry Center's mission is "to recognize excellence in books for young people." Previously published submissions only. Submissions made by author, author's agent or publisher. Must be published between January 1, 2000-December 31, 2001. Deadline for entries: March 15, 2002. SASE for contest rules and entry forms or visit website. Awards $500 for the author in either of 3 categories: PreK-Grade 3; Grades 4-6, Grades 7-12. Judging by a professional writer selected by the Poetry Center. Contest is open to any writer/illustrator.

PEN/NORMA KLEIN AWARD FOR CHILDREN'S FICTION, PEN American Center, 568 Broadway, New York NY 10012. (212)334-1660. Awarded triennially. Next award 2002. Estab. 1990. "In memory of the late PEN member and distinguished children's book author Norma Klein, the award honors new authors whose books demonstrate the adventuresome and innovative spirit that characterizes the best children's literature and Norma Klein's own work." Previously published submissions only. "Candidates may not nominate themselves. We welcome all nominations from authors and editors of children's books." Deadline for entries: December. Awards $3,000 which will be given in May. Judging by a panel of 3 distinguished children's book authors. Nominations open to authors of books for elementary school to young adult readers. "It is strongly recommended that the nominator describe in some detail the literary character of the candidate's work and how it promises to enrich American literature for children."

PENNSYLVANIA YOUNG READERS' CHOICE AWARDS PROGRAM, Pennsylvania School Librarians Association, 148 S. Bethelehem Pike, Ambler PA 19002-5822. (215)643-5048. Fax: (215)628-8441. E-mail: bellavance@erols.com. **Coordinator:** Jean B. Bellavance. Annual award. Estab. 1991. Submissions nominated by a person or group. Must be published within 5 years of the award—for example, for 2001-2002 books published 1997 to present. Deadline for entries: September 15. SASE for contest rules and entry forms. No entry fee. Framed certificate to winning authors. Judging by children of Pennsylvania (they vote). Requirements for entrants: currently living in North America. Reader's Choice Award is to promote reading of quality books by young people in the Commonwealth of Pennsylvania, to promote teacher and librarian involvement in children's literature, and to honor authors whose work has been recognized by the children of Pennsylvania. Three awards are given, one for each of the following grade level divisions: K-3, 3-6, 6-8.

N: PEN/PHYLLIS NAYLOR WORKING WRITER FELLOWSHIP, PEN, 568 Broadway, New York NY 10012. (212)334-1660. Fax: (212)334-2181. E-mail: jm@pen.org. Submit entries to: John Morrone. (Must have published 2 books to be eligible). Annual contest. Estab. 2001. To support writers with a financial need and recognize work of high literary caliber. Unpublished submissions only. Submissions nominated. Deadline for entries: January 14, 2002. Awards $5,000. Upon nomination by an editor or fellow writer, a panel of judges will select the winning book. Open to a writer of children's or young adult fiction in financial need, who has published at least two books, and no more than three during the past ten years.

PLEASE TOUCH MUSEUM® BOOK AWARD, Please Touch Museum, 210 N. 21st St., Philadelphia PA 19103-1001. (215)963-0667. Fax: (215)963-0424. E-mail: marketing@pleasetouchmuseum.org. Website: www.pl easetouchmuseum.org. **Open to students.** Annual award. Estab. 1985. Purpose of the award: "to recognize and encourage the publication of books for young children by American authors that are of the highest quality and will aid them in enjoying the process of learning through books. Awarded to two picture books that are particularly imaginative and effective in exploring a concept or concepts, one for children age three and younger, and one for children ages four-seven. To be eligible for consideration a book must: (1) Explore and clarify an idea for young children. This could include the concept of numbers, colors, shapes, sizes, senses, feelings, etc. There is no limitation as to format. (2) Be distinguished in both text and illustration. (3) Be published within the last year by an American publisher. (4) Be by an American author and/or illustrator." Deadline for entries: (submissions may be made throughout the year). SASE for award rules and entry forms. No entry fee. Judging by selected jury of children's literature experts, librarians and early childhood educators. Education store purchases books for selling at Book Award Celebration Day and throughout the year. Receptions and autographing sessions held in bookstores, Please Touch Museum, and throughout the city.

POCKETS MAGAZINE FICTION CONTEST, *Pockets Magazine*, The Upper Room, P.O. Box 340004, Nashville TN 37203-0004. (615)340-7333. Fax: (615)340-7267. (Do not send submissions via fax.) E-mail: pockets@upperroom.org. Website: www.upperroom.org/pockets. **Contact:** Patricia McIntyre, editorial assistant. The purpose of the contest is to "find new freelance writers for the magazine." Annual competition for short stories. Award: $1,000 and publication. Competition receives 600 submissions. Judged by *Pockets* editors and editors of other Upper Room publications. Guidelines available upon request and SASE or on website. Inquiries by e-mail and fax OK. No entry form. No entry fee. Note on envelope and first sheet: Fiction Contest. Submissions must be postmarked between March 1 and August 15. Former winners may not enter. Unpublished submissions. Word length: 1,000-1600 words. Deadline for entries: August 15. SASE for contest rules and entry forms. No entry fee. Awards $1,000 and publication. Judging by *Pockets*' editors and 3 other editors of other Upper Room publications. Winner published in the magazine.

MICHAEL L. PRINTZ AWARD, Young Adult Library Services Association, Division of the American Library Association, 50 E. Huron, Chicago IL 60611. Website: www.ala.org/yalsa/printz. The Michael L. Printz Award is an award for a book that exemplifies literary excellence in young adult literature. It is named for a Topeka, Kansas school librarian who was a long-time active member of the Young Adult Library Services Association. It will be selected annually by an award committee that can also name as many as four honor books. The award-winning book can be fiction, non-fiction, poetry or an anthology, and can be a work of joint authorship or editorship. The books must be published between January 1 and December 31 of the preceding year and be designated by its publisher as being either a young adult book or one published for the age range that YALSA defines as young adult, e.g. ages 12 through 18. The deadline for both committee and field nominations will be December 1.

N: [icon] THE PRISM AWARDS®, The Kids Netword, 1690 Warren Ave., Kimberley, British Columbia V1A 1R6 Canada. (205)427-2732. Fax: (250)427-7734. **Award Manager:** Lucy La Grassa. Annual award. Estab. 1989. Purpose of the award: Children have an opportunity to submit mss for review. Winners are chosen based on originality of ideas and self-expression. Unpublished submissions only. Deadline for entries: March. SASE for award rules and entry forms. Entry fee is $2. Award consists of $500 cash and editorial training and possible publication. Judging by independent judges. Requirements for entrants: a Native Indian, Canadian or landed immigrant in Canada, ages 7-14; story must be written solely by the submitter. No less than 4 pages, no more than 16 pages. Copyright only to winning ms acquired by The Kids Netword upon winning.

[icon] PRIX ALVINE-BELISLE, Association pour l'avancement des sciences et des techniques de la documenta-tion (ASTED) Inc., 3414 Avenue Du Parc, Bureau 202, Montreal, Québec H2X 2H5 Canada. (514)281-5012.

insider report

Careful research and SCBWI grant lead to book contract

There are many paths to success. Carla McClafferty's path veered toward success when she was named the recipient of the 1997 Society of Children's Book Writers and Illustrators (SCBWI) Unpublished Author Work-in-Progress Grant, which carried a $1,000 cash prize. Her book proposal had already been reviewed by an editor at Farrar, Straus & Giroux (FSG), who had requested the entire manuscript.

Carla McClafferty

"I was in the process of completing the manuscript when I found out I won," say McClafferty. "I wrote my editor a letter telling him the project was an SCBWI grant winner, reminding him that he had asked to see the manuscript when it was finished. By doing this, I hoped to create in him an excitement for the finished piece before he even saw it."

Scheduled for a fall 2001 release by FSG, the book, *The Head Bone's Connected to the Neck Bone: The Weird, Wacky and Wonderful X-Ray*, discusses the X-ray from its early days to present and explains how X-rays are used in science, industry, the arts and medicine. McClafferty has also had an adult inspirational book published, *Forgiving God* (Discovery House Publishers), and has had articles in *Cricket, German Life, Radiologic Technologist, Arkansas Times*, and *Sherwood Voice*. She recently signed a contract with FSG for a second book, this time about radium and Madame Curie.

How did the grant process help you become a better writer?
The grant process forced me to consider how to handle the research information about X-rays. I wanted to begin with the discovery of X-rays, but I also wanted to talk about how X-rays are used today. The information covered more than one hundred years and included many different topics. Preparing for the grant entry made me think about the best way to organize the unique material that research had uncovered. Instead of submitting pages of straight text to the committee, I developed a mini-book proposal geared toward the grant requirements.

My entry package consisted of the following:
- A *one-page career summary*. This was a bio of sorts that emphasized that I am a Radiologic Technologist who works in the field, which made me an expert on the subject. I listed my publishing credits about X-rays, which included articles in *Cricket* and my professional journal.
- A *one-page plan for how I would use the grant money.*
- A *two-page synopsis explaining the type of book I envisioned.* It would be illustrated with historical photographs and include a table of contents, index, glossary, and bibliography. I included examples of the funny, bizarre, and tragic anecdotal stories that would fill the book.

- *A one-page traditional bio.*
- *A seven-page chapter-by-chapter outline.* Here, I gave a one-paragraph explanation of each chapter and followed it with a one-paragraph sample of the anecdotal material for that chapter.

What inspired you to write nonfiction for kids?

One day I looked through a book of medical biographies and read the brief biography of Dr. Wilhelm Conrad Roentgen, the man who discovered X-rays. Dr. Roentgen had been expelled from school when he was a youth, but the biography didn't say why. I wanted to know why. I started digging around to find out and as I did, I found fascinating facts about the early days of X-rays that I had never heard before. I began to think that this would make a great children's book. I was hooked—I had to write that book!

What childhood experiences prepared you to be a writer?

I enjoyed reading. Although I read more nonfiction today, as a child I read fiction. I remember reading *The Tale of Peter Rabbit*, by Beatrix Potter and being relieved that Peter escaped Mr. McGregor. I can still remember the illustration that showed Peter's blue coat getting caught.

Even then I enjoyed having books of my own. In fact, my mother would bribe me: if I went to bed on time for a week, she would buy me a Little Golden book. I only had a small stack of books, but they were mine and I loved them. My school didn't even have a library. We had bookshelves underneath the windows in each classroom. To this day, I am impressed by a library.

How do you do research for your nonfiction titles?

The type of book I write requires a lot of research. I read many books, journals, newspapers, and articles relating to my subject. In addition, I also spend days looking through microfilm

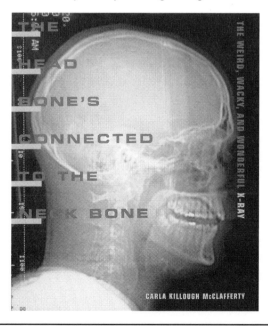

Writer Carla McClafferty received a $1,000 grant from SCBWI, helping her complete work on her book *The Head Bone's Connected to the Neck Bone: The Weird, Wacky and Wonderful X-Ray*, a 2001 release from Farrar, Strauss & Giroux. She's working on a subsequent book for FSG.

from *The New York Times*. I've found the most efficient way for me to work is to write down a fact I want to remember on an index card and note the location and page number where it was found. I learned the hard way that when I didn't write down where a fact came from, that was the one thing I needed to reread. Then I would have to look through a three-foot-high stack of research material to find it again. Now, I make a note card for everything, even if I have seen that fact before. The index card system works well for me when the time comes to actually begin writing.

Do you read other nonfiction titles?
Yes, I read lots of children's nonfiction. I'm especially drawn to longer nonfiction rather than picture books since that's the type book I write. My favorite authors are Russell Freedman and Jim Murphy. Their books are written with such skill that it makes it seem easy—which of course, it isn't.

Regardless of the subject, I'm drawn into each of their books because they have the ability to find the heart of the story and tell it with the right details in all the right places. I try to learn from their expertise as I read their work, by asking myself questions: How did he make this fact come to life? What makes this chapter work so well? How much detail is in the captions?

Do you have any advice for others considering entering contests?
Enter! Since the pool of entrants for these grants is relatively small, your chances of winning are pretty good. And if you do win, it will give your manuscript an advantage when you submit to an editor. And in this business you need every advantage you can get.
—*Darcy Pattison*

Fax: (514)281-8219. E-mail: info@asted.org. **Award President:** Micheline Patton. Award open to children's book editors. Annual award. Estab. 1974. Purpose of contest: To recognize the best children's book published in French in Canada. Previously published submissions only. Submissions made by publishing house. Must be published the year before award. Deadline for entries: June 1. Awards $500. Judging by librarians jury.

QUILL AND SCROLL INTERNATIONAL WRITING/PHOTO CONTEST, *Quill and Scroll*, School of Journalism, University of Iowa, Iowa City IA 52242-1528. (319)335-5795. Fax: (319)335-5210. E-mail: quill-scroll@uiowa.edu. Website: www.uiowa.edu/~quill-sc. **Contest Director:** Richard Johns. **Open to students.** Annual contest. Previously published submissions only. Submissions made by the author or school newspaper adviser. Must be published February 6, 2001 to February 4, 2002. Deadline for entries: February 5. SASE for contest rules and entry forms. Entry fee is $2/entry. Awards engraved plaque to junior high level sweepstakes winners. Judging by various judges. *Quill and Scroll* acquires the right to publish submitted material in the magazine if it is chosen as a winning entry. Requirements for entrants: must be students in grades 9-12 for high school division.

THE ERIN PATRICK RABORG POETRY AWARD, *AMELIA Magazine*, 329 E St., Bakersfield CA 93304-2031. (805)823-4064. Fax: (805)323-5326. E-mail: amelia@lightspeed.net. **Contact:** Frederick A. Raborg, Jr., editor. **Open to students.** Estab. 1992. Purpose of contest: To draw attention to childhood lifestyles and consequences. Also, to explore the humor as well as the pathos of childhood. Unpublished submissions only. Submissions made by author. Deadline for entries: December 1 annually. SASE for contest rules. Entry fee is $4 each entry. Award consists of $50 and publication in *AMELIA*. Judging is done in-house. Rights to winning material acquired: first North American serial only. "Be consistent within the form chosen." Sample copy $10.95.

RIP VAN WINKLE AWARD, School Library Media Specialists of Southeastern NY. (845)365-5556. **President:** Lois Parker-Hennion. Annual award. Purpose of award: given to reward an author, illustator or author/illustrator residing in the seven county SLMSSENY region (Dutchess, Putnam, Orange, Rockland, Sullivan,

Ulster and Westchester Counties, NY) for his/her outstanding contributions in the field of children's/young adult literature. Previously published submissions only. Submissions nominated by a person or group. Judging by Executive Board of Organization.

TOMÁS RIVERA MEXICAN AMERICAN CHILDREN'S BOOK AWARD, Southwest Texas State University, EDU, 601 University Dr., San Marcos TX 78666-4613. (512)245-2357. Fax: (512)245-7911. E-mail: jb23@academia.swt.edu. **Award Director:** Dr. Jennifer Battle. Competition open to adults. Annual contest. Estab. 1995. Purpose of award: "To encourage authors, illustrators and publishers to produce books that authentically reflect the lives of Mexican American children and young adults in the United States." Previously published submissions only. Submissions made by "any interested individual or publishing company." Must be published during the year of consideration. Deadline for entries: February 1 post publication year. Contact Dr. Jennifer Battle for nomination forms, or send copy of book. No entry fee. Awards $3,000 per book. Judging of nominations by a regional committee, national committee judges finalists. Annual ceremony honoring the book and author/illustrator is held during Hispanic Heritage Month at Southwest Texas State University.

SASKATCHEWAN BOOK AWARDS: CHILDREN'S LITERATURE, Saskatchewan Book Awards, 2311-12th Ave., Regina, Saskatchewan S4P 3Z5 Canada. (306)569-1585. Fax: (306)569-4187. E-mail: sk.bookaw ards@dlewest.com. Website: www.bookawards.sk.ca. **Award Director:** Joyce Wells. **Open to Saskatchewan authors.** Annual award. Estab. 1995. Purpose of contest: to celebrate Saskatchewan books and authors and to promote their work. Previously published submissions only. Submissions made by author, author's agent or publisher by September 15. SASE for contest rules and entry forms. Entry fee is $15 (Canadian). Awards $1,500 (Canadian). Judging by two children's literature authors outside of Saskatchewan. Requirements for entrants: Must be Saskatchewan resident; book must have ISBN number; book must have been published within the last year. Award-winning book will appear on TV talk shows and be pictured on bookmarks distributed to libraries, schools and bookstores in Saskatchewan.

WORK-IN-PROGRESS GRANTS, Society of Children's Book Writers and Illustrators, 8271 Beverly Blvd., Los Angeles CA 90048. Fax: (323)782-1892. E-mail: scbwi@juno.com. Website: www.scbwi.org. Annual award. "The SCBWI Work-in-Progress Grants have been established to assist children's book writers in the completion of a specific project." Five categories: (1) General Work-in-Progress Grant. (2) Grant for a Contemporary Novel for Young People. (3) Nonfiction Research Grant. (4) Grant for a Work Whose Author Has Never Had a Book Published. (5) Grant for a Picture Book Writer. Requests for applications may be made beginning October 1. Completed applications accepted February 1-May 1 of each year. SASE for applications for grants. In any year, an applicant may apply for any of the grants except the one awarded for a work whose author has never had a book published. (The recipient of this grant will be chosen from entries in all categories.) Five grants of $1,500 will be awarded annually. Runner-up grants of $500 (one in each category) will also be awarded. "The grants are available to both full and associate members of the SCBWI. They are not available for projects on which there are already contracts." Previous recipients not eligible to apply.

SHUBERT FENDRICH MEMORIAL PLAYWRITING CONTEST, Pioneer Drama Service, Inc., P.O. Box 4267, Englewood CO 80155-4267. Fax: (303)779-4315. E-mail: editors@pioneerdrama.com. Website: www.pion eerdrama.com. **Director:** Beth Somers. Annual contest. **Open to students.** Estab. 1990. Purpose of the contest: "to encourage the development of quality theatrical material for educational and family theater." Previously unpublished submissions only. Deadline for entries: March 1. SASE for contest rules and guidelines. No entry fee. Cover letter must accompany all submissions. Awards $1,000 royalty advance and publication. Upon receipt of signed contracts, plays will be published and made available in our next catalog. Judging by editors. All rights acquired with acceptance of contract for publication. Restrictions for entrants: Any writers currently published by Pioneer Drama Service are not eligible.

SKIPPING STONES YOUTH HONOR AWARDS, *Skipping Stones*, P.O. Box 3939, Eugene OR 97403-0939. (541)342-4956. E-mail: skipping@efn.org. Website: www.efn.org/~skipping. Annual award. Purpose of contest: "to recognize youth, 7 to 17, for their contributions to multicultural awareness, nature and ecology, social issues, peace and nonviolence. Also to promote creativity, self-esteem and writing skills and to recognize important work being done by youth organizations." Submissions made by the author. The theme "Internet's Impact on Multicultural Issues." Deadline for entries: January 20. SASE for contest rules. Entries must include certificate of originality by a parent and/or teacher and background information on the author written by the author. Entry fee is $3. Judging by *Skipping Stones*' staff. "Up to ten awards are given in three categories: (1) Compositions—(essays, poems, short stories, songs, travelogues, etc.) should be typed (double-spaced) or neatly handwritten. Fiction or nonfiction should be limited to 750 words; poems to 30 lines. Non-English writings are also welcome. (2) Artwork—(drawings, cartoons, paintings or photo essays with captions) should have the artist's name, age and address on the back of each page. Send the originals with SASE. Black & white photos are especially welcome. Limit: 8 pieces. (3) Youth Organizations—Tell us how your club or group works to: (a) preserve the nature and ecology in your area, (b) enhance the quality of life for low-income, minority or disabled or (c) improve racial or cultural harmony in your school or community. Use the same format as for compositions."

The winners are published in the September-October issue of *Skipping Stones*. The winners also receive "Honor certificates, five books and a subscription. Everyone who enters the contest receives the March-April issue featuring Youth Awards.

KAY SNOW WRITERS' CONTEST, Williamette Writers, 9045 SW Barbur Blvd. #5A, Portland OR 97219-4027. (503)452-1592. Fax: (503)452-0372. E-mail: wilwrite@teleport.com. Website: www.willamettewriters.c om. **Contest Director:** Elizabeth Shannon. Annual contest. **Open to students.** Purpose of contest: "to encourage beginning and established writers to continue the craft." Unpublished, original submissions only. Submissions made by the author or author's agent. Deadline for entries: May 15. SASE for contest rules and entry forms. Entry fee is $10, Williamette Writers' members; $15, nonmembers; free for student writers 6-18. Awards cash prize of $300 per category (fiction, nonfiction, juvenile, poetry, script writing), $50 for students in three divisions: 1-5, 6-8, 9-12. "Judges are anonymous."

✔ SPUR AWARDS, Western Writers of America, 386 Hwy. 124 West, Damascus AR 72039. (501)450-0086. **Award Director:** W.C. Jameson. Annual award. Estab. 1953. Previously published submissions only. Submissions made by author, author's agent or publisher. Must be published the year previous to the award. SASE for contest rules and entry forms. Awards plaque. Judging by panel of 3 published writers. Awards given in June 2002 at Wichita, Kansas.

THE STANLEY DRAMA AWARD, Stanley-Tomolat Foundation, Wagner College, One Campus Rd., Staten Island NY 10301. (718)390-3325. Fax: (718)390-3323. E-mail: tsweetwagner.edu. **Award Director:** Tanya Sweet. **Open to students.** Annual award. Estab. 1957. Purpose of contest: to support new works and playwrights. Unpublished submissions only. Submissions made by author. Deadline for entries: October 1. SASE for contest rules and entry forms. Entry fee is $20. Awards $2,000. Judging by committee. Award is to a full-length play or musical, previously unpublished and/or produced. One-act plays must be a full evening of theater; accepts series of one-acts related to one theme. "We will consider only one submission per playwright."

Ⓝ GEORGE G. STONE CENTER FOR CHILDREN'S BOOKS RECOGNITION OF MERIT AWARD, George G. Stone Center for Children's Books, Claremont Graduate University, 131 E. 10th St., Claremont CA 91711-6188. (909)607-3670. Fax: (909)621-8390. **Award Director:** Doty Hale. Annual award. Estab. 1965. Purpose of the award: to recognize an author or illustrator of a children's book or a body of work exhibiting the "power to please and expand the awareness of children and teachers as they have shared the book in their classrooms." Previously published submissions only. SASE for award rules and entry forms. Entries not returned. No entry fee. Awards a scroll. Judging by a committee of teachers, professors of children's literature and librarians. Requirements for entrants: Nominations are made by students, teachers, professors and librarians. Award made at annual Claremont Reading Conference in spring (March).

SUGARMAN FAMILY AWARD FOR JEWISH CHILDREN'S LITERATURE, District of Columbia Jewish Community Center, 1529 16th St. N.W., Washington DC 20036. (202)518-9400. Fax: (202)518-9420. E-mail: brett@jcc.org. **Award Director:** Brett Rodgers. **Open to students.** Biannual award. Estab. 1994. Purpose of contest: to enrich all children's appreciation of Jewish culture and to inspire writers and illustrators for children. Newly published submissions only. Submissions are made by the author, made by the author's agent. Must be published January-December of year previous to award year. Deadline: July 30, 2002. SASE for entry deadlines, award rules and entry forms. Entry fee is $25. Award at least $750. Judging by a panel of three judges—a librarian, a children's bookstore owner and a reviewer of books. Requirements for entrants: must live in the United States. Work displayed at the D.C. Jewish Community Center Library. Presentation of awards—October 2002.

SWW ANNUAL CONTEST, SouthWest Writers, 8200 Mountain Rd. NE, Suite 106, Albuquerque NM 87110. (505)265-9485. Fax: (505)265-9483. E-mail: SWriters@aol.com. Website: www.southwestwriters.org. Submit entries to: Contest Chair. Annual contest. Estab. 1982. Purpose of contest: to encourage writers of all genres. Previously unpublished submissions only. Submissions made by author. Deadline for entries: May 1, 2002. SASE for contest rules and entry forms. Entry fee. Award consists of cash prizes in each of over 15 categories. Judging by national editors and agents. Official entry form is required.

SYDNEY TAYLOR MANUSCRIPT COMPETITION, Association of Jewish Libraries, 315 Maitland Ave., Teaneck NJ 07666. Fax: (770)394-2060. E-mail: rkglasser@aol.com. Website: www.jewishlibraries.org. **Coordinator:** Rachel Glasser. **Open to students.** Annual contest. Estab. 1985. Purpose of the contest: "This competition is for unpublished writers of fiction. Material should be for readers ages 8-11, with universal appeal that will serve to deepen the understanding of Judaism for all children, revealing positive aspects of Jewish life." Unpublished submissions only. Deadline for entries: December 1. SASE for contest rules and entry forms must be enclosed. No entry fee. Awards $1,000. Award will be given at the Association of Jewish Libraries annual convention. Award winner will be notified on May 1, 2002, and the award will be presented at the convention in Denver, CO in June of 2002. Judging by qualified judges from within the Association of Jewish Libraries. Requirements for entrants: must be an unpublished fiction writer; also, books must range from 64 to 200 pages in length. "AJL assumes no responsibility for publication, but hopes this cash incentive will serve to encourage new writers of children's stories with Jewish themes for all children."

⊠⊠ THE TORONTO BOOK AWARDS, City of Toronto, 100 Queen St. W, 10th Floor, West Tower, Toronto, Ontario M5H 2M2 Canada. (416)392-8191. Fax: (416)392-1247. E-mail: bkurmey@city.toronto.onca. **Award Director:** Bev Kurmey. Submit entries to: Bev Kurmey, protocol consultant. **Open to students.** Annual award. Estab. 1974. Recognizes books of literary or artistic merit that are evocative of Toronto. Previously published submissions only in year prior to award year. Submissions made by author, author's agent or nominated by a person or group. Must be published the calendar year prior to the award year. Deadline for entries: last day of February annually. SASE for contest rules and entry forms. Awards $15,000 in prize money. Each short listed gets $1,000. Judging by committee. "The book has to be about Toronto or use Toronto as a reference."

TREASURE STATE AWARD, Missoula Public Library, Missoula County Schools, Montana Library Assoc., 301 E. Main, Missoula MT 59802. (406)721-2005. Fax: (406)728-5900. E-mail: bammon@missoula.lib.mt.us. Website: www.missoula.lib.mt.us. **Award Directors:** Bette Ammon and Carole Monlux. Annual award. Estab. 1990. Purpose of the award: Children in grades K-3 read or listen to a ballot of 5 picture books and vote on their favorite. Previously published submissions only. Submissions made by author, nominated by a person or group of people—children, librarians, teachers. Must be published in previous 5 years to voting year. Deadline for entries: March 20. SASE for contest rules and entry forms. No entry fee. Awards a plaque or sculpture. Judging by popular vote by Montana children grades K-3.

VEGETARIAN ESSAY CONTEST, The Vegetarian Resource Group, P.O. Box 1463, Baltimore MD 21203. (410)366-VEGE. Fax: (410)366-8804. E-mail: vrg@vrg.org. Website: www.vrg.org. Address to Vegetarian Essay Contest. Annual contest. Estab. 1985. Purpose of contest: to promote vegetarianism in young people. Unpublished submissions only. Deadline for entries: May 1 of each year. SASE for contest rules and entry forms. No entry fee. Awards $50 savings bond. Judging by awards committee. Acquires right for The Vegetarian Resource Group to reprint essays. Requirements for entrants: age 18 and under. Winning works may be published in *Vegetarian Journal*, instructional materials for students. "Submit 2-3 page essay on any aspect of vegetarianism, which is the abstinence of meat, fish and fowl. Entrants can base paper on interviewing, research or personal opinion. Need not be vegetarian to enter."

VFW VOICE OF DEMOCRACY, Veterans of Foreign Wars of the U.S., 406 W. 34th St., Kansas City MO 64111. (816)968-1117. Fax: (816)968-1149. Website: www.vfw.org. **Open to students.** Annual contest. Estab. 1960. Purpose of contest: to give high school students the opportunity to voice their opinions about their responsibility to our country and to convey those opinions via the broadcast media to all of America. Deadline for entries: November 1st. No entry fee. Winners receive awards ranging from $1,000-25,000. Requirements for entrants: "Ninth-twelfth grade students in public, parochial, private and home schools are eligible to compete. Former first place state winners are not eligible to compete again. Contact your participating high school teacher, counselor or your local VFW Post to enter."

⊠ VIRGINIA LIBRARY ASSOCIATION/JEFFERSON CUP, Virginia Library Association, P.O. Box 8277, Norfolk VA 23503. **Executive Director:** Linda Hahne. Award director changes year to year. Annual award. Estab. 1983. Purpose of award: to honor a distinguished biography, historical fiction, or American history book for young people, thereby promoting reading about America's past, and encouraging writing of U.S. history, biography and historical fiction. Previously published submissions only. Must be published in the year prior to selection. SASE for contest rules and entry forms. Judging by committee. The book must be about U.S. history or an American person, 1492 to present, or fiction that highlights the U.S. past; author must reside in the U.S. The book must be published especially for young people.

VSA (VERY SPECIAL ARTS) PLAYWRIGHT DISCOVERY PROGRAM, (formerly Very Special Arts Playwright Discovery), VSA, 1300 Connecticut Ave., NW, Suite 700, Washington DC 20036. (202)628-2800 or 1-800-933-8721. TTY: (202)737-0645. Fax: (202)737-0725. E-mail: playwright@vsarts.org. Website: www.vsart s.org. **Program Manager:** Dani Fox. Annual contest. Estab. 1984. "All scripts must document the experience of living with a disability." Unpublished submissions only. Deadline for entries: May 1, 2002. Write to Playwright Discovery Program Manager for contest rules and entry forms. No entries returned. No entry fee. Judging by Artists Selection Committee. Entrants must be students, grades 6-12. "Script will be selected for production at The John F. Kennedy Center for the Performing Arts, Washington DC. The winning play(s) is presented each fall."

THE STELLA WADE CHILDREN'S STORY AWARD, *Amelia* Magazine, 329 E St., Bakersfield CA 93304. (805)323-4064. **Editor:** Frederick A. Raborg, Jr. Annual award. Estab. 1988. Purpose of award: "With decrease in the number of religious and secular magazines for young people, the juvenile story and poetry must be preserved and enhanced." Unpublished submissions only. Deadline for entries: August 15. SASE for award rules. Entry fee is $7.50 per adult entry; there is no fee for entries submitted by young people under the age of

17, but such entry must be signed by parent, guardian or teacher to verify originality. Awards $125 plus publication. Judging by editorial staff. Previous winners include Maxine Kumin and Sharon E. Martin. "We use First North American serial rights only for the winning manuscript." Contest is open to all interested. If illustrator wishes to enter only an illustration without a story, the entry fee remains the same. Illustrations will also be considered for cover publication. Restrictions of mediums for illustrators: Submitted photos should be no smaller than 5×7; illustrations (drawn) may be in any medium. "Winning entry will be published in the most appropriate issue of either *Amelia*, *Cicada* or *SPSM&H*—subject matter would determine such. Submit clean, accurate copy." Sample issue: $10.95.

WASHINGTON POST/CHILDREN'S BOOK GUILD AWARD FOR NONFICTION, % Kathleen Karr, President of the Children's Book Guild of Washington, D.C., 15417 Merrifields Lane, Silver Spring MD 20906. Fax: (301)438-7602. E-mail: leggett@mindspring.com. Website: www.childrensbookguild.org. **President:** Karen Leggett. **Open to students.** Annual award. Estab. 1977. Purpose of award: "to encourage nonfiction writing for children of literary quality. Purpose of contest: "to call attention to an outstanding nonfiction author of several works, judged on the author's total output, to encourage authors to write nonfiction. Awarded for the body of work of a leading American nonfiction author." Awards are negotiated and include an engraved crystal paperweight. Judging by a jury of Children's Book Guild librarians and authors and a *Washington Post* book critic. "One doesn't enter. One is selected. Authors and publishers mistakenly send us books. Our jury annually selects one author for the award."

WE ARE WRITERS, TOO!, Creative With Words Publications, P.O. Box 223226, Carmel CA 93922. Fax: (831)655-8627. E-mail: cwwpub@usa.net. Website: members.tripod.com/CreativeWithWords. **Contest Director:** Brigitta Geltrich. Four times a year (April, May, June, September). Estab. 1975. Purpose of award: to further creative writing in children. Unpublished submissions only. Can submit year round on any topic. Deadlines for entries: year round. SASE for contest rules and entry forms. SASE for return of entries "if not on accepted entry." No entry fee. Awards publication in an anthology, on website if winning poem, and a free copy for "Best of the Month." Judging by selected guest editors and educators. Contest open to children only (up to and including 19 years old). Writer should request contest rules. SASE with all correspondence. Age of child and home address must be stated and manuscript must be verified of its authenticity. Each story or poem must have a title. Creative with Words Publications (CWW) publishes the top 100-120 manuscripts submitted to the contest CWW also publishes anthologies on various themes throughout the year to which young writers may submit. Request theme list, include SASE, or visit our website. "Website offers special contests to young writers with prizes."

WESTERN HERITAGE AWARDS, National Cowboy Hall of Fame, 1700 NE 63rd St., Oklahoma City OK 73111-7997. (405)478-2250. Fax: (405)478-4714. E-mail: editor@nationalcowboymuseum.org. Website: www.nationalcowboymuseum.org. **Director of Public Relations:** Lynda Haller. Annual award. Estab. 1961. Purpose of award: The WHA are presented annually to encourage the accurate and artistic telling of great stories of the West through 15 categories of western literature, television and film, including fiction, nonfiction, children's books and poetry. Previously published submissions only; must be published the calendar year before the awards are presented. Deadline for literary entries: November 30. Deadline for film, music and television entries: December 31. Entries not returned. Entry fee is $35. Awards a Wrangler bronze sculpture designed by famed western artist, John Free. Judging by a panel of judges selected each year with distinction in various fields of western art and heritage. Requirements for entrants: The material must pertain to the development or preservation of the West, either from a historical or contemporary viewpoint. Literary entries must have been published between December 1 and November 30 of calendar year. Film, music or television entries must have been released or aired between January 1 and December 31 of calendar year of entry. Works recognized during special awards ceremonies held annually at the museum. There is an autograph party preceding the awards. Awards ceremonies are sometimes broadcast.

JACKIE WHITE MEMORIAL NATIONAL CHILDREN'S PLAY WRITING CONTEST, Columbia Entertainment Company, 309 Parkade Blvd., Columbia MO 65202-1447. (573)874-5628. **Contest Director:** Betsy Phillips. Annual contest. Estab. 1988. Purpose of contest: to find good plays for over 20 theater school students, grades 8-9, to perform in CEC's theater school and to encourage writing production of large cast scripts suitable for production in theater schools. Previously unpublished submissions only. Submissions made by author. Deadline for entries: June 1. SASE for contest rules and entry forms. Entry fee is $10. Awards $250, production of play, travel expenses to come see production. Judging by board members of CEC and at least one theater school parent. Play is performed during the following season. 2001 winner to be presented during CEC's 2001-02 season. We reserve the right to award 1st place and prize monies without a production. All submissions will be read by at least three readers. Author will receive a written evaluation of the script.

LAURA INGALLS WILDER AWARD, Association for Library Service to Children, Division of the American Library Association, 50 E. Huron, Chicago IL 60611. (312)280-2163. E-mail: alsc@ala.org. Website: www.ala.org/alsc. Interim **Executive Director, ALSC:** Malore Brown. Award offered every 2 years. Purpose of the award:

to recognize an author or illustrator whose books, published in the US, have over a period of years made a substantial and lasting contribution to children's literature. Awards a medal presented at banquet during annual conference. Judging by Wilder Award Selection Committee.

PAUL A. WITTY SHORT STORY AWARD, International Reading Association, P.O. Box 8139, 800 Barksdale Rd., Newark DE 19714-8139. (302)731-1600. E-mail: exec@reading.org. or jbutler@reading.org. Website: www.reading.org. The entry must be an original short story appearing in a young children's periodical for the first time during 2001. The short story should serve as a literary standard that encourages young readers to read periodicals. Deadline for entries: The entry must have been published for the first time in the eligibility year; the short story must be submitted during the calendar year of publication. Anyone wishing to nominate a short story should send it to the designated Paul A. Witty Short Award Subcommittee Chair by December 1. Send SASE for guidelines. Award is $1,000 and recognition at the annual IRA Convention.

WOMEN IN THE ARTS ANNUAL CONTESTS, Women In The Arts, P.O. Box 2907, Decatur IL 62524-2907. (217)872-0811. Submit entries to Vice President. **Open to students.** Annual contest. Estab. 1995. Purpose of contest: to encourage beginning writers, as well as published professionals, by offering a contest for well-written material in fiction, essay and poetry. Submissions made by author. Deadline for entries: November 1 annually. SASE for contest rules and entry forms. Entry fee is $2/item. Prize consists of $30 1st place; $25 2nd place; $15 3rd place. Send SASE for complete rules.

ALICE LOUISE WOOD OHIOANA AWARD FOR CHILDREN'S LITERATURE, Ohioana Library Association, 274 E. First Ave., Suite 300, Columbus OH 43201. (614)466-3831. Fax: (614)728-6974. E-mail: ohioana@sloma.state.oh.us. Website: www.oplin.lib.oh.us/OHIOANA/. **Director:** Linda R. Hengst. Annual award. Estab. 1991. Purpose of award: "to recognize an Ohio author whose body of work has made, and continues to make a significant contribution to literature for children or young adults." SASE for award rules and entry forms. Award: $1,000. Requirements for entrants: "must have been born in Ohio, or lived in Ohio for a minimum of five years; established a distinguished publishing record of books for children and young people; body of work has made, and continues to make, a significant contribution to the literature for young people; through whose work as a writer, teacher, administrator, or through community service, interest in children's literature has been encouraged and children have become involved with reading."

CARTER G. WOODSON BOOK AWARD, National Council for the Social Studies, 3501 Newark St. NW, Washington DC 20016-3167. (301)588-1800, ext. 114. Fax: (202)966-2061. E-mail: excellence@ncss.org. Website: www.ncss.org. **Contact:** Manager of Recognition Programs. Annual award, named after Carter G. Woodson (1875-1950, a distinguished African-American historian, educator and social activist. Purpose of contest: to recognize books relating to ethnic minorities and authors of such books. NCSS established the Carter G. Woodson Book Awards for the most distinguished social science books appropriate for young readers which depict ethnicity in the United States. This award is intended to "encourage the writing, publishing, and dissemination of outstanding social studies books for young readers which treat topics related to ethnic minorities and race relations sensitively and accurately." Submissions must be previously published made by publishers because copies of the book must be supplied to each member and are of the committee and NCSS headquarters. Eligible books must be published in the year preceding the year in which award is given, i.e., 1997 for 1998 award. Books must be received by members of the committee by February 1. Rules, criteria and requirements are available at www.ncss.org/awards and are mailed to various publishers in December. Publishers that would like to be added to this mailing list should e-mail or mail their request to the contact information listed above, attention: Carter G. Woodson. No entry fee. Award consists of: a commemorative gift, annual conference presentation, and an announcement published in NCSS periodicals and forwarded to national and Council affiliated media. The publisher, author and illustrator receive written notification of the committee decision. Reviews of award-winning books and "honor books" are published in the NCSS official journal, *Social Education*. The award is presented at the NCSS Annual Conference in November. Judging by committee of social studies educators (teachers, curriculum supervisors and specialists, college/university professors, teacher educators—with a specific interest in multicultural education and the use of literature in social studies instruction) appointed from the NCSS membership at large.

WRITER'S BLOCK LITERARY CONTEST, *Writer's Block* Magazine, #32, 9944-33 Ave., Edmonton, Alberta T6N 1E8 Canada. Contest Director: Shaun Donnelly. Submit entries to: Shaun Donnelly, editor. **Open to students.** Biannual contest. Estab. 1994. Purpose of contest: to discover outstanding fiction/poetry by new writers for inclusion in *Writer's Block* magazine. Unpublished submissions only. Submissions made by author. Deadline for entries: March 30 and September 30. SASE for contest rules and entry forms. Entry fee is $5. Prize consists of publication, $100-150 cash, hardcover books in author's genre. Judging by independent judges (usually writers).

WRITER'S INT'L FORUM CONTESTS, Bristol Services Int'l., P.O. Box 2109, Sequim MA 98382. Website: www.bristolservicesintl.com. Estab. 1997. Purpose to inspire excellence in the traditional short story format and for tightly focused essays. "In fiction we like identifiable characters, strong storylines, and crisp, fresh endings.

Open to all ages." SASE or see website to determine if a contest is currently open. Only send a manuscript if an open contest is listed at website. Read past winning manuscripts online. Judging by Bristol Services Int'l. staff.

WRITING CONFERENCE WRITING CONTESTS, The Writing Conference, Inc., P.O. Box 27288, Overland Park KS 66225-7288. Phone/fax: (913)681-8894. E-mail: jbushman@writingconference.com. Website: www .writingconference.com. **Contest Director:** John H. Bushman. **Open to students.** Annual contest. Estab. 1988. Purpose of contest: to further writing by students with awards for narration, exposition and poetry at the elementary, middle school and high school levels. Unpublished submissions only. Submissions made by the author or teacher. Deadline for entries: January 8. SASE for contest rules and entry form or consult website. No entry fee. Awards plaque and publication of winning entry in *The Writers' Slate*, March issue. Judging by a panel of teachers. Requirements for entrants: must be enrolled in school—K-12th grade.

N: ⊠ WRITING FOR CHILDREN COMPETITION, The Writers Union of Canada, 40 Wellington St. E, 3rd Floor, Toronto, Ontario M6C 1C7 Canada. (416)703-8982, ext. 223. Fax: (416)504-7656. E-mail: twuc@the-wire.com. Website: www.writersunion.ca. **Contest Director:** Caroline Sin. Submit entries to: Caroline Sin, projects manager. **Open to students.** Annual contest. Estab. 1997. Purpose of contest: to discover, encourage and promote new writers of children's literature. Unpublished submissions only. Submissions made by author. Deadline for entries: April 23, 2002. Entry fee is $15. Awards $1,500 and submission of winner and finalists to 3 publishers of children's books. Judging by members of the Writers Union of Canada (all published writers with at least one book). Requirements for entrants: Open only to writers; illustrated books do not qualify.

YEARBOOK EXCELLENCE CONTEST, *Quill and Scroll*, School of Journalism, University of Iowa, Iowa City IA 52242-1528. (319)335-5795. Fax: (319)335-5210. E-mail: quill-scroll@uiowa.edu. Website: www.uiowa. edu/~quill-sc. **Executive Director:** Richard Johns. **Open to students.** Annual contest. Estab. 1987. Purpose of contest: to recognize and reward student journalists for their work in yearbooks and to provide student winners an opportunity to apply for a scholarship to be used freshman year in college for students planning to major in journalism. Previously published submissions only. Submissions made by the author or school yearbook adviser. Must be published between November 1, 2000 and November 1, 2001. Deadline for entries: November 1. SASE for contest rules and entry form. Entry fee is $2 per entry. Awards National Gold Key; sweepstakes winners receive plaque; seniors eligible for scholarships. Judging by various judges. Winning entries may be published in *Quill and Scroll* magazine.

⊠ YOUNG ADULT CANADIAN BOOK AWARD, The Canadian Library Association, 328 Frank St., Ottawa, Ontario K2P 0X8 Canada. (613)232-9625. Fax: (613)563-9895. Website: www.cla.ca. **Contact:** Committee Chair. Annual award. Estab. 1981. Purpose of award: "to recognize the author of an outstanding English-language Canadian book which appeals to young adults between the ages of 13 and 18 that was published the preceding calendar year. Information is available upon request. We approach publishers, also send news releases to various journals, i.e., *Quill & Quire*." Entries are not returned. No entry fee. Awards a leather-bound book. Requirement for entrants: must be a work of fiction (novel or short stories), the title must be a Canadian publication in either hardcover or paperback, and the author must be a Canadian citizen or landed immigrant. Award given at the Canadian Library Association Conference.

N: YOUNG READER'S CHOICE AWARD, Pacific Northwest Library Association, 101 Evans St., Missoula MT 59801. (406)542-4055. Fax: (406)543-5358. E-mail: monlux@montana.com. Website: www.PNLA.org. **Award Director:** Carole Monlux, chair YRCA. "This award is not for unsolicited books—the short list for this award is nominated by students, teachers and librarians and it is only for students in the Pacific Northwest to vote on the winner." YRCA is intended to be a Book Award chosen by students—not adults. It is the oldest children's choice award in US and Canada. Previously published submissions only (the titles are 3 years old when voted upon). Submissions nominated by a person or group in the Pacific Northwest. Deadline for entries: Febraury 1—Pacific Northwest nominations ony. SASE for contest rules and entry forms. Awards medal made of Idaho silver, depicting eagle and salmon in northwest. Native American symbols. Judging by students in Pacific Northwest.

"WE WANT TO PUBLISH YOUR WORK."

You would give anything to hear an editor speak those six magic words. So you work hard for weeks, months, even years to make that happen. You create a brilliant piece of work and a knock-out presentation, but there's still one vital step to ensure publication. You still need to submit your work to the right buyers. With rapid changes in the publishing industry it's not always easy to know who those buyers are. That's why each year thousands of writers and illustrators turn to the most current edition of this indispensable market guide.

Keep ahead of the changes by ordering *2003 Children's Writer's & Illustrator's Market* today! You'll save the frustration of getting your work returned in the mail stamped MOVED: ADDRESS UNKNOWN, and of NOT submitting your work to new listings because you don't know they exist. All you have to do to order next year's edition — at this year's price — is complete the attached order card and return it with your payment. Lock in the 2002 price for 2003 — order today!

Completely Updated Each Year

100% UPDATED'

Children's Writer's & Illustrator's Market

800+ EDITORS & ART DIRECTORS WHO BUY YOUR WRITING & ILLUSTRATIONS

150 new markets
250 book publishers
125 magazines
500 e-mail addresses
125 contests & awards
125 conferences & workshops

Over 80,000 copies sold!

2003 Children's & Illustrator's Market will be published and ready for shipment in January 2003.

More books to help you get published

Get Your Children's Stories Published
with Help from These Writer's Digest Books!

2002 Guide to Literary Agents
Your search for powerful representation and the perfect writer's contract begins here. Find the right agent to get your fiction, nonfiction or screenplay into the hands of the publishers who can make your dreams come true! With 100% updated listings of 570+ agents who sell what you write.
#10758-K/$22.99/400p/pb

The Writer's Guide to Crafting Stories for Children
This unique guide offers detailed information and an in-depth examination of storytelling and story structure. Using worksheets, exercises and checklists you'll discover how to capture and keep a young reader's attention, whether your topic is fact or fiction.
#10762-K/$16.99/192p/pb

Creating Characters Kids Will Love
Learn to develop vivid characters that come to life on the page and engage children. Includes characterization exercises, observation techniques and memory builders for incorporating experiences from your own childhood.
#10669-K/$16.99/208p/pb

Story Sparkers: A Creativity Guide for Children's Writers
Fire up your imagination! These easy-to-apply techniques will give your creativity a refreshing boost. You'll learn how to assess each new idea and use it to its fullest potential. Includes a guide to determine which formats will best showcase your ideas.
#10700-K/$16.99/208p/pb

How to Write and Illustrate Children's Books And Get Them Published
Advice and insider tips from some of the finest talents in children's publishing are collected in this must-have guide for success in writing and illustrating in the children's market. You'll find inspiring and insightful instruction from experts in the field to help you get your work published.
#10694-K/$19.99/144p/pb

You Can Write Children's Books
Tracey E. Dils, experienced author and faculty member of the Institute of Children's Literature, gives you insider tips and advice to help you see your work in print. You'll find out how to target the right age group, grab an editor's attention, and produce professional results. Perfect for first-time children's writers!
#10547-K/$12.99/128p/pb

Helpful Books & Publications

The editor of *Children's Writer's & Illustrator's Market* suggests the following books and periodicals to keep you informed on writing and illustrating techniques, trends in the field, business issues, industry news and changes, and additional markets.

BOOKS

AN AUTHOR'S GUIDE TO CHILDREN'S BOOK PROMOTION, by Susan Salzman Raab, 345 Millwood Rd., Chappaqua NY 10514. (914)241-2117. E-mail: info@raabassociates.com. Website: www.raabassociates.com/authors.htm.

N THE BUSINESS OF WRITING FOR CHILDREN, by Aaron Shepard, Shepard Publications. Website: www.aaronshep.com/kidwriter/Business.html. Available on www.amazon.com.

CHILDREN'S WRITER GUIDE, (annual), The Institute of Children's Literature, 95 Long Ridge Rd., West Redding CT 55104. (800)443-6078.

CHILDREN'S WRITER'S REFERENCE, by Berthe Amoss and Eric Suben, Writer's Digest Books, 1507 Dana Ave., Cincinnati OH 45207. (800)289-0963. Website: www.writersdigest.com.

CHILDREN'S WRITER'S WORD BOOK, by Alijandra Mogilner, Writer's Digest Books, 1507 Dana Ave., Cincinnati OH 45207. (800)289-0963. Website: www.writersdigest.com.

N THE COMPLETE IDIOT'S GUIDE® TO PUBLISHING CHILDREN'S BOOKS, by Harold D. Underdown and Lynne Rominger, Alpha Books, 201 W. 103rd St., Indianapolis IN 46290. Website: www.idiotsguides.com.

CREATING CHARACTERS KIDS WILL LOVE, by Elaine Marie Alphin, Writer's Digest Books, 1507 Dana Ave., Cincinnati OH 45207. (800)289-0963. Website: www.writersdigest.com.

FORMATTING & SUBMITTING YOUR MANUSCRIPT, by Jack and Glenda Neff, Don Prues and the editors of *Writer's Market*, Writer's Digest Books, 1507 Dana Ave., Cincinnati OH 45207. (800)289-0963. Website: www.writersdigest.com.

GETTING STARTED AS A FREELANCE ILLUSTRATOR OR DESIGNER, by Michael Fleischman, North Light Books, 1507 Dana Ave., Cincinnati OH 45207. (800)289-0963. Website: www.writersdigest.com.

☑ GUIDE TO LITERARY AGENTS, (annual) edited by Rachel Vater, Writer's Digest Books, 1507 Dana Ave., Cincinnati OH 45207. (800)289-0963. Website: www.writersdigest.com.

HOW TO PROMOTE YOUR CHILDREN'S BOOK: A SURVIVAL GUIDE, by Evelyn Gallardo, Primate Production, P.O. Box 3038, Manhattan Beach CA 90266, Website: www.evegallardo.com/promote.html.

HOW TO SELL YOUR PHOTOGRAPHS & ILLUSTRATIONS, by Elliot & Barbara Gordon, North Light Books, 1507 Dana Ave., Cincinnati OH 45207. (800)289-0963.

HOW TO WRITE A CHILDREN'S BOOK & GET IT PUBLISHED, by Barbara Seuling, Charles Scribner's Sons, 1230 Avenue of the Americas, New York NY 10020. (212)702-2000.

HOW TO WRITE AND ILLUSTRATE CHILDREN'S BOOKS AND GET THEM PUBLISHED, edited by Treld Pelkey Bicknell and Felicity Trottman, Writer's Digest Books, 1507 Dana Ave., Cincinnati OH 45207. (800)289-0963. Website: www.writersdigest.com.

HOW TO WRITE AND SELL CHILDREN'S PICTURE BOOKS, by Jean E. Karl, Writer's Digest Books, 1507 Dana Ave., Cincinnati OH 45207. (800)289-0963. Website: www.writersdigest.com.

HOW TO WRITE ATTENTION-GRABBING QUERY & COVER LETTERS, by John Wood, Writer's Digest Books, 1507 Dana Ave., Cincinnati OH 45207. (800)289-0963. Website: www.writersdigest.com.

HOW TO WRITE, ILLUSTRATE, AND DESIGN CHILDREN'S BOOKS, by Frieda Gates, Lloyd-Simone Publishing Company, distributed by Library Research Associates, Inc., Dunderberg Rd. RD 6, Box 41, Monroe NY 10950. (914)783-1144.

N IT'S A BUNNY-EAT-BUNNY WORLD: A Writer's Guide to Surviving and Thriving in Today's Competitive Children's Book Market, by Olga Litowinsky, 435 Hudson St., New York NY 10014. (212)727-8300. Website: www.walkerbooks.com.

LEGAL GUIDE FOR THE VISUAL ARTIST, 4th edition, by Tad Crawford, North Light Books, 1507 Dana Ave., Cincinnati OH 45207. (800)289-0963.

STORY SPARKERS: A Creativity Guide for Children's Writers, by Marcia Thornton Jones and Debbie Dadey, Writer's Digest Books, 1507 Dana Ave., Cincinnati OH 45207. (800)289-0963. Website: www.writersdigest.com.

A TEEN'S GUIDE TO GETTING PUBLISHED, by Danielle Dunn & Jessica Dunn, Prufrock Press, P.O. Box 8813, Waco TX 76714-8813. (800)998-2208.

TEN STEPS TO PUBLISHING CHILDREN'S BOOKS, by Berthe Amoss & Eric Suben, Writer's Digest Books, 1507 Dana Ave., Cincinnati OH 45207. (800)289-0963. Website: www.writersdigest.com.

THE ULTIMATE PORTFOLIO, by Martha Metzdorf, North Light Books, 1507 Dana Ave., Cincinnati OH 45207. (800)289-0963.

THE WRITER'S ESSENTIAL DESK REFERENCE, Second Edition, Writer's Digest Books, 1507 Dana Ave., Cincinnati OH 45207. (800)289-0963. Website: www.writersdigest.com.

N THE WRITER'S GUIDE TO CRAFTING STORIES FOR CHILDREN, by Nancy Lamb, Writer's Digest Books, 1507 Dana Ave., Cincinnati OH 45207. (800)289-0963. Website: www.writersdigest.com.

WRITING AND ILLUSTRATING CHILDREN'S BOOKS FOR PUBLICATION: Two Perspectives, by Berthe Amoss and Eric Suben, Writer's Digest Books, 1507 Dana Ave., Cincinnati OH 45207. (800)289-0963. Website: www.writersdigest.com.

WRITING BOOKS FOR YOUNG PEOPLE, Second Edition, by James Cross Giblin, The Writer, Inc., 120 Boylston St., Boston MA 02116-4615. (617)423-3157.

WRITING FOR CHILDREN & TEENAGERS, Third Edition, by Lee Wyndham and Arnold Madison, Writer's Digest Books, 1507 Dana Ave., Cincinnati OH 45207. (800)289-0963. Website: www.writersdigest.com.

WRITING FOR YOUNG ADULTS, by Sherry Garland, Writer's Digest Books, 1507 Dana Ave., Cincinnati OH 45207. (800)289-0963. Website: www.writersdigest.com.

WRITING WITH PICTURES: How to Write and Illustrate Children's Books, by Uri Shulevitz, Watson-Guptill Publications, 1515 Broadway, New York NY 10036. (212)764-7300.

YOU CAN WRITE CHILDREN'S BOOKS, by Tracey E. Dils, Writer's Digest Books, 1507 Dana Ave., Cincinnati OH 45207. (800)289-0963. Website: www.writersdigest.com.

N THE YOUNG WRITER'S GUIDE TO GETTING PUBLISHED, by Kathy Henderson, Writer's Digest Books, 1507 Dana Ave., Cincinnati OH 45207. (800)289-0963. Website: www.writersdigest.com.

PUBLICATIONS

☑ BOOK LINKS: Connecting Books, Libraries and Classrooms, editor Laura Tillotson, American Library Association, 50 E. Huron St., Chicago IL 60611. (800)545-2433. Website: www.ala.org/BookLinks. *Magazine published 6 times a year (September-July) for the purpose of connecting books, libraries and classrooms. Features articles on specific topics followed by bibliographies recommending books for further information. Subscription: $25.95/year.*

CHILDREN'S BOOK INSIDER, editor Laura Backes, 901 Columbia Rd., Ft. Collins CO 80525-1838. (970)495-0056 or (800)807-1916. E-mail: mail@write4kids.com. Website: www.write4kids.com. *Monthly news-*

letter covering markets, techniques and trends in children's publishing. Subscription: $29.95/year. Official update source for Children's Writer's & Illustrator's Market, *featuring quarterly lists of changes and updates to listings in CWIM.*

CHILDREN'S WRITER, editor Susan Tierney, The Institute of Children's Literature, 95 Long Ridge Rd., West Redding CT 06896-0811. (800)443-6078. Website: www.childrenswriter.com. *Monthly newsletter of writing and publishing trends in the children's field. Subscription: $26/year; special introductory rate: $15.*

THE FIVE OWLS, editor Dr. Mark West, 2004 Sheridan Ave. S., Minneapolis MN 55405. (612)377-2004. Website: www.fiveowls.com. *Bimonthly newsletter for readers personally and professionally involved in children's literature. Subscription: $35/year.*

THE HORN BOOK MAGAZINE, editor-in-chief Roger Sutton, The Horn Book Inc., 56 Roland St., Suite 200, Boston MA 02129. (800)325-1170. E-mail: info@hbook.com. Website: www.hbook.com. *Bimonthly guide to the children's book world including views on the industry and reviews of the latest books. Subscription: special introductory rate: $29.95.*

THE LION AND THE UNICORN: A Critical Journal of Children's Literature, editors Jack Zipes and Louisa Smith, The Johns Hopkins University Press, P.O. Box 19966, Baltimore MD 21211-0966. (800)548-1784 or (410)516-6987. Website: www.press.jhu.edu/press/journals/uni/uni.html. *Magazine published 3 times a year serving as a forum for discussion of children's literature featuring interviews with authors, editors and experts in the field. Subscription: $26.50/year.*

ONCE UPON A TIME, editor Audrey Baird, 553 Winston Court, St. Paul MN 55118. (651)457-6223. Fax: (651)457-9565. Website: http://members.aol.com/OUATMAG/. *Quarterly support magazine for children's writers and illustrators and those interested in children's literature. Subscription: $24.25/year.*

PUBLISHERS WEEKLY, editor-in-chief Nora Rawlinson, Bowker Magazine Group, Cahners Publishing Co., 249 W. 17th St., New York NY 10011. (800)278-2991. Website: www.publishersweekly.com. *Weekly trade publication covering all aspects of the publishing industry; includes coverage of the children's field and spring and fall issues devoted solely to children's books. Subscription: $189/year. Available on newsstands for $4/issue. (Special issues are higher in price.)*

RIVERBANK REVIEW of books for young readers, editor Martha Davis Beck, University of St. Thomas, 1000 LaSalle Ave., MOH-217, Minneapolis MN 55403-2009. (615)962-4372. E-mail: riverbank@stthomas.edu. Website: http://department.stthomas.edu/RBR/. *Quarterly publication exploring the world of children's literature including book reviews, articles and essays. Subscription: $20/year.*

SOCIETY OF CHILDREN'S BOOK WRITERS AND ILLUSTRATORS BULLETIN, editors Stephen Mooser and Lin Oliver, SCBWI, 8271 Beverly Blvd., Los Angeles CA 90048. (323)782-1010. Website: www.scbwi.org/bulletin.htm. *Bimonthly newsletter of SCBWI covering news of interest to members. Subscription with $50/year membership.*

Useful Online Resources

The editor of *Children's Writer's & Illustrator's Market* suggests the following websites to keep you informed on writing and illustrating techniques, trends in the field, business issues, industry news and changes, and additional markets.

AMAZON.COM: www.amazon.com
Calling itself "A bookstore too big for the physical world," Amazon.com has more than 3 million books available on their website at discounted prices, plus a personal notification service of new releases, reader reviews, bestseller and suggested book information. Be sure to check out Amazon.com Kids.

ASSOCIATION FOR LIBRARY SERVICE TO CHILDREN: www.ala.org/alsc/awards.html
This site provides links to information about Newbery, Caldecott, Coretta Scott King and Michael L. Printz Awards as well as a host of other awards for notable children's books.

AUTHORS AND ILLUSTRATORS FOR CHILDREN WEBRING: www.webring.org/cgi-bin/webring?ring=aicwebring;list
Here you'll find a list of link of sites of interest to children's writers and illustrators or created by them.

THE AUTHORS GUILD ONLINE: www.authorsguild.org/
The website of The Authors Guild offers articles and columns dealing with contract issues, copyright, electronic rights and other legal issues of concern to writers.

BARNES & NOBLE ONLINE: www.bn.com
The world's largest bookstore chain's website contains 600,000 in-stock titles at discount prices as well as personalized recommendations, online events with authors and book forum access for members.

BOOKWIRE: www.bookwire.com
A gateway to finding information about publishers, booksellers, libraries, authors, reviews and awards. Also offers frequently asked publishing questions and answers, a calendar of events, a mailing list and other helpful resources.

CANADIAN CHILDREN'S BOOK CENTRE: www3.sympatico.ca/ccbc/
The site for the CCBC includes profiles of illustrators and authors, information on recent books, a calendar of upcoming events, information on CCBC publications, and tips from Canadian children's authors.

THE CHILDREN'S BOOK COUNCIL: www.cbcbooks.org/
This site includes a complete list of CBC members with addresses, names and descriptions of what each publishes, and links to publishers' websites. Also offers previews of upcoming titles from members; articles from CBC Features, *the Council's newsletter; and their catalog.*

CHILDREN'S LITERATURE WEB GUIDE: www.ucalgary.ca/~dkbrown/index.html
This site includes stories, poetry, resource lists, lists of conferences, links to book reviews, lists of awards (international), and information on books from classic to contemporary.

CHILDREN'S PUBLISHERS' SUBMISSION GUIDELINES: www.signaleader.com/childrens-writers/
This site features links to websites of children's publishers and magazines and includes information on which publishers offer submission guidelines online.

CHILDREN'S WRITER'S AND ILLUSTRATOR'S RESOURCE LIST: www.pfdstudio.com/cwrl.html
Maintained by Peter Davis, this site includes lists of books on writing and illustrating, books on the business of illustration, organizations and periodicals and Internet resources.

CHILDREN'S WRITING SUPERSITE: www.write4kids.com
This site (formerly Children's Writers Resource Center) includes highlights from the newsletter Children's Book Insider; *definitions of publishing terms; answers to frequently asked questions; information on trends; information on small presses; a research center for Web information; and a catalog of material available from* CBI.

THE DRAWING BOARD: http://members.aol.com/thedrawing
This site for illustrators features articles, interviews, links and resources for illustrators from all fields.

EDITOR & PUBLISHER: www.mediainfo.com
The Internet source for Editor & Publisher, this site provides up-to-date industry news, with other opportunities such as a research area and bookstore, a calendar of events and classifieds.

INKSPOT: www.inkspot.com
An elaborate site that provides information about workshops, how-to information, copyright, quotations, writing tips, resources, contests, market information (including children's writers marketplace), publishers, booksellers, associations, mailing lists, newsletters, conferences and more.

INTERNATIONAL READING ASSOCIATION: www.reading.org
This website includes articles; book lists; event, conference and convention information; and an online bookstore.

KEYSTROKES: www.writelinks.com/keystrokes/
This online monthly newsletter for writers features articles on an array of topics, including topics related to writing for children. The site offers a years' worth of the newsletter.

ONCE UPON A TIME: http://members.aol.com/OUATMAG
This companion site to Once Upon A Time magazine offers excerpts from recent articles, notes for prospective contributors, and information about OUAT's 11 regular columnists.

PICTUREBOOK: www.picture-book.com
This site brought to you by Picturebook sourcebook offers tons of links for illustrators, portfolio searching, and news, and offers a listserv, bulletin board and chatroom.

PUBLISHERS' CATALOGUES HOME PAGE: www.lights.com/publisher/index.html
A mammoth link collection of more than 6,000 publishers around the world arranged geographically. This site is one of the most comprehensive directories of publishers on the Internet.

PUBLISHERS WEEKLY CHILDREN'S FEATURES: www.publishersweekly.com/childrensindex.asp
This is a direct link to Publishers Weekly articles relating to children's publishing and authors.

THE PURPLE CRAYON: www.underdown.org
Editor Harold Underdown's site includes articles on trends, business, and cover letters and queries as well as interviews with editors and answers to frequently asked questions. He also includes links to a number of other sites helpful to writers.

SLANTVILLE: www.slantville.com/
An online artists community, this site includes a yellow pages for artists, frequently asked questions and a library offering information on a number of issues of interest to illustrators. This is a great site to visit to view artists' portfolios.

SOCIETY OF CHILDREN'S BOOK WRITERS AND ILLUSTRATORS: www.scbwi.org
This site includes information on awards and grants available to SCBWI members, a calendar of events listed by date and region, a list of publications available to members, and a site map for easy navigation. Balan welcomes suggestions for the site from visitors.

UNITED STATES POSTAL SERVICE: www.usps.gov/welcome.htm
Offers domestic and International postage rate calculator, stamp ordering, zip code look up, express mail tracking and more.

VERLA KAY'S WEBSITE: www.verlakay.com
Author Verla Kay's website features writer's tips, articles, a schedules of online workshops (with transcripts of past workshops), a good news board and helpful links.

WRITERSDIGEST.COM: www.writersdigest.com
Brought to you by Writer's Digest magazine and Writer's Market, this site features a hot list, conference listings, markets of the day, and a searchable database of more than 1,500 writer's guidelines.

WRITERSMARKET.COM: www.writersmarket.com
This gateway to the Writer's Market online edition offers market news, FAQs, tips, featured markets and web resources, a free newsletter, and more.

Glossary

AAR. Association of Authors' Representatives.

ABA. American Booksellers Association.

ABC. Association of Booksellers for Children.

Advance. A sum of money a publisher pays a writer or illustrator prior to the publication of a book. It is usually paid in installments, such as one half on signing the contract; one half on delivery of a complete and satisfactory manuscript. The advance is paid against the royalty money that will be earned by the book.

ALA. American Library Association.

All rights. The rights contracted to a publisher permitting the use of material anywhere and in any form, including movie and book club sales, without additional payment to the creator. (See The Business of Writing & Illustrating.)

Anthology. A collection of selected writings by various authors or gatherings of works by one author.

Anthropomorphization. The act of attributing human form and personality to things not human (such as animals).

ASAP. As soon as possible.

Assignment. An editor or art director asks a writer, illustrator or photographer to produce a specific piece for an agreed-upon fee.

B&W. Black and white.

Backlist. A publisher's list of books not published during the current season but still in print.

Biennially. Occurring once every 2 years.

Bimonthly. Occurring once every 2 months.

Biweekly. Occurring once every 2 weeks.

Book packager. A company that draws all elements of a book together, from the initial concept to writing and marketing strategies, then sells the book package to a book publisher and/or movie producer. Also known as book producer or book developer.

Book proposal. Package submitted to a publisher for consideration usually consisting of a synopsis, outline and sample chapters. (See Before Your First Sale.)

Business-size envelope. Also known as a #10 envelope. The standard size used in sending business correspondence.

Camera-ready. Refers to art that is completely prepared for copy camera platemaking.

Caption. A description of the subject matter of an illustration or photograph; photo captions include persons' names where appropriate. Also called cutline.

Clean-copy. A manuscript free of errors and needing no editing; it is ready for typesetting.

Clips. Samples, usually from newspapers or magazines, of a writer's published work.

Concept books. Books that deal with ideas, concepts and large-scale problems, promoting an understanding of what's happening in a child's world. Most prevalent are alphabet and counting books, but also includes books dealing with specific concerns facing young people (such as divorce, birth of a sibling, friendship or moving).

Contract. A written agreement stating the rights to be purchased by an editor, art director or producer and the amount of payment the writer, illustrator or photographer will receive for that sale. (See The Business of Writing & Illustrating.)

Contributor's copies. The magazine issues sent to an author, illustrator or photographer in which her work appears.

Co-op publisher. A publisher that shares production costs with an author, but, unlike subsidy publishers, handles all marketing and distribution. An author receives a high percentage of royalties until her initial investment is recouped, then standard royalties.

Copy. The actual written material of a manuscript.

Copyediting. Editing a manuscript for grammar usage, spelling, punctuation and general style.

Copyright. A means to legally protect an author's/illustrator's/photographer's work. This can be shown by writing ©, the creator's name, and year of work's creation. (See The Business of Writing & Illustrating.)

Cover letter. A brief letter, accompanying a complete manuscript, especially useful if responding to an editor's request for a manuscript. May also accompany a book proposal. (See Before Your First Sale.)

Cutline. See caption.

Disk. A round, flat magnetic plate on which computer data may be stored.

Division. An unincorporated branch of a company.

Dummy. A loose mock-up of a book showing placement of text and artwork.

Electronic submission. A submission of material by modem or on computer disk.

E-mail. Electronic mail. Messages sent from one computer to another via a modem or computer network.

Final draft. The last version of a polished manuscript ready for submission to an editor.

First North American serial rights. The right to publish material in a periodical for the first time, in the United States or Canada. (See The Business of Writing & Illustrating.)

F&G's. Folded and gathered sheets. An early, not-yet-bound copy of a picture book.

Flat fee. A one-time payment.

Galleys. The first typeset version of a manuscript that has not yet been divided into pages.

Genre. A formulaic type of fiction, such as horror, mystery, romance, science fiction or western.

Glossy. A photograph with a shiny surface as opposed to one with a non-shiny matte finish.

Gouache. Opaque watercolor with an appreciable film thickness and an actual paint layer.

Halftone. Reproduction of a continuous tone illustration with the image formed by dots produced by a camera lens screen.

Hard copy. The printed copy of a computer's output.

Hardware. All the mechanically-integrated components of a computer that are not software—circuit boards, transistors and the machines that are the actual computer.

Hi-Lo. High interest, low reading level.

Home page. The first page of a website.

Imprint. Name applied to a publisher's specific line of books.

Internet. A worldwide network of computers that offers access to a wide variety of electronic resources.

IRA. International Reading Association.

IRC. International Reply Coupon. Sold at the post office to enclose with text or artwork sent to a foreign buyer to cover postage costs when replying or returning work.

Keyline. Identification, through signs and symbols, of the positions of illustrations and copy for the printer.

Layout. Arrangement of illustrations, photographs, text and headlines for printed material.

Line drawing. Illustration done with pencil or ink using no wash or other shading.

Mass market books. Paperback books directed toward an extremely large audience sold in supermarkets, drugstores, airports, newsstands and bookstores.

Mechanicals. Paste-up or preparation of work for printing.

Middle grade or mid-grade. See middle reader.

Middle reader. The general classification of books written for readers approximately ages 9-11. Also called middle grade.

Modem. A small electrical box that plugs into the serial card of a computer, used to transmit data from one computer to another, usually via telephone lines.

Ms (mss). Manuscript(s).

NCTE. National Council of Teachers of English.

One-time rights. Permission to publish a story in periodical or book form one time only. (See The Business of Writing & Illustrating.)

Outline. A summary of a book's contents in 5-15 double-spaced pages; often in the form of chapter headings with a descriptive sentence or two under each heading to show the scope of the book.

Package sale. The sale of a manuscript and illustrations/photos as a "package" paid for with one check.

Payment on acceptance. The writer, artist or photographer is paid for her work at the time the editor or art director decides to buy it.

Payment on publication. The writer, artist or photographer is paid for her work when it is published.

Photostat. Black & white copies produced by an inexpensive photographic process using paper negatives; only line values are held with accuracy. Also called stat.

Picture book. A type of book aimed at preschoolers to 8-year-olds that tells a story using a combination of text and artwork.

Print. An impression pulled from an original plate, stone, block, screen or negative; also a positive made from a photographic negative.

Proofreading. Reading a typescript to correct typographical errors.

Query. A letter to an editor designed to capture interest in an article or book you have written or propose to write. (See Before Your First Sale.)

Reading fee. Money charged by some agents and publishers to read a submitted manuscript.

Reprint rights. Permission to print an already published work whose first rights have been sold to another magazine or book publisher. (See The Business of Writing & Illustrating.)

Response time. The average length of time it takes an editor or art director to accept or reject a query or submission and inform the creator of the decision.

Rights. The bundle of permissions offered to an editor or art director in exchange for printing a manuscript, artwork or photographs. (See The Business of Writing & Illustrating.)

Rough draft. A manuscript that has not been checked for errors in grammar, punctuation, spelling or content.

Roughs. Preliminary sketches or drawings.

Royalty. An agreed percentage paid by a publisher to a writer, illustrator or photographer for each copy of her work sold.

SAE. Self-addressed envelope.

SASE. Self-addressed, stamped envelope.

SCBWI. The Society of Children's Book Writers and Illustrators. (See listing in Clubs & Organizations section.)

Second serial rights. Permission for the reprinting of a work in another periodical after its first publication in book or magazine form. (See The Business of Writing & Illustrating.)

Semiannual. Occurring every 6 months or twice a year.

Semimonthly. Occurring twice a month.

Semiweekly. Occurring twice a week.

Serial rights. The rights given by an author to a publisher to print a piece in one or more periodicals. (See The Business of Writing & Illustrating.)

Simultaneous submissions. Queries or proposals sent to several publishers at the same time. (See Before Your First Sale.)

Slant. The approach to a story or piece of artwork that will appeal to readers of a particular publication.

Slush pile. Editors' term for their collections of unsolicited manuscripts.

Software. Programs and related documentation for use with a computer.

Solicited manuscript. Material that an editor has asked for or agreed to consider before being sent by a writer.

SPAR. Society of Photographers and Artists Representatives.

Speculation (spec). Creating a piece with no assurance from an editor or art director that it will be purchased or any reimbursements for material or labor paid.

Stat. See photostat.

Subsidiary rights. All rights other than book publishing rights included in a book contract, such as paperback, book club and movie rights. (See The Business of Writing & Illustrating.)

Subsidy publisher. A book publisher that charges the author for the cost of typesetting, printing and promoting a book. Also called a vanity publisher.

Synopsis. A brief summary of a story or novel. Usually a page to a page and a half, single-spaced, if part of a book proposal.

Tabloid. Publication printed on an ordinary newspaper page turned sideways and folded in half.

Tearsheet. Page from a magazine or newspaper containing your printed art, story, article, poem or photo.

Thumbnail. A rough layout in miniature.

Trade books. Books sold strictly in bookstores, aimed at a smaller audience than mass market books, and printed in smaller quantities by publishers.

Transparencies. Positive color slides; not color prints.

Unsolicited manuscript. Material sent without an editor's or art director's request.

Vanity publisher. See subsidy publisher.

Word processor. A computer that produces typewritten copy via automated text-editing, storage and transmission capabilities.

World Wide Web. An Internet resource that utilizes hypertext to access information. It also supports formatted text, illustrations and sounds, depending on the user's computer capabilities.

Work-for-hire. An arrangement between a writer, illustrator or photographer and a company under which the company retains complete control of the work's copyright. (See The Business of Writing & Illustrating.)

YA. See young adult.

Young adult. The general classification of books written for readers approximately ages 12-18. Often referred to as YA.

Young reader. The general classification of books written for readers approximately ages 5-8.

Age-Level Index

This index lists book and magazine publishers by the age-groups for which they publish. Use it to locate appropriate markets for your work, then carefully read the listings and follow the guidelines of each publisher. Use this index in conjunction with the Subject Index to further narrow your list of markets. **Picture Books** and **Picture-Oriented Material** are for preschoolers to 8-year-olds; **Young Readers** are for 5- to 8-year-olds; **Middle Readers** are for 9- to 11-year-olds; and **Young Adults** are for ages 12 and up.

BOOK PUBLISHERS

Picture Books

Subject Index

This index lists book and magazine publishers by the fiction and nonfiction subject area in which they publish. Use it to locate appropriate markets for your work, then carefully read the listings and follow the guidelines of each publisher. Use this index in conjunction with Age-Level Index to further narrow your list of markets.

BOOK PUBLISHERS: FICTION

Nature/Environment

Problem Novels

BOOK PUBLISHERS: NONFICTION

Activity Books

Animal

MAGAZINES: FICTION

MAGAZINES: NONFICTION

Poetry Index

This index lists markets that are open to poetry submissions and is divided into book publishers and magazines. It's important to carefully read the listings and follow the guidelines of each publisher to which you submit.

Photography Index

This index lists markets that buy photos from freelancers, and is divided into book publishers, magazines and greeting cards. It's important to carefully read the listings and follow the guidelines of each publisher to which you submit.

General Index

Market listings that appeared in the 2001 edition of *Children's Writer's & Illustrator's Market* but do not appear in this edition are identified with a two-letter code explaining why the listing was omitted: (**NR**)—No (or late) Response to Listing Request; (**NS**)—Not Currently Accepting Submissions; (**RR**)—Removed by Request; (**UF**)—Uncertain Future.

GENERAL INDEX

Market listings that appeared in the 2001 *Children's Writer's & Illustrator's Market*, but do not appear in this edition are identified with a two-letter code explaining why the listing was omitted: **(NR)—No (or late) Response to Listing Request; (NS)—Not Currently Accepting Submissions; (RR)—Removed by Request; (UF)—Uncertain Future.**

Market listings that appeared in the 2001 *Children's Writer's & Illustrator's Market*, but do not appear in this edition are identified with a two-letter code explaining why the listing was omitted: (NR)—No (or late) Response to Listing Request; (NS)—Not Currently Accepting Submissions; (RR)—Removed by Request; (UF)—Uncertain Future.